Czech Republic

WORLD BIBLIOGRAPHICAL SERIES

General Editors:
Robert G. Neville (Executive Editor)
John J. Horton

Robert A. Myers   Hans H. Wellisch
Ian Wallace   Ralph Lee Woodward, Jr.

John J. Horton is Deputy Librarian of the University of Bradford and was formerly Chairman of its Academic Board of Studies in Social Sciences. He has maintained a longstanding interest in the discipline of area studies and its associated bibliographical problems, with special reference to European Studies. In particular he has published in the field of Icelandic and of Yugoslav studies, including the two relevant volumes in the World Bibliographical Series.

Robert A. Myers is Associate Professor of Anthropology in the Division of Social Sciences and Director of Study Abroad Programs at Alfred University, Alfred, New York. He has studied post-colonial island nations of the Caribbean and has spent two years in Nigeria on a Fulbright Lectureship. His interests include international public health, historical anthropology and developing societies. In addition to *Amerindians of the Lesser Antilles: a bibliography* (1981), *A Resource Guide to Dominica, 1493-1986* (1987) and numerous articles, he has compiled the World Bibliographical Series volumes on *Dominica* (1987), *Nigeria* (1989) and *Ghana* (1991).

Ian Wallace is Professor of German at the University of Bath. A graduate of Oxford in French and German, he also studied in Tübingen, Heidelberg and Lausanne before taking teaching posts at universities in the USA, Scotland and England. He specializes in contemporary German affairs, especially literature and culture, on which he has published numerous articles and books. In 1979 he founded the journal *GDR Monitor*, which he continues to edit under its new title *German Monitor*.

Hans H. Wellisch is Professor emeritus at the College of Library and Information Services, University of Maryland. He was President of the American Society of Indexers and was a member of the International Federation for Documentation. He is the author of numerous articles and several books on indexing and abstracting, and has published *The Conversion of Scripts and Indexing and Abstracting: an International Bibliography*, and *Indexing from A to Z*. He also contributes frequently to *Journal of the American Society for Information Science, The Indexer* and other professional journals.

Ralph Lee Woodward, Jr. is Professor of History at Tulane University, New Orleans. He is the author of *Central America, a Nation Divided*, 2nd ed. (1985), as well as several monographs and more than seventy scholarly articles on modern Latin America. He has also compiled volumes in the World Bibliographical Series on *Belize* (1980), *El Salvador* (1988), *Guatemala* (Rev. Ed.) (1992) and *Nicaragua* (Rev. Ed.) (1994). Dr. Woodward edited the Central American section of the *Research Guide to Central America and the Caribbean* (1985) and is currently associate editor of Scribner's *Encyclopedia of Latin American History*.

VOLUME 219

Czech Republic

Vlaďka Edmondson

with

David Short

Compilers

CLIO PRESS

OXFORD, ENGLAND · SANTA BARBARA, CALIFORNIA
DENVER, COLORADO

© Copyright 1999 by ABC-CLIO Ltd.

All rights reserved. No part of this publication may be reproduced, stored in any retrieval system, or transmitted in any form or by any means, electronic, mechanical, photocopying or otherwise, without the prior permission in writing of the publishers.

British Library Cataloguing in Publication Data

Edmondson, Vlaďka with Short, David
Czech Republic. – (World bibliographical series; v. 219)
1. Czech Republic – Bibliography
I. Title
016.9'437

ISBN 1–85109–304–4

ABC-CLIO Ltd.,
Old Clarendon Ironworks,
35A Great Clarendon Street,
Oxford OX2 6AT, England.

———

ABC-CLIO Inc.,
130 Cremona Drive,
Santa Barbara,
CA 93117, USA.

Designed by Bernard Crossland.
Typeset by Columns Design Ltd., Reading, England.
Printed in Great Britain by print in black, Midsomer Norton.

THE WORLD BIBLIOGRAPHICAL SERIES

This series, which is principally designed for the English speaker, will eventually cover every country (and some of the world's principal regions and cities), each in a separate volume comprising annotated entries on works dealing with its history, geography, economy and politics; and with its people, their culture, customs, religion and social organization. Attention will also be paid to current living conditions – housing, education, newspapers, clothing, etc. – that are all too often ignored in standard bibliographies; and to those particular aspects relevant to individual countries. Each volume seeks to achieve, by use of careful selectivity and critical assessment of the literature, an expression of the country and an appreciation of its nature and national aspirations, to guide the reader towards an understanding of its importance. The keynote of the series is to provide, in a uniform format, an interpretation of each country that will express its culture, its place in the world, and the qualities and background that make it unique. The views expressed in individual volumes, however, are not necessarily those of the publisher.

VOLUMES IN THE SERIES

1 *Yugoslavia*, Rev. Ed., John J. Horton
2 *Lebanon*, Rev. Ed., C. H. Bleaney
3 *Lesotho*, Rev. Ed., Deborah Johnston
4 *Zimbabwe*, Rev. Ed., Deborah Potts
5 *Saudi Arabia*, Rev. Ed., Frank A. Clements
6 *Russia/USSR*, Second Ed., Lesley Pitman
7 *South Africa*, Rev. Ed., Geoffrey V. Davis
8 *Malawi*, Rev. Ed., Samuel Decalo
9 *Guatemala*, Rev. Ed., Ralph Lee Woodward, Jr.
10 *Pakistan*, David Taylor
11 *Uganda*, Rev. Ed., Balam Nyeko
12 *Malaysia*, Rev. Ed., Ooi Keat Gin
13 *France*, Rev. Ed., Frances Chambers
14 *Panama*, Eleanor DeSelms Langstaff
15 *Hungary*, Thomas Kabdebo
16 *USA*, Sheila R. Herstein and Naomi Robbins
17 *Greece*, Rev. Ed., Thanos Veremis and Mark Dragoumis
18 *New Zealand*, Rev. Ed., Brad Patterson and Kathryn Patterson
19 *Algeria*, Rev. Ed., Richard I. Lawless
20 *Sri Lanka*, Vijaya Samaraweera

21 *Belize*, Second Ed., Peggy Wright and Brian E. Coutts
23 *Luxembourg*, Rev. Ed., Jul Christophory and Emile Thoma
24 *Swaziland*, Rev. Ed., Balam Nyeko
25 *Kenya*, Rev. Ed., Dalvan Coger
26 *India*, Rev. Ed., Ian Derbyshire
27 *Turkey*, Rev. Ed., Çiğdem Balım-Harding
28 *Cyprus*, Rev. Ed., P. M. Kitromilides and M. L. Evriviades
29 *Oman*, Rev. Ed., Frank A. Clements
30 *Italy*, Lucio Sponza and Diego Zancani
31 *Finland*, Rev. Ed., J. E. O. Screen
32 *Poland*, Rev. Ed., George Sanford and Adriana Gozdecka-Sanford
33 *Tunisia*, Allan M. Findlay, Anne M. Findlay and Richard I. Lawless
34 *Scotland*, Rev. Ed., Dennis Smith
35 *China*, New Ed., Charles W. Hayford
36 *Qatar*, P. T. H. Unwin
37 *Iceland*, Rev. Ed., Francis R. McBride
38 *Nepal*, John Whelpton
39 *Haiti*, Rev. Ed., Frances Chambers
40 *Sudan*, Rev. Ed., M. W. Daly
41 *Vatican City State*, Michael J. Walsh

42 *Iraq*, Second Ed., C. H. Bleaney
43 *United Arab Emirates*, Rev. Ed., Frank A. Clements
44 *Nicaragua*, Rev. Ed., Ralph Lee Woodward, Jr.
45 *Jamaica*, Rev. Ed., K. E. Ingram
46 *Australia*, Second Ed., I. Kepars
47 *Morocco*, Rev. Ed., Anne M. Findlay and Allan M. Findlay
48 *Mexico*, Rev. Ed., George Philip
49 *Bahrain*, P. T. H. Unwin
50 *Yemen*, Rev. Ed., Paul Auchterlonie
51 *Zambia*, Anne M. Bliss and J. A. Rigg
52 *Puerto Rico*, Elena E. Cevallos
53 *Namibia*, Rev. Ed., Stanley Schoeman and Elna Schoeman
54 *Tanzania*, Rev. Ed., Colin Darch
55 *Jordan*, Rev. Ed., Vartan Amadouny
56 *Kuwait*, Rev. Ed., Frank A. Clements
57 *Brazil*, Rev. Ed., John Dickenson
58 *Israel*, Second Ed., C. H. Bleaney
59 *Romania*, Rev. Ed., Peter Siani-Davies and Mary Siani-Davies
60 *Spain*, Second Ed., Graham Shields
61 *Atlantic Ocean*, H. G. R. King
62 *Canada*, Ernest Ingles
63 *Cameroon*, Rev. Ed., Mark W. DeLancey and Mark D. DeLancey
64 *Malta*, Rev. Ed., David M. Boswell and Brian W. Beeley
65 *Thailand*, Rev. Ed., David Smyth
66 *Austria*, Rev. Ed., Michael Mitchell
67 *Norway*, Leland B. Sather
68 *Czechoslovakia*, David Short
69 *Irish Republic*, Michael Owen Shannon
70 *Pacific Basin and Oceania*, Gerald W. Fry and Rufino Mauricio
71 *Portugal*, P. T. H. Unwin
72 *West Germany*, Donald S. Detwiler and Ilse E. Detwiler
73 *Syria*, Rev. Ed., Neil Quilliam
74 *Trinidad and Tobago*, Frances Chambers
75 *Cuba*, Jean Stubbs, Lila Haines and Meic F. Haines
76 *Barbados*, Robert B. Potter and Graham M. S. Dann
77 *East Germany*, Ian Wallace
78 *Mozambique*, Colin Darch
79 *Libya*, Richard I. Lawless
80 *Sweden*, Leland B. Sather and Alan Swanson

81 *Iran*, Reza Navabpour
82 *Dominica*, Robert A. Myers
83 *Denmark*, Rev. Ed., LeeAnn Iovanni
84 *Paraguay*, Rev. Ed., R. Andrew Nickson
85 *Indian Ocean*, Julia J. Gotthold with the assistance of Donald W. Gotthold
86 *Egypt*, Ragai N. Makar
87 *Gibraltar*, Graham J. Shields
88 *The Netherlands*, Peter King and Michael Wintle
89 *Bolivia*, Gertrude M. Yeager
90 *Papua New Guinea*, Fraiser McConnell
91 *The Gambia*, David P. Gamble
92 *Somalia*, Mark W. DeLancey, Sheila L. Elliott, December Green, Kenneth J. Menkhaus, Mohammad Haji Moqtar, Peter J. Schraeder
93 *Brunei*, Sylvia C. Engelen Krausse and Gerald H. Krausse
94 *Albania*, Rev. Ed., Antonia Young
95 *Singapore*, Stella R. Quah and Jon S. T. Quah
96 *Guyana*, Frances Chambers
97 *Chile*, Harold Blakemore
98 *El Salvador*, Ralph Lee Woodward, Jr.
99 *The Arctic*, H. G. R. King
100 *Nigeria*, Rev. Ed., Ruby Bell-Gam and David Uru Iyam
101 *Ecuador*, David Corkhill
102 *Uruguay*, Henry Finch with the assistance of Alicia Casas de Barrán
103 *Japan*, Frank Joseph Shulman
104 *Belgium*, R. C. Riley
105 *Macau*, Richard Louis Edmonds
106 *Philippines*, Jim Richardson
107 *Bulgaria*, Richard J. Crampton
108 *The Bahamas*, Paul G. Boultbee
109 *Peru*, John Robert Fisher
110 *Venezuela*, D. A. G. Waddell
111 *Dominican Republic*, Kai Schoenhals
112 *Colombia*, Robert H. Davis
113 *Taiwan*, Wei-chin Lee
114 *Switzerland*, Heinz K. Meier and Regula A. Meier
115 *Hong Kong*, Ian Scott
116 *Bhutan*, Ramesh C. Dogra
117 *Suriname*, Rosemarijn Hoefte
118 *Djibouti*, Peter J. Schraeder

119 *Grenada*, Kai Schoenhals
120 *Monaco*, Grace L. Hudson
121 *Guinea-Bissau*, Rosemary Galli
122 *Wales*, Gwilym Huws and D. Hywel E. Roberts
123 *Cape Verde*, Caroline S. Shaw
124 *Ghana*, Robert A. Myers
125 *Greenland*, Kenneth E. Miller
126 *Costa Rica*, Charles L. Stansifer
127 *Siberia*, David N. Collins
128 *Tibet*, John Pinfold
129 *Northern Ireland*, Michael Owen Shannon
130 *Argentina*, Alan Biggins
131 *Côte d'Ivoire*, Morna Daniels
132 *Burma*, Patricia M. Herbert
133 *Laos*, Helen Cordell
134 *Montserrat*, Riva Berleant-Schiller
135 *Afghanistan*, Schuyler Jones
136 *Equatorial Guinea*, Randall Fegley
137 *Turks and Caicos Islands*, Paul G. Boultbee
138 *Virgin Islands*, Verna Penn Moll
139 *Honduras*, Pamela F. Howard-Reguindin
140 *Mauritius*, Pramila Ramgulam Bennett
141 *Mauritania*, Simonetta Calderini, Delia Cortese, James L. A. Webb, Jr.
142 *Timor*, Ian Rowland
143 *St. Vincent and the Grenadines*, Robert B. Potter
144 *Texas*, James Marten
145 *Burundi*, Morna Daniels
146 *Hawai'i*, Nancy J. Morris and Love Dean
147 *Vietnam*, David Marr and Kristine Alilunas-Rodgers
148 *Sierra Leone*, Margaret Binns and Tony Binns
149 *Gabon*, David Gardinier
150 *Botswana*, John A. Wiseman
151 *Angola*, Richard Black
152 *Central African Republic*, Pierre Kalck
153 *Seychelles*, George Bennett, with the collaboration of Pramila Ramgulam Bennett
154 *Rwanda*, Randall Fegley
155 *Berlin*, Ian Wallace
156 *Mongolia*, Judith Nordby
157 *Liberia*, D. Elwood Dunn

158 *Maldives*, Christopher H. B. Reynolds
159 *Liechtenstein*, Regula A. Meier
160 *England*, Alan Day
161 *The Baltic States*, Inese A. Smith and Marita V. Grunts
162 *Congo*, Randall Fegley
163 *Armenia*, Vrej Nersessian
164 *Niger*, Lynda F. Zamponi
165 *Madagascar*, Hilary Bradt
166 *Senegal*, Roy Dilley and Jerry Eades
167 *Andorra*, Barry Taylor
168 *Netherlands Antilles and Aruba*, Kai Schoenhals
169 *Burkina Faso*, Samuel Decalo
170 *Indonesia*, Sylvia C. Engelen Krausse and Gerald H. Krausse
171 *The Antarctic*, Janice Meadows, William Mills and H. G. R. King
172 *São Tomé and Príncipe*, Caroline S. Shaw
173 *Fiji*, G. E. Gorman and J. J. Mills
174 *St. Kitts-Nevis*, Verna Penn Moll
175 *Martinique*, Janet Crane
176 *Zaire*, Dawn Bastian Williams, Robert W. Lesh and Andrea L. Stamm
177 *Chad*, George Joffé and Valérie Day-Viaud
178 *Togo*, Samuel Decalo
179 *Ethiopia*, Stuart Munro-Hay and Richard Pankhurst
180 *Punjab*, Darshan Singh Tatla and Ian Talbot
181 *Eritrea*, Randall Fegley
182 *Antigua and Barbuda*, Riva Berleant-Schiller and Susan Lowes with Milton Benjamin
183 *Alaska*, Marvin W. Falk
184 *The Falkland Islands*, Alan Day
185 *St Lucia*, Janet Henshall Momsen
186 *Slovenia*, Cathie Carmichael
187 *Cayman Islands*, Paul G. Boultbee
188 *San Marino*, Adrian Edwards and Chris Michaelides
189 *London*, Heather Creaton
190 *Western Sahara*, Anthony G. Pazzanita
191 *Guinea*, Margaret Binns
192 *Benin*, J. S. Eades and Chris Allen
193 *Madrid*, Graham Shields
194 *Tasmania*, I. Kepars
195 *Prague*, Susie Lunt

196 *Samoa*, H. G. A. Hughes
197 *St. Helena, Ascension and Tristan da Cunha*, Alan Day
198 *Budapest*, Mátyás Sárközi
199 *Lisbon*, John Laidlar
200 *Cambodia*, Helen Jarvis
201 *Vienna*, C. M. Peniston-Bird
202 *Corsica*, Grace L. Hudson
203 *Amsterdam*, André van Os
204 *Korea*, J. E. Hoare
205 *Bermuda*, Paul G. Boultbee and David F. Raine
206 *Paris*, Frances Chambers
207 *Mali*, Andrea Stamm, Dawn Bastian and Robert Myers
208 *The Maghreb*, Anthony G. Pazzanita

209 *The Channel Islands*, Vince Gardiner
210 *French Guiana*, Janet Crane
211 *Québec*, Alain-G. Gagnon
212 *The Basque Region*, Geoffrey West
213 *Sicily*, Valentina Olivastri
214 *Tokyo*, J. S. Eades
215 *Crete*, Adrian Edwards
216 *Croatia*, Cathie Carmichael
217 *Tonga*, Martin Daly
218 *Uzbekistan*, Reuel Hanks
219 *Czech Republic*, Vlad'ka Edmondson and David Short
220 *Micronesia*, Monique Carriveau Storie and William L. Wuerch
221 *Azores*, Miguel Moniz

Contents

PREFACE xv

INTRODUCTION xix

THE COUNTRY AND ITS PEOPLE 1

GEOGRAPHY AND GEOLOGY 8
General, physical and demographic   8
Regional   10
Maps and atlases   12

TOURISM AND TRAVEL GUIDES 14
Central and Eastern Europe   14
Czech Republic   15
Tourist events   18
Prague and regions   18
   Prague   18
   Regions   21

FLORA AND FAUNA 23
Flora   23
Fauna   25

PREHISTORY AND ARCHAEOLOGY 27

HERALDRY 30

HISTORY 32
General   32
   Central and Eastern Europe   32
   Czech Lands   34

Contents

Early mediaeval, mediaeval and early modern history   40
    General   40
    Reformation, Jan Hus, Hussitism   41
    George of Poděbrady   44
    Anabaptism and the Czech Brethren   44
Habsburg period (16th century to 1918)   45
    General   45
    16th to 19th century   47
    1900-18   52
Independence to Munich (1918-38)   54
    General   54
    Tomáš Garrigue Masaryk (1850-1937) and the Masaryk family   56
Munich and the Second World War (1938-45)   60
    The Munich crisis, Edvard Beneš   60
    Second World War and the Czech resistance abroad   62
Post-war period (1945-)   65
    General   65
    Prague Spring and Soviet intervention in 1968   69
    The Velvet Revolution of 1989 and the dissolution of Czechoslovakia   73
        General   73
        Václav Havel   75

NATIONALITIES AND MINORITIES   79
General and historical   79
The Roma (the gypsies)   81
The Jews   86
The Germans   89
Other nationalities and minorities   93

EXTRATERRITORIAL POPULATIONS   94

FOLKLORE AND FOLK ART   99

RELIGION AND THEOLOGY   102
General   102
Non-Roman Catholic denominations and ideological groups   107
The issue of the ordination of women   108
Religious orders   109
Modern theologians   110
Miscellaneous   111
Religious symbolism   112

SOCIAL CONDITIONS, WOMEN'S ISSUES, CHILDREN'S ISSUES,
    HEALTH AND WELFARE   113

Social conditions   113
Women's issues   118
Children's issues   121
Health care   122

EDUCATION 125
General   125
Comenius   128

STATISTICS 132

PHILOSOPHY 136

POLITICS 137
Political history   137
The Communist era, 1948-89   141
Contemporary: post-1989   144
General   144
Separation of Czechs and Slovaks, 1 January 1993   144
Czech Republic, 1993-   146

INTERNATIONAL RELATIONS 153
General   153
International security   159

CONSTITUTION AND LAW 161
Central and Eastern Europe   161
Czech Republic   164
Business law   165
Local government   166

ECONOMY 168
Reference   168
Economic history   170
Post-1989   173
Central and Eastern Europe   173
Czech Republic   178
The tax system   184
Doing business   185
Miscellaneous   186
Periodicals   187

BANKING AND FINANCE 189
Central and Eastern Europe   189
Czech Republic   192

Contents

General   192
The Stock Exchange   195

AGRICULTURE 197

INDUSTRY AND TRADE 200
General   200
Retailing and services   204
Industrial sectors   205

TRANSPORT 212

SCIENCE AND TECHNOLOGY 216

URBANIZATION AND HOUSING POLICY 220

THE ENVIRONMENT 225

SPORT AND RECREATION 229

LANGUAGE (Compiled by David Short) 235
General and historical   235
Dictionaries   236
   General   236
   Specialist   242
Grammars and textbooks   245
Miscellaneous   249

LITERATURE 253
Central and Eastern European   253
Czech   255
   History and criticism   255
   Translations and criticism of the works of individual writers   264
   Anthologies   277
Émigré literature   281
Literature of other nationalities   289
   German   289
      General   289
      Franz Kafka   290
   Other   296

THE ARTS 298
General   298
Visual arts   300
Applied arts   305

Theatre   308
Film   309
Architecture   313

MUSIC   321
General   321
Bedřich Smetana   324
Antonín Dvořák   325
Leoš Janáček   328
Bohuslav Martinů   333

FOOD AND DRINK   336

THE MEDIA AND PUBLISHING   338

NEWSPAPERS AND PERIODICALS   341
Czech-language newspapers and periodicals   341
English-language newspapers and periodicals   342
Scholarly journals   344
Business periodicals   346

ARCHIVES, LIBRARIES, MUSEUMS AND GALLERIES   348
Archives and libraries   348
Museums and galleries   351

BIBLIOGRAPHIES   355

INDEX OF AUTHORS   361

INDEX OF TITLES   375

INDEX OF SUBJECTS   403

MAP OF THE CZECH REPUBLIC   431

Preface

The task of preparing this bibliography was daunting from many aspects: I was aware of the magnitude of the quantity of publications on the subject which had appeared in recent years; David Short's *Czecho-slovakia* (volume 68, World Bibliographical Series, 1968), the book I was updating, is very highly regarded by its users, which gave the challenge another dimension; I abandoned the world of bibliography some years ago for freelance work, which fits in better with bringing up a family.

Looking back now, I realize that not for one moment have I regretted accepting the offer from the publisher. I derived immense enjoyment from browsing through books from such a variety of fields, with the common theme being the country to which I am inescapably committed and which I greatly respect. I renewed some old acquaintances from the national libraries and university world and was touched by the moral and practical support they offered. It was a surprisingly pleasurable journey back in time. Bibliography may be a dry subject to study but the work can be fascinating and seems to lead to dealing with the nicest people.

The core of the research was done in the British Library collections. This was hampered by the mammoth move which the institution undertook from Bloomsbury to St Pancras. Nevertheless, all of the frustration of having to wait for 'books on the move', for the Science Reading Rooms to open, the nostalgia for the gracious Reading Room in the British Museum, was overcome and forgotten during the last months of work in the efficient and pleasing environment of the new British Library.

The collections of the School of Slavonic and East European Studies, University of London were the second major source.

I have also used other collections, such as the library of the East European Trade Council, and the Czech Centre, both in London; I had a wonderful day browsing through bookshops in Wenceslas Square, looking for the latest English-language books published in Prague, and spent many a pleasant hour in the bookshops in Brno and visiting major London bookshops. Publishers' catalogues of US, UK and Czech provenance were researched, as well as those of specialist bookshops.

A contemporary bibliography inevitably becomes outdated on the day the manuscript is closed. There are other factors. David Short in the preface to the original *Czechoslovakia* admits that 'the final outcome may, despite the size, contain omissions which this or that user might deem indefensible. Such omissions will be a consequence in part of the semi-random pattern by which I found material surfacing, and in part of the need to pare down one or two of the sections, which were covered by large numbers of publications'. The same statement could be applied to this update.

Preference has been given to English-language material but there are entries for books published in German, French and Czech, and one or two in other languages. Most of these would have summaries in English or include papers in English. The majority of the material listed is books, on the principle that books are on the whole easier to trace and more accessible than periodical works. It is rare for any work cited not to have either a bibliography or references leading the reader to further study. In the areas where up-to-date information is of greatest significance, such as industry or the plight of the Roma, the sections rely heavily on articles. Articles are also included to complement book entries, such as reviews of translated fiction.

Some entries have been taken from the original *Czechoslovakia*, either because they are classics in their field or because they complete the coverage of a certain subject area. There is a small, inevitable overlap with the bibliography on *Prague* by Susie Lunt (volume 195 in the World Bibliographical Series, 1997).

In some subject areas, such as economy, politics and guidebooks, a fairly ruthless selection had to be made, due to the volume of material that has been published. It is useful to note, again, that most, if not all, books and articles listed contain bibliographical data, notes and references to lead the researcher to further reading.

Within the chapters, items are generally ordered approximately chronologically, where there is a historical dimension; in some sections, ordering represents a gradation downwards from the more to the less significant (the term 'less significant' should not be interpreted here as 'of lesser value'), or the arrangement is from general to particular (e.g. works on Central Europe generally would be listed before works specific to the Czech Republic only). The 'Bibliography' chapter lists mostly major general or national bibliographies. Subject bibliographies are included in specific chapters. The same rule was applied to English-language periodicals.

David Short had been very helpful well before becoming officially involved as co-author, with critical support and the first editing of a large section of the manuscript. I have received invaluable and extensive help from the Curator of Czech and Slovak Collections at the British Library, my former colleague and a friend of many years, Děvana Pavlík. Another former colleague and long-time friend, Tania Konn of Glasgow University, directed me to valuable research sources, and Vlasta Gyenes and Lenka Peacock went out of their way to be of assistance with research in the library of the School of Slavonic Studies, University of London. My gratitude goes to the editors of ABC-Clio Publishers: to Dr Robert G. Neville for his encouragement at the conception of this book, to Julia Goddard and to Anna Fabrizio, who edited the bibliography with great care and proved to be a most pleasant and understanding person to work with.

I thought originally that I would dedicate this book to my family. They assured me that they have in no way been influenced or affected by this addition to my already considerable workload. Being somewhat taken aback by this statement, I allowed it to germinate, thought of people or institutions I could dedicate the book to, before concluding that such a statement is a compliment. This book is, therefore, and after all, dedicated to my family.

Vlaďka Edmondson
1999

Introduction

While it was never strictly true that Czechoslovakia, forerunner of the Czech Republic when still united with Slovakia, was a small country of which we (the British in particular) knew little or nothing, it is eminently not at all true of the relatively young (and even smaller) Czech Republic itself. This improved profile is in no small way due to its intriguing, if not quite charismatic, first president, the dramatist, philosopher and former dissident Václav Havel.

Following the collapse of Communism in 1989 and the emergence of the new independent republic on 1 January 1993, the Czech Republic instantly became a major tourist destination for people from all over Western Europe and from further afield. For many it was simply the nearest of the former Iron-Curtain countries, while others went in the foreknowledge that Prague is undoubtedly one of the finest of European cities, perhaps a little unkempt through the previous regime's neglect, though in many respects preserved largely untouched by the wars of the 20th century. Such visitors were quick to discover, thanks in part to rapidly established town-twinning and other relations, that the same goes for scores of other towns and cities all over the country. And not only were foreign tourists (and, in time, film-makers) going *to* the country in droves, Czechs themselves became very conspicuous outside their own frontiers as travel restrictions disappeared overnight and foreign travel became something on which they could spend their often vast savings, accumulated during the last years of Communism when there had been little to spend money on at home.

The new political freedoms and the increasingly capitalist economic conditions brought with them a completely new outlook, which, for all the residual 'Eastern' patterns of thought and action, have drawn the country increasingly into Western, or West European spheres. Accordingly, the Czech Republic became one of the frontrunners among the ex-Soviet bloc countries to develop defence and economic ties with the West, through progressively closer cooperation with NATO and the

European Union in particular. The Czech Republic became a member of NATO in March 1999, and membership of the European Union and other bodies cannot be far off. Such closeness brings with it its downside, in that the country's internal problems impinge on, or overflow into, its new friendlier neighbours, whether in the consequences of an imperfect understanding of trade and business relations, or in the failure to cope promptly and adequately with its major minority 'problem', the gypsies, now known only as Roma.

The Roma are the only sizeable minority, and the numbers are growing thanks to migration westwards from Slovakia and the Balkans. Other groups trying to move westwards are also finding themselves trapped in the Czech Republic, including Albanians, Romanians, Kosovars, and even Kurds and others from further afield, though these do not yet constitute 'minorities' in any accepted sense; nor do the semi-permanent Russians and Ukrainians, or – arriving from the opposite direction – the Americans, Britons, Australians and Irish, for whom the country has provided a congenial place to engage in small business operations, or simply to drop out of the rat-race.

Genuine minorities living among the roughly ten million Czechs are the infinitesimal remnants of the former Jewish and German populations (respectively depleted during, and expelled after, the last war), relatively small pockets of Poles in the Silesian part of northern Moravia, a dispersed half-million or so Slovaks who elected to remain in (or move to) the Czech Republic in preference to Slovakia (whose post-independence political development did not, for many, inspire confidence), and a largish dispersed number of Vietnamese, beneficiaries under Communism of sundry fraternal aid programmes who have been allowed to stay on for the time being. They have proved to be agile small businessmen and market traders to whom the Czechs themselves have grown quite accustomed, and since they are seen more as a boon than as trouble-makers, they do not suffer the same kind of prejudice as encountered by the Roma.

Czechs themselves constitute minorities in various parts of the world. The internal migration which occurred within Austria-Hungary accounts for the fairly isolated communities in various parts of former Yugoslavia. There are also pockets across the border in Poland, and a dispersed population in Austria, especially Vienna. The Czechoslovak heritage means that there are also Czechs dispersed throughout Slovakia. Further afield, as a product of several waves of emigration for religious, economic or political reasons right through modern history, there are quite considerable populations in Canada, Nebraska, Texas and some of the large industrial cities of the United States. A large proportion of the once sizeable minority in Volhynia (Ukraine) has recently, since the Czech Republic's independence, 'come home', though not without some difficulties with reintegration.

The Czech Republic lies at the heart of Europe, a privilege also claimed by several of its neighbours. Prague, the capital, lies only fractionally north of the 50th Parallel, level with the Lizard Peninsular in Cornwall, and a line drawn due north-south through the city passes through the middle of Sweden and just misses Naples. It is about 645 miles east of London, about half-way to the Black Sea.

It is a small country of c. 30,450 square miles and a population of c. 10.3 million (1991 census). It consists of the historic Lands of the Bohemian Crown (Bohemia, Moravia and part of Silesia), still often referred to as 'the Czech Lands' (also within the present volume). Former Czechoslovakia consisted additionally of Slovakia, and between the wars, during the First Czechoslovak Republic, there was another province in the far east, then called Subcarpathian Ruthenia (lost at the onset of the Second World War and absorbed into Ukraine after the war).

During the Second World War Czechoslovakia ceased to exist. Slovakia became a quasi-independent state heavily dependent on its German allies, while the western part, minus its largely German-populated fringes (Sudetenland), became the German 'Protectorate of Bohemia and Moravia', that is, a reduced version of the modern state.

Since the war, but especially after February 1948 – then described by the Communists as Victorious February, after their seizure of power – Czechoslovakia fell firmly within the Soviet sphere of influence, economically as a member of Comecon, or the Council for Mutual Economic Assistance, and militarily as a member of the Warsaw Pact. These ties were rapidly loosened after the Velvet Revolution of 1989.

Further back in history, the mediaeval Kingdom of Bohemia was for many centuries the main power in Central Europe. Its kings became Holy Roman Emperors. Even after the Thirty Years' War (1618-48), which brought the Czechs under Habsburg control (after the Battle of the White Mountain in 1620), the Czechs did not simply disappear from history, though the traditional Czech label for the period which ensued, the Age of Darkness, indicates the sense of hiatus that lasted up to the National Revival at the end of the 18th, and the beginning of the 19th, century.

The Czech National Revival really marks the beginning of modern Czech history. Initially it was connected with a recodification of the standard ('literary') language (in fact based on an already obsolete model) and the deliberate provision of a corpus of original and translated literature in the language. This was the domain of such figures as Josef Dobrovský (the 'father of Slavonic studies') and Josef

Jungmann. Then followed efforts to equip the language with the vocabulary to cope with modern arts and sciences, the birth of a new generation of national historians and the writing of the nation's history by such writers as František Palacký. New 'national' music was written, by composers including Bedřich Smetana and, later, Antonín Dvořák. This new music was heavily coloured by the folk idiom and rather unfairly ignored the many earlier composers of Czech origin, contemporaries of Mozart, Beethoven and Schubert, who had been at the forefront of European mainstream music. In recent years, there has been a 'rediscovery' of works by Mysliveček – 'Il divino Boemo', Stamic, Dušek, Tomášek, Voříšek and others. Similar national trends showed themselves in painting and sculpture, with people like Antonín Mánes ('founder of the Czech landscape school'), his son Josef ('founder of Czech national painting'), and the latter's successor Mikoláš Aleš; the latter two belong to the generation which created the National Theatre (which opened in 1881, before burning down and being re-opened in 1883).

During the 19th century, though in fits and starts, and with some retreats, Czech schools became firmly established. Education has always carried a high premium with the Czechs, and they are very conscious that the 'father of modern education', Jan Ámos Komenský (known to the outside world as Comenius), was one of their number. A major event was the division, in 1882, of the Prague university into separate Czech and German institutions. Charles University (founded 1348), as it was originally called, after its founder Charles IV, and as it was renamed in 1920, is the country's premier institution of higher education. The first large national encyclopaedia was Rieger's *Slovník naučný* (1859-74. 10 vols. with later supplements), followed by the larger *Ottův slovník naučný* (1888-1901. 28 vols. also with supplements), a work so revered that it has recently seen a facsimile reprint.

The presidency is a function of great significance. It is currently held by Václav Havel, who adopted this mantle to universal acclaim shortly after the country's independence. Various actions have since then rather dented his popularity at home, although internationally he still enjoys considerable prestige, with countless foreign universities falling over each other to award him their honorary doctorates. The presidential office, and to an extent Havel himself, is seen as a continuation of the heritage of Tomáš Garrigue Masaryk, founder-president of Czechoslovakia, and his successor Edvard Beneš. Masaryk had been a somewhat Victorian liberal philosopher-politician who enjoyed immense personal prestige, almost reverence, even being referred to as 'tatíček' ('daddy' is the literal, but totally inadequate translation). Beneš had the unenviable task of coping with the onset, duration and aftermath of the

Second World War. In the eyes of many he failed in the end by not preventing the post-war squabbling which let the Communists in. Moreover, in the eyes of others he had failed at the beginning, by bowing to pressure from the appeasers instead of forcing their hand by offering armed resistance to Germany. Beneš died shortly after the Communist take-over in 1948, to be followed by Czechoslovakia's first 'worker-president', the hard-line Klement Gottwald. He was followed in turn by Antonín Zápotocký (1953-57) and Antonín Novotný (1957-68), the man under whom, though no thanks to whom, the 'thaw' set in. He is remembered for his moves to stem the thaw, his failure to understand the Slovaks, and as the man under whom the pre-1968 reformist trend eventually got underway. The economic and social reforms put forward in the mid- to late 1960s culminated in his removal from both the First-Secretaryship of the Communist Party and the presidency, to be replaced by the Slovak Alexander Dubček and General Ludvík Svoboda respectively. In this configuration the presidency lost much of its importance, though Svoboda himself was a popular figurehead and overseer of the reforms that continued beneath him. The period 1967-69, otherwise known as the 'Prague Spring' (after the annual Prague music festival), has been so extensively written about that nothing more need be said here, beyond the reminder that in August 1968 things came to an abrupt halt when Warsaw Pact troops intervened. Dubček was soon ousted, to be replaced by Gustáv Husák; President Svoboda served on until 1975, though a very sick man in his last years, after which time Husák once more combined the offices of First Secretary and President. Under Husák, Czechoslovakia became largely 'normalized', in the East European sense of the word, and the economy fairly stabilized, though not in a way that was sustainable in the long term. Opposition was largely silenced, though Charter 77 remained vociferous, if with but a modest following. Underground literature continued to be written, published either abroad or by *samizdat*, though its impact was not much greater than that of the underground religious, and later educational, activity as far as the silent majority was concerned. Nonetheless it was these spheres which maintained continuity with the 'Prague Spring', a continuity personified by Václav Havel. That period continues to have great resonance for the Czechs and is seen as a direct and moderately dynamic precursor of the events of 1989. For it not only brought a temporary loosening of the Communist Party's grip, but was also the period which saw the beginnings of Czech-Slovak federalism, though the country became federal in name only in 1990.

The complete break between Czechs and Slovaks may now seem to be merely the inevitable extension of the federalization process and a solution which, for different reasons, suited both sides. With other political leaders on each side it might perhaps not have happened, and there are plenty of people who to this day regret that it did. However, happen it did, and as the distance between the Czech and Slovak republics grows – with progressively tougher customs and excise regulations applying between them, with each treating the other as equally 'foreign' as any other third state, for instance in postal rates, and with the different rates at which they are 'approximating' to the European Union – it is extremely unlikely that the process will ever be reversed.

The de-Sovietized independence of Czechoslovakia and, soon after, of the Czech Republic, was greeted by a wave of popular enthusiasm. What was lacking, however, was a proper perspective on Western democracy, on political pluralism, on the market economy, on the rule of law. . . . Thus the failure of paradise on earth to arrive overnight led to profound disillusionment. Old attitudes, regarding work or welfare, for example, were slow to change; new legislation on, say, business or housing, was, or seemed to be, stitched together with a red-hot needle and burning thread, and was often reactive instead of proactive. Latent entrepreneurial skills found ample space to apply, and all too frequently misapply, themselves. Public and private corruption proved to be as prevalent as a kind of Parkinson's Law permitted it to be (filling every space opened up to it), to the dismay of those who had wishfully thought that their nation was more 'naturally good' and so not given to such practices. The weaknesses of what had been an apparently fairly solid economic (and legal) base eventually became revealed, so that after six or seven years numerous companies (and the remaining state enterprises) had found themselves in increasing, and sometimes terminal, difficulties. Despite all of this, however, there remains a hope that the tide will change, improvements will come, the work ethic will return, association with the European Union will, on balance, be a boon rather than a burden, and even the seemingly intractable Roma problem will be resolved. Most tellingly of all, few people really hanker after a return of the pre-1989 regime, in spite of the fact that opinion polls reveal that many sorely regret the passing of some of the social securities it guaranteed.

The country still enjoys a high reputation among tourists, though the peak has by now passed and the rise in cases where tourists have been, frankly, ripped off needs to be checked. This interest on the part of the foreign private individual has led to a boom in materials for learning the language; and more Czech literature is being translated than ever before. What might be described as 'official' interest in the country – no longer a potential enemy – focuses more on the social sciences, economics in particular.

Economic and political integration with the rest of western Europe will undoubtedly be achieved, if at the price of some nivelization and the loss of a little of what gives the Czechs their particular identity. The disappearance of the national inferiority complex, which is encapsulated in the phrase *malý český člověk* (the 'little Czech man'), often quoted with a kind of inverted pride, could only be beneficial, however. From this point of view, the smaller European populations – the Dutch, the Danes, the Irish and the Finns – constitute salutary targets of comparison. The country has already played its part in Bosnia, the Gulf and Kosovo, and it continues to make a positive impact in such fields as music, film and sport.

David Short
1999

The Country and Its People

1 **The Times guide to the peoples of Europe.**
Edited by Felipe Fernández-Armesto. London: Times Books, 1994.
416p. maps. bibliog.

The editor provides an introduction which seeks to define the European identity, followed by individual chapters on national identities. The criteria used for classification is geographic with the exception of the last chapter, twelve, 'Dispersed peoples', p. 385-400, on the Jews and the gypsies, their history, migratory patterns and culture. The Czechs are covered in chapter seven, 'The Carpathian region', p. 245-51, which gives a concise description of the land, history, religion, language, culture and trade and industry.

2 **Dějiny obyvatelstva českých zemí.** (A history of the inhabitants of the Czech Lands.)
Edited by Ludmila Fialová. Prague: Mladá Fronta, 1996. 399p. maps.

Claims to be the first complete publication on the demographic history of the Czech Lands, covering more than 1,000 years to the present day. Numerous researchers cooperated on this publication: an anthropologist, a historian, a sociologist, a demographer. Processing the data using the method of historical demography, archaeology and sociology, they map the demographic progress on the Czech territory: the settlement of the Czech Lands, the influence of wars and epidemics on the growth or decline of the number of inhabitants, the development of the family, birth rate and mortality rate as reflected in history, and migration from villages to towns. All this is well documented by maps, illustrations, photographs, charts and tables. The first census under the Austrian Empress Maria Theresa took place in 1754, and it was the first census of this type in Europe. There is a wealth of material for the last 200 years, which occupies the largest section of the book. The long-term demographic trends are aligned with general developments in Europe.

3 **The little Czech and the great Czech nation.**
Ladislav Holý. Cambridge, England: Cambridge University Press, 1996. 226p. bibliog. (Cambridge Studies in Social and Cultural Anthropology).
The author was a social anthropologist, born and educated in the Czech Republic. In the 1970s Holý joined Queen's University, Belfast and later the University of St Andrew's where he was promoted to the Chair of Anthropology in 1987. Thus, where Czech issues are concerned, he had the insight of an outsider, with a cosmopolitan perspective. The work on this study in Czech national identity, politics and culture was begun before the changes of 1989, and when the revolution came Holý was able to follow the developments in a theoretically informed way, concentrating on the symbolic ideas in Czech culture which, according to his deductions, were important in making the revolution a 'velvet' one. There is little material available in English on the gender issue in the Czech Republic and this book provides some well-researched information on modern Czech society. The issues of social equality, tradition, and the concept of culture, important to the Czechs, are highlighted as well as the issue of two separate nations and states, Czech and Slovak. The attitude of the natives to émigrés is also mentioned. The book is accessible, although inevitably it requires from the reader a fair knowledge of Czech affairs. The title refers to the 'Little Czech', or *malý český člověk*, or what is sometimes seen as the expression of the national inferiority complex.

4 **The coasts of Bohemia: a Czech history.**
Derek Sayer, translated from the Czech by Alena Sayer. Princeton, New Jersey: Princeton University Press, 1998. 442p. maps. bibliog.
Despite its subtitle, this is not a history book in the conventional chronological form, but a series of well-written studies of the cultural background of the Czechs. Sayer, a Professor of Sociology at the University of Alberta in Edmonton, utilizes his knowledge of historical sociology to tackle the complex dimensions of Czech culture, drawing on a multitude of literary, visual and documentary sources.

5 **Czechoslovakia.**
M. J. Burke. London: Batsford, 1976. 237p. (Batsford Travel Books).
This remained for a long time one of the best general works available on the Czech Lands. It is partly historical and partly geographical and contains a mass of information on many aspects of day-to-day life and the management of the country at that time. Designed more to attract than guide, it is a work which will be of interest to the general or academic reader, as well as tourists.

6 **Questions of identity: Czech and Slovak ideas of nationality and personality.**
Robert B. Pynsent. Budapest, London; New York: Central European University Press, 1994. 244p. bibliog.
'. . . This book discusses the prickly relationship between individual persons and nations and the world surrounding them.' Professor Pynsent identifies an example of nation-building, the creation of a Slav, as well as the Slovak, nation, in the work of Pavel Šafařík and Jan Kollár, two Slovak scholars. Their work on Pan-Slavism in the first half of the 19th century had great influence in Central and Eastern Europe, traces

2

of which are still in evidence today. The book is introduced by the chapter, 'The questions of identity and responsibility in Václav Havel', followed by an in-depth discussion on the Decadents, and concludes with a chapter on 'Czech self-definition through martyrs', a particularly Czech trait. St Wenceslas, Jan Hus, St John Nepomucene, Colonel Švec, Julius Fučík and Jan Palach are each given a section and represent various periods of Czech history. The author provides detailed bibliographical notes and an index.

7 Czech studies: literature, language, culture. České studie: literatura, jazyk, kultura.
Edited by Mojmír Grygar. Amsterdam; Atlanta, Georgia: Rodopi, 1990. 336p. map. bibliog.

This paperback, with a parallel Czech-English title, is a medley of subjects and forms, published on the occasion of the twentieth anniversary of the establishment of the department of Czech studies as a major subject at Amsterdam University. The contributions, which are in Czech, English and German, are from contemporary authorities on the Czech language from around the world. The range of subjects is wide: David Short writes on 'The vocative and its morphology in Czech and Slovak', Milan Jankovič on Bohumil Hrabal, and Robert Pynsent on Mácha's *May*; there are three articles on Jaroslav Hašek; and a historian from Olomouc, Libuše Hrabová (the contents page calls her Anna Hrabová), writes on the early mediaeval culture of the Slavs between the rivers Labe and Rhine.

8 100 perel Čech – 100 Perlen Böhmens – 100 pearls of Bohemia.
Edited by Oldřich Holan. Litvínov, Czech Republic: Dialog, [1993]. 105p. map.

This beautifully produced book in the coffee-table format is worth mentioning if only as a curio of post-Communist publishing. For it has no stated author, the authors in effect being the ten contributing photographers, of which the editor is one; that the usual publishing details are given only on the dust-jacket, which is the short-life part of any publication; and that unlike many luxury publications (and other cultural effects in the early post-Communist period) which were suddenly beyond the average Czech pocket, it was specifically published with sufficient commercial sponsorship for it to remain affordable. Another oddity is that a small statistical table (on the country's area, population structure, GDP) is included, but on the rear fly-leaf of the dust-jacket. It consists of 100 original (i.e. not hackneyed) photographs of many beautiful sites and sights from all over Bohemia, with trilingual thumbnail sketches of the relevant topography, history etc. (including such information as that Veltrusy chateau was used in the filming of Miloš Forman's *Amadeus*). One or two (Jáchymov, Sušice) are not wildly exciting, though in the main the pictures and annotations serve the purpose well. A map inside the front cover identifies the location of the places shown. The same publisher has also produced *100 pearls of Moravia*.

9 Czechoslovakia: the unofficial culture.
Roger Scruton, with additions by Barbara Day, Jiří Gruša, Jessica Gwynne, David Matthews. London[?]: The Claridge Press, [n.d.]. 226p. bibliog.

Prepared for the use of the trustees, visitors and friends of the Jan Hus Educational Foundation. The book starts with abridged Czech history from the introduction of

3

Christianity in the 10th century to 1939. A rather patchy survey of the culture and various art disciplines up to the 1980s follows; it is not easy to navigate owing to the incomplete list of contents, which puts the reader to arduous searching. The indexes do not make up for this deficiency. The text skips from the general to information which requires a well-informed reader. Of interest is Appendix II, p. 188-98, which lists books published in the underground Edice Petlice (Padlock Editions) from 1980-85.

10   **A thousand years of Czech culture: riches from the National Museum in Prague.**
Winston-Salem, North Carolina: Old Salem Inc.; Prague: National Museum, 1996. 166p. map. bibliog.

Published in conjunction with an exhibition of the same title at Old Salem and prepared jointly by the staff of the Museum in Old Salem and the National Museum (Národní museum) in Prague. The volume combines ten essays by Czech scholars with a foreword by Václav Havel, on history, art, Christianity, theatre, music, and folk art, which is so fundamental to Czech culture. Elegantly produced, the work contains numerous colour photographs of exhibits which provide a fair representation of the Czech nation's artistic, historical and cultural achievements. 'The cultural history of the Jews in the Czech Lands', by Lenka Kotrba-Novotná, is on p. 4-45.

11   **The Czechoslovak contribution to world culture.**
Edited by Miroslav Rechcígl, Jr.   The Hague; London, Paris: Mouton, 1964. 682p. bibliog.

Some of the fifty-six essays in this volume recount the contribution of Czechs and Slovaks to various disciplines, while other pieces are directly relevant to the country, the people, individual writers or scholars. The bibliography consists of 1,318 titles in various Western languages; the range of topics covered is broad and the volume also includes a bibliography of bibliographies. The whole work was published on behalf of the Czechoslovak Society of Arts and Sciences in America, which was at the time 'an academy in exile', known widely as SVU, from its Czech name.

12   **Czechoslovakia past and present.**
Edited by Miroslav Rechcígl, Jr.   The Hague; Paris: Mouton, 1968. 2 vols.

Very similar to the item above, the numerous articles in these two volumes offer a microcosmic view of émigré Czech and Slovak scholarly (and less scholarly) writings on many aspects of the country's history, culture, economics, society, arts and sciences. They are the product of the second congress of the Czechoslovak Society of Arts and Sciences in America, the SVU. The sections cover: Czechoslovakia up to the Second World War (seven papers); social and economic aspects of the First Republic (eight papers); the Second World War (five papers); political aspects of Czecho-slovakia under Communism (seven papers); social and economic aspects (nine papers); cultural aspects (seven papers); Czechoslovakia and its neighbours (eight papers, including separate papers on Czechoslovakia's relations with Austria, Hungary, Poland, Romania and what was then Yugoslavia); Czechoslovakia's relations with the Great Powers (four papers; separate attention being given to Germany, Britain and France); Czechs and Slovaks abroad (four papers, mostly on literature and journalism); literature (thirteen papers); linguistics (five papers); history (thirteen papers); music (four papers); fine arts (five papers); social sciences (ten papers);

4

physical, biological and behavioural sciences (nine papers); and a 1,384-entry bibliography of bibliographies and similar works pertaining completely, or partly, to Czechoslovakia. The sectional division is only a partial guide to what the collection includes, and the enquirer is advised to consult the entire contents pages for items that might well have appeared in more than one section.

13 **Czechoslovakia: crossroads and crisis, 1918-88.**
Edited by Norman Stone, Eduard Strouhal. Basingstoke, England: Macmillan; BBC World Service, 1989. 336p. maps. bibliog.

Norman Stone, Professor of Modern History at Oxford, provided an introduction to this collection of essays by various contributors, mostly Czech scholars living in the West. The main thesis of Stone's introduction is that the national characteristics and history of the Czechs are different to those of the Poles and that the Czechs should have fought in 1938, 1948 and 1968. The other editor of the volume, Eduard Strouhal, worked for the Czechoslovak section of the BBC World Service. The essays, which present varied viewpoints, are divided into five sections, the first four being the 'crossroads and crisis' in the modern history of the Czech Lands: the events of 1918 (the origins of Czechoslovakia); 1938 (the Munich crisis); 1948 (the advent of Communism); and 1968 (the Prague Spring and the Czechoslovak economic reforms of the 1960s). The essays assess various aspects of modern Czech history, the role of international relations in the independence of Czechoslovakia in 1918, the question of nationality, Czech Communists and Communism as such, and modern historiography. The fifth and final section covers the whole lifetime of Czechoslovakia, as a republic, to the date of compilation of this book, that is from 1918 to 1988, and consists of two essays: 'The Jews in Czechoslovakia between 1918-1968' by Erich Kulka (p. 271-96); and 'The vicissitudes of the Catholic Church in Czechoslovakia, 1918-1988' by Karel Skalický (p. 297-324). Some of the essays have their own bibliographies and the editors have provided some photographs from modern Czech history and an 'Index' (p. 325-36).

14 **Czechoslovakia: the heritage of ages past; essays in memory of Josef Korbel.**
Edited by Hans Brisch, Ivan Volgyes. Boulder, Colorado: East European Quarterly. Distributed by Columbia University Press, New York, 1979. 239p. bibliog. (East European Monographs, no. 51).

A collection of papers in memory of Josef Korbel, one of the most highly respected Czech émigré writers on history and political science, though his work was by no means confined to Czechoslovakia. The essays provide the student and general reader with a wide range of facts about the Czech Lands. In addition to historical articles on, for example, Hus, the First Republic, the Second World War, and three papers on the 'Prague Spring' period, there are essays on the economy, politics and justice, and 'the Czechoslovak tradition'. The last named, by Bruce Garver, considers the relations and similarities between the Czechs and Slovaks and their history, and also provides a brief historical account of Czechoslovak arts and letters, religion, agriculture and industry, science and technology, education and scholarship, and politics.

15 **Prozesse: Erfahrungen eines Mitteleuropaers.** (Trials: experiences of a Central European.)
Eduard Goldstücker, translated from Czech by Friedrich Uttitz.
Munich; Hamburg, Germany: Albrecht Knaus Verlag GmbH, 1989. 351p.
Eduard Goldstücker was born into a Slovak Jewish family. Twice he emigrated to England, in 1939 and again shortly after the invasion of Czechoslovakia by the Warsaw Pact countries in 1968. In the 1960s Goldstücker reached high academic recognition as a Prorector of Charles University, Prague, was instrumental in starting the rehabilitation of Franz Kafka and was the main initiator of the conference on Kafka in 1963. He headed the association of Czech writers, Svaz československých spisovatelů. He spent some years as an academic at the University of Sussex, England. His memoirs, complemented by a few photographs, provide an insight into the intellectual life of 20th-century Central Europe.

16 **Customs and etiquette in the Czech Republic.**
David Short. Folkestone, England: Global Books, 1996. 64p. (Simple Guides – Series 1).
This work deals with certain areas which are given little or no coverage in the major guidebooks. Its historical and geographical overview picks out facts and events that carry a particular resonance of which the visitor is wise to be aware. Examples of other sections are: 'The people', which deals with prejudices; 'Culture and customs'; 'Forms of address'; 'Visiting people'; 'Doing business'; and 'Getting about'. The book ends with a five-page section, entitled 'Did you know?', containing a curious range of less familiar facts about the Czechs.

17 **Czechs and balances.**
Benjamin Kuras. Prague: Baronet, 1998. 2nd ed. 191p. maps.
The Czech edition, *Češi na vlásku*, is subtitled 'Příručka národního přežívání' (Handbook for the nation's survival, which was translated as 'A nation's survival kit' in the first English-language edition, 1996). The book is a rarity in having been written and published first in English and only later translated by the author into Czech. The author is of Czech origin and went to Britain as a student in 1969, later working there for the BBC and in the theatre world. He is the author of several English plays. The book is a tongue-in-cheek (re)-assessment of the Czech character and Czech history. Kuras is earthy and robust in his expression and looks at the Czechs from the complex viewpoint of an expatriate. The resulting volume is similar in theme to Holý's *The little Czech and the great Czech nation* (q.v.), but is closer to the debunking spirit of *1066 and all that*.

18 **The liberation of women and nation: Czech nationalism and women writers of the Fin de Siècle.**
Robert B. Pynsent. In: *The literature of nationalism: essays on East European identity.* Edited by Robert B. Pynsent. Basingstoke, England: Macmillan, in association with the School of Slavonic and East European Studies, University of London; New York: St Martin's Press, 1996, p. 83-155.
Both titular subjects – Czech nationalism and the work of Czech women writers – have been paid little attention in English works. This relatively long contribution

discusses the diverse manifestations of nationalism and feminism in the works of well-or moderately well-known writers such as Božena Benešová, Růžena Jesenská, Marie Majerová, Helena Malířová, Teréza Nováková, Gabriela Preissová, Jiří Sumín, Růžena Svobodová, and Felix Tever, and such lesser (in some cases largely forgotten) writers as Marie Červinková-Riegrová, Popelka Bilianová, Pavla Buzková, Olga Fastrová (the first full-time Czech woman journalist), Anna Řeháková, and Božena Viková-Kunětická. Countless sub-topics feature, such as love and marriage, family life, marital fidelity, prostitution, exploitation, male and female eroticism, religion and spiritualism, convent education, attitudes to other Slav nations, and Jews, especially Jewish women. Several passages in the editor's 'Introduction' (p. 1-13) discuss Czech (and other) nationalism in a broader historical framework, going back as far as Jan Hus (1371-1415). The volume also includes David Short's 'The use and abuse of the language argument in mid-nineteenth-century "Czechoslovakianism": an appraisal of a propaganda milestone' (p. 40-65), which deals with a last-ditch attempt to prevent the Slovaks becoming divided from the Czechs linguistically. The 'milestone' of the title is the Slovak Jan Kollár's *Hlasové o potřebě jednoty spisovného jazyka pro Čechy, Moravany a Slováky* (Voices in support of the need for a common literary language for the Bohemians, Moravians and Slovaks) (written in Czech) (Prague: Kronberg a Řivnáč, 1846. 240p.), a major work in the 'Czechoslovak' dimension of Czech history.

19 **Cross Currents: a Yearbook of Central European Culture.**
Ann Arbor, Michigan: University of Michigan, Department of Slavonic Languages and Literatures, 1982-90 (vols. 1-9); New Haven, Connecticut; London: Yale University Press, 1990-92 (vols. 10-12). annual.

This discontinued annual publication used to have strong Czech representation. It carried translations of poetry, short stories, articles of literary and art criticism on past and contemporary works, and memoirs. For example, volume 11 (1992) contains: an article entitled 'Franz Kafka in Havel's Prague' by Ernst Pawel; 'Trends in Czech art after the Velvet Revolution' by Victor Miesel; poems by Frantíšek Halas; an article on Halas by Ludvík Kundera; a piece on T. G. Masaryk by H. Gordon Skilling; and an article on Czech, Polish and Hungarian cinema. The editorial board included distinguished translators, such as Paul Wilson, while the advisory committee included such personalities as Milan Kundera, H. Gordon Skilling and Josef Škvorecký.

20 **For better or for worse.**
Susie Lunt. *Geographical Magazine,* vol. 69, no. 5 (May 1997), p. 41-45. maps. bibliog.

The transition from Communism to a free democracy may be over in the Czech Republic but the dust has yet to settle. The resilient effects of the paternalistic, inefficient and bureaucratic recent past prevail and inhibit progress on a number of fronts. The gap in living standards has visibly widened over the last eight years. Susie Lunt is a freelance journalist, writer and bibliographer living in Prague.

21 **Pink tanks and velvet hangovers: an American in Prague.**
Douglas Lytle. Berkeley, California: Frog, 1995. 341p. bibliog.

Lytle's account of Americans in Prague, the city's major recent 'immigrant minority', looks at Prague culture and society in general, focusing on intellectual life. The book also describes the city's social and economic conditions.

7

Geography and Geology

General, physical and demographic

22 **Central Europe after the fall of the Iron Curtain: geopolitical perspectives, spatial patterns and trends.**
Edited by Francis W. Carter, Peter Jordan, Violette Rey.   Frankfurt, Germany: Peter Lang, 1998. 345p. maps. 2nd rev. ed. (Wiener Osteuropa Studien, Bd. 4).

A collection of essays on the geopolitical destruction, or re-construction, of a large section of the European continent. The book consists of two sections, as indicated in the subtitle: 'Geopolitical perspectives' and 'Spatial patterns and trends'. Topics covered are: the geopolitical scenarios for Central and Eastern Europe in a post-bipolar world; the transformation process; new regional processes; society and settlement systems; post-collectivist local societies in Central Europe; tourism; the environment; and migration. There is a specific chapter on 'Migration flows between the Czech and Slovak Republics – which forms of transition' by Nadine Cattan, Claude Grasland and Stanislav Řehák (p. 319-36), which is supported by a number of graphs and statistics.

23 **Boundaries and identities: the eastern frontier of the European Union.**
Edited by Malcolm Anderson, Eberhard Bort.   Edinburgh: University of Edinburgh, International Social Sciences Institute, 1996. 119p. maps. bibliog.

The proceedings of an international conference held at Tutzing, Germany, on 8-10 March 1996. These contributions on political geography, reproduced in German and in English, examine the issues of boundaries and identities, sovereignty and territory and prospects for the 21st century. Several papers deal specifically with cooperation on the Czech-German frontiers and with the way in which the Czech Republic is coping with the new political situation. The German-language papers are accompanied by English summaries.

8

24 **Human geography in Eastern Europe and the former Soviet Union.**
Ludwik Mazurkiewicz, with a foreword by R. J. Johnston. London:
Belhaven Press; New York; Toronto: Halsted Press, 1992. 163p.
bibliog.

An outline study of the human geography of the region, concentrating on 'ideas, concepts and approaches'. The problems of transformation from a Communist approach to human geography to Western-style discipline are also underlined. Czechoslovakia is referred to throughout the book, the topics being: agricultural geography, environmental determinism, population and settlement geography, and regional paradigms.

25 **Geography of Czechoslovakia.**
Jaromír Demek, Miroslav Střída. Prague: Academia, 1971. 330p.
maps. bibliog.

Even today this work is considered to be the best authoritative geography of the country in English, and relatively little in its separate chapters on structure and relief, climate, hydrology, soils, biogeography, population and settlements cannot still be taken as a reliable guide. This comprehensive volume is not always easy to obtain outside specialist libraries, and the same applies to a collection of papers edited by Miroslav Blažek, *Present-day Czech geography* (Brno, Czech Republic: Czechoslovak Academy of Sciences, 1971. 197p. maps). Blažek's work supplements Demek and Střída's volume by covering some additional topics and dealing more extensively with particular subjects such as cartography.

26 **The Czech Republic in brief.**
Milan Holeček, Josef Rubín, Miroslav Střída, Antonín Götz. Prague:
Publishing House of the Czech Geographical Society, 1995. 55p. maps.

A comprehensive, classic mini-geography of the republic providing basic information, and an outline of natural, social and economic conditions and the system of settlement. Compiled for the use of diplomats, business people and tourists, the geographical information is presented in a lucid text which is supported by numerous maps, charts and graphs. Several chapters are devoted to selected tourist attractions.

27 **Geofyzikální obraz ČSSR.** (Geophysical picture of the ČSSR.)
Jaroslav Ibrmajer, Miloš Suk. Prague: Nakladatelství Československé
akademie věd, Ústřední ústav geologický, 1989. 354p. maps. bibliog.

A modern picture of the country's geology, based on maps and a large volume of data, which provides information on deposits of raw materials, protection of the environment and agricultural land-use. The former Czechoslovakia had two main geophysical units: the Czech Massif, in the Czech Lands; and the Western Carpathians, in Slovakia. The petro-physical properties of the rocks of both units are summarized and geophysical methods evaluated. The book is supported by numerous charts, maps, tables and statistics.

28   **Soils of Czechoslovakia.**
      J. Pelíšek.   *Soil Science*, vol. 111, no. 3 (March 1971), p. 163-69.
The Czech Republic occupies a relatively small area, yet it has a great variety of
terrain, from fairly extensive lowlands to mountains, and the underlying fragmented
geology gives rise to a considerable mixture of soil types. This explains the significant
regional differences in patterns of agriculture.

29   **Czech demographic handbook.**
      Compiled by Milan Aleš et al, with an introduction by Karel Outrata,
      President, Czech Statistical Office.   Prague: Czech Statistical Office,
      1998. 376p. map.
This English-language edition was published at the same time as the original Czech-
language work. The handbook contains data on the Czech Republic up to 1995-96 and
data for former Czechoslovakia up to 1992. The information presented here has been
selected from regular population censuses and from 'intercensal' demographic
statistics. It also includes long-term series of population statistics interconnected
across time, some starting as far back as 1785. This A4 paperback handbook has the
standard layout for this type of publication and contains the following sections: 'Area
and population'; 'Houses and dwellings'; 'Families and households'; 'Retrospectives
of population changes'; 'Marriages'; 'Divorces'; 'Births'; 'Abortions'; 'Deaths';
'Migration'; and a 'Territorial' survey.

Statistická ročenka České republiky. (Statistical Yearbook of the Czech
Republic.)
See item no. 416.

Statistický lexikon obcí České republiky. (Statistical lexicon of communities in the Czech Republic.)
See item no. 419.

Regional

30   **An industrial geography of Prague: 1848-1921.**
      Francis William Carter.   PhD thesis, University College, University of
      London, 1979. Available from Ann Arbor, Michigan: University
      Microfilms International, 1984. 568 leaves. maps.
Carter's thesis covers the following topics: the role of inter-urban mobility in Prague's
industrial location patterns; the impact of rent on location and its linkage to Prague's
industrial structure; Prague's industrial growth from 1848 to 1921 and its recapitalization. Also examined are: the city's changing industrial structure, commerce
and industry, from the historical perspective of over seven decades of industrial
growth; Prague's industrialists; the 1848 revolution; the rights of industrial workers;
industrial conditions; and changes in Prague's urban areas. The thesis is accompanied
by charts, tables and statistics.

31 **Prague 1989, theatre of revolution: a study in humanistic political geography.**
Michael Andrew Kukral. Boulder, Colorado: East European Monographs; New York: distributed by Columbia University Press, 1997. 236p. maps. (East European Monographs, no. 472).
An unusual study in political and humanistic geography, focusing on Wenceslas Square as the scene of the Velvet Revolution, the development of this square and Prague in image, revolution and meaning.

32 **Plzeň. (Pilsen.)**
Delia Meth-Cohn. *Business Central Europe*, November 1994, p. 66.
One of the Czech Republic's largest cities is the subject of one of *Business Central Europe's* regular features, 'City Focus'. The article follows the style of the others in the series, analysing the town's infrastructure and business environment. Pilsen is coming back to life as an industrial centre.

33 **Mineral deposits of the Erzgebirge/Krušné hory (Germany, Czech Republic): reviews and results of recent investigations.**
Edited by Kurt von Gehlen, Dietrich D. Klemm. Berlin; Stuttgart, Germany: Borntraeger, 1994. 230p. maps. bibliog. (Monograph Series on Mineral Deposits, no. 31).
Krušné hory is a range of mountains which creates a natural border between Germany and the Czech Republic in the west. This book describes its mineral deposits in detail, and is intended for scientists and mineralogists. The text consists of translations from several languages.

34 **Brno.**
Joe Cook. *Business Central Europe*, May 1995. 74p.
This article provides information, supported by statistics, on the infrastructure, business, finance and politics of this city. Brno, the Czech Republic's second city after Prague in terms of population and importance, has a strategic location which should lead to strong growth. 'Brno-fair trading' (in *Business Europa*, April/May 1997, p. 15) provides a brief history of the city, concentrating on the history of the Brno trade fair and exhibition centre, and particularly on the annual engineering fair, which takes place in September.

35 **Czechoslovakia's North-Moravian region: a geographical appraisal.**
Francis W. Carter. *Revue Géographique de l'Est*, vol. 10, nos. 1-2 (1970), p. 65-86. maps. bibliog.
Although inevitably outdated, this is a comprehensive geography of the region, covering topics ranging from geological and physical features to industry, agriculture and population. In economic terms, the North-Moravian region is still one of the most important in the republic due to its deposits of black coal and the coal and metallurgical industries. The author describes the actual location of various industries and branches of agriculture, town by town and district by district. A separate subsection deals with road and rail transport in the region. The copious statistical information in the volume is now of historical value, for example, the population

11

growth of Ostrava, the major industrial city of the region. This region is also studied in *Dilemmas of regionalism and the region of dilemmas: the case of Upper Silesia,* edited by Mark S. Szczepanski (Katowice, Poland: Universytet Slaski, 1993. 176p. map).

36 **Largest cave system of the Czech Socialist Republic in the Moravský Kras (Moravian Karst).**
Edited by Jan Přibyl. Brno, Czechoslovakia: Czechoslovak Academy of Sciences, Institute of Geography, 1973. 83p. map. bibliog. (Studia Geographica, no. 35).
The wild and beautiful limestone cliffs and caves near the town of Blansko, northeast of Brno, are one of the major features of Moravian geography. The system of cliffs and caves, so popular with tourists, includes the famous Macocha chasm and caves, wreathed in local legends, and the underground river Punkva. Přibyl is also the author of *Paleohydrography of the caves in the Moravský Kras* (Studia Geographica, no. 28).

37 **Czechoslovak mineral springs.**
Jan Šilar. *Geotimes*, vol. 13, no. 5 (May-June 1968), p. 10-13.
Describes the many mineral springs which are a major feature of Bohemian and Moravian geography. The spa cult, which witnessed a boom in the 19th century, is still alive and well and the bottling of water from the springs and drinking of mineral water, either for health reasons or at the table, has a longstanding tradition. The consumption of bottled mineral water in the Czech Republic is very high.

Maps and atlases

38 **Atlas of Eastern Europe in the twentieth century.**
Richard Crampton, Ben Crampton. London; New York: Routledge, 1996. 297p. maps.
The major aid towards understanding the complexity of events and the disappearance of some countries in Eastern and Central Europe, presented in maps and diagrams. These are accompanied by extensive explanatory text and there is also a comprehensive glossary of major towns and rivers with their linguistic variants, and a multitude of graphs. The atlas has seven sections. The first section offers background information on the physical structure of the area, the ethnic and religious groups and the area of the three great European empires (Russian, Ottoman and Austro-Hungarian). The subject of the second section is the First World War and the treaties of 1919-20. The third section covers the years between the two world wars and also has a brief description of the politics, economics, population and religious denominations in individual countries, including Czechoslovakia. Section four covers the Second World War. Section five deals with the Communist era, being concerned chiefly with industrialization and trade. Part six illustrates population growth, economics and the issue of pollution. The last part inevitably deals with politics and economics in the region after the collapse of Communism in 1989. This is a most

welcome publication which will help the reader to comprehend the numerous territorial disputes in this region of Europe.

39 **Historical atlas of East Central Europe.**
Paul Robert Magocsi, cartographic design by Geoffrey J. Matthews.
Seattle, Washington; London: University of Washington Press, 1993.
89 maps. (A History of East Central Europe, vol. 1).
The atlas is organized on chronological lines, from the early 5th century to 1992. It contains eighty-nine colour photographs and accompanying text (more than can be found in the majority of similar publications) on the history of the region. Several maps interpret the changing political and administrative boundaries of the region at crucial moments in history and are interspersed with other maps that focus on similar changes within individual countries or specific areas. Thematic maps cover such subjects as economy, ecclesiastical structures, education and culture, demography and ethnicity, and military affairs. Numerous tables and lists provide related statistical and demographic material. The detailed index includes a multitude of variant place-names.

40 **A concise historical atlas of Eastern Europe.**
Dennis P. Hupchick, Harold E. Cox. Basingstoke, England:
Macmillan, 1996. 120p. bibliog.
Aimed at students and general readers, this atlas addresses the need to explain the political developments and the ethnic and cultural diversity of Eastern Europe. It presents fifty-two full-page maps, each illustrating in a comprehensible way the key moments in the history of the region, from the Middle Ages to the present. Individual maps are accompanied by a facing page of explanatory text.

41 **State Map Series.**
Prague: Czech Office for Surveying, Mapping and Cadastration, 1994.
This is a selection of maps produced by the Land Survey Office (Zeměměřický ústav) in Prague. The publisher, the Czech Office for Surveying, also produces a useful leaflet, published under the same title *State Map Series*, a list of available large-scale maps, the state map series, medium-scale basic maps, maps of landscape units, maps of administrative divisions, sheet lines at 1:500,000, the thematic state map series, road maps and others. If not available elsewhere, these maps can be purchased from Prodejna map – Map Sale Centre, Bryksová 1061, 198 00 Prague.

42 **Velký auto atlas. Česká republika. Slovenská republika.** (Large road atlas. Czech Republic. Slovak Republic.)
Prague: Kartografie Praha, a.s., 1996. 8th ed. 93p.
A comprehensive large-format colour road atlas of the two countries, which includes street plans of major towns (plus a small map of the Brno Grand Prix). The legend and indexes are in Czech, German, English, French and Italian.

Tourism and Travel Guides

Central and Eastern Europe

43 **Vanishing borders: the rediscovery of Eastern Germany, Poland and Bohemia.**
Michael Farr. London; New York: Viking, 1991. 272p. bibliog.
A number of travellers' accounts on Central and Eastern Europe appeared immediately after the Velvet Revolution. Farr has travelled widely in this region as a correspondent of various quality newspapers. This book represents mostly his impressions from the former Eastern Germany (GDR), but the articles on Bohemia are good: 'Southern Bohemia by bicycle'; 'The Bohemian spas: in Goethe's footsteps'; and 'Prague, the Golden City'. Two other journalists, Iris Gioia and Clifford Thurlow, produced an entertaining travel book, entitled *Brief spring: a journey through Eastern Europe* (London: Alan Sutton, 1992. 227p.), which presents a picture of the region 'in a process of rebirth'. Part three is on Czechoslovakia (p. 71-100). Anton Gill went mostly by train and by hired car from *Berlin to Bucharest: travels in Eastern Europe* (London; Glasgow; Toronto; Sydney; Auckland, New Zealand: Grafton Books, 1990. 328p. maps). In the Czech Republic he visited 'the Golden City' and took waters in the Czech spas. All three books have illustrations, mostly black-and-white photographs.

44 **Tourism and economic development in Eastern Europe and the Soviet Union.**
Edited by Derek R. Hall. London: Belhaven Press; New York: Halsted Press, 1991. 321p. maps. bibliog.
Now slightly outdated since the tourist boom to the Czech Republic has calmed down to a manageable, better quality level, this collection of essays looks at opportunities in Eastern Europe, advises on ways of overcoming certain restrictions imposed by the previous regime, and summarizes the history of tourism and its evolutionary pattern in this region. Chapter seven, 'Czechoslovakia' (p. 154-72), by Frank W. Carter, follows

14

the same framework as the general section but also looks at domestic tourism and recreation. It includes a number of graphs.

Czech Republic

45 **Welcome to the Czech Republic.**
    http://www.czech.cz/

This is the official homepage of the Czech Republic. At the time of writing there were several websites offering, amongst other things, information for tourists, including: 'Czech Information Center' (http://.muselik.com/), one of the best starting points for general information; 'CzechSite Home Page' (http://.czechsite.com/) which concentrates on Prague travel information; 'Lonely Planet guides' (http://.lonelyplanet.com/dest/eur/cze/htm), offering tourist information and basic facts on the Czech Republic in English; and 'Tourist update' (http://pis.eunet.cz/), which provides information in Czech and English on travel agencies and the services they offer. The traveller can find listings of cultural events in Prague and book tickets on-line at http://www.ticketsBTI.csad.cz or http://www.ticketpro.cz/index.html.

46 **Czechoslovakia.**
    Erhard Gorys, English version prepared by Sebastian Wormell.
    London: Pallas Guides, 1991. 462p. maps. bibliog.

An excellent guide, considered by many to be the best, translated from German and aimed at the more sophisticated traveller. A historical survey is followed by an account of a journey to Prague and descriptions of trips to ten regions and their capitals. It is appropriate that the emphasis is on history throughout the work. The volume contains small maps of the towns visited and old illustrations as well as modern photographs. Other features supplementing this splendid guidebook include: a chronology of the history of Czechoslovakia; statistical data; practical information, including notes on Czech pronunciation; an essential vocabulary in the Czech language; detailed indexes; and a bibliography, mainly of English-language works.

47 **Czech and Slovak republics: the Rough Guide.**
    Written and researched by Rob Humphreys, with additional research by
    Tim Nollen. London: Rough Guides, 1998. Distributed by the Penguin
    Group. 4th ed. 500p. maps. bibliog.

This is probably the most comprehensive guide available in bookshops. It has more than sixty maps, and begins with the most basic information, such as how to get there, before going on to provide further practical tips, such as those relating to health matters, what to do when in trouble with the police, and information for disabled travellers and vegetarians. There are notes on the language and pronunciation. The main part of the book is taken up with information on visiting individual regions. The 'Historical framework'(p. 461-78) starts at the very beginning, with the Celtic tribes at 500 BC, but it is strong on modern history. Interestingly, the guide has a chapter on 'Rommanies' (p. 478).

15

48 **Czech and Slovak republics.**
John King, Scott McNeely, Richard Nebeský. Hawthorn, Victoria,
Australia; Oakland, California; London, Paris: Lonely Planet
Publications, 1998. 2nd updated ed. 552p. maps.
Another very comprehensive guide, similar to the *Rough Guide* (q.v.). This guidebook
was first published in 1995. It contains ninety-seven maps and the layout and contents
follow other classical larger guidebooks.

49 **Fodor's new The Czech Republic and Slovakia: the complete guide
with great city walks and country drives.**
New York; Toronto; London; Sydney; Auckland, New Zealand: Fodor's
Travel Publications, Inc., 1997. 188p. maps. bibliog.
An authoritative guide which follows the format of other Fodor's guides, describing
walking tours in historic Prague, excursions into mediaeval villages, advice on
souvenir shopping (where to buy folk art, porcelain, crystal), where to stay, and where
to eat and drink. The research has been undertaken by present and former residents.
The historical section (p. 169-71), in the form of a chronology, is good. The guide has
seventeen pages of clear maps and suggestions for 'Further readings' (p. 172-73),
basic Czech-English phrases with pronunciation (p. 174-82) and a good index
(p. 183-88).

50 **Czech Republic: Berlitz pocket guides.**
Oxford; New York: Berlitz Publishing Co., Ltd, 1996. 144p. maps.
Probably the most popular of the pocket guides, this abridged Berlitz guide manages
to cover an amazing number of topics: the country and its people; a brief history;
places to visit; hotels; restaurants; shopping; a few useful expressions in Czech with
phonetics; communications; opening hours; money matters; embassies and consulates;
advice for disabled travellers; information for gays and lesbians; shopping; and
weights and measures.

51 **Essential Czech Republic: (with excursions into Slovakia).**
Michael Ivory. Basingstoke, England: AA Publishing, 1995. 128p.
maps.
Aimed at the independent traveller, this pocket guide follows the pattern of the AA
series. The tourist will find information on what to see in various places, the
countryside, food and drink, shopping, accommodation, night life, weather, language
and special events. Many guidebooks tend to be Prague-orientated, whereas this is
good on regions and minor towns.

52 **Culture shock: a guide to customs and etiquette.**
Tim Nollen. London: Kuperard, 1997. 208p. bibliog.
Aimed particularly at people who are relocating, this guide offers guidance on finding
a place to live, shopping, working environments and doing business in the Czech
Republic. The information is intended to help people to settle into the Czech lifestyle
quickly, and the emphasis is on people themselves. A section providing some brief
historical background is followed by descriptions of social organizations, family life
and standard business practices, and practical tips on finding a home, opening a bank

16

account, and starting at a new school. There is very little on the Czech language here. 'Further readings' is an annotated bibliography (p. 198-204) of fairly general books from various fields relating to the Czech Lands. The reader should also note David Short's volume, *Customs and etiquette in the Czech Republic* (q.v.).

53 Treasures from the past: the Czechoslovak cultural heritage.
Text by Jan Royt, photographs by Karel Neubert, translated from the Czech by Michael Hecht. Prague: Odeon, 1992. 205p.

This must have been one of the last picture-books on Czechoslovakia published before the division of the country on 1 January 1993. Indeed, the pictures illustrate the different historical and economic conditions prior to the unification of the two countries in 1918. Beautiful photographs of the capital towns of Prague and Bratislava form the main bulk of the town section but the other historical towns receive fair treatment. Thirty-six castles and country houses follow, the photographs being mostly of exteriors of the buildings in enviable settings in the countryside. There are a few photographs of the interiors, since in truth there are not many, due to the neglect of more than fifty years. The section on sacred monuments gives credit to another neglected area, the buildings of monasteries and convents, and the photographs justify their beauty. The book concludes with the smallest section, on vernacular architecture, a well-chosen selection of a few examples of rural architecture, avoiding the buildings or villages which are too heavily accented on folklore.

54 Spuren des "Realsozialismus" in Böhmen und der Slowakei: Monumente, Museen, Gedenktage. (Traces of 'realistic socialism' in Bohemia and Slovakia: monuments, museums, commemorative days.)
Vienna: Löcker, 1996. 190p. bibliog.

The cultural heritage of the Stalinist era was epitomized by the huge statue of Stalin, which dominated Prague and also dominates this book. This collection of articles by six historians is accompanied by numerous bibliographical notes and some photographs (including gruesome examples from the police museum in Prague).

55 Tourrets and tourists in Bohemia.
Greg Stevenson. *History Today*, vol. 46, no. 8 (August 1996), p. 7-10.

Reports on attempts to combine the interests of tourists and the efforts of conservationists. The castles in the Czech Lands are endangered by tourism.

56 Camping CZ.
Czech Tourist Authority. Prague: Marcom, 1994.

A fold-out map of 244 campsites in the Czech Republic. The traveller will find details of the sites on the reverse side of the map, including the location and name of the camp, opening hours and facilities. A brief text in English, French, Dutch and German supplies elementary information on travel documents, traffic rules, fuel, customs and import duties, shopping, medical care, public holidays and currency.

Customs and etiquette in the Czech Republic.
See item no. 16.

17

Tourist events

57 **Česká centrála cestovního ruchu.** (Czech Centre for tourism.)
http://www.visitczech.cz.
This homepage of the Czech Tourist Authority contains tourist information and a listing of all broadly cultural events. The information, which is still developing, is available in Czech, English and German. This website replaces an annual publication of the Czech Tourist Authority, *Calendar of tourist events – Czech Republic.*

58 **Kultura, sport.** (Culture, sport.)
http://www.travel-profi.cz
Provides regional information, in the Czech language, on cultural and sporting events which took place in the previous year. Since most of them look like regular events, it would be reasonable to plan a trip to a region around the information provided here. Examples of the kinds of events listed are brass band festivals, flower shows, folklore festivals, air shows, classic car rallies and sporting competitions. The telephone numbers of the organizers are given.

Prague and regions

Prague

59 **A guide to guides.**
Michael Ivory. *BCSA Newsletter*, 48 (April/May 1999), p. 8-9.
A thoughtful survey of many of the main contemporary guides to Prague by one who is himself the author of guides to the city, the Czech Republic and Slovakia. It includes reference to several major guides from the past, which are hard to get hold of but are still unrivalled in their particular category. A good selection of guides to Prague is to be found in Susie Lunt's *Prague*, which was published in this series in 1997 (q.v.). The following entries provide a selection of the most recent publications not cited in Lunt's work.

60 **Prague: an architectural guide.**
Radomíra Sedláková, translated from the Czech by Michal Schonberg.
Venice: Arsenale Editrice, 1997. 147p. maps. bibliog.
Claims to be the first architectural guide covering all styles. The chapters are entitled: 'Romanesque Prague'; 'Gothic Prague'; 'Renaissance Prague'; 'Baroque Prague'; 'Classicist Prague'; 'Architecture of 19th century'; and 'Architecture of 20th century'. The coverage of the last chapter goes up to the latest significant building, the Dancing House, alias the Fred and Ginger house on Rašínovo nábřeží (Rašín Quay), by architects Frank O. Gehry and Vlado Milunič, which was completed in 1996. Each chapter has a map giving the exact location of each of the buildings described. The guide has 208 illustrations of monuments and these are described both in historical

and architectural detail. The author also offers in-depth technical descriptions and, for the most important buildings, a planimetric map. The bibliography (p. 138-39) lists books and exhibition catalogues and is followed by an 'Index of Places' (p. 140-45) with references from English to Czech place-names and vice versa, and an 'Index of Names' (p. 146-47).

61 **Prague in black and gold: the history of a city.**
Peter Demetz. London: Allen Lane, The Penguin Press, 1997. 411p. maps. bibliog.

A beautifully produced, somehow moving history of this haunting and ambiguous city, which was the home town of the author until he left in 1949. Peter Demetz is Professor Emeritus of German and Comparative Literature at Yale University. Here he provides a map of ancient and early mediaeval archaeological sites, landmarks of Přemyslide Prague, landmarks and battlefields of Hussite Prague and an interesting map entitled 'Social topography of Prague in 1930'. The book has no other illustrations, except for those on the cover. The author provides 'A few suggestions on Czech pronunciation' (p. xvii-xviii) and a sizeable bibliography (p. 379-95) of mostly Czech and German sources. Some of the bibliographical entries have comments on the author, the work and its editions. There is also a good general index. The book is aimed at the English-speaking visitor to Prague and offers a very good authoritative history. Many Czechs returning to Prague after many years will share the author's mixed feelings in the final chapter, 'A difficult return to Prague' (p. 365-76).

62 **Pražský uličník: encyklopedie názvů pražských veřejných prostranství. I. díl A-N, II. díl O-Z.** (Prague street guide: encyclopaedia of the names of public open spaces in Prague. Part I A-N, Part II O-Z.)
Marek Lašťovka et al, introduction by Václav Ledvinka. Prague: Nakladatelství Libri, 1997. 2 vols.

Regrettably, only the enquirer with a knowledge of Czech can use this fascinating goldmine of the history of the names of Prague streets, squares, bridges etc. No street is omitted, and the entries trace and explain not only the origin of each extant name, but also all the names of a particular street through time, including, particularly for the central area, data going back hundreds of years. It is a valuable resource for recent political history, reflecting not only responses to Prague becoming part of Czechoslovakia as opposed to Austria-Hungary in 1918, but also changes wrought by the German occupation during the Second World War, the Communist takeover in 1948, and changes or reversions following the Velvet Revolution in 1989. A separate listing gives all defunct names, with cross-references to current names. The work is enhanced by old photographs and a black-and-white reference map. One oddity is Přemysl Filla's closing essay on the history of Prague street-cleaning and the removal of domestic refuse.

63 **Prague 100+100 cultural monuments guide.**
Ctibor Rybár. Prague: Libri, 1998. 246p. maps.

A pocket guide in which the author selected, from the large choice of architectural treasures, the buildings which the visitor should not miss and which are manageable on a short sightseeing tour on foot, with the aid of the Prague underground system. Each of the buildings mentioned in the text is numbered, and there is a corresponding

19

schematic plan for each section. The narrative is enlightened by Prague legends and numerous photographs and illustrations.

64 **Pražské zahrady.** (Gardens of Prague.)
Olga Bašeová, photographs by Ladislav Neubert.   Prague: Panorama, 1991. 247p. bibliog. (Edice Pragensia).
A coffee-table book which consists, as it should, mostly of photographs and illustrations. The text has a good English summary (p. 226-32), a German summary (p. 233-39) and a summary in Russian (p. 240-47). The publication is intended for the public at large, and it does not therefore venture deeply into the designs or into analysis and evaluation. The introductory text gives examples from the history of world horticultural art, before concentrating on Prague itself. The remainder of the volume is devoted to a chronologically arranged survey of historical and contemporary gardens and parks of Prague, such as monastic gardens, gardens of palaces and public gardens. Individual historical periods are represented by a selection of Prague gardens and parks. The gardens and parks are viewed here as a synthesis of several forms of art: architecture; sculpture; creative gardening and related crafts; and contemporary technology.

65 **Cafés in Prague: the 50 most interesting cafés.**
Oliver Heinl, Nicole Leopold, Libor Studnička, with a preface by Jiří Gruša, translated from German by Willfried Haubner.   Nuremberg, Germany: Art of Slide, 1996. 128p.
Art of Slide originally published this illustrated paperback in German, under the title *Cafés in Prag*, also in 1996. In the same year, the publisher also brought out Italian and Czech translations of this guide (*I caffe di Praga* and *Pražské kavárny*, respectively).

66 **The Golden Lane.**
Harald Salfellner.   Prague: Vitalis, 1998. 104p. bibliog.
The Golden Lane is in the surrounds of the Castle (Prague Castle). It has another name, 'The Lane of Alchemists', after the scientists at the court of Rudolf II. This small guidebook provides a history of this narrow, romantic lane. It describes its twenty houses and their individual history, which is interwoven with the history of Prague, and the immediate vicinity of the town. The volume contains many photographs and illustrations, old and new.

67 **Church of the Sacred Heart.**
Jože Plečnik, Ivan Margolius, photographs by Mark Flennes.   London: Phaidon Press, 1995. 60p. bibliog. (Architecture in Detail).
A history of a church in Prague (Kostel Nejsvětějšího Srdce Páně), a major 20th-century building, which was designed by the modernist Slovene architect Josip Plečnik (1872-1957), and of modern ecclesiastical architecture in Prague. The church has an extraordinary clock tower, and its brick exterior, with unusual patterning and a stone rim, are supposed to be a reference to the ermine cloak of Christ. This illustrated paperback includes a chronological survey.

68 **The Church of St. Nicholas.**
    Jan B. Lášek, translated by Peter Stephens, photographs by Jiří
    Všetečka.   Prague: V ráji – Náboženská obec Církve československé
    husitské, 1998. unpaged.

This is an English version of a Czech publication on a church in the Old Town (Staré
Město) of Prague (not to be confused with the grand baroque St Nikolas in the Small
Quarter). History and architecture are the core of this paperback, which was prepared
by the Czechoslovak Hussite Church.

Regions

69 **Hradec Králové.**
    Prague: S & D (Soukup & David), 1997. 73p. maps. (Guide to Bohemia,
    Moravia, Silesia).

The only guide to a provincial town published in English so far. Hradec Králové is a
town in northeast Bohemia, surrounded by pleasant countryside. It is rich in historical
monuments, and has unique architecture and many cultural opportunities. The
introduction to this slim, pocket-size guide provides a summary of the town's history
and notes on its architecture and famous people. Various walks are suggested, which
take in the town and its immediate surroundings. The guide also recommends places to
visit outside the town, such as the battlefield of Chlum where, on 3 July 1866, 400,000
men fought in the decisive battle of the Austro-Prussian War which resulted in the
victory of the Prussians over Benedek's Austrian army.

70 **Brno a okolí.** (Brno and its surroundings.)
    Dalibor Kusák, Jindřich Uher.   Prague: ČTK – Pressfoto, 1991. 246p.

Another pleasantly presented coffee-table book, which consists mostly of photographs
of the contemporary city of Brno, its architectural monuments, interiors and
surrounding countryside, by the well-known photographer Dalibor Kusák. The
narrative is by Jindřich Uher, who traces the history of the area back to the Great Bear
Cave near Brno, where Homo erectus lived half a million years ago. The modern town
of Brno is located at the confluence of the Svratka and Svitava rivers which was
originally inhabited 70,000 years ago. However, the book is mainly concerned with
the present, and it gives a fair presentation of life in this, the second most populated
city of the Czech Lands. The summaries offer much information and are in English,
German, French and Italian.

71 **Brno, výstaviště, Bitva u Slavkova.** (Brno, exhibition ground, the
    battle of Austerlitz.)
    František Zřídkaveselý, Vladimír Šmída, Dušan Uhlíř.   Brno: Šifra a.s.
    in cooperation with the Rapid advertising agency, 1993. (unpaged).

A successful 'propaganda' publication issued on the 750th anniversary of the city.
Brno was granted a charter of city privileges by King Wenceslas I in 1243, although
its history goes back more than 900 years. Now it is an industrial city with 400,000
inhabitants. The book is divided into three sections, as the title indicates. The first, on
Brno itself, provides a chronology of the history of the town which was home to
the founder of genetics Gregory Mendel and to the composer Leoš Janáček.

Unfortunately, these two giants, of science and of music, are dedicated only a short paragraph each. The authors are more concerned with the commercial success of the town and its reflection in architecture, which, after all, is what this pragmatic town is all about. The second section describes the Brno exhibition centre, where a large Engineering Fair takes place annually, being the most important of many international exhibitions which take place there. Some of the buildings which form the fairground are of considerable architectural interest. The last section is on the battle of Slavkov, or Austerlitz as it is known internationally, a small town northeast of Brno, at which Napoleon defeated the Austrian and Russian armies in 1805. The text is in Czech, English, German and French. The book lacks an index.

72 **Grand restoration of a humble birth place.**
J. Hendershott. *Financial Times*, 19 June 1998, p. 16.

The coaching inn in Kaliště near Jihlava, where Gustav Mahler was born, is being turned into an arts complex. This is a report on the project, which is considered a lesson in careful planning. English-language newspapers and periodicals frequently publish articles on places of interest in the Czech Lands, and this is one such piece. Another example, from quite a different type of printed media, is an illustrated quality article entitled 'The baroque theatre of Český Krumlov' in the regular 'Wonders of the world' section in *Hello!*, no. 553 (30 March 1999), p. 119-20.

73 **Guide to Bohemian Forest-Šumava.**
Radovan Rebstöck, translated by Michael Roth. Sušice, Czech Republic: Dr. Radovan Rebstöck, 1994. 63p. map.

A small guide, designed to fit into a pocket of a car, which suggests a one-week itinerary of trails across this beautiful range of hills on the Bohemian-Bavarian border and advice on daily routes by car or on foot, directing the tourist to places of interest in the region. The guide includes some black-and-white photographs of scenery and historic towns and basic tourist information, including 'Useful vocabulary' on p. 63. The English is awkward.

Flora and Fauna

Flora

74 **Květena České republiky.** (Flora of the Czech Republic.)
Edited by Slavomil Hejný, Bohumil Slavík. Prague: Academia,
1988- . irregular.

This major publication in the field of botany was originally published under the title
Květena České Socialistické Republiky (The Flora of the Czech Socialist Republic).
The current title dates from volume 2 (1990). The introduction is in English. The
Natural History Museum in London is a subscriber to this monographic series, which
should be completed in eight volumes and thus provide a complete and authoritative
work on the flora of the territory of the Czech Republic. Five volumes have been
published so far. The authors of the volumes are employees of the Academy of
Sciences of the Czech Republic, from the Institute of Botany in Průhonice, the highest
scholarly institution in the field.

75 **Nová květena ČSSR.** (The new flora of the Czechoslovak SR.)
Edited by Josef Dostál. Prague: Academia, 1989. 2 vols. map.

This volume is confused in book catalogues with the monographic series of *Květena
České Republiky* (q.v.). It is a separate publication, which covers flora in the whole of
former Czechoslovakia. The two volumes comprise a total of 1,548 pages with many
illustrations, thus providing a fully comprehensive work on Czech flora. The book is
available in major research libraries.

76 **The Hamlyn encyclopedia of plants.**
J. Tříska, edited by Helen L. Pursey. London; New York; Sydney;
Toronto: Hamlyn, 1975. 300p.

This book on European flora was a result of international cooperation. It was designed,
produced and printed in the Czech Lands, and the photographers were Dutch. Many
aspects of the book are typical of Czech culture, such as the wealth of information on

the uses of plants in folk medicine in the past and in the modern pharmaceutical industry. The tradition of the use of herbs, particularly herbal teas, has recently witnessed semi-official revival, as it has in the West. A related tradition is the frequent publishing of herbaria, quality books on the medicinal properties of plants, some of them of considerable antiquity. The encyclopaedia also gives information on protected plants. The best Czech artists specializing in nature subjects provided the illustrations. The book gives a fair representation of Czech flora.

77 **Urban ecology: plants and plant communities in urban environment.**
Edited by H. Sukopp, S. Hejný, co-editor I. Kowarik. The Hague: SPB Academic, 1990. 282p. maps. bibliog.

A collection of essays on plants and vegetation in the cities. References to Czechoslovakia are numerous and several essays deal specifically with this country: 'Comparison of the vegetation and flora of the West Bohemian villages and towns', by P. Pysek and A. Pysek (p. 105-12); 'Natural and semi-natural plant communities of the city of Prague, Czechoslovakia', by J. Kubíková (p. 131-39); and 'Changes of vegetation and pollen respiratory tract allergies on Prague sample', by K. Kopecký (p. 267-72). Each article is accompanied by its own bibliography and the book contains a 'Subject index' and a 'Species index'.

78 **Gardens in Central Europe.**
Patrick Bowe, photographs by Nicolas Sapieha. New York: M. T. Train/Scala Books, 1991. 215p. bibliog.

A coffee-table book, which the visitor can study and enjoy, offering a brief history of gardens and landscape gardening in the countries of Central Europe. Czechoslovakia, with its reputable history of garden design, is discussed on pages 77-131. Landscaping is placed in relation to architectural styles, and the Czech Republic is home to examples from almost every period. Of these, the baroque heritage is the most prominent.

79 **Forests of Czechoslovakia.**
L. Hružík et al. Prague: Ministerstvo lesního a vodního hospodářství, 1960. 223p. maps.

Although published many years ago, this publication is still an important source of information on the state of afforestation of the Czech Republic. Forests and woods are important to the quality of life of the Czechs. 'Going into the woods' with the family on Sunday or in the holidays is, as in the Scandinavian countries, an inseparable part of Czech culture and a pleasant pastime. The book describes the distribution of forests and state management practices, many of which are still applied. Some of the forests are now privately owned, but the state still has a degree of control over the forests and their management.

80 **Mushrooms and other fungi.**
Aurel Dermek, translated by Darina Reguliová. Leicester, England: Galley Press (W. H. Smith), 1982. 223p.

A popular handbook on mushrooms and fungi which grow, and can be found, in most European countries, including Britain and the Czech Republic. The general mycological sections are not specific to any country, but the recipe section includes many Czech dishes and involves many more species than just the field mushrooms trusted by the English. *The Czech and English names of mushrooms* by Josef Hladký has been published by a university publisher in Brno (Brno, Czech Republic: Nakladatelství Masarykovy univerzity, 1996. 320p.).

Fauna

81 **Fauna ČR a SR.** (Fauna of the Czech Republic and Slovak Republic.)
Prague: Academia, [1967?]- . irregular.

A Czech-language monographic series which was previously published as *Fauna ČSSR* and which causes headaches for cataloguers in libraries. The issues are irregular, a feature common to many fauna series, and deal with specific zoological and entomological subjects. For example the latest of these monographs which reached the library in the Natural History Museum in London is vol. 28/1 and 28/2, the subject being 'Mihulovci a ryby – Petromyzontes a Osteichthyes', i.e. lampreys and fish. The pagination of the two parts is 698p., which is an indication of the readership the series is aiming at. It is the most important Czech series in the field.

82 **Ptáci-aves.** (Birds.)
Karel Hudec et al. Prague: Academia, 1972-83. 3 vols. maps. bibliog.
(Fauna ČSSR).

A monograph from the *Fauna ČR a SR* series (q.v.), this scholarly work comprehensively covers Czech birdlife. Although it is in Czech, it is comprehensible to non-Czech readers for comparative purposes, due to its maps, statistical data and many illustrations. This large opus (over 1,000 pages and over 600 illustrations) provides: various names for each species; a full account of their distribution; information on sub-species; and various statistical data. It also deals with means of recognition, significance to man, any relevant legislation, and the incidence of avian parasites. It has synopses in German. Karel Hudec is also the author of a book on European birds entitled *A guide to birds* ([London]: Treasure Press, 1992. 294p.), which includes birds from the Czech Lands.

83 **Where to watch birds in Eastern Europe.**
London: Hamlyn, in association with Birdlife International, 1994. 214p. maps. (Hamlyn Birdwatching Guides).

The guide is divided by country, with the Czech Republic on p. 44-67. The core of each country section is a catalogue of birdwatching sites. Each entry in the catalogue provides information on a particular site's location, a description of the site, a calendar (advising on when to visit and the best time for watching), a list of species found there and details of access to the site.

84 **Songbirds.**
Karel Šťastný.   London; New York; Sydney; Toronto: Hamlyn, 1960.
216p. maps.
Originally published in Czech as a handbook on songbirds, this was only slightly
adapted for the British amateur ornithologist. This is an indication that the basic range
of birds found in the Czech Lands is nearly identical to that of the British Isles. This is
demonstrated again in another book by Karel Šťastný, *Birds of Britain and Europe: a
comprehensive illustrated guide to over 360 species* (London: Hamlyn, 1990; London:
Sunburst, 1995) and, where freshwater birds are concerned, in his *Birds of sea and
fresh water* (London: Hamlyn, 1985).

85 **Freshwater fishes.**
Karel Vostradovský, with illustrations by Jakub Malý, translated by
D. Coxon.   New York; London; Sydney; Toronto: Hamlyn, 1978.
252p.
This is another mutation of a Czech book and as such gives a good representation of
the fish found in the Czech Lands. It is of interest to note that the first ever Czech
book translated into English was on fish farming, by a monk named Dubravius (1486-
1553).

86 **Seznam motýlů České a Slovenské Republiky. Checklist of
lepidoptera of the Czech and Slovak Republics.**
Zdeněk Laštůvka et al.   Brno, Czech Republic: Konvoj, 1998. 118p.
An authoritative catalogue of butterflies and moths published in a hardback form. It
may not be easy to obtain, however; at the time of writing the book was not available
in the natural history libraries in London.

Prehistory and Archaeology

87 **Archaeology in Bohemia: 1981-1985.**
Edited by Radomír Pleiner, Jiří Hrala, translated into English by Petr
Charvát. Prague: Archaeological Institute of the Czechoslovak
Academy of Sciences, 1986. 357p. bibliog.

This collection of articles on major finds and sites covers periods from Neolithic to
mediaeval archaeology, and illustrates the research activities of the archaeological
institutions in the Czech Lands.

88 **Czechoslovakia before the Slavs.**
Evžen Neústupný, Jiří Neústupný, translated by Lewis Ducke.
London: Thames & Hudson, 1961. 225p. maps. bibliog. (Ancient
Peoples and Places).

A richly illustrated and fully annotated introduction to the prehistory of the Czech and
Slovak lands, which manages to strike a happy balance between the popular and the
scholarly. The authors describe the old migration routes, the general topographical
background and the contemporary archaeological evidence available. Evidence is
presented relating to the period from the Lower Palaeolithic right up to the appearance
of the Slavs, and some cultures (Hallstatt, La Tène, Celtic, Teuton and Roman) are
shown to be of considerable importance. A tentative chronology of early finds is
included, together with a good periodized bibliography containing many references to
Western European-language sources that are more accessible than those in many other
bibliographies.

89 **Bohemia from the air: seven decades after Crawford.**
Martin Gojda. *Antiquity*, vol. 67, no. 257 (December 1993), p. 869-75.
maps. bibliog.

It is more than seventy years since O. G. S. Crawford, founder of *Antiquity*, was given
air photographs from southern England which led him to realize their potential for
archaeology. Leo Deuel's book, *Flights into yesterday*, was translated into Czech in

27

1979, providing a first impetus to the new programme of work in Bohemia which is presented here, a programme made possible by the new freedom to fly and photograph that followed the revolution of 1989.

90   A site in history: archaeology at Dolní Věstonice/Unterwisternitz.
     Silvia Tomášková.   *Antiquity*, vol. 69, no. 263 (June 1995), p. 301-16.
     map. bibliog.

The archaeological site of Dolní Věstonice in southern Moravia has long been considered a crucial place for understanding human settlement in glacial Europe. In this article the author looks at Věstonice as a place in the Central European zone where national boundaries have moved many times; ideologies and attitudes have transposed the place, each leaving its mark. Věstonice is crucial to, and alive in, history as well as prehistory.

91   Upper Palaeolithic fibre technology: interlaced woven finds from
     Pavlov I, Czech Republic, c. 26,000 years ago.
     James M. Adovasio, Olga Soffen, Bohuslav Klíma.   *Antiquity*, vol. 70,
     no. 169 (September 1996), p. 526-34. map. bibliog.

The later Palaeolithic sites in Moravia continue to be a source of new noteworthy material. The archaeological sites Dolní Věstonice and Pavlov are particularly famous for art mobilier, such as bones and carved stones, such as the figurine of Venus, for which Věstonice is known. However, recent discoveries at these sites have also revealed evidence of the technology of groundstone, the technology of ceramics and new woven materials, and interlaced basketry or textiles of a kind which is associated with a much later era.

92   Cave bears and modern human origins: the spatial taphonomy of
     Pod Hradem Cave, Czech Republic.
     Robert H. Gargett.   Lanham, Maryland; London: University Press of
     America, 1996. 265p. maps. bibliog.

A scientific monograph on the taphonomic and spatial analysis of Upper Pleistocene bear bone accumulation in a cave near Brno. The cave was excavated by Moravské museum in Brno in the 1950s. This is heavy reading for a lay person, but is interesting for anyone with even a superficial interest in palaeontology, cognitive processes behind behaviour, or the region of Brno, where the author spent considerable time. Spatial analysis has the potential to help resolve questions about the origin of modern humans. As would be expected, the monograph contains numerous tables and illustrations, a huge bibliography of references (p. 239-58) and an index.

93   Analysis of the Czech Neolithic pottery: morphological and
     chronological structure of projections.
     I. Pavlů, M. Zápotocká.   Prague: Archaeological Institute, 1978. 217p.
     bibliog.

A highly specialized work which presents descriptions of the various types of surface projections on the large corpus of Neolithic finds in the Czech Lands. The text proper is supported by appendices listing all the linear and stroked pottery finds, statistical and other relevant tables and many illustrations.

94 **Viereckschanzen in Czechoslovakia.**
C. G. Cumberpatch. *Scottish Archaeological Review*, no. 9/10 (1995), p. 80-87. maps. bibliog.

There exists a wealth of archaeological data concerning Celtic religion and ritual practices which has not been integrated into the broader scheme of studies of the Iron Age in Europe. This article looks at enclosures called Viereckschanzen, which occur particularly in the former Czechoslovakia and date from the end of the Middle La Tène, focusing on their archaeological and historical context and connection with ritual sites.

95 **Central Europe in 8th-10th centuries. Mitteleuropa in 8-10 Jahrhundert.**
Edited by Dušan Čaplovič. Bratislava: Ministry of Culture of the Slovak Republic and the Slovak Academy of Sciences, 1997. 212p. maps. bibliog.

Comprises papers, in German, English and Russian, from an international conference in Bratislava which took place in 1995. This A4 paperback contains a number of illustrations and maps, e.g. of archaeological sites.

96 **Moravia Magna: the Great Moravian Empire, its art and times.**
Ján Dekan, with an introduction by Josef Poulík, translated by Heather Trebatická. Minneapolis, Minnesota: Control Data Arts, 1979. 166p.

Written by a prominent Slovak archaeologist, this work was first published in Slovak, as *Veľká Morava: doba a umenie* (Bratislava, Czechoslovakia: Tatran, 1976 and 1980), and again by the same publisher in German in 1980, as *Grossmahren: Epoche und Kunst*, and subsequently in English (as above), Czech (Prague: Odeon, 1980), Polish, Hungarian and Russian. With this work Czechoslovakia celebrated the 1,100th anniversary of the Great Moravian Empire, which was marked by many exhibitions and publications. The text takes us from the earliest known prehistory of the region, through the fall of the Roman Empire, the misty realm of 7th-century Samo (the first state on the territory), to Great Moravia itself, providing an account of the cultural, spiritual and economic life of the most highly developed state of 9th-century Central Europe. The work is illustrated by countless superbly reproduced colour photographs (unpaginated) and other illustrative material from the whole period, representing all the major archaeological sites, some quite far from the centre of the Empire. Broader information on the early history of Central Europe can be obtained from *Franks, Moravians and Magyars: the struggle for the middle Danube, 788-907*, by Charles R. Bowlus (Philadelphia: University of Pennsylvania Press, 1995. 420p. bibliog. Middle Ages Series).

Heraldry

97 **Lines of succession: heraldry of the royal families of Europe.**
Tables by Jiří Louda, text by Michael Maclagan. London: Orbis,
1981. 308p. maps. Reprinted, 1984. Rev. eds., London: Macdonald,
1991; 1995.

Jiří Louda is an internationally recognized illustrator, specializing in coats of arms.
This beautifully produced book starts with a good lengthy introduction to heraldry
before focusing on individual European countries. Chapter twenty-one, on Bohemia
(p. 167-71) contains: the genealogies and coats of arms of the rulers of the Lands of
the Bohemian Crown from the original House of Přemysl, through the house of
Luxemburg and Jagellon; and a genealogical table and family tree of the Winter King,
Frederick, Elector Palatine, King of Bohemia (elected 1619). The general overview
starts with Břetislav I, the ruler of Bohemia from 1034, and concludes with Charles I,
the last Emperor of Austria-Hungary. Inevitably, there is an overlap with chapters on
Austria, Hungary, Poland and other countries; their histories are interwoven.

98 **Království české: erby a rodokmeny vládnoucích rodů. Kingdom of
Bohemia: arms and pedigrees of reigning houses. Königreich
Böhmen: Wappen und Genealogie der regierenden Häuser.
Royaume de Bohême: armoiries et généalogie des maisons
souveraines.**
Jiří Louda. Havířov, Czech Republic: Petr Pavlík, 1996. 122p.
12 plates.

This huge book (the format is 38 cm by 54 cm and it weighs 5 kg), beautifully bound
in dark blue velvet, will not be easy to obtain. The British Library has a copy and the
author presented copies to several genealogical and heraldic institutions in England.
Enquiries relating to heraldry from the public and researchers are many. Jiří Louda's
Lines of succession: heraldry of the royal families of Europe (q.v.) is available in most
reference sections of larger public libraries. The Czech text in this book has been
translated into English, French and German. It is a remarkable book which contains
basic biographical data on all Czech rulers, from the Prince Bořivoj (c. 894) to the last

30

Austrian emperor Charles I. The coats of arms of all rulers are also provided from the beginnings of heraldry in the Bohemian Lands, that is from the 12th century. Jiří Louda had completed the book in 1948, but it would have been difficult to publish in the Communist era and even in the new market economy such a publication was not considered commercially viable. It took Louda some time to find a brave publisher and a sponsor. He is the designer of the Czech Republic's emblem and of the Czech presidential standard, and a member of heraldic societies in Britain and in France.

99 **Erbovník, aneb Kniha o znacích i osudech rodů žijících v Čechách a na Moravě podle starých pramenů a dávných ne vždy věrných svědectví.** (Heraldry, or a book of the armorial bearings and the fortunes of the families living in Bohemia and Moravia according to the ancient sources and bygone, not always reliable testimonies.)
Milan Mysliveček. Prague: Horizont, 1993. 159p. + 63p. of plates.
The new post-Communist era revived interest among the Czechs, abroad and at home, in the old Bohemian and Moravian families. But for the country's unfortunate history there would be more of them. This colourful book, which is even available in some libraries in Britain, contains: 63 pages of plates, some in colour; English, French and German summaries; and an index. Of more limited interest is *Biskupové Čech, Moravy a Slezska po roce 1918 a jejich znaky* (The bishops of Bohemia, Moravia and Silesia since 1918 and their coats of arms), by Pavel R. Pokorný with illustrations by Jiří Hanáček (Ostrava, Czech Republic: Genealogická agentura, 1992. 67p.).

100 **Městské znaky v českých zemích.** (The coats of arms of towns in the Czech Lands.)
Jiří Čarek. Prague: Academia, 1985. 453p. + 146p. of illustrations.
This large tome starts with the general history of heraldry in relation to towns. The second part is a codex of coats of arms of towns in the Czech Lands, with a description of each crest. The arrangement is alphabetical. The description of each crest is in some detail, since the information is intended not only for heraldists and historians, but also for use by local authorities and institutions. For that reason the principles of heraldry are also explained. Each annotation provides a brief history of the town and village, followed by a description of the crest and a listing of available documents and sources. The last section of the book consists of 146 pages in colour of all the known coats of arms. *Pražská heraldika* (Prague heraldry) by Jakub Hrdlička (Prague: Public History, 1994) is a Czech publication which deals specifically with Prague.

History

General

Central and Eastern Europe

101 **Central and Eastern Europe.**
John Dornberg. Phoenix, Arizona: Oryx Press, 1995. 238p. maps.
bibliog. (International Government and Politics Series).
This contemporary history of Central Europe is divided into two sections. The first
section addresses: the changes and developments in the area since the miracle of 1989;
the issues of the revival of ex-Communists and nationalism; the break-up of
Czechoslovakia and Yugoslavia; the religious and ethnic conflicts; and social changes
such as setbacks for women. The second section deals with individual countries.
Chapter twelve, 'The Czech Republic and Slovakia' (p. 111-28), provides: statistical
profiles; a common history of the Czechs and Slovaks before 1918; a history of
Czechoslovakia from 1918-93; an account of the political developments of the 1990s;
and a study of the economy since 1989. The book contains a glossary and an excellent
index. It offers a very good general introduction to contemporary Central Europe with
an accent on the economy.

102 **The making of Eastern Europe.**
Philip Longworth. Basingstoke, England; London: Macmillan Press
Ltd, 1994. 320p. maps. bibliog.
An important historical analysis, adopting a bold, 'provocative' approach in search of
the origins of the region's current problems. Longworth works his way back, from
1989 to the year 324. This first-rate study is intended for students and general readers,
leaning towards readers with an Anglo-Saxon background: the references are mostly
to English-language material and comparisons with the West are made. The early
history of Central Europe is also the subject of a study by Charles R. Bowlus, *Franks,
Moravians and Magyars: the struggle for the middle Danube* (Philadelphia:
University of Pennsylvania Press, 1995. 420p. bibliog.).

103 **The Slavs in European history and civilisation.**
Francis Dvornik. New Brunswick, New Jersey: Rutgers University
Press, 1962. 2nd paperback printing. 688p. maps. bibliog.
Acknowledges the key role played by early Bohemia before and after its kings became
Holy Roman Emperors and thus covers Czech history, especially the mediaeval
period, in fair detail. The author, however, stresses the unity of the Slavs, based on
'common traits in their political history, their civilization, their national character, and
language'; and it is perhaps as well that he uses no stronger word than 'traits' here.
While some sections pick out the Czechs for nominally separate discussion, the fact
that this is often barely possible is tacitly acknowledged in the constant recognition of
inter-Slav or international factors necessarily involved in the nation's history. The
end-point of the account is the Slav Congress of 1848 and its later echoes.

104 **The other Europe: Eastern Europe to 1945.**
E. Garrison Walters. New York: Dorset Press, 1988. 430p. maps.
bibliog.
A general history of Eastern Europe from earliest times to the end of the Second
World War. The arrangement is chronological, focusing on the major events, pre-
dominantly revolutions and wars. Walters highlights the phenomenon of nationalism
and its various manifestations and the distinctive cultural heritages of the various
countries. The study is intended both for students and non-specialist readers.

105 **East European history: selected papers of the Third World
Congress for Soviet and East European Studies.**
Edited by Stanislav J. Kirschbaum. Columbia, Ohio: Slavica
Publishers, 1988. 183p.
A selection from more than 600 papers presented or distributed at the Congress, which
took place in Washington, DC from 30 October to 4 November 1985. Two papers
have a Czech theme: 'People's democracy: the emergence of a Czech political concept
in the late nineteenth century' by Eva Schmidt-Hartmann (p. 125-40); and
'Dependence or independence? Relations between the Red Unions and the Communist
Party of Czechoslovakia' by Kevin McDermott (p. 157-84).

106 **Historical reflections on Central Europe: selected papers from the
Fifth World Congress of Central and East European Studies,
Warsaw, 1995.**
Edited by Stanislav J. Kirschbaum. Basingstoke, England: Macmillan
Press Ltd; New York: St. Martin's Press, Inc., 1995. 245p.
The titles of the contributions with a Czech theme are an indication of the diversity of
the papers presented: 'T. G. Masaryk's *Nová Evropa*: a reinterpretation' by Francesco
Leoncini (p. 65-73); 'Czechoslovakia and the anti-Hitler emigrants, 1933-1939' by
Frank Hahn (p. 74-90); 'Václav Havel and the ideal democracy' by Marie L. Neudorfl
(p. 116-37); 'Social and political contributions of theatre to the Czechoslovak
revolution of 1989' by Janet Savin (p. 138-61); and 'Social partnership in the Czech
Republic' by Zdenka Mansfeldová (p. 207-18).

107 **Historians as nation builders: Central and South-East Europe.**
Edited by Dennis Deletant, Harry Hanak. Basingstoke, England:
Macmillan, in association with the School of Slavonic and East
European Studies, University of London, 1988. 245p. bibliog. (Studies
in Russian and East European History).
A collection of studies in historiography dedicated to the memory of Hugh Seton-
Watson, Professor of Russian History at the University of London School of Slavonic
and East European Studies from 1951-83. Hugh Seton-Watson died in 1984. Some of
the contributions deal with East European historiography in general, but two have a
specifically Czech theme: Harry Hanak's 'Czech historians and the end of Austria-
Hungary' (p. 70-86); and Robert Pynsent's 'Žalud-Vysokomýtský: a Czech rebel
historian of 1848-9' (p. 174-205). Žalud-Vysokomýtský was the author of *Početí roku
1620 a sledí jeho* (The conception of 1620 and its sequel), published in Litoměřice in
1849, which was banned under Austria-Hungary, the main reason being the stand the
author took against the German elements and against the Roman-Catholic church.
Each paper contains a separate 'Notes' section and there is a common name and
subject index on p. 238-45. Chapter thirteen is a 'Bibliography of works of Hugh
Seton-Watson' (p. 216-37), by John C. K. Daly.

Czech Lands

108 **The Columbia history of Eastern Europe in the twentieth century.**
Edited by Joseph Held. New York: Columbia University Press, 1992.
435p. maps. bibliog.
Presents papers from a conference held at Rutgers University in February 1990. The
collection starts with a very detailed, sometimes even day-by-day, 'Chronology of
events in Eastern Europe, 1918-1990' (p. xi-lxix). This is followed by articles on
individual countries. 'Czechoslovakia' (p. 119-63) is by Sharon L. Wolchik. The book
has a selective 'Bibliography' (p. 405-16) of sources used. There are also notes on the
'Contributors' (p. 417-18) and an 'Index' (p. 419-35).

109 **Czechoslovakia.**
William V. Wallace. Boulder, Colorado: Westview Press; London;
Tonbridge, England: Benn, 1976. 374p. maps. bibliog.
A major, highly readable modern history of the Czech Lands which reaches back to
the middle of the 19th century and ends with the reform movement of the 1960s. The
book offers an account of demographic, economic and social change, and of the
international dimension behind all the country's major turning points, especially in
1938, 1948 and 1968. The book contains an extensive periodized bibliography, an
index of names, and an interesting selection of thirty-two photographs depicting
people, places and events. A wealth of detailed historical information can be found in
Twentieth century Czechoslovakia: the meaning of its history, by Joseph Korbel (New
York: Columbia University Press, 1977. 346p. bibliog.). Korbel, an émigré of the
1948 generation, is solidly pro-Masaryk, whom he sees as the country's ideal
statesman and proponent of his nation's freedom and social justice.

110 **R. W. Seton-Watson and his relations with the Czechs and Slovaks: documents 1906-1951.**
Edited by Jan Rychlík, Thomas D. Marzik, Miroslav Bielik. Prague: Ústav T. G. Masaryka; Martin, Slovakia: Matica Slovenská, 1995-96. 2 vols. bibliog.

This collection of documents is based on: the R. W. Seton-Watson Papers in the archives of the School of Slavonic and East European Studies, London; the diaries and private letters which are the property of his younger son Christopher; and some documents which were chosen from archives in the Czech and Slovak republics. R. W. Seton-Watson held the Masaryk Chair of Central European Studies in London from 1922 and the Chair of Czechoslovak Studies at Oxford University from 1945-49. This is a multilingual work: the preface and introduction are in English and in Czech or Slovak, and these languages are used alternately in the abstracts of the documents and in the captions, explanations, footnotes and notes. The first volume contains the documents which, although selected, span from Seton-Watson's first encounter with his future Slovak friend Anton Štefánek in 1906, to the death of Seton-Watson in 1951 and illustrate both his personal and official relations with the two nations. The majority of the documents are reprinted in the language in which they were written, this being mostly English; a few are in German, Czech, Slovak or French. Each document is introduced by a brief abstract in English and in either Czech or Slovak, and the place of origin and date are given. Beneath the text is information as to the type of document and its location. The documents are arranged by date of origin, and volume one contains a few historical photographs. Volume two has a chronological register of the documents presented in volume one and the text of the abstract of the document, in English and in Czech or Slovak. This is followed by: 'Itineraries of R. W. Seton-Watson in Central and Eastern Europe 1905-1946' (p. 57-58); 'Bibliography of R. W. Seton-Watson's main publications relating to Czechs and Slovaks' (p. 59-60); and a substantial, useful 'Name index' in English (p. 61-135) and in Czech/Slovak (p. 137-223). The 'Geographical Index' (p. 225-41) concludes this reference volume. The editors state that the book is intended for Czechs and Slovaks and for a wider English-reading public. The publication has been long overdue, the documents on Seton-Watson's relations with Romanians and Southern Slavs having been published many years ago. This work gives expanded space to these important documents, which the status of Seton-Watson among Slavists deserves. The documents offer a new depth to Anglo-Czechoslovak relations and an original perspective on Czech and Slovak history in the first half of this century.

111 **The making of a new Europe: R. W. Seton-Watson and the last years of Austria-Hungary.**
Hugh Seton-Watson, Christopher Seton-Watson. London: Methuen, 1981. 459p. bibliog.

In essence this is a biography of Scotus Viator, as Seton-Watson was known. The volume contains a great deal of valuable material concerning the birth of Czechoslovakia, including Seton-Watson's contribution to Tomáš Masaryk's thinking and his influence on the British government and its policies towards Central Europe generally. The book contains generous quotations from Seton-Watson himself.

35

112 **Historical dictionary of the Czech state.**
Jiří Hochman. Lanham, Maryland; London: The Scarecrow Press, 1998. 203p. map. bibliog. (European Historical Dictionaries, no. 23).
This basic reference book offers a 'Note on spelling' and pronunciation (p. xi), a chronology of Czech history, and a brief description of the country which covers: geography, the population, education, the economy, transport and communications, and the political system. The dictionary proper is encyclopaedic in form and consists of entries for various major figures (with the accent on modern and contemporary), institutions, places, historical events, political parties and movements. Each entry has a commentary. Hochman himself was a journalist and the book was obviously compiled for the use of journalists, librarians and information workers. Although valuable for being up to date, it is not actually comprehensive and for a scholar it is far too abridged. There is a list of Czech princes, kings and presidents, the text of Charter 77 and the Charter of fundamental rights and freedoms. The bibliography is substantial; it is divided by subject and lists major journals published in the main fields (e.g. philosophy, Slavic studies, biology). This is preceded by a list of academic libraries and academic information centres with addresses and e-mail addresses, where available.

113 **Bohemia: an historical sketch.**
Francis von Lützow. London: J. M. Dent & Sons Ltd, 1939. rev. ed., with a new section by H. A. Piehler. 379p. bibliog. maps. (Everyman's Library).
Count von Lützow (1849-1916), who divided his home between Žampach in Eastern Bohemia and London, was a Czech nobleman, diplomat and historian, who was also active in politics at the Austrian court in Vienna. He was a supporter of the movement for Czech self-government and an advocate of Czech-British cultural relations and social contacts. This book was first published by Dent in 1896 and remained for a long time the only complete history of Bohemia available in English translation. The book is still appreciated by the enlightened English visitor; it helps to comprehend Prague, a phenomenon steeped in history, and somehow has the quality which enables the English reader to relate the events from Czech history to the parallel events in Britain, thus bringing the geographically distant Czech past closer and making various issues easier to understand. Lützow deals with the period from AD 100 to 1879, in an apparently congested, yet readable text. This is continued by H. A. Piehler's 'Outline of the history of the Czech nation from 1879 to 1939', starting on p. 351. This edition has an introduction by President T. G. Masaryk. The book does not have a separate bibliography but rich footnotes refer to books for further reading. The appendix on p. 372 lists the princes (the rulers up to 1230) and subsequent kings of Bohemia and the presidents of Czechoslovakia. This is followed by a brief index on p. 373-79.

114 **A history of the Czechs and Slovaks.**
R. W. Seton-Watson. London; New York; Melbourne: Hutchinson, 1943. Reprinted, Hamden, Connecticut: Archon Books, 1965. 413p. maps. bibliog.
According to Polišenský (q.v.), who is widely regarded as the foremost expert on Anglo-Czech relations, this is the most accessible of the general histories of Czechs and Slovaks and is still widely considered the best, a classic written by one who came to be regarded as a competent foreign spokesman for the two nations. The study was

36

first published nearly sixty years ago. Polišenský considers *The spirit of Bohemia: a survey of Czechoslovak history, music and literature* by Vladimír Nosek (London: George Allen & Unwin, 1926. 379p. bibliog.) of lesser value. It provides a comprehensive view of Czech literature and music, although half of the book is heavily weighted towards religious history, or history as carried forward largely by the great religious, or at least religion-based, controversies of the 14th-17th centuries. Kamil Krofta's *Short history of Czechoslovakia* (London: Williams & Norgate, 1935) has the disadvantage that it was written primarily for Czech readers. More notable is R. J. Kerner's *Czechoslovakia* (Berkeley, California; Los Angeles: University of California Press, 1940).

115 **History of Czechoslovakia in outline.**
    J. V. Polišenský. Prague: Bohemia International, 1991. 2nd ed. 142p.
    bibliog.

Professor Polišenský is *the* Czech expert on Anglo-Czech relations. This book is based on three lectures given in London in 1946 and as such is intended primarily for the English reader. The introduction is dated 1947 and is by R. R. Betts, Masaryk Professor of Central European History, School of Slavonic and East European Studies, London University. This basic but excellent first introduction to Czech history is supplemented by: a note on English-language books on Czech history; a note on Czech pronunciation; a detailed index; a useful and interesting comparative chronology of Great Britain and Czechoslovakia; and a fair amount of illustrations.

116 **A history of the Czechs.**
    A. H. Hermann. London: Allen Lane, 1975. 324p. maps.

A concise summary of Czech history which devotes most attention to the 20th century. It underlines the Western framework of the Czechs' cultural and political traditions, and relates the major turning points in Czech history to international events. The Czechs are seen as a major factor in the history of Austria, and Austria is presented as having been a safe haven for the Czechs between the giants of Russia and Prussia to the east and west. Very importantly, attention is drawn to the significance of cultural and literary activity, especially in the 20th century, although art, literature and politics have always been more inseparable among the Czechs than in many other nations.

117 **The stones of Prague.**
    Mary R. Anderson. Dubicko, Czech Republic: INFOA, 1998. 92p.
    bibliog.

A pocket-size, elegant book, inspired by the author's admiration of Prague, which offers a brief, illustrated history of the Czech Lands, from the arrival of Celtic tribes in the country in the 4th century BC to the present. The book has two sections: the first part sets Czech history into a European context, and the second highlights important Czech historical events and personalities.

118 **Czechoslovakia at the crossroads of European history.**
    Jaroslav Krejčí. London; New York: I. B. Tauris & Co., 1990. 255p.
    map. bibliog.

A philosophical, unconventional history book researching the influence and impact the Czechs had over 1,000 years on the course of European political, economic and

37

cultural history. Three times in their history the Czechs 'stood in the forefront of conflagration stretching far beyond their borders; their country became the place of opposition against mightier forces in their surroundings'. The first time was during the Hussite revolution in the 15th century, when they opposed the Roman Church and the Roman Empire, the second time in 1618 when the Protestant Bohemian Estates revolted against their Catholic king and thus started the Thirty Years War. On the third occasion, the Munich Agreement in 1938 and the Czech lack of defiance postponed the Second World War by a year. The narrative follows the headlines of history, covers all issues and aims to provide the background to explain why the Czech experience of democracy was unique in Central and Eastern Europe.

119 **Geschichte Böhmens: von der slavischen Landnahme bis zur Gegenwart.** (History Bohemia: from the annexation by the Slavs to the present.)
Jörg K. Hoensch. Munich: Verlag C. H. Beck, 1997. 3rd enlarged ed. 588p. maps. bibliog. (Beck's Historische Bibliothek).

The bulk of this beautifully produced book is made up of indexes, notes and a bibliography, while the narrative itself is fairly brief. A few illustrations would have made this volume, which is after all meant to be a popular Czech history in German, more digestible for the general reader. The time-scale is broad, which makes it one of the most up-to-date histories. Beginning in the 9th century, the coverage ends with the new, separate Czech Republic in 1996.

120 **Toulky českou minulostí.** (Wanderings through the Czech past.)
Petr Hora-Hořejš. Prague: Baronet, 1993- . maps.

Volume one was published by Bonus Press, Prague. At the time of writing the latest volume published was number six, taking the reader to the time of the National Revival in the 19th century. These 'wanderings' through history, which start in the Stone Age, skip from facts to legends, from history to the history of art and literature. The books, which are handsomely produced in A4 format, are intended for a general audience and are rich in illustrations and maps.

121 **Československé dějiny v datech.** (Czechoslovak history in data.)
Prague: Svoboda, 1986. 2nd enlarged ed. 714p. maps. bibliog.

This volume is intended for quick reference, and as such the work has little narrative. The main section of this history is a chronological list of historical events, each with a short explanation. The appendixes are numerous, comprising: a list of the heads of states in Central Europe from 830 to the date of publication; a chronology of church hierarchy; a list of Austrian and later Czechoslovak governments; election results from 1907-81; basic data from historical demography; and a quantity of maps.

122 **Czech history: chronological survey.**
Jaroslav Krejčíř, Stanislav Soják, translated by Jan Mynařík. Dubicko, Czech Republic: INFOA, [1996]. 150p. maps.

Widely available in Czech bookshops due to its suitability for tourists, this publication suffers from bad grammar and strange syntax and expressions. The facts, however, are accurate and there are plenty of them. The chronology of Czech history has a wealth of illustrations and numerous appendixes, listing: sovereigns and heads of state of neighbouring countries; popes; Czech governments; and architectural styles in the Lands of the Bohemian Crown.

123 Fundamentals of Czech history.
Petr Čornej, translated by Todd Morath. Prague: Práh, 1992. 46p.

A very brief introduction to Czech history, presumably intended for tourists or foreigners relocated to the Czech Republic, which starts from primeval times and goes up to 1989. The main virtue of this publication is that it is concise, has a fair amount of illustrations and, being strictly chronological, it is handy for orientation, despite the lack of any index and the awkward language of the translation from Czech. A good, modern, succinct summary of Czech history in good English has still to be published.

124 Rulers of the Czech Lands.
Petr Čornej, Jiřina Lockerová, Pavel Major. Prague: Fragment, 1997. 64p. (The Legacy Edition).

This illustrated large-format book 'attempts, in a brief but complete review, to portray all the historically proved rulers of the Czech lands and make their faces known'. The illustrator had to improvize greatly with the early rulers whose images are not known. The book starts with Samo, the Frankish merchant, who after 620 AD organized a political unit which included Bohemia and Moravia, and ends with the present president Václav Havel. As such it provides a simple history of the Czech Lands. The illustrations are the main features; on most pages they take up more space than the text. The book is available widely in Czech bookshops and is intended for older children and tourists.

125 Bibliografie k dějinám měst České republiky. (A bibliography of the history of the towns in the Czech Republic.)
Compiled by Jaromír Kubíček, with an introduction by Jaroslav Pánek. Brno, Czech Republic: Sdružení knihoven ČR, 1997. 275p. maps.

This publication is part of an international programme on municipal and urban history. It is a selective bibliography – one of the inclusion criteria is that the publication must have more than sixteen pages. The selection of towns corresponds to the current administrative structure and the citation follows the rules of historical bibliography. The list is arranged into large geographical units and within these the towns are listed alphabetically. The name of the town is followed by basic data (the number of inhabitants in 1861, 1900, 1950 and 1991, the first written record and when the status of town was obtained) prior to the relevant bibliographical entries. The text is in Czech and German.

Early mediaeval, mediaeval and early modern history

General

126 **East-Central Europe in the Middle Ages: 1000-1500.**
Jean W. Sedlar. Seattle, Washington; London: University of Washington Press, 1994. 556p. bibliog. (A History of East-Central Europe, vol. III).

A much needed and excellent first systematic study and overview of the lands between the Labe (Elbe) and Ukraine in the Middle Ages, aimed at the general reader as well as the historian. The book is organized thematically and comparisons between nationalities are drawn. Examples of the topics covered are: early migration; state formation; monarchies; social structure; religion and churches; governments and judicial systems; ethnicity and nationalism; culture; and education. Sedlar's writing is fluent and lucid. The book has a number of appendixes (chronologies, lists of monarchs, place-names equivalents) and a bibliography in the form of an essay (p. 497-527).

127 **Good King Wenceslas: the real story.**
Jan Rejzl. Norwich, England: 1st Choice Publishing, 1995. 108p. maps.

Written in the style of Czech history textbooks, in that it is packed with data which are bound together by rather stilted English. It is difficult to decide what type of readership it is aimed at: probably at expatriate Czechs. It is too factual for a general English reader and not scholarly enough for an academic. The story of Wenceslas is described in great detail, going well into his background, his times and the lasting influence of this saint. The author obviously loved the subject and takes his reader on a pilgrimage to a number of places connected with Wenceslas and Czech history. The volume is very well documented by old and modern drawings, sketches, plans of churches and castles and photographs.

128 **Essays in Czech history.**
Reginald Robert Betts. London: Athlone Press, 1969. 315p. bibliog.

A posthumous collection of scattered essays which, taken together, offer a partial history of mediaeval Bohemia including its scholarship (two essays on the University of Prague, founded in 1348) and philosophy (political ideas and religious reform: the Hussite movement). There are also short monographs on Jan Hus, Jerome of Prague and Peter Payne (the English 'heretic', better known in Czech, than English, history; other aspects of English influence are discussed in another essay). Two further papers look at mediaeval society, and the last one provides an analysis of Masaryk's philosophy of history.

129 **Charles IV., the king from golden cradle.**
Eduard Petiška. Prague: Martin, 1994. 92p.

A brief biography of Charles IV (1316-78), the emperor and king of Bohemia, who made Prague the capital of the Holy Roman Empire. The book includes a section

entitled 'Tales from Karlštejn', Charles' favourite castle, which he had specially built
to house the Bohemian crown jewels. This is a slim, nicely produced paperback with
numerous, mostly old, black-and-white illustrations, including a gallery of Bohemian
rulers.

130 **L'Empéreur Charles IV: l'art en Europe au XIVe siècle.** (Emperor
     Charles IV: art in Europe in the 14th century.)
     Karel Stejskal, translated from the Czech into French by Jean Karel,
     Renée Karel.   Paris: Grund, 1980. 230p.

Written for a more sophisticated reader than Petiška's book (see previous entry).
Charles IV was an exceptional ruler, who had a great impact on the development of
the Czech Lands. Stejskal analyses such topics as the legacy of the Přemyslide
dynasty, the arts in the Czech Lands at the time (St Vitus' cathedral in Prague receives
special attention here), and the position of Prague as the capital of an empire. This
well-researched book is rich in illustrations and includes plans, a descriptive
catalogue, a genealogical tree of Charles IV, a chronology and an index.

Reformation, Jan Hus, Hussitism

131 **Jan Hus.**
     Eva Kantůrková.   Prague: Melantrich, 1991. 466p. bibliog.

Although published in Czech and therefore not easily accessible, this study has the
right balance of biographical information on Jan Hus, his teaching, general theological
discourses, and the politics and culture of mediaeval Bohemia and Central Europe.
There has been a renewed interest in the major figures of Czech history since the
Velvet Revolution, and this work reflects the interest in Jan Hus. The selective
bibliography lists Czech sources only, which have been used for the compilation of
this study.

132 **John Hus: a biography.**
     Matthew Spinka.   Princeton, New Jersey: Princeton University Press,
     1968. 344p. maps. bibliog.

After thirty years this work remains a major work on Hus in English. Spinka sets his
analysis of the life and work of John Hus, the 15th-century Czech Protestant reformer,
in historical and theological context. He starts with an account of the reigns of Charles
IV and Wenceslas IV and of the precursors of Hus, and includes, at the appropriate
point, a description of the opposition to Hus's reforming efforts. Spinka goes on to
summarize the events that followed Hus's burning at the stake in 1415 and recounts
details of the lives of the preachers known as Hus's successors. The volume includes
an analysis of Hus's major works and many useful snippets, such as the translation, in
the epilogue, of the best-known Hussite battle-hymn, *Ktož sú boží bojovníci.*

History. Early mediaeval, mediaeval and early modern history. Reformation, Jan Hus, Hussitism

133 **Jan Hus as a general linguist, with special reference to Česká nedělní postila.**
David Short. In: *Essays in Czech and Slovak language and literature.* London: School of Slavonic and East European Studies, University of London, 1996, p. 1-15.

Adapted from a paper given at a conference on heresy, held at the School of Slavonic and East European Studies, London in 1994. It is intended for linguists and historians, the objective being to confirm on the basis of Jan Hus's *Česká nedělní postila* (Czech postilla for Sundays) that he was a linguist of 'considerable breadth and even, for his time, sophistication'. He is here interpreted as lexicologist, onomast, lexicographer and etymologist, practising translator, speech therapist and nascent aspectologist. Hus's general contribution to the external history of Czech – his purism, stylistics and the introduction of diacritics – has long been acknowledged.

134 **From Oxford to Prague: the writings of John Wycliffe and his English followers in Bohemia.**
A. Hudson. *Slavonic and East European Review*, vol. 75, no. 4 (October 1997), p. 642-57. bibliog.

Hudson provides an account of how, in 1406-07, two Czech friends, Mikuláš Faulfis and Jiří Kněhnic, spent time in Oxford copying 'De ecclesia' and 'De dominio divino', written by the English religious reformer John Wycliffe, and searching for authoritative copies of works on theories which were already known in Bohemia. Mikuláš Faulfis is thought to have been a colourful character.

135 **The magnificent ride: the first Reformation in Hussite Bohemia.**
Thomas A. Fudge. Aldershot, England; Brookfield, Vermont; Singapore; Sydney: Ashgate, 1998. 315p. bibliog. (St Andrews Studies in Reformation History).

The social and religious dimensions of the Hussite revolutionary movement are examined and reconstructed. 'The book is concerned chiefly not with telling the narrative history of the Hussite story but rather in coming to terms with the Hussite phenomenon as a historical reality in the sense of a popular social and religious movement' comprising a reformation in its own right' (p. 2). The bibliography lists manuscripts in various European archives and books. The selection of books gives priority to titles in English and lists only essential Czech titles.

136 **The Hussite revolution: 1424-1437.**
František Michálek Bartoš, English edition prepared by John M. Klassen. Boulder, Colorado: East European Monographs. Distributed by Columbia University Press, New York, 1986. 204p. bibliog.

This abridged version of a Czech original deals with the second half of the Hussite wars, after the death of the Hussite military leader Jan Žižka in 1424. Although the narrative is short, it provides plenty of historical detail and goes well beyond the year 1437, pondering on the echoes and achievements of this revolution. The greatest Czech historian, Jan Palacký, called the Hussite movement the culminating epoch of Czech history. The book is well documented by detailed 'Notes', which include bibliographical notes. It is often referred to and cited in other English publications.

42

137 **The Hussite revolution.**
Jiří Kejř, translated by Till Gottheinerová. Prague: Orbis, 1988.
159p. maps. bibliog.

Although richly documented by illustrations, photographs and maps, this volume offers only a superficial history of the greatest Czech anti-feudal movement, which was the culmination of the deep crisis in society in the first half of the 15th century and has had a major impact on the Czechs over the last 500 years. The book is not aimed at scholars, but is rather a coffee-table book. The English translation is lacking in smoothness.

138 **John Žižka and the Hussite revolution.**
Frederick G. Heymann. Princeton, New Jersey: Princeton University Press, 1955. 521p. maps. bibliog.

Jan Žižka of Trocnov (1360?-1424) was one of the main Hussite leaders and the eventual controller of much of Bohemia, having fallen out with the Taborites (a radical religious group within the Hussite movement). This book is a mixture of history and biography of the first quarter of the 15th century. Žižka was one of the foremost generals of the Hussite wars and part of his renown resides in some of the military techniques which he invented and which were so successful as to have been adopted by many others far away in time and space. This is one of the best accounts of the role of Žižka, a one-eyed military leader who, to this day, is a revered figure in the Czech firmament of religious and political militancy whenever it surfaces.

139 **The nobility and the making of the Hussite revolution.**
John Martin Klassen. Boulder, Colorado: East European Quarterly. Distributed by Columbia University Press, New York, 1978. 186p. map. bibliog. (East European Monographs, no. 47).

A collection of essays, which only partially amount to a consecutive history. Klassen analyses the role of both Catholic and Protestant nobility during the Hussite revolution. In theory he sees the importance of nobility as dispensers of patronage over priests' livings and parish economies, and in practice as positive defenders of the Hussite cause around the time of Hus's death and during the years immediately following. The concluding essay describes the short- and long-term advantages that accrued to the nobility in the aftermath of the Hussite revolution.

140 **Great revolutions compared: the outline of a theory.**
Jaroslav Krejčí. New York; London: Harvester Wheatsheaf, 1994. 302p. bibliog.

A revised and updated edition of a classic which examines the causes, origins, types and range of social changes throughout history, focusing particularly on political and cultural aspects. Bohemia (1403-58), on p. 47-71, is the first of the main case-studies. There are also references to the Hussite revolution in the general introduction and conclusion and there is a graph and a chronology accompanying a morphological model of the Hussite revolution on p. 192-94. The bibliography at the end of the book is substantial and there are 'Notes' at the end of the 'Bohemia' case-study, on p. 69-71, discussing books and articles published on the subject, mostly in English.

43

History. Early mediaeval, mediaeval and early modern history. Anabaptism and the Czech Brethren

George of Poděbrady

141 **The Hussite king: Bohemia in European affairs 1440-1471.**
Otakar Odložilík. New Brunswick, New Jersey: Rutgers University Press, 1965. 375p. maps. bibliog.

George of Poděbrady, the 'Hussite king' (1458-71), is widely perceived as one of the best rulers the Czechs have ever had, due to his genuine and far-felt statesmanship. The extent of his impact on contemporary affairs means that this biography is simultaneously a history of Bohemia and at least a partial history of the adjacent states and provinces and some more distant ones, notably France. After dealing with the wars at the end of George's reign, the author traces the next half-century of political and religious developments, including the destiny of George's children, many of whom became Catholics.

142 **George of Poděbrady: king of heretics.**
Frederick G. Heymann. Princeton, New Jersey: Princeton University Press, 1965. 671p. map. bibliog.

The book is a sequel to *John Žižka and the Hussite revolution* (q.v.). Heymann enlarges on the view that developments under this king were parallel to what was happening elsewhere in Europe – a 'vigorous if short-lived development of "Tudorism" in Bohemia'. The quinquecentennial celebration of George of Poděbrady, supported by UNESCO, saw the publication of *The universal peace organization of King George of Bohemia: a fifteenth century plan for world peace 1462-1464*, edited by the respected historians František Kavka, Vladimír Outrata and Josef Polišenský (Prague: Publishing House of the Czechoslovak Academy of Sciences, 1964. 122p.). The volume is in two parts: a historical essay on George of Poděbrady's proposals for a league of Christian nations by Václav Vaněček; and a transcript of the original Latin text of the proposal, edited by Jiří Kejř, together with modern translations into English, Russian, French and Spanish.

Anabaptism and the Czech Brethren

143 **The political and social doctrines of the Unity of Czech Brethren in the fifteenth and early sixteenth centuries.**
Peter Brock. The Hague: Mouton, 1957. 302p. bibliog.

Even forty years after its conception this remains an important work for an understanding of religious and hence social and political development in the Czech Lands after Jan Hus. It includes an account of the Unity of Czech Brethren (a reformed church founded in 1457 by separation from Utraquists), not only of the evolution of its ideology, based originally on strict inner discipline, voluntary poverty and non-resistance to aggression (the teaching of Chelčický) and the main split in the movement, but in particular an appraisal of the life and work of Petr Chelčický, the precursor of the Brethren and one of the main figures of Czech religious and political history.

44

144 **The anabaptists and the Czech Brethren in Moravia 1526-1628: a study of origins and contacts.**
Jarold Knox Zeman, foreword by Jaroslav Pelikán. The Hague: Mouton, 1969. 407p. bibliog.

A major contribution to Moravian, hence Czech, religious history, this is a detailed and documented study of Czech anabaptists, with whom the Brethren had not only negotiated for a merger, but had also engaged in some serious theological polemics. Incorporated in the account is a record of other religious influences at work, especially those from Germany and Switzerland. An important academic contribution of this work is the detailed historical topography showing the times when, and places where, individuals of the many religious sub-groupings could have been in contact.

Habsburg period (16th century to 1918)

General

145 **The Habsburg Empire 1790-1918.**
C. A. Macartney. London: Weidenfeld & Nicolson, 1968. 886p. map. bibliog.

A history of the whole period of the monarchy, in wide use as a standard text. The emphasis is on political, social, economic and national development, and in all of these areas specific measures and other changes originating at the centre had direct consequences for the Czechs.

146 **The decline and fall of the Habsburg Empire: 1815-1918.**
Alan Sked. London; New York: Longman, 1989. 295p. maps. bibliog.

The subject of this study is very broad – and not only in the geographical sense – but it is very relevant to Czech development in the later part of the 19th century and early part of the 20th century. The sequence of chapters is chronological, each accompanied by a substantial bibliography. Appendixes are on 'Chronology of events', 'Habsburg Foreign Ministers' and 'Population and nationalities in the empire'. The maps are also a valuable adjunct, in particular 'Nationalities of the Empire' on p. 284.

147 **Die tschechische Gesselschaft 1848 bis 1918.** (Czech society from 1848-1918.)
Otto Urban, translated from the Czech by Henning Schlegel. Vienna; Cologne, Germany; Weimar, Germany: Böhlau Verlag, 1994. 2 vols. bibliog. (Anton Gindely Reihe zur Geschichte der Donaumonarchie und Mitteleuropas, herausgegeben von Gerald Stourzh, 2).

A political, social and cultural history. The author systematically handles Czech society's demographic, economic, social and cultural evolution. Volume one is the narrative proper, a vast tome of 930 pages. Volume two consists of a chronology, an extensive bibliography of mostly German and Czech sources, a name index and notes.

148 **Intellectuals and the future in the Habsburg monarchy, 1890-1914.**
Edited by László Péter, Robert B. Pynsent. Basingstoke, England: Macmillan, in association with the School of Slavonic and East European Studies, University of London, 1988. 196p. bibliog.

The editors state in their 'Introduction' that 'the culture of Austria-Hungary at the turn of the century has done as much or more than any other culture to shape the thinking of Twentieth-century European man. This collection of essays is intended to lay bare some of the roots of that phenomenon' (p. 12). The collection contains three articles which concern the Czech Lands directly: 'The decadent nation' by Robert B. Pynsent from the School of Slavonic and East European Studies (p. 63-91); 'The meaning of Czech history' by Karel Brušák from Cambridge University (p. 92-106); and 'National sensualism' by Tomáš Vlček from Prague (p. 107-28). To be fully accurate, the essay on 'Sigmund Freud' by Brian Farrell should be included in this list, since Freud was born in Příbor in Moravia. However, Freud has always been considered an Austrian and as such he falls outside the purview of this bibliography. Pynsent's essay on the Czech decadent trend has an explanatory subtitle: 'The politics of Arnošt Procházka and Jiří Karásek ze Lvovic'. These two decadent writers founded and edited *Moderní Revue*, a magazine published between 1894 and 1925, which greatly influenced Czech literature. Pynsent recognizes the relevance of Karásek's homosexuality for the comprehension of his work. The issue of 'Czechness', which is of interest to Pynsent, is raised again. The subtitle of Brušák's essay is 'Pekař versus Masaryk'. Josef Pekař (1870-1937) was a historian who re-evaluated several periods of Czech history and some Czech historical personalities. 'The meaning of Czech history' (1927) is a study by Pekař and 'concerns the very idea of looking for the meaning of history'. Masaryk's thesis was that the meaning of Czech history lies in a religious idea; according to Pekař the force in Czech history was nationalism. Vlček gave his essay the subtitle 'Czech *Fin-de-Siècle*' and chose several genres for his examination, e.g. literature (Julius Zeyer, Jaroslav Hašek), sculpture (František Bílek), graphic art (Vojtěch Preissig). Each essay is accompanied by meticulous bibliographical 'Notes' and the book has an 'Index' (p. 191-96).

149 **Decadence and innovation: Austro-Hungarian life and art at the turn of the century.**
Edited by Robert B. Pynsent. London: Weidenfeld & Nicolson, 1989. 258p.

A selection of papers from an international conference on *fin-de-siècle* Austria-Hungary, which was held at the School of Slavonic and East European Studies, University of London, in December 1986. Professor Pynsent lists in the introduction

46

all the papers which were presented at the conference (p. x-xiii). The contributors were British, American, German, Austrian, Czech, Hungarian and Polish scholars and the fields covered were literature, philosophy, psychology, music and visual arts. The selection is intended for scholars. Each paper has its own explanatory notes and the book has one joint index (p. 249-58). Notes on the authors of the papers selected for this volume are on p. vii-viii. R. B. Pynsent is the author of 'Conclusory essay: decadence, decay and innovation' (p. 111-248), the final paper and longest contribution. The author 'attempts to outline the main elements of fin de siècle culture in Austria-Hungary on the background of contemporaneous English and French culture' (p. 111). The essay concludes with a brief comparison of the turn of the century and the 1960s as phenomena.

16th to 19th century

150 **Crown, church and estates: Central European politics in the sixteenth and seventeenth centuries.**
Edited by R. J. W. Evans, T. V. Thomas. London: Macmillan, in association with the School of Slavonic and East European Studies, University of London, 1991. 321p. map. bibliog.

A collection of revised papers from an international conference held at the School of Slavonic and East European Studies, 5-8 January 1988. The papers provide a survey of contemporary research into this decisive period of European history, on which there is a lack of English publications, hence the particular value of this contribution. As the title suggests, the three points of the triangle of the Habsburg crown, the estates of Austria, Bohemia and Hungary, and the church, are examined in their mutual relationships. 'The more specific topics . . . included the nature and workings of the system of crown and estates; the relations between the Habsburgs and the church; the character of Habsburg absolutism; the connection between protestantism and the defence of rights of the nobility; and the relationship between religion and politics during the upheaval of the sixteenth and seventeenth centuries'.

151 **King and estates in the Bohemian lands, 1526-1564.**
Kenneth J. Dillon. Brussels: Editions de la Librairie Encyclopédique, 1976. 206p. maps. bibliog. (Studies Presented to the International Commission for the History of Representative and Parliamentary Institutions, no. 57).

The period considered here goes from the anarchy that preceded the election of Ferdinand of Habsburg to the Bohemian throne (the first Habsburg in a line that ended in 1918, though by then the Bohemian throne had long been a semi-ignored appendage to that of Austria) to his death in 1564. It was a period of continuous religious dispute, marked by royal attempts to cut back the old privileges of the estates and by the lurking threat posed by the Turks. The ambivalent relationship between crown and estates – mutual reliance and mutual distrust – is illustrated by four central aspects of the history of the period: the Turkish wars; finance (dealt with throughout the volume in considerable detail); religion; and internal political control.

152 **The making of the Habsburg Monarchy, 1550-1700: an interpretation.**
Robert J. W. Evans. Oxford: Clarendon Press; Oxford University Press, 1979. 531p. maps. bibliog.

The history of the Czechs is inseparable from that of the Austro-Hungarian Empire, and therefore this volume is of unquestionable relevance to the history of the Czech Republic. As the title indicates, this is not an account of history in terms of 'wars and armies, diplomacy and foreign relations', but in terms of social and intellectual evolution and change. Religion has always been a part of the background in this region, and a great deal hinged on the changes from peaceful coexistence between Protestants and Catholics to the recatholicization of the Counter-Reformation. For Bohemia a major consequence of this was the change in landownership, loyal nobility being rewarded with land confiscated from the disloyal. Evans contests that the decline of Czech culture was due to the cosmopolitanism of the newly promoted nobility rather than to the dominant influence of Austria. Useful appendices include a political and military chronology, a genealogy of the Habsburgs and a multilingual glossary of place-names.

153 **Rytíři renesančních Čech.** (The knights of Renaissance Bohemia.)
Václav Bůžek. Prague: Acropolis, 1995. 156p. bibliog.

Presents life stories of Czech knights, the lesser nobility, from the second half of the 16th century to the first decades of the 17th century. The book is inevitably of limited interest but it provides a good picture of social development, economy, politics, education and culture in that era. The substantial bibliography, unfortunately of works in Czech only, leads to further reading. The books and articles listed here are indication of the recent surge in interest in the Czech nobility.

154 **Rudolf II and Prague: the court and the city.**
Text by James M. Bradburne, Beket Bukovinská, Jaroslava Hausenblasová, Michal Šroněk, edited by Eliška Fučíková. London: Thames & Hudson; Milan, Italy: Skira, 1997. 792p. bibliog.

Follows the interest in Emperor Rudolf II after the exhibitions on him and his times in 1988 in Essen and Vienna and a recent exhibition in Prague, of which this book is a catalogue and companion. It contains 1,500 illustrations and one of its strong features is the way in which it reveals how the court of Rudolf used the arts, particularly the visual arts, to advance science and learning. The book was reviewed by T. K. Rabb in *The Times Literary Supplement*, no. 4950 (13 February 1998), p. 18-19, under the title, *The heart of Kunstkammer: Prague's Golden Age and the eclecticism of Rudolfine aesthetics*. The review is critical of the book's lack of coherent purpose; it argues that although there are 30 introductory essays covering nearly 400 pages, it is difficult to find related objectives and themes. A sister volume is *Rudolf II and Prague: the Imperial Court and residential city as the cultural and spiritual heart of Central Europe*, edited by Eliška Fučíková, James M. Bradburne, Beket Bukovinská, Jaroslava Hausenblasová, Lubomír Konečný, Ivan Muchka and Michal Šroněk (Prague: Prague Castle Administration; London: Thames & Hudson; Milan: Skira, 1997. 392p.).

155 **Rudolf II and his world: a study in intellectual history 1576-1612.**
Robert J. W. Ewans. Oxford: Clarendon Press, 1984. 340p. map.
bibliog.

Many important contributions on this period have been written over the last twenty
years, yet scholars frequently return to this classic, which was first published by
Clarendon Press in 1973. The intellectual history of the title is largely tied up with the
many scholars with whom Rudolf surrounded himself (Tycho de Brahe, Kepler and
others) and the religious question.

156 **Tragic triangle: the Netherlands, Spain and Bohemia 1617-1621.**
Josef Polišenský. Prague: Charles University, 1991. 258p.

As well as being the foremost Czech authority on Anglo-Czech relations, Professor
Polišenský is also the authority on 17th-century Czech history. This is a successful
attempt to demonstrate the thesis that the 'Thirty Years' War was a military-political
conflict rooted in the past, in which two models of European civilisation confronted
one another: those represented by the lands in which development toward a modern
capitalist society has been halted, and the lands in which this development has been
allowed to proceed'. Although this is a scholarly publication which contains inches of
footnotes, it is very readable. An index is included.

157 **The Thirty Years War.**
Josef V. Polišenský, translated by Robert Evans. London: Batsford,
1971. 305p. map. bibliog. Paperback edition, London: NEL books,
1974. 314p.

This is another period on which many books have been written and it is one of the
periods which are felt to be of key significance in Czech history, as many of the major
events took place on Czech soil: the second Prague Defenestration, 1618; the Battle of
the White Mountain, 1620; the colourful career of the Habsburg general, later traitor,
Wallenstein, who was murdered by Scots and Irish in 1634; and the Swedish siege of
Prague in 1648. This history of one of the longest European wars, by a highly
respected Czech historian, is well served by Polišenský's English colleague, the
translator.

158 **The Czech renascence of the nineteenth century: essays in honour
of Otakar Odložilík.**
Peter Brock, H. Gordon Skilling. Toronto: University of Toronto
Press, 1970. 345p. bibliog.

Well established as *the* authority in English on this period in Czech history. The
Czech renaissance, or National Revival, marks the beginning of modern Czech
history. Its importance to the state of the modern Czech language, the shaping of the
modern literary classics, and the nation's political identity, culminating in the birth of
the Czechoslovak Republic a century later, is only one aspect of a rich and varied set
of processes.

159 **Origins of the Czech national renascence.**
Hugh le Caine Agnew. Pittsburg, Pennsylvania; London: University of Pittsburg Press, 1993. 338p. bibliog. (Russian and East European Studies, 18).
The book provides background to the current resurrection of nationalism as manifested by the dissolution of Czechoslovakia. The National Revival of the early to mid-19th century, so important to the Czechs, has its intellectual roots in the Enlightenment, according to Hugh Agnew's thesis. The main themes of the book are the revival of an antiquated standard language to replace the period vernacular, the rediscovery and reassessment of Czech history and the cultivation of ethnic culture and consciousness and of Pan-Slavism. This work started as a doctoral thesis many years ago. Agnew drew on numerous sources, mostly Czech, German and English, as reflected in his 'Notes', and provides a substantial bibliography of archival material, books, monographs and articles (p. 3-24), as well as an index. Agnew is a Professor of History and International Affairs at George Washington University.

160 **Czech nationalism in the nineteenth century.**
John F. N. Bradley. Boulder, Colorado: East European Monographs. Distributed by Columbia University Press, 1984. 153p. bibliog. (East European Monographs, no. 157).
The author's main concern is with the evolution, as he sees it, of Czech political nationalism out of cultural nationalism and its manifestations, negative and positive, in social and religious life, including responses to pan-German trends and attitudes to the Catholic church. The book relies heavily on archival material from Vienna, the details of which are incorporated as a set of appendices. The best example of cultural nationalism was the building of the Czech National Theatre, as recorded in a study by Stanley Buchholz Kimball, based on extensive archival sources, *Czech nationalism: a study of the national theatre movement 1845-1883* (q.v.).

161 **Austerlitz 1805: battle of three emperors.**
David G. Chandler. London: Osprey Publishing Limited, 1990. 96p. maps. bibliog. (Osprey Military Campaign Series, 2).
Dedicated to the Napoleonic Association of Great Britain, this book is intended for the amateur enthusiast in military history. Approximately half of the book is text, while the other half is taken up with illustrations, maps, charts and colour plates. This concise account adopts the classical framework for a book on a military campaign: plans and preparations; profiles of opposing commanders; descriptions of the opposing armies; the course of the battle itself; its aftermath; and the battlefield today. There is a short but useful list of further reading (p. 90), which includes details of contemporary accounts (memoirs of generals etc.). David G. Chandler, a historian of international repute, is the general editor of the Osprey Military Campaign Series and is the head of the Department of War Studies at Sandhurst Military Academy.

162 **Bitva tří císařů: Slavkov/Austerlitz.**
Dušan Uhlíř. Brno, Czech Republic: AVE, 1995. 135p. maps. bibliog.
It is a pity that the text of this coffee-table book is in Czech only, but the book is pleasingly produced, containing many pictures (portraits, scenes from the battle, maps,

50

charts). The Battle of Austerlitz took place on 2 December 1805 not far from the town of Slavkov, near Brno, and was later remembered by Napoleon with great nostalgia. This book is made up of brief biographies of a number of the French, Austrian and Russian commanders, descriptions and illustrations of the soldiers' uniforms and legends surrounding the battle. The account of the battle itself does not go into great detail, so that the drawings of various formations are of greater value than the text. The publication is aimed at the general public, and at the amateur military historian. The bibliography on p. 132 is a brief, multilingual list of the most important books on the Battle of Austerlitz.

163 **The Prague Slav Congress of 1848.**
Lawrence D. Orton. Boulder, Colorado: East European Quarterly. Distributed by Columbia University Press, New York, 1978. 187p. bibliog. (East European Monographs, no. 46).

The Prague Slav Congress of 1848 intended to resolve or clarify many of the issues which united and divided the disparate Slavonic nations. The study traces 'the genesis, organization, deliberations and results of the congress' and 'focuses attention especially on those issues which . . . dominated contemporary evaluations and which have influenced subsequent historical judgements of the congress'. The year 1848 is of considerable importance in Czech history. *The Czech revolution of 1848* by Stanley Z. Pech (Chapel Hill, North Carolina: University of North Carolina Press, 1969. 386p. bibliog.) is based on an impressive range of archival sources including the contemporary press and publications.

164 **Palacký: the historian as scholar and nationalist.**
Joseph Frederick Zacek. The Hague: Mouton, 1970. 137p. bibliog. (Studies in European History, no. 5).

František Palacký is the father of modern Czech historiography and is to many the uncontested leader of the 19th-century Czech National Revival. This biography brings together these two threads in his work and draws on the existing literature and his own analyses of primary sources.

165 **Karel Havlíček (1821-1856): a national liberation leader of the Czech renascence.**
Barbara K. Reinfeld. Boulder, Colorado: East European Quarterly. Distributed by Columbia University Press, New York, 1982. 135p. bibliog. (East European Monographs, no. 98).

Karel Havlíček, usually known by his agnomen, Borovský, was a major, almost purely political, writer of the National Revival. He was a satirist, independent journalist and editor of his own newspapers, who was eventually sent to trial over the contents of one of his publications before being dispatched to internal exile at Brixen. The study includes a history of National Revival politics and publications, books and serials, as the background to Havlíček's life and work. This study gives more space to Borovský's journalistic work than to his later satirical literature.

166 **The Young Czech Party 1874-1901 and the emergence of a multiparty system.**
Bruce M. Garver. New Haven, Connecticut; London: Yale University Press, 1978. 568p. bibliog.

A complete history of the entire political climate out of which sprang the Young Czech Party, 'the dominant Czech political party during one decade and . . . a leading force in three others, with achievements for the most part constructive'. The party largely lost its relevance after the birth of Czechoslovakia in 1918.

1900-18

167 **The coming of the First World War.**
Edited by R. J. W. Evans, Hartmut Pogge von Strandmann. Oxford: Clarendon Press, 1990. 289p. maps. bibliog.

Incorporates some amendments to the first edition, published in 1988. There is still much research to be done on the First World War. The main purpose of this collection of excellent articles by prominent academics – in addition to the editors, these were Michael Howard, Z. A. B. Zeman, D. W. Spring, Richard Cobb and Michael Brock – is 'to provide a concise and accessible account for the general reader of the circumstances which led directly to war'. Czech indifference towards the conflict and the fate of members of the Emperor's family is illustrated by an extract from Hašek's novel *Good soldier Švejk* (q.v.), when the protagonist Švejk is informed by his landlady of the assassination of Archduke Ferdinand (p. 44-45), the event which triggered the war. In this well-known humorous dialogue, Švejk is trying to pinpoint which of the Ferdinands he knows (and most of them are far from having noble backgrounds), has been killed.

168 **The Czechs during World War I: the path to independence.**
H. Louis Rees. Boulder, Colorado: East European Monographs. Distributed by Columbia University Press, New York, 1992. 170p. bibliog. (East European Monographs, no. CCCXXXIX).

Focuses on the domestic situation by describing the activities of political leaders in Prague and Vienna, which are placed 'within the economic, social and political context in which they were carried out' (p. vi). That context includes the October Revolution in Russia, the establishment of a democratic republic and parliamentary government after the predicted collapse of Austria-Hungary and the issue of the dominance of Czech language and culture in this future republic. The study pays particular attention to the final two years of the war, when these issues gained in significance. The bibliography lists archival collections, published documents, memoirs, books and unpublished sources, mostly in English, some in Czech or German.

169 **The Czechoslovak legions in Russia: 1914-1920.**
John F. N. Bradley. Boulder, Colorado: East European Monographs.
Distributed by Columbia University Press, New York, 1991. 156p.
(East European Monographs, no. 321).
The involvement of the Czechoslovak legions in the Russian civil war is still obscure
despite the quantity of historical sources concerning this war. The war has not been
previously studied objectively, and where the legions are concerned research was
hindered by the ideological prejudices in the successor states of the First World War.
The Czech and Russian archives have only recently been opened to a non-Communist
historian. This study, which was originally a doctoral thesis, provides a good account
of Czech involvement in the Russian civil war. Maps of the movements of the legions
and an index of names and places would, however, have helped general readers to find
their way through the confusion of times and events. Of interest to a philatelist would
be *The field post of the Czechoslovak and Allied Forces in Russia, 1918-1920: an
anthology*, produced by W. A. Page ([London]: Czechoslovak Philatelic Society of
Great Britain, 1991. Publications of the Society, no. 9).

170 **Revolutionary war for independence and the Russian question:
Czechoslovak army in Russia 1914-1918.**
Victor M. Fic. New Delhi: Abhinav Publications, 1977. 270p.
bibliog.
A detailed history of the origins of the legion, from all the problems associated with
their formation, disunity and conflicting interests, through the Russian Revolutions of
1917, to a discussion of the Czechoslovak army's actual and possible roles up to the
evacuation of the Ukraine in 1918. Fic continues the history of the legion in *The
Bolsheviks and the Czechoslovak legion: the origin of their armed conflict March-May
1918* (New Delhi: Abhinav Publications, 1978. 495p. map. bibliog.), set against
contemporary Allied policies, the internal politics of the Czechoslovaks and developments within the immature Soviet state, ending with Soviet interpretations of the
events. The appendix contains English-language texts of a number of contemporary
British, Russian and Czech documents and a broadly classified bibliography, including
many early English-language publications.

171 **The Great War's forgotten front: a soldier's diary and a son's
reflections.**
Jan F. Triska. Boulder, Colorado: East European Monographs.
Distributed by Columbia University Press, New York, 1998. 182p.
maps. bibliog.
This cameo, based on a soldier's memoirs from the First World War, is a vivid and
moving account by an ordinary Czech soldier on the Italian front. The soldier changed
allegiance and joined the newly formed Czechoslovak legions in Italy. His son, Jan
Triska, a distinguished political scientist, provides commentaries on the soldier's
background and his experiences and a frame of reference for the times, places and
events, particular to this individual soldier's war, thus placing this record in the
broader context of the Great War. The soldier's son also appends his own reflections
on the meaning of the First World War in the present day. A selective bibliography (p.
177-82) broadly covers the First World War. Triska included some interesting private
photographs and several maps of Central Europe.

Independence to Munich (1918-38)

General

172 **Der Legionär: ein deutsch-tschechischer Konflikt von Masaryk bis Havel.** (The legionnaire: the German-Czech conflict from Masaryk to Havel.)
Wilhelm Muschka. Frankfurt, Germany; New York: Peter Lang, 1995. 317p.

This medium-weight biography presents another perspective on the Czech involvement in the upheavals in Russia between 1917 and 1921. The pivotal figure is the legionnaire general, Josef Kroutil. The volume contains many photographs and a name index (p. 309-17).

173 **The United States, revolutionary Russia, and the rise of Czechoslovakia.**
Betty Miller Unterberger. Chapel Hill, North Carolina; London: University of North Carolina Press, 1989. 463p. maps. bibliog.
(Supplementary Volume to "The Papers of Woodrow Wilson").

The American perception of the origin of Czechoslovakia is presented in this substantial volume which 'endeavours to present a history of the role of the United States in the dissolution of the Austro-Hungarian empire and the rise of the most cataclysmic events of the twentieth century – the First World War and the Bolshevik revolution'. The book is also an excellent study of the Czechoslovak legions in Russia. Unterberger's book is supplemented with photographs, copious notes, a bibliography and an index.

174 **The genesis of Czechoslovakia.**
Josef Kalvoda. Boulder, Colorado: East European Monographs. Distributed by Columbia University Press, New York, 1986. 673p. bibliog. (East European Monographs, no. 209).

The book starts with 'The Czechs and Slovaks and their leaders on the eve of the [First World] war', and continues with a detailed account of the activities of the Czech leaders abroad during the First World War, the build-up of the Czechoslovak army and its activities and conflicts in Russia in 1917-18. Kalvoda devotes well-informed attention to: Czechoslovakia's quest for recognition and the Declaration of Independence; the activities of T. G. Masaryk, E. Beneš, M. Štefánik and K. Kramář; and the new state, represented by Beneš, at the Paris conference after the end of the First World War. The book is documented by notes, an extensive bibliography on all types of material, mostly from the 1920s, and an index.

175 **Vznik Československa: 1918.** (The origin of Czechoslovakia: 1918.)
Antonín Klímek. Prague: Ústav mezinárodních vztahů, 1994. 440p. (Dokumenty československé zahraniční politiky).

The objective of the diplomatic activities of the Czech political resistance abroad was to achieve Allied recognition of its leading body, the Czechoslovak National Council

54

(Československá národní rada), as the representative of the country and later as the Czechoslovak government abroad. The documents in this volume illustrate the events in 1918 which resulted in the declaration of the Czechoslovak state on 28 October 1918. The Czech, French, English and Russian documents are arranged chronologically, and supplemented by: a synopsis of the main events in 1918 which were relevant to the Czech resistance; and a list of the documents included, accompanied by abstracts and an index of persons whose names occur in the documents, with a few words of explanation on each person's role.

176 **On the emergence of Czechoslovakia.**
Jaroslav Opat. In: *Czechoslovakia 1918-88: seventy years from independence.* Edited by Gordon H. Skilling. Basingstoke, England; London: Macmillan Academic and Professional Ltd, in association with St Antony's College, 1991, p. 41-52. bibliog.

Although the text of this paper was submitted to a conference held in Toronto in 1989, the author was not allowed by the Czechoslovak authorities to attend. Jaroslav Opat disputes the official interpretation of forty years that the 1917 October Revolution in Russia was the decisive factor in the liberation of the Czechs and Slovaks in 1918, having contributed to the break-up of Austria-Hungary. The volume contains bibliographical notes.

177 **The Czechoslovak Declaration of Independence: a history of the document.**
George J. Kovtun. Washington, DC: Library of Congress, 1985. 59p. bibliog.

The Declaration was published in Washington on 18 October 1918. Documents which illustrate the history of this most important declaration are examined here as well as the role of several American citizens in its creation. This well-produced and handsomely printed study is supplemented by photographs of documents, articles and personalities. The appendices contain: Masaryk's Czech-language draft of the Declaration; a translation of Masaryk's draft; the preliminary text of the Declaration which was sent to US Secretary of State Lansing; and the final version of the Declaration.

178 **East Central Europe between the two world wars.**
Joseph Rothschild. Seattle, Washington; London: University of Washington Press, 1992. 7th ed. 420p. maps. bibliog. (A History of East Central Europe, 9).

The first edition of this book was published in 1974 and the number of subsequent editions indicates the quality of the book. Chapter three, 'Czechoslovakia' (p. 73-135) is a social and political history up to the loss of independence in 1939, and it serves as the author's paradigm for an account of the political problems which arise from multi-ethnicity. The chapter includes population tables by province, mother tongue, religion, economic sectors, urban rural residence and illiteracy, as well as election results for 1920, 1925 and 1929. Equally well regarded as one of the best surveys of inter-war Eastern Europe is Hugh Seton-Watson's *Eastern Europe between the wars, 1918-1941*, which also saw numerous editions (Cambridge, England: Cambridge University Press, 1945; Hamden, Connecticut: Shoe String Press, 1963. 3rd ed. 442p.).

179 **A history of the Czechoslovak Republic 1918-1948.**
Edited by Victor S. Mamatey, Radomír Luža. Princeton, New Jersey: Princeton University Press, 1973. 534p. maps. bibliog.

Even now widely regarded as providing the best picture in English of Czechoslovakia's history up to the Communist takeover in 1948, this book was compiled as a response to the resurgence of interest in Czechoslovakia in 1968. It is not a typical linear account, but a collection of essays on separate aspects which are partly parallel chronologically. It is organized in three parts: the [first] Czechoslovak Republic, 1918-38; occupation, war and liberation, 1938-45; and Czechoslovakia between East and West, 1945-48. Aspects covered include: the nature and development of democracy in Czechoslovakia; the Germans and other minorities; foreign policy; the Munich crisis; exile politics; and resistance movements. There are thirteen illustrations, five maps, an impressive 'selected' bibliography, and a comprehensive index. The latest work on the period 1918-39 is 'The rise and fall of a democracy' by Robert Kvaček in *Bohemia in history*, edited by Mikuláš Teich (Cambridge, England: Cambridge University Press, 1998, p. 244-66).

180 **The Czech and Slovak experience: selected papers from the Fourth World Congress for Soviet and East European Studies, Harrogate, 1990.**
Edited by John Morison. Basingstoke, England: The Macmillan Press; New York: St. Martin's Press, 1992. 235p. bibliog.

The Congress was the first of its kind to take place in Britain and was the largest and most complex congress of Soviet and East European studies that had so far taken place. Further distinctions are that it was held shortly after the revolutionary events in the Soviet Union and Eastern Europe and that it was duly attended by a large number of scholars from the region. The essays in this book deal mostly with the modern history of Czechoslovakia between the two world wars. The exception is an essay on serfdom in 18th-century Bohemia, 'The odd alliance: the underprivileged population of Bohemia and the Habsburg court, 1765-1790' by George Svoboda. Each essay has a separate bibliography.

Tomáš Garrigue Masaryk (1850-1937) and the Masaryk family

181 **T. G. Masaryk (1850-1937).**
Edited by Stanley B. Winters (vol. 1), Robert B. Pynsent (vol. 2), Harry Hanak (vol. 3). Basingstoke, England: Macmillan, in association with the School of Slavonic and East European Studies, University of London, 1989-90. 3 vols. bibliog. (Studies in Russia and East Europe).

An important attempt to revive and re-appraise Masaryk's work. The essays in these three volumes represent a broad range of critical and positive assessments, and they overlap thematically. In volume one, 'Thinker and politicians', Winters states, 'The essays in this volume are thematically heterogeneous and leave many gaps in Masaryk's career and ideas, some of these will be filled by essays in the two volumes that follow'. This first collection deals with the middle years of Masaryk's life, up to 1914. The essays were originally commissioned by the editor who was subsequently invited to merge his efforts with those of the organizers of the London conference, 'T. G. Masaryk (1850-1937)'. A list of T. G. Masaryk's writings, giving the Czech titles with English translations and the date of publication, can be found on p. XIII-XVI. Volume two, 'Thinker and critic', contains revised versions of papers delivered at the above-mentioned conference organized by the School of Slavonic and East European Studies in December 1986. Volume three, 'Statesman and cultural force', follows on from the second volume. The conference commemorated Masaryk's death half a century ago and simultaneously the seventeenth anniversary of his speech inaugurating the School of Slavonic and East European Studies in October 1915, following his appointment as a lecturer in Slavonic literature and sociology. Each of the chapters in the three volumes has bibliographical notes and there is a joint index at the end of each volume.

182 **Odkaz T. G. Masaryka.** (T. G. Masaryk's legacy.)
Prague: Práce, 1990. 110p.

Published on the occasion of the 140th anniversary of the birth of Masaryk. The publication consists mostly of photographs. A brief summary in English is on p. 109.

183 **T. G. Masaryk against the current: 1882-1914.**
H. Gordon Skilling. Basingstoke, England: Macmillan, in association with St Antony's College, Oxford, 1994. 248p. bibliog.

A critical re-appraisal of Masaryk's work prior to the First World War and his life in Prague between 1882 and 1914, when, at the age of sixty-four, Masaryk went into exile. This work is based primarily on Masaryk's own writings and arranged by theme, not chronologically. Thus there are chapters on Masaryk's views on: Czech academic life; political dissent; anti-Semitism; religious heresy; and women's rights. The author provides copious bibliographical notes and an index. As the title indicates, Masaryk often went against the majority opinion. The book is prefaced by the thoughts of historians and philosophers, of which the philosopher Jan Patočka's is the most recent (from 1977) and apt: 'Not by cringing, adjusting and serving that which forms a momentary wave on the surface, but by thought, radically penetrating into the depth, can we gain insight into what is, and into its meaning, and hence an orientation in the chaos and storms of todays and tomorrows.' Another noteworthy quotation is from 1910, by the French historian Ernest Denis, who specialized in Czech history: 'Masaryk fears neither traditions, nor majorities, nor prejudices. It sometimes happens that he errs, but he never fears to express what he considers to be the truth. He belongs to that sublime class of heretics, and it is just the heretics who bring about progress.'

184 **The spirit of Thomas G. Masaryk (1850-1937): an anthology.**
Edited by George J. Kovtun, foreword by René Wellek. Basingstoke, England: Macmillan, in association with the Masaryk Publications Trust, 1990. 267p. bibliog.

Masaryk's writings are very little known in the West, and they have been subject to popularization and simplification in the Czech Republic, during the First Republic and in the mushrooming of Masarykiana in the 1990s. The contributions in this book present Masaryk as a philosopher, dissecting individual works which were often controversial as he was a catalyst of opinions. These contemporary discussions on Masaryk's work follow this vein, in that they are also controversial. The book contains: a 'Chronology of Masaryk's life and work' (p. XVIII-XX); a selected biographical glossary (p. 249-60); a bibliography of Masaryk's writings quoted in the book (p. 261-62); suggested further readings (p. 263); and a name index (p. 264-67).

History. Independence to Munich (1918-38). Tomáš Garrigue Masaryk (1850-1937) and the Masaryk family

185 **T. G. Masaryk: the problem of small nations.**
George J. Kovtun. In: *Czechoslovakia 1918-88: seventy years from independence.* Edited by Gordon H. Skilling. Basingstoke, England; London: Macmillan Academic and Professional Ltd, in association with St Antony's College, 1991, p. 25-40.
Presented at a conference held in Toronto in 1989, this paper analyses the conflicts and paradoxes of Masaryk as a politician and philosopher, whilst on the whole applauding his personality and achievements. The author quotes heavily from various literary sources and provides numerous bibliographical notes. The 'small nation problem' was the subject of Masaryk's inaugural lecture at the foundation of the School of Slavonic and East European Studies, London, in 1945.

186 **Masaryk: religious heretic.**
H. Gordon Skilling. In: *The Czech and Slovak experience: selected papers from the Fourth Congress for Soviet and East European Studies, Harrogate, 1990.* Edited by John Morison. Basingstoke, England: The Macmillan Press; New York: St. Martin's Press, 1992, p. 62-88. bibliog.
Skilling's paper informs us that Masaryk's religious views met with hostility and misunderstanding. Masaryk himself evolved from Roman Catholicism to Protestantism but was critical of both doctrines. He knew that religious differences were one of the factors which could endanger the new Czechoslovak state and expected a separation of church from state and from the schools, in order to foster freedom of thought. His own approach to religion was basically ethical and practical.

187 **On Masaryk: texts in English and German.**
Edited by Josef Novák. Amsterdam: Rodopi, 1988. 398p. bibliog. (Studien zur Österreichischen Philosophie, Band 13).
This collection of scholarly articles by various authors describes and evaluates the work of T. G. Masaryk (1850-1937), mainly as a philosopher, but also as a sociologist and statesman. The philosophy of Masaryk is assessed in relation to Austrian philosophy and he is compared with his peers. The volume contains bibliographical notes and an index.

188 **Talks with T. G. Masaryk by Karel Čapek.**
Karel Čapek, edited with a substantially new translation by Michael Henry Heim. New Haven, Connecticut: Catbird Press, 1995. 256p. bibliog.
This new translation of the famous biographical 'talks' consists of two books and a section entitled 'Silence with Masaryk' which has not been published in English before. Čapek interviewed Masaryk over a number of years, starting in the early 1920s. The two books have self-explanatory titles: 'Youth' and 'Life and work'. Having been compiled by Karel Čapek, a skilful writer, they are readable and represent a good starting point for anyone interested in Masaryk's life and thought. They convey Masaryk's views on a number of moral and political issues. The chronology of Masaryk's life can be found on p. XII, and 'Notes' on p. 250-52 provide basic information on the various figures and events mentioned for the reader

58

with no knowledge of Czech history or culture. Indeed, one does not need to know anything about Masaryk or the Czechs, or for that matter about history or philosophy, to enjoy this popular read. There is also a bibliography of works written by, and about, T. G. Masaryk in English translation (p. 253-54).

189   **The Masaryks: the making of Czechoslovakia.**
      Zbyněk A. B. Zeman.   London; New York: I. B. Tauris & Co. Ltd,
      1990. 230p.

Originally published in London by Weidenfeld & Nicolson in 1976, this is a combined biography of Tomáš Masaryk and his son Jan, who ultimately became Czechoslovakia's foreign minister, and it covers a century of Czechoslovak history. The background of the break-up of great European empires (Russian and Austrian), great military conflicts (the two world wars) and the birth of Czechoslovakia itself (due in great part to Tomáš Masaryk) makes the book an alternative history of the country as well as a political biography. Zeman also looks at the friends and family life of the Masaryks. The absence of a bibliography is compensated for by footnotes and by references in the introduction.

190   **The Masaryk case: the murder of democracy in Czechoslovakia.**
      Claire Sterling, with an afterword by Adam B. Ulam.   Boston,
      Massachusetts: David R. Godine, 1982. 374p. bibliog.

Jan Masaryk (1886-1948), the charismatic son of T. G. Masaryk, was a Czechoslovak diplomat and politician with a known zest for living. Between the wars he was the Czechoslovak ambassador to the United States and later on to the United Kingdom, and was a strong opponent of appeasement. During the Second World War he was the Minister of Foreign Affairs in the Czech government-in-exile, retaining this function after the war, in Prague. In February 1948 he accepted a ministerial position in the new, Communist government and became the object of reactionary attacks from the West. The official story was that he succumbed to depression and committed suicide by jumping out of his bathroom window in the Černín Palace, the seat of the Ministry of Foreign Affairs, on 9 March 1948. He was a popular figure, both at home and abroad, both as the son of the first president and in his own right, and at any time when there was a relaxation from Communist rule, in 1968 and 1989, the manner of his death was re-examined by investigative reporters. This book was first published in 1969 and traces in detail the events surrounding Masaryk's suicide/assassination, providing a list of the persons involved (p. xi-xvii), many of whom were interviewed by Claire Sterling. The description of surviving members of the Masaryk family in Prague has a charming intimacy. The book draws on Bruce Lockhart's *Jan Masaryk: personal memoir* (London: Dropmore Press, 1951. 80p.). It contains photographs, bibliography and an index.

191   **Alice Garrigue Masaryk, 1879-1966: her life as recorded in her
      own words and by her friends.**
      Compiled by Ruth Crawford Mitchell, special editing by Linda Vlasak,
      with an introduction by René Wellek.   Pittsburg, Pennsylvania:
      University Center for International Studies, 1980. 251p. bibliog.

A biography of Masaryk's daughter: political prisoner in 1915; president of the Czechoslovak Red Cross in the First Republic; teacher and social worker; and émigrée during the war and again after 1949. As suggested in the subtitle, the biographical narrative is interlaced with letters and depicts her as a feminist, patriot and practical adherent of her father's social philosophy.

Munich and the Second World War (1938-45)

The Munich Crisis, Edvard Beneš

192 **Czechoslovakia between Stalin and Hitler: the diplomacy of Edvard Beneš in the 1930s.**
Igor Lukeš. New York; Oxford: Oxford University Press, 1996. 318p. map. bibliog.

The author had access to newly opened archives in Prague and his objective was to illustrate how the escalating crisis of the 1930s appeared from a Czech perspective, thus filling a gap in a field which has been well researched. The author did not have access to the Russian archives. 'The crisis of 1930s, especially the Four Power Agreement signed at Munich in September 1938, provoked a vast amount of writing . . . It is safe to say that we now have a high resolution picture of the British, French, German, Hungarian and Polish dimensions of the crisis. This cannot be said about the roles played by the Prague government and the Kremlin.' The scope of the book is inevitably somewhat narrow, focusing on not yet fully researched Czechoslovak and Soviet views. The author lists the archives he researched in Prague (p. 278-79) and the published documents and collections of diplomatic documents, mostly German and British, which he consulted (p. 279-80). These collections are in English, Czech, German, Russian and Polish. The extensive 'Selected literature' (p. 281-309) gives sources used in the book as well as those that might be consulted for further research. The book has an index and each chapter has detailed notes. The book includes photographs, mostly from private collections.

193 **Mnichov 1938. (Munich 1938.)**
Vojtěch Blodig et al. Prague: Svaz protifašistických bojovníků, 1988. 3 vols.

A paperback collection of contributions from the Symposium held in Cheb on the occasion of the fiftieth anniversary of the Munich Diktat on 14 and 15 April 1988. The majority of the contributors were academics, from the Department of Philosophy of Charles University in Prague and from the Institute of Marxism and Leninism of the Central Committee of the Communist Party. The papers still represent the Marxist view on Munich. A contemporary view on Munich is represented in 'Le mythe de Munich. Mythos München. The myth of Munich' by Christiane Brenner, *Bohemia*, vol. 39, no. 2 (1998), p. 431-33.

194 **Appeasement and the Munich crisis.**
Peter Mantin. Brighton, England: Spartacus, 1988. 36p. (Turning Points in History).

Published in the 'Turning Points in History' series, which makes extensive use of source material and is written with GCSE students in mind, in the form of questions and answers. The Munich Agreement, which allowed Germany to annex the border areas of Czechoslovakia where the German minority lived, was signed on 29 September 1938 by Neville Chamberlain for Great Britain, Édouard Daladier for France, Benito Mussolini for Italy and Adolf Hitler for Germany, and was the result of Germany's policy of aggressive expansion and the British and French policy of appeasement. The Agreement was preceded by several months of campaigning by Hitler's Germany and its agent in Czechoslovakia, the Sudetendeutsche Party, against Czechoslovakia for the alleged oppression of the three million Germans in the border areas. This slim volume is illustrated by period photographs, pictures, statements and first-hand accounts.

195 **Jawaharlal Nehru and the Munich betrayal of Czechoslovakia.**
Zdeněk Trhlík. Prague: Orbis Press Agency, 1989. 89p. bibliog.

Nehru and his daughter Indira came to Czechoslovakia in August 1938 on an unofficial, but hectic, visit during which they met a number of people of consequence and visited the Sudeten area. The book may not be easy to obtain but it is a worthwhile document, being full of quotations by Nehru from his articles and speeches which evince the shrewd intuition of an outside observer who found the acceptance of fascist blackmail without struggle unthinkable.

196 **The Czechoslovak partial mobilization in May 1938: a mystery (almost) solved.**
Igor Lukeš. *Journal of Contemporary History*, no. 32, vol. 4 (October 1996), p. 699-720. bibliog.

The author used newly available archive material for his research. His thesis is that the Czechoslovak mobilization was based on disinformation. The Prague government was intentionally misled into thinking that Germany was going to attack. The truth is that Hitler had no intention of conducting an offensive at that stage. The article concludes that neither Prague nor Berlin were factors in the May 1938 crisis, but it does not identify the source of the deception.

197 **Beneš between East and West.**
Walter Ullmann. In: *Czechoslovakia 1918-88: seventy years from independence.* Edited by Gordon H. Skilling. Basingstoke, England; London: Macmillan Academic and Professional Ltd, in association with St Antony's College, 1991, p. 55-61. bibliog.

This contribution to a conference held in Toronto in 1989 describes the activities and tribulations of Beneš from 1939 to 1948, when he was truly caught between the Soviet Union and the Western powers. The paper is supplemented by bibliographical notes.

198 **The life of Edvard Beneš, 1884-1948: Czechoslovakia in peace and war.**
Zbyněk Zeman, with Antonín Klimek. Oxford: Clarendon Press, 1997. 293p.

1998 marked the fiftieth anniversary of the death of Beneš, the second president of Czechoslovakia and 'one of the most problematic and complex figures in Czech history'. This is the first full-length biography of Edvard Beneš in English and the first major work on Beneš to be published in forty-five years. Zeman's book starts with childhood: Beneš was the tenth child of elderly parents, an easy target for bullying being small and on the fat side (Havel shared this fate). The personality traits of a solitary, puritanical individual who achieves by working hard, not by brilliance, and is withdrawn, ascetic, even prudish, take shape. He was a poor judge of people, and the stress he suffered was the result of being a high achiever who never learned to delegate authority. Often described as a tragic figure, he went into exile twice – during the first and second world wars – and lost out at Munich (when he did not get the support he had hoped for in the face of German claims on the Sudetenland) and again to Gottwald in February 1948 (having become president of Czechoslovakia again after the Second World War, he was outwitted by the Communist Prime Minister Klement Gottwald; the country went Communist, Beneš resigned and Gottwald became president). 'Beneš lived in a state of constant stress. As long as stress was lightened by success, Beneš managed to carry the burden well.' He suffered his first stroke in 1947 and died in September 1948. The book is readable and accessible to an English reader with a moderate knowledge of modern history. It does not have a bibliography, but on the first page of the introduction (p. 1), previous biographies of Edvard Beneš, in Czech and English, are quoted. An important political biography of Beneš, by a man who knew him at first hand and who was familiar with the politics of the war period, is Edward Taborsky's *President Edvard Beneš: between East and West 1938-1948* (Stanford, California: Hoover Institution Press, 1991. 299p. bibliog.); it is of necessity also a history of the Czechoslovak wartime government-in-exile.

Second World War and the Czech resistance abroad

199 **Czechoslovak-Polish negotiations on the establishment of confederation and alliance: 1939-1944.**
Edited by Ivan Šťovíček, Jaroslav Valenta. Prague: Carolinum and the Institute of History of the Academy of Sciences of the Czech Republic, 1995. 450p. map.

A collection of mainly diplomatic documents in Czech, Polish and French. The introduction is in English. The text proper is supplemented by a list of the documents and an index of names occurring in the documents and the text, with a brief summary of the career of each person named.

200 **On all fronts: Czechs and Slovaks in World War II.**
Edited by Lewis M. White. Boulder, Colorado: East European
Monographs. Distributed by Columbia University Press, New York,
1991, 1995. 2 vols. map. bibliog.

A collection of war stories dealing with the actions of Czech and Slovak soldiers on
the Western Front: in France, Great Britain and Tobruk, Libya. Brief biographies of
individual airmen and photographs of the men of arms and of the locations where the
Czech and Slovaks were posted supplement the book. Unfortunately it lacks an index
of names and places. General Ludvík Svoboda, later a prominent figure in Czech
politics – a patriot or a Communist collaborator? – is given special attention in two
articles. This work was published under the auspices of the Czechoslovak Society of
Arts and Sciences, which was founded in Washington, DC, in 1956.

201 **Československý odboj na Západě (1939-1945).** (The Czech
resistance in the West, 1939-45.)
Eduard Čejka. Prague: Mladá fronta, 1997. 534p. bibliog.

The first survey of Czech political and military resistance in the West after the Munich
Agreement of 1938 and up to the end of the war in May 1945. The author follows: the
fortunes of individuals and their dramatic escapes from the country under occupation;
the problems surrounding the foundation of resistance centres in Poland, France, Great
Britain, the United States, the Soviet Union, Yugoslavia and other places; Czech
participation in the Battle of Britain, the Battle of the Atlantic, the 1944 invasion, the
battlegrounds of the Middle East and Northern Africa; and participation in resistance
movements in Italy and France. The political resistance receives equal attention, from
the establishment of the Czechoslovak National Council (Československý národní
výbor) in Paris to the work of the government-in-exile in London and the Moscow
negotiations of spring 1945. The bibliography covers periodicals published by the
resistance movement and books, mostly in Czech. These include memoirs, some of
which are specimens of vanity publishing, often difficult to trace. *The Czechoslovak
Air Force in Britain, 1940-1945* is a PhD thesis submitted by Alan Brown to the
University of Southampton in May 1998. The abstract and synopsis of the thesis can
be found on http:www.netsite.co.uk/airforce.

202 **The Czechoslovak army in France: 1939-1945.**
Roy E. Reader. Dartford, England: Czechoslovak Philatelic Society
of Great Britain, 1987. 46p. bibliog.

Surveys the postal aspects of the Czechoslovak army's stay in France during the
Second World War. The survey includes postal stationery and a listing of the army's
postmarks and date stamps. It also provides a history of this Army and the location of
its troops. A bibliography is included on p. 44-45. A *Supplement to the Czechoslovak
army in France: 1939-1945*, was published in 1992, and edited by W. A. Page
(Dartford, England: Czechoslovak Philatelic Society of Great Britain, 1992. 45p.).

History. Munich and the Second World War (1938-45). Second World War and the Czech resistance abroad

203 **The German occupation of Sudetenland: 1938.**
W. A. Dawson, edited and produced by W. A. Page. Dartford, England: Czechoslovak Philatelic Society of Great Britain, 1988. 71p. bibliog. (Monographs of the Society, no. 6).

This brief historical and political summary of events prior to the Munich Agreement in 1938 also provides a list of post offices affected by the changes of the frontiers. The Czechoslovak Philatelic Society also published *The occupation of Czechoslovak frontier territories by Beck's Poland from the postal history view-point*, by Jiří Neumann, translated from the Czech (London: Czechoslovak Philatelic Society, 1989. 43p. maps. bibliog. Monographs, Czechoslovak Philatelic Society of Great Britain, no. 8). The Czechoslovak stamps ceased to be valid in the territories which were subject to gradual occupation under the Munich Diktat in October 1938. The impact of the 1938-39 changes on the postal services is examined in detail and as such would be of interest to the specialist only.

204 **Jews in Svoboda's army in the Soviet Union: Czechoslovak Jewry's fight against the Nazis during World War II.**
Erich Kulka. Lanham, Maryland: University Press of America, 1987. 432p. bibliog.

The direct involvement of Jews in armed resistance has great significance. This book was previously published in Hebrew in 1977 by the Institute of Contemporary Jewry, Yad Vashem and Moreshet and a shorter version was published in Toronto in 1979 by Sixty-Eight Publishers in Czech, and again in Czech in Prague by Naše vojsko in 1990, under the title *Židé v československé Svobodově armádě*. The work is part of a broad research project into the history of armed opposition by Jews during the Holocaust by the Institute of Contemporary Jewry and is the result of seven years' work. The relationship between the Jews and the Czechs and Slovaks is highlighted and as such the book provides a contribution to the minorities issue. This edition, unlike the others, does not have photographs, but it has several indexes, appendixes, a bibliography and detailed footnotes.

205 **Prague in the shadow of the swastika: a history of the German occupation 1939-1945.**
Callum MacDonald, Jan Kaplan. London: Quartet Books, 1995. 215p. maps. bibliog.

The German army occupied Czechoslovakia, or what remained of it after the Munich Agreement, on 15 March 1939. The occupation lasted six years and afterwards the history of those years was distorted to suit Communist propaganda. There are more photographs than text in this publication, documenting these six years, the remarkable photographs coming from the collections of Kaplan and MacDonald, and from other private collections.

206 **Hitler's gift: the story of Theresienstadt.**
George E. Berkley. Boston, Massachusetts: Branden Books, 1993. 308p. bibliog.

The town of Terezín in northern Bohemia was given to the Jews by the Führer in 1941, to become a paradise ghetto. The indigenous residents were evacuated. Older German and Austrian Jews were sent to Terezín, as were Jews who distinguished themselves in the First World War, Jews from mixed marriages to Aryans, Jewish

64

people of prominence and, later on, Jews from Denmark and the Netherlands. These people were sent to Terezín as a privilege, as opposed to the 'East', which meant Auschwitz and other harsher concentration camps. Terezín was liberated by the Russian army in 1945. This is a very readable and informative account but, as with other books on concentration camps, it is quite harrowing. Of interest are the relations between the Czech Jews and German-speaking Jews. *Terezín memorial book: Jewish victims of Nazi deportations from Bohemia and Moravia 1941-1945*, edited by Miroslav Karný (Prague: Melantrich, Nadace Terezínská iniciativa, 1996. 128p.), is a guide to the Czech original with a glossary of Czech terms occurring in the lists.

207 **Pobyt americké armády v Plzni v roce 1945: (dobové fotografie a dokumenty); The story of the American Army in Pilsen in the year 1945: (period photos and documents).**
Lenka Jandová. Pilsen, Czech Republic: Západočeské museum v Plzni, 1995. 133p. bibliog.
A chronicle of the US Army's stay in Pilsen from 6 May to 1 December 1945. The work is divided into two sections: the 'official' part, a collection of black-and-white photographs and documents, arranged chronologically, on the course of the official events of the Americans' stay; and the second, 'everyday' part, depicting the overall atmosphere in the town, the good relations between the US soldiers and the citizens of Pilsen and leisure activities. This section, which is in no particular order, is obviously livelier, covering sporting events, dances, concerts (e.g. with Marlene Dietrich and artists from the Metropolitan Opera) and simple picnics. The text and the title are in Czech and English. There is a short bibliography of the sources used: printed material, negatives and other sources of photographs.

Post-war period (1945-)

General

208 **Dictionary of East European history since 1945.**
Joseph Held. Westport, Connecticut: Greenwood Press, 1994. 509p. maps. bibliog.
A guide for serious students and the only one of its type so far, which covers major events, personalities and policies. The arrangement is country-by-country (Czechoslovakia is on p. 126-74) and within the country section the entries are arranged alphabetically. These entries have their own mini-bibliographies of sources, books and articles for further study, mostly in English and published in the United States. Each country section is preceded by general information and a chronology of the years 1944-93. The content relates to politics after the Second World War above all, rather at the expense of cultural, social or other issues. Unfortunately, the diacritics in the text, which are so vital to the Czech language, are absent, owing to technical difficulties, which is inexcusable in 1994, when so many versatile word processing and typesetting programmes are available. The book has one general index (p. 500-09).

65

209 **Central Europe since 1945.**
Paul G. Lewis. London; New York: Longman, 1994. 352p. maps. bibliog. (The Postwar World).
Not intended for the specialist and thus accessible, this volume provides an outline of the major events of the last fifty years, from the pre-Communist period to the new phase of post-Communism in Czechoslovakia, Poland, East Germany and Hungary. The attention focuses on progress under Communism, and the crucial role of the Soviet Union and its instruments is traced and highlighted. Each chapter is supplemented by notes and references and the final bibliography is substantial. The maps are fairly simple. The target readership is students of modern European history, politics and international relations.

210 **East European revolution.**
Hugh Seton-Watson. New York: Praeger, 1955. 3rd ed. 435p. bibliog. (Praeger Publications in Russian History and World Communism).
This is in essence the direct sequel to Seton-Watson's *Eastern Europe between the wars 1918-1941* (Cambridge, England: Cambridge University Press, 1945; Hamden, Connecticut: Shoe String Press, 1963. 3rd ed. 442p.), and covers the period 1941-49, long enough to take in the Communist revolution of all states in the area, including then Czechoslovakia. Like all Seton-Watson's works it is highly readable, with a wealth of factual information.

211 **The establishment of Communist regimes in Eastern Europe, 1944-1949.**
Edited by Norman Naimark, Leonid Gibianskii. Boulder, Colorado; Oxford: Westview Press, a division of Harper Collins Publishers, 1997. 319p. bibliog.
A collective effort by scholars from Russia, the United States and Europe, drawing on the newly accessible archives in Russia and Eastern Europe. This collection of essays is the result of a project entitled 'The establishment of Communist Regimes in Eastern Europe', the objective of which was to provide a re-evaluation of that period of history and a new historical analysis of the post-war Communist takeover. The papers were presented at the Project's conference in Moscow on 29-31 March 1994. Two parallel, but not identical, volumes were to be published, one of them in Russian. This, the other volume, features the papers by American contributors. The notes on historiography in the East and West contain due reference to Czechoslovakia and there are also two specific entries: chapter ten (p. 191-216), 'Communist higher education policies in Czechoslovakia, Poland and East Germany', by John Connelly from the University of California, Berkeley; and chapter twelve, 'The Czech road to Communism' by Igor Lukes from Boston University (p. 243-65). Lukes assesses the causes of Czechoslovakia's movement to the Left and provides bibliographical 'Notes' (p. 259-65). The book contains 'Notes on Contributors' (p. 313) and an index (p. 315-19).

212 **The rise and fall of Communism in Eastern Europe.**
Ben Fowkes. Basingstoke, England: Macmillan, 1995. 2nd ed. 232p.
bibliog.

First published in 1993, this is a good historical study of the period between 1945 and
1989 (that is, the period of Communist rule), concerned generally with society and
politics. Of the many good books on aspects of Communism in the area this one stands
out, although it is slightly biased towards Poland. The author's intention was to
complement Joseph Rothschild's *Return to diversity: a political history of East
Central Europe since World War II* (q.v.). Communist rule in Central and Eastern
Europe 'consists of long stretches of event-free monotony punctuated by dramatic
catastrophes, flashes of lightning'. One of those flashes occurred in 'Czechoslovakia in
1968: climax and defeat of Reform Communism' (p. 118-41). The study focuses on
the dramas, but the persistent structural features are not ignored. The author provides
tables, pages of explanatory notes and a good general index (p. 22-32).

213 **The Cold War.**
Katherine A. S. Sibley. Westport, Connecticut; London: Greenwood
Press, 1998. 212p. bibliog.

Written for A-level and university students of contemporary history, this work offers a
concise overview of the Cold War, from 1945 to 1991, in a world, rather than merely
European, framework. It is concerned with the impact of the Cold War on the nations
directly affected and on the world in general. The key element in the book is the areas
of Cold War conflict and there is some new material on the Cold War in Europe. The
bibliography is annotated and also lists videos and web sites.

214 **A history of Czechoslovakia since 1945.**
Hans Renner. London; New York: Routledge, 1989. 200p. bibliog.

Translated from the Dutch and frequently referred to in other publications. Hans
Renner was born and educated in Czechoslovakia and left the country as a student in
1968. Thus he has more insight into the contemporary history of the country than
some Western historians, even though he conducted his research from outside
Czechoslovakia. The focus is on the reform movement, the Prague Spring of 1968 and
the subsequent twenty years. The book has a bibliography, an index and extensive
'Notes' (p. 162-92), chronologically documenting the historical events.

215 **Czechoslovakia: anvil of the Cold War.**
John O. Crane, Sylvia Crane, foreword by Corliss Lamont. New
York; Westport, Connecticut; London: Praeger, 1991. 325p. bibliog.

John Crane was research and press secretary to T. G. Masaryk. His work as a historian
was completed and posthumously published (he died in 1982) by his wife Sylvia, also
a historian. This valuable contribution to 20th-century history is dedicated 'to the
spirit of T. G. Masaryk'. The Crane family were friends of the Masaryks and the
friendship stretched over two generations. The Cranes supported the Masaryks and
their cause prior to, and during, the First World War and the book contains cameos in
the form of personal memoirs. Three critical events inform this book: the founding of
Czechoslovakia in 1918; the Munich crisis and betrayal in 1938; and the Communist
take-over in 1948. The authors are critical of the attitude of the West towards
Czechoslovakia during the Communist years and were particularly anguished by the
Munich betrayal. John Crane was a close friend of Jan Masaryk and he believes in the
suicide theory, with which the book concludes. The book has an index.

216   **The short march: the Communist takeover in Czechoslovakia:
1945-1948.**
Karel Kaplan.   London: C. Hurst & Co., 1987. 207p. map. bibliog.

The Czechoslovak Communists succeeded in installing a totalitarian regime in
February 1948 with the support of a large part of the population. Kaplan himself
joined the Czechoslovak Communist Party in 1948 and was an ardent, idealistic
activist. This study in Communist power politics examines the ease with which power
was seized and with which Czechoslovakia was linked to the Soviet bloc. The roots of
the strong support which the Communists enjoyed and which was peculiar to the
Czechoslovak case, are examined and discussed. The book has a good bibliography, a
register of names/functions of the people involved (p. 201-04), and a brief index
(p. 205-07).

217   **The unbearable burden of history: the Sovietization of
Czechoslovakia.**
Ivan Sviták.   Prague: Academia, 1990. 3 vols. bibliog.

A trilogy by a historian and philosopher. The first volume, 'From Munich to Jalta',
covers the critical period between 1938 and 1945, after which the Czechs started their
fateful balancing act between East and West, to end up in the Soviet camp. The second
volume, 'Prague Spring revisited', covers the following two decades 'when the dream
about socialist democracy resulted in the harsh reality of bureaucratic dictatorship'.
The third paperback, 'The era of abnormalization', i.e. the following two decades,
'analyzes the bitter decades of Soviet socialism, the emergence of dissent and the
growth of opposition movements, which resulted in Central European democratic
revolutions'. A concise history of this period is 'Czechoslovakia behind the Iron
Curtain (1945-1989)', by Milan Otáhal, in *Bohemia in history*, edited by Mikuláš
Teich (Cambridge, England: Cambridge University Press, 1998, p. 306-23). 'Czechs
and Slovaks in modern history', by Dušan Kováč, is from the same publication (p. 364-79).

218   **Political persecution in Czechoslovakia: 1948-1972.**
Karel Kaplan.   Cologne, Germany: Index e.V., 1983. 50p. (Crisis in
Soviet-type Systems, study no. 3).

Deals with 'the role of the mechanism of political and police surveillance of society'
and provides concrete historical facts. The connection between various methods of
political discrimination and the various phases in the development of the crisis of the
system are discussed.

219   **Report on the murder of the General Secretary.**
Karel Kaplan.   London: I. B. Tauris & Co. Ltd, 1990. 232p. bibliog.

Kaplan is a contemporary historian who lived in exile in Western Europe and wrote
several books on political persecution in Czechoslovakia. The book was published
first in Italian in 1987 by Valerio Levi Editore in Rome and subsequently in Prague by
Mladá Fronta in 1992. It is a full and factual, perhaps the best, published account of
the most publicized of the 1952 show trials. These witch hunts were organized under
Soviet pressure in the 1950s and were reminiscent of the Moscow trials of 1936-38. In
this trial, eleven leading Communist Party officials, including the General Secretary
himself, Rudolf Slánsky, were sentenced to death. The trial was closely followed by
the media, which also reported the 'voice of the people': the public was supposed to
have been deeply shocked by the crimes of the traitors, so anti-Semitism and

denunciation were given free rein. The political institutions, police and courts cooperated admirably. Kaplan had access to secret documentary material in 1968-69, when he was a secretary of a special rehabilitation commission, established by the Central Committee of the Communist Party of Czechoslovakia to investigate in full the circumstances of the Slánský trial. Slánský himself was rehabilitated in 1963. This is an important book for students of modern European history and should be found in university libraries. The appendixes consist of the biographies and final letters of those condemned and lists of names of the persons tried, which reveal a number of Jewish names. Kaplan provides detailed 'Notes' to the text, an index of names and photographs.

220 **The Prague trial: the first anti-Zionist show trial in the Communist Bloc.**
Meir Cotic. New York: Herzl Press; New York; London; Toronto: Cornwall Books, 1987. 281p. bibliog.

Another study, more orientated towards the anti-Semitic factors, of the 1952 trial in which fourteen members of the government and leaders of the Communist Party, eleven of them allegedly Jewish, were charged with high treason. Cotic considers the background to the trial, the political atmosphere, and the manipulation of the judicial system under the guidance of Soviet advisors. The accounts of survivors document the methods used by the prosecutors to obtain prisoners' cooperation (moral coercion, brain-washing, utter humiliation). Feelings in Israel are also highlighted, and in the 'Epilogue' Cotic considers the problems of Soviet Jewry at the time of writing. The book includes photographs, a list of key figures in the Slánský affair, a chronology of events from 1945 to 1969, and an index. The 'Select bibliography' (p. 276-77) lists books on the trial and books on Jewish-Soviet relations.

221 **The overcoming of the regime crisis after Stalin's death in Czechoslovakia, Poland and Hungary.**
Cologne, Germany: Index e.V., 1986. 119p. bibliog. (Research Project Crisis in Soviet-type Systems, study no. 11).

The crisis in the Soviet bloc from 1953-57 impacted on the whole of society, affecting politics, economics and culture. This paperback is concerned mostly with the political and economic spheres and identifies the roots of the crisis. The study is well researched and the text has generous annotations.

Prague Spring and Soviet intervention in 1968

222 **The Prague Spring: a mixed legacy.**
Edited by Jiří Pehe. New York: Freedom House, 1988. 223p. bibliog. (Perspectives on Freedom, no. 10).

Warsaw Pact armies, led by the Soviet Union, invaded Czechoslovakia on 21 August 1968, suppressing a movement which was hoping to democratize socialism, to establish, as the saying went, 'socialism with a human face'. This movement, the Prague Spring, suffered humiliating defeat and left behind a mixed legacy of ideas. This volume is a collection of articles by distinguished names from a variety of fields: Jan Vladislav, František Janouch, Jiří Hochman, Radoslav Selucký, Jiří Loewy,

Vladimír Škutina, Pavel Tigrid, Eva Kantůrková, Jan Kavan, Josef Škvorecký, Otto Ulč, the editor Jiří Pehe, Antonín Liehm and Ivan Sviták. The collection is rather better than the first impression given by its dull exterior and the missing diacritics in the Czech words. Some of the articles are eyewitness accounts of the invasion, some reflect on the cultural, mainly literary, movement which was part of the 1968 ideology, and some focus on life after the invasion. (This includes Josef Škvorecký's article on Sixty-Eight Publishers, the Czech émigré publishing house in Toronto which was established after the invasion of 1968, p. 131-41). Some articles draw parallels between the Prague Spring and Gorbachev's Perestrojka in the Soviet Union. Of interest are the short biographies of the contributors (p. 201-09). There is a chronology of Czech history from 400 BC to March 1988 (p. 189-200) and a chronology of 1968 (p. 194-98).

223 **The Prague Spring and its aftermath: Czechoslovak politics, 1968-1970.**
Kieran Williams.   Cambridge, England: Cambridge University Press, 1997. 270p. bibliog.

Kieran Williams of the School of Slavonic and East European Studies, University of London, justifies his work in a field which appears to be already adequately covered by 'the change of perspective made possible by the passage of three decades'. This means not merely the length of time since the invasion of Czechoslovakia by Warsaw Pact armies, but above all the fundamental changes which occurred in Czechoslovakia, such as the revolution in November 1989, the end of Soviet supremacy in Central Europe and the realization that Communism was simply not amenable to reform. In addition to this change of perspective, the author had access to newly available documents and archival sources, e.g. the archives of the Central Committee of the Czechoslovak Communist Party. Some of these documents were previously classified. The study has two sections. The first is an analysis of the political situation from the standpoint of political science. The second provides a meticulous, sometimes even hour-by-hour, account, based on archival documents, of the period between January 1968 and December 1970. Martin Brown writes in *BCSA Newsletter* August/September 1998 (p. 9): 'Dr. Williams resists apportioning blame and instead seeks a deeper, more objective approach, free of partisan conclusions, resulting in a truly excellent study'. The book does not uphold the popular interpretation of the Warsaw Pact invasion, as a monster of aggression, but reveals the incompetence of, and the divisions within, the Czechoslovak Communist Party, Prague and Moscow, and the Warsaw Pact itself. The author provides numerous footnotes referring to the sources used, mostly archival, a selective bibliography of books and articles and an index. Kieran Williams also explained his thesis in *New sources on Soviet decision making during the 1968 Czechoslovak crisis, Europe-Asia Studies,* vol. 48, no. 3 (May 1996), p. 457-70. bibliog. The article is based on new material released from the archives of several countries between 1990 and 1993 and on certain Russian archive sources released later. Williams assesses the material and develops new theories on the change in Soviet policy after 3 August 1968.

224 **Soviet intervention in Czechoslovakia, 1968: anatomy of a decision.**
Jiří Valenta.   Baltimore, Maryland; London: Johns Hopkins University Press, 1979. 208p. bibliog.

This work is an exercise in intellectual analysis, reconstructing the thought processes behind the final Soviet decision to intervene, and is based in part on documents published at the time and partly on interviews with first-hand participants. A revised edition was published in 1991.

225 **The Prague Spring '68: a national security archives documents reader.**
Compiled and edited by Jaromír Navrátil, with Antonín Benčík, Václav Kural, Marie Michálková, Jitka Vondrová, preface by Václav Havel, translated by Mark Kramer, Joy Moss, Ruth Tosek. Budapest: Central European University Press, 1998. Distributed by Plymbridge Distributors Ltd, Plymouth, United Kingdom. Distributed in the United States by Cornell University Press, New York. 596p. map. bibliog.
The editors were members of a commission appointed by Václav Havel to investigate the events of 1967-70. They had the advantage of being able to research the previously inaccessible archives of individual members of the Warsaw Pact, as well as having access to previously highly classified US documents from the National Security Council, the CIA and other intelligence bodies. The book also presents documents from the highest level: the council of the Kremlin Politburo; multilateral meetings of the Warsaw Pact, which led to the decision to invade Czechoslovakia; and transcripts of KGB records of telephone conversations between Alexander Dubček and Leonid Brezhnev. The book is accessible to the reader and each section is introduced by an essay in which the editors provide the historical and political context. There is additional background information in the 'Chronology', 'Glossary' and 'Bibliography'. The volume has an index and the inside front cover has a map of the Warsaw Pact's Operation Danube, which gives the positions of the various corps, divisions and units of the invading forces. A different dimension to the events of 1968 is provided by a collection of photographs, a photographic history of the time, by the renowned Czech photographer Josef Koudelka, published under the title *Prague, 1968* (Paris: Centre national de la photographie, 1990). This moving photographic record is annotated by Petr Král.

226 **Czechoslovakia: the plan that failed.**
Radoslav Selucký, introduction by Kamil Winter. London: Nelson, 1970. 150p.
A number of books were generated by the events of 1968-69 and published immediately after and it is difficult for a non-historian to forage his way through this mass of literature. This volume is one of the early ones which continue to enjoy a reputation and are widely re-quoted. Its primary concern is with the economic reforms which lay behind the 'Prague Spring', and the political and economic crisis which preceded them in the aftermath of the Stalinist 1950s and de-Stalinization. The author had a first-hand involvement in the reform of economic thinking and is portrayed in the introduction as having made, through his lucid writings, a significant contribution to public understanding of the impending changes.

227 **Czechoslovakia's interrupted revolution.**
H. Gordon Skilling. Princeton, New Jersey: Princeton University Press, 1976. 924p. bibliog.
One of the most detailed analyses of the 1968 crisis. It starts with the historical background and continues with an almost blow-by-blow record of events and the responses to them by different sectors and interested parties. The major issues of rehabilitation of the victims of Stalinism, the new economic proposals, and federalization are each given a reasoned appraisal. After dealing with the Soviet intervention, Skilling discusses whether the events that led to it had represented

reform, revolution or counter-revolution, and explores some of the views that had been expressed.

228 **Srpen '69: edice dokumentů.** (August '69: edition of documents.) Oldřich Tůma: Prague: Ústav pro soudobé dějiny AVČR v nakladatelství MAXDORF, 1996. 344p. maps. bibliog.

The invasion of Czechoslovakia in August 1968 started the period of normalization, when there was a return to socialism and Communism in the old sense, rather than the pre-1968 interpretations of 'Communism with a human face'. These documents testify to the first anniversary of the invasion, when unrest occurred in some towns. The documents cover the measures taken by official bodies, that is the police, the Communist Party etc., and the leaflets of underground organizations. The critical days of 19-22 August 1969 are described in chronological order, and there are photographs which were taken in the cities of Prague, Brno and Liberec. These show that the anniversary was fairly uneventful: they record minor incidents, police activity and a few demonstrators.

229 **Dubček: Dubček and Czechoslovakia 1968-1990.** William Shawcross. London: Hogarth, 1990. 244p. bibliog.

First published by Weidenfeld & Nicolson in 1970, this was generally regarded as the best of several biographies of Dubček published at the time. It is a detailed personal and political biography of the man who nominally headed the reform movement known as the 'Prague Spring', the Slovak Communist Alexander Dubček. In this edition the author took out some passages which had become less relevant in retrospect. The chapter on the Soviet invasion of Czechoslovakia in 1968 has been supplemented and a short epilogue has been added on what happened to Dubček in the difficult last twenty years of his life; he died in a car crash in 1992. At the time of writing the first edition the author had not fully realized that 'socialism with a human face' was impossible since it is a contradiction in terms. The book contains photographs up to 1989, a short bibliography, references to primary and secondary sources and an index.

230 **Hope dies last: the autobiography of Alexander Dubcek.** Edited and translated by Jiří Hochman. Tokyo; New York; London: Kodansha, 1993. 354p. maps.

This detailed autobiography starts with Dubček's childhood in Slovakia and the Soviet Union, the return of the family to Slovakia and the young Dubček's activities in the resistance and the 1944 Slovak Uprising. The period between 1945 and 1967, the years of his activities as a rising Communist activist, are treated rather scantily, whereas 1967 and 1968, when Dubček became one of the most important men in the world, are described in great detail. The complete text of the Program of the Communist Party of Czechoslovakia, dated April 1968 is on p. 287-335. In 1989 Dubček was a vital influence in the united democratic forces which caused the fall of Communism. He also strove for the preservation of the unity of the Czechs and Slovaks, but Czechoslovakia was dissolved into two countries a year after his death. Dubček was killed in 1992 in a car crash and did not complete his autobiography. Jiří Hochman, a journalist, completed the book and wrote an editorial postscript after Dubček's death.

231 **Dubček speaks: Alexander Dubček with Andras Sugar.**
Alexander Dubček, Andras Sugar. London; New York: L. B. Tauris & Co. Ltd, 1990. 110p.

Reproduces the full text of Alexander Dubček's interviews with Andras Sugar for Hungarian television which were broadcast on 17 and 26 April 1989, that is, prior to the overthrow of Communism in November 1989. At the time the Czech media were critical of the interviews and Andras Sugar had a battle, which he won, to have the text published in Hungary. The interviews describe the events of 1968. Although a Communist, Dubček enjoyed considerable popular approval. Some ninety per cent of Czechs backed him in 1968, supporting his programme of democratic socialism, and only five per cent wished for a return to capitalism. The interviews lack an index.

232 **Dubček: profily vzdoru. Profiles of defiance. Profile des Trotzes. Les portraits de l'obstination.**
Bratislava: Smena, 1991. 176p.

Presents parallel texts in Slovak, English, German and French. The text is in fact brief, the book consisting mostly of photographs, many of them from Dubček's private life. Some of them are touching, particularly those from the difficult years after 1968, when Dubček was demoted and worked for the Slovak forestry commission.

233 **Gustáv Husák, President of Czechoslovakia: speeches and writings.**
Oxford: Pergamon Press, 1986. 267p. (Leaders of the World).

At the time of publication Husák had been president of Czechoslovakia for seventeen years, having been appointed in 1969, at the time of dissension and turmoil. This hagiography, a coffee-table book, has an introduction by Robert Maxwell, an interview with Husák conducted also by Robert Maxwell and a short biography of the President. The speeches and writings themselves are fairly run-of-the mill party-line communications and there are photographs of President Husák with various world leaders.

The Velvet Revolution of 1989 and the dissolution of Czechoslovakia

General

234 **The uses of adversity. Essays on the fate of Central Europe.**
Timothy Garton Ash. Cambridge, England: Granta Books in association with Penguin, 1989. 305p.

Contains a collection of essays written between April 1984 and May 1989 by one of the most sensitive and independently minded specialists in contemporary history in the West. The chapters 'Pre-spring' and 'Prague advertisement' on pages 192-217 are specifically concerned with the movement against the establishment in Czechoslovakia. The author visited the country in 1988 to attend a meeting of Charter 77. The book was written many years after the Prague Spring and the invasion of the Warsaw Pact countries, but before the Velvet Revolution. For that reason some of the

History. Post-war period (1945-). The Velvet Revolution of 1989 and the dissolution of Czechoslovakia. General

deliberations and conclusions, which would have made essential and interesting reading at the time, are now outdated; despite this, the essays are considered classics and Garton Ash is often quoted. The work lacks a contents page, but does have an index. Penguin are preparing another, paperback edition of this work, to come out in September 1999. Garton Ash published another collection of essays on even more contemporary history, *History of the present: essays, sketches and despatches from Europe in 1990s* (London: Allen Lane, 1999).

235 We the people: the revolution of '89 witnessed in Warsaw, Budapest, Berlin and Prague.
Timothy Garton Ash.   Cambridge, England: Granta Books in association with Penguin, 1990. 256p.

At the time of writing the author had been studying the situation in Central Europe for ten years and was a well-informed observer. He was with the Civic Forum, a Czech political movement founded in November 1989 which united opposition against the totalitarian Communist regime and was the main force behind the Velvet Revolution, and Václav Havel as the events of November 1989 unfolded. The chapter entitled 'Prague: inside the Magic Lantern' gives a participant's account of this important moment in the political history of Europe. A new, paperback edition of this work is expected in September 1999. Timothy Garton Ash is one of the distinguished academics who contributed to *Between past and future: the revolutions of 1989 and their aftermath* (Budapest: Central European University Press, 1999. 500p.). The publication, edited by Soriun Antohi and Vladimir Tismaneanu, will be published in the autumn of 1999, on the tenth anniversary of the collapse of Communism in Central and Eastern Europe.

236 The rebirth of history: Eastern Europe in the age of democracy.
Mischa Glenny.   Harmondsworth, England: Penguin, 1993. 2nd ed. 274p. map.

With his background as the Central European correspondent of the BBC and former *Guardian* journalist covering Southeastern Europe, Mischa Glenny, a Czech speaker, is one of the best informed individuals where this part of Europe is concerned. His insight and knowledge makes this frequently cited book a very valuable contribution to the region's recent history. The first edition was published in 1990.

237 The crisis of Leninism and the decline of the Left: the revolutions of 1989.
Edited by Daniel Chirot.   Seattle, Washington: University of Washington Press, 1991. 245p. bibliog.

Contributions to this collection of essays cover events in Eastern Europe, the Soviet Union, China and Korea and attitudes to these events in the West, particularly in the United States. The year 1989 redefined the world and its impact is compared in the introduction with the events of 1789. The contributors explain the decades of political, economic and social change, and the forces which were at work and resulted in the collapse of Communism in Eastern Europe in 1989. The future is examined, although not predicted, with consideration of the issue of NATO and the prospects for Communism.

74

History. Post-war period (1945-). The Velvet Revolution of 1989 and the dissolution of Czechoslovakia. Václav Havel

238 **Deset pražských dnů, 17.-27. listopadu 1989: dokumentace.** (Ten Prague days, 17-27 November, 1989: documentation.) Prague: Academia, 1990. 672p.

These ten days in November 1989, which were turbulent, yet not violent, decided the fate of the Czechs and Slovaks. In the first part of the book there is a chapter on each day, containing documents grouped by theme. This collection of declarations, articles, proclamations and speeches is intended for the general reader as well as for the researcher. Each document has a heading which gives the day, the time of day or sometimes even the hour. All documents are from Prague. The second part of the book, 'Rozhovory', contains interviews with political representatives about the revolutionary events. These interviews are a valuable resource, since they capture the unforgettable atmosphere of those November days.

239 **The Velvet Revolution: Czechoslovakia 1988-1991.** Bernard Wheaton, Zdeněk Kaván. Boulder, Colorado; San Francisco; Oxford: Westview Press, 1992. 255p. bibliog.

A fairly detailed description of the social and political changes of which Bernard Wheaton was one of the few Western observers. The appendices are of interest since they include actual documents of the revolution (statements, resolutions and declarations), the slogans which represented the voice of the street, a survey of public opinion during the Velvet Revolution and a biographical cameo of Václav Havel. The work is well documented by photographs, political cartoons, detailed notes on written sources and a bibliography. Bernard Wheaton is a historian and Zdeněk Kaván a specialist on international relations.

240 **Central and Eastern Europe: problems and prospects.** Edited by Charles Dick, Anne Aldis. Camberley, England: The Strategic and Combat Studies Institute, in association with the Conflict Studies Research Centre, 1998. 236p. (The Occasional, Number 37).

The theme of this study is the change from the era when the Communist bloc was a threat to the Western world to the era when this region was a zone of danger, of potential local conflict and civil war. The study looks at language and national identity, the present state of the economy and the potential for conflict. The Czech Republic is specifically dealt with in two chapters: 'Poland and Czech Republic' on p. 24-25; and 'Czech Republic' on p. 174. The enlargement of NATO and EU are also discussed. This good collection of essays is handicapped by the lack of an index.

Václav Havel

241 **After the Velvet Revolution: Václav Havel and the new leaders of Czechoslovakia speak out.** Edited by Tim D. Whipple. New York: Freedom House, 1991. 328p. (Focus on Issues, no. 14).

Presents interviews, speeches and articles from newspapers, journals and magazines in which the new leaders of Czechoslovakia put forward their own analyses of the contemporary situation and their aspirations for the future. Photographs and cartoons

75

History. Post-war period (1945-). The Velvet Revolution of 1989 and the dissolution of Czechoslovakia. Václav Havel

illustrate the 'velvet', and also merry, revolution of November 1989. A chronological commentary of events from 1968 to 1989 introduces the collection, the greatest attention being given to events in November 1989 in which all the contributors played major roles.

242 **Disturbing the peace: a conversation with Karel Hvížďala.**
Václav Havel, translated from the Czech and with an introduction by Paul Wilson. London; Boston, Massachusetts: Faber & Faber, 1990. 228p.

This biography of Václav Havel is distinguished from the others, and there are many, by its origin. The Czech title is 'Long distance interrogation', because it is an interview by Karel Hvížďala, dated 1985-86, when Hvížďala was living in Germany, and sent his questions to Havel, then still locked, by choice, in Communist Czechoslovakia. The biographical section is brief and although the interview does convey Havel's philosophy and a section dwells on his work for the stage, most of the questions relate to his political activities in the late 1970s and 1980s and to Charter 77. To a general reader the interviews convey an ordinary being, the first among equals, a politician and a literary person. The Glossary, p. 207-18, which provides concise information on various key figures from the Czech political and cultural world of the second half of the 20th century, serves both journalists and general readers well. Paul Wilson lived in Czechoslovakia for ten years teaching English and was expelled in 1977 during the campaign the regime waged against Charter 77.

243 **The reluctant president: a political life of Václav Havel.**
Michael Simmons. London: Methuen, 1991. 229p. bibliog.

A straightforward, accessible biography. The author undertook substantial research on the subject but there is evidence of lack of depth in his knowledge of the Czech situation and there are some inaccuracies, albeit very minor. The author admits he drew on Havel's *Letters to Olga: June 1979-September 1982* and *Disturbing the peace: a conversation with Karel Hvížďala* and the essays from *Living in truth* (qq.v.). He tried to 'get to grips' with Czechoslovakia under Communism and on the whole he succeeded. Although the subject is Havel and the book is mostly on Havel, much of the narrative is on the Czech situation generally. Perhaps because Simmons is an outsider he makes some refreshing observations. The Czech names have no diacritics, which is surprising in a book published by such an august publisher. The biography has sixteen photographs, a 'Chronology' of Czech history from 1918-91 (p. XX-XXII), a bibliography of Havel's work published in English (p. XXIII), a 'Bibliography' of books consulted (p. 219-20) and an index.

244 **Václav Havel: la biographie.** (Václav Havel: biography.)
Eda Kriseová, translated from the Czech by Jan Rubeš in collaboration with Catherine Daems, preface by Jiří Gruša. [La Tour d'Aigues, France]: Édition de l'Aube, 1991. 380p.

This official, authorized biography was published in Czech in Brno, Czech Republic, by Atlantis in 1991, and in English in New York by St. Martin's Press in 1993 (313p. 16 plates). It has been criticized by some in the Czech Republic as being written in haste, superficial and more about Kriseová than about Havel. Yet this is a well-written book, which provides a better explanation of Havel's background and youth than many other biographies of the man. The book has some delightful period

76

photographs of Václav and his brother Ivan when the family lived in Havlov, their country retreat in Žďárec in Moravia, during the war. This retreat is difficult to translate into English terms, being neither a cottage nor a country house. It is more of a sizeable and comfortable chalet built in the beautiful part of Moravia from which some of Havel's ancestors came. Unfortunately, the reproductions of the photographs in the French edition are not as good as in the original Czech edition. Kriseová is a journalist and writer, of the same generation as Havel, and is well qualified to write on the difficulties encountered by the children of middle- and upper-class families in the 1950s and early 1960s and on the Prague cultural scene of the 1970s and 1980s. There are 'Notes' and an annotated name index (p. 369-78).

245 **Letters to Olga: June 1979-September 1982.**
Václav Havel, translated from the Czech with an introduction by Paul Wilson.   London; Boston, Massachusetts: Faber & Faber, 1988. 397p. bibliog.

These letters, well translated here by Paul Wilson, were first published as *Dopisy Olze (červen 1979-září 1982)* in 1983 by arrangement with Rowohlt Taschenbuch Verlag GmbH, Reinbeck bei Hamburg in Germany and subsequently published by the same publisher in German in 1984 as *Briefe an Olga.* Sixty-Eight Publishers in Toronto published the letters again in Czech in 1985. The first English edition appeared simultaneously in 1988 in the United States and Canada, published by Alfred A. Knopf Inc. in New York and Random House of Canada Limited, Toronto. This is the first edition in the United Kingdom and contains the majority of the 144 letters which Havel wrote to his wife Olga when he was in prison both as a signatory to Charter 77 and for assembling, copying and distributing in Czechoslovakia and abroad indictable material (mainly material on unjust judicial and extra-judicial procedures and practices in that country). Havel was allowed to write to one person only from his prison; his sentence was originally four-and-a-half years. None of Olga's letters to Havel are included. The letters are philosophical as well as of a practical nature, the philosophical element something of a continuation of Havel's polemics with Jan Patočka, the Czech dissident philosopher. They betray Havel's worries and anxieties, the main one being at 'being cut off from the community of friends and colleagues'. The Letters have explanations in the 'Glossary of names' (p. 381-85) and 'Notes' (p. 377-80), which are a necessary adjunct to the text. There is also an index and the introduction includes some explanatory bibliographical notes (p. 2).

246 **Questions of identity and responsibility in Václav Havel.**
Robert B. Pynsent.   In: *Questions of identity: Czech and Slovak ideas of nationality and personality.*   Budapest, London; New York: Central European University Press, 1994, p. 1-42.

The author traces Havel's philosophy with regard to the concept of identity and nationalism through biographical notes on Havel and through Havel's literary works, which opposed the collective pseudo-identity of Communist doctrine, and speeches. '. . . Havel's central conception of identity is that it consists in the sum of one's responsibilities. In other words he comes close to the medieval perception: one is what one does'.

History. Post-war period (1945-). The Velvet Revolution of 1989 and the dissolution of Czechoslovakia. Václav Havel

247 **Václav Havel and the Velvet Revolution.**
Jeffrey Symynkywicz. Parsippany, New Jersey: Dillon Press, 1995. 184p. map. bibliog. (A People in Focus Book).

This book is intended for a reader who has very little knowledge of modern Central European history. It is the story of Havel's life with some general background on Czechoslovakia. The font is larger then usual and there are numerous historical photographs. The tone is slightly patronizing; presumably it is meant to be read as a fairy-tale. For example, 'Appendix one' (p. 173-74) offers explanations of such terms as bourgeois, capitalist and parliamentary democracy. There are some minor inaccuracies but on the whole the book was well researched. It contains a chronology of Havel's life in Appendix two, 'Václav Havel: A time line' (p. 175-79). The 'Selected bibliography' (p. 180-81) lists some of the key literature. The book has an index. In summary, this book is a general history of Czechoslovakia, incorporating a biography of Havel, intended for the general reader.

Nationalities and Minorities

General and historical

248 **Contemporary nationalism in East Central Europe.**
Edited by Paul Latawski. Basingstoke, England: Macmillan, 1994. 200p. bibliog.

A collection of papers on modern nationality issues which questions the definition of nationality, the nation and the nation state in East Central Europe and examines it in its historical context. 'The road to separatism: nationalism in Czechoslovakia' (p. 67-85) is by John Morison. A small table of the ethnic composition of that country in the years 1930, 1950, 1970 and 1987 is on p. 74.

249 **Minorities in politics: cultural and language rights.**
Edited by Jana Plichtová. Bratislava: Czechoslovak Committee of the European Cultural Foundation, 1992. 285p. bibliog.

This collection of papers from an international symposium held in Bratislava, which attracted speakers from many countries including Britain, is divided into several even sections. The first section, on 'Nationalism and minorities – central and eastern Europe', raises the issue of whether this region, with its turbulent history, can achieve a society where people respect each other, whatever their ethnic origin, and whether a political state can exist here. The nation and the state, nationality and citizenship are discussed. The other sections are concerned with the ethnic structure of Central Europe, providing the relevant historical background, and with the protection and implementation of cultural rights, in particular language rights and language laws, and the problems of identity. A paper on Croatian settlements in Moravia is in the section on minorities with suppressed identity. There is a separate section on the Jews.

250 **Průvodce právy příslušníků národnostních menšin v České republice.** (A guide to the rights of members of national minorities in the Czech Republic.)
Hana Frištenská, Andrej Sulitka. Prague: Demokratická aliancia Slovákov v ČR, 1995. 2nd ed. 95p.

This important handbook offers an overview of the then Czech policy on minorities and a summary of the Czech legislative framework from 1993, the year when the Czech Republic became a separate political entity. The authors provide data on national minorities in the country, on mother-tongue education (there is a survey of Polish schools in the districts of Karviná and Frýdek-Místek in Northern Moravia), culture and media and the use of the mother tongue in official contacts. One section is on international agreements and pacts, bilateral agreements between the Czech Republic and neighbouring states, the Czech constitutional acts, and the legislative standards concerning national minorities. Some of these are reproduced in the book.

251 **The politics of ethnicity in Eastern Europe.**
Edited by George Klein, Milan J. Reban. Boulder, Colorado: East European Quarterly. Distributed by Columbia University Press, New York, 1981. 279p. (East European Monographs, no. 93).

Reban's contribution, 'Czechoslovakia: the new federation', has prophetic traits. At the time, the author considered Czechoslovakia second only to Yugoslavia in terms of mixed ethnicity in Eastern Europe, thanks to the existence of the substantial Slovak nation and some not insignificant minorities, especially Germans, within its original frontiers. When this book was being compiled, the main watershed as regards Slovaks had been in 1968-69 at the time of the country's federalization, which for the time being solved the Slovaks' aspirations of the 1960s, when nationhood was their primary concern. The Czechs, on the other hand, were more concerned with economic reform at this stage. The article looks at the history of official Czechoslovak attitudes to the Slovaks and Slovakia and at some of the workings of the new federal state. An account is also given of the condition and status of the national minorities within the federation, pinpointing the problematic nature of the relevant statistics (the fact that there were no separate figures for Jews and only an uncertain estimate for the Romany population, in addition to some general discrepancies).

252 **Eastern European national minorities, 1919-1980: a handbook.**
Stephen M. Horak et al. Littleton, Colorado: Libraries Unlimited, 1985. 375p. bibliog.

The book has two chapters (one and three), which constitute a very comprehensive account of the recent state of minorities in the Czech Lands. The chapters are: Stephen Horak's 'Eastern European national minorities 1919-1980' (p. 1-34); and Josef Kalvoda's (with the assistance of David Crowe) 'National minorities in Czechoslovakia, 1919-1980' (p. 108-59). The chapters start with a historical summary, supported by statistical tables, and trace the main demographic changes, in most cases associated with the approach of war and war itself, and any relevant changes of frontier. The main minorities in the former Czechoslovakia with which the authors are concerned are the Ukrainians, Russians, Poles, Hungarians, Germans, gypsies (Roma) and Jews; the Greeks, who are mentioned in the Polish section of the book and came to Czechoslovakia at the same time and for the same (political) reasons, are not mentioned. Each section of the book has an annotated bibliography.

80

253 **The multinational empire: nationalism and national reform in the Habsburg Monarchy 1848-1918.**
Robert A. Kann. New York: Octagon Books, 1950. 2 vols. bibliog.
This book has been reprinted several times. The entire work needs to be known by anyone wishing to consider the early history of the minorities problem in the Czech Lands, which has its roots in the multinational nature of Austria-Hungary and the quirks of national frontiers. Volume one has a separate section giving the cultural and political history of the Czechs (*inter alia*) as a national group with an independent national political history (p. 15-220). The views of such leading figures as Palacký and Masaryk are outlined at relevant points in both volumes. Of particular value is the wide range of references in both the bibliography and the footnotes to each chapter. Kann is an authority on Habsburg history.

254 **Ethnic national minorities in Eastern Europe 1848-1945.**
Raymond Pearson. London: Basingstoke, England: Macmillan, 1983. 249p. maps. bibliog. (Themes in Comparative History).
This study constitutes an introduction to the demographic background of the whole area, showing where the minorities originated and how they evolved into nations – in the 'luckier' cases. By its general nature, including its history of emergent states and shifting frontiers, the work covers both the non-Czech minorities within the Czech Lands and Czech minorities outside the country. A subject to which the author pays particular attention is the effect of war on minorities. The thematic section of the bibliography is excellent. This is essential reading on the subject.

The Roma (the gypsies)

255 **Historical dictionary of the gypsies (Romanies).**
Donald Kenrick, with the assistance of Gillian Taylor. Lanham, Maryland; London: The Scarecrow Press, 1998. 231p. bibliog. (European Historical Dictionaries, no. 27).
This excellent dictionary, 'designed to be a tool for all those working in education, culture, civil rights and politics', has entries on significant persons, events, institutions and organizations. Of particular importance are the entries on Romany clans and groups and the countries in which they live. The Czech Republic and Czech Romany are well covered. The bibliography is large (p. 194-230) and includes web sites.

256 **Gypsies: a multidisciplinary annotated bibliography.**
Diane Tong. New York; London: Garland Publishing, 1995. 399p.
Based on the collections of the New York Public Library, the Texas Romany Archives and the Boston Athenaeum, this very useful and well-produced bibliography has 1,075 entries and subject and name indexes. The main section is divided by subject and includes works written by, and about, gypsies, extracted from all forms of printed media. The Czech element is well represented. From the UK comes *A gypsy bibliography* compiled by Dennis Binns (Manchester, England: Dennis Binns) which

81

Nationalities and Minorities. The Roma (the gypsies)

was originally published in 1982 and included 1,306 references, not annotated, of mostly British origin and published after 1914. Two supplements have been issued, of similar size: volume two in 1986 and volume three in 1990. The most relevant of other gypsy bibliographies is *Zigeneur in Osteuropa: Eine Bibliographie zu den Ländern Polen, Tschechoslowakei und Ungarn* (The gypsies in Eastern Europe: bibliography of Poland, Czechoslovakia and Hungary) (Munich: K. G. Saur, 1983).

257 **The gypsies.**
Angus M. Fraser. Oxford; Cambridge, Massachusetts: Blackwell, 1992. 359p. maps. bibliog.

An accessible, well-researched and illustrated 'story of a wandering people', which looks at all aspects of the gypsy issue, past and present. 'Bohemia, Poland-Lithuania and the Ukraine' is covered on p. 111-12. The book has twenty pages of bibliography (p. 319-39) and an index.

258 **A history of the gypsies of Eastern Europe and Russia.**
David M. Crowe. London; New York: I. B. Taurus, 1995. 317p. map. bibliog.

This book started as an annotated bibliography but developed into a study of the Roma, as gypsies prefer to be called. It is well researched, and the author used a wide range of sources. The 'Introduction' and 'Conclusion' discuss generally the 'bittersweet' history of this ethnic minority, which came originally from Northern India. The author seeks to balance the romantic and critical views on this ethnic group and concentrates on its history, which, unfortunately, is largely one of persecution. Each country is accorded its own chapter; 'Czechoslovakia' is on p. 31-67. Again, the accent is on the history of the Roma, in the Czech Lands and in Slovakia. The book is suitable for the general reader who is interested in Roma history and issues. The author provides extensive bibliographical 'Notes' (p. 239-90) and a large 'Bibliography' (p. 291-301) of articles and books. The articles are specifically on the Roma issue and the books included in the bibliography are on Eastern Europe generally.

259 **The gypsies of Eastern Europe.**
Edited by David Crowe, John Kolsti, with an introduction by Ian Hancock. Armonk, New York; London: M. E. Sharpe, 1991. 194p. bibliog.

Josef Kalvoda contributed the chapter, 'The gypsies of Czechoslovakia' (p. 93-115), in which he looks at the history of this socio-ethnic group in Bohemia, Moravia and Slovakia. Kalvoda focuses on culture and religion, education, the economic status of the gypsies, demography and assimilation. He quotes extensively from contemporary gypsy scholars, such as Eva Davidová and Milena Hübschmannová. The essay was completed before the revolution of 1989 and the author added a postscript on the manifestations of racial intolerance, and its causes, in 1990.

260 **Gypsies in Czechoslovakia.**
E. Davidová. *Journal of the Gypsy Law Society*, vol. 49, part 3-4 (1970), p. 84-97.

An excellent study of the gypsies in the Czech Lands, their history and socio-economic conditions. Davidová describes the three gypsy groups in the then

82

Czechoslovakia – nomadic, semi-nomadic and sedentary – and the gypsy language and its dialects. She provides a fairly detailed study of their historical development, from the first historical record dated 1399, the legislative efforts of Maria Theresa and Joseph II, the constitutional recognition under the first republic, and the persecution during the Second World War. The author provides data from Czechoslovak censuses over fifty years, without being able to explain fully the dramatic rise in the number of gypsy citizens.

261 **Struggling for ethnic identity: Czechoslovakia's endangered gypsies.**
New York; London: Human Rights Watch, 1992. 152p. (Human Rights Report).

The word gypsy, or the Czech word *cigáni*, are both considered derogatory by this ethnic group and indeed neither term is accurate and the connotations are disreputable. Yet it is used in the title of this booklet, which just illustrates the complexity of the issue. The name chosen by this ethnic group is Romany/Roma. There is confusion as to the number of Roma living in the Czech Lands because many of them ticked Czech nationality on census forms. Romany was recognized as a language in Czechoslovakia only in 1989 and there were attempts to set up Romany kindergartens and schools, mostly in Slovakia where the majority of Roma lived at the time. One of the unforeseen problems was that the children in these schools did not acquire a sufficient command of Slovak to be able to progress into higher education. Most Roma children, from whatever school and for a variety of reasons, end up in special schools for children with learning difficulties. Another topic examined is the sterilization of women. In the Communist era some women were offered financial incentives to be sterilized. Housing, employment, relations with the police and the criminal justice system are also scrutinized. The State Scientific Library (Štátna vedecká knižnica) in Košice, Slovakia, has maintained a Roma database since 1994.

262 **Geschichte der Roma in Böhmen, Mähren und der Slowakei.**
(History of the Roma in Bohemia, Moravia and Slovakia.)
Bartoloměj Daniel, edited and with a preface and conclusion by Joachim S. Hohmann, introduction by Milena Hübschmannová.
Frankfurt, Germany: Peter Lang, 1998. 221p. map. bibliog. (Studien zur Tsiganologie und Folkloristik, Bd. 23).

A detailed study of the wanderings of the Roma tribes, their arrival in the Czech Lands in the 14th century, their sojourn in the region and their confrontations with the indigenous population and establishment. Daniel is of Slovak-Roma origin, studied at the university in Prague and was one of the founders of the museum of gypsy culture in Brno. The bibliography (p. 211-21) includes numerous early sources. The study is spoiled by occasional errors in Czech words (missing accents) and a few inaccuracies (Hübschmannová's first name is Milena, not Helena as given on the back page of the book).

263 **Československí Romové v letech 1938-1945.** (Czechoslovak Roma in the years 1938-45.)
Ctibor Nečas. Brno, Czech Republic: Masarykova Univerzita, 1994. 220p. bibliog. map.

There is a shortage of informed publications on the Roma. This important volume may not be too difficult to obtain at a larger university library or via interlibrary loans from special collections. The author is a well-known and respected authority on the Roma and the book merits inclusion here, despite being published only in Czech. It has credible statistics on the demographic trends among the Roma prior to the Second World War and refers to legislation affecting gypsies (e.g. legislation curbing their nomadic lifestyle). It is interesting to note the emigration of German gypsies to Czechoslovakia, immediately after Hitler's ascent to power, where they sought better treatment from the government as well as from the population. The largest section of the book is given over to the 'second, unknown Holocaust', the extermination of the gypsies in concentration camps. The author provides an index of places, chronological appendices and a bibliography. A collection of haunting poems, in English and Czech, was published by Paul Polanský (Prague: G plus G, 1998. 125p.), translated by Miluš Kotišová under the title *Living through it twice: poems of the Romany holocaust (1940-1997). Dvakrát tím samým: básně o romském holocaustu (1940-1997).*

264 **Notes sur le destin des Tsiganes tchèques.** (Notes on the fate of the Czech gypsies.)
Ctibor Nečas. *Études Tsiganes*, vol. 26, no. 3 (1980), p. 8-11.

This is a response to a French edition (Paris: Calmann-Levy, 1974) of Donald Kenrick and Grattan Puxton's *The destiny of Europe's gypsies* (London: Chatto-Heinemann Educational for Sussex University Press, 1972. 256p. bibliog. Columbus Centre Series: Studies in the Dynamics of Persecution and Extermination). It adds to the book a great deal of statistical and geographical data, specific to the Czech gypsies, on: the numbers involved in the 'final solution'; the whereabouts and nature of different camps; dates for when gyspies were transported; and their forced employment in industry. The then new data came from recently accessible archival material.

265 **Gypsies.**
Photographs by Josef Koudelka, text by Willy Guy. New York: Aperture Foundation, 1975. unpaginated.

A collection of beautiful, melancholic black-and-white photographs by the world renowned Czech photographer. The photographs were taken in settlements in East Slovakia during 1962-68. Many of these gypsies moved gradually to the west, to the more prosperous Czech Lands where, in the 1970s, the conditions for gypsies were improving. Willy Guy's text is a history of the gypsy tribe, from their departure from their original homeland in northern India in 1000 AD, through their gradual progress through Europe until they arrived in the Czech Lands in the 14th century, down to the present day. Koudelka's photographs project a distressing picture of rural and urban poverty and squalor and the conclusions of Willy Guy are not optimistic: three-quarters of Czechoslovak gypsy children failed, at the time, to complete their basic education. The result will be a continuation of bleak job prospects and low social status.

266 **Můj svět. My world.**
www.radio.cz/romove/mujsvet
The Human Rights Educational Association initiated an exhibition of photographs taken by gypsy children in 1998. The spontaneous, unstylized pictures capture typical gypsy locations in the Bohemian and Moravian towns of Ústí na Labem, Chánov, Ostrava, Brno, Rokycany, Pardubice and Blansko. The children took pictures of their own environment, family, friends and relatives. The exhibition, which travelled around the Czech Republic, was intended as part of 'Romany Holocaust and Romany Present', a project which was being prepared at the time of writing. Ninety-six of these photographs were published in book form under the same title, *Můj svět. My world* (Prague: Fedor Gál, 1998). The text in the book and in the web site is bilingual, English and Czech.

267 **In the ghetto.**
L. Grant. *The Guardian*, 25 July 1998, 'Weekend', p. 16-17, 19, 21-22.
During the Second World War practically all the gypsies in the Czech Lands were exterminated in the Holocaust. After the war the Slovak gypsies were forcibly deported to the Czech regions. Now, after the Velvet Revolution, the new generation is facing racial attacks, menace and possible enclosure into segregated, walled areas.

268 **Strangers in their own land.**
H. Judah. *Independent*, 6 August, 1998, 'Review', p. 8.
The Czech Republic enjoys a civilized image and its president is known worldwide for his liberal attitudes. Yet the country has some of the worst skinhead problems in Europe and the racist attacks against the Roma citizens, which increased after 1989, are symptoms of a violent and ugly fascism. However, since this article, and many others on this theme, appeared in Britain, more encouraging news began to come from the Czech Republic. In 1999, for example, the first Roma newscaster, Ondrej Gina, was appointed by Czech television.

269 **Gypsy malady.**
D. Campbell, K. Connolly. *The Guardian*, 20 November, 1997, 'Supplement', p. 1-2, 7.
This report from Prague addresses the difficult issue of what to do with the Czech gypsies. Many came to the United Kingdom, hoping to solve their problems by emigrating, but the locals and skinheads in Britain made sure that they did not feel welcome.

270 **Babel: the Roma.**
Index on Censorship, 27(1), (January/February 1998), p. 156-61.
Presents the views of several groups of people. Czech and Slovak gypsies explain why they are seeking refuge in Britain, and the citizens of Dover, in the UK, present their viewpoint. In the Czech Republic the Roma and the neo-Nazi skinheads tell their stories. These are excerpts from a 'World in Action' programme produced for Granada Television, UK.

271 **The model mother to Prague's forgotten children.**
P. Keating. *The Times*, 4 April 1998, 'Weekend', p. 3.
Czech supermodel Teresa Maxová established a foundation which sought Western families wishing to adopt Czech orphans. About eighty per cent of these children are of Roma origin, mostly abandoned. This situation is explained by the disintegration of traditional gypsy family values, a direct consequence of seventy years of state persecution.

The Jews

272 **Jewish identities in the new Europe.**
Edited by Jonathan Webber. London; Washington, DC: Published for the Oxford Centre for Hebrew and Jewish Studies [by] Littman Library of Jewish Civilization, 1994. 307p.
This collection of scholarly essays by Jewish and non-Jewish authorities originated from a symposium held at Oxford in 1992, when the 'New Europe' was forming. None of the essays is specifically on the Czech situation but the book has universal relevance and the reader will find comments on anti-Semitism in the Czech Lands and on the position of Jews there in the inter-war liberal democracy. Among the distinguished contributors to this timely book are Professor Lord Beloff and Rabbi Jonathan Sacks.

273 **The Jews of Czechoslovakia: historical studies and surveys.**
Compiled by the Jewish Publication Society of America. New York: Society for the History of Czechoslovak Jews, 1968, 1971. 2 vols. bibliog.
This major work, with a total of almost 1,300 pages, emphasizes the democracy of the First Republic and asserts that the Jews had never been able to flourish in the same way before, or since. The various studies in volume one concern the early history of, and differences between, the Jews in the different provinces of pre-war Czechoslovakia, their legal position, social organization, religious life, welfare, education, art and emigration. Volume two deals with major Jewish leaders, Czechoslovak Zionism, economics, literature, press and publishing and Jewish music. The coverage in some sections is extremely detailed and the essays taken together constitute an encyclopaedic range of information on Czechoslovak Jewry between the wars. Each chapter has its own bibliography.

274 **The making of Czech Jewry. National conflict and Jewish society in Bohemia, 1870-1918.**
Hillel J. Kieval. Oxford: Oxford University Press, 1988. 288p. bibliog. (Studies in Jewish History).
A study of the social and cultural history of the Jews in the Czech Lands. The multicultural character of the region is underlined, as well as the linguistic dexterity

and cultural ambiguity of the Jews. The Czech-Jewish movement, an attempt at cultural and linguistic assimilation, and Prague Zionism, an alternative to German and Czech assimilation, are given special attention, as well as the background to Jewish attitudes and behaviour at the onset of the Second World War. Although, as the title implies, the book concentrates on the second half of the 19th century and the first years of the 20th century, it provides a reasonable body of information on the Jews in the Czech Lands over the last 500 years.

275 **The Jewish community of Prague during the inter-war period.**
Nancy M. Wingfield. In: *The Czech and Slovak experience: selected papers from the Fourth World Congress for Soviet and East European Studies, Harrogate 1990.* Edited by John Morison. Basingstoke, England: The Macmillan Press; New York: St. Martin's Press, 1992, p. 218-29. bibliog.

About half of Bohemian Jewry lived in Prague before the Second World War, and at the beginning of the 18th century it was the largest urban Jewish community in Europe. This essay gives a brief survey of the long and important history of Jews in the Czech Lands before concentrating on the acculturization of the German-speaking Jews to Czech society which began in the late 19th century and culminated in 1938.

276 **Jewish sights of Bohemia and Moravia.**
Jiří Fiedler, introduction by Arno Pařík. Prague: Sefer, 1991. 224p. map.

This guidebook provides information on the state of the synagogues and cemeteries of selected Jewish communities in Bohemia, Moravia, Silesia and Bratislava. It contains 138 encyclopaedic entries, alphabetically arranged by place-name. This list is preceded by an abstract of the history of Jewish religious communities in these places from the early Middle Ages. The guide also lists significant personalities, whose lives have been linked with the communities, and includes: notes on 500 vanished Jewish communities and their architecture; details of synagogues and cemeteries destroyed during the Holocaust and in the post-war period; and information on concentration and labour camps and mass graves of Jewish victims. The general Czech population, despite the broad Czech education, knows very little about Jewish customs, and is barely aware of monuments they may be passing daily, so that an inquisitive tourist would not get much help by asking a passer by. The guidebook contains 200 illustrations and a good description of architectural detail. The author offers a useful 'Explanation of terms' (p. 211) and an 'Index of places' (p. 224).

277 **Židovské památky Brna: stručná historie židovského osídlení Brna.** (Jewish monuments in Brno: a brief history of Jewish settlement in Brno.)
Jaroslav Klenovský. Brno, Czech Republic: Moravské zemské museum, 1993. 56p. map. bibliog.

This slender pamphlet, published on the occasion of the 750th anniversary of Brno being given town privileges, may not be easy to obtain but it has a good English summary on p. 53-56 followed by 'Legend to figures', meaning English-language captions to the many illustrations. Jewish history in Brno is traced back to the beginning of the 13th century, but the largest increase in the Jewish population of the town happened in the religiously emancipated second half of the 19th century (in 1848 there were 445 Jews living in Brno, by 1900 the figure increased to 8,200) and Brno became one of the most important centres of Jewish culture in Central Europe. The multilingual bibliography on p. 52 offers good leads for further study.

278 **A socialist remembers.**
Max Adler, foreword by Norman Stone. London: Duckworth, 1988. 174p. maps.

This book could have been included in several sections of this present bibliography – under history, literature or politics – yet it provides above all a picture of the life of a member of an ethnic minority, a German Jew who was born in 1905, in the first half of this century in Central Europe. Max Adler and his wife Janka lived in England from 1938, where Max became a successful linguist and economist. This compelling memoir, which is of interest to the modern historian, was published posthumously. Max Adler's background was in more ways than one very similar to that of Franz Kafka: his father's occupation (an affluent shopkeeper in Pilsen); a Jewish-German background with some infusion of Czech-Jewish blood; and exposure to – and here Adler is powerful – endemic anti-Semitism and the resulting lack of identity: does a Jew in truth belong anywhere? Max Adler describes his dislocated schooling and his studies in Vienna, which were concluded by a doctoral thesis on Czechoslovak nationality problems, and his activities as secretary of the German Social Democratic Party in Slovakia. He is critical of the Czech 'colonial' rule of Slovakia between the two world wars and even more of the Czech domination of backward Ruthenia. This section is of particular interest since Adler, being neither Czech nor Slovak, viewed the situation from the neutral standpoint of a (socialist) outsider. The memoir includes first-hand testimony on the union of Austria with Germany and on the final collapse of Czechoslovakia in 1939. The book has an index.

279 **Jewish customs and traditions.**
Text by Jana Doleželová, Alexandr Putík, Jiřina Šedinová, translated by Till Gottheinerová, photographs by Dana Cabanová and Archives of the Jewish Museum in Prague. Prague: Jewish Museum in Prague, 1994. 101p.

This well-produced, large-format publication comprises four studies: 'Judaism and its sources'; 'The synagogue'; 'Divine service: weekday, Sabbath and festivals'; and 'The course of life and Judaism (Birth, marriage, the family and death as reflected in the collections of the Jewish Museum in Prague)'. The coloured illustrations of ceremonial objects and Jewish personalities from the past are plentiful.

280 **Crossing the Yabbok: illness and death in Ashkenazi Judaism in the sixteenth- through nineteenth-century Prague.**
Sylvie-Anne Goldberg, translated by Carol Cosman. Berkeley, California; Los Angeles; London: University of California Press, 1996. 303p. bibliog.

This is a study in historical anthropology, of the 'permanence and evolution of the Jewish conception of death' (p. 2). It is an academic work, translated from the French, on illness and death, on the history of ideas and social practices, and on philosophy and religion. The book is included here because, although strictly academic, it is

88

written in a style which is accessible. It contains pictures, appendixes, pages of explanatory 'Notes' and a multilingual bibliography (p. 273-92) of manuscripts and books on the history of Judaism. The bibliography has no time limitation: a number of entries carry publication dates from the 16th and 17th centuries, but there are also plenty of fairly recent publications. There is also an 'Index' (p. 293-303).

The Germans

281 **The politics of ethnic survival: the Germans in Prague, 1861-1914.**
Gary B. Cohen. Princeton, New Jersey: Princeton University Press, 1981. 344p. maps. bibliog.

An impressive account of a fascinating period in Czech history, when Prague had ceased to be an almost solidly German city with a Czech lower-class minority and had become a Czech city, with a majority Czech council, Czech finance houses and a dwindling, but by no means insignificant, German minority. It is the period which saw the split of the university into two linguistically separate institutions, and the culmination of the Czech National Revival. The author realizes that much has been written about the rise of the Czechs, but little work has emerged about the decline of the Germans, a study of which should contribute to an understanding of the fate of the Austrian monarchy. Involved in the story are the various socio-political manifestations of 'Czechdom', such as: the rise of the Sokol movement (a large gymnastics association founded in 1862); the status of the Jews; political parties and other groupings; and religious affiliation. The work uses much archival material and statistical analyses. For a related paper see the same author's 'Ethnicity and urban population growth: the decline of the Prague Germans, 1880-1920' in *Studies in East European Social History*, edited by Keith Hitchins (Leiden, the Netherlands: E. J. Brill, 1981, vol. 2, p. 3-26).

282 **Castles on the landscape: Czech-German relations.**
Ronald M. Smelser. In: *Czechoslovakia 1918-88: seventy years from independence.* Edited by Gordon H. Skilling. Basingstoke, England; London: Macmillan Academic and Professional Ltd, in cooperation with St Antony's College, Oxford, 1991, p. 82-104. bibliog.

Professor Smelser is an authority on 20th-century German history. This contribution to a conference questions the impossibility of the two nations living in modern times in reasonable concord. Most attention is given to the period of the founding of Czechoslovakia in 1918. The paper is supplemented by bibliographical notes. The American view is researched in 'Die "Sudetendeutsche Frage" und die Historiker in den USA' (The question of Sudeten Germans and the US historians) by Eva Hahnová, *Bohemia*, vol. 39, no. 2 (1988), p. 435-37.

283 **Sudetoněmecký problém: obtížné loučení s minulostí.** (The Sudeten German problem: the difficulties of leaving the past.)
Eva Hahnová. Prague: Prago Media, 1996. 276p. bibliog.
An important, well-researched contribution which follows the Sudeten German question from 1918 to the present day, seeking to achieve objectivity regarding this confusing and highly charged issue. German and Czech attitudes to the Jews are given considerable attention. The character of Czech nationalism is also scrutinized. Also concerned with the relationship between the Czechs and Germans is an English-language paperback entitled *Czechs and Germans: yesterday and today* by Milan Hauner (Washington, DC: Woodrow Wilson International Centre for Scholars, 1991. 32p. East European Studies, no. 30).

284 **T.G. Masaryk a vztahy Čechů a Němců: sborník příspěvků přednesených od listopadu 1993 do června 1995 v rámci Masarykovy společnosti na FFUK v Praze.** (T. G. Masaryk and relations between the Czechs and Germans: collection of papers given between November 1993 and June 1995 within the framework of the Masaryk Society at the Faculty of Philosophy, Charles University in Prague.)
Prague: Masarykova společnost, 1997. 297p.
Masaryk considered the Czech-German problem a key issue and the conciliation of the Czechs with the Germans in the new Czech state was, in his own words, his life-long task. The speakers in this cycle of lectures make up a list of distinguished academic names: Miroslav Bednář, Eva Broklová, Koloman Gajan, Josef Harna, Zdeněk Kárník, Martin Kučera, Robert Kvaček, Šimona Lowensteinová, Věra Olivová, Karel Pichlík, Josef Polišenský, Jaroslav Šebek, Zdeněk Šolle and Miroslav Tejchman.

285 **Dr Edvard Beneš and Czechoslovakia's German minority: 1918-1943.**
Mark Cornwall. In: *The Czech and Slovak experience: selected papers from the Fourth World Congress for Soviet and East European Studies, Harrogate 1990.* Edited by John Morison. Basingstoke, England: The Macmillan Press; New York: St. Martin's Press, 1992, p. 167-202. bibliog.
A detailed account of the political activities of Edvard Beneš, a fervent nationalist, from before the First World War until the expulsion of about a million 'untrustworthy' Germans from Czechoslovakia after the Second World War, an act which Beneš thought was fundamental to the future of Czechoslovakia. The author questions some of Beneš's objectives and beliefs. The Czechoslovak minority treaty, which was signed on 10 September 1919, is included as an appendix.

286 **'National reparation'? The Czech land reform and the Sudeten Germans 1918-38.**
Mark Cornwall. *Slavonic and East European Review*, no. 75, 2 (April 1997), p. 259-80. bibliog.
Mark Cornwall analyses the stages of the Czech land reform from 1918-38 and draws specific conclusions. The plan for land reform in the Czech Lands and the way in which these reforms were implemented had a greater element of nationalism than

90

many historians have appreciated. The reform should have had no nationalistic meaning, but due to the development of Czech history since 1620 the large number of landowners were German-speaking nobility. This made the nobility resent the new republic even more, and many of them sympathized with the Sudeten Germans. Some of the Czechs who were instrumental in the programme considered it a continuation of the nationalism of 1918, when Czechoslovakia was created, or as an act of reparation for German culpability through history.

287 **The German Social Democratic Party of Czechoslovakia: 1918-1926.**
Fred Hahn. In: *The Czech and Slovak experience: selected papers from the Fourth World Congress for Soviet and East European Studies, Harrogate 1990.* Edited by John Morison. Basingstoke, England: The Macmillan Press; New York: St. Martin's Press, 1992, p. 203-17. bibliog.

A contribution to the study of German attitudes to the new Czechoslovak Republic, which was formed after the First World War. The author points out the missed opportunities for concord on both sides, Czech as well as German.

288 **Minority politics in a multinational state: the German Social Democrats in Czechoslovakia: 1928-1938.**
Nancy Merriweather Wingfield. New York: Columbia University Press, 1989. 238p. map. bibliog.

A well-researched account of the economic situation in the Sudetenland, the political parties and internal politics in Czechoslovakia, and of the larger European situation at this time. At the time of the formation of Czechoslovakia in 1918 there were more Germans living in the region than Slovaks. The book contains numerous notes, tables and glossaries.

289 **Odsun Němců z Československa: 1945-1947.** (The transfer of the Germans from Czechoslovakia, 1945-47.)
Tomáš Staněk. Prague: Academia & Naše vojsko, 1991. 536p. map. bibliog.

Staněk's thesis is that the post-war fate of the German minority in Czechoslovakia was determined by purely 20th-century forces. In the inhuman atmosphere of the Nazi dictatorship, these forces established a historical situation when enforced pseudo-collectivism backfired and left every German tarred with blame for the war and the crimes which accompanied it. This publication is perhaps the most comprehensive book on the subject and aims at objectivity. It is well documented and includes tables and statistics on the treatment of the German-speaking population of Czechoslovakia immediately after the Second World War. The book covers not only the transfer, but also: international reactions to the transfer; the position of German 'anti-fascists' living in Czechoslovakia; areas where nationalities were not sharply defined; persons from mixed marriages; Austrians; Jews; and persons of value to the economy, such as highly qualified specialists and key individuals. There is also a chapter on confiscated property. The book has a summary in German (p. 521-29) and also includes some photographs, for example of the assembly points and of the transportation itself, a transportation card, and a notice of the penalty for anyone caught helping Germans. There are many pages of notes and references (p. 383-500), a bibliography ('Prameny a literatura', p. 502-20) of archive sources, documents, articles, statistical sources and books, mostly in Czech and German, and a name index (p. 530-36).

91

290 **Odsun Němců: výbor z pamětí a projevů doplněný edičními přílohami.** (The transfer of the Germans: selection from memoirs and speeches with supplements.)
Edvard Beneš, edited by Věra Olivová. Prague: SEB – Společnost Edvarda Beneše, in collaboration with Český svaz bojovníků za svobodu, 1995. 103p. (Knižnice Společnosti Edvarda Beneše, vol. 8).

The purpose of this publication is to disperse somewhat the shadow which has been hanging over the relationship between Germany and the Czech Lands since the expulsion of the Germans, a direct result of the Second World War. The additional purpose is a re-assessment of President Beneš and his actions. Most of the frontier of the present Czech Republic is with German-speaking countries and in the new, post-1989 international situation long-standing, entrenched sentiments have come to the surface. The extracts from Beneš's memoirs, speeches and letters show how painful he found some of the decisions he had to make. The editorial supplements are period documents, such as the text of the Munich Agreement, the decree of Adolf Hitler on the occupation of the Czech Lands and the establishment of the Protectorate of Bohemia and Moravia, and the post-war plan for the transfer of the Germans. The collection rehabilitates Beneš. The transfer of the Germans happened half a century ago and it was part of a historical process, spanning generations. One question which the documents and the editors do not answer is: why, fifty years on, these Germans do not feel at home in Germany.

291 **Češi, Němci, odsun: diskuze nezávislých historiků.** (The Czechs, the Germans, the transfer: discussions of independent historians.)
Edited by Bohumil Černý, Jan Křen, Václav Kural, Milan Otáhal.
Prague: Academia, 1990. 368p.

The only monograph published before 1990 was Radomír Luža's *The transfer of the Sudeten Germans: a study of Czech-German relations, 1933-1962* (London: Routledge & Kegan Paul, 1964. 365p. maps. bibliog.). The present publication has assembled articles, letters and other texts dating from 1967 to 1990 and written by various historians, journalists and public figures. The editors' intention was to produce a historical document, a testimony to national thinking on the subject. No discussion was previously allowed, this (taboo) episode in Czech history having had a veil drawn over it. The outlook of the contributors varies, but the overall picture the editors sought to present is one of civic maturity, responsibility and openness. The contributions may be broadly divided into two overlapping approaches: the specialist, or technical approach, which justifies the transfer on the basis of facts and causes; and the moral approach, capturing the politico-moral responsibility and consequences for the Czech nation, giving a moral judgment on history. It is frustrating for the reader that the book has no index.

292 **Die Zerstörung der Bilder: unsentimentale Reisen durch Mähren und Böhmen.** (The destruction of images: an unsentimental journey through Moravia and Bohemia.)
Ilse Tielsch. Graz, Austria: Verlag Styria, 1991. 166p.

Ilse Tielsch is an Austrian novelist and poet who was born in Czechoslovakia and left with her parents, as Germans, after the Second World War. She visited Czechoslovakia in 1990 and this is a record of her reminiscences and impressions from the visit to her former homeland.

Other nationalities and minorities

293 **Ruská, ukrajinská a běloruská emigrace v Praze: Adresář.**
Russian, Ukrainian and Belorussian emigration in Prague:
directory.
Compiled by Anastasia Kopřivová. Prague: Národní knihovna České
republiky, 1995. 30p.

The text of the directory is in Czech, Russian and English and it contains the Prague
addresses of various institutions and organizations. The introduction stresses the
importance of this evidence of the extensive and ever-changing political, social and
cultural life of Russian immigrants in Czechoslovakia between the two world wars, in
particular during the first years of emigration from Russia after the 1905 and 1917
revolutions.

294 **Ruská, ukrajinská a běloruská emigrace v Praze: Katalog výstavy.**
(Russian, Ukrainian and Belorussian emigration in Prague: catalogue
of an exhibition.)
Compiled by Jiří Vacek, introduction by Zdeněk Sládek. Prague:
Národní knihovna České republiky, 1995. 53p. + supplements.

A sister volume to the previous entry. The introduction to this volume is in Czech and
Russian. The main part of the publication is an annotated list of institutions, periodicals, newspapers, organizations, groups, political parties and movements, museums,
associations, educational establishments and publishing houses, with annotations in
Czech, Russian and English. This list is followed by a selection of reprinted
documents, which are mostly official correspondence.

Extraterritorial Populations

295 Czechs abroad.
http://cech.cesnet.cz/welcome.shtml.
One of the subsections of the above web site provides access to serious, as well as frivolous, information. Examples of the serious sites and pages are: Czech Happenings (New York), Czech Service Center (Washington, DC) CZECH Info Center (Canada and United States). The site of Jan Čulík from Glasgow University provides a variety of quality information.

296 **Adresář českých a československých krajanských organizací, společností přátel České republiky, dalších organizací se vztahem k Čechům v zahraničí, krajanského tisku k 1.1.1997.** (Directory of Czech and Czechoslovak expatriate organizations, societies of friends of the Czech Republic, other organizations with an interest in Czechs abroad, expatriate press as of 1 January 1997.)
Compiled by M. Miková. Prague: Ministerstvo zahraničních věcí, odbor krajanských a nevládních styků, 1996/97. 112p.
A simply arranged reference book which should be available at embassies or consulates. It consists of two sections: organizations and press. Within these two sections the arrangement is alphabetical by country. The entries give the name of the institution, a translation of the name where necessary, occasionally a brief description of its activities, followed by the address, contact name, telephone number and e-mail address, where applicable. The publication is intended to be updated on an annual basis.

94

297 **Czechs and Slovaks in North America: a bibliography.**
Esther Jerabek. New York: Czechoslovak Society of Arts and
Sciences in America; Chicago: Czechoslovak National Council of
America, 1976. 448p.

Although this may appear outdated due to its date of publication, it remains an invaluable tool for research into the history of Czech immigration in North America. The list of 7,609 entries – books and relevant periodicals – on the history of immigration, distribution of immigrants, and artistic and scientific achievements of the Czechs and Slovaks in North America, is arranged by subject, starting with 'agriculture' and ending with 'travel'. The text is enhanced and supported by a comprehensive index.

298 **The Czech Americans.**
Stephanie Saxon-Ford. New York; Philadelphia: Chelsea House
Publishers, 1988. 110p. maps. bibliog. (The Peoples of North
America).

A brief 'official' history of the Czech émigrés in North America which highlights the successes of the Czechs in their adopted country, culminating with the story of Martina Navrátilová. Were the book published today, it would have been Madeleine Albright. The various waves of emigration are explained by historical events at home. The illustrations are plentiful.

299 **History of Czechs in America.**
Jan Habenicht, with a foreword to the English edition by Paul M.
Makovsky, translated by Miroslav Koudelka. St. Paul, Minnesota:
Czechoslovak Genealogical Society International, 1996. 581p. maps.

Originally published in 1910 in Czech under the title *Dějiny Čechův Amerických*, the narrative starts with the life story of the first-known Czech emigrant to America, one Augustin Heřman who was born in Prague in 1608, and describes the fortunes of several émigré families. Subsequently the Czechs in different states of the United States in the second half of the last century are described. The Czech Catholic clergy and their activities are given special attention. The many photographs are of interest, as are the maps of states with the greatest number of Czech inhabitants during the early 1900s. There is also an index of surnames and a geographical index. A treatise on Heřman by M. Norma Svejda, *Augustine Heřman of Bohemia Manor*, can be found in *The Czechoslovak contribution to world culture*, edited by Miroslav Rechcígl, Jr. (The Hague; London, Paris: Mouton, 1964, p. 500-04). This valuable collection of articles also includes: 'Trends in Czech and Slovak economic enterprise in the New World', by Vojtěch Erven Andic (p. 523-27. bibliog.); 'The Czechs in Texas' by John M. Skřivánek (p. 510-15); and 'The Czechs and Slovaks in Latin America', by Milič Kybal (p. 516-22).

300 **The Čechs (Bohemians) in America: a study of the national,
cultural, political, social, economic and religious life.**
Thomas Čapek. Westport, Connecticut: Greenwood, 1970. 293p.

Thomas Čapek had exceptional knowledge of the subject, having been called 'the historian of American Czechs'. Despite its age (this is a reprint of the original 1920 edition), the work offers many insights into Czech emigration to the United States. The book contains a distributional map of Czechs in America.

95

301 **The Czechs and Slovaks in America.**
Joseph S. Roucek. Minneapolis, Minnesota: Lerner Publications, 1967. 71p. (In America Series).
A slim volume, which is one of a series on minority emigrant communities which aims to educate young Americans. It provides a concise history, supported by photographs, describing the waves of immigration into the United States, the causes of the exodus from the home country, the areas of Czech concentration in America, their cultural and spiritual life and the Czech contribution to politics, arts and sciences in the new country. This includes the foundation in 1960 of the Czechoslovak Academy of Arts and Sciences in America.

302 **Panorama: a historical review of Czechs and Slovaks in the United States of America.**
Cicero, Illinois: Czechoslovak National Council of America, [1970]. 328p.
A much larger tome than the previous entry, which includes biographies of many well-known Czech immigrants and their descendants. Another book, even more dated, which nevertheless provides valuable historical detail and statistics on the major centre for Czechs in the United States, is *The Czechs of Cleveland* by Eleanor E. Ledbetter (Cleveland, Ohio: Americanization Committee, 1919. 40p.).

303 **Our brothers across the ocean: the Czech Sokol in America to 1914.**
Claire E. Nolte. *Czechoslovak and Central European Journal*, vol. 11, no. 2 (1993), p. 15-37.
The first comprehensive study of the initial stage of the Czech gymnastic movement Sokol in the United States. The movement took root among the Czech immigrants as early as the 1860s. The more congenial and agreeable political climate in the United States made it possible for the American Sokols to establish a central organization as early as 1878, while in the Czech Lands the Sokols had to wait until 1889. The survey looks at the organizational and ideological development of the American Sokol, its internal differentiations, liaison with the Sokol in the Czech Lands up to the First World War, and the socio-political coherence of the movement. The article is supplemented by many photographs.

304 **Studies in ethnicity: the East European experience in America.**
Edited by Charles A. Ward, Philip Shashko, Donald E. Pienkos. Boulder, Colorado: East European Quarterly. Distributed by Columbia University Press, New York, 1980. 254p. maps. bibliog. (East European Monographs, no. 73).
The four contributions relevant to the Czech community cover mostly the United States, only touching on Canada in the article by Josef Škvorecký, 'The East European émigré as writer: some personal observations' (p. 225-31), an argument against the theory of artistic decline in exile. The state of Czech teaching and research topics and some areas of English-Czech contrastive study are discussed in 'Czech linguistics in the United States' by Henry Kučera (p. 27-37). Karel D. Bicha's 'Community of cooperation? The case of the Czech Americans' looks at the well-known tendency for Czechs not to stay together in cohesive communities abroad. The last relevant paper,

'Geographic patterns of ethnic and linguistic groups in Wisconsin' (p. 39-67), by Barbara Borowiecki, includes, with the help of statistical tables and maps, among other ethnic groups, the distribution of Czechs in Wisconsin.

305 **The forgotten Czechs of the Banat, Zapomenutí Češi v Banátu.**
Iva Zímová. Prague: Köcher & Köcher s. r. o., 1996. 52p.
The Banat region in southern Romania has several Czech settlements. This short text, in Czech and English, is supplemented by black-and-white photographs by the author. References to Czechs in Romania can be also found in *National minorities in Romania: change in Transylvania*, by Elmér Illyés (Boulder, Colorado: East European Quarterly. Distributed by Columbia University Press, New York, 1982. 355p. maps. bibliog. East European Monographs, no. 112). *East European national minorities: 1918-1980. A handbook* (q.v.) contains accounts of the extraterritorial population of Czechs in: 'Poland' by Kenneth V. Farmer (p. 35-65); 'Hungary' by Martin L. Kovacs (p. 160-74); 'Yugoslavia' by Toussaint Hočevar (p. 216-41); and 'Bulgaria' by Peter John Georgeoff (p. 274-85). The book has a general chapter on the nationality research centres in various countries by Theodor Veiter (chapter ten, p. 314-26), which also gives an account, albeit incomplete, of facilities available to the ethnic groups, such as broadcasting, the press, schools and publishing.

306 **A bibliography of sources concerning the Czechs and Slovaks in Romania.**
Z. Salzmann. *East European Quarterly*, vol. 13, no. 4 (winter 1979), p. 465-88.
The relatively tiny and scattered Czech and Slovak communities in Romania have given rise to quite a corpus of work on their origins, their place in politics and economics, and their language and folklore, drawn together in this list of over 175 entries, dating from 1857 to the present. It is unfortunate that the listing is solely alphabetical by author, with no subdivision by subject.

307 **Volhynian Czechs.**
Leos Satava. *Contact*, winter 1985, p. 22-24.
This unique socio-ethnic group arose in the 1860s as one of the movements away from the Czech Lands driven by economic reasons. They settled in Ukraine around the towns of Rovno, Dubno and Luck in the Volhynia region. However, this extraterritorial population returned practically *en bloc* at the end of the Second World War, to resettle, as an ethnic minority *sui generis*, largely in the border areas vacated by the Germans (a point not made in this paper); their main centre was, however, at Žatec, in northwestern Bohemia. By the 1950s they are deemed to have been more or less fully re-integrated, though they retained certain distinctive features of language, diet, dress and religion (two of their Orthodox churches are illustrated). The author predicts that few signs of this once unique community will survive the end of the century. The article also describes the group's sufferings at the hands of the Nazis and their contribution to the expatriate war effort.

308 **Minority culture in a capital city: the Czechs in Vienna at the turn of the century.**
Monika Glettler. In: *Decadence and innovation: Austro-Hungarian life and art at the turn of the century.* Edited by Robert B. Pynsent. London: Weidenfeld & Nicolson, 1989, p. 49-60. bibliog.

Professor Glettler of Munich University is a specialist on ethnic minorities and emigration. This paper was a contribution to an international conference in London. The second half of the 19th century witnessed a sharp increase in horizontal mobility of the inhabitants of the Czech Lands. Many Czechs were attracted to what was then their capital city, Vienna. According to the census, at the turn of the century the Czech population in Vienna was officially just over 100,000 out of Vienna's population of more than 1.5 million. Unofficially though, a fifth of the population were supposed to be Viennese Czechs and this figure included Slovaks. Glettler looks into their employment, social conditions, social structure and class division, and their assimilation in the capital. She pays particular attention to education, political organizations and national consciousness. Monika Glettler is the author of a huge, major treatise on the subject, published in German, which indicates the magnitude of the historical process of the integration of Viennese Czechs, *Die Wiener Tschechen um 1900* (Vienna Czechs around 1900) (Vienna: Oldenbourg Verlag, 1972. 628p. bibliog. Veröffentlichungen des Collegium Carolinum, no. 28). About a third of the book consists of supporting material, such as documents, tables and a bibliography.

309 **Triumph of hope: from Theresienstadt and Auschwitz to Israel.**
Ruth Elias, translated from the German by Margot Bettauer Dembo. New York; Chichester, England: John Wiley & Sons, published in association with the United States Holocaust Museum, 1998. 274p. map.

An autobiography of Ruth Elias, who grew up in Ostrava, Moravia. She was initially in hiding with her family during the Second World War, and was eventually imprisoned in the Theresienstadt and Auschwitz concentration camps. At the end of hostilities, after a brief sojourn in Prague, she left with her husband in 1949 for Israel. The last chapter of her book describes the life of Czech Jewish immigrants, old and new, in the villages of Israel.

Folklore and Folk Art

310 **Tales from Bohemia.**
Karel J. Erben, illustrations by Artuš Scheiner, translated by Vera
Gissing. London: Macdonald & Company (Publishers) Ltd, 1987.
141p. (A Purnell Book).
Presents thirteen popular fairly-tales, a genre which is taken seriously by the Czechs.
This selection is handsomely produced (it was printed and bound in Czechoslovakia),
illustrations are stylized, reminiscent of Art Nouveau. Because these tales are intended
for children, the text has been adapted and is in modern English, and the Czech
personal names have been anglicized. K. J. Erben, a poet and historian, collected folk
songs and stories of the Slavonic nations in the middle of the 19th century. This is a
good selection of tales of kings and princesses, criminals and wizards, rewritten with
the milder taste of the English reader in mind: the more brutal stories are omitted.

311 **Fairy tales from Czechoslovakia.**
Božena Němcová, translated by Ludmila Ondrůjová. Rockville,
Maryland: Kabel Publishers, 1987. 268p.
This book contains thirty-six fairy-tales, translated and published in a limited and
numbered edition, but in the uninspiring form of a textbook or lecture notes. It is
obviously intended for an adult readership, for connoisseurs of fairy-tales.

312 **Folk and fairy tales from Bohemia.**
Jiří Horák, Jane Carruth, translated from the Czech by Alice Denešová,
illustrated by Jiří Trnka. London; New York: Hamlyn, 1973. 186p.
This book is one of the products of the years of collaboration between the publishing
house, Hamlyn, and Czechoslovakia's printing and publishing industries. It is
included here not merely as another representative collection of fairy-tales, but
because of the illustrator, Jiří Trnka, who was, and still is, one of the best-known and
best-loved of Czech artists specializing in pictures for children, especially book
illustrations and animated films. Another very popular collection is the illustrated

Pověsti českých hradů a zámků (Tales from Czech castles and country houses), by Josef Pavel and Adam Jist, which is unfortunately available in Czech only (Prague: Melantrich, 1995. 3rd rev. ed. 381p.).

313 Moravian tales, legends, myths.
Karel Absolon. Rockville, Maryland: Kabel, 1984, 1985. 2 vols.

Absolon has collected stories handed down through his family, émigrés in North America. The first volume of tales relates to the Macocha chasm and the underground river Punkva, in the legend-rich Moravian Karst. One of the Absolon family, also Karel Absolon (1887-1960) was a Czech zoologist, speleologist and palaeoanthropologist who studied the underground fauna of the Moravian Karst and was one of the great popularizers of the natural sciences. Volume two contains tales connected with other localities, including the haunted Pernštejn Castle.

314 Golem.
Eduard Petiška, translated by Jana Švábová. Prague: Martin, 1991. 92p. maps.

This paperback consists of two sections: a collection of stories about the ghetto of old Prague and the famous Rabbi Löw (1520-1609); and a guide to Jewish Prague. Löw founded the Talmud school of Prague, was known for his pansophism (the idea of the possibility of universal knowledge) and wisdom and his name is wreathed in myth. Golem, a creature created by Löw, is thought to be the predecessor of Frankenstein's monster. Petiška is a popular children's writer and here he has rewritten about twenty of the Jewish legends in a simple form, suitable both for adults and children, and added a history of the Jewish town of Prague, chapters on Prague synagogues and the old Jewish cemetery, the latter two with maps.

315 Jewish anecdotes from Prague.
Vladimír Karbusický, translated by David R. Beveridge, photographs by Jiří Všetečka. Prague: V ráji Publishers, 1998. 2nd rev. ed. 112p.

The first edition was published in Freiburg, Germany, by Herder Verlag in 1993. The anecdotes are on various topics and are divided accordingly. There are predictable sections on wealth and poverty, business dealings, marriage and on Christians and Jews. Less common themes are covered in anecdotes on the Jewish attitude to music, on 'the general relativity of life', love, and on life under socialism.

316 Česká přísloví: soudobý stav konce 20. století. (Czech proverbs: the current state at the end of the 20th century.)
Dana Bittnerová, Franz Schindler. Prague: Karolinum, 1997. 315p. bibliog.

The research on this collection was based on F. L. Čelakovský's *Mudrosloví národů slovanských* (Proverbial wisdom of the Slavonic nations), published in 1852. Out of 11,000 sayings, 5,738 were selected, which characterize the current knowledge of proverbs among the Czechs. The proverbs are arranged in groups and graded according to their significance today, starting with the more common and ending with the obscure. These groupings take up approximately half of the book; the second half is an alphabetical index of the topics covered by the proverbs, with various linguistic and statistical appendixes. The Czech language is rich in proverbs and many are genuinely alive and in daily use. Inevitably, it is difficult to do justice to them in translation.

317 Folk art of Czechoslovakia.
Věra Hasalová, Jaroslav Vajdiš, translated by Ivo Dvořák.   London; New York; Sydney; Toronto: Hamlyn, 1974. 296p. map. bibliog.
The text, which starts with a historical survey of the country and evolves into a geographical guide with commentary on prevailing art forms and their typical features, is interlaced with 235 illustrations, many in colour, showing samples of uniquely Czech art and architecture. The art coverage includes all manner of farm and household items and their decoration, folk costumes, toys and devotional objects. The variety is too vast for an adequate impression to be given here. Each illustration carries a brief caption, but more details of, for example, source and location are given at the back of the book. The bibliography is divided into Czech and English titles, the latter mostly emanating, like this title, from Prague via one or other of the British publishers with strong commercial links with Czechoslovakia.

318 Dances of Czechoslovakia.
Mila Lubínová, translated by G. B. Smith.   London: Max Parish, 1949. 40p. map. bibliog.
A brief outline of the characteristics of types of Czech and Slovak folk dances and the music that accompanies them, with a description of the occasions when dancing was traditional, and of some of the costumes (partially illustrated). This is followed by a technical guide to performing a selection of the best-known dances (this section was edited by Kathleen P. Tuck).

319 An egg at Easter: a folklore study.
Venetia Newall.   London: Routledge & Kegan Paul, 1971. Reprinted, 1973. 423p. bibliog.
The tourist in the Czech Republic, whatever the time of year, will be able to include among his souvenirs some of the very finely decorated Easter eggs produced in a variety of styles all over the country. Their production is now more a minor money-spinning industry than a folk craft, though its latter function is by no means dead. Although the coverage of this book is world-wide, it contains some superb illustrations of many of the Czech types. The text provides a complete account of the calendar-related background, associated legends and beliefs, methods of production and general Easter frolicking connected more or less directly with eggs, as well as other spring-time folk customs, such as 'carrying death out of the village'. The book is comparative, but the Czech items can be located via the index (there are entries on Bohemia, the Czechs and Moravia) which will also lead to coverage of the country's German minority.

Religion and Theology

General

320 Conscience and captivity: religion in Eastern Europe.
Janice Broun, Grazyna Sikorska. Washington, DC: Ethics and Public Policy Center, 1988. Distributed by arrangement with University Press of America, Lanham, Maryland. 376p. maps. bibliog.

Janice Broun is a well-informed journalist who writes on religion in the former Communist countries. Chapter five of this book is entitled 'Czechoslovakia' (p. 67-101). The Czechs were disillusioned with religion and Czech history answers for the feeble resistance of the Church to Communism. Under Communism all eighteen recognized churches were under the state Office for Religious Affairs, which dictated every aspect of the life of the Church: finance; administration; training of clergy; and religious education at schools. In modern history, the role of the largest denomination, the Roman Catholic Church, has officially been considered reactionary and obstructive to progress. Thus the numbers of clergy were dwindling, as were the numbers of believers, who were discriminated against in employment under Communism. The Roman Catholic Church is, rightly, given the most attention here. The volume describes the Vatican policy towards Czechoslovakia, the effect of the Polish Pope John Paul II, who was elected in 1978, the persecution of various clergymen (e.g. cardinal František Tomášek), and the activities and confrontations of this clergy. A more recent newspaper article by Janice Broun was 'The Catholic clergy in the Czech Republic: progress or regress?' (*Month*, vol. 26, no. 11, November 1993, p. 460-63). Among earlier publications on the theme, the researcher should note *Discretion and valour: religious conditions in Russia and Eastern Europe*, by Trevor Beeson (London: Collins, 1974. 348p. map. bibliog.). The chapter on Czechoslovakia is on p. 190-226.

321 **Catholicism and politics in Communist societies.**
Edited by Pedro Ramet. Durham, North Carolina; London: Duke
University Press, 1990. 454p. (Christianity under Stress, vol. 2).
A collection of studies examining the changes in the relationship between the Roman
Catholic Church and Communist and socialist societies. The essays are today of
historical value. Catholic traditions and hierarchy, the politics of co-existence under
Communism, and Catholic social teaching are examined first, followed by chapters on
individual countries. Of interest are chapters on: papal policy, eastern diplomacy and
the Vatican apparatus; and Karol Wojtyla (the current Pope) and Marxism. The
'Church in Czechoslovakia' by Milan J. Reban (p. 142-55), a factual account of the
Catholic Church, is now outdated. The difficult times for the Roman Catholic Church
after the Second World War, up to 1955, are documented in a first-hand account by
Ludvík Němec, *Church and state in Czechoslovakia, historically, juridically and
theologically documented* (New York: Vantage Press, 1955. 577p.).

322 **The Vatican and the red flag: the struggle for the soul of Eastern
Europe.**
Jonathan Luxmoore, Jolanta Babiuch. London; New York: Geoffrey
Chapman, 1999. 351p. bibliog.
The book goes further into history than the title suggests, starting with the
confrontations of the Catholic Church at the time of the French Revolution. The
book's strength is its coverage of the period after the Second World War, and this
makes up the largest part of the work. The Polish theme prevails and much of the
narrative centres on Pope John Paul II. However, the reader will also find much
information on the Roman Catholic Church in the Czech Lands and on the actions of
its leaders during the Communist era, which would be difficult to trace in English
elsewhere.

323 **Politics and religion in Central and Eastern Europe: traditions and
transitions.**
Edited by William H. Swatos, Jr. Westport, Connecticut; London:
Praeger, 1994. 230p. bibliog.
A collection of essays on: the problems and prospects for religion in Eastern Europe;
the values of young people; and the Church, politics and society in post-Communist
countries. Some of the essays deal with specific countries; the Czech Republic is only
referred to, though frequently and in depth, in the general articles.

324 **Politics and religion in Eastern Europe: Catholicism in Hungary,
Poland and Czechoslovakia.**
Patrick Michel, translated by Alan Braley. Oxford: Polity Press,
1991. 321p. bibliog.
A theoretical work which was completed, in French, in 1987. The English edition has
a postscript, written from the post-1989 perspective. The treatise analyses, 'with help
of specific examples, the relationship between politics and religion within the specific
framework of Soviet-type systems'. It also provides an analysis of such theoretical
problems as the relationship between religion and national identity and the issue of
forms which Catholicism has adopted through history. The study challenges the
Western theory that politics is an independent sphere by analysis of the relationship

between politics and religion. One of the supplements is a chronology of developments between 1945 and 1990 (p. 251-310).

325 **The origins of Christianity in Bohemia: sources and documents.**
Marvin Kantor. Evanston, Illinois: Northwestern University Press, 1990. 299p.

A scholarly work with an interesting layout by an authority on mediaeval Slavonic literature and mediaeval Slavonic hagiography. Part one deals with 'Church Slavonic fragments and hymns'; part two, the core of the book, is on 'Church Slavonic works about Wenceslas and Ludmila'; part three is 'Other Church Slavonic works', which includes the life of St Vitus; and part four is on 'Latin works about Wenceslas and Ludmila', with a brief account of St Cyril and St Methodius and the Christianization of Moravia and Bohemia. The Czech translation of the Bible is one of the oldest translations into a European national language. Only French and Italian translations appeared earlier. 'Czech translation of the Bible' is an essay by Jaroslava Pečírková, in *Interpretation of the Bible. Interpretation der Bibel. Interprétation de la Bible. Interpretacija svetega pisma* (Ljubljana, Slovenia: Slovenska Akademija znanosti a umetnosti; Sheffield, England: Sheffield Academic Press, 1998, p. 1,167-99).

326 **The Penguin dictionary of saints.**
Donald Attwater with Catherine Rachel John. London: Penguin, 1995. 3rd ed. 382p. bibliog.

There are many reference works on hagiology; this one is easy to come by and has more international coverage then some. Among the Bohemian and Moravian saints covered are: Adalbert (Vojtěch) of Prague; Clement Hofbauer (originally named Jan Dvořák); Wenceslas (this sizeable entry includes his grandmother St Ludmila); and the apostles Cyril and Methodius. In May 1995 Pope John Paul II canonized, in Olomouc, two more saints: Zdislava of Lemberk (née of Křižanov); and, to profound disquiet among the non-Catholics, Jan Sarkander. The British broadsheets covered the event at the time.

327 **The lives of St. Wenceslas, St. Ludmila and St. Adalbert.**
Eduard Petiška, translated by Norah Hronková. Prague: Martin, 1994. 94p.

These three names are the most important saints from the dawn of Czech history and are linked to the beginning of Christianity in Bohemia. The legendary duke St Wenceslas (907-935?) is the patron saint of Bohemia. His grandmother, St Ludmila, is claimed to have been strangled on the orders of Wenceslas' mother Drahomíra. St Adalbert (Vojtěch in Czech), was the second bishop of Prague, between 982 and 994. He died as a missionary in Prussia and was canonized in 999. Petiška is a good storyteller and his narrative reads well. In this slim paperback, the text is accompanied by old drawings, some of which have not been published for centuries.

328 **Staat und Kirche in der Tschechoslowakei: die kommunistische Kirchenpolitik in den Jahren 1948-1952.** (State and Church in Czechoslovakia: Communist policy towards the Church 1948-52.)
Karel Kaplan. Munich: R. Oldenbourg Verlag, 1990. 293p. bibliog.

Kaplan's book starts with the first conflicts between the Church and the state in March 1948, after the Communist takeover of Czechoslovakia. The new policy of the state towards the Church was formulated in 1948-49 and Kaplan describes the oppression suffered by the Church in 1950 and 1951. He also summarizes the situation in the years between 1953 and 1956, despite the time-frame given in the book's title. This is a scholarly work, well supplied with copious footnotes and pages of documentation: protocols from the meetings of the Party presidium; letters of politicians; directives; and records from meetings between politicians and representatives of the Church. The short bibliography (p. 290) lists articles, books, protocols and manuscript documents in Czech and German. On the same page Kaplan also lists periodical publications, mostly ecclesiastical, but some general, which appeared in Czechoslovakia between 1949 and 1968. There is also a name index (p. 291-93). The book was subsequently published in Czech by the Academy of Sciences under the title *Stát a církev v Československu v letech 1948-1953* (Prague: Ústav pro soudobé dějiny AV ČR, 1993).

329 **Katolická církve a pozemková reforma 1945-1948: dokumentace.**
(The Catholic Church and the land reform 1945-48: documentation.)
Prepared by Milena Janisová, Karel Kaplan. Prague: Ústav pro soudobé dějiny AV ČR v nakladatelství Doplněk, 1995. 400p. bibliog.

This publication will be of limited interest, particularly since it is available in Czech only. However, it does provide valuable source-based information on the modern history of the Catholic Church and on its relationship with the state. The list of documents is also given in English. Another, much shorter publication, concerning the property of the Church, alas also only in Czech, deals with the reverse (and vexed) problem – the restitution of ecclesiastical property after 1989. *Církev a majetek: k restituci majetku církví a náboženských organizací* (The church and property: restitution of the property of the churches and religious organizations), edited by Jaromír Žegklitz (Prague: Občanský institut, 1993. 27p.).

330 **The soul of Czechoslovakia: the Czechoslovak nation's contribution to Christian civilization.**
Arthur Stuart Duncan-Jones. London: Herbert Baker, 1941. 63p.

A history of Czech theology which pays close attention to early Hussitism and its debt to Wycliffe's teaching, thereby addressing the English reader. The other period which is given particular attention is the National Revival of the 19th century, the spiritual and intellectual movement out of which rose the gymnastic organization Sokol. The work and the career of political journalist Karel Havlíček Borovský is given due prominence. In the sections on the modern period the author stresses the high democratic values of the young Czechoslovak state and its exceptionally good record in the treatment of ethnic minorities – this was very much the period perception.

331 **The philanthropic motive in Christianity: an analogy of the relations between theology and social services.**
Frank Martin Hník, translated from the Czech by M. Weatherall, R. Weatherall. Oxford: Basil Blackwell, 1938. 328p. bibliog.

A long treatise in social theology and a history of Christian attitudes to charity. It is of significance here because it provides an insight into Czech social and theological thinking up to the Second World War. Part five (p. 287-328) is specifically concerned with the 'socially theological basis of charity in the Czechoslovak Church', in which Hník was a leading figure.

332 **Religion and atheism in the USSR and Eastern Europe.**
Edited by Bohdan Bociurkiw, John W. Strong. London: Macmillan,
1975. 412p.

By now of historical interest, this collection of essays considers the differences
between the official atheist doctrine of Communist states and the traditions of
Christianity in Central and Eastern Europe. Peter A. Toma and Milan J. Reban are the
authors of 'Church-state schism in Czechoslovakia' (p. 273-91), an article which is
rich in statistics. It contains an account of the two periods which were particularly
inimical to the church's survival, post-1948 and post-1968, when the state exerted
exceptional pressure on the Church.

333 **Prague Winter: restrictions on religious freedom in
Czechoslovakia twenty years after the invasion.**
Washington, DC: Puebla Institute, 1988. 60p. map.

Of historical value now, this slim book was prepared by the Puebla Institute, a Roman
Catholic human rights group. It looks at the various forms of state restrictions on
religious expression: persecution of the clergy; control of religious organizations and
literature; and travel restrictions. Contemporary religious activities in the country are
described, together with attendance figures at different churches and information on
the legislation pertaining to religious groups.

334 **Bohemia sacra: das Christentum in Böhmen 973-1973. Ecclesia
universalis, ecclesia magistra, ecclesia.** (Holy Bohemia: Christianity
in Bohemia 973-1973. Universal Church, Church the Master, Church.)
Edited by Ferdinand Seibt. Düsseldorf, Germany, 1973. 645p. map.
bibliog.

Published to commemorate the millennium of the Prague bishopric, this collection of
German essays discusses successive periods, the condition of the Church and churches
in each, with separate sections on relevant linguistic, literary, artistic or architectural
themes. The emphasis is on the Church in the 19th and 20th centuries and the
influences of nationalism and politics. Good black-and-white photographs and
coloured plates taken by Werner Neumeister illustrate buildings, manuscripts and
statues.

335 **The Catholic Church in the Czech Republic.**
Text and maps by Miroslav Krejčír, photographs by Antonín Bína,
illustrated by Zdirad Čech. Dačice, Czech Republic: Karmelitánské
nakladatelství, 1998. unpaginated. maps.

A practical source of information on the representatives of the Roman Catholic
Church in the land: the apostolic nunciature and all bishoprics (accompanied by
photographs of the bishops and cathedrals, with addresses and telephone numbers).
The slim paperback also provides basic historical and statistical data.

336 **Acts of faith.**
Ian Traynor. *The Guardian*, 2 November 1998, 'Weekend', p. 28-30, 34, 37.

The Roman Catholic priests who were ordained in secret during Communist rule when the Czech Church was underground were hoping for recognition of their courage by the Vatican when democracy arrived. Instead they seem to be on the receiving end of a different type of persecution, and their ordination is not recognized.

Non-Roman Catholic denominations and ideological groups

337 **Protestantism and politics in Eastern Europe and Russia: the Communist and post Communist eras.**
Edited by Sabrina Petra Ramet. Durham, North Carolina; London: Duke University Press, 1992. 441p. (Christianity Under Stress).

Comprises essays, edited by a leading authority on the subject, which stress the special political features of Protestantism within the Communist system and provide many examples of the adaptation of theological doctrine and adjustment to political reality. An essay specific to the Czech situation is 'Protestantism in Czechoslovakia and Poland' (p. 73-106) by Paul Bock and there are also fact sheets (p. 105-06) on the numbers of adherents, churches and pastors in the land.

338 **The Reformation in Eastern and Central Europe.**
Edited by Karin Maag. Aldershot, England: Scolar Press, 1997. 235p. maps.

A collection of essays which draws on broad-based archival research, yet aims to be accessible to the general reader. The essays have copious footnotes, black-and-white illustrations and graphs. 'Protestant literature in Bohemian private libraries *circa* 1600' (p. 36-49) is by Jiří Pešek of Charles University in Prague.

339 **The Czechoslovak heresy and schism: the emergence of a national Czechoslovak Church.**
Ludvík Němec. Philadelphia: American Philosophical Society, 1975. 78p. (Transactions Series, vol. 65, part 1).

A comprehensive history of the Czechoslovak Church, which was born out of the situation after 1918, when the Roman Catholic Church was considered to be old-fashioned and discredited by close association with the Austro-Hungarian establishment. Further details on the origin of this church can be found in an earlier publication, *Czechoslovak Church* by Frank M. Hník, Frank Kovář and Alois Spisar (Prague: Central Council of the Czechoslovak Church, 1937. 101p.). Some aspects of the Czechoslovak Church give it affinity with the Anglican Church and the Unitarian Churches of Britain and the United States.

340 **Zeal for truth and tolerance: the ecumenical challenge of the Czech Reformation.**
Jan Milič Lochman. Edinburgh: Scottish Academic Press, 1996. 78p. (The Cunningham Lectures).

Based on a lecture given at New College, University of Edinburgh. Lochman won a scholarship in 1946 to study theology at the University of St Andrews. The theme of his lecture is the history of the Czech Reformation and related theological issues.

341 **Church in a Marxist Society: a Czechoslovak view.**
Jan Milič Lochman. London: SCM Press, 1970. 198p.

A professional theologian of the Czech United Brethren Church provides the background to Czech Protestantism and a debate between Christianity and Marxism, on the symbiosis between Church and state under socialism. The author was a committed socialist. The book also summarizes the distribution of Christian denominations throughout Eastern Europe.

342 **Prague and Viennese Freemasonry, the Enlightenment, and the operations of the Harmony Lodge in Vienna.**
R. William Weisberger. In: *Speculative Freemasonry and the Enlightenment. A study of the craft in Paris, Prague and Vienna.* Boulder, Colorado: East European Monographs, 1993, p. 109-57. bibliog.

Masonic lodges first appeared in Prague in 1726. In this study, which is based on the author's dissertation at the University of Pittsburg in 1980, the organization, rituals and cultural activities of the Freemasons of Prague at the time of the Enlightenment in the 18th century are described. Weisberger scrutinizes the Prague Lodge of the Three Stars; the Masonic aristocratic élites; anti-masonry; philanthropy; and religion generally in the Habsburg empire of the time. A more substantial work on the history of Freemasonry in Bohemia, but available only in Czech, is by Jiří Beránek, *Tajemství lóží: svobodné zednářství bez legend a mýtu* (The secret of the lodges: Freemasonry without the legends and myth) (Prague: Mladá fronta, 1994. 308p.). A smaller study by František Maslan, *Dějiny svobodného zednářstvi v Čechách* (History of Freemasonry in Bohemia), which was originally published in 1923, was recently republished (Prague: Kawana, 1993. 48p.).

The issue of the ordination of women

343 **The priest Rome can't embrace.**
Peter Stanford. *The Independent*, 10 April 1998, p. 15.

It is said that several women and several married men were ordained under Communism in Czechoslovakia, to ensure the survival of the church, which was under threat of being suppressed. Ludmila Javarová, who lives in Brno, is the only one who has spoken about it and is considered to be the Catholic Church's first woman priest in modern times. She was ordained in the 1970s by bishop Felix Davídek, and her dispute with Rome as to her recognition is at the core of her interview with Peter Stanford: should tradition be sacrificed for survival? Married men and women were least suspected of being priests, and, for example, prisoners, who included nuns, were denied access to priests and the sacraments by the authorities. Javarová's primary role was to visit women prisoners. This is a sad interview with a sixty-eight-year-old person who is accepted neither as a priest, nor as a woman and who has learned not to trust anyone. A version of this interview appears in Peter Stanford's *The She-Pope: a quest for the truth behind the mystery of Pope Joan* (London: Heinemann, 1998. 205p.).

344 **Women's ordination in the Czech silent church.**
P. Fiala, J. Hanuš. *Month*, vol. 31, no. 7 (July 1998), p. 282-88.
The clandestine Czech Roman Catholic bishop Felix Davídek ordained several women in the first half of the 1970s. This was done within an unofficial ecclesiastical organization which Davídek founded after his return from prison in the late 1960s. This was an alternative body, with bishops and priests who were secretly consecrated and a carefully thought-out system of education which took full account of the relevant issues of theology, philosophy and history.

345 **The gender agenda.**
Ivana Dolejšová. *Month*, vol. 30, no. 5 (May 1997), p. 176-79.
The Czechoslovak Hussite Church split from Rome in 1920. Women have been ordained in this Church for the last fifty years, but many tangential issues have not been resolved. The author has an insider's knowledge of the problems faced by women active in the Church.

Religious orders

346 **Církevní řády a kongregace v zemích českých.** (Religious orders and congregations in the Czech Lands.)
Luděk Jirásko. Prague: Klášter premonstrátů na Strahově, 1991. 173p. bibliog.
Information on the churches in the Czech Republic is fairly scarce, hence the inclusion here of this slim, nicely produced and illustrated paperback. The author starts with the history and development of the religious orders and congregations in the Czech Lands. He also provides a simple chronological table (p. 19-23). Then follows a catalogue of the individual orders, all Roman Catholic, each entry accompanied by a history of the order, its formal structure, philosophy and mission, its activity past and present in the Czech Lands and a drawing of its coat of arms. Wherever possible, photographs or drawings of the order's habits are included. The author provided two indexes: of the religious orders, congregations and societies themselves (p. 159-62); and of places and names (p. 163-71).

347 Prémonstrés en Bohème, Moravie et Slovaquie. Premonstráti v Čechách, na Moravě a na Slovensku. Premonstratenser in Böhmen, Mähren und der Slowakei. Premonstratensians in Bohemia, Moravia and Slovakia.
Bernard Ardura, Karel Dolista. Prague: Karolinum, 1993. 61p.

A guide to the Premonstratensian abbeys in the Czech Lands and Slovakia, published as one of the cultural itineraries sponsored by the Council of Europe. The guide gives a brief chronology of this Catholic order for men, from 1143 to 1993, covering its background and origins, structure and rules, and its history within the Czech Lands. The individual abbeys are subsequently described – Strahov in Prague, Želiv in Southern Bohemia, Teplá in Western Bohemia, Nová Říše in Southern Bohemia and Jasov in Slovakia – all with pictures of the buildings and interiors, the latter being mostly of the churches and libraries. The Strahov monastery was the first Premonstratensian monastery in Prague, having been founded in 1140. Today it houses the Memorial of Czech Literature (Památník národního písemnictví), the Strahov library, which dates back to the 12th century, and a vast literary archive. The guide has parallel texts in Czech, French, German and English.

348 On the way to Jesus: Czech Jesuits during the Communist oppression.
Jan Pavlík, translated from the Czech by Pavel Kolmačka. Velehrad, Czech Republic: Refugium Velehrad-Roma, 1998. 57p.

A slim paperback on the recent history of the Jesuit order in Czechoslovakia. The association of the order with the Czech Lands in the distant past and their activities there have not been considered by historians and the general public to have been beneficial to the Czech nation. The name of one Jesuit preacher, the Counter-Reformation fanatic Antonín Koniáš (1691-1760) who burned about 30,000 Protestant books during his life-time, has become a by-word for bigotry. A full history of the Jesuit order in the Czech Lands has been written by Ivana Čornejová and published in Czech (Prague: Mladá fronta, 1995) under the title *Tovaryšstvo Ježíšovo: Jesuité v Čechách* (The Society of Jesus: the Jesuits in Bohemia).

Modern theologians

349 Breaking out of fortress church.
Tim Noble, Václav Malý. *Month*, vol. 30, no. 6 (June 1997), p. 224-47.

Bishop Václav Malý was one of the signatories of Charter 77. As a consequence he spent some time as a political prisoner, but was free in time to be one of the active figures in the events of the Velvet Revolution in 1989. This article is an interview with Bishop Malý in which he answers questions on the current position of the Roman Catholic Church in the Czech Lands and on the relations of the Church with society.

350 **Laveur des vitres et archevêque. Biographie de Mgr Miloslav Vlk (Prague).** (Window cleaner and archbishop. A biography of Mgr Miloslav Vlk [Prague].)
Alain Boudre, preface by Václav Havel. Paris: Les éditions nouvelle cité, 1994. 208p. map. bibliog.

Miloslav Vlk (born 1932) became Archbishop of Prague and Primate of Bohemia in 1991. This book is his biography, covering his childhood and, as the title suggests, his varied career. Miloslav Vlk was ordained during the Prague Spring in 1968 and continued his work after the Soviet invasion, inevitably in a clandestine manner. The biography includes a chronology of his life. A monograph on the previous leader of the Czech Catholics, Cardinal František Tomášek, is available in Czech only: *Kardinál Tomášek* (Prague: Zvona Aeterna, 1994), compiled by Jan Hartmann et al.

351 **Thoughts of a Czech pastor.**
Josef Hromádka, translated by Monica Page, Benjamin Page.
London: SCM Press, 1970. 117p. bibliog.

This autobiography of a Moravian Lutheran theologian, the best-known and most influential Protestant leader in Central Europe in the era after the Second World War, presents his views on many religious and philosophical issues. Lutheranism is discussed within the context of Protestantism and in relation to Catholicism. The book also provides an outline of Czech theological history.

Miscellaneous

352 **Reflections of heresy in Czech fourteenth- and fifteenth-century rhymed compositions.**
K. Brušák. *Slavonic and East European Review*, vol. 76, no. 2 (April 1998), p. 241-65. bibliog.

Profesor Brušák traces the earliest mention of heresy in Czech vernacular literature to the Dalimil chronicle, which was composed in rhymed verse in around 1314. He then expands the coverage to the last years of the 14th century and the first decades of the 15th century and points out where the heretical ideas of the Czechs were reflected in verse compositions.

Religious symbolism

353 **The Holy Infant of Prague.**
Josef Forbelský, Jan Royt, Mojmír Horyna, photographs by Karel
Neubert, Ladislav Neubert, translated by Kateřina Hilská. Prague:
Aventinum, 1992. 95p. bibliog.

Miraculous powers have been attributed to the 300-year-old wax effigy (presented to
the church by Polyxena of Lobkowicz in 1628) in the Carmelite Church of Our Lady
Victorious (Panna Marie Vítězná) in Prague. The Infant has been an object of
pilgrimage and has accumulated a vast selection of donated clothes, which are
frequently changed by nuns. Susie Lunt cites four books on the effigy in her
bibliography on *Prague* (Oxford; Santa Barbara, California; Denver, Colorado: Clio
Press, 1997, p. 69, 71), which is some indication of its fame and popularity. The
books, including this one, also act as illustrated guidebooks to the whole church. A
much larger, older publication is *The Infant of Prague: the story of the Holy Image
and the history of the devotion* by Ludvík Němec (New York: Benziger, 1958. 304p.).

Social Conditions, Women's Issues, Children's Issues, Health and Welfare

Social conditions

354 **Czechoslovakia, 1918-92: a laboratory for social change.**
Jaroslav Krejčí, Pavel Machonin. Basingstoke, England; London:
Macmillan, 1996. 266p. map. bibliog.
Written for English speakers, this is a documentary account of the Czechoslovak
experiment in building a multi-ethnic nation within a political structure which is not
too complex. The book has three parts. The first two parts, 'Ethnopolitics' and 'The
economic context', were written by Jaroslav Krejčí, an Emeritus Professor at
Lancaster University. The Czech-Slovak partnership, its history, the respective roles
of the two nations and the squabble over power sharing are the main topic. The Czech-
German issue, the Magyars, Jews, Poles and the case of Ruthenia are looked at from
the angle of the four dimensions of the complex and long process of creating a nation:
geographical, cultural, political and psychological. The third, largest part, 'Social
metamorphoses' by Pavel Machonin, who has a distinguished career in sociology in
the Czech Republic, offers an overview of social changes from the birth of
Czechoslovakia in 1918 to the dissociation of the Czechs and Slovaks in 1993. The
book has a number of tables, explanatory notes and a substantial bibliography.

355 **Social reform in the Czech Republic.**
Edited by Stein Ringen, Claire Wallace. Prague: Prague Digital Arts,
1994. 68p. bibliog. (Prague Papers on Social Responses to
Transformation, vol. 2).
This slim paperback contains papers which were presented at a workshop on social
transition held at the Central European University in Prague from 14 to 16 May 1993:
a forum for social scientists to discuss empirical research on social transition. The
papers document the movement towards social reform, which was considerable, and
responses to changes. The titles of the papers are: 'Income support system in Central
and Eastern European transition' by Igor Tomeš (p. 1-20); 'The development of

113

Social Conditions, Women's Issues, Children's Issues, Health and Welfare.
Social conditions

pension schemes in the Czech Republic' by Jana Klimentová (p. 21-24); 'Current social policy developments in the Czech Republic. The case of health service' by Martin Potůček (p. 25-29); 'Social problems and coping strategies' by Jiří Večerník (p. 41-58); and 'The Czech family in transition. From social to economic capital' by Ivo Možný (p. 59-69).

356 **Markets and people: the Czech reform experience in a comparative perspective.**
Jiří Večerník. Aldershot, England; Brookfield, Vermont; Hong Kong; Singapore; Sydney: Avebury, 1996. 294p. bibliog.

This academic study considers the socio-economic transition as viewed by individuals and households. The period studied is from 1989 to 1995 and the focus is on earnings, secondary resources, household incomes, expenditures, hardship and poverty. Večerník uses data both from economics and sociology, and from national and cross-national surveys. His conclusions are that the Czech transformation is an 'active, energetic and determined process, with, however, many pitfalls and uncertainties'. He provides a substantial bibliography (p. 273-85), mostly of recent articles and reports.

357 **Societies in transition: East Central Europe today. Prague papers on social responses to transformation.**
Edited by Stein Ringen, Claire Wallace. Aldershot, England; Brookfield, Vermont; Hong Kong; Singapore; Sydney: Avebury; Brookfield, Vermont: Ashgate; with the Central European University, Budapest and Prague, 1994. 224p. bibliog.

Presents papers from a series of workshops held at the Central European University in Prague in May 1992. The focus was on the social impact of political and economic transformation. The papers concerning unemployment (transient or permanent?) and economic justice have many references to Czechoslovakia. Martin Potůček contributed an essay entitled '"Quo Vadis." Social policy in Czechoslovakia', (p. 129-36), in which he looks at the tradition of social policy in Czechoslovakia, development since 1989 and its alternative future. Igor Tomeš is the author of 'Social policy and protection in ČSFR since 1989', (p. 137-47), an essay in which he analyses the aims of the social reform scenario: the employment policy, income policy and social security. Tomeš also writes about relevant Acts which were passed in 1990 and 1991. The book has tables and charts.

358 **Eastern Europe in transformation: the impact on sociology.**
Edited by Mike Forrest Keen, Janusz Mucha. Westport, Connecticut; London: Greenwood Press, 1994. 208p. bibliog.

A collection of articles by various authors. 'Ups and downs in Czech sociology' (p. 79-87) by Edvard Urbánek, Professor of Sociology at Charles University, is a brief summary of the subject, from its origins in the Czech Lands, which are linked to T. G. Masaryk. Masaryk was a professor of philosophy and referred to sociology as 'practical philosophy'. After the establishment of the Czech Republic in 1918, the development of sociology was intense. This development was quantitative as well as qualitative, and was interrupted by German occupation in 1939. The Communist doctrine considered sociology a bourgeois pseudo-science and the subject disappeared from universities. It was only in 1965 that lectures were reintroduced and the

114

Social Conditions, Women's Issues, Children's Issues, Health and Welfare.

Social conditions

Sociological Institute was founded at the Czechoslovak Academy of Sciences. The Velvet Revolution of 1989 brought new challenges in the process of transition. Sociology must participate in the solution of problems of social integration. The conclusion is that the 'totalitarian regimes adopt a highly disparaging and negative stance towards sociology . . . sociology can exist and flourish only in a pluralistic and democratic society'. The book has an index and a bibliography (p. 177-95).

359 **Class structure in Europe: new findings from East-West comparisons of social structure and mobility.**
Edited by Max Haller. Armonk, New York; London: M. E. Sharpe, 1990. 271p. bibliog.

A collection of comparative studies, most of which were contributions to an international conference on 'Societies at borderlines. Social structure and social consciousness in East and West Europe' which took place in Graz, Austria in 1987. The conference was also a Tenth Biannual Meeting of the Austrian Sociological Association. Three of the papers mention the Czech situation specifically. 'Family background and educational attainment in Czechoslovakia and the Netherlands: the analysis of cultural and economic sources of inequality in comparative perspective' is by Petr Matějů and Jules L. Peschar (p. 121-49); 'Social mobility in Austria, Czechoslovakia and Hungary, an investigation of the effects of industrialization, socialist revolution and national uniqueness' is by Max Heller (p. 153-97), Tamás Kolosi and Petér Róbert; and 'Transition to socialism and intergenerational class mobility. The model of core social fluidity applied to Czechoslovakia' is by Marek Boguszak (p. 233-60). Each paper has its own bibliography.

360 **The constant flux: a study of class mobility in industrial societies.**
Robert Erikson, John H. Goldthorpe. Oxford: Clarendon Press, 1993. 429p. bibliog.

There are references to Czechoslovakia throughout the book, in the text as well as in tables. A specific chapter on 'Czechoslovakia' is on pages 167-69. The book is based on secondary analysis and the authors provide a large bibliography of modern material and name and subject indexes.

361 **Equality and inequality in Eastern Europe.**
Pierre Kende, Zdeněk Strmiska, in collaboration with Jean-Charles Asselain et al, translated from the French by Françoise Read.
Leamington Spa, England; Hamburg, Germany; New York: Berg, 1987. Distributed in the USA and Canada by St. Martin's Press. 421p.

A collection of scholarly studies, written before the collapse of Communism in Eastern Europe, by authors from several disciplines, which provide data on economic and social inequality and compare the old and new types of inequalities. The authors look closely at distribution of incomes, division of resources in the area of consumption, housing, personnel hierarchy in companies, social mobility and social differentiation, political power and social inequality, the education ethos and the meritocratic ethos and the paradoxes of socialist distribution.

Social Conditions, Women's Issues, Children's Issues, Health and Welfare.
Social conditions

362 **Prague sprung: notes and voices from the New World.**
David Leviathin. Westport, Connecticut; London: Westpoint, 1995.
142p.
A study of intellectual life, politics and government in the Czech and Slovak republics
in the form of interviews, focusing on the socio-historical aspects. The book is written
in a lively style. Leviathin is a Harvard academic and a Fulbright lecturer teaching
American Studies at Charles University.

363 **Unemployment in capitalist, Communist and postcommunist
countries.**
J. L. Porket. Basingstoke, England: Macmillan, in association with
St Antony's College, Oxford; New York: St. Martin's Press, 1995.
230p. bibliog.
A scholarly study, providing useful background reading for an understanding of the
Czech situation since it makes extensive use of Czech sources in most chapters. The
Czech Republic also figures in tables and charts. By the same publisher is *Employment
policies in the Soviet Union and Eastern Europe* which was edited by Jan Adam
(Basingstoke, England: Macmillan, 1997. 224p.)

364 **Living standards and social conditions in Czechoslovakia.**
Oto Ončák. Prague: Orbis Press Agency, 1986. 47p.
This superficial study, which was written still in the defence of the socialist system,
offers basic information on economics, social security, care for the elderly and health
care in Czechoslovakia generally, before the political changes of 1989. It is translated
from Czech. The volume lacks statistics or charts.

365 **Unemployment in the Czech and Slovak republics.**
Jan Švejnar, Katherine Terrell, Daniel Munich. In: *The Czech
Republic and economic transition in Eastern Europe.* Edited by Jan
Švejnar. San Diego, California: Academic Press, 1995, p. 285-316.
A comparative study on the evolution of unemployment in the two republics since
1990, when the rate for both was 0.1 per cent. By 1993 the gap between the two
countries had grown considerably and in each of the countries unemployment has been
concentrated in certain areas and districts. The authors analyse the dynamics of
unemployment and the different factors which affect inflows and outflows. The
processes of inflows and outflows are examined in some detail. The article includes:
tables of unemployment rates by region and budget allocation to employment
programmes; a correlation matrix for the annual data of the republics; and
characteristics of the annual district data. Not only is the Czech Republic's rate of
unemployment less than in Slovakia, but its rate of growth of unemployment is also
slower.

116

Social Conditions, Women's Issues, Children's Issues, Health and Welfare.

Social conditions

366 The social legacy of Communism.
Edited by James R. Millar, Sharon L. Wolchik. Washington, DC: Woodrow Wilson Center Press; Cambridge, England; New York: Cambridge University Press, 1994. 404p.

Although mostly concerned with Russia, this book provides some information on the situation in the Czech Republic, on topics which are otherwise not easy to access in book form. An example of this is the issue of drug abuse in Central Europe. The work also covers general health and mortality, ethnicity and nationalism in Central and Eastern Europe. The book has tables and a rich index.

367 Social consequences of a change in ownership: two case studies in industrial enterprises in the Czech Republic, spring 1993.
Ivo Možný, Libor Musil, Petr Mareš, Ivo Řezníček, Tomáš Sirovátka. Brno, Czech Republic: Masarykova Univerzita, 1993. 154p. bibliog.

Examines two industrial plants – 'Mechanica Corporation' and 'Domus Factory' – both of medium to upper medium size. The enquiry is from the view of economists as well as sociologists. Both plants were privatized: one via privatization which was based on the voucher method; the other one was a direct sale. It may not be easy to obtain this publication outside the Czech Republic, but it has value in offering an insight into attitudes of employees which may not be easy to interpret by an outsider. The authors' understanding of the subject is apparent in the several concrete examples which they include – mini life stories of employees, which illustrate the complexity of the situations and regional influences and peculiarities. Most of the text is in English, some is in Czech. The sizeable bibliography lists books, articles, reports etc. in Czech and English.

368 Paying the price: the wage crisis in Central and Eastern Europe.
Edited by Daniel Vaughan-Whitehead. Basingstoke, England: Macmillan Press, 1998. 418p.

The first ever assessment of wage policies in post-Communist parts of Europe. The studies examine the evolution of wage levels and wage structures since 1989 and provide a direct assessment of wage policies in terms of both social protection and economic efficiency. The conclusions are underpinned by the most recent data in dozens of tables. 'The true effects of wage regulations in the Czech Republic' was written by Jiří Rusnok and Martin Fassmann (p. 140-81).

369 The Czech household sector in transition.
Marie Vavrejnová, Irena Moravčíková. In: *The Czech Republic and economic transition in Eastern Europe.* Edited by Jan Švejnar. San Diego, California: Academic Press, 1995, p. 317-29.

Between 1989 and 1993, in the first four years of economic transition, significant changes were brought about in the amount and structure of incomes, expenditures and savings of the population in the Czech Republic. The authors draw heavily on the statistical data and provide tables on: the evolution of nominal and real incomes; the aggregate balance sheet of household incomes, expenditures and savings; average monthly household cash incomes; the nominal value and structure of the average monthly household cash expenditure; and bank deposits.

117

370 **Changes in expenditure and household inequality in the Czech and Slovak Republic.**
Thesia Garner, Martina Lubyová, Katherine Terrell. In: *The Czech Republic and economic transition in Eastern Europe.* Edited by Jan Švejnar. San Diego, California: Academic Press, 1995, p. 331-75.
The article examines the extent of the impact made by the economic reforms on the distribution of income in the two republics. The authors used for their analysis both income and expenditures as criteria for measuring the welfare of citizens. They explain their methodology; provide definitions; and illustrate their conclusions on a number of tables and charts such as tables on the mean income of various groups of workers and pensioners, cost of living indexes, expenditures, and differences in inequality of expenditures.

371 **The re-formation of the managerial elite in the Czech Republic.**
Ed Clark, Anna Soulsby. *Europe-Asia Studies*, vol. 48, no. 2 (March 1996), p. 285-303.
A study based on several large privatized state enterprises. The authors look at a number of individual managers, and analyse how far the composition of the managerial elite has been influenced by the changes since 1989, and the relationship of the present managers with the pre-1989 elite. They explain the changes in the social structure in the Czech Republic and investigate whether economic power on a local level has changed. The sociological concept of a social elite is applied to show how the former, so-called nomenclature managers manoeuvred themselves after 1989, not only to satisfy the requirements and institutional conditions in the wake of the death of state socialism, but also to be influential in defining these requirements and conditions.

Statistická ročenka České republiky. (Statistical Yearbook of the Czech Republic.)
See item no. 416.

The family in the mother of towns. Today's Prague portrayed in statistical data.
See item no. 421.

Review of the labour market in the Czech Republic.
See item no. 575.

Women's issues

372 **Women and politics worldwide.**
Edited by Barbara J. Nelson, Najma Chowdhury. New Haven, Connecticut; London: Yale University Press, 1994. 818p. map. bibliog.
This substantial tome is alphabetically arranged by country. 'Czechoslovakia (former)' (p. 208-25) commences with political, demographic, educational and economic data. It

is a pity that there are spelling errors in the text. The collection of data is followed by 'Women's issues in Czechoslovakia in the Communist and postcommunist periods' by the expert on gender issues in Central Europe, Sharon L. Wolchik. This contribution has its own bibliography on p. 223-25. Wolchik concentrates on women's political role, demographic trends and policies, employment policies and religious rights. She concludes that, 'Although focusing on women's political engagements regarding demographic, employment and religious practice policies illustrates some of the ways in which politics and policy making in Communist political systems differ from those in democratic states, it also demonstrates the importance of factors other than political structure and values in shaping women's relationship to politics. Women's experiences with politics in Czechoslovakia during the Communist and early post-Communist periods highlight how gender roles in other areas, patterns of social and family relations, and economic policies have affected women's political activities and how women use existing political resources'.

373 **Women's work and women's lives: the continuing struggle worldwide.**
Edited by Hilda Kahne, Janet Z. Giele.   Boulder, Colorado; Oxford: Westview Press, 1992. 324p. bibliog.

'Women and work in Communist and post-communist Central and Eastern Europe' on p. 119-39 is by Sharon L. Wolchik. The article has its own excellent and extensive bibliography on p. 135-39. During the Communist period the level of female employment was high due to policies towards women and broader economic and political imperatives. These policies led to an increase in women's educational access. The levels of employment outside home have been higher in the more developed northern countries, which includes the Czech Republic. This is illustrated in a table on p. 121. The striking characteristic was the high level of outside employment during childbearing ages.

374 **Women, the state and development.**
Edited by Sue Ellen M. Charlton, Jana Everett, Kathleen Staudt.   New York: State University of New York Press, 1989. 248p.

'Women and the state in Eastern Europe and the Soviet Union' by Sharon Wolchik (p. 44-65) is of historical value by now. Wolchik looks at the pre-Communist legacy, political change and the effects of change in this region, at gender relations, the state sponsorship of gender equality, cultural changes and the renewed importance of motherhood.

375 **Women in the politics of postcommunist Eastern Europe.**
Edited by Marilyn Rueschemeyer.   Armonk, New York; London: M. E. Sharpe, Inc., 1998. rev. and expanded ed. 308p. bibliog.

Sharon Wolchik contributed an essay entitled 'Women and the politics of transition in Czech and Slovak Republics' (p. 116-41). Wolchik goes back to the role of women in politics in the Communist period and analyses the pattern of women's political participation in the post-Communist period. She looks at women's organizations, the Communist legacy, the impact of economic transition after 1989 and future possibilities. The women's issue has been pushed back by the more important political and economic reforms and there seems to be even a rejection, caused mainly by economic circumstances, of the Communist crede of gender equality. Several times,

Social Conditions, Women's Issues, Children's Issues, Health and Welfare.

Women's issues

Wolchik draws a parallel with the situation in Latin America. The essay has very detailed and informative bibliographical 'Notes' and the whole collection of essays has a 'Select bibliography' (p. 298-300) and an index (p. 301-08).

376 **Lidská práva, ženy a společnost.** (Human rights, women and society.) Edited by Hana Havelková. Prague: Evropské středisko UNESCO, 1992. 96p. bibliog.

A selection of papers, with summaries in English, given at a seminar in Pečky in November 1991 on the position of women in the society in transition. Of special interest are articles on the history of the women's movement in Czechoslovakia and on the social position of women in Czechoslovak society. The individual papers have good explanatory notes and bibliographical references. There is not much up-to-date material on the gender issue and this collection of papers is welcomed. More specific issues were the subject of a Czech-Ukrainian conference which took place in Prague, 27-28 November 1977, under the title 'Obchod se ženami v postkomunistických zemích střední a východní Evropy – Traffic in women in Postcommunist countries of Central and Eastern Europe'. A collection of papers was published under the same title (Prague: La Strada, 1998. 183p.).

377 **Do Czech women need feminism? Perspectives of feminist theories and practices in Czechoslovakia.** Jiřina Smejkalová-Strickland. In: *Women's Studies International Forum*, vol. 17, no. 2/3 (March-June 1994), p. 277-82.

The article points out the obstacles, for both Czech women and men, which stand in the way of communication with current Western feminist theories. The current feminist theories cannot be separated from the development of post-war Western thinking and writing about society and culture.

378 **Czech women in the labour market: work and family in the transition economy.** Nicole Kozera. Prague: Institute of Sociology, Academy of Sciences of the Czech Republic, 1997. 45p. bibliog. (Working Paper WP 97:6).

This paper examines the effects of the transition from a planned economy on women's integration of family and work responsibilities by comparing the following variables from before and after 1989: labour force participation rates; occupational segmentation; wage differences; social policy regarding working women and families; discrimination in the labour market; and women's attitudes to family and work. Kozera concludes that no fundamental changes occurred for Czech women in the labour market. The main source of data for this study were journal articles, working papers, surveys by sociological institutions and personal interviews conducted by the author.

379 **Czech and Slovak women and political leadership.** Sharon Wolchik. *Women's History Review*, vol. 4, no. 5 (1996), p. 525-38. bibliog.

Reviews the history of women's role in public life, and the women's movement in the 19th century and in the Communist era. Wolchik also looks at the longstanding political and cultural contacts between the Czech Lands and Slovakia, which continue today, even though the two countries are separate states. The influences which restrict

120

Czech and Slovak women and limit their interest in political life on a higher level are identified.

380 **Feminism meets socialism: women's studies in the Czech Republic.**
Marianne Grunell. *Journal of Women's Studies*, no. 2, 1 (February 1995), p. 101-11. bibliog.
An account of women's studies in the Czech Republic. Since the Velvet Revolution, a Gender Studies Centre has been established. The article looks generally at feminism and the intellectual and social climate in the Czech Republic.

381 **Women of Prague. Ethnic diversity and social change from the eighteenth century to the present.**
Wilma A. Iggers. Oxford; Providence, Rhode Island: Berghahn Books, 1995. 381p. bibliog.
A study of twelve women, from the turn of the 18th/19th century to the present day, their roles in history, the social conditions and ethnic relations. Iggers chose diverse personalities: from the writer Božena Němcová (1820-62), founder of modern Czech prose, to Dr Milada Horáková who was executed in the first years of Communist rule. The book has illustrations, including engravings and photographs.

382 **Young women of Prague.**
Alena Heitlinger, Susanna Trnka. Basingstoke, England: Macmillan Press Ltd, 1998. 187p. bibliog.
A worthwhile contribution to modern gender studies, this volume presents fourteen interviews with fourteen 'ordinary' Czech women, born in the 1970s, who came of age in the aftermath of the Velvet Revolution of November 1989. They are of similar age and education but each have varying work, marital and childbearing experiences. They are allowed to speak for themselves and come across as personalities. The interviews are preceded by a chapter mapping the social and historical agents that have influenced these women's lives. The interviews are analysed and conclusions are made. Three additional chapters outline how the study was planned. Common themes emerge from the interviews, linking them to both the legacies of Communism and the current post-Communist transition.

Children's issues

383 **Childhood as a social phenomenon: national report – Czechoslovakia.**
Jiří Kovařík, translated from Czech. Vienna: Europaische Zentrum für Wohlfartspolitik, 1992. 66p. bibliog. (Eurosocial Report, 36/14).
A paperback concerned with the rights of children in the former Czechoslovakia, the social position of children and social conditions in Czechoslovakia generally. It includes a note on the author.

384 **Europe's sex supermarket.**
D. Campbell, K. Connelly. *The Guardian*, 17 December 1997, p. 8-9.
At the time this article was published, the former Radio 1 disc jockey Christopher
Denning was awaiting a trial in Prague on paedophilia charges. Central Europe has
become the latest destination for wealthy people from the West searching for children,
who are ready to sell their bodies for money.

385 **Sexual abandon.**
Michael Woodhead. *The Times*, 9 November 1996, 'Magazine',
p. 17.
Reports on the abandoned children of prostitutes who operate on the borders between
the Czech Republic and Germany. Their trade is flourishing, but the children are not
cared for. The article is illustrated.

Health care

386 **Health care reform in the Czech Republic.**
Randall K. Filler, Jaromír Vepřek, Olga Výborná, Zdeněk Papeš, Pavel
Vepřek. In: *The Czech Republic and economic transition in Eastern
Europe.* Edited by Jan Švejnar. San Diego, California: Academic
Press, 1995, p. 395-411.
The transformation of the Czech health sector from being controlled by the state to
being privately run is the subject of this article. In terms of the health status of the
Czech population relative to other countries, Czechoslovakia experienced a significant
deterioration between the mid-1960s and early 1990s. The two major features during
the transition have been the privatization of the suppliers of the nation's health care
and the transfer of payment for health from the state budget to private insurance
companies. The privatization of the suppliers involved mainly the small- and medium-
sized health care institutions. The next step, in the near future, will be the privatization
of larger establishments, such as hospitals and clinics and the preparation and
realization of additional insurance schemes for those citizens who wish to be covered
for more, either in the scope or in the quality of the services, than the 'basic package'
of insurance has to offer.

387 **The health care system in the Czech Republic.**
Basle, Switzerland: Pharmaceutical Partners for Better Health Care;
London: National Economic Research Association, 1996. 160p.
bibliog.
The first chapter of this report offers a profile of the health care system, an analysis of
individual sectors and of risk-adjustments in the Czech Republic. Chapter two is a
projection of health care needs and funding and a summary of the reform of the health
care system, a reform which constitutes fundamental changes. The report recommends
further reforms. It contains many tables and charts, a bibliography of mostly reports

and articles, unfortunately in many instances with inadequate citation, and a list of people interviewed during the preparation of this study.

388 **Health care and the pharmaceutical industries of the Czech Republic and Slovakia.**
Nicholas Saunders, Nick Sljivic. London: FT Pharmaceuticals & Health Care Publishing, a division of Pearson Professional Limited, 1996. 118p. (FT Management Report).

An account of economic, political and demographic aspects, historical as well as current, precedes a description of the pharmaceutical sector in each of the two countries. Under Communism, until 1989, health care was fully under state management. Economic reforms led to enforced reforms within the health care system with regard to financing, with insurance companies being set up, and the changes are ongoing. Appendixes on p. 103-17 provide addresses of general contacts (ministries, associations, pharmaceutical companies and health care providers).

389 **Risk-adjustment and its implications for efficiency and equity in health care systems. Examples from the Czech Republic, England, Germany, the Netherlands, Switzerland, the United States of America.**
Thomas McCarthy, Keith Davies, John Gaisford, Ulrich Hofmeyer. Basle, Switzerland: Pharmaceutical Partners for Better Healthcare; London: National Economic Research Association, 1995. 254p. bibliog.

A comprehensive report on the mechanisms that ensure equity of health insurance coverage regardless of health status 'within the framework of competitive health insurance market'. The Czech Republic is at present experiencing a total overhaul of its health care system. 'Risk-adjustment in the Czech Republic' (p. 79-98) looks at the current structure of the insurance sector and highlights the needs which will have to be addressed in the future. The chapter has several charts and its own bibliography (p. 98).

390 **Reproduction, medicine and the socialist state.**
Alena Heitlinger. Basingstoke, England: Macmillan, 1987. 318p. bibliog.

The study is concerned mostly with Czechoslovakia, with the social and individual management of reproduction in a state socialist society, the process of reproduction being defined as 'transition to motherhood'. It is a comparative study, the main issue being individual reproductive rights and choices, between socialist and capitalist societies, which highlights many similarities and reveals some differences. This treatise is scholarly, yet accessible, and it is supplemented by statistics and a sizeable bibliography of mostly Czech and English sources (p. 280-303) and an index. At the time of writing, the Central European University Press was preparing *Towards better reproductive health in Eastern Europe: concern, commitment and change*, edited by WHO Scientific Working Group on Reproductive Health Research (Budapest, 1999. 170p.).

391 **Homosexuality, society and AIDS in the Czech Republic.**
Džamila Stehlíková, Ivo Procházka, Jiří Hromada. Prague: Orbis
Publishing House, 1996. 140p. bibliog.
The aim of this study is to evaluate the knowledge, attitudes and behaviour of
members of the Czech gay community in relation to HIV and AIDS and to draw
conclusions for future preventative strategies. This study was supported by the
Ministry of Health of the Czech Republic and the Swiss National Fund for the Support
of Scientific Research in Bern. The research was carried out by SOHO (Association of
Organisations of Homosexual Citizens) between 1994 and 1997. The aims and
methods of the study are explained and based on numerous charts, graphs and
statistics. It investigates the current knowledge and beliefs regarding HIV and AIDS,
attitudes towards social conditions, sexuality, interpersonal relations and the risks of
HIV and AIDS and the sexual behaviour of gay men.

392 **National Institute of Public Health, Prague, Czech Republic, in
1995-2000.**
J. Kříž. *Central European Journal of Public Health*, vol. 3, no. 4
(1995), p. 186-88.
The National Institute of Public Health in Prague is responsible for public health and
disease prevention. Kříž looks at trends in development, the structure of the institute,
its objectives and goals, activities and cooperation with other public health institutions
in the Czech Republic.

Zdravotnická ročenka České Republiky. (Czech Republic Health Statistics
Yearbook.)
See item no. 420.

124

Education

General

393 **Education and economic change in Eastern Europe and the former Soviet Union.**
Edited by David Phillips, Michal Kaser.   Wallingford, England: Triangle Books, 1992. 138p. bibliog.
The basis of the majority of articles in this collection is a comparative analysis of the restructuring of education in the formerly Communist countries. The other topics are education and the economy and education and religion. Each paper has a separate bibliography or notes. 'Education and economic change in Czechoslovakia' (p. 71-82), by Vlastimil Pařízek, offers a brief historical overview before expanding on the current issues and on the present state of primary, secondary and university education in Czechoslovakia and the issue of quality education in a market economy. In conclusion, the author, who is a professor of education at Charles University in Prague and was involved in the education reforms in the Czech Republic, highlights the stagnation and relative neglect of education in recent decades and indicates that education does not have to be influenced by the economy. The short bibliography accompanying this article is on p. 82.

394 **Higher education reform process in Central and Eastern Europe.**
Edited by Klaus Hufner.   Frankfurt, Germany; Bern; New York: Peter Lang, 1995. 254p. bibliog. (Ökonomische Theorie der Hochschule, Bd. 7).
This paperback is concerned with the reforms of tertiary, mostly university, education in the post-Communist countries. Some of the contributions were translated from Czech, Swedish and French.

125

395 **Reviews of national policies for education: Czech Republic.**
Paris: Organisation for Economic Cooperation and Development
(OECD), 1996. 196p. bibliog.
Nineteen Czech specialists contributed the background information for this work,
which was originally a report submitted to an OECD and Czech Ministry of Education
conference held in Prague on 14-15 May 1996. The report was updated and provides
statistical data and information on developments in education up to the middle of
1996. The review has two parts: part one, 'Transforming education'; and part two,
'Examiner's report', which is a report by OECD specialists. The Czech Republic was
the first economy in transition to have acceded to the Organisation for Economic
Cooperation and Development. The review is concerned primarily with education
policy, relating to primary and secondary schools, general as well as vocational, and to
a lesser extent with the continuing education of adults.

396 **Higher education in the Czech Republic, 1998.**
Prague: Ministry of Education, Youth and Sports of the Czech
Republic and the Centre for Higher Education Studies, 1998. 80p. map.
A comprehensive, useful reference book on tertiary education, to which approximately
twenty-five per cent of Czech eighteen-year-olds are admitted. This large, A4
paperback publication with colour photographs is a first edition, but there is no
indication that the content will be updated regularly. Part one starts with a history of
education in the Czech Lands and goes on to deal with practical matters, such as
financing, management of such institutions, membership of international organizations
and international cooperation. Part two is a catalogue of twenty-seven institutions,
starting with the venerable Charles University in Prague and concluding with the
Police Academy of the Czech Republic, also in Prague. Each entry covers the history
of the institution, its structure, organization of studies and student services, and this is
complemented by a photograph, usually of the main building. Part three provides
addresses of the institutions, phone and fax numbers and websites.

397 **Higher education in the Czech and Slovak Federal Republic: guide
for foreign students.**
Edited by Mária Hrabinská, Dana Tollingerová, Ladislav Haberštát.
Bratislava: Institute of Information and Prognosis of Education, Youth
and Sports, 1992. 279p. map.
This publication may not be easy to obtain, but it provides compressed, factual
information which would otherwise have to be researched from several sources. As
the title indicates, it is intended for foreigners interested in studying in an institution
of tertiary education in the Czech or Slovak Republic. The information contained is
similar to what one would find in prospectuses of British universities: full address of
the institution, its history, organization of studies, student services, student
organizations, admission requirements, additional information for foreign students.
Each department is subsequently described in moderate detail. The language of the
narrative is not perfect: the English would have benefited from some editing. There
were twenty-three institutes of higher education in the Czech Republic in 1991, all
state institutions. The New Higher Education Act no. 172/90 was passed in 1990. An
update of this publication, written in better English, is *Higher education in the Czech
Republic: guide for foreign students* (Prague: Center for Higher Education Studies,
1996. 364p. map).

126

398 **Communist higher education policies in Czechoslovakia, Poland and East Germany.**
John Connelly. In: *The establishment of Communist regimes in Eastern Europe, 1944-1949.* Edited by Norman Naimark, Leonid Gibianskii. Boulder, Colorado; Oxford: Westview Press, a division of Harper Collins Publishers, 1997, p. 191-216.

Connelly, of Boston University, provides an account of the history of higher education in the Czech Lands and goes back to 1939, when the universities in the Protectorate of Bohemia and Moravia were closed as a result of anti-Nazi demonstrations initiated and led by the students. Connelly highlights some features of the Czech situation. In the Czech Lands the administration of education was traditionally centralized. In 1948 most of the power rested with the Communist students. The purges in academia after the Communist takeover in 1948 were not as serious as, for example, in East German universities. The author concludes in his comparative essay that the Communist Party somehow did not alter the constitution of the student body: on the whole the students of 1968 or 1989 had a very similar social background to the students of 1938 or 1948 and their anti-totalitarian ideology was similar. They played a vital part in the restoration of democratic systems in the country.

399 **Foundry engineering in the Czech Republic.**
M. Horáček. *Foundry Trade Journal*, no. 170 (3517) (April 1996), p. 142-44.

The profile of a graduate in foundry engineering. The article looks into the relevance of this education to the current needs of the Czech foundry industry.

400 **Ekonomika a cudzie jazyky. Economy and foreign languages. Ökonomie und Fremdsprache.**
Edited by Rudolf Muhr, Katarína Miková. Banská Bystrica, Slovakia: REPRO-HUPE, 1998. 363p.

On the state of teaching foreign languages and languages for specific purposes in Central and Eastern European countries. It is a medley of articles in various languages, mostly on teaching English, and would be of interest to a linguist, TEFL (teaching English as a foreign language) teacher or a business person. Examples of topics are: teaching legal English to students of economics; the use of newspapers in teaching communication; metaphors in English for business purposes; and interpreting skills for managers.

401 **The Czech Republic.**
Robert Lynes. In: *Teaching English in Eastern and Central Europe. Finding work, teaching and living in Eastern and Central Europe.* Brighton, England: In Print Publishing, in association with International House, 1995, p. 84-146. map.

The boom in English-language teaching after 1989 in the Czech Republic occurred on several levels: from conditions in schools after Russian ceased to be compulsory, to the needs of top management in the more Western orientated economic environment. This work provides a wealth of information on living in the Czech Republic, how to find teaching work, accommodation, how to make most of living there, useful

127

addresses and telephone numbers. It includes the specific features of teaching Czech, with examples of grammar teaching and classroom technique.

402 Universitas Carolina. (Charles University.)
http://www.cuni.cz/

This Czech- and English-language website welcomes the researcher to the oldest university in Central Europe. The site provides information on the history of this ancient institution and on its current structure and has a search facility for the names of the academic staff. Further information services cover newspapers, libraries, catalogues and the Charles University Press. The section called 'Study' is also intended for foreign consumption, given its coverage of Czech-language courses for foreigners and medical studies at Charles University.

403 Charles University.
Compiled by Helena Justová. Prague: Charles University, 1995. 198p.

A small, landscape-format guide to Charles University in Prague, which offers both a history and a profile of the institution as it is today. This is followed by a description of individual departments of the university and addresses and contact numbers of the management and administrative bodies.

404 Alma Mater Carolina Pragensis: výbor svědectví cizích návštěvníků. Charles University and foreign visitors.
Prague: Univerzita Karlova, 1988. 231p.

Opens with comments on Prague university by an Italian humanist, Uberto Decembrio, who came to Prague in 1399. A gallery of distinguished visitors to the oldest university in Central Europe progresses through the centuries and finishes with the inscription in the Carolinum visitors' book by the Secretary General of United Nations, Javier Pérez de Cuellar, in 1984. The book has many illustrations and photographs of the university and its visitors, and an index. The title page is in Czech and English, and the text is in Czech, English and Russian.

Statistická ročenka České republiky. (Statistical Yearbook of the Czech Republic.)
See item no. 416.

Comenius

405 Comenius: a critical reassessment of his life and work.
Daniel Murphy. Blackrock, Republic of Ireland: Irish Academic Press, 1995. 294p. bibliog.

This modern study is a post-1989 reappraisal of the Czech educator Jan Amos Komenský (Comenius). It rejects some of the Marxists' interpretations of his teaching.

128

The life of Comenius is reviewed, to illustrate his doctrine that a teacher should be an 'exemplar', as are the influences which helped to form his ideas and which were new at the time, and the principles of his liberal pedagogical philosophy. The leading principle was that the primary objective of education is the moral and spiritual formation of the individual. Murphy starts with a biographical portrait of Comenius and traces the cultural and historical roots of his educational ideas. Subsequently the author focuses on the legacy of the great educator: the vision of universal education; learner-centred methods of teaching; language education; and education as a lifelong process. The emphasis is on the unity and integrity of Comenius's educational ideas, which are derived from a liberal Christian faith. Murphy is well acquainted with contemporary Czech culture, refers frequently to the philosophy of Havel, the Czech president, and quotes from his speeches (Havel, in turn, is fond of quoting from Comenius), and to writers, thinkers and personalities such as Milan Kundera, Ivan Klíma and Josef Škvorecký. The conclusion offers an assessment of the importance of Comenius's ideas for the modern age and evaluates their significance in the context of contemporary, moral, religious, social, educational and political concerns. Murphy teaches education at Trinity College, Dublin. The book includes copious notes to the text and an index. A complete bibliography on Comenius would be massive and the author has selected books and articles dealing with education, either by Comenius himself or by scholars writing on his life and work (p. 288-90). *Panorthosia or Universal Reform* by Comenius has been translated by A. M. O. Dobbie (Sheffield, England: Sheffield Academic Press, 1995).

406   J. A. Comenius and the concept of universal education.
John Edward Sadler.   London: George Allen & Unwin, 1966. 318p. bibliog.

A very accessible description and interpretation of the basic theories and central concepts of the founder of modern education. These are here identified as: the 'Good Man'; encyclopaedic knowledge of the world about us and of ourselves; the 'Good Society'; and the didactic process. Comenius's philosophy of language is also described as are his ideas on the practical side of education, the nature and needs of schools and teachers, and textbooks. The bibliography has a number of references to earlier works on the Moravian educator.

407   Comenius.
Olivier Cauly.   Paris: Éditions du Félin, 1995. 342p. maps. bibliog.

This detailed yet accessible French biography in a classical, chronological format offers a modern assessment of Comenius as educator, Protestant theologian, philosopher and Czech patriot. Cauly calls the great educator the Galileo of modern education. The author includes several historical maps and illustrations and provides a bibliography and index.

408 **Jan Amos Comenius 1592-1992: theologische und pädagogische Deutungen.** (Jan Amos Comenius 1592-1992: theological and pedagogical interpretations.)
Edited by Klaus Gossmann, Christoph Th. Scheilke. Gütersloh, Germany: Gütersloher Verlagshaus Gerd Mohn, 1992. 167p. bibliog.
A collection of lectures published on the occasion of the 400th anniversary of the birth of Comenius. As the title indicates, the subject is the work of Comenius in the field of theology and education. The last chapter is on Comeniana in the 20th century.

409 **Homage to J. A. Comenius.**
Edited by Jaroslava Pešková, Josef Cach, Michal Svatoš. Prague: Karolinum, Publishing House of Charles University, 1991. 363p. bibliog.
Contributions to this homage are divided into two main sections: 'Comenius and the Czech and world culture'; and 'The traditions of pedagogical comeniology'. This collection of essays, all of which are in English, has been prepared by a number of Czech scholars to mark the 400th anniversary of the birth of Comenius in 1592. The book contains many photographs and illustrations. Some of the contributions have bibliographies appended.

410 **Johannes Amos Comenius (1592-1670): exponent of European culture?**
Edited by P. van Vliet, J. A. Vanderjagt. Amsterdam; Oxford; New York; Tokyo: Royal Netherlands Academy of Arts and Sciences, 1994. 115p. bibliog. (Koninklijke Nederlandse Akademie van Wetenschappen, Verhandelingen, Afd. letterkunde, Nieuwe reeks, deel 160).
The proceedings of a colloquium held in Amsterdam on 14 and 15 May 1992 in the presence of HM Queen Beatrix and commemorating the quatercentenary of the birth of Comenius. The contributing scholars were from the Czech Republic, the Netherlands, Germany and Switzerland. Approximately half of the papers are in English and the other half are in German. The themes of the lectures were: Comenius's pedagogy and its historical context; and Comenius's utopian bent and his place in the cultural history of Europe. There is a note on 'Contributors' (p. 3) and each paper has its own bibliography.

411 **Symposium Comenianum 1986: J. A. Comenius's contribution to world science and culture.**
Edited by Marie Kyralová, Jana Přívratská. Prague: Academia, 1989. 320p.
The majority of the papers presented at a symposium which took place at Liblice, Czechoslovakia on 16-20 June 1986, organized by the Comenius Institute of Education of the Czechoslovak Academy of Sciences and the Czechoslovak Committee for UNESCO. Seventy-six scholars from eleven countries took part; the papers were presented in English, German and Russian and they are reprinted here as such.

130

412 **Comenius 1592-1670: European reformer and Czech patriot, an exhibition.**
Oxford: Bodleian Library, 1992. 5p.

A guide to an exhibition of books by Comenius and the 'Map of Moravia' by Comenius. The introduction and comments are by the foremost specialist on 17th-century Central European history, Professor R. J. W. Evans of Oxford. The manuscript collection of the British Library houses a translation of an article by Jos. Volf: 'Pavel Eugene Layritz and his (In) Defence of Comenius', translated by V. Edmondson, *Časopis Musea Královstí českého*, vol. XCIV (1920), p. 177-90. The work of Layritz was published in 1742 and was frequently referred to by Palacký in his works on Comenius.

131

Statistics

413 **Labour statistics for a market economy: challenges and solutions in the transition countries of Central and Eastern Europe and the former Soviet Union.**
Edited by Igor Chernyshev. Budapest, London; New York: Central European University Press, 1994. 339p.
Prepared for the International Labour Office and written by leading international and national specialists, this publication is aimed at students and statisticians, explaining how and why the statistics are collected and what still has to be done to make the data from Central and Eastern Europe compatible with the rest of the world. 'The labour force survey in Czechoslovakia' (p. 111-18) is by B. Mejstřík and J. Kux, and 'Wage and labour costs statistics' (p. 179-82) by J. Kux. 'Annex 5' is 'Labour force sample survey in Czechoslovakia' (p. 299-314).

414 **Information dissemination and access in Russian and Eastern Europe: problems and solutions in East and West.**
Edited by Rachel Walker, Marcia Freed Taylor. Amsterdam; Berlin; Oxford; Tokyo; Washington, DC: IOS Press, in cooperation with NATO Scientific Affairs Division, 1997. 228p. bibliog. (NATO Scientific Series. Series 4: Science and Technology Policy, vol. 26).
The outcome of a workshop that took place at Essex University on 15-19 August 1997. The theme is social science networking, European cooperation, data and information transfer between Eastern and Western Europe, issues and challenges in the wider Europe, and development strategies. 'The collection and dissemination of social science information in the Czech Republic' is by Petr Matejů and Aviezer Tucker (p. 158-63).

415 **The quality and availability of statistical data.**
Jaroslav Jílek. In: *The Czech Republic and economic transition in Eastern Europe.* Edited by Jan Švejnar. San Diego, California: Academic Press, 1995, p. 103-18.

The author describes the changes in the methodology of statistical data collecting after the political changes of 1989, comparing them with the pre-1989 methods of data gathering and assessing the impact of the changes on the quality of the information produced by the official Czech statistical offices. The process of economic transition and the division of Czechoslovakia into two republics had, from the statistical viewpoint, considerably complicated the performance of the governments' statistical services, although despite countless problems they were able to supply regular statistical information. The available data have many weaknesses but these shortcomings are known and are being corrected. Meanwhile, the user must consider the strong and weak points of the information available. The article looks in particular at foreign trade statistics, price statistics, statistics on employment and unemployment and statistical forecasts. The author points out that the extent of the hidden economy in this country has not so far been systematically investigated.

416 **Statistická ročenka České republiky.** (Statistical Yearbook of the Czech Republic.)
Prague: Český Statistický úřad, 1993- . annual.

Previously published as *Statistická ročenka České a Slovenské federativní republiky* (Statistical Yearbook of the Czech and Slovak Federal Republic), this is the major source of statistical information on the republic. The textual apparatus in the tables and maps and the index are in Czech and English. Most of the data in the twenty-eight chapters are taken from the previous five years and offer 'basic indicators of national economy, area and climate, environment'. The yearbook is particularly strong on the environment. It is always a sizeable publication, the 1998 edition having 743 pages, and includes maps. Details of the coverage of the 1996 edition are listed below.

Section 2 (p. 48-61) is on area and climate and offers a brief description of the location of the land-locked country, its municipalities, fauna and flora and soils. The tables provide mostly climatic data.

Section 3 (p. 66-88) is on the environment and provides statistics on: investment in environmental pollution control projects; various polluters; public water supply; and sewage systems. A list of protected areas is given.

Section 4 (p. 89-118) is on population. The tables are based on the census; and statistics are taken from registries and various health and other institutions, such as the Institute of Health Information. The information is mostly in tables and charts and gives: the structure of the population by sex, age and marital status; life expectancy; marriages by age; divorces; birth statistics and reproduction rates; mortality rates; and the internal and external migration of the population.

Sections 1 (p. 26-47) and 5-21 (p. 119-530) deal with the economy, which forms the largest part of the yearbook. In Section 1 (p. 26-47), the reader will find the basic indicators of the economy. Sections 5-21 (p. 119-530) cover: the national accounts; finance; currency; prices; income; expenditure and consumption of the population; labour; tangible fixed capital; research and development; agriculture; forestry; industry and energy; construction; transport; communications; external trade; internal trade; tourism; market services; privatization; and organizational structure of the national economy. The text and descriptions in tables and maps and the index are in Czech and English. The data used are from the previous five years.

Sections 13 and 14 (p. 326-67) are on agriculture and forestry. The farm is the basic unit for records in the area of agricultural statistics and in this yearbook the figures on farms are divided into three categories: cooperative, private and others. The statistics provided are on: gross agricultural output; land use; sowing areas; harvest of main crops; fruit trees; livestock; fish husbandry; sales of agricultural products; and consumption of fertilizers. The forestry section is concerned with forest land, tree species, afforestation and reforestation, timber removal, pollution damage to forests, gamestock and hunting.

Section 15 (p. 368-401) covers industry and energy and provides the basic indicators for industry: industrial output; structure of industrial enterprises; industry finance; employees in industry and their wages; labour productivity in selected products; energy processes; power generation; and fuel consumption.

Section 22 (p. 532-57) is on education and gives a good account of the education system of the Czech Republic, explaining the types of schools, from pre-school education to university. The explanation of the system of secondary schools is useful, since this varies in many countries and Czech vocational training is particularly admired. Tables on both state and local education budgets are included.

Section 23 (p. 558-71) is on culture and sport. The information in the tables was supplied by the Ministry of Culture, Youth and Sports and the Institute for Information in Education. The tables analyse the membership structure of sport organizations and state allocation and expenditures. The medals won by Czechs at world and European championships are listed. The statistical data on culture, provided by the Ministry of Culture and the Institute for Information and Education, cover the activities of theatres, state orchestras, libraries, museums, galleries, observatories, planetariums and press. Statistics on Czech radio and television broadcasting are also given.

Section 24 (p. 573-89) provides brief information on: public health; infant mortality; beds in hospitals; the occurrence of infectious diseases; government and non-governmental health establishments; hospitals; pharmaceutical care establishments; physicians practising under the Ministry of Health, listed by main branch or activity; expenditure on health service; and selected financial indicators of health insurance companies.

Section 25 (p. 590-608) is on social security. The social security programme is divided into: pension security; sickness insurance and sickness benefits; assistance to mother and child; and social care. All these sections are represented by statistics and tables.

Section 26 (p. 603-27) comprises data relating to justice, crime and accidents. The information is based on figures and texts provided by the Ministry of Justice of the Czech Republic and the Ministry of Interior. The tables cover cases dealt with by district and regional courts of law, results of criminal proceedings and sentences in effect. Traffic accidents and fires are also analysed in tables.

417 Monthly Statistics of Czech Republic.
Prague: Czech Statistical Office, 1997- . monthly.

Published in Czech as a quarterly publication from 1964, as a monthly publication from 1967, and as a bilingual Czech-English monthly from 1997 onwards. The journal offers basic statistical data on the Czech Republic on a variety of topics, such as its external trade, consumer price index development, cost-of-living index numbers, industry, construction, job applicants and financial institutions.

418 **Fakta o sociální situaci v České republice.** (Facts about social conditions in the Czech Republic.)
Prague: Český statistický úřad, 1997. 372p.

The objective of this publication is to offer a statistical survey of the main areas of Czech society between 1975 and 1995. It does not claim to be comprehensive. It contains chapters on the following subjects: population; marriages; families; households; housing; environment; health and health care; education; social security; economic activity of the population; incomes and expenditures; and criminality and the protection of citizens. It is a large-format volume with numerous graphs, tables and explanatory text.

419 **Statistický lexikon obcí České republiky.** (Statistical lexicon of communities in the Czech Republic.)
Prague: Český statistický úřad, in cooperation with Ministerstvo vnitra ČR, 1994. 895p.

Based on the census dated 3 March 1991 and the administrative division of the territory in December 1991, this is a lexicon of regions, districts and communities (civil parishes) in the Czech Republic. The lexicon is divided into two main parts: the systematic section, which is a list of communities according to districts; and an alphabetical section. The names of towns and villages which are used are the official names currently in force. The census of March 1991 gives a breakdown of houses and flats, the structure of the population and its economic activity, and numbers of households, permanently inhabited dwellings and recreational homes. It also gives details of the areas surrounding villages, lists the relevant authorities and registry offices, the postal code and the nearest post office.

420 **Zdravotnická ročenka České republiky.** (Czech Republic Health Statistics Yearbook.)
Prague: Ústav zdravotnických informaci a statistiky, 1991. 162p. maps.

Originally published as *Zdravotnická ročenka ČSFR*. The publication is an annual series, with parallel Czech and English text, published by the Prague Institute of Health Information Statistics, and combines information from Czech statistical and health information bodies as well as from international institutions, such as the World Health Organization. The topics covered are: demography, people's health status, health establishments, their network and activity, manpower and financial data. The text is supplemented by maps, charts and figures.

421 **The family in the mother of towns. Today's Prague portrayed in statistical data.**
Prague: Statistical Office of Prague, 1994. 70p.

Published on the occasion of the United Nations' international 'Year of the Family' in 1994. The statistics analyse the age structure of the city, provide details of the marriage rate, birth rate, abortion rate and what is termed as substitute families, all with some historical background. Further information is on family stability, divorce and crime rate. Education is allocated a large section, as is family and households. The text is supplemented by humorous illustrations and good colour tables and diagrams.

135

Philosophy

422 **Slovník českých filozofů.** (Encyclopaedia of Czech philosophers.)
Edited by Jiří Gabriel, Josef Krob, Helena Pavlincová, Jan Zouhar.
Brno, Czech Republic: Masarykova univerzita, 1998. 700p.
The first Czech bio-bibliographical directory of philosophers, from earliest times to
the present, compiled from contributions by dozens of contemporary scholars. The
entries are 'philosophical profiles', which provide basic biographical data and information on the directions of each philosopher's work. Each profile is followed by a
bibliographical section which covers the author's monographs, transactions, articles,
prefaces, epilogues and editorial work. The directory includes foreign philosophers
who had connections with the Czech Lands, either biographical or through their work,
and entries for Slovak philosophers. This is due to the seventy years during which
Czechs and Slovaks lived in one state, but it is also recognized that the contacts
between the two countries cannot be limited to the period when Czechoslovakia was
in existence. The Slovak entries are written in Slovak and were compiled by Slovak
contributors. As to the subject coverage, the editors include philosopher-scientists,
theologians and artists, but the coverage of sociologists, particularly of contemporary
sociologists, is limited.

423 **Velvet philosophers.**
B. Day. *The Times*, 20 August 1998, p. 18.
British philosophers and academics played a crucial part in supporting the independent
spirit of the demoralized Czech academics and students in Communist Czechoslovakia
in the 1970s and 1980s. The British academics took part in unofficial seminars on
philosophy in the so-called Czechoslovak Underground University in Prague.

Politics

Political history

424 **The political history of Eastern Europe in the 20th century: the struggle between democracy and dictatorship.**
Sten Berglund, Frank Aarebrot. Cheltenham, England: Edward Elgar, 1997. 196p. maps. bibliog.

A study in comparative political science and micro-sociology. It is intended for political scientists and does not include much factual information, the stress being on comparative analysis. The authors identify several paradoxes: Eastern Europe has a substantial and stabilizing middle class, which is the result of, and is dependent upon, a modern educational system. The second paradox is the creation of a strong secular state and the third paradox is identified as 'electoral potential for mobilization along religious and nationalistic lines'. There are numerous references to the Czech Republic throughout the book and the authors provide many maps, charts, tables and indexes of names and subjects.

425 **National conflict in Czechoslovakia: the making and remaking of a state, 1918-1987.**
Carol Skalnik Leff. Princeton, New Jersey: Princeton University Press, 1988. 304p. bibliog.

'Czechoslovak history is almost a museum for the major political options of the twentieth century: parliamentary democracy, fascism and socialism.' The secondary political component of this history has been the unyielding Slovak quest for greater recognition. This studious treatise in nationalism takes the reader through the times when the republic was vulnerable – situations which were persistently used by the Slovaks to gain greater autonomy or complete independence – concentrating on the liberal First Republic, from 1918-38, and on the Communist state, which came into being in 1948. The book was published before the events which culminated in the separation of the Czechs and Slovaks, and the federal solution, instituted from 1969 as

137

a concession to Slovak demands, is here prophetically considered not to be the final stage which would pacify the national tensions. The volume includes tables, bibliographical references and an index.

426   **Czechoslovakia 1918-88: seventy years from independence.**
      Edited by H. Gordon Skilling.   Basingstoke, England; London:
      Macmillan Academic and Professional Ltd in association with
      St Antony's College, Oxford, 1991. 232p. bibliog.
      (St Antony's/Macmillan Series).

Presents contributions from two conference sessions, organized at the University of Toronto on 28 and 30 October 1988, the first date being exactly seventy years from the declaration of independence in Prague, the second date seventy years from the declaration by which Slovakia joined the new state. There was supposed to have been a parallel meeting in Prague, which the Czech police prohibited. The papers offer a scholarly re-examination of seventy years of history from the political, cultural and economic viewpoints. The ethnic conflicts between the Slovaks and the Czechs and the Czechs and the Germans are introduced and there is also a paper by Paul Robert Magocsi on Hungarians and Ruthenians. The appendixes are various contemporary documents. Each contribution is accompanied by separate bibliographical notes.

427   **Political culture – continuity and discontinuity.**
      Frederick M. Barnard.   In: *Czechoslovakia 1918-88: seventy years
      from independence.*   Edited by Gordon H. Skilling.   Basingstoke,
      England; London: Macmillan Academic and Professional Ltd in
      association with St Antony's College, Oxford, 1991, p. 133-53.
      bibliog.

This philosophical contribution to the Toronto conference in 1988 (see entry no. 426) looks back over the seventy years of the republic's existence. Barnard concludes with his belief in the continuity of political culture amidst change and despite change and his belief in the recovery of Masaryk's philosophy and ethical values. The author provides extensive bibliographical notes.

428   **Czechoslovakia between the wars: democracy on trial.**
      Z. A. B. Zeman.   In: *The Czech and Slovak experience: selected
      papers from the Fourth Congress for Soviet and East European
      studies, Harrogate, 1990.*   Edited by John Morison.   Basingstoke,
      England: The Macmillan Press; New York: St. Martin's Press, 1992,
      p. 163-66. bibliog.

By analysing language regulations and land reform in the First Republic, this short essay demonstrates that not all was perfect in the new democracy. The author writes that the new republic discriminated against the German minority at least as much as the Czechs had been discriminated against in the Habsburg Empire.

429   **Politické vzpomínky.** (Political memoirs.)
      Ladislav Feierabend.   Brno: Atlantis, 1994. 2nd ed. 2 vols.

These rather sorrowful memoirs of a Czech politician and patriot were first published by the author himself in 1965 and 1966 in Washington, DC. They cover the years between 1938 and 1948 and were assessed by political historians as an objective account by a person in high office. Feierabend was one of the captains of the Czech financial and industrial scene before the war. After Munich he was called by president Beneš into the government as a minister. In exile he was a member of all governments, but he resigned in February 1945, owing to disagreement with government policy, against the wishes of Beneš. The two volumes are entitled 'Ve vládách druhé republiky, srpen 1938 – běezen 1938' (In the governments of the Second Republic, August 1938 to March 1939) and 'Na londýnské frontě: od ustavení vlády v exilu až do napadení Sovětského svazu Hitlerem' (On the London front: from the establishment of the government in exile to the invasion of the Soviet Union by Hitler). The value of the memoirs rests in the account of the activities of the government in exile. Not much has been written about the Czech government in exile from 1943-45. Feierabend returned to Prague as a private person in 1945 but left again, for his second, permanent exile in 1948. He published other memoirs in Czech in exile publishing houses, but this collection is the most significant.

430 **The Czechoslovak government and its disloyal opposition: 1918-1938.**
Věra Olivová. In: *The Czech and Slovak experience: selected papers from the Fourth Congress for Soviet and East European studies, Harrogate, 1990.* Edited by John Morison. Basingstoke, England: The Macmillan Press; New York: St. Martin's Press, 1992, p. 89-101.
Olivová stipulates nationalism, republicanism and Communism as the main classification of the political thought of inter-war Czechoslovakia. She recognizes the influence of Masaryk in making the republic's pluralistic democracy viable.

431 **History of elections in Bohemia and Moravia.**
Oskar Krejčí. Boulder, Colorado: East European Monographs. Distributed by Columbia University Press, 1995. 425p. bibliog.
This rather dry contribution to the discussion on the importance of elections in democracy explains the concept of democracy and electoral choices before working its way from the parliamentarianism of the Estates in Bohemia and Moravia, starting with the assemblies at the time of the Přemyslide dynasty in the 9th and 10th centuries, to the 1992 elections in the Czech Republic, analysing and explaining its results. The latest election is given the greatest attention and the narrative is supported by charts, tables and graphs.

432 **The Czech fascist movement: 1922-1942.**
David Kelly. Boulder, Colorado: East European Monographs. Distributed by Columbia University Press, 1995. 243p. maps. bibliog.
There has been a fair amount written on the Czech fascist movement, but very little, if any, of this has been in English. The fear of Communism, anti-Semitism and resentment towards Masaryk and Beneš were the main reasons for the rise of the extreme Right in Czechoslovakia. Fascism has been consistently rejected from the very birth of the state and by the end of 1930s it was impossible to be a Czech patriot and a fascist at the same time. This book is aimed at a wide readership, not merely the modern historian. It includes copious notes, several tables, a substantial bibliography of primary and secondary sources and an index.

139

433 **The Czech red unions, 1918-1929: a study of their relations with the Communist Party and the Moscow International.**
Kevin McDermott. Boulder, Colorado: East European Monographs. Distributed by Columbia University Press, 1988. 350p. bibliog. (East European Monographs, no. CCXXXIX).

The general consensus in the West used to be that, in the 1920s, Stalin and the Soviet leadership increasingly ruled all activities of the world Communist movement. This book attempts to prove that the 'red trade unions' were not simply subjects of the Communist Party and of the Soviets but, on the contrary, managed to maintain a level of self-government and national differences. McDermott concentrates on the Czech Social Democratic and Communist trade unions and on the 'stormy relationship' between the International All Trade Union Organisation and the Communist Party of Czechoslovakia. The study is well researched and offers pages of explanatory notes, eight tables, a bibliography of archival and other sources consulted, and lists of: newspapers and periodicals; reports and proceedings of trade union and political party congresses; Comintern, Profintern and IFTU (International Federation of Trade Unions) sources; secondary sources; books and articles published in Czech and subsequently in English; and both published and unpublished doctoral dissertations dealing with the subject. The book also has an index.

434 **Lions or foxes: heroes or lackeys?**
H. Gordon Skilling. In: *Czechoslovakia 1918-88: seventy years from independence.* Edited by Gordon H. Skilling. Basingstoke, England; London: Macmillan Academic and Professional Ltd in association with St Antony's College, Oxford, 1991, p. 3-22.

This contribution to the Toronto conference (see entry 426) surveys seventy years of the political leadership of the Czechoslovak Republic. T. G. Masaryk, the founder of the republic, is predictably given the greatest attention, although all major Communist and non-Communist leaders are noted. The paper ends on an optimistic note, welcoming the 1989 election of Václav Havel as president, 'a leader of intellect and courage in the mould of Masaryk'. The paper is supplemented by bibliographical notes.

435 **Václav Klofáč and the Czechoslovak National Socialist Party.**
Bruce Garver. In: *The Czech and Slovak experience: selected papers from the Fourth Congress for Soviet and East European studies, Harrogate, 1990.* Edited by John Morison. Basingstoke, England: The Macmillan Press; New York: St. Martin's Press, 1992, p. 102-23. bibliog.

In the 1890s Václav Jaroslav Klofáč was one of the founders of the Czech (later Czechoslovak) National Socialist Party, of which he later became leader; he was a supporter of Masaryk. The party was influential in coalition governments and championed women's rights and social welfare.

140

436 **Antonín Švehla: master of compromise.**
Daniel E. Miller. In: *The Czech and Slovak experience: selected papers from the Fourth Congress for Soviet and East European studies, Harrogate, 1990.* Edited by John Morison. Basingstoke, England: The Macmillan Press; New York: St. Martin's Press, 1992, p. 124-35. bibliog.

Antonín Švehla was the leader of the Czech Agrarian Party in the last days of the Austro-Hungarian Empire, the leader of the Republican Party in the new Czechoslovak Republic and the prime minister of three coalition governments. The author appraises Švehla's friendly personality and influence and his successful endeavours in achieving political compromises and continuity.

The Communist era, 1948-89

437 **Cold War Europe, 1945-1991: a political history.**
John W. Young. London: Arnold, 1996. 2nd ed. 292p. map. bibliog.

The first edition was published by Arnold in 1991. This edition has been expanded to give a more detailed account of the events in Central and Eastern Europe after 1989, and social and economic development in Europe after 1989. It is a general study of forty years of tension, its rise and decline, the solidarity of Western Europe and the decomposition of Communism in Central and Eastern Europe. The book is intended for students of Europe and is readable and well organized, with a sizeable bibliography and index. Czechoslovakia is frequently mentioned *passim*.

438 **Return to diversity: a political history of East Central Europe since World War II.**
Joseph Rothschild. New York; Oxford: Oxford University Press, 1993. 2nd ed. 299p. maps. bibliog.

Highly thought of by many contemporary historians, this is a continuation of *East Central Europe between the two world wars* (q.v.) by the same author. The book starts with a good background section on the inter-war period and a chapter on the Second World War. In terms of content the author leans strongly towards the Second World War and its immediate sequel. A distilled, but factual and laborious political history follows, with numerous references to the situation in Czechoslovakia throughout the book. The final chapter, 'Epilogue', is in a cautiously positive vein. The author provides notes to chapters, maps, bibliography and an index.

439 **Politics in Czechoslovakia: 1945-1990.**
John F. N. Bradley. New York: Columbia University Press, 1991. 137p. bibliog. (East European Monographs, Boulder CCCXV).

Divided into two sections, part one is a history concerned mostly with the years from 1945-68, up to the Prague Spring, while part two is a valuable analysis of the constitutions and parliaments, the central government under Communism and the judicial system in Czechoslovakia.

440 **Culture, identity and politics.**
Ernest Gellner. Cambridge, England: Cambridge University Press, 1987. 189p. bibliog.

There are references to Czech nationalism throughout this book, but the chapter on 'The captive Hamlet of Europe' (p. 123-33) is specifically concerned with the Czechs after the suppression of the Prague Spring in 1968, the 'Hamlet' being the Czech intelligentsia, writers, teachers and thinkers. The basis of the chapter is a book by Milan Šimečka, *Obnovení pořádku* (The restoration of order), which was originally published in Germany (Cologne, Germany: Index, 1979). Šimečka was a dissident and philosopher, who continued to live in Czechoslovakia. His book is an account of Communism as a social form which existed in Czechoslovakia in the 1970s and which, however ugly, was viable and stable, and, at the time of his book's publication, seemed permanent.

441 **Political culture and Communist studies.**
Edited by Archie Brown. London: Macmillan, in association with St Antony's College, Oxford, 1984. 211p.

Two papers in this volume deal with the political culture of former Czechoslovakia: H. Gordon Skilling's 'Czechoslovak political culture: pluralism in an international context' (p. 115-33); and David W. Paul's 'Czechoslovakia's political culture reconsidered' (p. 134-48). Together they constitute a debate on the topic, with Skilling making references to Paul's earlier work, and Paul responding in part to the Skilling paper. Both consider the continuity, or otherwise, of pluralism in Czech and Slovak political culture, with relation to interior and exterior forces.

442 **Civic freedom in Central Europe: voices from Czechoslovakia.**
Edited by Gordon H. Skilling, Paul Wilson. Basingstoke, England: Macmillan Academic and Professional Ltd, 1991. 152p.

Eighteen Czech signatories of Charter 77 replied to Gordon Skilling's questionnaire sent out during 1986 and 1987. The questions were as follows: 1) Do you think the term 'Independent society' is relevant and meaningful under present conditions in your country?; 2) If so, what would you include as being essential features of an independent society?; 3) What are the immediate purposes of the independent activities and organizations thus conceived?; and 4) What are the long term implications and possible consequences of such an independent society?. The book contains 'Notes on the contributors' on p. xii-xiv. Appendix I is the 'Manifesto of the movement, civic freedom' (p. 135-43), and Appendix II (p. 148) consists of a list of Samizdat periodicals and a note on Samizdat series. The replies were translated by Paul Wilson. The book has an index.

443 **The Charta 77 Foundation: twenty years.**
Preface by František Janouch, articles by Antonín Hošťálek, Květa Jechová, Eva Kantůrková. Brno, Czech Republic: Atlantis, 1998. 144p.

Three personalities of contemporary Czech life – a journalist, a historian and a writer, plus a theoretical physicist (Janouch) – view the Charta 77 Foundation (Charter 77 Foundation), since the conception of this humanitarian institution in 1978. The Foundation initially received funds mainly from George Soros and supported publishing (a list of these publications is included in this bibliography), later diversifying into other fields, such as medical equipment. The articles draw on the archives of the Foundation in Prague and in Sweden – Janouch was the founder and chairman of the Charter 77 Foundation in Sweden. Kantůrková was one of the activists of Charter 77. The book lacks an index, which would have helped the reader to cross-reference names and events.

444 **The Communist Party in power: a profile of party politics in Czechoslovakia.**
Karel Kaplan, edited and translated by Fred Eidlin. Boulder, Colorado; London: Westview Press, 1987. 231p. (Westview Special Studies on the Soviet Union and Eastern Europe).

According to the author, the book '. . . seeks to describe the main features of internal life and functioning of a communist party. It reflects both the results of a historian's research and the long years of experience of a communist official and party aparatchik'. The Communist Party of Czechoslovakia was founded in 1921 and until the Second World War was one of the strongest political parties in Czechoslovakia. After the war it became the strongest party in the country and in February 1948 it became the party of power. The author provides tables and charts illustrating the structures of the party apparatus on various levels and an index.

445 **Human rights in Czechoslovakia.**
Prepared by the Czechoslovak Helsinki Committee, Prague, March 1989. New York; Washington, DC: US Helsinki Watch Committee; Vienna: The International Helsinki Federation for Human Rights, 1989. 115p.

This pamphlet is a period piece. Of interest is the chapter entitled 'Freedom of religion' (p. 27-29), since information about the churches in Czechoslovakia is not easy to find. There are short biographies and photographs of the members of the Czechoslovak Helsinki Committee. Some of them played significant roles in the events of November 1989 and in the new establishment.

446 **The making and breaking of Communist Europe.**
Zbyněk A. B. Zeman. Oxford: Basil Blackwell, 1991. rev. ed. 364p. map. bibliog.

The first edition was published in 1989 by Chatto & Windus under the title *Pursued by a bear*. It is an essay on the long rise of Communism in Europe and its sudden dissolution. The aim is to explain to the reader why Eastern Europe drew apart from Western Europe in the 20th century and why the partition between the two did not remain in place. Zeman does not claim to present a comprehensive account of 20th-century history in Eastern Europe; he is deliberately selective, avoiding the Holocaust and the crimes of Stalinism, and trying to focus instead on the circumstances which made these possible. Czechoslovakia, Russia, Poland and Germany and their leaders play the main roles in the narrative.

Contemporary: post-1989

General

447 **Revolution and change in Central and Eastern Europe: political,
economic and social challenges.**
Minton F. Goldman, with a foreword by Karel W. Ryavec. Armonk,
New York; London: M. E. Sharpe, 1997. 497p. maps. bibliog.

On the roots and causes of the collapse of Communism in the, now twelve, countries
of Central and Eastern Europe and the problems of post-Communist development.
'From Czechoslovakia to the Czech and Slovak Republics' (p. 113-54) concludes that
a smooth transition from the Communist system to democratic pluralism is attributable
to: an already established democratic opposition; the non-violent tendencies of the
Czechs and Slovaks; and the indifference of the Soviet Union. The most serious
problem is considered to be the revival of inter-ethnic prejudices between the Czechs
and Slovaks, which led to the split of the country. An extensive bibliography of
newspapers, documents, monographs, articles, reports and unpublished papers is on
p. 453-69.

448 **Czechoslovakia's Velvet Revolution: a political analysis.**
John F. N. Bradley. Boulder, Colorado: East European Monographs.
Distributed by Columbia University Press, New York, 1992. 140p.
bibliog.

Bradley gives a brief but informed historical background to the turbulent year of 1989,
starting from 1900, before embarking on a more detailed breakdown of the last twenty
years from a political point of view. The ten days of November 1989, the Velvet
Revolution, are the high point. The book then covers several subsequent months,
examining the political and legislative framework of the new state. Documentary
support is provided in a number of appendixes (declarations, speeches) but the book
lacks an index.

Separation of Czechs and Slovaks, 1 January 1993

449 **Slovaks and Czechs: an uneasy coexistence.**
Edita Bosák. In: *Czechoslovakia 1918-88: seventy years from
independence.* Edited by Gordon H. Skilling. Basingstoke,
England; London: Macmillan Academic and Professional Ltd in
association with St Antony's College, Oxford, 1991, p. 65-81. bibliog.

Professor Bosák provides a retrospective view of the seventy-year-old marriage and
beyond of the Czechs and Slovaks, and of attempts to create a Czechoslovak language.
She describes the differences as well as the similarities between the two nations. The
cautious hope which she puts forward in the conclusion – that the marriage might have
a future in a more open and democratic state – proved to be over-optimistic.
Czechoslovakia split into the separate states of the Czech Republic and Slovakia on 1
January 1993. The paper ends with bibliographical notes.

Politics. Contemporary: post-1989. Separation of Czechs and Slovaks, 1 January 1993

450 **The end of Czechoslovakia.**
Edited by Jiří Musil. Budapest, London; New York: Central European University Press, 1995. 283p. map. bibliog.

Written by eleven Czech and Slovak experts and by Sharon Wolchik from the United States and Jacques Rupnik from France, this publication is a result of three workshops organized by the Center for the Study of Nationalism of the Central European University, which was at that time in Prague (it is now in Hungary and Poland, with administrative offices in Budapest). Martin Brown reviewed this book in *BCSA Newsletter*, August/September 1998 (p. 9): 'Collectively, the essays are an insightful and well researched examination of the social dynamics at work in Czechoslovak society. However, the book contains an intrinsic weakness, one that excludes the possibility of it reaching concrete conclusions: the very proximity of the original workshops to the events they sought to investigate. As a result it lacks the overreaching perspective that only time can bestow. This is not a fatal flaw but one that is evident throughout the work and one that weakens its impact.' Wolchik's contribution is on the politics of the transition and Jacques Rupnik's is on the international context of the separation. The Czech and Slovak contributors assess the demographic, economic and social aspects of the split and the history of Czech-Slovak relations. The sections on demography and economics are supported by a number of charts and tables. Some of the contributions have individual bibliographies or bibliographical notes. The complete book has an index. The editor's conclusion in the introduction is that 'once more, on the Slovak as well as on the Czech side, liberal and democratic sources were taken aback by an outburst of nationalism'.

451 **Le divorce Tchéco-Slovaque: vie et mort de la Tchécoslovaquie 1918-1992.** (The Czech-Slovak divorce: the life and death of Czechoslovakia 1918-92.)
Fréderic Wehrle. Paris: L'Harmattan, 1994. 302p. maps. bibliog. (Collection 'Pays de l'Est').

A painstakingly researched study in geopolitics, nationalism and dualism as a political experiment, which leads the reader from the formation of Czechoslovakia in 1918, through the First Republic (1918-38), the Second Republic (1938-39), the war years (1939-45), the Third Republic (1945-48), the subsequent years of socialism, the Prague Spring of 1968 and the subsequent years of normalization to the years of the transition to democracy in 1989-92. This richly documented book contains numerous and detailed footnotes, tables, charts, an index and a bibliography of periodicals, articles, archive material, documents, statistical and reference material and books. The 'Chronologie succinte (1918-1992)' (Brief chronology, 1918-92) (p. 287-89) is of great interest and relevance.

452 **Czecho-Slovakia in transition: from federation to separation.**
Judy Batt. London: Royal Institute of International Affairs, 1993. 47p. bibliog. (RIIA Discussion Papers, 46).

The background to the split is investigated from the creation of Czechoslovakia in 1918 to the events of 1989 and their aftermath. The greatest attention is, however, accorded to domestic politics prior to the separation of the Czech Lands and Slovakia on 1 January 1993. The international dimensions of the split are examined and the statistics of the election results are analysed.

145

453 **Transition, fragmentation, recomposition: la Tchéco-Slovaquie en 1992.** (Transition, fragmentation, recomposition: Czechoslovakia in 1992.)
Compiled by Violette Rey. Fontenay-St. Cloud, France: ENS éditions, 1994. 194p. maps. bibliog.
A collection of articles printed in both English and French. The introductory article and the conclusion are by Violette Rey. The abstracts in English are on p. 177-80. Numerous maps, charts, tables and references document the evolution of the Republic of Czechoslovakia from 1990 to 1 January 1993, when it split into two, the Czech Republic and Slovakia. This political devolution is considered from a variety of angles: population migration; religious structure; economics; social factors; and geographical aspects.

454 **The structuring of political cleavages in post-Communist societies: the case of the Czech Republic and Slovakia.**
G. Evans, S. Whitefield. *Political Studies*, no. 46, 1 (May 1998), p. 115-39.
After their separation on 1 January 1993 the Czech Republic and Slovakia were faced with specific challenges in rebuilding their states. The countries have experienced different economic fortunes and different social problems, which have had an inevitable impact on party politics and the behaviour of the electorate in the respective countries.

Czech Republic, 1993-

455 **Who's who of Czech politicians.**
Compiled by Trade Links. Prague: Trade Links, 1998. 288p.
The directory was reviewed in *BCSA Newsletter*, no. 47 (February/March 1999), p. 9, by Angela Spindler-Brown. It lists the majority of current Czech politicians: the members of the government and the shadow cabinet and deputies and senators according to their party affiliation. Each entry is a brief biography. The coverage is not even; some senior politicians from recent history are omitted. The coverage of the directory also highlights certain specific features of Czech politics, such as the large number of senators, or the under-representation of women in politics. Wider coverage can be found in a little known volume, entitled *Kdo je kdo v České republice na přelomu 20. století* (Who is who in the Czech Republic at the turn of the 20th century) (Prague: Agentura Kdo je kdo, 1998. 734p.). The title is misleading – it should be 21st century – but this reference book is at present the most complete dictionary of contemporary Czech personalities.

456 **Czech Parliament.**
http://www.psp.cz/
An excellent site in terms of information provision, albeit in Czech only. The information offered is on members of parliament, parliamentary party clubs, documentation and the library, the parliament office and general news regarding the house.

457 **Reform of the socialist system in Central and Eastern Europe.**
Edited by Martin J. Bull, Mike Ingham. Basingstoke, England:
Macmillan Press Ltd, 1997. 208p. bibliog.

The complexity of transition, recent developments and current problems are examined
in this collection of articles. The economics of transition and the political changes are
the main theme. Other topics are civil society and civic life, ethnicity and nation,
Western aid, privatization processes and elections. The largest section of the book is
devoted to changes in the former Soviet Union. Most of the articles have their own,
sizeable bibliographies and the book has a common, detailed index.

458 **Why did the socialist system collapse in Central and Eastern
European countries? The case of Poland, the former
Czechoslovakia and Hungary.**
Jan Adam. Basingstoke, England; London: Macmillan; New York:
St. Martin's Press, 1995. 244p. bibliog.

Examines the reform process in Central Europe and the economic reasons for the
collapse of socialism in 1989. The initial successes of socialism are defended and a
viable alternative to capitalism is deemed possible. The combination of economic,
political, psychological, social and external factors contributed to the breakdown in
Central and Eastern Europe and in the former Soviet Union. The book is readable and
the references are useful.

459 **Czechoslovakia in transition: politics, economics and society.**
Sharon L. Wolchik. London; New York: Pinter Publishers, 1991.
390p. bibliog.

Begins with an outline of the modern history of Czechoslovakia, mostly of the 20th
century, and continues in fair detail with political developments since November
1989. The description of political life is factual and technical and the reader will find
information on the structure of the governments, the political parties, the presidency,
the armed forces, the ethnic composition of the population, gender issues and religion.
The text is supported by tables. The same approach applies to the chapters on the
economy and on environmental and education policies. The bibliography is large but
there are some regrettable spelling errors in Czech names.

460 **Citizenship and democratic control in contemporary Europe.**
Edited by Barbara Einhorn, Mary Kaldor, Zdeněk Kaván.
Cheltenham, England; Brookfield, Vermont: Edward Elgar Publishing,
1996. 239p. bibliog.

Zdeněk Kaván contributed 'Democracy and nationalism in Czechoslovakia' (p. 24-39)
to this collection of essays, the result of seminars organized by the University of
Sussex, where most of the contributors were active in the early 1990s. The essays are
divided into three sections: politics and nationalism; economics, privatization,
economic transition and the European Union; and social conditions, communications
and the media. Most of the essays contain references to the Czech situation.

461 **The Czech and Slovak republics: nation versus state.**
Carol Skalnik Leff.   Boulder, Colorado: Westview Press, 1997. 295p.
maps. bibliog.

Leff refers to this complicated topic as 'triple transition': the democratization, marketization and the national transformation of post-Communist Czechoslovakia, which ultimately culminated in the paradoxical disintegration of a state that most of its citizens wished to preserve. At the time of publication, this was a compelling, definitive review of post-Communist Czechoslovakia. The book also relates to the situation in the whole of contemporary Central and Eastern Europe which makes it of importance to those seeking a better understanding of that entire region. Leff's account is clear and objective and, like all of her books, it is carefully researched. There is an index, as well as maps and a bibliography. This is a serious contribution to political science.

462 **Political changes in Eastern Europe since 1989: prospects for liberal democracy and a market economy.**
Robert Zuzowski.   Westport, Connecticut; London: Praeger, 1998.
165p. bibliog.

Chapter five, 'Czech Republic: Czechs are different' (p. 97-118), is a comparative study, explaining why the Czechs had made more progress than the other East European countries. In economic, as in political terms, the Czechs only had to do a U-turn to a 'not too distant and well remembered past' and were able to re-establish a stable liberal democracy with a workable economic system founded on market forces. The reader is offered further information in a sizeable 'Select bibliography' (p. 149-60) of articles and books, all recent. The book has an index.

463 **Eastern European development and public policy.**
Edited by Stuart S. Nagel, Vladimir Rukavishnikov.   Basingstoke,
England: St. Martin's Press, 1994. 244p. bibliog.

On the political and economic transformation in post-Communist European countries. Other topics dealt with are environmental issues, social policy and social conditions, and economic conditions. The book has a subject index.

464 **Innovations in public management: perspectives from East and West Europe.**
Edited by Tony Verheijen, David Coombes.   Cheltenham, England:
Edward Elgar Publishing Limited, 1998. 432p. bibliog.

The reform of public administration in the post-Communist countries was judged by the politicians to be a minor issue and not enough attention was paid to the importance of its efficiency. Economic activity in a market economy requires a proper framework of state administration; an inefficient one can be a grave obstacle to the reform of the economy. Although none of the contributions deals specifically with the Czech Republic, this collection of papers assesses the considerable difficulties encountered by the post-Communist countries in redefining and redesigning their administrations, and questions whether the experiences and models of Western Europe can be used and applied in Central and Eastern Europe to provide answers to the problems. Some of the papers have their own bibliographies and there is a common index (p. 427-32).

465 **Institutional design in new democracies: Eastern Europe and Latin America.**
Edited by Arend Lijphart, Carlos H. Waisman. Boulder, Colorado; Oxford: Westview Press, a division of Harper Collins Publishers, 1996. 265p.

A collection of essays by American, Central European and Latin American scholars on the process of political and economic liberation. The two systems compared are dissimilar and the contributors seek to explain why there are different constitutional choices in the trends towards democracy in Latin America and Eastern and Central Europe and to foresee the impact of these changes on the final forms of democracy. There is not much specifically on the Czech Republic, but the concept of comparing diverse systems is new and interesting. Each essay has bibliographical 'Notes', and the volume has notes 'About the editors and contributors' (p. 251-53) and an index (p. 255-65).

466 **Forging ahead, falling behind.**
With an introduction by J. F. Brown. Armonk, New York; London: M. E. Sharpe, 1997. 428p. maps. (The OMRI Annual Survey of Eastern Europe and the Former Soviet Union, 1996).

This is the OMRI's second annual survey of political developments in the countries of the former socialist bloc. The Czech Republic section (p. 10-20) has the following sub-chapters: 'Maverick Czech reformers get bogged down' by Jiří Pehe; 'Czech secret police scandal – a storm in a teacup?' by Steve Kettle; 'Collapse of Czech Kreditní Banka turns criminal – and political' by Ben Slay; and 'Czech parties' views of the EU and NATO' by Jiří Pehe.

467 **Party formation in East-Central Europe: post-Communist politics in Czechoslovakia, Hungary, Poland and Bulgaria.**
Edited by Gordon Wightman. Aldershot, England: Edward Elgar Publishing Company, 1995. 270p. maps. bibliog. (Studies of Communism in Transition).

Several articles deal specifically with the Czech Republic. Chapter four, 'The development of party system and the break up of Czechoslovakia', is by G. Wightman (p. 59-98). Chapter five is on 'Changing party allegiances in a changing party system: the 1990 and 1992 parliamentary elections in the Czech Republic', by Tomáš Kostelecký (p. 79-106). This article includes a number of maps showing the constituencies in the Czech Republic for the 1990 and 1992 parliamentary elections and electoral support for the various parties. Chapter ten questions the 'Impediments to the development of democratic politics: a Czech perspective' and is by Zdeněk Zbořil (p. 202-16). The book has a good, sizeable multilingual 'Bibliography' (p. 252-62).

468 **The security policy of the Czech Republic.**
Prague: Institute of International Relations, 1997. 103p. bibliog.

A research report on security, defence and the protection of the citizens of the Czech Republic. The country's security policy contains three fundamental components: foreign policy in respect of security concerns; the defence and military policy of the state; and internal security and public order. The publication will be of interest to journalists and it provides useful statistics; for example, 'The development of crime in the Czech Republic 1989-1995' (p. 95-100) reveals a threefold increase in criminal offences in this period.

469 **Postcommunist elites and democracy in East Europe.**
Edited by John Higley, Jan Pakulski, Wlodzimierz Wesolowski.
Basingstoke, England: Macmillan Press Ltd; New York: St. Martin's Press, Inc., 1998. 301p. bibliog.

'Czech and Slovak political and parliamentary elites' by Lubomír Brokl and Zdenka Mansfeldová (p. 131-40) analyses the elections in Czechoslovakia, and the successor Czech Republic, since 1945. The book itself concludes: 'The extremely sudden and comparatively comprehensive collapse of the "frozen" Czechoslovak Communist regime during the first days in November 1989 produced significant elite discontinuities. There were enough new elite groups with an interest in sharpening their anti-Communist images and credibilities to make a relatively serious programme of decommunization possible, though only for a brief period and only with limited practical consequences'.

470 **Struggling with the Communist legacy: studies of Yugoslavia, Romania, Poland and Czechoslovakia.**
Edited by P. W. Klein, A. W. Helweg, B. P. McCrea. Boulder, Colorado: East European Monographs. Distributed by Columbia University Press, 1998. 256p. maps. bibliog. (East European Monographs, no. DX).

This collection of studies would appear from its title to be relevant to research in contemporary Czech politics. In fact it is mostly concerned with the Yugoslav situation and there is only one contribution, out of nine, on Czech politics. However, this paper is by Carol Skalnik Leff who has a unique knowledge of Czech society: 'Elite transformation in Post-Communist Eastern Europe: the case of disappearing dissidents' (p. 191-221).

471 **Postnational identity: critical theory and existential philosophy in Habermas, Kierkegaard and Havel.**
Martin J. Matuštík. New York; London: The Guilford Press, 1993. 329p. bibliog. (Critical Perspectives: A Guilford Series).

A response to Havel's characterization of the end of the Communist era as an 'existential revolution', meaning 'the awakening of human responsibility, spirit and reason'. The play on the stage of the world has changed from competition between the politics and economics of two systems – capitalist and Communist – to issues of national identity, religion and fundamentalism. From this summary it is obvious that the study, which brings together critical theory and existential philosophy, is intended for the serious reader. It is supplemented by painstakingly compiled 'Notes', a bibliography of primary sources cited (p. 265-71), a large 'Bibliography of secondary works' (p. 307-20) and an index.

472 **The art of the impossible: politics and morality in practice.
Speeches and writings, 1990-1996.**
Václav Havel, translated from the Czech by Paul Wilson et al. New
York; Toronto: Alfred A. Knopf, 1997. 273p.

Represents a selection of thirty-five speeches and articles by Václav Havel, translated
from the hundreds written and delivered during his presidency up to 1996, along with
some which were selected from a collection published privately by Havel himself. The
speeches are in chronological order and start with the first of Havel's annual
presidential New Year's addresses on 1 January 1990 and his address to the United
States Congress in February 1990. The latest speeches included were given at Trinity
College, Dublin, on 28 June 1996, and at the Academy of Performing Arts in Prague
on 4 October 1996. The criteria for selection were, in Havel's own words: 'the
fundamental questions of our civilisation, questions I have tried to answer . . . more as
an inhabitant of this planet than as a representative of my country'. The translations of
the speeches and writings are excellent and the book is well produced. The 'Notes'
contain comments on each of the entries as to the venue and timing, the reasons for
the speech or article and on the translation. The index (p. 265-73) is comprehensive.

473 **Summer meditations: on politics, morality and civility in a time of
transition.**
Václav Havel, translated from the Czech by Paul Wilson. London;
Boston, Massachusetts: Faber & Faber; New York: Alfred A. Knopf,
Inc.; Toronto: Alfred A. Knopf Canada, 1992. 149p.

This book was originally published in Czech as *Letní přemítání* in Prague by Odeon in
1991. The title and the headings of the individual chapters indicate the theme of the
meditations: 'Politics, morality and civility'; 'In time of transition'; 'What I believe';
'The task of independence'; and 'Beyond the shock of freedom'. Among other points,
Havel argues the question of national rivalries, the traumas of change and the
transition. His conclusions are considered by many as being unique to political life,
but he demonstrates ethical and political consistency. For example, he answers the
question, which a politician might be expected to avoid, whether being a politician has
caused him to modify and abandon his ideals as they developed in his life and in his
writings. These ideals were influenced by his youth, his imprisonment and harassment
by the police under Communism, but did not fundamentally change when Havel
became president. Paul Wilson added a 'Translator's preface' (p. ix-xi), in which he
explains how this edition differs from the original, and valuable explanatory
'Background notes' (p. 133-49), providing a key to words, phrases and names in the
text. Havel himself wrote the 'Foreword' to the English edition. The translation is
particularly good.

474 **The work of Václav Havel.**
Robert B. Pynsent. *Slavonic and East European Review*, vol. 73,
no. 2 (April 1995), p. 269-81. bibliog.

Discusses Havel's speeches and essays from 1992 and 1993 and compares the views,
therein expressed, with his earlier literary work, particularly plays and essays. The
accent now is on the contemporary issue of national and political identity. Havel's
former literary work was satirical, demonstrating his appreciation of anecdote, but
there is little sign of this in his current work. Havel stopped writing plays and his
essays are written to complement his duties as President of the Republic.

475 **Living within the truth.**
Peter Phillips. *Month*, vol. 26, no. 9/10 (September-October 1995), p. 368-72. bibliog.

Another philosophical assessment of Havel's work, on the manner in which he addresses his fellow countrymen in times of trouble and on the contemporary plight of Western society. Each human being has lines of conflict running right through him and Havel maintains that living in truth is the only possible way to create an environment within which we can be proud of what it entails to be human.

476 **The moral leader of Europe.**
Timothy Garton Ash. *The Independent*, 21 October 1998, 'The Wednesday Review', 'Comment', p. 5.

The subtitle is 'Havel has the breadth of vision and skill to remind us of the larger issues'. This article was written on the occasion of the second state visit of Václav Havel as President of the Czech Republic to the United Kingdom. This visit was fairly low-key and little reported by the media. Ash is one of the best qualified journalists in Britain on the subject of Havel, whom he has known for a long time, and on Czech-British relations. This article is included here because it is an excellent summary of both. Havel is portrayed as a writer and politician who, despite adversity, consistently holds moral standards. Ash provides a sketch of Czech-British relations in the past and produces some apt and perceptive observations on the present.

477 **Empty victory for conqueror of tyranny.**
Christopher Lockwood. *The Daily Telegraph*, 19 October 1998, p. 10.

This article was also written on the occasion of Havel's four-day state visit, starting on 19 October 1998. Lockwood introduces Havel as the giant on the European stage, with remarkable political longevity, and assesses the playwright-president's career. The role of the President in the Czech Republic is largely ceremonial, but carries great moral weight. The article is included here because it highlights Havel's current dilemma: under Communism his aim was the defence of the individual against the mighty state; now, the economically successful country appears to be in the hands of people whose main concern is their personal advancement. This attitude is widespread in the country. Freedom and unbridled individualism have their own costs and Havel, the philosopher, may eventually consider himself a failure. This is not the most informed article, but it is an interesting one. It includes a photograph of Havel and his second wife, Dagmar.

478 **The tragedy of king Havel.**
J. Keane. *The Sunday Times*, 19 April 1998, section 5, p. 10.

Václav Havel, the President of the Czech Republic, appears to be exhausted physically and politically. Over the twelve months prior to the publication of this article, he had been admitted to hospital four times. His other ailment is one which is common to many politicians, that is, failure to realize that his time is up. Havel's problems are here considered symbolic of the universal Czech malaise.

International Relations

General

479 **The international politics of East Central Europe.**
Adrian Hyde-Price. Manchester, England; New York: Manchester University Press, 1996. Distributed exclusively in the USA and Canada by St. Martin's Press. 300p. maps. bibliog.

Intended for the student of international relations, European politics and international history. East Central Europe is understood in this work as Hungary, Poland and the Czech and Slovak lands. Hyde-Price, who teaches politics and international relations at Southampton University, analyses the changes which have occurred in the region since the collapse of Communism in 1989 from the point of view of international relations: the altering bilateral relationships and the prospects of multilateral cooperation and conflict. The author highlights the influence of history, national identity and geopolitics and examines relations with the Western countries and with the newly formed states to the east of the region. Inevitably, security issues are also analysed. The author expects the 'return to Europe' of these countries to have a significant impact on, and implications for, internal politics and issues of national identity, and looks into the next century, when the dynamics of European integration and the international system may be considerably changed. The textbook is supplemented by: pages of bibliographical notes to each chapter; a good 'Select bibliography' (p. 289-92) of recently published books; simple maps; and an index (p. 293-300).

480 **International migration in Central and Eastern Europe and the Commonwealth of Independent States.**
Edited by Tomas Frejka, with the assistance of Rosina Bisi. New York; Geneva: United Nations, 1996. 143p. bibliog. (United Nations Economic Commission for Europe. United Nations Population Fund. Studies no. 8).

In the introduction Frejka identifies the reasons for the recent increased level of international emigration in Central and Eastern Europe. Chapter five, on the 'Czech Republic', by Jarmila Marešová (p. 49-56), provides a brief history of emigration from Czechoslovakia from 1918, before focusing on migration after 1989. Marešová looks at the migration movement by geographical area, at the structural characteristics of migrants, at information on the migration processes, and the role of policies and politics. The chapter has tables on emigration and immigration and a list of 'References' (p. 55-56). At the time of writing, the Central European University Press was preparing for publication *Safe third countries: extending the EU asylum and immigration policies to Central and Eastern Europe* by Sandra Lavenex (Budapest, 1999. 200p.). The book has three chapters: part one, 'Refugees and international relations'; part two, 'Emergence of a European refugee regime'; and part three, 'Extension of the European refugee regime'.

481 **Refugees in inter-war Europe: the emergence of regime.**
Claudena M. Skran. Oxford: Clarendon Press, 1995. 324p. bibliog.

Identifies the origins of the refugee movement in the 1920s and 1930s and assesses the international response to the phenomenon. The concept of international 'regime', which continues to have impact on refugee policy to this day, is understood as the efforts of governments, the League of Nations and private organizations. The first international refugee law was developed during the period this book is concerned with and the refugee issues, explored here, are as highly relevant as ever to contemporary international politics. The Czechs and the Czech Jews are mentioned throughout the book, and so is Czechoslovakia, its relations with the League of Nations and its own attitude to refugees. This excellent study is complemented by a good bibliography (p. 297-314) which lists archive collections, League of Nations documents (official records, reports by the High Commissioner for Refugees 1921-30), other official sources, newspapers and periodicals, contemporary publications and modern published material. Incidentally, this inter-war period witnessed the largest emigration wave, the majority of emigrants being economic migrants, due to high levels of unemployment, from Slovakia. Most of the migrants departed for the United States and Canada, and fairly large flows went to Romania and Yugoslavia.

482 **Británie a Česká republika. Britain & the Czech Republic.**
London: Foreign & Commonwealth Office, 1996. 37p. + 16p.

A glossy official publication produced on the occasion of the state visit of Her Majesty The Queen and His Royal Highness The Duke of Edinburgh to the Czech Republic, March 1996. The introduction is by The Prince of Wales. The text was published as Czech and English versions, but only the Czech version has illustrations and photographs; the English reader is referred to the Czech version for these. The book starts with the history of Czech-British relations, stressing the royal links, and continues with the current commerce and investment situation, academic and cultural links and language teaching. Several personalities with Czech-British connections contributed their life stories (John Tusa, Geraldine Mucha, Joy Kadečková). Also included is a history of the beautiful building of the British Embassy and the Ambassador's Residence in Prague, the Thun Palace, and a list of relevant contact addresses in the Czech Republic and in the United Kingdom (embassies, the British Council, commercial organizations and expatriate organizations).

483 **A history of British-Czech relations.**
Jaroslav Peprník. *Perspectives*, no. 7 (summer/autumn 1996), p. 12-21.

This is perhaps the best recent survey of this topic, starting with the mediaeval ecclesiastical (positive) and secular (less positive) contacts and ending with Elizabeth II's visit to Prague in 1996 (the trigger for this article in the British Council's Prague-published journal). The less positive secular contact refers to the defeat of John of Luxemburg, King of Bohemia, by Edward III at the Battle of Crécy in 1346; its sequel was the appearance of the eagle feathers from King John's helmet as the ostrich feathers on the emblem of the Prince of Wales. Much is made of the story of the Winter Queen, Elizabeth, daughter of James II. The article covers the numerous journeys between the two countries by alchemists, artists, theologians, musicians, journalists, grammarians, politicians and academics (T. G. Masaryk combined both of these latter roles). Contacts and cooperation came in trade and warfare, historiography and literary translation, and in the teaching of the respective languages and culture. One obvious omission from this (as from most earlier surveys) is the role of (St) Edmund Campion who was – as an Englishman in Bohemia – probably as important on the Catholic side as his non-Catholic predecessors had been during the Reformation and earlier.

484 **Britain and Czechoslovakia: a study in contacts.**
Josef V. Polišenský. Prague: Orbis, 1968. 2nd rev. ed. 98p. bibliog.

The 'contacts' of the title have a long and respectable history, though the first of many fascinating facts in this slim volume does not count as a contact proper; this is Alfred the Great's *Anglo-Saxon Chronicle*, in which he writes about the Slavs. As Polišenský says in the introduction, there are many manifestations of contact, but he concentrates, in the space available, on 'a mixed company of medieval princes and princesses, bishops and revolutionaries, industrial pioneers, diplomats, scholars and politicians'. He also includes an outline of indirect contacts, i.e., the picture of each country in the other's literature. The book ends (p. 86-92) with a useful comparative chronology of the two countries, and the work contains some relevant illustrations.

485 **Grossbritannien, die USA und die bömischer Länder 1848-1938: Vorträge der Tagung des Collegium Carolinum in Bad Wiessee, vom 2. bis 6. November 1988. Great Britain, the United States and the Bohemian lands 1848-1938.**
Edited by Eva Schmidt-Hartmann, Stanley B. Winters. Munich: R. Oldenbourg Verlag, 1991. 392p. bibliog. (Forschungstelle für die Böhmischen Länder, Band 16).

Papers from this international symposium cover the broad, multi-faceted relations between Bohemia and the United States and Britain. The topics are varied: Jews from the Bohemian lands in the United States; Czech and Slovak musicians in the United States; the British concept of Bohemia and the Czechs; Czech literature in Britain; the Anglo-American influence on Czech economics; the development of English studies in Czech universities; politics; and diplomacy. The contributors, mostly British, American, Czech and German scholars, are leading names in Czech studies: Fred Hahn, Harry Hanak, James Naughton, David Short, Nancy M. Wingfield, Stanley B. Winters (on the Czech historian Otakar Odložilík), Victor Mamatey, Mark Cornwall, Yeshayahu Jelinek (on T. G. Masaryk), Christopher Seton-Watson (on his father, R. W. Seton-Watson) and Peter Drews. This collection of contributions has bibliographical footnotes and an index. Vilém Prečan's study, 'British attitudes towards Czechoslovakia, 1944-45', *Bohemia*, Bd. 29, Heft 1 (1988), p. 73-87, is concerned with the last years of the war.

486 **Canada and Czechoslovakia.**
Josef Vincent Polišenský, translated from the Czech by Jessie
Kocmannová. Prague: Orbis, 1967. 60p. bibliog.

Examines Canadian-Czechoslovak relations from prehistoric times to the mid-19th century (relations of a frequently but understandably tenuous nature), the involvement of North American Czechs and Slovaks in the movement for Czechoslovak independence, and political, cultural and commercial relations between the two states. Illustrations and a comparative chronology of the histories of the two countries are included.

487 **Češi a Slováci ve 20. století.** (Czechs and Slovaks in the 20th century.)
Jan Rychlík. Bratislava: Academic Electronic Press, 1997, 1998.
2 vols.

Based on archival sources, many of which are reprinted in the books, this is an analysis of Slovak politics in relation to Czechs and Czechoslovakia. The author's original intention, based on realization of the general Czech lack of knowledge of Slovak history, was to acquaint the Czech reader with Slovak attitudes. The theme, therefore, was the different standpoints of Czech and Slovak communities on constitutional arrangements and principles of Czechoslovakia. The second volume suffers, as the author himself acknowledges, from lack of time distance from the recent events, such as the devolution of Czechoslovakia. Volume one is entitled 'Česko-slovenské vztahy: 1914-1945' (Czech-Slovak relations: 1914-45) and volume two is 'Česko-slovenské vztahy: 1945-1992' (Czech-Slovak relations: 1945-92).

488 **Die Sowjetunion und die Verteidigung der Tschechoslowakei
1934-1938: Versuch der Revision einer Legende.** (The Soviet Union
and the defence of Czechoslovakia 1934-38: an attempt at a
reassessment of a myth.)
Ivan Pfaff. Cologne, Germany: Bohlau, 1996. 510p. bibliog.

The author is trying to shed new light on the foreign policy of the Soviet Union in the crucial years between 1934 and 1938 and on the relationship with Czechoslovakia. The causes and origins of the Second World War are reexamined in this vast volume.

489 **The Soviet Union in Eastern Europe: 1945-89.**
Edited by Odd Arne Westad, Sven Holtsmark, Iver B. Neumann.
New York: St. Martin's Press; Basingstoke, England: Macmillan Press
Ltd, 1994. 234p. bibliog.

A collection of articles, translated from various languages, on the international
relations of the Soviet Union in Central and Eastern Europe from the end of the
Second World War in 1945 until the end of Communism in 1989. The general articles
describe the stages of Soviet control, the various regimes, and the return to diversity in
the late 1980s. The articles also address some secondary issues, for example: the role
of the mass media; and civil resistance in the East European and Soviet revolutions of
1989-91. 'Czechoslovakia, the Soviet Union and the Marshall Plan' (p. 9-25) is by
Karel Krátký.

490 **Češi a Němci: ztracené dějiny? Tschechen und Deutsche: verlorene
Geschichte?** (The Czechs and the Germans: the lost history?)
Prague: Nadace Bernarda Bolzana, 1995. 406p.

Presents papers from the fourth Czech-German conference on current problems of
mutual relations which took place in Jihlava, Czech Republic in the spring of 1995.
The theme of this conference was Czech-German relations in the fifty years after the
end of the Second World War and in the five years after the radical changes in Central
Europe. All the papers are published here in Czech as well as in German. The
contributors were prominent politicologists, historians, sociologists and the clergy.

491 **Czechs and Germans: a study of the struggle in the historic
provinces of Bohemia and Moravia.**
Elizabeth Wiskemann. London; Melbourne; Toronto: Macmillan;
New York: St. Martin's Press, 1967. 2nd ed. 299p. maps. bibliog.

Although written in the heat of the events leading up to the war (the first edition was
published in 1938), this work is still regarded by many as a classic. It traces the full
history of the rivalries, animosities and perfidies between the two nations and the
conflicting claims and counter-claims to dominance in the Lands of the Czech Crown,
from the prehistoric movements of the Germanic tribes to the 20th century. It is
factually sound and, for the modern age, is based on the author's broad range of
contacts among both communities. The author presents a wide-ranging picture,
portraying economic and cultural, as well as political, aspects. Wiskemann is also
frank in admitting doubts as to the correctness of some of the information she was
given – doubts which were not misplaced.

492 **Czechoslovak-Polish relations, 1918-1939: a selected and annotated
bibliography.**
Chester Michael Nowak. Stanford, California: Hoover Institution
Press, 1976. 219p. (Hoover Institution Bibliographical Series, no. 55).

An annotated bibliography of 869 publications up to 1972. It is a good source for
works relating not just to the ups and downs of the two countries' political and
economic relations, but also to individual border areas (such as Teschen) that have
mixed populations on both sides of the frontier.

493 **A radiant future: the French Communist Party and Eastern Europe: 1944-1956.**
Richard Sacker, edited and with a preface by Michael Kelly. Bern; Berlin; Frankfurt, Germany; New York; Paris, Vienna: Peter Lang, 1999. 344p. bibliog.

A study of one of the strongest of the Communist movements which influenced international politics in Europe. The chapter on show trials in Eastern Europe in 1948-52 has a section on 'The Slansky trial' (p. 85-90) and there is also a chapter on 'The French Communist party and the uprisings in Czechoslovakia and East Germany (1953)' (p. 129-66). Sacker draws on original sources and archive material and the book has a sizeable bibliography (p. 319-44), but the study lacks an index to guide the reader to names and events.

494 **Italy and East-Central Europe: dimensions of the regional relationship.**
Vojtech Mastny. Boulder, Colorado; Oxford: Westview Press, 1995. 131p. bibliog.

Published in cooperation with the Bologna Center of the Johns Hopkins University, Paul Nitze School of Advanced International Studies. The papers collected here were originally prepared for a conference held in Bologna in 1992, but were updated two years later. Italy was expected to play a major part in helping the ex-Communist countries to re-integrate into Europe. The essays examine the diverse aspects of the contacts between Italy and, among the other ex-Communist countries, Czechoslovakia. Vojtech Mastny, a professor at Johns Hopkins University, provides the historical background, focusing on the Risorgimento, the Habsburgs and the First World War. The other papers are concerned with the Italian Communist Party, with ethnic strife and with the European Union. Each chapter has bibliographical 'Notes', and the book contains several tables, notes 'About the editors and contributors' (p. 121-22) and an index (p. 123-31).

495 **Československo a Izrael, 1945-1956: dokumenty.** (Czechoslovakia and Israel, 1945-56: documents.)
Edited by Marie Bulínová, Jiří Dufek, Karel Kaplan, Vladimír Šlosar. Prague: Institute for Contemporary History AV ČR in cooperation with the Czech Army Historical Institute and the Central State Archives, 1993. 399p.

Comprises sources from the Central State Archives, the Archives of Military History, archives of the President's Office and of the Ministry of Interior and other archives of state bodies and of the Communist Party. Czechoslovakia supported the demands of Jewish and Zionist organizations to divide the former Palestine into two states. It was also one of the first countries to recognize, in May 1948, the state of Israel and to establish diplomatic relations. This collection of documents in Czech has a chronology of events (p. 369-76), a 'List of published documents' (p. 381-92) in English and a name index (p. 393-99).

496 Československo a Izrael, 1947-1953: studie. (Study on Czechoslovakia and Israel, 1947-53.)
Jiří Dufek, Karel Kaplan, Vladimír Šlosar. Prague: Institute for Contemporary History, 1993. 203p.

Compiled from archival sources by Czech historians, this study examines Czechoslovak-Israeli relations, the emigration of Czech Jews to Israel and the material and technical aid Czechoslovakia provided to Israel: armaments, military training and the voluntary brigade. The study has English 'Summary' by Karel Kaplan (p. 199-203).

International security

497 East European security reconsidered.
Edited by John R. Lampe, Daniel N. Nelson, in collaboration with Roland Schonfeld. Washington, DC: Woodrow Wilson Center Press, distributed by John Hopkins University Press, 1993. 217p. bibliog. (Woodrow Wilson Center Special Studies).

The book originated in a conference, 'Redefining regional society and the new foreign policy in Eastern Europe', held in Potsdam, Germany, on 23-26 June 1992, at the site of the 1945 Allied Conference. The articles cover a broader spectrum than the title suggests: domestic change and international relations; the position of Germany, as newly defined in relation to Central Europe; the security viewpoints; the process of change in the military in the region; the Višegrad Triangle (Czech Republic, Poland, Hungary, Slovakia) and the western lands of the CIS (Commonwealth of Independent States – former Soviet Union); minority problems and politics. Each paper has rich bibliographical notes and the book has a joint index.

498 New forms of security: views from Central, Eastern and Western Europe.
Edited by Pál Dunay, Gábor Kardos, Andrew J. Williams. Aldershot, England; Brookfield, Vermont; Singapore; Sydney: Dartmouth, 1995. 165p.

A collection of commentaries, divided into three sections, with self-explanatory titles: 'On rethinking of military security', 'Rethinking of economic security' and 'Rethinking of humanitarian security'.

499 **Economic development and reforms in cooperation partner countries: the role of the state with particular focus on security and defence issues: Colloquium 17-19 June 1998, Ljubljana, Slovenia.**
Brussells: NATO Office of Information and Press, 1998. 301p.

Thirty-two speakers, unfortunately none of whom were from the Czech Republic, represented the business world, academia and governmental institutions at this colloquium. The speeches and discussions were on pertinent issues concerning the role of the state in transition economies (industrial restructuring, budgetary policies, social networks, shadow economy and foreign economic relations). The emphasis was on defence and security-related issues.

500 **NATO's Eastern dilemmas.**
Edited by David G. Haglund, S. Neil MacFarlane, Joel J. Sokolsky.
Boulder, Colorado; San Franciso; Oxford: Westview Press, 1994. 231p.

Although this focuses on the Yugoslav question, some of the chapters are relevant to Czech issues, such as the American response to European nationalism, NATO's *Ostpolitik* in post-Cold War Europe and the transformation of civil-military relations in Central Europe.

501 **Česká zahraniční politika: Česká republika v Radě bezpečnosti OSN: 1994-1995.** (Czech foreign policy in the United Nations Security Council: 1994-95.)
Prague: Ústav mezinárodních vztahů, 1997. 109p.

The Czech Republic was elected to the Security Council and became a member of the United Nations in the first year of its existence in 1945. This brochure defines the role and activities of the Czech Republic in the Council and reproduces the speeches of Czech delegates.

502 **Growing the alliance.**
Javier Solana Madariaga. *The Economist*, vol. 350, no. 8110 (13-19 March 1999).

Javier Solana, the Secretary General of NATO, played a leading role in NATO's expansion. In this leading article, published on the day of the Czech Republic's entry into NATO in 1999, he argues that the alliance's expansion, at this stage to include the Czech Republic, Hungary and Poland, will help to reshape Europe's security system for the 21st century. All quality British newspapers covered this event.

503 **NATO handbook: a companion volume to the 50th anniversary edition of the NATO handbook, 1998.**
Brussells: NATO Office of Information and Press, 1998. 90p.

The Czech Republic, Poland and Hungary became members of NATO on 12 March 1999. Published to accompany *NATO handbook: 50 anniversary edition* (Brussells: NATO Office for Information and Press, 1998. 400p.), the chronology in this volume takes the researcher from 1949, the year of NATO's establishment, to 11 November 1998. This small pamphlet records the world events effecting NATO, the activities of NATO, visits of state dignitaries (the latest Czech visit being the visit to NATO by the Prime Minister of the Czech Republic Miloš Zeman), agreements and negotiations.

Constitution and Law

Central and Eastern Europe

504 **Constitution making in Eastern Europe.**
Edited by A. E. Dick Howard. Washington, DC: Woodrow Wilson Center Press, distributed by The Johns Hopkins University Press, 1993. 215p.

Chapter three, 'Czecho?Slovakia: constitutional disappointments' by Katarina Mathernová (p. 57-92), is concerned with the constitutional development of the federation of Czechs and Slovaks. This article was written in January 1992 but was reviewed during the year and a few lines were added after the 'velvet divorce' of Czechs and Slovaks on 1 January 1993. There are references to the Czech and Slovak Federal Republic in most of the other chapters of the book. The book is well documented and has an index. *East European Constitutional Review* offers a country-by-country update on constitutional policies in Eastern Europe and the ex-USSR. The latest one is in vol. 7, no. 2-3 (1998), p. 2-42.

505 **Parliaments in transition: the new legislative politics in the former USSR and Eastern Europe.**
Edited by Thomas F. Remington. Boulder, Colorado; San Francisco; Oxford: Westview Press, 1994. 246p. maps. bibliog.

The transformation of governments in Eastern Europe into democratic systems started with a series of parliamentary elections and in some countries these elections had the function of a referendum on ending Communist rule. Some of the contributions in this collection of essays are general and deal mostly with Russia and Czechoslovakia among the other countries. There is a specific chapter, 'The sundered state, federalism and parliament in Czechoslovakia' (p. 97-123) by David M. Olson, Professor of Political Science at the University of North Carolina. His essay concentrates on the last periods of the Federal Assembly, from the first democratic elections in 1990, after the Velvet Revolution, to the 'sundering' of the state on 1 January 1993, when

161

Czechoslovakia broke in half, into the Czech Republic and the Slovak Republic. It is mainly a comparative study of various parliamentary systems, but the bicameral system, based on the former federal state, its structure and composition, unicameralism and tricameralism, legislative rules procedures, their sources, elections and political parties are described in fair detail. Each chapter has its own 'References'. Olson's, on p. 120-23, is a sizeable bibliography of books, articles and reports from the early 1990s. The book has a section 'About the contributors' (p. 233-35) and an 'Index' (p. 237-46).

506 **Transforming East European law: selected essays on Russian, Soviet and East European law.**
Kaj Hobér. Uppsala, Sweden: Justus Forlag, 1997. 550p.

Kaj Hobér is Adjunct Professor of East European Commercial Law at Uppsala University. His essays are mostly in English and the majority are concerned with legislation in the former Soviet Union. However, there are several short articles specifically on Czech constitutional law (p. 478-80, 493-94, 498-99, 502-03), but these are in Swedish. The whole book should be of interest to practising lawyers, who are currently confronted with practical legal issues in that area, and it should help them to comprehend the legal systems in Eastern Europe and the profound changes these systems are undergoing. An academic lawyer might use the book as a teaching and research tool. The articles cover a period of almost ten years and address a wide variety of areas of law, ranging from legal regulations of the planned economy to privatization legislation, the civil code and constitutional law. At the time of writing the Central European University Press was preparing for publication *Administrative law in Central and Eastern Europe*, edited by Denis J. Galligan and Daniel M. Smilov, both of University of Oxford (Budapest: Central European University Press, 1999. 350p.).

507 **Central and East European legal materials.**
General editor Vratislav Pechota. Ardsley-on-Hudson, New York: Transnational Juris Publications; London: Graham & Trotman; Dordrecht, the Netherlands: Kluwer Academic, 1990- . 7 vols. + bi-monthly supplement.

The volumes publish acts, laws and other legal material concerning trade, commerce and business generally. The books are divided by country. The 1990 volume covers, in the Czechoslovakia section, the following material: 'Act on Economic Relations with Foreign Countries, 19. April 1990'; 'Law on State Enterprise of April 19, 1990'; 'The Enterprise with Foreign Property Participation Act of April 19, 1990'; 'The Foreign Stock Companies Act'; and 'Czechoslovakia-USA: Agreement on Trade Relations between Czechoslovakia and the United States of April 12, 1990'.

508 **East-Central European states and the European communities: legal adaptations to the market economy.**
Edited by Peter Christian Muller-Graff. Baden-Baden, Germany: Nomos, 1993. 235p. (ECSA-Series, vol. 2).

A collection of essays, translated from various languages, on economic transformation in the Czech Republic, Poland and Hungary after 1989. The focus is on legislation and legislative compliance with the directives of the European Union.

162

509 **Privatization in Eastern Europe: legal, economic and social aspects.**
Edited by Hans Smit, Vratislav Pechota.   Dordrecht, the Netherlands: Martinus Nijhoff Publishers; Irvington-on-Hudson, New York: Transnational Juris Publications, 1994. 255p. bibliog.

The Czech element is strong in this first-class collection of essays. One of the introductory articles is a 'Luncheon address delivered by former Prime Minister of the Czech Republic', by Petr Pithart (p. 18-20). The concepts, objectives, modalities and methods of privatization are dealt with in the first section. The second section of the book is on the subsidizing and financing of the privatization. The subsection on voucher privatization includes 'The development and regulation of investment funds in the Czech and Slovak Republics: a case study on the use of intermediaries in the privatization process' by Kristine DeKuiper (p. 74-88). Part three, on the practical aspects of privatization, has a large subsection on 'Privatization in the successor states of former Czechoslovakia', which contains four essays by various authors. One 'Annex' of the book is a 'List of privatization laws' (the Czech Republic is covered on p. 244), another is 'Bibliography on privatization in Eastern Europe' (p. 247-55), a listing of mostly articles from juridical and economic journals.

510 **Intellectual property rights in Central and Eastern Europe: the creation of favourable legal and market preconditions.**
Edited by Elmar Altvater, Kazimiera Prunskiené.   Amsterdam; Berlin; Oxford; Tokyo; Washington, DC: IOS Press, 1998. 187p. (NATO Science Series, Series 4: Science and Technology, vol. 25).

This is a collection of scholarly studies on the protection of intellectual property, industrial property and technology, intellectual property laws and patent laws. 'Industrial property protection and technology licencing in the Czech Republic in 1998' is by V. Husáková (p. 121-25).

511 **Promises, promises: contracts in Russia and other post-Communist economies.**
Paul H. Rubin.   Cheltenham, England; Northampton, Massachusetts: Edward Elgar, 1997. 85p. bibliog.

'The Czech Republic, Hungary and Poland' is on p. 27-30. Czechoslovakia had more of its legal system adapted to Communism than most of the other Communist countries. The Czech and Slovak Federal Republic adopted a new civil code and a new commercial code in 1991. This monograph applies legal and economic scholarship to the issue of succeeding in achieving efficient, meaning wealth-maximizing, methods of enforcing agreements and in this way facilitating exchanges with post-Communist countries.

163

Czech Republic

512 The Constitutional Court of the Czech Republic.
http://libra.concourt.cz/.
This website, in English, provides a general description and contact information, plus cases and legal materials.

513 Legal guide, Czech Republic: general report.
London: DTI Export Publications, 1997. 73p. bibliog. (URN 97/6234).
Prepared by Cameron McKenna, a major international law firm which has offices in Prague. This reference work, which starts with a country fact file, contains an introduction to the civil law and to business law and gives advice on setting up a company in the territory of the republic. There are chapters on foreign investment, privatization, agency distribution and franchise agreements, property, planning and construction law, taxation, employment and pensions, dispute mechanism, settlement and arbitration, and on future directions and European Union harmonization. In common with all Department of Trade and Industry guides, the publication provides lists of information sources in the Czech Republic, information sources in the United Kingdom and a list of related DTI publications (p. 70). A treatise on *Criminal law reform in the Czech Republic in the interdisciplinary perspective* has been published in Brno, Czech Republic (Masarykova universita, 1997).

514 Commentary on the Czechoslovak Civil Code.
Th. J. Vondracek. Dordrecht, the Netherlands; Boston, Massachusetts; Lancaster, England: Martinus Nijhoff, 1988. 473p. bibliog. (Law in Eastern Europe, no. 37).
Provides a translation of, and commentary on, the Civil Code of Czechoslovakia. The format is the text of the statute with an extensive annotation by the author – the commentary smoothly combines judicial and scholarly opinion. It has numerous references to court cases. Czechoslovakia had strict partition between civil law and economic law, the former sphere being that of the private life of the citizen. This civil code was ideologically socialist and was changed after 1989. Fundamentally, though, Czechoslovakia was a former member of Austria-Hungary and its civil law is historically closely tied to the legal world of Central Europe, despite the temporary ideology due to belonging to the Soviet bloc. Above all, this civil law may be socialist, but it has definite Czechoslovak features. The Czech law is succinct and comprehensible to a person with average education. The author provides an index.

515 Human rights and democratization in the Czech Republic.
Prepared by the Staff of the Commission on Security and Cooperation in Europe, Washington, DC. Washington, DC: Commission on Security and Cooperation in Europe, 1994. 32p. map. (Implementation of the Helsinki Accords).
The title is self-explanatory. This paperback investigates the Czech Republic's progress with regard to human rights, the achieved level of democracy and the general relationship between society and politics.

Statistická ročenka České republiky. (Statistical Yearbook of the Czech Republic.)
See item no. 416.

Business law

516 **Czech Republic: businessman's guide to Czech legislation in 1995-96.**
Compiled by Trade Links. Prague: Trade Links, 1995. 182p. map.
A useful paperback which starts with an introduction to the geography, history and constitution of the Czech Republic. The main section of the guide is concerned with: economic reforms; foreign direct investment; the commercial code; the trades licensing act; the foreign exchange act and financial legislation; taxation; accounting; labour-related legislation; social security and health insurance; foreign trade and the customs code; the public procurement act; anti-trust legislation; and the bankruptcy and composition act.

517 **Business law guide to the Czech Republic.**
Jennie Mills, David Roach, Ian Rowbotham. Bicester, England: CCH Editions Limited, 1994. 329p.
Published under the auspices of Norton Rose, the major international law firm, and Price Waterhouse, one of the largest organizations of accountants and consultants, this provides comprehensive information about the legal system in the Czech Republic and summarizes and discusses the main areas of Czech law, the cut-off date being 31 May 1994. This very good book in hardback format and with a substantial, quality index is intended for business people but should also be of interest to the legal and tax profession. Jennie Mills is an expert on the European Union and has published articles on Czech law.

518 **Tschechisches und slowakisches Wirtschaftsrecht: ausgewahlte Gebiete.** (Czech and Slovak business law: selected areas.)
Jan Dědič, Christian Baumgartner. Vienna: Service Fachverlag, 1994. 233p. bibliog. (Schriftenreihe des FOWI, Bd. 5).
Considers the commercial law of the Czech Republic and legislative provisions concerning business. Another publication in German, offering help with the legal side of business for foreign partners, is *Wirtschaftspartner Tschechische Republik* (Business partner Czech Republic), edited by Hans-Wolfgang Arnst, Peter Jäger and Peter Kutschera (Bonn: Economica, 1995. 135p.). A more comprehensive volume which also covers other Central and East European countries is the large *Handbuch Wirtschaft und Recht in Osteuropa* (Handbook of business and law in Eastern Europe), edited by Stephan Breidenbach (Munich: C. H. Beck, 1994. 2,232p.).

519 **A wolf in sheep clothing: the 1996 Amendments to the Czech Commercial Code.**
Prague: Allen & Overy, 1996. 21p.

Concerns the key points of the most radical amendments to Czech corporate law since 1989, the year of the Velvet Revolution, which were published in May 1996. The amendments represent a major overhaul of Czech company law and introduce the bases of the takeover code. The sweeping legislation combines changes to the law governing public disclosure rules, mergers and acquisitions, shareholder's agreements, minority shareholder protection and director's liability. The Act brings Czech legislation in the corporate field into line with legislation in the European Union countries.

520 **Immobilienerwerb in der Tschechischen Republik.** (Property business in the Czech Republic.)
Gerhard Schmidt, Johannes Prinz Lobkowicz. Cologne, Germany: RWS Verlag, 1996. 96p. (RWS-Skript, 281).

An explanation of the Czech laws concerning real estate.

Local government

521 **Local government in Eastern Europe: establishing democracy at the grass roots.**
Edited by Andrew Coulson. Aldershot, England: Edward Elgar, 1995. 291p. maps.

A collection of essays intended for students of politics, as background material and basic information for visitors and consultants who may encounter local state officials, but also for politicians, administrators and academics in Eastern Europe, to help them to understand how others are tackling problems similar to their own. The book starts with an overview of contemporary local governments of Central European countries and continues with 'a series of specialist studies, focusing on local government, finance, management skills, local economic development, housing and the relationship between the elected and appointed government'. Chapter three, 'The Czech and Slovak Republics', by Kenneth Davey of the University of Birmingham, traces the history of local government in the Czech and Slovak republics to the system in former Austria-Hungary, summarizes the Communist system of local administration, and outlines the principles of reform and the new structures. The subchapters in the book are also relevant to the student of the Czech situation because they provide general coverage of local government finance, municipal enterprises and property and the management of services.

522 **Local government and market decentralization: experiences in industrialized, developing and former Eastern Block countries.**
Edited by Robert J. Bennett. Tokyo; New York; Paris: United Nations University Press, 1994. 506p. maps. bibliog.

This is a detailed examination of the former Eastern Bloc, the possibilities for decentralization and the limitations of such a move. Section four, 'Central-local relations under the new Czechoslovak constitutional law' (p. 67-75) by Pavel Zarecký, evaluates the significance of local government, describes the 1990 reforms of the local government, the division of the country into administrative areas, sectoral bodies and the basic level of government.

Economy

Reference

523 **Kompass: Czech Republic 1997, company information, products and services: directory of industry and commerce of Czech Republic.**
Prague: Kompass Czech Republic a.s., 1997. 6th ed. 1,480p.
A volume which is similar to that produced by Kompass for British companies. It is published by a part of Kompass International, which started publishing in Switzerland in 1944. As such it provides company information in a uniform manner, the classification system covering 50,000 products and services. This sixth updated Czech edition has data collected up to 31 January 1997 on more than 11,000 companies. This Kompass database is available in all types of media: in the form of a catalogue, as described here; on CD-ROM; in the data network Dialog; on the Internet; and, for the Czech Republic, in the data network PVT. The electronic form is updated monthly and is available in various languages, including English. The book form is published in April each year; the CD-ROM is updated in August and December.

524 **Inform katalog 93/94: katalog českých podniků. Directory of Czech companies.**
Brno, Czech Republic: Inform Katalog, 1994. 4th ed. 2 vols. maps.
Published in Czech, English and German, this has become a standard reference work which offers, in volume one, profiles of nearly 15,000 Czech companies, in alphabetical order. This is followed by a list of companies by region, the entries again being arranged alphabetically within the region entry. Volume two is an index of products and services by subject.

168

525 **Inform, katalog, export 1995: Czech trade and investment promotion.**
Brno, Czech Republic: Inform Katalog, 1995. 3rd ed. [unpaged]. maps.
An English-language publication which consists of several distinct sections. The first section has articles by leading Czech economists on the development of Czech foreign trade, the liberalization and harmonization of import and export legislature, quality guarantees, export customs procedures and Czech customs tariff systems, licensing procedures, VAT and excise duty. The second section is an index of products and services, and the third and largest section is a subject catalogue of leading Czech exporters. The last section is an alphabetical index of the companies. Inform Katalog also published *Czech exporters and importers 98* (Prague: Inform Katalog, 1997. unpaginated).

526 **The Prague Post 1998 book of business list: key business and financial data on more than 1,500 top Czech companies.**
Prague: The Prague Post, 1998. 4th ed. 142p. map.
Intended for use by the business community to search for new clients and to analyse investment potential, this book, which has been published annually since 1995, provides an overview of market sectors and specific industries. It is published in English, but some of the headings are also in Czech, and it is heavily dependent on advertising. The main section, in which companies are arranged by subject, is supplemented by an alphabetical list of companies.

527 **Grosse und mittelständische Unternehmen in der Tschechischen Republik. 1996.** (Large and medium-size enterprises in the Czech Republic, 1996.)
Prague: Hoppensted Bonner Information, 1996. 3rd ed. 1,039p. + 126p. (supplement).
A handbook published in German and English. Its introductory section includes an alphabetical list of companies, giving their location. The main part of the handbook consists of entries providing brief company profiles. This section is arranged alphabetically, by place-name. The last section of this reference book lists the companies by their products. The English of this handbook is awkward, but this should not distract the user of this otherwise sound reference tool.

528 **Eastern Europe market atlas.**
Researched by Corinne Yee. Hong Kong: The Economist Intelligence Unit, 1994. 206p. maps.
While there are a few maps in this atlas, by far the largest part of the publication consists of graphs and charts on: economy, finance, investment, agriculture, energy, industry, trade, banking, stock markets, tourism, retailing, consumers, cost of living, operational costs, labour, population and health, education and information, environment, government, defence, infrastructure, transport and communications. A good political and economic survey of the region is provided by *Eastern Europe and the Commonwealth of Independent States, 1999* (London: Europa Publications Ltd, 1999. 4th ed. 1,004p. Regional Surveys of the World). This vast volume contains country surveys, the Czech Republic being covered on p. 300-30.

169

Statistická ročenka České republiky. (Statistical Yearbook of the Czech Republic.)
See item no. 416.

Economic history

529 **Central Europe in the twentieth century: an economic history perspective.**
Edited by Alice Teichova. Aldershot, England; Brookfield, Vermont: Ashgate, 1997. 1,174p. maps. bibliog. (Eastern Europe in Transition).

Alice Teichova, a leading specialist on Central European economic history, contributed the introduction and a general article on 'Economic development during the Interwar and Postwar period' (p. 5-27). Michael C. Kaser wrote 'Property rights and debt in East-West European relations' (p. 147-57). The other articles in this collection deal with the individual countries. Václav Průcha, Professor of Economic History at the Economics University in Prague and President of the Czech Economic History Association, is the author of 'Continuity and discontinuity in the economic development of Czechoslovakia 1918-91' (p. 23-41). Each article has its own explanatory notes and some have lists of further reading. The book has a number of tables, 'Notes on Contributors' (p. viii-ix) and a general 'Index' (p. 161-74) for all the articles.

530 **The Czechoslovak economy: 1918-1980.**
Alice Teichova. London; New York: Routledge, 1988. 178p. map. bibliog. (Contemporary Economic History of Europe).

An outline of the economic history of Czechoslovakia by an Emeritus Professor of Economic History at the School of Economic and Social Studies, University of East Anglia. Teichova lived in Czechoslovakia for twenty years and left in 1968. After the introduction the text is divided into two sections: part one, Czechoslovakia: 1918-45, and part two, Czechoslovakia after the Second World War. The first section is a standard economic history, surveying the structure and growth of the population, migration, minorities, distribution of employment, social class and social mobility, and education, before proceeding to analyse individual sectors of the economy and the state's economic policy. The second section is a more challenging description of the reconstruction after the Second World War: the change from multinational to binational state, from free economy to centrally planned economy. Teichova provides tables for the various topics mentioned above and offers a 'Select bibliography' (p. 154-66) of books and articles which shows the scarcity of English material on the Czech economy at the time this book was being prepared. There is also an 'Index' (p. 167-78). This work was also published in German as *Wirtschaftsgeschichte der Tschechoslowakei 1918-1980* (Vienna: Böhlau, 1988).

531 **The Czechoslovak economy 1948-1988: the battle for economic reform.**
Martin Myant. Cambridge, England: Cambridge University Press, 1989. 316p. bibliog. (Soviet and East European Studies, no. 65).

The book was compiled before the political changes in Czechoslovakia took place in 1989 and only reflects on the restructuring which Gorbachev was introducing in the Soviet Union in the late 1980s. The economic performance of Czechoslovakia over those forty years was not disastrous, but economic growth was slower than in neighbouring countries. This comparison is not a true indicator of the situation, however, since between the wars the national income per capita in Czechoslovakia was considerably higher than that, for example, in Hungary and Poland. Particular attention is given to the creation of the new socialist economic system in the early 1950s and to the reforms of 1968. The work is well documented by notes, tables, an extensive bibliography and an index.

532 **From capitalism to socialism.**
Radoslav Selucký. In: *Czechoslovakia 1918-88: seventy years from independence.* Edited by Gordon H. Skilling. Basingstoke, England; London: Macmillan Academic and Professional in association with St Antony's College, Oxford, 1991, p. 154-73. bibliog.

A contribution to a conference in Toronto in 1988 by a professor of economics, which starts further back than the scope of the conference, from before 1918, and continues until the 1970s, providing a good, brief summary of the country's economy from an international perspective. The author provides bibliographical notes.

533 **The Council for Mutual Economic Assistance – the new tasks.**
Zdeněk Chalupský. *Czechoslovak Economic Digest,* no. 6 (September 1989), p. 52-64.

A Czech economist summarizes the Council for Mutual Economic Assistance's progress towards economic integration up to the early 1980s, then discusses in greater detail the work of the 43rd (Extraordinary) and 44th CMEA Session and the 1987 Working Meeting. He argues that closer coordination and cooperation is needed in order to complete the transfer to 'a modern economy of intensive type', and that 'the strategy of socio-economic development must be based above all on the internal resources of the socialist community with simultaneous use of all possibilities for effective participation in the worldwide division of labour [...]'. Similar arguments are used in František Stránský's 'Greater integration is the solution', *Czechoslovak Economic Digest,* no. 3 (May 1989), p. 16-20; he stressed that 'the CMEA possessed unique sources of fuel and raw materials, a numerically strong scientific-technological base, a labour force of average qualification, and unique reserves in the use of materials capities [sic] and labour'; what it lacks is an effective economic system.

171

534 **Reforms in the foreign economic relations of Eastern Europe and the Soviet Union: proceedings of a Symposium conducted in association with Osteuropa-Institut Munich and Sudost-Institut, Munich.**
Edited by Michael Casper, Aleksandar M. Vacic. New York: United Nations, 1991. 199p. (United Nations Economic Commission for Europe. Economic Studies, no. 2).
The papers in this indispensable volume were completed in August-September 1990. Chapter three, 'Economic relations with CMEA countries', includes a paper on Czechoslovakia by Vratislav Válek. Each paper provides some historical background, surveys current intra-CMEA (Council for Mutual Economic Assistance) relations and presents plans and ideas for economic cooperation with other (former) socialist states in the future. The papers are discussed by three Western experts: Jozef M. van Brabant, Marie Lavigne and Wolfram Schrettl. The whole debate was remarkably frank, even acrimonious, lively and sometimes emotional, revealing a wide range of opinions over the need to retain some form of regional cooperation after the collapse of the CMEA.

535 **The external relations of the Council for Mutual Economic Assistance.**
Arie Bloed. Dordrecht, the Netherlands: Martinus Nijhoff, 1988. 257p. bibliog.
Bloed provides a detailed and authoritative analysis of the legal aspects of the CMEA's external relations. Topics covered include the CMEA's decision-making process, the legal character of CMEA resolutions and the increasing importance of the CMEA's external relations. Chapter five is a detailed investigation of the controversy over the CMEA's powers in the field of external relations, and the following chapter deals with the competent organs and procedural aspects. Chapter seven covers relations with third states (including those with observer status) and relations with other international organizations, both socialist and non-socialist. Chapter eight is a thorough survey of the most important legal issues in the relations between the CMEA and the European Community.

536 **National income and outlay in Czechoslovakia, Poland and Yugoslavia.**
Jaroslav Krejčí. London: Macmillan, 1982. 122p. bibliog.
This book is a comparative and quantitative analysis of socio-economic systems, their structural aspects and development. Heavily based on statistics, this analysis focuses on GNP and concentrates mainly on the division of national income and on living standards. The numerous tables in the text and in the appendix span the period between 1961 and 1978.

Post-1989

Central and Eastern Europe

537 **The political economy of transition: coming to grips with history and methodology.**
Jozef M. van Brabant. London; New York: Routledge, 1998. 559p. bibliog. (Routledge Studies of Societies in Transition).

A theoretical treatise explaining the nature of the process of transition towards political democracy and a market economy in Central Europe and the sustainability of this transition. It is an extremely detailed study in which the components of the transformation agenda are analysed: stabilization; internal and external liberalization; privatization and the market economy; the role of institutions in the market economy; transformation and the socio-political consensus; the evolving role of the state during the transition; integration into the world economy; and international assistance. A comprehensive bibliography of books, reports and articles can be found on p. 508-39. The latest theoretical work on the subject is by Martin Potůček, Professor of Sociology at Charles University in Prague: *The role of the market, government and civic sector in the development of postcommunist societies* (Budapest: Central European University Press, 1999. 250p.).

538 **Remaking Eastern Europe – on the political economy of transition.**
Jozef M. van Brabant. Dordrecht, the Netherlands; Boston, Massachusetts; London: Kluwer Academic Publishers, 1990. 223p. bibliog. (International Studies in Economics and Econometrics, vol. 23).

Brabant draws on his long experience of studying East European economics and the Council for Mutual Economic Assistance (CMEA) in particular to discuss developments in the area in the late 1980s. He then considers the problems of transition to a market economy, looking in particular at assistance from the West and the idea of a new 'Marshal Plan'; property rights and privatization; and the place of the planned economies in transition (PETs) in the world economy. He argues that the CMEA should be retained in some form because of: the existing dependencies in Eastern Europe (trading partners, oil, infrastructure); the lack of a flexible trade and payments system that would enable quick switching of markets at a tolerable socio-economic and political cost; and the exploitation of static and dynamic comparative advantages, some of which derive from there being an active CMEA. This is an excellent analysis of the last year of the CMEA and the options for its future.

539 **The transformation of economic systems in Central Europe.**
Herman Willem Hoen. Cheltenham, England; Northampton, Massachusetts: Edward Elgar Publishers, 1998. 203p. bibliog. (Studies in Comparative Economic Systems).

A theoretical approach to the process of economic transformation and integration in Central Europe, which is different to the approach taken in Brabant's book (see previous entry). 'Transformation in the Czech and Slovak Republics: liberal rhetoric versus populist disgrace' (p. 47-76) explains how the Czech Republic did not adopt a

173

shock approach to transition, as Prime Minister Václav Klaus claimed, but introduced important elements of a gradual approach to transformation with the Czech government intervening extensively. The merits of 'shock versus gradualism' are one of the main topics of this theoretical study, which has a large bibliography on p. 181-93.

540 **Winds of change: economic transition in Central and Eastern Europe.**
Daniel Gros, Alfred Steinherr. Harlow, England; New York: Longman Group, 1995. 544p. bibliog.

A compendious study of economic conditions and policy in the region. It examines the economic transformation of the countries concerned and their growing enterprise sector, analyses income policy, employment and unemployment, financial sector reform and the macroeconomy, and fiscal policy. The cost of restructuring the whole region is considered, as are the trade arrangements in the new Europe. In the mid-1990s numerous books were published on the Central European economy. The following two books have many references to the Czech situation: *Markets, states and democracy: the political economy of postcommunist transformation*, edited by Beverley Crawford (Boulder, Colorado; San Francisco; Oxford: Westview Press, 1995. 278p. bibliog.) – the index is on p. 269-78; and *Privatization in Eastern Europe: is the state withering away?* by Roman Frydman and Andrzej Rapaczynski (Budapest, London; New York: Central European University Press, 1994. 221p. bibliog.), in which the index is on p. 217-21.

541 **The integration of the European Community and third states in Europe: a legal analysis.**
Andrew Evans. Oxford; New York: Clarendon Press, 1996. 413p. bibliog.

The legal frameworks that encompass European integration are analysed in detail. The future problem areas concerning the composition of agreements with, for example, Central Europe, are identified.

542 **Creating capital markets in Eastern Europe.**
Edited by John R. Lampe. Washington, DC: Woodrow Wilson Center Press, distributed by John Hopkins University Press, 1992. 114p. bibliog. (Woodrow Wilson Center Special Studies).

A representative selection of papers given at a conference on 'Creating capital markets in Eastern Europe', held in Sofia, Bulgaria, on 20-22 September 1991. In addition to the development of capital markets in transition, the papers also embrace: foreign investment in Eastern Europe prior to privatization; company management; and, in a paper by Alice Teichova, inter-war capital markets in Central and Southeastern Europe – this will be of interest to the economic historian. The book has an index.

174

543 **Restructuring Eastern Europe: the microeconomics of the transition process.**
Edited by Soumitra Sharma. Cheltenham, England: Edward Elgar Publishing Limited, 1997. 195p. bibliog.

A collection of papers on some of the major issues of restructuring after the fall of Communism: industrial restructuring; technological integration; corporate governance and decision-making; public investment expenditure and regional development; foreign direct investment; and the banking sector. Chapter five, 'Efficiency under restructuring from a microeconomic perspective', by Vladimír Beňáček, Dmitri Shemetilo and Alexei Petrov (p. 58-71), is on the Czech microeconomic miracle. This chapter, like most of the others, has its own small bibliography on p. 71. Also of interest is chapter seven, 'Policies for control of air pollution in Central and Eastern Europe' (p. 82-96), by Jennifer Steedman. There is a composite index for the whole book (p. 189-95).

544 **Transition report 1998: financial sector in transition.**
London: European Bank for Research and Development, 1998. 234p; Transition report update, April 1998. 73p.

The 'Transition reports' have been published since 1994: the main report comes out in November, with the update appearing in the April of the following year. This report draws on the expertise of the European Bank for Research and Development (EBRD) as an investor in twenty-six countries of Central and Eastern Europe, the Baltic States and the Commonwealth of Independent States, and offers extensive coverage of macroeconomic developments and structural reform. The Czech Republic is well covered in this unique report, which is intended for investors, policy-makers and researchers.

545 **What markets can and cannot do: the problem of economic transition in Central-Eastern European countries.**
Edited by Milan Sojka, Stefano Zamagni. Prague, Rome: Charles University/Nova Spes International Foundation, 1992. 186p.

A collection of papers from a seminar held in Prague on 6-7 March 1992 by the Institute of Economic Sciences of Charles University and the Nova Spes International Foundation. The situation in Czechoslovakia is referred to in most of the papers and two papers are specific to that country: 'The Czechoslovak economy in transition: the metamorphosis of ownership structures' (p. 119-36), by Lubomír Mlčoch; and 'Czechoslovak economic reform: perspectives for co-operation' (p. 165-80) by Pavel Mertlík.

546 **The end of central planning? Socialist economies in transition: the cases of Czechoslovakia, Hungary, China and the Soviet Union.**
Edited by David M. Kemme, Claire E. Gordon. New York; Boulder, Colorado: Institute for East-West Security Studies, 1990. 112p.

Presents revised and edited versions of papers which were originally presented at a meeting of the Working Group on International Economic Change and Restructuring in Athens in April 1990. Czechoslovakia was chosen as a case-study. Milan Čižkovský and Mikolaj Ordnung's paper, 'Economic transition of Czechoslovakia: realities, intentions and goals' (p. 11-31), presents the basic programme as an unqualified transition to a market economy and discusses the integration of the reforming socialist countries in the world economy and the pluralistic structure and external conditions for transition.

547 **Privatization in the Visegrad countries: a comparative assessment.**
Michael Borish, Michael Noel. *World Economy*, vol. 20, no. 2 (March 1997), p. 199-219. bibliog.

As the title indicates, the article reviews the strengths and weaknesses of the Czech Republic, Slovakia, Hungary and Poland, and the macroeconomic environment and enabling environments, assessing privatization and private sector development up to 1997. Conclusions are drawn as to the performance of each country and its progress towards European Union accession.

548 **Moving to sustainability: how to keep small business development centres alive. Studies on centres in Poland, Hungary and the Czech Republic.**
Edited by Daniel S. Fogel, Monika Edwards Harrison, Frank Hoy.
Aldershot, England; Brookfield, Vermont; Hong Kong; Singapore; Sydney: Avebury, 1995. 104p.

A report on a conference held at the Czech Management Centre in Čelákovice in April 1995, covering the major themes discussed and also including key presentations. In 1990 the US Congress passed legislation creating the Central European Small Business Enterprise Development Commission with the purpose of assisting the governments in Poland, Hungary and the Czech Republic to promote the growth and development of small businesses. This book is one component of that assistance. 'Small business and the SBDC in Czech Republic', by Miroslav Foret and Miroslav Doležal, both of the Masaryk University in Brno, is on p. 53-57.

549 **Firm behavior in emerging market economies: cases from the private and public sectors in Central and Eastern Europe.**
Edited by Daniel S. Fogel. Aldershot, England; Brookfield, Vermont; Hong Kong; Singapore; Sydney: Avebury, 1995. 193p. map. bibliog.

Considers three periods: the socialist system in its pure form; reform periods; and post-reform, or the current condition. There are references to Czech companies throughout the book and two companies were selected as case-studies: 'Zetor tractor: from central planning to market economy' p. 55-70) by Karen L. Newman and Stanley D. Nollen of Georgetown University; and 'Valuation in a transition economy: the case of Spolana Chemicals' (p. 113-35) by Archana N. Hingorani of the Bombay stock exchange and Anil. K. Makhija of the University of Pittsburg. Some aspects of the changes in the Czech public art sector are summarized in 'Managing the transition: financing culture in the Czech Republic' (p. 161-78) by Jeffrey D. Straussman of Syracuse University.

550 **The economic impact of new firms in post-socialist countries: bottom-up transformation in Eastern Europe.**
Edited by Horst Brezinski, Michael Fritsch. Cheltenham, England; Brookfield, Vermont: Edward Elgar, 1996. 273p. bibliog.
Presents discussions, based on the latest empirical data, on the emergence and contribution of new entrepreneurs in the transition economies. 'Small entrepreneurs in the society of employees' (p. 217-226), by Richard Růžička, is on the situation in the Czech Republic and stresses the social value of small private businesses. The author provides tables and charts. 'Poland and Czech Republic: privatization from above versus privatization from below or mass privatization versus generic private enterprise building' (p. 175-88) is by Krzysztof J. Ners. The article has its own bibliography on p. 188.

551 **Co-operatives in Central and Eastern Europe: self-help in structural change.**
Edited by Andreas Eisen, Konrad Hagedorn. Berlin: Ed. Sigma, 1998. 219p. bibliog. (Berliner Schriften zur Kooperationforschung. Berlin Cooperative Studies).
These country reports offer a comprehensive description of the development of cooperatives in Central and Eastern Europe, and were presented at the 13th International Congress on Co-operative Sciences in September 1996 in Berlin. 'Co-operative systems in transformation: Poland, the Czech Republic and Slovakia' (p. 11-20) is by Johann Brazda, and 'Co-operatives in the Czech Republic' (p. 21-48) is by Yohanan Stryjan and Zdeněk Linhart. The topics of the latter paper are: background and legislation; consumer cooperatives; housing cooperatives; worker (producer) cooperatives; and agricultural cooperatives. One of the conclusions is that the highly regulated transformation process in fact inhibited true adaptation. The article has a good multilingual bibliography (p. 46-47), although the majority of material listed is in English and relates mostly to agriculture.

552 **Eastern Europe in crisis and the way out.**
Edited by Christopher T. Saunders. Basingstoke, England: Macmillan, in association with The Vienna Institute for Comparative Economic Studies, 1995. 526p. bibliog.
Based on the proceedings of the fifteenth Workshop on East-West European Interaction and Integration, which was organized by the Vienna Institute for Comparative Economic Studies and the Dr. Karl Renner Institute, and held in Vienna from 21-25 November 1993. The theme was a critical assessment of the transformation of the East European economies, from 1989-93, and the ways out of the crisis. Thus these contributions deal with countries which are still in deep recession caused by the transformation. Several of the chapters are concerned specifically with the Czech Republic. In the section on the reforms of the financial sector there is a contribution by Judita Štouračová and Alojz Neustadt: 'Foreign trade in the process of economic transformation, with special references to Czech experience' (p. 229-42). In the section on the social problems of transformation is an article by Karel Kouba, 'Systematic changes in the Czech economy' (p. 451-65). Some of the articles have bibliographies. There is a 'List of participants' (p. 511-16) and a joint 'Index' (p. 517-26). This collection of articles will be useful to business people and to students of contemporary economics.

553 **Eastern Europe's emerging cities: operating outside the region's capitals.**
Vienna: The Economist Intelligence Unit, 1998. 205p. maps. (Research Report).
Chapter four is on the Czech Republic (p. 35-47), represented here by Brno, České Budějovice, Liberec, Nový Jičín, Ostrava and Plzeň. The introduction explains the advantages of the regions over Prague (proximity to other markets and lower costs) and compares the six cities. This is followed by a profile of each, the focus being on foreign investments and acquisitions, retailing and industry. The findings are supported by graphs and charts.

Czech Republic

554 **The break-up of Czechoslovakia: an in-depth economic analysis.**
Oldřich Dědek et al. Aldershot, England: Avebury, 1996. 208p. bibliog.
A collection of articles by a number of economists, the majority of whom are researchers in the Economic Institute of the Czech National Bank. The book therefore represents the financial perspective of macroeconomists. The format is based on chronology. The first part reviews the influences on economic relations between the Czechs and Slovaks from the foundation of the Republic in 1918 to the fall of Communism in 1989. The second part surveys the most important economic and political events after 1989. The core of the book rests in the final part, which deals with the main actions taken to reduce the traumas that resulted from the gradual collapse of a highly integrated economic system. The fourth part attempts to examine the economic consequences of the break-up of the state for the successor republics and how social and economic development might be managed. Teachers and students of economics should benefit from reading this book. It has a number of tables and a bibliography, mostly of articles.

555 **Die Teilung der ČSFR: eine österreichische Perspective.** (The division of the ČSFR [Czechoslovak Federal Republic]: an Austrian perspective.)
Jan Stankovsky. Vienna: Österreichisches Institut für Wirtschaftsforschung, 1993. 110p. bibliog.
Although of interest mainly to Austrian economists, this book is worth inclusion here because of the good statistical tables on foreign trade and investment which it includes; trade with Austria is highlighted. Published in May 1993, the multilingual bibliography (p. 109-10) lists works, mostly on economics, published between 1990 and 1993.

556 **The Czech Republic and economic transition in Eastern Europe.**
Edited by Jan Švejnar. San Diego, California: Academic Press, 1995. 434p. bibliog.
A collection of articles which offers a comparative view of economic development and assesses political systems in relation to economic transition, the quality and

availability of statistical data in the new republic, the macroeconomic situation there and the money demand. Several of the contributions are on the privatization process, the largest transfer of property in modern history. There are articles on the voucher privatization, corporate governance, and manufacturing in transition. Social and environmental issues, such as unemployment, the impact of the changes on household incomes, health care reforms and the impact of the transition on the environment are also analysed. All of the chapters are richly documented by statistical tables and charts and the reader is directed to further sources of information. There is a sizeable bibliography ('References', p. 413-26) of reports, articles, acts and books, mostly in English, with some in Czech. The collection has a list of contributors (p. ix) and a simple index (p. 427-34). It was also published in Czech as *Česká republika a ekonomická transformace ve střední a východní Evropě* (Prague: Academia, 1997).

557 **The Czech Republic: the quest for integration with the West.**
Zdenek Cervenka. London: Economist Intelligence Unit, 1996. 88p. map.

A follow-up to Cervenka's report, *Czechoslovakia in transition* (London: Economist Intelligence Unit, 1990), this provides a good overall account of the political scene in the Czech Republic, its foreign policy, economic achievements and shortcomings, enterprise ownership, management and the sustainability of the Czech economic miracle.

558 **Managing in emerging market economies: cases from the Czech and Slovak republics.**
Edited by Daniel S. Fogel. Boulder, Colorado; San Francisco; Oxford: Westview Press, 1994. 233p. maps. bibliog.

Intended for academics, students and business people, this volume presents the difficulties companies face in the transition from a command to a market economy and the management of the transformation. It includes diverse case-studies, for example, the issue of pricing for Czechoslovak Airlines in the market environment, the privatization options in the glass industry and downsizing in steel companies. There are short biographical sketches of the managers of the Harvard Group and a write-up on its founder, the young entrepreneur Viktor Kožený (p. 149-65), who considerably rocked the boat of the Czech financial scene. The book has a fair number of tables, charts and graphs but lacks an index.

559 **Conditions for business activities of foreign investors in the Czech Republic.**
Prague: Joint Venture Club, 1995. 3rd ed.

This ample publication consists of several sections, each with separate pagination. These are: the Czech Republic, its geographical location and political and economic orientation; opportunities for foreign investors to conduct business in the Czech Republic; main steps in establishing a business company in the Czech Republic; operation of a firm; termination of company activities; and basic provisions of the banking, stock exchange and insurance company acts. The book provides a condensed description of all the legal acts, passed up to the time of publication, which business people must comply with in their activities in the Czech Republic. It also contains nineteen appendixes, mostly lists of relevant institutions or examples of contracts.

560 **The Czech and Slovak republics at a glance.**
Compiled by Trade Links. Prague: Trade Links, 1994. 157p. maps.
This very general guide to the two republics, intended for visiting businessmen, offers key facts and straightforward summaries of geography, history, politics and culture, before focusing on the current economic situation. This last section, the largest, is supported by a number of statistical tables.

561 **Investing, licencing and trading in the Czech Republic: 1997.**
New York: The Economist Intelligence Unit, 1997. 33p.
The book presents information available up to August 1997. It is an independent survey, divided into eleven chapters: 'The operating environment'; 'Organising an investment'; 'Incentives'; 'Licensing'; 'Competition and price policies'; 'Exchanging and remitting funds'; 'Corporate taxes'; 'Personal taxes'; 'Capital resources'; 'Human resources'; and 'Foreign trade'. Each chapter begins with an overview of the particular field and then dissects the subject in subchapters.

562 **Czech Republic: a business and investment guide.**
Prague: Coopers & Lybrand, 1997. 35p.
This document, published in the autumn of 1997, provides a brief introduction to foreign investment in the Czech Republic. It was prepared by one of the world's leading providers of accounting, auditing, tax and consulting services and as such also offers an introduction to Coopers & Lybrand and its services in the Czech Republic. The document looks at: investment context; investment vehicles; forms of business representation; registration procedures; corporate and personal taxation; VAT; and other taxes and charges.

563 **Metamorphosis in the Czechoslovak economy: the Stamp Memorial Lecture 26. November 1991.**
Václav Klaus. London: University of London Press, 1996. 15p.
This paperback is of historical value now, but at the time Klaus, an admirer of Margaret Thatcher's reforms in Britain, was the Prime Minister of Czechoslovakia. The country was only two years into its economic reforms and Klaus was highly thought of by Western economists and politicians. The volume includes a list of international awards and prizes conferred on Václav Klaus.

564 **The transformation of Czech society, retrospect and perspect.**
V. Klaus. *Economic Affairs*, vol. 17, no. 4 (December 1997), p. 44-47. bibliog.
At the time this article was published Václav Klaus was still the Prime Minister of the Czech Republic. Here he acknowledges his intellectual debt to the economist Friedrich von Hayek, expands on the gap between expectations and reality in the post-Communist Czech Republic and meditates upon the advice Hayek might give in the current situation. Klaus concludes that Hayek would probably take a long-term, not short-term position and would recommend continued deregulation, liberalization and privatization.

565   Czech Republic: country profile.
Prague: QplusQ, 1997. 40p.
Issued on behalf of the Ministry of Industry and Trade of the Czech Republic for foreign trading partners. The available information goes up to July 1997, is basic but concise and to the point and concerns economic development, the economic environment, the institutional framework and foreign investments. Annexes list: the members of the Prague stock exchange; issues of shares, units and bonds with the highest total trade value in 1996; banks which were awarded a banking licence in the Czech Republic; and members of the Czech Association of Insurance Companies.

566   Successful transformations? The creation of market economies in Eastern Germany and the Czech Republic.
Martin Myant, Frank Fleischer, Kurt Hornschild, Růžena Vintrová, Karel Zeman, Zdeněk Souček.   Cheltenham, England; Brookfield, Vermont: Edward Elgar, 1996. 267p. bibliog.
The Czech Republic and East Germany were the best-placed countries for the transition from a command, to a demand, economy. Their GDP per capita was the highest in the Eastern bloc. Chapter four outlines the microeconomic policy framework in the Czech Republic; chapter five is an essay on changes in the Czech economic structure; chapter six is on changes within enterprises, based on a number of case-studies; and chapter seven is on the sectoral structure of Czech industry. The economies of the Czech Republic and Eastern Germany are compared. This is perhaps the best study on the current economic situation in the Czech Republic. The authors support their findings with statistical tables, charts and a bibliography.

567   Privatization in the Czech and Slovak republics.
Compiled by Trade Links.   Prague: Trade Links, 1993. 218p. maps.
This handbook provides brief information on the Czech and Slovak privatization process. The privatization of sections of the economy, in a country where nearly all was national property and the economy was centrally planned, started in 1989. The main body of legislation on restitution and privatization was adopted in 1990-91. There have been amendments to this legislation since the publication of this book, which renders some of the information out of date. The publication offers key facts on the two countries, and in addition to sections on privatization, it has summaries of foreign investment, investment companies and investment funds, the stock exchange and securities. Trade Links also provides a list of major companies in the First Wave of voucher privatization, another of companies ear-marked for the Second Wave and for Standard Privatization, lists of investment funds and share funds, and a list of Prague stock exchange members.

568   The privatisation process in East-Central Europe: evolutionary process of Czech privatisation.
Edited by Michael Mejstřík.   Dordrecht, the Netherlands; Boston, Massachusetts; London: Kluwer Academic Publishers, 1996. 330p. bibliog.
The team of contributing authors, mostly economists, see the evolutionary process of the Czech privatization as a prototype for the other countries of the region. This privatization was a 'critical complement to the Standard International Monetary Fund

181

restructuring and adjustment package (anti-inflationary macroeconomic policy, liberalisation of prices, and foreign trade)'. The Czech experience is unique owing to its combination of the mass privatization of large companies, which dominated the economy, and individual privatizations that resulted in the rapid evolution of a capital market.

569 **Moving beyond assistance: final report of the IEWS Task Force on Western assistance to transition in the Czech and Slovak Federal Republic, Hungary and Poland.**
Krzysztof Ners, Arjan van Houwelingen, Michael Palmer, Kate Storm Steel. New York: Institute for EastWest Studies, 1992. 80p.

An assessment of Western assistance to the three countries since 1989. The report includes tables, graphs and figures and analysis of various aids and fundings. The main objective of the first phase of transition, stabilization, had been achieved. The second phase, structural transformation, was likely to last until the countries concerned achieved membership of the European Union.

570 **Facts on foreign trade of the Czech Republic.**
Prague: Ministry of Industry and Trade, Czech Statistical Office, Czech Trade Promotion Agency, 1997. 249p.

Detailed statistical data on the status, dynamics and structural changes of Czech foreign trade are presented, mostly in table form, in this well-arranged work. This reference work starts with notes on the methodology of foreign trade statistics and continues with a break-down of the foreign trade (e.g. with European Union countries, developing countries, CEFTA countries) and goes on to deal with imports of selected commodities according to the Standard International Trade Classification. The largest section is a list of countries, grouped under continents, giving the principal commodities of trade with the Czech Republic.

571 **Export promotion in the Czech Republic.**
Prague: Ministry of Economy of the Czech Republic, 1995. 103p.

Published in cooperation with the Ministry of Foreign Affairs and the Ministry of Industry and Trade and described as a practical manual for exporters. The content covers the legislative conditions for the support of exports, organizations (state as well as non-govermental) which promote export and render services to exporters, and organizations that provide corporate information on foreign and domestic bodies.

572 **Finance, investment and trade with Czechoslovakia: Prague 7th & 8th November 1991.**
London: Financial Times Conference Organisation, 1991. 69p.
(Financial Times Conferences).

The papers, which were given by important speakers, including the then Czech ministers from various sectors of the economy, international bankers, advisers and industrialists, deal with current problems and the prospects for Czechoslovak economic reform.

182

573 **Czech industry and investment: Financial Times Survey.**
Vincent Bolan, Kevin Done. *Financial Times*, 14 May 1997, p. 1-6.
A rather gloomy collection of articles, mostly on the economic reforms which were
still to be completed. The era of low unemployment appeared to be coming to an end.
The industrial infrastructure had suffered decades of neglect and under-investment and
a series of frauds concerning investment funds had reduced investors' confidence.
This illustrated supplement also includes profiles of companies: the engineering
company ČKD Praha Holding; Léčiva pharmaceuticals; Škoda; Daewoo Avia; and the
bank Investiční a Poštovní banka. A year later *Financial Times* carried out another
survey, 'Czech Republic – industry and investment', *Financial Times*, 14 May 1998,
supplement, p. I-IV. This survey of the Czech economy suggests the need for
economic reforms and describes the situation in the capital markets and in banking.
The industrial city of Brno features strongly.

574 **Organizational changes in post-Communist Europe: management
and transformation in the Czech Republic.**
Ed Clark, Anna Soulsby. London; New York: Routledge, 1999. 249p.
bibliog. (Routledge Studies of Societies in Transition).
A scholarly study of organization and management change. The authors look back at
enterprise and management under state socialism and at the Czech historical
inheritance before progressing to an analysis of the emergence of post-Communist
management, organizational transformation, enterprise and institutional change and
the re-definition of Czech management and enterprise. The authors provide figures, a
sizeable bibliography of books and articles in English (p. 234-45) and an index.

575 **Review of the labour market in the Czech Republic.**
Paris: OECD & Center for Cooperation with Economies in Transition,
1995. 143p. maps. bibliog.
This slim paperback 'analyzes the main factors underlying the Czech success story
and discusses the challenges ahead'. The study assesses the role of the labour market
and social policies in preventing further reductions of labour supply, the reduction in
inflatory pressures associated with labour market imbalances, and ways to avoid the
marginalization of a hard-core group of long-term unemployed.

576 **Czech Republic: Financial Times survey.**
Robert Anderson, Kevin Done. *Financial Times*, 1 December 1997.
6p. map.
1997 was a year of economic difficulties and growing uncertainty. This collection of
articles covers: politics; preparations for the membership of the European Union and
the membership of NATO; banking and the stock market; recovery after the 1997
floods in the north of the country; and the steel industry.

577 **The Czech Republic.**
Financial Times, 22 November 1995, p. 15-18. map.
Provides a general survey of the current economic and political situation in the Czech
Republic at the time, with the focus on the forthcoming election and the prospective
membership of the European Union. The tourist sector is flourishing, but tough new
methods have been introduced into banking and the fund managers are under siege.

The article offers a profile of the ceramics company, Chlumčany Ceramics Works, and of a television company, Nova TV.

578 **Czech Republic.**
The Times, 2 May 1995, supplement, p. 2-15. maps.
A series of articles presenting a picture of the economic programme in the Czech Republic since the Velvet Revolution in 1989. The topics are: trade and industrial opportunities for international partners; government budgets; commercial banks; tourism; and an interview with the mayor of Prague. The conclusions are that the Czech technical and entrepreneurial skills and industrial traditions are held in high esteem by international investors. Foreign business and tourists are pouring into the capital and into the country.

The Czech Republic: Financial Times survey.
See item no. 615.

The tax system

579 **Tax reform in Czechoslovakia.**
Christopher Heady, Mark Pearson, Najma Rajah, Stephen Smith.
London: Institute for Fiscal Studies, 1992. 35p. bibliog.
The objective of the 1992 reform of the federal tax system was to complete the transition from the arbitrary tax structures of the centrally planned economy to a taxation system fitted to a market economy of the Western style. Income tax, capital gains tax and taxes on goods and services are the three main fields of taxation which are also the main sources of revenue.

580 **Fiscal system in transition: the case of the Czech income tax.**
Fiona Coulter. *Europe-Asia Studies*, vol. 47, no. 6 (September 1995), p. 1,007-23. bibliog.
The Czech tax reform of 1993 is examined and the reasons for the change from the old system and its consequences are evaluated. The article then concentrates on one component of this reform, personal income tax, comparing it to the system of income taxes in Western Europe. Czech personal income tax creates relatively little revenue, and in fact it raises a lower percentage of fiscal revenue than under the old system. The role of the new income tax within the overall fiscal system in the Czech Republic is analysed.

Doing business

581 **Doing business in the Czech Republic.**
Edited by Adam Jolly. London: Kogan Page, 1997. 232p. map.
bibliog.
Various contributors, representatives of corporate bodies involved in business with the Czech Republic, provide sound advice on how to determine and exploit the opportunities there. The appendices which are included are also in a practical vein, on sources of grants and aid, contact addresses and addresses where further information can be obtained. The general accent is on market potential and on setting up a company in the Czech Republic.

582 **Doing business in the Czech Republic.**
New York: Ernst & Young, 1994. 102p. map. bibliog.
There are several advisory booklets on the Czech Republic, published by various bodies, offering a quick overview of the investment climate, taxation, forms of business organization, business and accounting practices in the Czech Republic. This booklet reflects information available at the end of 1993. At that time Ernst & Young had offices in Prague, Brno, Ostrava, Pardubice, Plzeň and in Ústí nad Labem.

583 **Doing business in Czechoslovakia.**
London: Kogan Page, 1991. 392p. bibliog.
Published under the auspices of the Confederation of British Industry. The contributors were the accounting firm KPMG Peat Marwick McLintock, the City law firm S. J. Berwin & Co. and National Westminster Bank. All three have a long association with Czechoslovakia. The book is now outdated but the bibliography is still of value.

584 **Doing business in the Czech Republic.**
London: Price Waterhouse, 1995. 176p.
Available from any local Price Waterhouse office, this edition supersedes the 1993 edition and 1994 supplement. It is one of a series on business conditions in countries where Price Waterhouse is represented. The material was assembled in 1995 but because of the rapid changes in the investment climate it quickly became outdated. The accent is on taxation which is likewise subject to changes.

585 **Doing business in the Czech Republic: 1997/1998.**
Prague: PP Agency, 1998. 138p. maps.
This handsome publication, prepared in cooperation with the Czech Ministry of Trade and Industry, Ministry of Foreign Affairs and Ministry of Finance and various other Czech organizations, relies heavily on advertising, which is of good quality. Its contents follow other, similar publications, outlining the business climate, but also provides very down-to-earth information on such topics as internal transport, maps, dialling codes and a host of important addresses.

586 **Doing business with the Czech Republic.**
London: The Foreign and Commonwealth Office & The Department of
Trade and Industry, 1995. 57p. map. bibliog.
Provides concise information on sectors of the Czech economy (agriculture, industry,
services, communications), establishment costs, distribution channels, terms of
payment, foreign investment legislation and financing. Pages 43-52 offer 'Further
sources of information in the UK', and pages 53-56 contain 'Further sources of
information in the Czech Republic'.

Miscellaneous

587 **Czech Republic: the property, construction and building materials
markets.**
London: Foreign and Commonwealth Office & the Department of
Trade and Industry, 1997. 75p. bibliog.
A guide intended primarily for British companies and individuals operating in
property investment and development, construction or building material supply and
looking for business opportunities. It provides a general introduction to the Czech
Republic and to the economy, including the tax regime and banking, before focusing
on the three named sectors. The publication was prepared by Gleeds International
Property and Construction Consultants, which has offices in the Czech Republic. The
guide includes a list of sources of information in the Czech Republic, sources of
information in the UK and a list of related DTI publications (p. 73).

588 **Four years on.**
J. Dee Hill, Anthony Griffin. *Business Europa*, April/May 1997,
p. 7-18.
Four years refers to the time since the previous general election; the Czech Republic,
according to this collection of surveys and interviews, had made enormous strides
during his time. Changes in the pattern of Czech trade are examined, as well as trends
in foreign trade (the Czech Republic has successfully re-orientated itself after the
collapse of Comecon, trade with the European Union now accounting for 56.1 per
cent), and the realities of the Czech tourism industry.

589 **Bohemia's fading rhapsody.**
Economist, no. 343, 8019 (31 May 1997), p. 87-88, 91.
Since 1996 the Czech economy, which had been considered a lively model of success
in Central Europe, showed signs of serious difficulties. At the time this article was
written, the account deficit, driven by a large trade deficit, was among the highest in
the world (at 8.6 per cent of GDP). Czech industry had still not been restructured and
the economic position of the country was becoming unsustainable.

590 **Is a Czech era ending?**
Economist, no. 345, 8046 (6 December 1997), p. 47-48.
Václav Klaus presided over the Czech economic reforms from 1993 onwards. He was
voted out in the autumn of 1997, and this article looks at the implications of this

change in leadership. It need not mean an immediate end to market reforms but this article predicts that it will mean the end of the sharp, combative approach which Klaus represented. The article hopes that the corruption and lack of transparency in business, which had infected dealings in recent years, will stop, and that investments, which had become leaner, will recover.

Construction and property in the Czech Republic: 1994-2000.
See item no. 712.

Periodicals

591 **Prague Economic Papers. Quarterly Journal of Economic Theory and Policy.**
Prague: Institute of Economics, Czechoslovak Academy of Sciences, 1990- . quarterly.
A scientific journal from the sphere of economic theory and Czechoslovak economic policy. The quarterly publication includes book reviews, articles and an index.

592 **Prager Wirtschafts- und Sozial- Historische Mitteilungen. Prague Economic and Social History Papers.**
Prague: Charles University, Department of Philosophy, 1994- . annual.
The issues present collections of scholarly studies and reports, either in German or in English, the majority of them with an international theme. The journal also includes reviews of books on economy or social history.

593 **The Economist Intelligence Unit Business Report Czech Republic and Slovakia.**
London: Economist Intelligence Unit, 1996- . quarterly.
This quarterly has a wide subject coverage of key facts: the business environment; infrastructure and key sectors; investment; land; labour; business services and contacts; import information; sales distribution and marketing etc. The Economist Intelligence Unit also publishes *Country Reports, Country forecasts, Country risk services, Investing, Licencing and trading conditions abroad, Financing foreign operations, Country profiles* and *Business newsletters.*

594 **Consumer Eastern Europe.**
London: Euromonitor PLC, 1992- . annual.
This publication consists mostly of tables; it provides regional overviews, country-by-country, of demography, economic indicators, standard of living, household characteristics, advertising and media access, retail distribution, consumer expenditure, consumption rates, service industries and consumer market.

595 Czech Business and Foreign Trade.
Prague: PP Agency, 1994- . monthly
The journal has a quarterly supplement, *Czech Industry*. The readership aimed at is foreign trading partners, the business, financial and manufacturing world, state bodies and institutions interested in cooperation with the Czech Republic. The publication relies heavily on advertising.

Banking and Finance

Central and Eastern Europe

596 **Universal banking in the twentieth century: finance, industry and state in north and Central Europe.**
Edited by Alice Teichova, Terry Gourvish, Agnes Pogány. Aldershot, England; Brookfield, Vermont: Edward Elgar, 1994. 308p.
A collection of articles which deal mostly with individual countries. Part one, 'Continuity and discontinuity in historical perspective', has an article by Jan Hájek on 'Origins of the banking system in Czechoslovakia' (p. 22-31). Part two, 'Central banks, the state and universal banks', has a contribution by Charlotte Natmessnig, 'The establishment of Anglo-Czechoslovak Bank: conflicting interests' (p. 96-115). Part three is on 'Universal banks and industry' and includes 'Banking system changes after the establishment of the independent Czechoslovak Republic' by Vlastislav Lacina (p. 131-41). All articles are well documented by tables and charts and each article has its own explanatory notes. The book has notes on 'Contributors' and an 'Index' (p. 295-308).

597 **Eastern European banking.**
James Essinger. London: Chapman & Hall, 1994. 406p.
The aim of this book is to provide a comprehensive survey of the Central and East European banking industry after the collapse of Communism in 1989. The Czech Republic is frequently referred to and there is a separate chapter on 'Obtaining security for funds advanced in the Czech Republic' (p. 56-60). The reference section has profiles of each country's economy with addresses of its banking institutions: the Czech Republic is on p. 109-20.

189

598 **Central European handbook: a guide to financial markets in Central and Eastern Europe.**
Haywards Heath, England: Euromoney, 1995- . annual.
Contains articles on various aspects of finance and relating to specific financial institutions. The 1997/98 issue has articles on: investment banking and international trade finance, by employees of RZB Austria; custody, by the Dutch ING Baring; privatization, by Investment Bank Austria; correspondent and commercial banking, by BNP-Dresdner Bank; Russia in the international capital markets, by West Merchant Bank in London; and depository receipts, by an employee of The Bank of New York.

599 **The Euromoney: Central and Eastern Europe financial resources book.**
London: Euromoney Publications, 1998. 312p.
This complete guide to commercial and investment banking in Central and Eastern Europe is divided into three parts: 'Cross-border reviews'; country-by-country 'Market reviews' (Czech Republic is on p. 65-73); and, the largest section, a 'Directory'. The cross-border review considers local currency trading, the EMU (European Monetary Unit) and its implications for the region, cross-border mergers and acquisitions and privatization. The directory lists the leading Eurobond and equity issuers and book-runners, regional funds, finance ministries, exchanges, corporates, banks, etc.

600 **Banking in transition economies: developing market oriented banking sectors in Eastern Europe.**
John Bonin, Kálmán Mizsei, István Székely, Paul Wachtel.
Cheltenham, England: Edward Elgar Publishing Limited, 1998. 195p. bibliog.
The findings and conclusions from a project on Comparative Privatisation, carried out by the Institute for EastWest Studies. The project was supported by the World Bank, European Bank for Reconstruction and Development (EBRD) and the United Nations Development Program. The findings and conclusions here are from the final stage of the project, which concentrated on establishing, as the title says, market-oriented banking sectors. The book summarizes the policy recommendations on: market oriented banking for the economies in transition; bank privatization; the role of foreign banks in economies in transition; regulation of bank failures; and retail banking in Central and Eastern Europe generally. Several subchapters deal specifically with the Czech Republic and there are also a number of tables. The 'References' section (p. 187-90) provides a bibliography, listing contemporary books and articles. The book has an index.

601 **The development and reform of the financial system in Central and Eastern Europe.**
Edited by John P. Bonin, István P. Székely. Aldershot, England: Edward Elgar, 1994. 364p.
An overview and discussion of the development of bank privatization, bankruptcy, banking regulations and the consequences of financial liberalization. The Czech Republic is dealt with specifically in the section, 'Reform of the banking sector in the Czech Republic', by Miroslav Hrnčíř (p. 221-56).

602 **Financial reform in Central and Eastern Europe.**
Edited by Stephany Griffith-Jones, Zdeněk Drábek. Basingstoke,
England: Macmillan, 1995. 256p. bibliog.
A collection of articles, some of which were translated from Czech, Polish and
Hungarian, on the financial reforms in three post-Communist countries: the Czech
Republic, Poland and Hungary. Privatization in the Czech Republic, the largest
property transfer in modern history, is appraised. The book has a subject and name
index.

603 **Global trends and changes in East European banking.**
Edited by Eva Miklaszewska. Cracow, Poland: Jagellonian
University, 1998. 405p. bibliog.
This collection of essays by academics from many countries is concerned mainly with
Polish banking, but there are enough contributions on the East European situation as a
whole, business strategies, usage of banking services, European Monetary Unit and
financial intermediation to make the book relevant for anyone probing the Czech
situation. Among the case-studies are two essays on Czech banking specifically:
'Finance and investment in transition: Czech enterprises 1993-1994' (p. 280-305) by
Ronald Anderson and Chantal Kegels; and 'Fuzzy analysis of the short-term credit
market in the Czech Republic' (p. 306-13) by Mirko Dohnal from Brno University and
L. Nejezchleb. Each essay has its own bibliography but the complete book does not
have an index, which would have helped the search for topic and country references.

604 **The evolution of the state-owned banking sector during transition
in Central Europe.**
M. Borish, Wei Ding, M. Noel. *Europe-Asia Studies*, vol. 49, no. 7
(November 1997), p. 1,187-208. bibliog.
The countries of Central Europe must transform their financial sectors, which have
been slowly and gradually liberalized, to be able to integrate into the European Union.
The large state-owned commercial banks make the private banks insignificant where
deposits, loans and nominal assets are concerned. The article reviews the break-up of
the mono-bank system, the role of the state-owned banks and bank privatization in
Central Europe up to 1996.

605 **Rebuilding the financial systems in Central and Eastern Europe.**
Edited by Philip L. Cottrell. Aldershot, England: Scolar Press, 1997.
177p. bibliog.
Comprises essays written by former bankers, government advisors and historians
which were published to celebrate the seventieth anniversary of the National Bank of
Hungary. The historian Vlastislav Lacina contributed 'The financial system following
the establishment of Czechoslovakia' (p. 115-22), i.e. after 1918. The bibliography
covers only major works on the subject and books.

606 **Economic performance and financial sector reform in Central and Eastern Europe: capital flows, bank and enterprise restructuring.**
Edited by Andrew W. Mullineux, Christopher J. Green. Cheltenham, England; Northampton, Massachusetts: Edward Elgar, 1999. 320p.

A critical examination of the progress made on macroeconomic stabilization and financial sector reform in the transition economies of Europe. The microeconomic experiences are related in the wider macroeconomic context of reform. The study emphasizes that macro reform is underpinned by micro and institutional reform, especially in the sphere of finance. Two articles are specific to Czech issues: 'Fixed exchange rate regime in the stages of transition: lessons from the Czech case' (p. 185-220, bibliog.), by Miroslav Hrnčíř; and 'Stabilization of capital inflows in transition economies: an econometric investigation of the Czech and Polish cases' (p. 256-74) by Eric Girardin and Jan Klacek.

Czech Republic

General

607 **Banking and nationality conflict in the modernization of the Bohemian Crown Lands.**
F. Gregory Campbell. In: *Studies in East European social history.* Edited by Keith Hutchins. Leiden, the Netherlands: E. J. Brill, 1981, p. 88-105.

This essay examines the growth of competitive banking among the Czechs in the 19th century as part of the urbanization process. It includes a history of the important Živnostenská banka, which survived, in name at least, right through the Communist era, and is now a 'normal' bank once more.

608 **Financing operations in the Czech Republic, 1997: a guide to finding, managing and moving money.**
New York: The Economist Intelligence Unit, 1997. 33p.

A reference guide to financing techniques and banking services available to foreign businesses, governments and international organizations. This issue has special features on the top ten domestic-owned banks and top foreign-owned bank subsidiaries.

609 **Banking and financing.**
In: *Doing business in the Czech Republic, 1997/98.* Prague: PP Agency, 1998, p. 56-61. maps.

Concerned with the Czech banking system in 1996 and banking products. The aim of the currency policy is stability. This is illustrated by a survey of the exchange rate of the Czech Crown after 1989 and its effect on trade relations.

610 **Czech Republic: presented on the occasion of the EBRD Annual Meeting Business Forum, London, 12-15 April.**
London: EBRD, 1997. 40p. map.

As expected, this presentation is concerned mostly with the activities of the European Bank for Reconstruction and Development (EBRD) in the Czech Republic and with the investment climate there: Foreign Direct Investment (FDI); macroeconomic data for the Czech Republic; advice on establishing businesses; taxation; customs; currency; banking and insurance; securities; and the stock exchange. The book provides addresses of trade contacts, and of ministries, industrial and professional associations. It also contains information on CzechInvest (an agency set up by the Ministry of Industry and Trade for the express purpose of assisting the foreign investor) and the Association for Foreign Direct Investment.

611 **Czech Republic.**
Financial Times, 'Survey'. 'Annual country review', 19 January 1991, p. 19-22.

'Urgency of reform reflects problems within the sector' by Stefan Wagstyl (p. 21) is the most important from this collection of articles on the Czech Republic. It concerns the current situation in the banking sector and the attitude of the recently elected government. The author concludes that the Czech 'authorities are convinced that only a firm hand will restore domestic and foreign confidence in Czech finance'. The other articles in this latest survey are on: maintaining the momentum of the restructuring of the industry; the first true recession in the country (a small article, offering a profile of the heavy industrial city of Ostrava, where unemployment has risen to 12.5 per cent compared to the national average of 7 per cent); the engineering sector; and how the Czech government is tackling the problems which prompted many Romanies to seek asylum abroad.

612 **The web of cross-ownership among Czech financial intermediaries: an assessment.**
Peter Kenway, Eva Klvačová. *Europe-Asia Studies*, vol. 48, no. 5 (July 1996), p. 797-809. bibliog.

The article examines the situation concerning investment privatization funds and the allied cross-ownership within the ownership framework in the Czech Republic. The article is based on assembled data and questionnaires, which are described and analysed.

613 **Československá obchodní banka, a.s.: annual report 1996.**
Prague: published by ASCo for ČSOB, a.s., 1997. 117p.

Československá obchodní banka (ČSOB) is the major bank in the Czech Republic. This is a standard annual report which covers: the consolidated three-year financial summary for 1996, 1995 and 1994; the chairman's and directors' reports; major macroeconomic factors which influenced the activities of the bank during 1996; goals of the bank for 1997; the auditor's report; notes on shareholders of ČSOB in the Czech Republic and the Slovak Republic; senior executives of ČSOB; and the sponsorship activities of ČSOB.

614 **UK joint venture activity in the Czech Republic: motives and uses.**
Eleanor M. M. Davies, Brian Kenny, Robert R. Trick. *European Business Review*, no. 96, 6 (1996), p. 22-29. bibliog.
Presents the initial findings of an ongoing survey, which has more than transitory value. The study was looking into joint ventures by British investors in the Czech Republic, their motives and uses. The British investors were comparatively hesitant and slow, and were not among the top investors. The data from the study indicate that investors from the UK prefer to own their overseas operations fully, rather than work with local partners. The technological needs of the ex-Communist countries are examined, as well as the different modes of entry and the function of investment as applied by UK firms.

615 **The Czech Republic: Financial Times survey.**
Vincent Bolan, Anthony Robinson. *Financial Times*, 6 December 1996. supplement. 6p. maps.
The articles in this *FT* Survey interpret the impact of the 1996 Czech elections, which changed the dominant position of the Prime Minister Václav Klaus. The core of this article covers the serious banking problems and worrying trade deficit of the country. An interview with Zdeněk Bakala, chairman of Patria Finance, sheds some light on the issues. Other topics covered are: industrial financing; notes on the construction company IPS Praha; housing policy; the steel industry, which seems to have made a fresh start; the wait to join the ranks of NATO; and the Sudeten question.

616 **Stability through monetary integration in Eastern Europe: a scenario for the Czech Republic.**
Reutlingen, Germany: Institut für Europäische Wirtschaftstudien, 1995. 97p. bibliog.
This slim book claims that the Czech Republic has made the greatest economic transformation since 1989 among the countries of Eastern Europe and argues for its monetary integration within the European Union. The Czech government achieved remarkable monetary stability and this thesis is supported by many tables and a sizeable bibliography of recent books, articles and reports (p. 86-97).

617 **Czech finance and investment.**
Financial Times, 26 April 1998. supplement. 6p. map.
A general survey of Czech finance and investment which focuses on the following topics: efforts to bridge the wealth gap; the country's successful record of economic progress and consequent good reputation; increased flexibility in exchange rate policy; the headache of problem loans for the banks; consolidation in capital markets; the Prague stock exchange; the National Property Fund, foreign investment and the future of European transport networks.

618 **Czech Republic.**
Poole, England: Barclays Economics Department, 1997. 8p. (Barclays Country Reports).
Barclays Bank has been active and strong in the Czech Republic for some time. This report from May 1997 summarizes key economic indicators, trends and outlooks,

194

structural features, general politics and monetary and fiscal policies, foreign trade and foreign debt. A few addresses, useful for doing business in the Czech Republic, are included.

619 Money demand and seignorage in transition.

Nina Budina, Jan Hanousek, Zdeněk Tůma. In: *The Czech Republic and economic transition in Eastern Europe.* Edited by Jan Švejnar. San Diego, California: Academic Press, 1995, p. 137-50.

A comparative study of four countries, the Czech Republic, Poland, Romania and Bulgaria, which probes into the relationship between inflation and money growth during the economic transition. The analysis confirmed that Poland and the Czech Republic were the most stable of the economies undergoing transformation in the region. It further confirmed that, in the Czech Republic in particular, the initial upset, or disequilibrium, and resulting inflation were comparatively minor. The basis of the analysis was the money demand function and a model of seignorage and the growth of money. The Czech government, like the governments of the other countries investigated here, was aware that just printing money would not result in a successful transformation of the economy.

620 Payment systems in the Czech Republic.

Basle, Switzerland: Bank for International Settlement, 1997. 64p.

The Committee on Payment and Settlement Systems of the central bank of the Group of Ten Countries periodically publishes a reference book on payment systems in the G-10 countries, the so-called 'Red Book', to help the general understanding, at the domestic and international level, of payment and settlement arrangements. The main chapters are headed: 'Institutional aspects'; 'Payment instruments'; 'The interbank payment system'; 'The special use of interbank transfer systems for international and domestic financial transactions'; and 'The role of the central bank in the wider bank payment system'. The guide is supported by comparative tables and a glossary of terms and abbreviations which is useful for the layperson.

621 Focus.

Prague: Coopers & Lybrand, 1994- . monthly.

A newsletter for professionals in international firms working in the Czech Republic. It advises on tax law amendments, accounting developments, international trade fairs and exhibitions.

The Stock Exchange

622 Czech stockmarket guide: October 1997-September 1998.

Prague: ASPEKT kilcullen, 1998. 133p. annual.

Published under the auspices of a Czech bank, Komerční banka, which is a founding member of the Prague stock exchange. A regular feature covers 100 profiles of leading decision-makers from companies traded on the Prague stock exchange and a list of broking houses. This issue also has an article on preparation for a derivatives market and the development of tax consultancy in the Czech Republic.

623 **Stock exchanges.**
In: *Doing business in Czech Republic, 1997/98.* Prague: PP Agency, 1998, p. 62-66.

Act no. 229/1992 on Commodity Exchanges, which was amended by Acts Nos. 216/1994 and 105/1995, enabled Czech entrepreneurs to participate in exchange trading in the same way as in developed countries. The Prague exchange opened in April 1993, after a forced recess of more than half a century. This article explains the principles of commodity exchange in the Czech Republic, the corporate bodies, the aims of the Prague stock exchange, the Brno commodity exchange, and the Bohemia-Moravia Commodity Exchange Kladno. The Brno exchange trades mostly in crop and animal products and products from their processing, whilst the Kladno exchange trades in minerals, oil refining, and construction materials.

624 **Securities and the stock exchange.**
In: *Czech Republic: presented on the occasion of the EBRD Annual Meeting Business Forum, London 12-15 April.* London: European Bank for Reconstruction and Development (EBRD), 1997, p. 24-25.

A survey of the securities market and the Prague stock exchange. Trading systems, clearing and settlement, membership, regulation and off-stock exchange trading are all covered. The Prague stock exchange re-opened on 6 April 1993 with twelve monetary institutions and five brokerage firms as its founding shareholders. In 1993 the average daily trading volume was US$ 8.1 million; in 1996 it was US$ 57.8 million.

Agriculture

625 **Policy and institutional reform in Central European agriculture.**
Edited by Johan F. M. Swinnen. Aldershot, England; Brookfield,
Vermont; Hong Kong; Singapore; Sydney: Avebury, 1994. 236p.
A collection of essays offering a good overview of the subject. 'Agricultural reform
and transformation in the Czech Republic' (p. 107-37) by Josef Kraus, Tomáš
Doucha, Zdeněk Sokol and Bohumil Prouza attempts to shed some light on the
complicated and difficult situation in Czech agriculture, after two years of economic
reforms. The text is supported by tables on farm structure and production, food
consumption and price development.

626 **The agrarian economies of Central and Eastern Europe and the
Commonwealth of Independent States: situation and perspectives,
1997.**
Csaba Csaki, John Nash. Washington, DC: The World Bank, 1998.
144p. (The World Bank Discussion Paper, 387).
This study offers a brief review of agricultural economies of a region which holds a
substantial part of the world's agricultural resources. The overall analysis is followed
by a country-by-country analysis and a statistical annex on food and agriculture in
Central and Eastern Europe and the Commonwealth of Independent States (CIS).
Surprisingly, the Czech Republic is the only ex-Communist country not listed under
the country analysis but, as a member of CEFTA (Central European Free Trade
Association) and a country which is in the European Union succession process, the
Czech statistics are incorporated into the statistical annex. The source for all the tables
in this section is FAOstat (statistics published by the Food and Agriculture
Organization).

627 **Review of agricultural policies: Czech Republic.**
Paris: Organisation for Economic Cooperation and Development, 1995.
298p.

This study has been carried out under the 'Partners in Transition' programme of the
Center for Cooperation with Economies in Transition and has a sister review on
industry, *Industry in the Czech and Slovak Republics* (q.v.). The intention of the
programme is to help in the process of integration of the Czech Republic into the
Committee for Agriculture of OECD. The review is divided into five parts. Part one,
'Economic and agricultural environment', is a summary of recent macroeconomic
developments. Part two, 'Privatisation and restructuring of agriculture and food
industries', deals with the main structural changes, which include the process of
restitution of land and other agricultural properties, the transformation of collective
farms, the privatization of state farms and the effects of privatization on industry. Part
three, 'Agriculture and food policies, objectives and measures', examines the support
policies, but also research and development, training, taxation policies, consumer
subsidies and environmental measures. Part four, 'Evaluation of support to agriculture', includes an analysis of Czech agriculture between 1986 and 1994. The final
part, five, deals with agricultural trade relations, and the implications of the Uruguay
Round Agreement and of Czech membership of the European Union. The review
includes many graphs and charts.

628 **Agriculture of the Czech Republic.**
Prague: Ministry of Agriculture of the Czech Republic, 1995. 50p.

This is an official brief survey of agriculture in the Czech Republic, supported by
many tables and graphs, and as such it offers a good, simple yet comprehensive guide
to its development from 1989 to 1995. Czech agriculture was heavily subsidized by
the state under Communism. In the new, post-Communist era, agriculture will have to
undergo the upheaval of readjustments. There has been a decline in livestock and crop
production and the percentage of people working in agriculture has shrunk. The
coverage is as complete as it can be, starting with charts of the land fund,
privatization, subsidies to agriculture, markets and market regulations and foreign
trade in agricultural commodities. The largest section, on agricultural production, is
broken down into subsections on cereals, sugar beet (an important commodity in this
country), potatoes, rapeseed, vines, fruit, vegetables, milk, red meat, poultry, fish,
rabbits and honey. There are further major sections on forestry, water, environment
and alternative agriculture. The last page (p. 50) lists the addresses of institutions
connected with agriculture.

629 **Czechoslovakia's agriculture, situation, trends and prospects:
document.**
Luxembourg: Office for Official Publications of the European
Communities, 1991. 206p.

A fairly detailed analysis of Czechoslovakia's agricultural sector, agricultural policies
and development needs, potentials and obstacles to economic reform. Approximately
half of the study consists of charts, tables and indexes, some going back to the 1950s.
The study is now of historical interest.

630 **Privatization in rural Eastern Europe: the process of restitution and restructuring.**
Edited by David Turnock. Cheltenham, England: Edward Elgar, 1998. 427p. maps. bibliog. (Studies of Communism in Transition).

A collection of essays dealing with the complex East European situation. The book has a sizeable introduction, which is followed by essays on individual countries. In the Czech Republic, where cooperatives and state farms were central to the socialist system, the rural transition after 1989 meant radical change. Chapter four, 'Czech Republic' (p. 93-119), is by Ivan Bičík and Antonín Götz, both from Charles University. It covers changes in farm ownership and production, employment in agriculture, conservation, changes in rural settlement, recreation in the countryside and commuting. In one of the general chapters, 'Aspects of farm diversification', there is a chapter on 'Beer and other beverages' (p. 318-20) which contains a well-informed summary of the contemporary Czech brewing industry. Each chapter has its own separate bibliography and the references given after the general sections ('Introduction', 'Aspects of farm diversification', 'Conclusion') are numerous but, as with the references in the 'Czech Republic' chapter, they indicate the scarcity of printed material on the subject of Czech agriculture, particularly material published outside the republic. The detailed index (p. 401-27) covers all chapters. The studies were written for academics with an interest in agricultural and transitional economies and for businessmen interested in Central and Eastern European agriculture, food processing and farm machinery.

631 **La transition post-collective: mutations agraires en Europe central.**
(Post-collective transition: changes in Central European farming.)
Marie-Claude Maurel. Paris: Editions l'Harmattan, 1994. 365p. maps. bibliog. (Pays de l'Est).

A study not intended for the general reader. It traces the history of agriculture in Central Europe in the 20th century, describes the collectivization in the late 1940s and in the 1950s, and discusses the contemporary dilemma of neo-collectivism and post-collectivism. The Czech Republic is the country most frequently referred to in the narrative and there are several subchapters which deal specifically with this country. The author provided numerous figures, tables and charts and a bibliography (p. 355-58) listing yearbooks, reports, journals, books and articles.

632 **Zemědělská technika: katalog výrobců, dovozců a prodejců zemědělské techniky.** (Agricultural machinery: catalogue of producers, importers and sellers of agricultural machinery.)
Brno, Czech Republic: ZeT Sdružení výrobců zemědělské techniky, 1996. 38p.

The text is in Czech, English and German and the coverage is the Czech Republic and Slovakia. After several introductions by leading Czech and Slovak agricultural figures, the catalogue proper is divided into a list of companies (with codes indicating production, trade, services, research and membership of associations) and a list of addresses of the companies. Inevitably, the publication is heavily supported by adverts.

Statistická ročenka České republiky. (Statistical Yearbook of the Czech Republic.)
See item no. 416.

199

Industry and Trade

General

633 **The industrialisation of a Central European city: Brno and the fine woollen industry in the 18th century.**
Herman Freudenberger.   Edington, England: Pasold Research Fund Ltd, 1977. 220p. map. bibliog.
This work has been written as a contribution to the understanding of economic development in the Habsburg monarchy. It is also a good study of industrial growth within a region. The study is detailed and fairly scholarly, and contains graphs, tables and a large bibliography, which includes archival sources, and an index. It is interesting to note that 19th-century Brno has been called the Manchester of Austria.

634 **Sectoral changes in industry after WWII.**
Edited by Waltraud Falk, Václav Průcha.   Prague: Institute of History of the ČSAV, 1991. 347p. bibliog.
Published on the occasion of the tenth International Economic History Congress in Leuvain. The article by Václav Průcha on 'Changes in the structure of the manufacturing industry in the countries of Central-East and South-East Europe after the Second World War' (p. 255-84) contains some interesting statistical data which also cover Czechoslovakia.

635 **Industry in the Czech and Slovak Republics.**
Paris: Organisation for Economic Cooperation and Development, 1994. 139p. bibliog.
A sister volume to a publication on agriculture, *Review of agricultural policies: Czech Republic* (q.v.), this study was undertaken in 1993 in the context of the 'Partners in Transition' programme of the OECD. The chapters deal with the legacies of the Communist period, liberalization, stabilization and privatization, the restructuring of

industry, and the general industrial policy of the Czech Republic. The issues raised by the division of the Czechoslovak Federal Republic in 1993 are also addressed. The report is documented by tables. The bibliography, which lists recent books and articles on the economy, is an indication of how little has been published specifically on industry.

636 **The future of industry in Central and Eastern Europe.**
Hans van Zon. Aldershot, England; Brookfield, Vermont; Hong Kong; Singapore; Sydney: Edward Elgar, 1996. 164p. bibliog.

Assesses the factors determining the future competitiveness of the industry of the region and acknowledges the relative success of the Czech reforms. Of the Czech industries, the author selected for closer inspection the textile and clothing, pharmaceutical and canning industries. The book has an extensive bibliography (p. 145-56) with much of the material listed relating to the Czech situation.

637 **Promoting cleaner and safer industrial production in Central and Eastern Europe.**
Paris: OECD, Center for Cooperation with the Economies in Transition, 1995. 144p. (OECD Documents).

Based on papers presented at the seminar on 'Auditing to improve safety, environmental performance and economic efficiency', held at Kiev, Ukraine, in October 1993. The focus was on auditing as applied to the chemical industry. This report describes the objectives and methodology of environmental audits and the results achieved in Western, Central and Eastern Europe.

638 **Hints to exporters visiting Central Europe: Czech Republic, Hungary, Poland, Slovak Republic, Slovenia.**
London: The Foreign and Commonwealth Office & The Department of Trade and Industry, 1998. 236p. maps.

The introductory section of this pocket-size publication offers advice on: travel; help available from DTI Country desks and various other institutions; and the British commercial representatives in the region. The chapter on 'Czech Republic' (p. 22-45) provides maps of the country and of Prague, general information in the form of key facts, and information on trade, hotels, restaurants, tipping, communication systems, economic factors and exchange control regulations.

639 **Changing foreign trade patterns in post-reform Czech industry (1989-1995): empirical evidence.**
F. Stolze. *Europe-Asia Studies*, vol. 49, no. 7 (November 1997), p. 1,209-35. bibliog.

Examines the degree to which the competitiveness of the various branches of the Czech manufacturing industry may be determined by their intensity and changes in endowments or input prices. The paper analyses in detail the relation between the input structure of Czech manufacturing industries and their position on international markets.

640 **Competitiveness of industry in the Czech Republic and Hungary.**
D. M. W. Hitchens, J. E. Birnie, J. Hamar, K. Wagner, A.
Zemplinerová. Aldershot, England: Avebury; Brookfield, Vermont:
Ashgate Publishing Company, 1995. 360p. bibliog.

A study of transition in the two countries with the most favourable conditions for that process. This comparative study is divided into three sections: part one deals with the Czech Republic, part two with Hungary and part three gives the results of the 'matched firm comparisons' of the authors and summarizes the implications of these comparisons for companies in former East Germany and Northern Ireland. Part one, on the Czech Republic, covers recent performance and developments there, with a summary of its labour market, before considering several branches of manufacturing, such as engineering, food, clothing and textiles, and furniture. The book is a report on the outcome of a two-year project (1992-94). The text is documented by a number of tables and has a substantial bibliography (p. 351-60), but, unfortunately, no index.

641 **Corporate governance in Central Eastern Europe: case studies of firms in transition.**
Josef C. Brada, Inderjit Singh. Armonk, New York; London: M. E.
Sharpe, 1999. 340p. bibliog. (The Microeconomics of Transition Economies).

An account of experiences of transition, the focus being explicitly on corporate governance. The objective was to determine whether the new owners are capable of exerting meaningful influence on their managers. The Czech companies investigated are: Glavunion, a leading flat glass producer with a large Belgian investment (p. 80-99); CS-12, which is a pseudonym for a major Czech producer of pharmaceutical products who wished to remain anonymous; ZVU, a heavy engineering and manufacturing joint-stock company; Veba Broumov, a cotton processing firm; and CSAO Teplice a.s., a middle-sized company engaged in truck and car maintenance.

642 **Sourcing czech-up.**
Peter Parry, Peter Marsh, Rodney Yeadon. *Supply Management*,
18 September 1997. 4p. (unpaginated).

'This article looks at the opportunities and obstacles for sourcing from this most western of the east European countries.' The Czech Republic has been most successful in attracting inward investment but it is still an unknown quantity for most UK purchasers. The authors work for consultancies, one in the UK and one in the Czech Republic, which will identify a potential supplier, support the tendering and negotiation process and contract preparation.

643 **Czech Republic.**
The Times, 10 July 1995, supplement, p. 2-14, 16-14. maps.

A separate supplement dedicated to the Czech Republic which looks at foreign investment and investors, how to preserve the best Czech industrial traditions and how to support foreign sales of manufacturing industries. The two serious, long-standing problems have been coal-fired power stations, which are being gradually phased out, and communications, which need to be improved quickly. Brno, the second largest metropolis, is given space, as of course is Prague, but a number of smaller country towns are also considered.

644 **Evolution and efficiency of concentration in manufacturing.**
Alena Zemplinerová, Josef Stíbal. In: *The Czech Republic and economic transition in Eastern Europe.* Edited by Jan Švejnar. San Diego, California: Academic Press, 1995, p. 233-54.
The authors examine the question of 'how quickly the transferring economies would be able to establish competitive conditions that would be conducive to economic efficiency'. They provide statistics and tables and calculate the concentration ratio and Herfindahl index for twenty-three industries. Industrial concentration was greatly reduced owing to the exceptionally high growth of new enterprises, the decomposition of existing firms and the entry of the Czech economy into world trade.

645 **Past glory, shaky future.**
Business Central Europe, July/August 1997, p 37-50.
'To all appearances, the Czech Republic has been spared the high social and economic costs of reform. In reality, it has only put them off – but the bills are coming due.' After a general survey of the Czech industrial past, this collection of articles continues with essays on heavy engineering, the Ostrava steelworks, the glass industry and investment banking.

646 **Performance of manufacturing.**
Marie Bohatá, Petr Hanel, Michal Fischer. In: *The Czech Republic and economic transition in Eastern Europe.* Edited by Jan Švejnar. San Diego, California: Academic Press, 1995, p. 255-83.
Surveys the development of the manufacturing industry during the transition. The authors make some valuable observations and examine the reasons for the following conclusions: the industries producing research and development had a more difficult time replacing their lost Comecon markets than industries exporting intermediate goods based on national resources; Czech industry also suffered a significant decline in sales; and the first few years of transition witnessed a disparity in the performance of successful and unsuccessful companies.

647 **The future of the defence industries in Central and Eastern Europe.**
Edited by Ian Anthony. Oxford; New York: Oxford University Press, 1994. 142p. (SIPRI Research Report, no. 7).
Looks at the conditions created by the collapse of the Warsaw Treaty Organization and the emergence of a new European security environment, both of which left the defence industries of the countries of Central and Eastern Europe with over-capacity. The topics covered are: military expenditure; the restructuring of the defence industry and its international dimensions; and arms exports. The Czech Republic is well represented both in the text and in the tables; the Czech jet trainer is cited as a specific product, an exception which should continue to sell.

Statistická ročenka České republiky. (Statistical Yearbook of the Czech Republic.)
See item no. 416.

Czech Republic: Financial Times survey.
See item no. 576.

Czech industry and investment: Financial Times survey.
See item no. 615.

Retailing and services

648 **The internalization of retailing in Czech and Slovak Republics.**
Tomáš Drtina. *Service Industries Journal*, vol. 15, no. 4
(October 1995), p. 181-203.

Drtina presents a brief summary of the recent history of the Czech and Slovak
retailing trade: retailing had a small number of selling areas; the retail structures were
inconvenient; the consumer was in an inferior position and did not have the upper
hand. The transition from a command economy to a demand economy and
privatization resulted in a fragmented retail network. The process of reconcentration
has started. These developments are parallel with the alteration in the quality of goods
supplied in retail outlets and are helped by the entry of foreign retail chains.

649 **Distribution and retailing in Eastern Europe: supplying the new**
consumers.
James Arnold. Vienna: The Economist Intelligence Unit, 1998. 102p.
maps. (Research Report).

A very good study of the retail revolution in post-Communist countries. Even the most
advanced retail sectors from these countries, such as the Czech Republic's, are in
many aspects behind the West. The distribution sector is frail and the retail sector
fragmented; the wholesale and retail prices are uneven. Consumer purchasing power is
still fairly low and retailers have been slow to adapt to the new technology. The study
and its conclusions are based on statistics, in which the Czech Republic is very well
represented.

650 **Small privatization: the transformation of retail trade and**
consumer services in the Czech Republic, Hungary and Poland.
John S. Earle, Roman Frydman, Andrzej Rapaczynski, Joel Turkewitz.
Budapest, London; New York: Central European University Press,
1994. 301p. (CEU Privatization Reports, vol. 3).

Information on Czech retail trade in book form is hard to come by. This paperback
does, however, have nearly 100 pages on the substantial changes in retailing and
consumer services in the Czech Republic. The text is supported by tables and graphs.
The chapter is divided into three sections. The first, now of historical interest only, is a
detailed account of the conditions under Socialism, in the centrally planned Czech
economy. The second part is of greater relevance, dealing with the privatization of
the retail trade and consumer services. This includes: the complex process of the
restitution of properties nationalized after 1948, which was introduced after 1989; the

'small privatization' programme; the 'large privatization' programme; and the transformation of consumer cooperatives. These sections are asset-orientated, and overall the focus of the book is on the legal and economic aspects of the main issues. Some of the Czech legislation referred to has been amended since the book's completion.

Industrial sectors

651 **Brewing row puts Czech regulators in spotlight: Bass and IPB are each hoping that the competition authorities will back their plan for the republic's second biggest brewer.**
Robert Anderson. *Financial Times*, 24 December 1997, p. 27.
In 1997 the second biggest brewer in the Czech Republic, Radegast, was the target of takeover bids by the UK brewer Bass and by IPB, a bank which at that stage was in the process of being taken over by Nomura, a Japanese bank. The Czech media took up the cudgels and various executives of the two companies gave long interviews to the press.

652 **A case of Czech beer: competition and competitiveness in the transitional economies.**
P. T. Muchlinski. *Modern Law Review*, vol. 59, no. 5 (September 1996), p. 658-74. bibliog.
The Czech brewing industry has great business potential. It is an example of an area which should expand into international markets, and it offers an opportunity for investment because the demand for high-quality lagers is on the increase worldwide. The Czech breweries have been either privatized or are in the process of privatization. Budějovické pivovary, which produces the famous Czech Budvar, or Budweiser Budvar, is examined here. This company has been the focus of attention from Anheuser-Busch, the US-based largest brewery in the world. The Internet has various, and numerous, websites offering information on Czech beer.

653 **Skoda overtakes Fiat in Eastern Europe: VW investment has helped the Czech carmaker become biggest producer in the region.**
Kevin Done. *Financial Times*, 3 February 1998.
Škoda, now under the control of Volkswagen, has become the leading car producer in Central Europe. Output increased in one year by 35.8 per cent and further growth is predicted. The company has been radically restructured and has absorbed VW technology. The workforce has grown and the plants are expanding. The Czech government retained a 30 per cent stake, which means that the state coffers are expecting substantial dividends. Some of the history of VW's interest in Škoda is repeated by Kevin Done in 'Harmony under the bonnet', *Financial Times*, 8 November 1994, p. 17. At the time, the German company Volkswagen had been negotiating for fourteen months with Škoda, the Czech carmaker. An agreement was imminent. A large amount of information on Škoda can be found on the website: http://www.skoda.cz.

654 Czech and Slovak steel industries.
Tim Smith. *Steel Times*, 221, 9 (September 1993), p. 395-98. maps.
The United Nations Economic Commission for Europe sponsored a study tour of the major steel plants in the Czech and Slovak republics; generally it revealed realism in the size of the market available to the industry. By the mid-1990s the annual Czech production was expected to be cut. However, the split of the former Czechoslovakia caused an imbalance in the types of production, with all wide-strip production taking place at Košice in Slovakia, and all long production and some narrow-strip production taking place in the Czech Republic.

655 Responding to changing conditions.
Foundry International, vol. 18, no. 1 (March 1995), p. 33-40.
A reasonably optimistic forecast for the Czech foundry industry, which expects it to be an important feature on the European, and even the world, market. The two important factors are management's rapid acquisition of the skills required to run a commercial enterprise in a free economy and the established engineering expertise of the Czechs. Up to 1989 the foundry industry operated in quite different situations to those which exist today. 'The Czechoslovak foundry industry – past, present and future' by J. Sedlák, *Foundryman*, 85, 8 (October 1992), p. 312-17, reached similar conclusions.

656 Investment engineering: February 1998.
Prague: ASPEKT kilcullen, 1998. 136p.
An analysis of the sector which supplies complete engineering units for such industries as energy, chemicals, food, metallurgy, extraction and transport. The publication consists mostly of tables, in which companies are compared by selected indexes and company profiles. The outlook, owing to increasing competition which is diminishing opportunities in traditional sectors and areas, is not rosy for investment engineering.

657 Something clunky out east.
Economist, no. 334, 7902 (18 February 1995), p. 88-89.
There is a second large company in the Czech Republic called, like the motor car producer, Škoda. This article describes this engineering company as a crucible of Czech engineering talent. In 1992 it was technically bankrupt, but now, two-and-a-half years later, things are improving. The company is now fully in private ownership, reorganized into separate divisions and with a workforce which has been reduced by a third. It has also signed several joint-venture agreements with foreign companies. This article, however, still questions the ability of the company to finance its ambitions.

658 Opportunities and incentives in a newly emerging market.
M. Doherty. *Energy World*, no. 248 (April 1997), p. 19-21.
Since 1989 there have been changes in the energy policy of the Czech Republic. This article examines electricity generation, the independent power sector, natural gas, oil, energy efficiency and environmental considerations and discusses the opportunities for the United Kingdom in the energy sector of the Czech economy.

659 **The history of Czechoslovak nuclear energy and the future of nuclear power in the Czech Republic.**
P. Otčenášek. *Nuclear Engineer*, vol. 34, no. 5 (September/October 1993), p. 130-34.

The article broadly covers the following topics: Czech uranium; the beginning and development of nuclear power; the first Czechoslovak nuclear power stations; new technology for Czech nuclear power; the nuclear fuel cycle; and public relations.

660 **Government cautious over future of gas.**
T. Land. *Gas World International*, no. 199 (4901) (February 1994), p. 33-35.

The energy sector has a crucial role in the restructuring of the national economy. This article looks into the issue of privatization of the gas industry and the problems of rehabilitating the natural environment.

661 **Energy, water and the environment in the Czech Republic: an overview.**
M. Daněk. *Proceedings of the Institution of Civil Engineers: Water, Maritime and Energy*, no. 112, 3 (September 1995), p. 260-67. maps.

Surveys the changes which the use of energy has undergone over the last few years. There has been a decline in the percentage of electricity produced from coal; gas and nuclear energy are taking over. The only domestic source for the short-term development of energy output is nuclear energy because the hydroelectric potential of relatively small rivers is almost fully exhausted. The water management authorities are aware of the issues of river water quality, drinking-water supply and waste-water management and are taking anti-pollution measures. Atmospheric pollution is still critical in some areas.

662 **Thinking small: mountain streams power micro-hydro plants.**
P. Novák, V. Jirsák. *International Water Power and Dam Construction*, vol. 48, no. 10 (October 1998), p. 16-18.

There are four small hydroelectric power stations already running in the Czech Republic. This illustrated article describes the design and operation of these automated electric plants, their capacity, the types of turbine and power outputs and their hydraulic system.

663 **Pharmaceuticals in Central and Eastern Europe.**
Chichester, England: Espicom Business Intelligence, 1997. 2 vols.

Probably the most detailed English-language survey of the region's pharmaceutical industry. The arrangement is simply by country, with the Czech Republic covered in volume one, p. 59-121. The main topics are: basic health indicators; social and environmental causes of mortality and morbidity; health care management; the financing of health care; and the pharmaceutical industry (pharmaceutical supplies, regulations, domestic production and manufacture, imported medicines and distribution, paying for medicines). This reference book also includes a contact directory of relevant government and trade organizations, producers and manufacturers, wholesalers and distributors and importers.

664 **Chemicals, pharmaceuticals and rubber: December 1996.**
Prague: ASPEKT kilcullen, 1997. 90p.
This was the first in the sequence of analyses of various sectors by Aspekt to be published in English. It was originally in Czech and the translation lacks finesse. These reports are considered by some to be the major suppliers of corporate and financial information in the Czech capital market. Twenty-six companies in the chemical, pharmaceutical and rubber sector are analysed and compared here, with the help of numerous charts and tables, the main focus being the financial aspects of their operations.

665 **A man for all seasons.**
Economist, 346 (8052) (24 January 1998), p. 82.
Chemapol is one of the largest Czech companies. It specializes in importing oil, chemicals and drugs. The eleven core chemical businesses are planning to merge into a unified company. It is hoped that one day it may become the equivalent of Britain's ICI in Eastern Europe. The article outlines the problems the company is facing in achieving this goal.

666 **Construction I: October 1997.**
Prague: ASPEKT kilcullen, 1997. 69p.
Analyses one of the most important industrial sectors in the Czech Republic, which has also a high standing on the capital market. The report gives details of the activities of twenty-one construction companies, their financial results from 1993 to the first half of 1997 and their share prices. The companies are compared using a range of financial indexes. The future of the construction industry is dependent on many factors: political, economic and legislative. The publication consists mostly of charts and tables. *Czech and Slovak Construction Journal* (Prague: Roberts Publishing, 1996- . monthly) is a glossy magazine which includes company profiles, labour issues, legal developments and building material.

667 **Nástin vývoje textilní výroby v českých zemích v období 1781-1848. Abriss der Geschichte der Textilindustrie in den Böhmischen Landern.** (An outline of the development of the textile industry in the Czech Lands in the period 1781-1848.)
Jana Macháčková, Jiří Matějček. Opava, Czechoslovakia: Slezský ústav ČSAV v Opavě, 1991. 3 vols. bibliog. (Práce Slezského ústavu ČSAV v Opavě, Řada B: hospodářské a sociální dějiny).
This work may be difficult to obtain, but the textile industry was a key one in the industrial revolution in the Czech Lands. Volume three has a summary in German (p. 644-76). This volume also has an extensive bibliography of periodicals, books and articles, some in German but mostly in Czech (p. 688-722). The content of volume one is general conditions, production and employment, distribution of production, market and sales. Volume two is concerned with raw materials and technology, and volume three is on social development.

208

668 **The Czech textile industry.**
R. Innes. *Textile Horizons*, vol. 13, no. 4 (August 1993), p. 46-49.
A review of textile-manufacturing machinery currently being constructed in the Czech Republic.

669 **Czech firearms and ammunition: history and present.**
Vladimír Dolínek, Vladimír Karlický, Pavel Vácha. Prague: Radix, 1995. 191p. bibliog.
The English terminology in this field owes something to the Czech language: the words 'pistol' and 'houwitzer' owe their origin to mediaeval Czech and there is the more specific, more recent hybrid word Bren gun. The Czech armaments industry is well known and this book should perhaps find a publisher in Britain or the United States. The book is well introduced by the editor of a Czech shooting magazine, Zdeněk Faktor, who hails the small firearm as a technological wonder of its own and highlights famous Bohemian and Moravian gunsmiths and designers from the past (such as the gunsmith Bedřich Brandejs or the designer Karel Krnka) and the last of the great designers (Emanuel Holek, brothers Josef and František Koucký). The text proper is a chronological survey of firearms from their origins to 1995. This is followed by a summary of the contemporary Czech arms works and their products (namely Zbrojovka Brno, a.s.; Česká Zbrojovka Uherský Brod, a.s.; Zbrojovka Vsetín, a.s.) and the production of ammunition (Sellier & Bellot, a.s.). The book contains dozens of good, colour photographs of guns and ammunition; an 'Index of place names' (p. 167-69), which, among other things, gives the names of designers; an 'Index of companies' (p. 170-77); an 'Index of arms' (p. 172-75); and an 'Index of ammunition' (p. 176-77). The bibliography is an 'Index of selected technical literature' (p. 183-88), which lists books, articles, lectures, periodicals, archives, collections and corporate documentation.

670 **Adapting to a free market: the task faced by a Czech pump manufacturer.**
R. Dopita. *World Pumps*, no. 326 (November 1993), p. 26-30.
Describes how a long established and large pump manufacturer, Sigma Lutín, must meet the new challenges of competing in a free market. The sudden collapse of the organized markets of the Eastern Bloc caused many problems to industry management.

671 **Changes in Czech.**
O. Obermeier. *Dairy Industries International*, vol. 58, no. 11 (November 1993), p. 29, 31.
Describes the current state of the Czech dairy industry. The conclusion is that it presents a unique opportunity for foreign investment.

672 **Czechoslovakia – difficult times after divorce.**
International Sugar Journal, no. 97 (1154) (February 1995), p. 54.
A general report on sugar production in the Czech Republic and Slovakia.

673 **Czechoslovakia.**
Paper, no. 217 (7 April 1992), p. 30-32, 34-35.
A general survey of the Czechoslovak papermaking industry. The data predate the break-up of the country. The following article deals with the printing industry, in which Czech printers are meeting the demands of western publishers and offering consistent levels of quality: 'Quality Czechs' (*Printing World*, no. 248[8], November 1994, p. 442-43).

674 **Czech Republic country report.**
European Plastics News, vol. 23, no. 7 (July/August 1996), p. 39, 41-42.
An illustrated survey of the Czech plastics industry.

675 **A guide to Czech and Slovak glass.**
Diane E. Foulds.   Prague: European Community Imports, 1993. 208p. maps. bibliog.
A directory of Czech and Slovak glass production for commercial use and for tourists. The paperback starts with basic information on glass, the definition of crystal, information on how to ship glassware, and how to care for quality glass. Parts two and three of the directory are dedicated to the history of Czech and Slovak glassmaking and glassmaking in the 20th century. Part four is on shopping for glass, both new and antique. The largest section, part five, is on major glassworks in the two republics. A number of companies are listed here, including producers of both industrial and technical glass and decorative and ornamental glass. The entry for each company gives its address, telephone and fax numbers. This is followed by: a fairly detailed history of the company; information for visitors to the company; and information on retail outlets. The last section in the directory is on resources and offers information on museums and on influential contemporary artists in glass (with illustrations of their work). There is also a glass vocabulary, in English, Czech and Slovak, and glossary (both on p. 201-03), a bibliography (p. 204-05) and an index (p. 206-08).

676 **Czech industry grows despite heavy debts.**
Glass, vol. 73, no. 8 (August 1996), p. 323-24.
A review of the Czech glass industry over the previous year. The narrative is supplemented by tables. Two other articles on this industry were published earlier in *Glass*, no. 69 (June 1992): 'Czechoslovakian glassmakers' (p. 219-20); and 'Glassmaking trends in Czechoslovakia' (p. 221).

677 **Brave new world for Czech glassmakers.**
M. Synek.   *Glass*, vol. 70, no. 8 (August 1993), p. 327-29.
The article describes Czech studio glass activity as shown by the work of three companies: Artcristal Bohemia, Beránek Glassworks and Art Glass Studio Svoboda.

678 **Perlen aus Gablonz: Historismus, Jugendstil. Beads from Gablonz: historicism, art nouveau.**
Waltraud Neuwirth. Vienna: Waltraud Neuwirth, 1994. 560p. map.
Jablonec nad Nisou, or, as it is called here in German, Gablonz, is a medium-sized district town in northern Bohemia, at the foot of the beautiful Jizerské hory mountains. The town has a long tradition in the glass industry, specializing in costume jewellery. This illustrated book, which has parallel German and English texts, looks at the technology and history of making beads in Jablonec and at various styles which were subject to fashion as dictated by artistic trends in Central Europe, not all of them sublime. As with other art objects from the Czech Lands, the costume jewellery from the art nouveau period has a particular stamp of elegance. The glassworks in Jablonec also produces Christmas decorations. The costume jewellery and Christmas decorations are exported all over the world.

679 **New Glass Review.**
Prague: Efect Co. Ltd, 1993- . monthly.
This magazine was originally published in 1945, for foreigners, in English, German, French and Russian, as *Czecho-Slovak Glass Review*. It was considered perhaps the most beautiful magazine ever published in the former Czechoslovakia. Today it is a glossy, bilingual (English and German) magazine, which is privately owned. The publisher's address is Bardounova 2140, Prague 4. The articles offer an overview of Czech and Slovak glass industries and their developments. Full-page colour illustrations are supplied by leading glass photographers and the magazine publishes surveys of novelties, new trends and technologies, exhibitions and designs, and important business deals.

Czech Republic: Financial Times survey.
See item no. 576.

Czech Republic: the property, construction and building materials markets.
See item no. 587.

The Czech Republic: Financial Times survey.
See item no. 615.

Transport

680 Prospect for East-West European transport.
Paris: ECMT, distributed by the OECD Publications Services, 1991. 561p.

A report from an international seminar held in Paris on 6 and 7 December 1990 setting out broad guidelines for a pan-European transport policy and preparing the ground for future analysis and concrete steps to exploit the considerable potential for the movement of trade and for tourism. The book has tables and graphs.

681 Road strengthening in Central and Eastern European countries.
Paris: OECD, 1993. 150p.

A report prepared by a group of OECD scientific experts which deals with short-term strategies and technologies for road strengthening and providing policy advice and technical recommendations. Upgrading the existing road infrastructure and overcoming the maintenance backlog are the key problems of the area. The study was carried out within the work programme of the OECD Centre for Cooperation with European Economies in Transition.

682 Czech Republic.
Edited by Sue Moody. In: *FTA international road transport guide.*
Tunbridge Wells, England: Freight Transport Association, 1996, p. 99-101.

The Czech Republic section contains information on conditions within the country. This covers vehicle weights and dimensions, prohibitions and particularly useful addresses.

683 CzechSite.
http://www.czechsite.com/

An English-language web-site intended for tourists going to Prague, with one section providing information on international passenger transport. The facilities of Prague

212

Ruzyně airport are described, including information on transport from the airport into the city and on the airlines using the airport. Czech international train and coach services are also covered in this section of the website, although not in great detail.

684 **Thomas Cook airports guide to Europe.**
Peterborough, England: Thomas Cook Ltd. 3 times yearly.
The guide includes Ruzyně, the Prague airport, which has recently been greatly expanded and improved. The publication is revised three times a year and as such provides up-to-date information on flights, the airport code, telephone numbers, location (with a map showing the airport's position in relation to Prague), transport connections, car parking and car hire, major airlines and representatives, and information on hotels.

685 **The steam locomotives of Eastern Europe.**
A. E. Durrant. Newton Abbot, England: David & Charles, 1972.
160p. bibliog. 2nd ed. (David & Charles Locomotive Studies).
There cannot be many steam enthusiasts who do not have this excellent book in their library. Steam engines were ousted from services in Czechoslovakia in the 1960s. The chapter on this country (p. 90-105) offers an outline history of all types of steam engines ever employed, information on the builders of locomotives, cooperation with foreign manufacturers and details on in-service use. The article has photographs, technical diagrams and a table of the main dimensions of the major classes. The name of Škoda, an important Czech locomotive builder, appears in many places in the rest of the book.

686 **Parní symfonie.** (A steam symphony.)
Photographs by Zdeněk Bauer, Jiří Bouda, Jaroslav Kocourek, Miroslav Petr, Ondřej Řepka, Bohumil Skála, Karel Zeithammer, text by Karel Soukup. Prague: Nakladatelství dopravy a spojů, 1988. 239p.
For steam enthusiasts, this is an ode to steam locomotives, their era, and the superiority of a lever over a push button, of a vibrating, pulsating machine over a smoothly running electric train, acknowledging the appeal the steam engine still has to men young and old. Of the 229 black-and-white photographs, all of Czechoslovak provenance, some are very good, while some are deliberately grained. Unfortunately the reproduction does not do justice to the artistic value of the pictures. There is a one-page 'Résumé' of the text, in Russian, German, English and French.

687 **Czech and Slovak trolleybus and tram guide.**
Martin Harák. London: Rapid Transit Publications, 1996. 96p. maps. bibliog.
It will be of interest to British readers that vehicles in the old Austria-Hungary and in Czechoslovakia ran on the left-hand side of the road, until the German occupation of Czechoslovakia on 15 March 1939. Prague and Brno have sizeable museum collections of tramcars, trolleybuses and motorbuses. The Prague collection is strictly for vehicles which have been used in Prague; the collection in Brno includes vehicles from all towns of the Czech and Slovak republics. There are also transport museums at Liberec, Olomouc, Ostrava and Pilsen. Tramways were built at great speed in the

213

Transport

Czech Lands at the end of the 19th century and in the first decades of the 20th century. Some of the systems for small towns, of meter gauge, were replaced by trolleybuses in the 1940s and 1950s. Trolleybuses first appeared in the Czech Lands under Austrian rule, in Southern Bohemia. The Czech Republic is still a builder and supplier to other countries, of both tramcars (built by ČKD-Tatra in Prague) and trolleybuses (Škoda at Pilsen). This slim paperback gives a brief history of these modes of transport in the Czech Lands, the dimensions of the vehicles, fares and a glossary of relevant terms in English, German, Czech and Slovak. The author then describes the city transport of Brno, České Budějovice, Chomutov-Jirkov, Hradec Králové, Jihlava, Liberec, Mariánské Lázně, Most-Litvínov, Olomouc, Opava, Ostrava, Pardubice, Pilsen, Prague, Teplice, Ústí nad Labem and Zlín-Otrokovice. Each entry gives the address of the municipal transport authority, general information on the town (population, industry), a brief history of its public transport, brief technical specifications of the vehicles, fares and information on where to purchase tickets. There is at least one map of the routes for each town.

688 **Tramways of Czechoslovakia. Pt. 1.**
Jan Linek. *Light Rail and Modern Tramway*, no. 55 (658) (October 1992), p. 259-65, 268. maps.

Tramways of Czechoslovakia. Pt. 2. Brno, Opava, Teplice and Praha.
Jan Linek. *Light Rail and Modern Tramway*, no. 55 (660) (December 1992), p. 311-17. maps.

A general survey of the tramway industry and transport in the Czech Republic. Both articles have illustrations, tables and maps.

689 **The standard approach in Eastern Europe.**
J. Linek. *Light Rail and Modern Tramway*, no. 58 (689) (May 1995), p. 132-34. maps.

An article on the conversion of metre-gauge tramways into standard 1.435m-gauge tramways in the Czech Republic and Slovakia. Conversion in the cities of Bratislava and Liberec is described in greater detail.

690 **Pražské metro.** (The Prague metro.)
Josef Křivánek, Jaromír Vítek. Prague: Nakladatelství dopravy a spojů, 1987. 149p. map.

The authors start with an overview of the history of urban transport. The first horse-drawn public transport appeared in Prague in 1875, the first electric tram in 1891. The underground, or Metro, as the Praguers call it, was already being considered in 1898, but it was not until 1967 that things started moving and the Prague city council issued clear directives to launch the building of the underground. This development and plans for the future are examined, followed by detailed descriptions of individual stations of the Metro. Then follows a chapter, 'What a traveller should know', on the underground systems of other world cities and in the then Soviet Union, and full information on the connections from the Metro to tram, bus and coach routes. There is also a chapter on the funicular leading to Petřín hill in Prague, technical details of the Metro, the depth of the lines and stations, and operational terminology. General tourist

214

information is also supplied: important telephone numbers, hotels, shops, cultural establishments, all in Prague.

691 **Linky městské hromadné dopravy v Praze: 1829-1990.** (The Prague city transport routes: 1829-1990.)
Prague: Společnost městské dopravy, 1992. 164p. maps.

On the development of the system of public transport in Prague. The starting point was the omnibus service of Jakub Chocenský in 1829. Public transport is here understood as including the horse-drawn and electric tram, bus and trolleybus routes and the underground, all of which are described exhaustively. Supplementary types of public transport are described selectively, these being omnibus routes, some horse-drawn road transport, minibus services, taxi routes and funiculars. The list of connections between these means of transport is supplemented by maps of the routes described. The book has hardly any narrative, consisting merely of a list of routes described and the various changes that have occurred over time. The description proper of each route is arranged chronologically, giving a verbal description of the line, the main stops and termini.

692 **The transport problems of a new state: Czechoslovak rivers, 1918-38.**
Ivan Jakubec. *Journal of Transport History*, vol. 17, no. 2 (September 1996), p. 116-32. map.

The newly formed Czechoslovakia faced huge transport problems as a consequence of the break-up of the Austro-Hungarian empire. The initial difficulties and dislocations were serious and this slowed down the economic development of the new country. It took some time before new official bodies and connections were in operation.

Science and Technology

693 The Academy of Sciences of the Czech Republic.
http://www.cas.cz

This website, in Czech and in English, is still developing. At the time of writing the latest update (December 1998) offered information on the structure of the Academy of Science of the Czech Republic (ASCR), with an alphabetical list of the institutes, the scientific divisions, services, joint establishments of the ASCR and universities and on associations of institutes. Further information was on the library of the ASCR and on journals published by the ASCR.

694 Centenary of Czech Academy of Sciences and Arts.
Jiří Beran, translated from the Czech by Jaroslav Tauer. Prague: Academia, 1991. 50p. (+32p. of plates).

The Bohemian Academy of Sciences, Literature and Arts of Emperor Francis Joseph was founded in 1891, the location then being the National Museum in Prague. From 1918 this august institution was called the Czech Academy of Sciences and Arts. This paperback, translated into the English of Central European intellectuals, which will be slightly puzzling to many first-language English speakers, surveys the origin of the Academy in its historical context, its work and philosophy (referred to as 'idealistic profile' in the text), activities and their impact, its structure and how this structure has evolved. The main section of the text, written by Jiří Beran, is supplemented with short contributions by prominent Czech academics. The pictures (plates) are of interest: the charter of the Academy, issued by Emperor Francis Joseph; and photographs of the buildings where the Academy was housed at various times, and of its past presidents and distinguished members.

695 Czech Republic's strengthened academy.
A. Abbott. *Nature*, no. 372 (6507) (15 December 1994), p. 601-04.

The article looks at industrial research in the Czech Republic.

216

696 **Czechoslovak engineering until the Second World War.**
Joseph Z. Schneider. In: *The Czechoslovak contribution to world culture.* Edited by Miloslav Rechcígl, Jr. The Hague; London, Paris: Mouton, 1964, p. 477-81.

The essay takes an historical approach and provides an account of the first Czech technical colleges (still in existence), sundry 'firsts' in Czech industry associated with Czech innovations in engineering and technology, and engineering endeavours by Czechs in North America. The old Czech industries are well represented here and the article has data on malt, hops and sugar beet.

697 **Czech Republic.**
Ann B. Francis. In: *Electronics in Central and Eastern Europe: the market for IT, consumer products and domestic appliances.* London: Pearson Professional, 1996, p. 43-80. (Financial Times Management Reports).

Computers, software and other IT office equipment, consumer electronics and domestic appliances are identified here and the market is assessed. The book contains a directory and trade details.

698 **Czechoslovak armoured fighting vehicles: 1918-1945. Development for Czechoslovakia. Exploitation by Germany.**
Charles K. Kliment, Hilary Louis Doyle. Watford, England: Argus Books Ltd, 1979. 139p. bibliog.

On the history, development and war-time use of armoured fighting vehicles of advanced Czechoslovak construction and manufacture. These vehicles were exported to many countries and played a significant role in the first two years of the Second World War, being used mostly by the Germans and their Axis partners. This book describes the three major manufacturers, Škoda, ČKD Praha and Tatra Kopřivnice, and the organization of armoured units of the Czechoslovak army, before dealing with the actual vehicles, their development and use. Chapter thirteen (p. 92-130) gives specifications of the vehicles while chapter fourteen offers scale drawings of the vehicles. The bibliography on p. 90-91 is a simple list of titles which include text on, or photographs of, vehicles of Czech origin. The provenance, construction, composition and use in action of Czechoslovakia's armoured trains are described in detail in Paul Catchpole's *Steam and rail in Slovakia* (Birmingham, England: Paul Catchpole Ltd, 1998, p. 63-67). They saw service chiefly in Slovakia, during the 1919 hostilities with Hungary and again during the 1944 Slovak National Uprising.

699 **Gregor Mendel: the first geneticist.**
Vítězslav Orel, translated by Stephen Finn. Oxford; New York; Tokyo: Oxford University Press, 1996. 363p. bibliog.

Mendel (1822-1884) was an abbot of the Augustinian monastery in Brno and is considered to be the founder of modern genetics. This major biography describes Mendel's origins and childhood, his studies and early career as teacher and monk. Orel expects the reader to have some conception of genetics, which he considers the pivotal science and primary focus of contemporary natural philosophy, and explains how Mendel's research brought together ideas from various scientific disciplines, the most important and decisive being physics. The book describes how Mendel's theories were received by contemporaries at home and abroad, and in his preface and in the last chapter Orel touches on the rehabilitation of genetics after 1950, its development to the present day and the quest for a more detailed explanation of the impact of Mendel's research on the origin and development of genetics. The multilingual bibliography of a variety of printed sources (p. 323-53) starts with natural history well before Mendel and covers genetics generally. The book is only sparcely illustrated; there is an index. Vítězslav Orel is Emeritus Director of the Mendelianum in Brno.

700 Mendel (1822-1884) in 90 minutes.
John and Mary Gribbin. London: Constable, 1997. 78p.

A brief biography from a series on major scientists which is aimed at students and non-scientists. The text skims superficially over Mendel's origins, studies and his career in teaching and the church. The book is concerned more with Mendel's life than his discoveries and the authors have managed to correct some of the notions relating to this 'obscure Austrian monk'. This obscurity is possibly due to the fact that Darwin never learned of Mendel's work, and, although their respective theories complement each other, they never merged. Although Mendel's origin was fairly humble, his education had the incredible breadth and depth of the Austrian system and Mendel finally became the abbot of an important monastery in Brno, a job which carried with it membership of the Moravian provincial assembly and other prestigious duties and privileges. Mendel's papers were published in 1865. The book has a chronology, 'A brief history of science from 2000 BC to 1966', but lacks an index. It is very much an introduction to the subject, an easy read couched in simple language and printed in a largish font.

701 The Mendelian revolution: the emergence of hereditarian concepts in modern science and society.
Peter J. Bowler. London: Athlone Press, 1989. 207p. bibliog.

A study of current thinking on the origins of Mendelism, intended for the non-specialist. The author introduces himself as a non-specialist and asserts that the book is neither a biography nor a history of genetics in the conventional sense. The aim is to present a history of the initial stages in the development of modern genetics. Inevitably, Gregory Mendel and his laws are mentioned throughout the study. The bibliography of books and articles (p. 185-200) is vast and has depth. There is also a short index.

702 Theories of life: Darwin, Mendel and beyond.
Wallace Arthur. Harmondsworth, England: Penguin, 1987. 214p. bibliog.

This Penguin book is intended for the general reader with an interest in nature and in scientific theories. It is written in comprehensible English, avoiding difficult scientific terms. Such unavoidable scientific expressions as are used are explained in chapter three, a separate basic biology course, which can be skipped by biology undergraduates or readers with a biological background. This is not a biography of the two scientists but a book on their theories, in the case of Mendel his theory of heredity and the nature of the advance he made over the then prevailing dominant views on inheritance. In 1986 Gregory Mendel described the formula which is the basis of almost all inheritance in the living world. This popular science book has a short bibliography and a brief index.

703 **J. E. Purkyně and psychology: with a focus on unpublished manuscripts.**
Edited by J. Brožek, Jiří Hoskovec. Prague: Academia, 1987. 137p. bibliog.

Presents transcriptions of manuscripts of Jan Evangelista Purkyně (1787-1869), the physiologist, psychologist and philosopher who discovered the cells, fibres and phenomena that now bear his name (Purkinje cells etc). His contribution to psychology has not yet been fully appreciated. The majority of the text is in German; the section written in Czech has been translated into English. The introduction, editor's foreword and the summary are also in English.

704 **Jan Evangelista Purkyně in science and culture: scientific conference, Prague, August 26.-30. 1987.**
Edited by Jaroslav Purš. Prague: Ústav československých a světových dějin československé akademie věd, 1988. 2 vols. bibliog.

The preface and contents and some of the papers are in English, other papers are in Czech, German or Russian. The topics of the conference were Purkyně and Czech society, Purkyně and the world of science, Purkyně and the scientific community, Purkyně's scientific achievements and the relation of these achievements to modern science, and Purkyně's life and his philosophy. Of interest is the paper by Monica Vetter, 'The reception of Purkyně's scientific studies by British scientists during the first half of the nineteenth century' in volume one (p. 402-22).

219

Urbanization and Housing Policy

705 **European cities, planning systems and property markets.**
Edited by James Berry, Stanley McGreal. London; Glasgow;
Weinheim, Germany; New York; Tokyo; Melbourne; Madras: E & FN
Spon, 1995. 417p. bibliog.
On the interaction of the planning systems of European cities, property markets and
real estate investment and planning. 'Prague' (p. 321-44), by Luděk Sýkora, examines
the historical development of the city's structure, the consequences of transition to
market priorities and urban planning. The article has its own bibliography (p. 367-70).

706 **The reform of housing in Eastern Europe and the Soviet Union.**
Edited by Bengt Turner, József Hegedus, Iván Tosics. London; New
York: Routledge, 1992. 362p.
Various aspects of housing reform are highlighted in this collection of essays. They
include, for example: rehabilitation, private initiatives, housing quality, welfare
requirements and home-ownership. 'Czechoslovakia: an introduction' is by Ola Siksö,
'Housing in Czechoslovakia: past and present problems' is by Peter Mihalovic and
'Recent changes in the housing system and policy in Czechoslovakia: an institutional
approach' is by Jiří Musil.

707 **Economic restructuring of the former Soviet Union: the case of
housing.**
Edited by Raymond J. Struyk. Aldershot, England; Brookfield,
Vermont; Hong Kong; Singapore; Sydney: Avebury, 1996. 373p.
bibliog.
This collection of studies opens with an overview of macroeconomic developments
(decentralization and privatization, housing construction, prices, remodelling of
housing finance, reform of the rented sector), before concentrating on individual
countries. 'The Czech and Slovak Republics: housing as a *second stage* reform' by G.
Thomas Kingsley and Maria Mikelsons (p. 175-218) follows the same content

220

structure as the general section, but applies it in detail and to these countries only. The article has its own bibliography (p. 217-18).

708 **Toward a market-oriented housing sector in Eastern Europe: developments in Bulgaria, Czechoslovakia, Hungary, Poland, Romania and Yugoslavia.**
Jeffrey P. Telgarsky, Raymond J. Struyk. Washington, DC: The Urban Institute, 1990. 258p. bibliog. (Urban Institute Report 90-10).
Opens with a summary of centrally planned economies and reform, population and urbanization, and the housing sector, that is, occupancy, production and demand, before focusing on individual countries. 'The housing policy in Czechoslovakia' (p. 141-61) covers demographic trends, an economic overview, the system of financing, prices and fiscal policy, housing stock, construction and the building materials industry, housing allocation and tenure, housing finance and future directions in housing reform.

709 **The pillars of Central Europe: the roles of cities in the process of transformation.**
Interdisciplinary Centre for Comparative Research in the Social Sciences, Vienna, edited by Jiří Musil, Ronald Pohoryles, Liana Giorgi. Aldershot, England: Avebury, 1995. 300p. (Contemporary Trends in European Social Sciences).
This study of urban development with analysis of the process of transition in Prague, Vienna, Kraków and Budapest is based on case-studies. The level of interaction between, and among, the cities is examined. The topics assessed are: public transport; telecommunications; privatization; tourism; and the geopolitical situation of the towns now and in the past.

710 **The Czech and Slovak republics.**
East 8. In: *Real estate development in Eastern Europe.* London: Interforum Publications, 1993, 3rd ed., p. 6-11. maps.
Covers the economy of the two republics generally, rents, development control, the construction industry, tourism and hotels, air, road and rail transport, industrial offices, retail and residential property. The study also provides information on Czech company law and real-estate law.

711 **The Czech housing system in the middle of transition.**
Jiří Musil. *Urban Studies,* vol. 32, no. 10 (December 1995), p. 1,679-84.
A critical analysis of changes in the housing system in the Czech Republic since the demise of Communist rule in 1989. The country lacks a market model against which to establish an even housing economy. This has resulted in the adoption of a pragmatic approach and first attempt at creating a system of housing finance. A new form of cheaper, affordable, state-run or social housing is required for low-income households.

712 **Construction and property in the Czech Republic: 1994-2000.**
Carsten Lehrskov, Michael Sander Loua. Copenhagen: European
Construction Research, 1994. 139p. maps.

This report provides information on the Czech construction industry: Czech
companies, architects and ministries; housing construction and the housing market;
office construction and the market in office and shop properties; and hotel and
industrial construction. The report further looks into construction techniques,
materials and their distribution, approvals, regulations and building permits,
construction prices, civil engineering generally, the road system, car parks, railways
and road traffic, with additional information on the environment, water, energy,
tourism, privatization, investment and joint ventures, setting up companies, local
taxes, banks, currency, financing and mortgages, duty and VAT charges, accounts and
land registry. The report lists addresses and sources.

713 **Local urban restructuring as a mirror of global processes: Prague
in the 1990s.**
Luděk Sýkora. *Urban Studies*, vol. 31, no. 7 (August 1994),
p. 1,149-66. bibliog.

The major systemic transformation in the changing post-Communist economy enabled
global forces to impact on local urban restructuring. The re-allocation of resources and
authority has created the preconditions for secondary transformations. In consequence
there are serious implications for geographically uneven development.

714 **Prague. Avenir d'une ville historique capitale.** (Prague. Future of a
historic capital city.)
Allesandro Anselmi, Miroslav Baše, Oriol Bohigas, Nancy Bouché,
Vittoria Calzolari, Françoise Choay, Jacques Derrida, Antoine
Grumbach, Karel Firbas, Pavel Havlík, Ivo Hlobil, Peter Krikovszki,
Dobroslav Líbal, Zdeněk Lukeš, Petr Kratochvíl, Alexandro
Melissinos, Vlado Milunič, Jiří Novotný, Ivo Oberstein, Michel Parent,
Josef Polišenský, Leon Pressouyre, Zdeněk Rajmš, Jean-Eudes
Roullier, Jan Sedlák, Eliška Součková, Hein W. Struben, Marie
Švábová, Ivan Vavřík, Aleš Vosahlík, edited by Jean Viard. La Tour
d'Aigues, France: Édition de l'aube, 1992. 299p. maps. (Monde en
Cours).

Historians, architects and urban specialists, drawn from eight countries, consider
questions of the urban life and development of Prague. Issues dealt with include: the
philosophy of the city and its heritage; the place of Prague in European society; the
history and current problems of urban patrimony; ancient Prague; the current and
future protection of its historic districts; its problems in the face of the market
economy; urban politics in Prague and the achievements of Prague City Council;
private capital and foreign investment; the social aspects of the renovation of historic
quarters, with focus on the rebuilding of Old Town Square; and cooperation of the
town inhabitants on architectural projects. This valuable French-language study
contains some black-and-white photographs.

715 **Concentrated Prague.**
Francis W. Carter. *Geographical Magazine*, vol. 40, no. 7 (July 1974), p. 537-44. 6 maps.

In an article as concentrated as its title, Carter provides a good introduction to the city's evolution, in terms of its great architectural variety, its pattern of industrial spread and its transport and demographic changes. The agricultural and recreational facilities of the surrounding region are also described, as important adjuncts to the life of this city of over a million inhabitants. At the time, pollution and industrial planning were among the problems faced by what the photographs show is a truly beautiful city.

716 **Prague and Sofia: an analysis of their changing internal city structure.**
Francis W. Carter. In: *The Socialist city: spatial and urban policy.* Edited by R. A. French, F. E. Ian Hamilton. Chichester, England; New York; Brisbane; Toronto: John Wiley, 1979, p. 425-59. maps. bibliog.

The author provides a potted architectural history of Prague and examines the sale and rental of dwellings, inward migration from rural areas and such more obvious topics as (then) recent developments in architecture, the location of industry, the adaptation of a mediaeval and capitalist city to modern (socialist) requirements and the elaboration of master-plans. The description of the city's contemporary features is as in 1975 and includes an account of the problems being faced at the time, many of which remained unresolved or only partially resolved: shortcomings in building practice; vandalism and rubbish dumping; and the restoration of long-neglected buildings. Many of the plans have materialized since, such as the inner ring-road, the metro and various sectoral amenities.

717 **Conservation problems of historic cities in Eastern Europe.**
Francis W. Carter. London: University College Department of Geography, 1981. 44p. maps. (Department of Geography, University College London, Occasional Papers, no. 39).

Against its more general background, this paper contains a separate case-study of Prague. The maps show the location of national and regional conservation areas and a table gives the distribution of the different architectural periods represented at various protected centres.

718 **Pollution in Prague: environmental control in a centrally planned socialist country.**
Francis W. Carter. *Cities*, vol. 1, no. 3 (1984), p. 258-73.

This is a more detailed case-study of the issues raised in the previous entry. Of the many types of pollution, only air pollution is seen as having improved since peaking in 1966; before then, with no legislation, the increase had been dramatic. Noise and water pollution continue to give cause for concern.

719 **Prague '93: metropolitan area report; urbanistic development of the town.**
Ivan Plicka. Prague: City Architect's Office of Prague, 1993. 131p. maps.

A detailed study of the urban development of Prague, prepared for the Unesco World Heritage Convention, which is supplemented with twenty pages of maps and charts. These range from maps from before 1230 AD to environmental charts showing the current levels of nitrous oxides in the city air. The text documents the city's evolution and development, town planning, population and its density, housing, public amenities, distribution of space, green spaces, sports and recreation, transport and public utilities.

720 **The nature of urbanism.**
V. Sahai. *Architectural Review*, no. 198, 1181 (July 1995), p. 84-88.

An illustrated analysis of elements of urbanism which shows how they combine to create new visual pleasures. The city of Prague is used as an example.

721 **Prague: some contemporary growth problems.**
Francis W. Carter. *Bulletin of the Société Royale de Géographie d'Anvers*, vol. 81 (1970), p. 197-218. maps.

The problems described in this study (by no means overcome now, despite the age of this item) relate to: the ability of the agricultural hinterland to satisfy the city's demands for food; effects of the concentration of industry in the city; the demands placed on a geographically (railways) and climatically (rivers) constrained transport network; the city transport authority's struggle to cope with increasing passenger numbers; and population growth, migration and density. The solutions suggested are necessarily a product of the era, but the paper remains valuable for the wealth of statistical information, the details on the distribution of industry and agriculture, and the problems' historical dimension. A similar paper, but which concentrates more on the history and the physical and economic geography and geology of the city, is 'Prague et la Bohême centrale: quelques problèmes de croissance' (Prague and Central Bohemia: some problems of growth), *Annales de Géographie*, vol. 82, no. 450 (March-April 1973), p. 165-92.

The Environment

722 **Environmental problems in Eastern Europe.**
F. W. Carter, D. Turnock. London; New York: Routledge, 1996.
291p. bibliog. maps. 2nd updated ed.
Chapter four, 'Czechoslovakia' (p. 63-88) by F. W. Carter describes the country as
one of the most polluted in Europe. The author provides case-studies and graphs and
looks at air and water pollution, soil and vegetation pollution, nuclear power, the issue
of pollution and health and green politics. The overall picture is distressing. The last
chapter in the book (chapter ten, p. 206-51) is a general work on the whole of the area,
'A review of environmental issues in the light of the transition', by F. W. Carter and
D. Turnock. The first edition of this work was published by Routledge in 1993.

723 **La crise de l'environnement à l'Est.** (The crises of the environment
in the East.)
Edited by Krystyna Vinaver. Paris: Editions L'Harmattan, 1993.
190p. bibliog.
A collection of articles identifying the problems, economic factors, attitudes of governments, activities of non-governmental organizations and international responsibility
and cooperation. There are references to Czechoslovakia throughout the book and
'Tchécoslovaquie' (Czechoslovakia) (p. 69-95), has contributions by two Czechs and
a Slovak: Jaroslav Stoklasa, Jiří Šembera and Juraj Mesik.

724 **La question énergétique en Europe de l'Est.** (The energy problems
of Eastern Europe.)
Catherine Locatelli. Paris: L'Harmattan, 1992. 255p. maps. bibliog.
(Collection Pays de l'Est).
This serious study offers many tables and charts, most of them featuring
Czechoslovakia. It is a fairly detailed, valuable analysis of the sources of energy used
in Central Europe and the Soviet Union, showing consumption over the last fifty years
(focusing on the last twenty years). The accent is on the importance of energy sources

225

for the economy. A selective bibliography of statistical sources, periodicals, books and articles is to be found on p. 233-37. The author also provides a thematic and geographical index. The same topic is studied by Jeremy Russell in *Energy and environmental conflicts in East/Central Europe: the case of power generation* (London: Royal Institute of International Affairs and World Conservation Union, 1991. 77p. map. Environmental Issues in Eastern Europe). Czechoslovakia is well represented here in numerous figures and tables.

725 **Investor's environmental guidelines: Bulgaria, Czech Republic and Slovak Republic, Estonia, Hungary, Latvia, Lithuania, Poland, Romania.**
Developed by the European Bank for Reconstruction and Development (EBRD) and the European Communities PHARE Programme.
London: Graham & Trotman; Martinus Nijhoff, 1994. 540p.
(Environmental Library, 1).

This set of reports was prepared by the EBRD to provide information for investors in Central and Eastern Europe. The work was part of a wider programme of research on the implications of the harmonization of environmental legislation and regulations between Western and Eastern Europe. The book is divided by country. 'Czech and Slovak Republics' (p. 77-164) provides an overview of the environmental situation and includes specific sections on: environmental liability; environmental audits; land-use planning; environmental impact assessments; integrated permitting requirements applicable to the operation of industrial and commercial facilities; air emission requirements; water requirements; noise requirements; hazardous and non-hazardous waste management; and chemical storage, handling and emergency response. The chapter has several annexes, the important ones being the list of key legislation and the list of proposed legislation and environmental standards. Further information on the subject can be found in *Environmental impact legislation: Czech Republic, Estonia, Hungary, Latvia, Lithuania, Poland, Slovak Republic, Slovenia*, also published in London by Graham & Trotman in 1994 (Environmental Library, 2). The full *Environmental laws of the Czech Republic* have been published in English, in four volumes (Prague: Ministry of the Environment of the Czech Republic, 1993-94. Editor in chief Václav Vacek, translation editor Madeleine Štulíková).

726 **Market opportunities brief: Czech Republic.**
[London]: Joint Environmental Markets Unit (JEMU); Technology Partnership Initiative, 1998. 35p.

This JEMU country brief investigates the opportunities for UK environmental companies in the Czech Republic. The report looks at the general background to the economic and environmental situation, environmental problems and environmental policy, lists the short-term priorities, and summarizes the legislation and regulations, market drivers, sources of funding and the competitive position of the United Kingdom. The main core of the publication is information for specific business sectors: air pollution control; water and waste water treatment; waste management; contaminated land remediation; energy management; environmental services; noise and vibration control; and renewables/cleaner technology. The study includes a list of essential contacts in the Czech Republic.

226

727 National environmental protection funds in Central and Eastern
Europe: case studies of Bulgaria, the Czech Republic, Hungary,
Poland, and the Slovak Republic.
Edited by Patrick Francis. Budapest: Regional Environmental Center
for Central and Eastern Europe, 1994. 78p.
This paperback publication summarizes information on the protection of the environment
in Eastern and Central Europe and on the funds which are available for this huge task.

728 Ministerstvo živtního prostředí České republiky. The Ministry of
the Environment of the Czech Republic.
http://www.env.cz/
The official website of the Ministry of the Environment of the Czech Republic is
published in Czech and English. At the time of writing, the English pages were still
under construction and some links were not yet available. The content was: 'The
Ministry'; 'Service organization'; 'Co-operation'; 'State of the environment in the
Czech Republic'; and 'Hot News'.

729 Environmental Yearbook of the Czech Republic.
Prague: Ministerstvo životního prostředí České republiky; Český
ekologický ústav; Český statistický úřad, 1991- . annual.
The Cabinet of the Czech Republic adopted a National Environmental Policy, a key
strategy document, on 23 August 1995. This Yearbook became the information
instrument of national environmental policy. The articles cover the causes and factors
of environmental changes, environment and health, and the environmental policy.
Two separate editions are published, one in Czech and one in English. It is a highly
detailed source of data, to which many Czech institutions contribute, such as the
Environmental Institute, Statistical Office, the Ministry of Health, the Ministry of
Agriculture, the Hydrometeorological Institute, the Geological Institute, the Institute
for Nature Conservation and the Research Institute for Water Management.

730 State of the environment in Czechoslovakia.
Prague: Vesmír, 1992. 119p. maps. bibliog.
Produced by the Federal Committee for the Environment, this work provides a brief,
general geographical and economic outline with the focus on environmental issues and
environmental policy. The Czech Republic has grave environmental problems. The
quality of air is poor, due to emissions of harmful substances and deposit release, the
impact of technological processes, transport and poor maintenance within towns.
Other topics are: the quality of water supplies; deterioration of the health, gene pool
and reproductive ability of the population; and environmental management strategy.
The slim book has a proportionate number of tables, graphs and maps.

731 Economic transformation and the environment.
Alena Černá, Eva Tošovská, Pavel Cetkovský. In: The Czech
Republic and economic transition in Eastern Europe. Edited by Jan
Švejnar. San Diego, California: Academic Press, 1995, p. 377-94.
The authors look into the impact of the economic transition on the main environmental
elements. The article starts with a general survey of the environmental situation prior

227

The Environment

to the revolution of 1989 and continues with an analysis of two areas which, during the transition, have been considered the most important and have received most attention: water quality and air pollution. The authors provide tables, on, for example: air pollution emissions per capita; investment in the environment, and the structure of this investment in the Czech Republic; the pollution produced and discharged into Czech waterways; the water and sewerage rates; the decrease in emissions; and a comparative table of the energy balance of the Czech Republic and some countries of the European Union and the Organisation for Economic Co-operation and Development (OECD).

732 **Interaction between agriculture and nature conservation in the Czech and Slovak republics. IUCN European Programme.**
M. Kundrata, J. Löw, J. Ungerman. Cambridge, England: Gland, 1995. 123p. map. bibliog. (Environmental Research Series, 8).
A report on conservation issues prepared by a Czech and Slovak team of specialists. Other titles published as part of the IUCN European Programme, dealing with the Czech Republic among other Central European countries, are: *Tanks and thyme: biodiversity in former Soviet military areas in Central Europe* (Cambridge, England: Gland, 1996. 136p. maps. bibliog. Environmental Research Series, 10); and *The mountains of Central and Eastern Europe* (Cambridge, England: Gland, 1995. 139p. maps. bibliog. Environmental Research Series, 9).

733 **National report on the Czech and Slovak Federal Republic: United Nations Conference on Environment and Development, Brazil June 1992.**
Prepared under the direction of B. Moldan. Prague: Czechoslovak Academy of Science and Environment, 1992. 141p. maps.
Numerous contributors cooperated on this report, an environmental analysis of Czechoslovakia, the core of which is natural resources and commercial activities, environmental concerns and – the most important – planning for sustainable development. A number of maps, charts and tables are included.

734 **Report on the environment of the Czech Republic in 1996.**
Prepared by the editorial team of the Ministry for the Environment.
Prague: Ministerstvo životního prostředí, 1997. 138p.
The primary objective of the report is to describe the changes in the conditions of the environment from 1995-96. The changes during that year were the result of the developments during 1990-96. The report focuses in particular on 1992-96, and indicates anticipated future trends. The secondary objective was to incorporate the environmental situation in the Czech Republic into the international context and to inform on the progress in carrying out the priority measures, which were undertaken by the state with regards to the environmental policy.

Statistická ročenka České republiky. (Statistical Yearbook of the Czech Republic.)
See item no. 416.

228

Sport and Recreation

735 **ČSTV.**
http://www.cstv.cz

A website of Český svaz tělesné výchovy (Czech Association for Physical Education), a national institution for activities relating to sport, physical education and tourism. The site is in Czech and provides information on subjects such as the history of this institution, its constitution, committees, institutional members, regional bodies, sporting activities and sport centres. Many of the general Czech Republic websites offer excellent information on sport and current sporting events in English. Many have specific subsections on sport, which are further subdivided into individual disciplines or refer to other websites.

736 **Turistický server. Travel profi. Kultura, Sport.** (Tourist server. Travel profile. Culture and sport.)
http://www.travel-profi.cz

The information on this website, in both Czech and English, is divided by county (kraj) and lower regional entities and covers only events outside the capital and other big towns. The web-site is still developing; not all regions have been processed as yet and they are being added gradually. It lists even fairly minor, not to say whimsical, cultural and sporting events and pursuits, which took place the previous year. The website gives the telephone numbers of the organizers of these happenings.

737 **Sport v království českém.** (Sport in the Kingdom of Bohemia.)
Václav Pacina.   Prague: Mladá fronta, 1986.

Sport has been associated with the issue of Czech national identity since the mid-19th century. The Sokol, a mass movement for physical training founded in 1862 by Miroslav Tyrš, is given special attention, as well as the introduction of cycling and, inevitably, the Czech successes in international competitions up to 1920.

738 **Sport under Communism: the USSR, Czechoslovakia, the GDR, China, Cuba.**
Edited by James Riordan. London: C. Hurst, 1981. 2nd ed. 181p.
This account is now a history, but it is the best one on the subject, by a writer who has long studied it. The book covers both the political and practical aspects of the organization and performance of sport. Sport played an important part in Czech life under Communism, for ideological as well as health reasons.

739 **Czechoslovakia and Olympic Games.**
Jan Kotrba, Zdeněk Illman, Jiří Kossl, translated by Libor Trejdl.
Prague: Orbis Press Agency, 1984. 143p.
A Czech, Jiří Guth, was one of the founding members of the International Olympic Committee. The first part of this book gives an account of the involvement of Czechs in the Olympic movement from its modern conception to the 1980s. The book recognizes the strong tradition of physical culture among the Czechs. The authors go as far back as the *Panorthosia* of the Moravian educator Comenius, in which he advocated the re-introduction of the Olympic Games. The second part of the book consists of photographs, a gallery of Olympic sportsmen from the Czech Lands and Slovakia and of other sporting events. The third part gives brief sketches of nineteen Czech and Slovak individuals or teams, medal winners, their careers and achievements. The last section is a chronological table of successes achieved by Czechoslovaks from 1948 to 1980. The book is not enhanced by the translation which seeks to imitate the style of English sports journalism. Slightly more recent information on Czechoslovak Olympic competitors can be obtained from a publication in Czech, *Zátopek a ti druzí: galerie čs. olympijských vítězů* (Zátopek and the others: a gallery of Czechoslovak Olympic winners), by Zvonimír Šupich (Prague: Olympia, 1986).

740 **Sokol: the Czechoslovak national gymnastic organization.**
F. A. Toufar. London: George Allen & Unwin, 1941. 61p.
This historical work looks back beyond the foundation of Sokol in 1862 to the times and events that followed 1848. Its evolution is traced from its conception up to the Second World War. It is also a biography of the founder of Sokol, Miroslav Tyrš (1832-84). Other celebrated members are also described, as well as associated organizations among Czech émigrés abroad, the insignia of Sokol, its slogans, and the music played at the displays.

741 **'Every Czech a Sokol': feminism and nationalism in the Czech Sokol movement.**
Claire E. Nolte. *Austrian History Yearbook* (Center for Austrian Studies, University of Minnesota), vol. 24 (1993), p. 79-100.
On the role of the Sokol organization in the emancipation efforts of Czech women up to the First World War. The American author, who has a longstanding research interest in the history of the Sokol movement, looks at the activities of the Sokol, evaluates the importance of the foundation in 1869 (at the instigation of the founder of Sokol itself, Miroslav Tyrš) of the Prague Ladies and Girls Gymnastic Club (Tělocvičný spolek paní a dívek pražských), which contributed to the emancipation of women by involving them in physical training and education, alas separately from the activities of men. The author notes the obstacles and prejudices which made the participation of women in Sokol difficult. This was achieved only at the beginning of

the 20th century, when for the first time 800 women took part in the fourth Sokol Slet (mass gymnastics display) in 1901. Nolte points out the military dimension to the Sokol movement's mission, which was used in the debate on the position of women within the movement as an argument against their participation in its organizational bodies right up to 1913.

742 **The Czechoslovak Spartakiad 1985.**
Zdeněk Lipský, translated by Alžběta Rejchrtová. Prague: Orbis Press Agency, 1984. 48p. map.

After the Communist takeover of Czechoslovakia, Spartakiads replaced the Sokol slety, or gymnastic displays. Spartakiads were five-yearly displays of physical education which took place in Prague and involved more than 150,000 people. Each event was the culmination of mass preparations and regional run-ups, in which most schoolchildren and hundreds of thousands of adults took part. Spartakiads were heavily promoted by the state; this was an area where sport and politics met. A larger publication came out after the 1980 display, which bore the slogan 'festival of peace and socialism'. *Československá Spartakiáda 1980* (Czechoslovak Spartakiad 1980) was edited by Július Chvalný with text by sports writer Zvonimír Šupich (Prague: Olympia; Bratislava: Šport, 1981. 176p.). The text is in Czech, but there is a summary of the events in Russian, English, German, French and Spanish. Both publications provide statistical information and photographs, which illustrate the magnitude and complexity of these mass gymnastic displays.

743 **Století fotbalu: z dějin československé kopané.** (One hundred years of football: from the history of Czechoslovak football.)
Josef Pondělík, Jindřich Pejchar. Prague: Olympia, 1986. 412p. bibliog.

As might be expected, nearly half of this book is made up of photographs. They include the oldest photograph of a football team from the Czech Lands, dated 1893, and the gallery ends with a photograph of the team which took part in the 1986 World Cup in Mexico. The sequence of the text is chronological, from 1891 to c.1985, and highlights the successes of Czech football. The documentary section lists various championships, cups and important matches.

744 **Kronika českého fotbalu do roku 1945.** (Chronicle of Czech football up to 1945.)
Miloslav Jenšík, Jiří Macků. Prague: Olympia, 1997, 1998. 2 vols.

The two sizeable volumes were compiled by two football journalists, regular contributors to the Czech weekly *Gól* (Goal). The work is arranged by date, as a chronicle should be, and supported by a wealth of historical material. Although it offers plenty of data, the core of the work is its rich narrative.

745 **The quiet Karel amid the clamour.**
Michael Walker. *The Guardian*, 9 August 1996, p. 4-5.

A profile of Karel Poborský, one of the most popular players in the 1996 European Championship football tournament, held in England, in which the Czech Republic came second. The twenty-four-year-old Czech Republic international joined Manchester United at Old Trafford later that year but subsequently left.

231

Sport and Recreation

746   **Český hokej.** (Czech hockey.)
      Karel Gut, Jaroslav Prchal.   Prague: Olympia, 1998. 159p.
In terms of the relative popularity of spectator sports, in the Czech Republic (and
former Czechoslovakia) ice hockey is on the same level as football. The long list of
memorable international successes achieved by the Czech national hockey team was
topped by a gold medal from the 1998 Winter Olympics in Nagano, Japan. This
colourful, large-format book, which has many commercial advertisements, looks at the
ninety years (from 1908) of hockey in the Czech Lands. This narrative is summarized
in German and English on p. 158. However, the main section of the book consists of
photographs, in colour and black-and-white. The supplement is 'Statistika' (p. 145-
55), which is a chronology of major events, from the European Championship in 1910
to the World Championship in Switzerland in 1998.

747   **Náš hokej.** (Our ice hockey.)
      Compiled by Vladimír Dobrovodský, Stanislav Halásek, text by
      Václav Pacina.   Prague: Olympia, 1985. 2nd updated ed. 176p.
This publication is outdated since it is a portrait of the then Czechoslovak context of
the game and its players, but it includes over 100 mostly colour photographs, which
give the book its enduring interest. It has résumés in English, German and Russian.

748   **Martina Navrátilová.**
      Julia Holt.   London: Adult Literacy and Basic Skills Unit, 1994. 16p.
      (Real Lives).
Published within a series of simple readers about the fifteen most famous personalities
from the world of sport. Navrátilová is considered the most successful woman tennis
star of all time. This book has clear, easy-to-read text, contains a number of
photographs and seeks to interest readers of all ages.

749   **Martina: an ace of an autobiography from the greatest women's
      tennis player the world has ever known.**
      Martina Navrátilová, with George Vecsey.   New York: Fawcett Crest,
      1986. 321p.
This autobiography was also published in London (Collins, 1985) under the title *Being
myself*, and translated into other languages. The book is true to the title of the English
edition and is more about Navrátilová than her tennis. The public in general, and many
of the newspaper articles published on her, seem to be interested more in
Navrátilová's private life than in her astonishing performance (her shots were timed at
90 miles per hour and she won Wimbledon nine times). This autobiography of
Navrátilová includes photographs from her childhood in Czechoslovakia (she was
born in 1956), notes on tennis in Czechoslovakia and on other Czech players. *Love
match: Nelson vs. Navrátilová*, by Sandra Faulkner with Judy Nelson (New York:
Carol Publishing Group, 1993), was written in cooperation with Navrátilová's former
female lover of six years. A biography of a contemporary outstanding Czech woman
player, alas not of Navrátilová's calibre, was published in Czech only, *Hana
Mandlíková*, by Vladimír Škutina (Prague: Olympia, 1991).

232

750 **Net result.**
Helen Oldfield. *The Guardian*, 18 January 1995, supplement, p. 12-13.

A profile of the tennis player Martina Navrátilová, who came from Prague and became one of the most successful sportswomen ever. She has now retired from the grass courts, at the age of thirty-eight, and muses on her future.

751 **Serenity greets the ultimate athlete reborn.**
Simon Barnes. *The Times*, 23 January, 1995. 31p.

An interview with Martina Navrátilová, now retired and happily in charge of her own future. There were numerous articles on Martina around this time, the two listed here are a quality profile (see previous item) and an interview.

752 **Martina Navrátilová.**
M. Macdonald. *Observer*, 14 June 1998, Life section, p. 14-16, 18.

Another interview with the ex-queen of the tennis courts. This one catches up with what she has been doing since her retirement as a professional player, three-and-a-half years previously.

753 **Chata and Chalupa: recreational houses in the Czech Socialist Republic.**
Lawrence C. Herold. *Social Science Journal*, vol. 18, no. 1 (January 1981), p. 51-68.

Traditionally, urban Czechs, Praguers and citizens of Brno in particular, have sought recreation at the second homes which so many of them possess. This paper describes the then prevailing pattern of *chata* (roughly: 'chalet') and *chalupa* (roughly: 'cottage') ownership, when the system was at its height. In part things are unchanged, though the extent of ownership and use of such second homes has dropped for economic reasons, including taxation and the sheer cost of travelling to them since petrol price increases of several hundred per cent.

754 **Fish and fishermen.**
Text by Stanislav Lusk, photographs by Jiří Vostradovský, translated by Elizabeth Kindlová. London: Sunburst, 1995. 184p.

Published first in Czech by Artia in Prague (1986), this book on fishing in Europe has many pictures from the Czech Republic and Slovakia. The fine colour illustrations of rivers, lakes, ponds and reservoirs and activities related to angling are accompanied by text on water environment, fish families, distribution of fish species, the protection of fish, fish breeding and the fish industry.

755 **Fishing in the Czech Socialist Republic.**
Government Committee for Tourism of the Czech Socialist Republic and the Czech Fishing Association. Prague: Merkur, 1983. 23p. [unpaginated]. map.

An introduction to the riverscapes and fishponds of the Czech Lands for tourists who would like to try fishing, with an outline of provisions for angling in the country and how to obtain the necessary permits. The pamphlet gives reasonably detailed information on the distribution of twelve species of fish which are found there and a physical description of each. An insert of sixteen pages provides a list of the best fishing grounds for individual types of fish and gives statistical tables for sizes of catches per annum and individual record catches. It is a publicity brochure for tourists which is normally available through official agencies.

756 **Checkmate in Prague: memoirs of Luděk Pachman.**
Luděk Pachman, translated by Rosemary Brown. London: Faber & Faber, 1975. 216p.

The best-known Czech chess player, Luděk Pachman, is the author of numerous books on chess for players of all standards and on the application of computer systems to chess (published by Routledge & Kegan Paul). He starts his memoirs with the Nazi occupation and continues through the Prague Spring, his own imprisonment and subsequent emigration to the then West Germany. His opposition to the Communist regime won him considerable notoriety at the time. The autobiography is also an account of Pachman's career as a chess player, giving insights into the organization of the game and information on some of the tournaments in which he took part.

Statistická ročenka České republiky. (Statistical Yearbook of the Czech Republic.)
See item no. 416.

234

Language
Compiled by David Short

General and historical

757 The Slavonic languages.
Edited by Bernard Comrie, Greville G. Corbett.   London; New York:
Routledge, 1993. 1,078p. bibliogs.

Several chapters in this volume are relevant: chapter one, 'Introduction' (by the editors, p. 1-19. map. bibliog.), which describes the salient features of Slavonic languages generally; chapter two, 'Alphabets and transliteration' (Paul Cubberley, p. 20-59. bibliog.), with subsections on alphabets in use, or created, in Bohemia (p. 30, 42-43); and chapter nine, 'Czech' (David Short, p. 455-532. bibliog.), which gives a fairly detailed discursive survey of the contemporary language (with tables), including sections on the language's history and dialects. The whole volume is conceived as a practical and comparative compendium (the layout of the language chapters has a common format to aid comparison) and is widely perceived as superseding R. G. A. de Bray's *Guide to the Slavonic languages* (Columbus, Ohio: Slavica Publishers, 1980. 3rd ed. 3 vols. bibliog.), in which the Czech section is in volume two. A work devoted specifically to Czech orthography is Comrie's section on 'Languages of eastern and southern Europe', in Peter T. Daniels and William Bright's *The world's writing systems* (New York; Oxford: Oxford University Press, 1996, p. 663-89), especially p. 663-65, 668 and 673-74.

758 The Slavonic literary languages.
Edited by Alexander M. Schenker, Edward Stankiewicz.   New Haven,
Connecticut: Yale Concilium on International and Area Studies, 1980.
287p. bibliog.

The section on Czech (Robert Auty, p. 163-82. bibliog., p. 271-74), though ageing, remains a good general history. Auty presents the patterns of historicizing conservatism and waves of purism as the main trends to have given Czech its present shape, and relates the religious history of the nation to the history of its language.

Reference is made to the development of the alphabet, the early grammars and the formation of the lexicon. The bibliography contains a number of references to his own earlier works dealing with specific topics in greater detail.

759 **An introduction to the study of the Slavonic languages.**
Karel Horálek, translated from the Czech, amended by Peter Herrity.
Nottingham, England: Astra Press, 1992. 587p. (in 2 vols.). bibliogs.

For all the textual evidence of its being a translation, the evidence of incomplete (defective) word-processing and some mistranslations, this work is a useful introduction to all the Slavonic languages, with countless apposite sections on Czech and its evolution *passim*. In its own right, Horálek's work is also a key example of Czech scholarship in historical linguistics.

760 **Czech historical grammar.**
Stuart E. Mann. Hamburg, FRG: Helmut Buske Verlag, 1977. rev. ed. 183p.

This revised edition of a 1957 work (London: Athlone Press, 1957. bibliog.) is the only complete history of the language available in English. The author, unlike the authors of competing Czech works, deals with different segments of the grammar in turn, rather than providing a consecutive history. The work draws heavily on etymologies and the prehistoric periods of evolution, in accordance with generally accepted reconstructions. The book also contains a summary account of the modern dialects, notes on Old Czech textual sources, some illustrative Old Czech literary extracts and a note on the composition of the Czech vocabulary; the revised edition has no bibliography.

Dictionaries

General

761 **Slovník spisovného jazyka českého.** (Dictionary of the Czech literary language.)
Compiled by the lexicography team of the Institute of the Czech Language of the Czechoslovak Academy of Sciences, led by Bohuslav Havránek, Jaromír Bělič, M. Helcl, Alois Jedlička, Václav Křístek, František Trávníček. Prague: Academia, 1989. 8 vols.

A handier, smaller-format reprint of the work that originally appeared in four large volumes in 1971. For all its signs of in-built obsolescence, and in the absence of any comparable dictionary, this is *the* basic modern lexicon. It is descended from the nine-volume *Příruční slovník jazyka českého* (Reference dictionary of the Czech language) of 1935-57, which was equally without competition. Though these works are not easy to obtain, major Slavonic libraries will have them. The obsolescence, made worse by the political changes of 1989 onwards, is partially overcome by the following title.

762 **Slovník spisovné češtiny pro školu a veřejnost.** (Dictionary of literary Czech for school and public.)
Edited by Josef Filipec, František Daneš, Jaroslav Machač, Vladimír Mejstřík. Prague: Academia, for the Institute of the Czech Language, 1998. 2nd rev. ed. 647p.

Amazingly, when the first edition of this work appeared (1978) the Czechs had been without a single-volume dictionary of their language for over quarter of a century, the last having been a 1952 edition (heavily redolent of the post-1948 period of its publication) of the 1937 *Slovník jazyka českého* (Dictionary of the Czech language) by Pavel Váša and František Trávníček. The present dictionary, without a serious competitor, has evolved over time, each successive edition and printing being a revision of its predecessor. It is readily available. Although the title contains the problematic word here translated (traditionally) as 'literary', the reference is really to the modern *standard* language generally. Unlike the two predecessor works (*Slovník spisovného jazyka českého* [q. v.] and *Příruční slovník jazyka českého*), this one recognizes the shift in the language's centre of gravity from the high literary to the (semi-)technical. The first edition contained much of a theoretical nature, relating to lexicography in general and recent changes in the Czech language; these sections have been somewhat reduced since.

763 **Akademický slovník cizích slov.** (Academy dictionary of foreign words.)
Věra Petráčková, Jiří Kraus, Bohuslav Havránek, Jaromir Bělič, M. Helcl, Alois Jedlicka, Václav Křístek, Frantiek Trávníček.
Prague: Academia, 1995. 2 vols.

These two volumes, paginated through to p. 834, give a specialist, compendious and comprehensive picture of the wealth of loan-words in modern Czech. It is an item which would be found in a library, rather than one which would be bought by the common enquirer, who is adequately served by the following item.

764 **Slovník cizích slov.** (Dictionary of foreign words.)
Compiled by the authors and consultants of Encyklopedický dům.
Prague: Encyklopedický dům, 1996. 366p.

This dictionary is perhaps marred by its failure to indicate the source language of the loan-words listed (total not given), on the grounds that it is not a specialist linguistic publication. It seeks to be as up-to-date as possible, recognizing that many new items had entered the language, in the media and commerce especially, since all similar previous works. It is unusual in that it gives numerous words that are so new that their final written form in Czech is not established; these are given in both the orthography of the source language (usually English) and in a phonetic rendering equivalent to how the native perceives the foreign item. Where a word has become established, the orthography follows the latest Academy standard (1993-94). This volume largely supersedes Lumír Klimeš's *Slovník cizích slov* (Prague: Státní pedagogické nakladatelství, 1981. 791p. bibliog.), which does offer some information on the source of the loan-words listed.

237

765 **Nová slova v češtině: slovník neologismů.** (New words in Czech: a dictionary of neologisms.)
Compiled by Olga Martincová et al. Prague: Academia, 1998. 336p. bibliog.

Mainstream Czech dictionaries (few as there are) are notorious for slowness in adapting to the latest usages. This academic publication draws on a wide range of then recently published books and periodicals to provide a comprehensive list of new words in most spheres of life. The problem for the foreign user is being able to predict whether any word unknown to him is to be sought in the mainstream dictionary, or in a publication like this; in an ideal world the two corpora should be merged into one work as soon as possible – notwithstanding the transitory nature of some neologisms. This work opens with the politically correct *abilympiáda* (a competitive olympiad for those with disabilities, based on their particular *abi*lities) and closes with *žralokárium*, a grotesque hybrid based on *žralok* ('shark') and 'aquarium', and the established *žurnalistika* ('journalism'), cross-referenced to *investigativní*.

766 **Co v slovnících nenajdete.** (What you will not find in dictionaries.)
Zdeňka Sochová, Běla Postolková. Prague: Portál, 1994. 204p.

This dictionary of neologisms opens with a linguistic and lexicological introduction relating above all to the information explosion (and social change) of the years since 1989 and its impact on contemporary Czech – part of the broader 'westernising' processes going on in all Central and Eastern European societies. This often means the mechanical adoption, with minimal adaptation, of all manner of alien words, though there is also no shortage of such Czech novelties as *erosenka*, defined as 'a professional sexual worker in a massage parlour' ('massage parlour' itself translates back from Czech as 'erotic bar'). As a detail of interest, this listing also opens, like the previous entry, with *abilympiáda*, but it also contains an alternative, *abiolympiáda*.

767 **Slovník české frazeologie a idiomatiky: přirovnání.** (Dictionary of Czech phrases and idioms: similes.)
Compiled by František Čermák, Jiří Hronek et al. Prague: Academia, 1983. 492p.

A dictionary of all manner of idioms, most still in active modern usage, ordered by the 'obvious' nominal key-word. Each entry contains the phrase's syntactic range, an explanation of its origins, examples, and specimen (though not necessarily all-purpose) translations in English, German, French and Russian. The similes volume set the pattern for later volumes on *Výrazy neslovesné* (Non-verbal expressions) (1988. 511p.) and *Výrazy slovesné* (Verbal expressions) (1994. 2 vols.). Yet another volume based on other word-classes is in preparation by this publisher.

768 **Pravidla českého pravopisu.** (The rules of Czech orthography.)
Compiled by Zdeněk Hlavsa et al. Prague: Academia, 1993. 391p.

A handbook of this kind has appeared regularly for a century or so, updating the changing orthographic standard and offering guidance on punctuation, capitalization, the appropriate handling of the latest loan-words etc. This edition is included in preference to any later ones (and to any published by provincial publishers) since it included the text (p. 390-91) of the Appendix ordered by the Czech Ministry of Education and summoned forth in reaction to the popular disquiet caused by a particular innovation in the orthographic standard. The disquiet was allayed by an official sanctioning of both the previous and the new standard.

769 **Slovník českých synonym.** (Dictionary of Czech synonyms.)
Karel Pala, Jan Všianský. Prague: Nakladatelství Lidové noviny,
1994. 435p.

Supersedes J. V. Bečka's *Slovník synonym a frazeologismů* (Dictionary of synonyms
and phrasal units) (Prague: Vydavatelství Novinář, 1979. 431p.), from which it differs
in a variety of respects. There are no Latin or English tags, and the synonyms to the
entry-words are clearly grouped according to the part-meanings of polysemic items.
The dictionary also gives antonyms. The theoretical background on the structure and
use of the dictionary (p. 5-9) is given only in Czech.

770 **Etymologický slovník jazyka českého.** (Etymological dictionary of
the Czech language.)
Václav Machek. Prague: Academia, 1971. 3rd ed. 866p. bibliog.

The standard, now classical etymological dictionary. In it, prefixed words do not
usually appear, so a knowledge of basic forms, even if obsolescent, is essential. It
contains a wealth of peripheral words – regional, dialectal, Slovak and various types
of interjections – in addition to the core native word-stock. A language-by-language
list of all words referred to in the etymological glosses is provided (p. 733-866).
Although widely accepted as authoritative, Machek's *magnum opus* is the subject of
constant revisions and reappraisal and revised etymologies frequently appear on the
pages of *Naše řeč* (Our Language) (Prague: Institute of the Czech [previously
Czechoslovak] Language of the Czech Academy of Sciences, 1917- . 10 issues per
year) and other Czech philological journals.

771 **Stručný etymologický slovník se zvláštním zřetelem k slovům
kulturním a cizím.** (Concise etymological dictionary with special
reference to cultural and foreign words.)
Josef Holub, Stanislav Lyer. Prague: Státní pedagogické
nakladatelství, 1978. 2nd rev. ed. 483p. bibliog.

This work complement's Machek's classic work (see previous entry) and contains, for
the most part, words whose foreign origin has been obliterated, more recent loans that
are on the way to full domestication, often in the absence of an adequate native
synonym, and a proportion of the 'international' vocabulary essential to everyday life.
The introduction outlines the structure of the Czech word-stock and the evolution of
Indo-European. This provides the background to the systematic cross-referencing
between entries to reveal interrelations between loans across language boundaries, e.g.
both *mykorrhiza* and *ředkev* are cross-referenced to *radikál*. The work reappeared in
unnumbered reprints.

772 **Retrográdní morfematický slovník češtiny.** (Reversing morphemic
dictionary of Czech.)
Eleonora Slavíčková. Prague: Academia, 1975. 645p.

A valuable aid to the study of the language, this *a tergo* dictionary differs from many
in being compiled using morphemes, rather than graphemes, as base. It contains
inventories of root, prefixal and suffixal morphemes as well as the main list. The
theoretical introduction is in English, Czech, Russian and French.

773 **Český slovník věcný a synonymický.** (Czech dictionary of subjects and synonyms.)
Compiled by Jiří Haller. Prague: Státní pedagogické nakladatelství, 1969-77. 3 vols.

This is still the only Czech thesaurus to go beyond lists of synonyms. The vocabulary is classified by semantic fields, all relevant items brought together irrespective of, for example, word class. The classification evolves in a logical sequence, as follows from the contents table. Work on the thesaurus was arrested by the death of the compiler and several of the members of the editorial committee.

774 **Anglicko-český – česko-anglický slovník.** (English-Czech – Czech-English dictionary.)
Josef Fronek. Prague: LEDA, 1998. 1,277p.

This is beyond doubt the best two-way dictionary to have appeared since lexicography, like other areas of publishing, was released from the straightjacket of central planning. Unlike many of its predecessors from the Communist era, it takes full account of both the Czech and the anglophone user, the theoretical apparatus in the preliminary pages being in both languages and grammatical and other glosses being both adequate and transparent. It has a wealth of grammatical glosses in both halves. The 'most recent expressions', whose inclusion makes this book so much better than its competitors, include, for example, *cot death* and *zonked*, but not, say, *security risk* or *code of practice*. In structure it is a merging – but with numerous improvements in every respect – of the same author's innovative *Anglicko-český slovník s nejnovějšími výrazy* (English-Czech dictionary with the most recent expressions) (Voznice, Czech Republic: LEDA, 1996. xxix + 1,204p.) and his rather less successful earlier *Česko-anglický slovník* (Czech-English dictionary) (Prague: SPN, 1993. 708p.); in the latter case he enjoyed the collaboration of Margaret Tejerizo.

775 **Velký anglicko-český slovník.** (Large English-Czech dictionary.)
Karel Hais, Břetislav Hodek. Prague: Academia, 1991-93. 2nd ed. 4 vols.

When the first edition of this work appeared (1984-85. 3 vols.), it was the first large work of its kind to appear since 1911. The second edition is merely a smaller-format and better bound reprint. The work seeks to enable the Czech user to cope with idiomatic English (of various geographical kinds) from the 18th century to the present (i.e. the 1980s), thus it has a good stock of phrasal and other idiomatic expressions in the generous exemplification. The English-speaking user is more likely to detect the occasional flaws, and query the need for the inclusion of several items. Each entry is glossed for pronunciation, and any necessary grammatical, stylistic or other indicators are given as appropriate (American vs. British usage, for example). The vocabulary of various specialist or technical fields is fairly well represented. Generous appendixes (volume four, p. 401-552) cover English-language abbreviations, the administrative subdivisions of English-speaking countries, weights and measures, British and US military ranks (but not their Czech equivalents), and personal and geographical names (again, without their Czech equivalents; these sections are an aid to pronunciation for the Czech user).

776 **Anglicko-český výkladový slovník.** (English-Czech defining dictionary.)
Prepared, printed and distributed with the authorization of HarperCollins Publishers Ltd. Prague: Lidové noviny, 1998. 1,174p. + 12 unpaginated pages of picture dictionary.
Combines the features of a bilingual (translating, *překladový*) and monolingual (defining, *výkladový*) dictionary. Six different translators contributed to the task of re-rendering a classic English dictionary into a valuable, multi-purpose tool for learners, translators and other practitioners in the two languages. Not only are the headwords translated, as in a conventional bilingual dictionary, but the entire apparatus of an entry-word's definitions and examples are given in both English and Czech.

777 **Czech-English dictionary.**
Ivan Poldauf, in cooperation with Robert Pynsent. Prague: SPN, 1986. 1,133p.; Prague: WD Publications, 1996. 3rd ed. 1,187p.
This was the first post-war dictionary to benefit from collaboration with an Anglo-Saxon co-author. Its coverage is broad, but traditional, from the high literary to the coarse colloquial, but excluding many semi-technical items that are, after all, in daily use. The layout and nesting are often irritating, but this is due to the publisher's late demand for space-saving cuts. The introductory apparatus is entirely in Czech (and includes a list, p. 24, of its predecessors going back to 1876), while the survey of Czech grammar at the back is in English. One obvious curiosity is the absence from the main corpus of the very word *český*, which can only be found in the 'Differential glossary of proper names' (p. 1,085-99). The pirate third edition has been 'modernized' (if only to a limited extent) and otherwise modified by Sinclair Nicholas, who has also produced a *Velký americko-český slovník* (Large American-Czech dictionary) (Prague: WD Publications, 1998, distributed in North America by Hippocrene Books, New York).

778 **Anglicko-česky – česko-anglický slovník.** (English-Czech – Czech-English dictionary.)
Ivan Poldauf, Jan Caha, Alena Kopecká, Jiří Krámský. Prague: SPN, 1994. 9th rev. ed. 1,014p.
Among the better one-volume two-way dictionaries, this is much improved in comparison with its earlier editions, to the extent that it is worth saying earlier versions should be avoided; it is also completely re-set.

779 **Slovník amerikanismů.** (Dictionary of Americanisms.)
Jaroslav Peprník. Prague: SPN, 1982. 612p.
This useful supplement to the usual English-Czech dictionaries covers all modern American English, literary and non-literary, and is almost entirely reliable. It also includes a US-British differential glossary and differences of pronunciation.

241

780 **Oxford photo dictionary anglicko-český. Praktická cvičení pro potřebu škol a samouků.** (Oxford English-Czech photo-dictionary. Practical exercises for the needs of schools and self-teachers.) Edited by Jane Taylor. Oxford: Oxford University Press, 1992. 141p.
Although intended by the publishers as an aid to Czechs learning English, the book is also available in some British bookshops. The high-quality colour photographs contain some 24,000 bilingual entries, where the translation equivalents are usually reliable. Its shortcomings arise from the assumption of merely one-to-one equivalences (except where differing British and American usage is acknowledged), and from some difficulties arising from certain simple, but striking cultural differences between the Czech and English environment (such as in cuisine). There are separate Czech and English word-lists and fifteen pages of mixed exercises (with a key). Revised editions of this work have been published since 1992.

781 **Czech-English idioms and figurative expressions.** Libushe Zorin-Obrusníková. Prague: JTP, 1997. unpaginated.
This collection was originally assembled privately and not intended for publication. It has a number of curious inappropriate equivalents and unaccountable omissions, not to mention uncorrected misprints, but as Juliet Kepl said (*ITI Bulletin*, 20 August 1998): 'With a revision of the English part and some indication of the origin of the expressions, it could become not only good reading, but a useful tool'.

782 **English-Czech dictionary of idioms.** Břetislav Kroulík, Barbora Kroulíková. Prague: Svoboda, 1993. 2nd ed. 203p.
This is a reprint, much improved in printing and layout, of the first edition (Toronto: Czechoslovak Association of Canada, 1986. 515p.), which may still be available in places. The 'idioms' contained are a broad and unpredictable medley of metaphorical and other phrases and idiomatic uses of sundry phrasal verbs, generally provided with good translation equivalents and illustrated by examples in whole sentences.

Specialist

783 **Česko-anglický ekonomický slovník.** (Czech-English economics dictionary.) Alberto Caforio. Prague: Encyklopedický dům, 1996. 583p.
The new conditions of a market economy have bred numerous specialist dictionaries in almost every sphere. Most have appeared in the Czech Republic and their quality is very mixed. This is one of the better examples, which, perhaps oddly, can be used with greater certainty by the English user: the frequent strings of (apparent) synonyms have no glosses to indicate to the Czech user which item is appropriate to a particular context.

784 **Anglicko-český ekonomický slovník s výkladem a výslovností.**
(Czech-English economics dictionary with explanations and pronunciation.)
J. H. Adam. Voznice, Czech Republic: LEDA, 1995. 652p.

This is a translation (Jiří Elman) of the second edition of the *Longman dictionary of business English*, in which the explanation and exemplification of the meanings of the many concepts which were genuinely new in the Czech business environment is no less important than the translation equivalents. Some of the latter may prove to be transitory and it is more than likely that the book's agile publisher will be mindful of the need for updates. Within its 13,000 entries, some 17,000 terms in banking, stocks and shares, taxation, insurance, management, accountancy, advertising, tourism, public finance and others are defined and translated. By the nature of the agreement with the Longman Group, this book is licensed for sale in the Czech and Slovak republics only.

785 **Anglicko-český ekonomický slovník.** (English-Czech economics dictionary.)
Jiří Elman, Kamila Šemberová. Prague: Victoria Publishing, 1996. 2 vols. 1,241p.

Intended for economists, bankers, brokers, computer operators, lawyers, translators and universities, this dictionary of over 100,000 entries, covering both US and UK usage, is not only fairly comprehensive and generally reliable, but particularly user-friendly, since it overtly avoids nesting. Appendixes include abbreviations (p. 1,185-1,227), the world's currencies and the main bank codes for them, weights and measures, abbreviations of the states of the United States, and guidelines for writing (English) business letters.

786 **Čtyřjazyčný slovník práva Evropských společenství.** (Quadrilingual dictionary of the law of the European Communities.)
Luboš Tichý, Richard Král, Jiří Zemánek, Pavel Svoboda. Prague: Linde, 1997. 202p.

This English-Czech-French-German dictionary, produced through the European Union PHARE programme in the context of harmonizing Czech law with that of the EU, apparently draws only on one English and two French glossaries emanating from the European Commission. Occasionally, then, some items one might need are simply not included; in other words it is only as good as far as it goes in terms of both range and cut-off point in time ('subsidiarity' is in, 'degressivity' came too late). Furthermore, while it might be assumed to be indicative of the approved 'European' jargon, the evidence of the Czech press is that there is still no uniform practice for a number of expressions. For obvious reasons, regular updated reprints will be eminently desirable, though their appearance remains to be seen.

787 **Anglicko-český právnický slovník – English Czech law dictionary.**
Marta Chromá. Prague: LEDA, 1995. 341p.

A useful general-purpose legal dictionary, which also contains a section on legal abbreviations and acronyms (p. 333-41). Some entries reveal evidence of the compiler's own attempts to supply terms for which she failed to find established English equivalents.

243

788 **English-Czech technical dictionary – Anglicko-český technický slovník.**
Jiří Elman, Václav Michálek. Prague: Sobotáles, 1998. 1,317p. + 6 unpaginated appendices.
A good general technical dictionary of 120,000 entries, covering all domains of science and technology and economics. Any older, similarly titled dictionaries, by different authors and from different publishers, were generally as good, but in principle, given the speed of technological developments, it only makes sense to cite and use the latest.

789 **Anglicko-český lékařský terminologický slovník.** (English-Czech medical terminological dictionary.)
Jonathan P. Murray. Prague: H & H, 1995. 339p.
A sectional, or classified, rather than alphabetical, dictionary which recognizes the different 'social, cultural and historical determinants' which may occasionally be problematical in the search for equivalents. It opens with 'parts of the body' (p. 7-10), while, for example, 'descriptive words for a child's mental state or behaviour' (p. 168-71) contains a rich and varied range of adjectives. In the course of the six main sections, there are twenty 'cases' presented as doctor-patient dialogues, which are coincidentally excellent specimens of good 'free', but accurate, translation. The dictionary also contains bilingually glossed diagrams of the human skeleton and sundry key organs. For a fairly good general medical dictionary, compiled on the basis of materials supplied by ten specialists in individual medical disciplines, see *Lékařský slovník anglicko-český česko-anglický* (English-Czech Czech-English medical dictionary), compiled by Jarmila Paroubková (Prague: Avicenum, 1992. 2nd ed. 693p.). Published at a time when the new Czech Republic was finding new ways in all spheres, this dictionary includes a comprehensive introduction (in Czech) to the National Health Service and medical research and training in the United Kingdom, including a list of UK medical degrees and diplomas (p. 8-23).

790 **Anglicko-český chemický slovník – English-Czech chemical dictionary.**
Karel Bláha et al. Prague: SNTL, 1988. 550p.
A fine modern dictionary of chemical terminology, with special preliminaries on 'General instructions for the translation of the names of chemical compounds', 'The nomenclature of organic compounds' and 'The nomenclature of inorganic compounds', which appear in both Czech (p. 11-60) and English (p. 61-111). A companion Czech-English volume was also produced by the same publisher (1989).

791 **Anglicko-český výkladový slovník výpočetní techniky.** (English-Czech defining dictionary of computer technology.)
Oldřich Minihofer. Prague: SNTL, 1990. 2nd ed. xviii + 228p. bibliog.
A fairly comprehensive dictionary which combines the advantages of definition and translation, important in a field in which so many items are thoroughly new and therefore, in languages other than (generally) English, some invention of new terms or latter-day metaphorization of existing expressions is unavoidable. Despite the work that went into the theoretical introduction (in Czech and English), experts in the field

are often dismissive of many of the innovations in this particular field and are quite content to use mere modifications of an English source-word. The companion Czech-English work also saw a second edition in the same year.

Grammars and textbooks

792 **Grammaire de la langue tchèque.** (Grammar of the Czech language.)
André Mazon. Paris: Institut d'études slaves, 1952. 3rd rev. ed. 252p.
A once highly regarded, now classical but dated reference grammar, which nevertheless remains a useful resource.

793 **An outline of modern Czech grammar.**
Stanislav Kavka. Uppsala, Sweden: Slaviska Institutionen, Uppsala Universitet, 1988. 93p.
An A4-format descriptive grammar, intended primarily as a university textbook and prepared by a Czech linguist during his period as *lektor* in Sweden. In addition to the discursive text, in reasonable English, but couched very much in Prague School terms, it has a fairly wide range of reference tables, including one on the individual syntactic structures dictated by particular verbs. For a more recent description of the language, see David Short's 'Czech' in *The Slavonic languages* (q.v.).

794 **Contemporary Czech.**
Michael Heim. Columbus, Ohio: Slavica Publishers, 1982. 2nd ed. 271p. bibliog. (UCLA Slavic Studies, no. 3).
This very dense course in fourteen lessons and fourteen review lessons is intended for university study; it does not lend itself to self-instruction. While not specifically intended for those with a prior knowledge of Russian, it does cater for them with notes *passim* on specific areas of similarity or contrast. The exercises (no key) are more generous than in many course books and there are useful appendices (grammar tables). The pilot edition of this work was published in 1976 by the Slavic Department of the University of Michigan.

795 **Czech through Russian.**
Charles E. Townsend. Columbus, Ohio: Slavica Publishers, 1981. 263p.
A knowledge of one Slavonic language makes it possible for most of the others to be learnt more easily. Townsend's book recognizes that, traditionally, most people have acquired Russian first, and it proposes that a knowledge of Russian is the first step towards acquiring a good working knowledge of Czech. This is both a serious comparative study and a workable course book. The comparisons are made at all levels of analysis and in the recognized problem areas of Slavonic grammar. Examples abound and a fair number of exercises and a reasonable vocabulary are included.

796 **Czech: a complete course for beginners.**
David Short. London: Hodder & Stoughton, 1993. 3rd ed. Reprinted,
1998. 346p.; Lincolnwood (Chicago), Illinois: NTC Publishing Group,
1994. 346p. bibliog. (Teach Yourself Books).
This third edition of *Czech* in the 'Teach Yourself' series bears no relation to the first
and second editions, by W. R. Lee and Z. Lee (first published in 1959). Its twenty
entirely new, graded lessons are intended to be as user-friendly as possible in the case
of a language which is widely perceived as 'difficult', and the whole work seeks to
meet the Council of Europe's Threshold guidelines. It includes exercises (with key)
and reference tables and can also be obtained in a pack containing the book with an
accompanying cassette. Although intended for the self-teaching learner, it is in wide
use at evening classes and by private tutors. Numerous revisions have been
incorporated into successive printings.

797 **Colloquial Czech.**
James D. Naughton. London; New York: Routledge & Kegan Paul,
1999. 2nd ed. 372p.
This replaces not only J. Schwartz's *Colloquial Czech* (first published in 1943 by the
same publisher) but also Naughton's own first (1987) edition, of which the second is
an almost complete rewrite, 'with a broader range of themes and settings' and
according more obvious recognition to 'the needs of the non-specialist learner'. It has
the chief merit over the original Schwartz course of reflecting more literally a
colloquial version of the language; there is greater realism in the stories used to
introduce each of the twenty graded lessons and an improved range of vocabulary. All
the basic grammar is covered. Like *Czech: a complete course for beginners* (q.v.), it
has tables, a vocabulary and is available in a pack containing the book and a two-hour
cassette.

798 **Czech in three months.**
Elisabeth Billington. Woodbridge, England: Hugo's Language
Books, 1995. 224p. Distributed in the United States by Hunter
Publishing Inc., Edison, New Jersey (Hugo's Simplified System).
The course was assembled by a member of the publisher's staff on the basis of
material supplied 'raw' from Prague by Eva Roubalová. 'Three months' may or may
not be a realistic target for the language to be learned by this means, even with the aid
of the optional cassettes (as marketed, with the book, as *Hugo's Czech cassette
course*). Some areas of the grammar (verbal aspect, verbs of motion) are presented
somewhat idiosyncratically, while the attention paid to individual features of the
language reveals a degree of disproportion. The eighteen lessons have a variety of
exercises, with keys.

799 **Czech: a multi-level course for advanced learners.**
František Čermák, Jan Holub, Jiří Hronek, Milan Šára, David Short.
Brno: Masaryk University (in cooperation with Charles University,
Prague, and the School of Slavonic and East European Studies,
University of London), 1993. 624 + 343p.
The 'advanced learners' of the title are people with considerable language-learning
experience, who are capable of coping with the copious linguistic (in the Prague

School vein) apparatus and terminology which is used throughout. Each lesson consists of a basic section of new material, a section with more on the same topic ('for those who want to know more'), and a section based on thematically focused vocabulary building; hence the 'multi-level' reference of the title. Each lesson has masses of drill-like exercises (with key). Unusually, this course proceeds basically from semantics and syntax to morphology, rather than vice versa. The second volume consists of twenty text-based lessons, some consisting of dialogue, some introducing aspects of Czech history and culture. Volume two also contains all the reference material – glossary and reference tables, the latter covering far more than mere paradigms.

800 **A modern Czech grammar.**
William E. Harkins. New York: King's Crown Press, 1960. Reprint of 1st ed., 1953. 338p. (Columbia Slavic Studies).

One of the post-war generation of textbooks, still used in some places and occasionally still found on sale. It introduces the grammar in thirty lessons through reading passages, fairly conservatively selected, from Czech literature. The vocabulary that is introduced is fairly limited.

801 **Czech for you.**
Milena Kelly. Prague: Angličtina Expres, 1993. 168p. + 8 cassettes.

One of the better and more usable products from Prague, this combines the modern communicative approach with some of the traditional aspects of the presentation of Czech as a foreign language by Czechs. Structured in nine lessons, it contains: copious drills, reproduced on the cassettes; a good range of vocabulary; and grammar reference tables, including a list of verbs and their peculiarities. This is intended for classroom use (a teacher's manual may be obtained separately) or self-instruction.

802 **Czech for foreigners.**
Olga Parolková, Jaroslava Nováková. Prague: Published privately, 1993. 2nd ed. 154p. + separately paginated pictorial appendices.

Structured in ten lessons and widely used at summer courses and language schools for foreigners, the course contains many drills, a glossary and some texts for reading-comprehension. A cassette is also available, as are a set of tests. This is more appropriate for classroom use than for self-instruction.

803 **Čeština pro cizince.** (Czech for foreigners.)
Karla Hronová, Milada Turzíková. Prague: Státní pedagogické nakladatelství, 1993. 479p.

This textbook is solely usable for classroom purposes, since the entire text is in Czech; English, along with French and Spanish, only figures in the translations to the glossary. However, it has, in its twenty-five lessons, a wide range of types of exercises, with keys, and the texts of an optionally available audio-oral course. This work is worthwhile, but since the collapse of the publishers it may be harder to obtain than some others from Prague.

804 **Spoken Czech. Situational dialogues for intermediate level students.**
Thomas Dickins. Wolverhampton, England: University of Wolverhampton, 1993. 34 + 36 + 65 + 18p.

This work, which has an accompanying video-cassette, is really two works in one. Chapter one is a scholarly history of the Czech literary language, with footnotes, appendixes (maps) and bibliography, as the background to the key polar versions of the contemporary Czech language (literary and Common Czech); the main oppositions are not only described and explained, but illustrated by tables. Chapter two consists of exercises based on previous watching of the video-cassette. They are set against a wide range of common situations and provide some introduction to authentic Czech. Chapter three gives transcriptions of the video dialogues, with language notes and the relevant vocabularies. Chapter four contains the key to the exercises in chapter two.

805 **Mluvte s námi česky! Audiovizuální kurs.** (Speak Czech with us. An audio-visual course.)
Josef Fronek, Světlana Obenausová, David Bickerton. Glasgow: Department of Slavonic Languages and the Language Centre of the University of Glasgow, 1995. book (unpaginated) + video-cassette and audio-cassette.

The ten lessons, for intermediate learners, rely on simultaneous use of the book, video and audio cassette. The scenes (set in the university environment, theatre, shops, railway stations, the countryside etc.) were filmed in Olomouc and the whole course benefits from close cooperation between the universities of Glasgow and Olomouc. Exercise material (with a key between the lessons and the appendices) is based closely on each scene, with cross-referencing to the immediately relevant sections of the survey grammar at the rear of the book. This includes morphological tables and a glossary.

806 **Czech phrase book travel pack.**
Zuzana Zrůstová, consultant Daniel Freeland. London: BBC Books, 1996. 192p. + cassette.

The market is awash with phrase books for the common traveller, each with a slightly different focus, usually with a potted Czech grammar, pronunciation guide, a mixture of phrases likely to be seen, heard or needed, and a vocabulary, all of which applies here (where the English-Czech 'mini-dictionary' has 3,000 entries). The well produced sixty-minute cassette, tailored for pre-travel practice purposes, contains its own transcript; it is presented by John Newton, Zuzana Zrůstová, Benjamin Kuras and Jitka Kolářová. Another good phrase book is that which has appeared in various mutations and under various imprints from materials prepared by Lexus Ltd and Václav Řeřicha.

Čeština jako cizí jazyk II. Výběrová blbiografie příruček češtiny jako cizího jazyka. (Czech as a foreign language II. Selective bibliography of handbooks of Czech as a foreign language.)
See item no. 1157.

Miscellaneous

807 **Český národní korpus.** (Czech national corpus.)
http:\\mathesius.ff.cuni.cz\

The internet address for access to the Czech National Corpus, a vast database of the contemporary Czech language, which grows vaster by the day as an ongoing project. Without full registration, the public can only access a limited number of incidences (in strings of up to sixty characters) of any particular item, though the total number of occurrences recorded is stated. This is a goldmine for the linguistic researcher.

808 **A description of spoken Prague Czech.**
Charles E. Townsend. Columbus, Ohio: Slavica, 1990. 151p. bibliog.

This is one of the few English-language works on a specific dialect of Czech, in this case the most central version of Common Czech – or Czech as it has evolved without the constraints of linguists – based on Prague and Central Bohemia. Townsend recognizes most of the problems of setting out as 'rules' the forms etc. of a language which has no agreed standard, and succeeds in producing a generally sound overview of the version of Czech which most fascinates the foreign learner (who is, of course, advised against trying to use it actively). The main distinctive features of phonology, morphology and syntax are set contrastively against the equivalent areas of Standard Czech. Perhaps the least reliance should be placed on the evaluation of the lexical section, which is more open to further refinement than the grammatical sections. A review article, 'Living Czech: the language of the he(a)rd', *Slavonic and East European Review*, vol. 69 (1991), p. 502-10, by David Short, not only expands on some of the specific issues raised by this description of one version of modern spoken Czech, but also lists a number of other (Czech) studies on the speech of several other Czech towns and cities.

809 **Borders of language and identity in Teschen Silesia.**
Kevin Hannan. New York; Washington, DC; Baltimore, Maryland; Berne; Frankfurt, Germany; Berlin, Vienna, Paris: Peter Lang, 1996.
xx + 255p. (Berkeley Insights in Linguistics and Semiotics).

A wide-ranging, well-researched study of speech communities in the former Duchy of Teschen, now in the Czech Republic and astride the Polish-Czech linguistic border. It is of interest to dialectologists, ethnolinguists, anthropological linguists and sociolinguists. An exemplary study of language change as a social phenomenon, it also contains the history of the populations that have met in Teschen and discusses the interface between language, religion and ethnicity. It not only provides an account of the main dialect of the area, but also analyses adjacent Polish, Czech and Slovak dialects. The book provides a rare introduction in English to the local ethnic group of Lachs (or Lachians) and the nearby Wallachs (or Wallachians), sheep-farming folk with a distinctive culture, whose remoter origins look back to Wallachia in present-day Romania.

810 **Essays in Czech and Slovak language and literature.**
David Short. London: School of Slavonic and East European Studies, University of London, 1996. 215p.

This miscellaneous collection of articles is directed towards an academic readership, some of the language items being rather narrowly specialist. Of more general interest is the final item, on the instant impact of West European languages, English in particular, on post-1989 Czech. The first five items focus, sometimes narrowly, elsewhere more generally, on works by Jan Hus, Karel Matěj Čapek-Chod, Karel Čapek, Alena Vostrá and Vít Stuchlý.

811 **Praguiana: some basic and less known aspects of the Prague linguistic school.**
Selected, translated and edited by Josef Vachek, Libuše Dušková, with an introduction by Philip A. Luelsdorff. Amsterdam; Philadelphia: John Benjamins, 1983. xxxi + 321p. (Linguistic and Literary Studies in Eastern Europe, vol. 12).

It is impossible not to include in a bibliography of this nature at least something on the Prague School, to which Luelsdorff's introductory essay, 'On Praguian functionalism and some extensions', is just one suitable background source. The papers herein are all key texts; all have their own bibliographical notes, and there is an index of persons (p. 303-08) and index of subjects (p. 309-21). The former reveals that, by 1983, one key figure, Roman Jakobson, could at least be quoted (the volume was prepared in Prague, where it was separately published by Academia *hors série* and where Jakobson had for a time been 'unmentionable'), but no Jakobson text is included. More Prague School classics, including one where Jakobson does figure as co-author, are included in Peter Steiner (ed.), *The Prague School: selected writings, 1929-1946* (Austin, Texas: University of Texas Press, 1982. 219p. University of Texas Press Slavic Series, no. 6). This collection also contains key texts in the Prague School's theoretical approach to literature and aesthetics.

812 **Reader in Czech socio-linguistics.**
Edited by Jan Chloupek, Jiří Nekvapil. Amsterdam; Philadelphia: John Benjamins, 1987. 344p. bibliog. (Linguistic and Literary Studies in Eastern Europe, vol. 23).

The series of which this volume is a part was an important outlet in the West for current East and Central European linguistic scholarship, which at times found it hard to win an outside readership. The nature of the agreement with the Dutch publisher meant that while the Czech edition of the same work, published by Academia for the Czechoslovak Academy of Sciences, preceded the Dutch chronologically, being dated 1986, its actual publication was delayed until 1988, after the Dutch company had secured the sales. The essays herein cover topics such as the socially conditioned nature of language, urban speech (on which countless monographs, covering various towns and cities, have appeared in Czech), the changing dichotomy between informal and formal utterances, linguistic geography, slang, and historical sociolinguistics. Each contribution has notes or bibliographical references.

813 **Varieties of Czech. Studies in Czech sociolinguistics.**
Edited and with an introduction by Eva Eckert. Amsterdam; Atlanta, Georgia: Rodopi, 1993. 285p.

This volume contains a variety of contributions on many key issues regarding the current condition of the Czech language. Most notably, the first section (five contributions) is concerned with the relationship between Standard and 'Common' Czech and the fraught topic of normal everyday usage and codification. Other areas covered are stylistics and translation, dialects, and versions of extraterritorial Czech (e.g., in Texas, Chicago, Canada, Vienna and the former Yugoslavia). One contribution considers aspects of the relationship between Czech and Slovak. The contributions are by both Czech and American scholars. The distortions in the Czech used in Chicago are also discussed by Jaromira Rakusan in 'A case of Chicago Czech: on the bookshelf and on the stage', in *Writing vs. speaking. Language. Text. Discourse. Communication*, edited by Světla Čmejrková, František Daneš and Eva Havlová (Tübingen, Germany: Gunter Narr Verlag, 1994, p. 373-81). The Czech of Texas is the subject of two articles – Lida Dutkova's 'Texas Czech of Texas Czechs: an ethnolinguistics perspective on language use in a dying language community', and Eva Eckert's 'Language variation in an immigrant community: language and community maintenance' – in *Brown Slavic Contributions*, edited by Alexander Levitsky and Masako Ueda (Providence, Rhode Island: Department of Slavic Languages, Brown University, p. 2-10, 11-37. Brown Slavic Contributions XI – A Special Issue of *Czech Language News*). The remainder of this volume contains a variety of papers on various aspects of Czech language and literature.

814 **Spoken Czech in literature. The case of Bondy, Hrabal, Placák and Topol.**
Karen Gammelgaard. Oslo: Faculty of Arts, University of Oslo and Scandinavian University Press, 1997. 272p. bibliog. (Acta Humaniora no. 18).

The history of sub-literary, sub-standard features of Czech in works of literature is long and complex. In modern times, increasing numbers of writers have 'dared' to put such features to artistic effect. This study looks at one work by each of four post-war writers – some better known than others – against a theoretical presentation of the relations among the main versions of Czech. Prospective readers will probably need an a priori appreciation of the general, let alone the specific, questions at issue, some of which are addressed in Gammelgaard's *Two studies on written language* (Oslo: University of Oslo, Slavonic-Baltic Department, 1996. 74p. bibliog. Meddelelser, Nr. 74). The first study, 'Derrida, Vachek and spoken *vs.* written language' (p. 7-21), is the more theoretical and, incidentally, reveals the political problems that could beset Czech linguists; the second, 'Dobrovský's Czech standard language norm', summarizes the historical background to the contemporary opposition between standard and sub-standard Czech, including an appraisal of 'The sociolinguistic situation in the Czech lands in Dobrovský's lifetime (ca. 1770-1820)' (p. 23-25).

251

815 **Variation in language: code-switching in Czech as a challenge for sociolinguistics.**
Petr Sgall. Amsterdam; Philadelphia: John Benjamins, 1992. 368p. (Linguistic & Literary Studies in Eastern Europe, vol. 39).
Perhaps the most widely quoted work in English on the overlap and interference between the two fundamental poles of contemporary Czech: the standard language and 'Common Czech', a social dialect, forms from which penetrate increasingly into neutral and higher registers.

816 **Morfill and the Czechs.**
James D. Naughton. *Oxford Slavonic Papers*, vol. 17 (1984), p. 62-76.
Richard Morfill (1834-1909) was one of the first English scholars with a strong interest in Czech affairs. This essay offers a scholarly bio-bibliography of Morfill, especially concerning the period scholars with whom he was in contact, or dispute, not to mention the many writers and historians with whom he was in contact or met during visits to Prague. Morfill was a Czechophile who was in turn appreciated by the Czechs, who ultimately honoured him by granting him corresponding membership of the Royal Learned Society of Bohemia in 1905. This was despite their having found fault, with justification, with his *Grammar of the Bohemian or Čech language* (1899), the first major work of its kind in English. Naughton's text and footnotes provide an interesting period bibliography of Czech studies, especially in England.

817 **Historio de la Esperanto-movado en Čehoslovakio: iom da historio kaj iom da rememoroj.** (History of the Esperanto movement in Czechoslovakia: some history and some reminiscences.)
Stanislav Kamarýt. Prague: Český esperantský svaz (Čeĥa Esperanto-Asocio), 1983. 256p. bibliog.
The history of Esperanto in Czechoslovakia dates back to before the country was even born; the first textbook was produced as early as 1890 and the Prague Esperanto club was founded in 1902. The present history was compiled from the author's manuscript materials (he died in 1956) under the editorship of Jan Werner. It traces the history of the movement from 1887 to 1969; the period from 1956 onwards is written up by the editors. Of some interest to the international Esperantist community is the periodical *Auroro* (1926-), published in Braille for foreign blind Esperantists.

Czech Language News.
See item no. 1117.

Literature

Central and Eastern European

818 **Traveller's literary companion to Eastern and Central Europe.**
Edited by James Naughton, series foreword by Margaret Drabble.
Brighton, England: In Print Publishing, 1995. 456p. maps. bibliog.
(Traveller's Literary Companions).

The reader-traveller is given a sympathetic country-by-country guide to literary luminaries and the places associated with them. The Czech Republic is represented by the editor's own chapter (p. 50-135), consisting of: a potted literary history from earliest times (to p. 73); 'literary landmarks' (to p. 81), of which over half are in Prague; an eleven-page booklist of translations (from both Czech and Bohemian-German literature), including a handful of titles of secondary literature; twenty-two literary extracts in translation (p. 91-115); and a selection of brief biographies of some major and/or much translated writers. It makes a good introduction to the totally uninitiated traveller.

819 **The Everyman companion to East European literature.**
Edited by Robert B. Pynsent with the assistance of S. I. Kanikova.
London: J. M. Dent, 1993. 605p. map.

The term, East European literature, is understood here to mean the fiction written in the language native to a given East European country. Accordingly, the companion does not include, for example, Franz Werfel, Max Brod or Franz Kafka, who all lived in Prague but wrote in German. Professor Karel Brušák of Cambridge, and Robert B. Pynsent, Professor of Czech and Slovak literature at the School of Slavonic and East European Studies, University of London, contributed the Czech entries. The companion has a general historical introduction, followed by the core of the book, 'Authors: alphabetical entries'. The entries are of varied length. A maximum of three works is given in the list of translations from a given author and no more than three critical items on a given author or work, these being in English, French, German or

253

Italian. The alphabetical author entries are followed by 'Anonymous, collective and oral tradition texts', which covers texts which were important for the development of an individual genre of literature, and so translations of the Bible feature prominently. Then follows 'Brief histories of East European literature, alphabetically arranged according to language'. 'Czech', by R. B. Pynsent, is on p. 519-21. The book's indexes are a major asset. 'Index A: Listed authors according to language' (p. 559-67) gives the name of the author, his date of birth and, where applicable, date of death. 'Index B: Anonymous, collective and oral tradition works' is on p. 568; the most useful, 'Index C: General index, including cross-references' (p. 569-605), lists authors given in the main section, as well as authors who do not have an entry of their own, but are mentioned in the text, as well as movements, groups, trends and periodicals.

820 **The heart of Europe: essays on literature and ideology.**
Joseph Peter Stern. Oxford; Cambridge, Massachusetts: Blackwell, 1992. 415p. bibliog.

A collection of outstanding essays by a scholar and expert on German literature, philosophy and modern history. The majority of the essays are concerned with people or events in the Czech Lands, demonstrating the importance and influence of the Czech environment for the intellectual life of this part of Europe. There are essays on the philosopher and mathematician Bernard Bolzano, on Prague German literature, on the writer Jaroslav Hašek and on Václav Havel. An essay on 'The gypsies' (p. 224-26) is of topical interest. Bibliographical notes, references and acknowledgements of sources are numerous.

821 **Two paradoxes of Czech literary evolution.**
George Pistorius. In: *The Czechoslovak contribution to world culture.* Edited by Miroslav Rechcígl, Jr. The Hague, London, Paris: Mouton, 1964, p. 39-43.

Pistorius seeks to discover why Czech literature, unlike even Danish, Portuguese and other literatures of small nations, has failed to become a part of universal literature. In essence the argument is that: Czech literature has always been weighed down by non-literary considerations (such as the service of national emancipation); the search for style has in part stifled the search for ideas; and while foreign borrowings (translations) have been readily admitted, the influences they might have brought to the formation of a native system of values have been lost beneath the weight of the 'patriotic emancipative function' of literature and were irrelevant to an undemanding readership. Accordingly, there is little of value to export, or re-export. This evaluation is a little harsh, as a perusal of some of the other works listed here may demonstrate.

822 **Ex-Communists in post-Communist societies.**
Lesley Chamberlain. *Prospect*, no. 8 (May 1996), p. 61-63.

A survey of the unique literary philosophical tradition which Communism created in Central Europe, both before and after the collapse of the Communist system. Ivan Klíma and Milan Kundera are discussed here, the author's preference being for the work of Klíma.

823 **Post Stalinist Central European drama on the British stage.**
Peter P. Muller. *History of European Ideas*, vol. 20, nos. 1-3
(January 1995), p. 25-29. bibliog.
An important article since it provides a synopsis of 140 reviews and essays written on
British productions of contemporary Central European drama in the United Kingdom.
Václav Havel is identified as one of the most frequently produced foreign dramatists
in Britain.

Czech

History and criticism

824 **Traditions of Czech literature: curses and blessings.**
Igor Hájek. In: *Czechoslovakia 1918-88: seventy years from
independence.* Edited by Gordon H. Skilling. Basingstoke,
England: Macmillan Academic and Professional Ltd, in association
with St Antony's College, Oxford, 1991, p. 177-95. bibliog.
Igor Hájek translated English and American authors into Czech. The curses and
blessings in this conference contribution are the result of a dichotomy which has been
historically symptomatic to Czech literature, that of ethics and aesthetics. Hájek
describes it as 'a schism between national, religious, social and political duty and the
artist's obligation to art'. The degree to which Czech culture, including literature, is
coloured by, and is in the service of, politics and political aspiration is striking.
Artistic values appear to be secondary and this may explain Czech literature's lack of
success abroad. The paper is supplemented by bibliographical notes.

825 **The native literature of Bohemia in the fourteenth century.**
A. H. Wratislaw. London: George Bell & Sons, 1878. 165p.
The four popular lectures contained in this work still remain a fascinating curio. They
give an outline of many works of Old Czech literature with, importantly, copious
sections in English translation, in verse where relevant. The wealth of Old Czech
literature, prose and verse chronicles, satire, disputations and theological writings, is
well represented. Where an English dimension can be found, it is duly pointed out.

826 **Anne's Bohemia: Czech literature and society 1310-1420.**
Alfred Thomas, foreword by David Wallace. Minneapolis,
Minnesota; London: University of Minnesota Press, 1998. 193p.
bibliog. (Medieval Cultures, vol. 13).
An accessibly written comparative overview of mediaeval culture in Bohemia.
Thomas reflects on Czech literature and society from 1310, the year in which the
foreign count John of Luxemburg was crowned King of Bohemia, to 1420, when the
Pope declared a Catholic crusade against the Hussite reformers. The central figure of
the study is Anne of Bohemia, who married Richard II, and for that reason this period

255

is of particular importance to the study of mediaeval England. The book has pages of bibliography and notes, as well as an index.

827 **A history of Bohemian literature.**
The Count Lützow. London: Heinemann, 1907. 437p. (Short Histories of the Literatures of the World, no. 7).
This is another curio of similar antiquity to Wratislaw's *The native literature of Bohemia in the fourteenth century* (q.v.), but covers the literature right up to the 18th century. Like later literary historians, Lützow notes the extent to which Czech literature, more than some others, is bound up with the nation's general and religious history. Many quotations are given in translation. The work is of sufficient significance to have merited reprinting by Kennikat Press in 1970.

828 **The labyrinth of the word: truth and representation in Czech literature.**
Alfred Thomas. Munich: R. Oldenbourg Verlag, 1995. 174p. bibliog.(Veröffentlichungen des Collegium Carolinum, Bd. 78).
A philosophical enquiry into the concept of 'truth', so important to the Czechs. 'One of the most tenacious self-images fostered by Czech writers – from Masaryk to Havel – is of a society unified from generation to generation by its commitment to freedom and truth' (p. 13). Thomas considers: Dalimil's *Chronicle*, the first history of Bohemia in the Czech language (c. 1314); the allegorical *Tkadleček* (The little weaver, 1407/1409); the most important work of Comenius, a baroque allegory *Labyrint světa a ráj srdce* (The labyrinth of the world and the paradise of the heart, 1623); and the romantic poem *Máj* (May) by Karel Hynek Mácha (1836). From the turn of the century Thomas chose two neglected writers: a representative of Decadence in literature and a homosexual, the writer Jiří Karásek ze Lvovic (1871-1951) and his *Legenda o Sodomovi*; and Richard Weiner, whom he describes as 'introverted, enigmatic, difficult', and his *Netečný divák* (The indifferent observer). The next work is Karel Čapek's *Kniha apokryfů* (Apocryphal stories), which were originally published as a column in a newspaper between 1920 and 1938. Among contemporary writers Thomas selects Milan Kundera and his *Kniha smíchu a zapomění* (The book of laughter and forgetting) and finally Václav Havel's *Largo desolato*, the play which largely inspired this study. The author makes frequent comparisons with other literature. The book has numerous bibliographical footnotes, a large separate bibliography and an index.

829 **The Czech chivalric romances Vévoda Arnošt and Lavryn in their literary context.**
Alfred Thomas. Goppingen, Germany: Kummerle Verlag, 1989. 312p. bibliog. (Goppinger Arbeiten zur Germanistik, no. 504).
A dissertation on two 14th-century Czech verse romances, both being adaptations of German works. It is regrettable that the publisher could not rise to the use of a font with Czech diacritics; the latter appear to have been added by hand, which is detrimental to the appearance of the text. The multilingual bibliography of books and articles is vast.

830 **A sacred farce from medieval Bohemia. Mastičkář.**
Jarmila F. Veltruský. Ann Arbor, Michigan: Horace H. Rackham
School of Graduate Studies, University of Michigan, 1985. 396p.
bibliog.

Mastičkář is the best known of Czech mediaeval plays, though practically only among
speakers of Czech. Veltruský concludes that, had it been an English work, it would
have become much better known, and to overcome at least the language barrier, she
includes full transcriptions *and* parallel English translations of both extant fragments
of the play (p. 332-76). The rest of the book is a history of mediaeval drama. There is
also a literary, linguistic, dramatic and semantic analysis of the play, and an account
of the role of farce and laughter in the mediaeval religious context. Comparisons are
drawn throughout with some better known English and French plays of similar
antiquity.

831 **The romantic hero and contemporary anti-hero in Polish and
Czech literature: great souls and grey men.**
Charles S. Kraszewski. Lewiston, New York; Lampeter, Wales: The
Edwin Meller Press, 1998. 325p. bibliog.

The introduction summarizes, 'the critical method employed in Great Souls and Great
Men is that of close readings of certain key texts of the literature of the Czech and
Polish Romantic and the post-Second World War periods. The lion's share of the
present study is devoted to the Romantic period in order to illustrate as completely as
possible the 19th-century intellectual bedrock which forms such an integral part of the
cultural make up of the contemporary artists . . .' (p. 3). Czech Romantics discussed
include Karel Hynek Mácha and his *Máj* (May) and Josef Kajetán Tyl's historical
drama *Jan Hus*. Later developments are represented by Karel Havlíček Borovský and
his ironic epic *Tyrolské elegie* (Tyrolean elegies), Karel Jaromír Erben's *Svatebni
košile* (The spectre's bride) from his collection of ballads *Kytice* and Božena
Němcová's novel, *Babička* (Grandmother). The two latter works here represent the
decline of Romanticism. The examples of contemporary anti-heroic texts herein are:
the Catholic poet Jan Zahradníček's *Znamení moci* (The sign of power), published in
Australia by Thomas Bourke in 1980 in translation by Thomas Bourke and Josef
Horny; Vladimír Holan's verse *Noc s Hamletem* (Night with Hamlet) (London: Oasis
Books, 1980, translated by Jarmila and Ian Milner); and a play by Václav Havel,
Vyrozumění (The memorandum) (New York: Grove Press, 1980, translated by Vera
Blackwell with an introduction by Tom Stoppard).

832 **Czech literature.**
Arne Novák, translated from the Czech by Peter Kussi, edited with a
supplement by William E. Harkins. Ann Arbor, Michigan: Michigan
Slavic Publications, under the auspices of the Joint Committee on
Eastern Europe, American Council of Learned Societies, 1976. 375p.
(Joint Committee on Eastern Europe, Publications Series, no. 4).

The text selected here for translation is a posthumous edition (1946) of Novák's
classic, prepared for publication by Antonín Grund, who also brought the text up to
that date. Harkins' supplement then follows Czech literature up to 1976. The work
seeks to be a complete history, within the limitations of space, from the earliest extant
texts right down to the present, and it largely succeeds. In the absence of any other
complete history of Czech literature in English one is grateful that it exists, but it is

257

nevertheless marred by certain omissions – a consequence of its triple authorship at the points where the sections meet – and the translation contains a number of malapropisms, mostly fairly transparent, and some serious mistranslations of the Czech titles of works. However, even as it stands it is a useful introduction and has the added benefit of a section on folk literature.

833 **Essays on Czech literature.**
René Wellek, introduced by Peter Demetz. The Hague: Mouton, 1963. 214p. bibliog. (Slavic Printings and Reprintings, no. 43).

A classic collection of essays, some of the survey type, others dealing with specific narrow problems. The interpretations were not all received without criticism, and some are openly polemical, such as the one on K. Čapek and T. G. Masaryk's philosophy and its literary dimensions. There are also highly instructive studies on, for example, Bohemia in English literature, where the coverage extends from the 9th to the 19th centuries, or Mácha and English literature, which explores the 'Byron problem' in relation to K. H. Mácha, perhaps the best Czech poet of all time. There is also a sober history of Czech-German literary contacts. Each essay is accompanied by its own bibliography.

834 **Narrative modes in Czech literature.**
Lubomír Doležel. Toronto: University of Toronto Press, 1973. 152p. bibliog.

A set of specialist literary essays by a leading scholar, providing detailed structuralist accounts of several major works in Czech literature by writers who all merit translation, though some are still waiting attention: J. A. Comenius, Karel V. Rais, Karel Čapek, Vladislav Vančura and Milan Kundera. Another structuralist essay, on the cycles and circles in Jaroslav Hašek's life and the structure of his novel, is Doležel's 'Circular pattern: Hašek and the Good Soldier Švejk' in *Poetica Slavica: studies in honour of Zbigniew Folejewski*, edited by J. Douglas Clayton and Gunter Schaarschmidt (Ottawa: University of Ottawa Press, 1981, p. 21-28).

835 **The significance of Czech Fin-de-siècle criticism.**
Jiří Kudrnáč. In: *Decadence and innovation: Austro-Hungarian life and art at the turn of the century*. Edited by Robert B. Pynsent. London: Weidenfeld & Nicolson, 1989, p. 88-101.

The author is a Czech academic and specialist in Czech *fin-de-siècle* literature. In this scholarly contribution to an international conference he 'focuses on the semantics of Czech fin-de-siècle literature by identifying keywords which link literary and extraliterary contexts' (p. 88). The general key words are criticism and functional syncretism of Czech turn-of-the-century literature, the other key words concern specific features, such as 'naturalness' or 'justifiability'. Kudrnáč looks at various artistic, but mostly literary, groups.

836 **The images of the prostitutes in Czech *fin de siècle* literature.**
Kathleen Hayes. *Slavonic and East European Review*, vol. 72, no. 2 (April 1997), p. 234-58. bibliog.

Draws comparisons between the image of the fallen woman as frequently depicted in period newspaper articles and essays by Czech intellectuals interested in the women's

258

movement with the image presented by literature. In the latter the fallen woman is not portrayed as a victim, although the theme of man's exploitation of women is present. Kathleen Hayes analyses a number of literary texts by *fin-de-siècle* writers and intellectuals, including examples from Josef Svatopluk, Růžena Jesenská, Petr Kles, Marie Majerová, Julius Zeyer and Karel Matěj Čapek-Chod.

837 Magic Prague.
Angelo Maria Ripellino, translated from Italian by David Newton-Marinelli, edited by Michael Henry Heim. London: Macmillan, 1994. 333p. maps.

Written in 1973, this is an intensively researched work on Prague, which is explored as a city riddled with poets, writers and painters, criminals, madmen and magicians, from Rudolf II to Kafka, and culminating in the Communists of the 1970s. The book is illustrated by forty-nine black-and-white photographs. Ripellino, a novelist and poet, was a lecturer in Czech Language and Literature at the University of Rome. He was certain he lived in Prague in a previous incarnation.

838 Daydreams and nightmares: Czech Communist and ex-Communist literature 1917-1987.
Peter Hrubý. New York: Columbia University Press, published jointly with the Czechoslovak Society of Arts and Sciences (SVU), distributed by Columbia University Press, 1990. 362p. bibliog. (East European Monographs, no. 290).

The author calls these essays a 'personal review of selected Czech writers, who at least for some time followed the Bolshevik star and as members of the Communist Party of Czechoslovakia devoted their literary talents and energies to working for it in words and deeds'. The book has two historical chapters, in which the roots of Czech socialism and Pan-Slavism are traced and which take the reader past the Second World War, through the disillusionment and humiliation of the Communist era. Of the writers who 'went through a process of enchantment and disenchantment with communism', Hrubý selected the poet Josef Hora (1891-1945). In the third part of the book the author further selected 'Jaroslav Hašek, the nihilist anarchist', Ivan Olbracht, Vladislav Vančura, Jan Drda, the women writers Marie Majerová, Marie Pujmanová, Jarmila Glazarová and, among contemporary writers, Milan Kundera, Ivan Klíma and Ludvík Vaculík. They all, for a time at least, believed in the Communist ideal and were members of the Communist Party. The manuscript of this book was completed in 1988, one year before the Velvet Revolution. That has not, however, invalidated many of its conclusions or the data on which they are based. Instead of a formal bibliography the author provides notes (p. 312-56) to the text and there is also a name index (p. 357-62).

839 Der Poetismus: das Programm und die Hauptverfahren der tschechischen literarischen Avantgarde der zwanziger Jahre.
(Poetismus: the programme and main progressions of the Czech literary avant-garde in the 1920s.)
Vladimír Müller. Munich: Verlag Otto Sagner, 1978. 215p. bibliog.

The movement known as Poetism, which is claimed by the Czechs as belonging uniquely to them, has received more attention from German than English scholars.

Poetism was actually broader than just a literary movement, being represented in music, painting and architecture, and in the performing arts. It 'was based on the principle of pure poetry . . . poetry that did not serve the purposes of actual existence and that scornfully rejected all tendentiousness: it was a poetry that cultivated sheer playfulness, plunged headlong into inventive fantasy in order to heighten the delights of hedonistic existence, reached with the magic of carefully selected words, oxymoronic concepts and paradoxical images of an esthetic intensity hitherto unknown' (Novák). Many of these characteristics are picked out by Müller and are exemplified and analysed in great detail; he concentrates on four central figures: Karel Teige, Vítězslav Nezval, Konstantin Biebl and Jaroslav Seifert.

840 **Der Naturalismus in der tschechischen Literatur.** (Naturalism in Czech literature.)
Wolfgang Hobland. Munich: Verlag Otto Sagner, 1991. 177p. bibliog. (Marburger Abhandlungen zur Geschichte und Marburger Abhandlungen zur Kultur Osteuropas, Band 29).

Written as a dissertation for the Philipps-Universität in Marburg an der Lahn. Hobland gives a general survey of Czech literature and the Czech literary scene in the first decades of the 20th century. The core covers the works of Czech writer Karel Matěj Čapek-Chod (1860-1927) (*Kašpar Lén mstitel, Antonín Vondrejc* and *Turbína*). The dissertation has an index of names. This major, but underrated, writer is discussed from many aspects in *Karel Matěj Čapek-Chod: proceedings of a symposium held at the School of Slavonic and East European Studies*, edited by Robert B. Pynsent (London: School of Slavonic and East European Studies, University of London, 1985. 276p. bibliog. SEES Occasional Papers, no. 3). The symposium was unusual in that it was held outside its subject's home territory, and benefited from balanced treatment by both Western and Eastern European scholars. The papers place the author in both his Czech and European context and consider him in his own right, from both the literary and linguistic angle.

841 **Otokar Březina: zur Rezeption Schopenhauers und Nietzsches im tschechischen Symbolismus.** (Otakar Březina: on the reception of Schopenhauer and Nietzsche in Czech symbolism.)
Urs Heftrich. Heidelberg, Germany: Universitats Verlag C. Winter, 1993. 502p. bibliog.

An academic study of the lyricist and essayist Otokar Březina, which assesses him as a poet and philosopher. 'Dichter oder Denker?' (poet or thinker?) is the theme. The study draws substantially on Březina's correspondence with, among many others, the minor Moravian feminist philosopher and poet Anna Pammrová, and through these letters gives a profound picture of Moravian intellectual life in the first decades of the 20th century. The study is supplemented by detailed notes ('Anmerkungen', p. 342-67), notes on the work of Schopenhauer, Nietzsche and Březina himself (p. 468-74), and an excellent bibliography ('Literaturverzeichnis', p. 475-92) of the works of Březina, Schopenhauer and Nietzsche and published letters, books and articles on the subject in Czech, German and English. There is also an index of names, 'Register' (p. 493-502).

842 **Czech writers and politics, 1945-1969.**
Alfred French. Boulder, Colorado: East European Quarterly,
distributed by Columbia University Press, New York, 1982. 435p.
(East European Monographs, no. 94).
'The social importance of the intelligentsia in Czechoslovakia was not only due to the
traditionally high role conceded by public opinion to the artist and writer. At a time
when no opposition politics were permitted – when no official opposition was deemed
to exist – then its place was taken, in the eyes of the public, by the officially tolerated
opposition of artists and intellectuals.' Against the background of the periodized post-
war history of the country, from the Communist take-over, through Stalinization to the
reformist experiment of 1968, thence to the renewed stiffening of orthodoxy, Czech
literary output is followed in readable essay form. The work of many writers is traced,
and various works, especially those open to allegorical interpretation, are described in
detail, with generous quotations.

843 **Slovník českých spisovatelů: pokus o rekonstrukci dějin české
literatury 1948-1979.** (A dictionary of Czech writers: an attempt to
reconstruct the history of Czech literature 1948-79.)
Compiled by Jiří Brabec (editor), Jiří Gruša, Igor Hájek, Petr Kabeš,
Jan Lopatka. Toronto: Sixty-Eight Publishers, 1982. 537p.
The word 'reconstruction' in the title refers to the reinstatement, in a reference work,
of those many authors, some living in Czechoslovakia at the time of compilation,
many abroad, who had fallen foul of the Communist régime. In other words, it seeks
to provide a complete biography and bibliography of all émigré and dissident writers
and those who, while denying dissidence, were, or had been, denied the opportunity to
publish. Manuscripts and other inedita are included with appropriate annotations,
coverage being broad enough to include, for example, literature proper, criticism,
travel writing and theological writings. The work was based on the second edition of
the Prague underground version. In addition to the writers' careers, details of
professional and political affiliations are included (such as being a signatory to
Charter 77). Given the specific range of authors included, the 'reconstruction' cannot
be complete, since it excludes those writers who had never been involved in
controversy, which of itself does not disqualify them from a place in literature. Three
pre-1989 dictionaries from inside Czechoslovakia also need to be noted: the *Slovník
českých spisovatelů* (Dictionary of Czech writers) (Prague: Československý spisovatel,
1964. 625p.); the sequel to this, *Slovník české literatury 1970-1981* (A dictionary of
Czech literature, 1970-1981), edited by Vladimír Forst (Prague: Československý
spisovatel, 1985. 502p. bibliog.); and *Čeští spisovatelé literatury pro děti a mládež*
(Czech writers of literature for children and young people) by Otakar Chaloupka and
others (Prague: Albatros, 1985. 476p.). The latest addition to this gallery of directories
is *Čeští spisovatelé – Czech writers* (Prague: Ministerstvo kultury ČR, 1999. 123p.) by
Pavlína Kubíková and Petr Kotyk. This bilingual publications lists sixty-three
contemporary writers and their works.

844 **Czech literature since 1956: a symposium.**
Edited by William E. Harkins, Paul I. Trensky. New York:
Bohemica, 1980. 161p. (Columbia Slavic Studies).
Described by one reviewer (R. B. Pynsent) as an omnium gatherum of eulogies for
post-Thaw writing, this collection of ten essays by six authors contains a lot of

information that is unavailable elsewhere and it is therefore a useful supplement to the other literary histories quoted here. Survey essays discuss: the Czech novel since 1956 (W. E. Harkins); the playwrights of the Krejča Circle (P. I. Trensky); Czech culture and politics in the 1960s (Antonín J. Liehm); and Czech poetics and semiotics in the 1960s (Thomas G. Winner). Individual writers whose works are discussed include: Bohumil Hrabal (George Gibian); Vladimír Páral (W. E. Harkins); Milan Kundera (Antonín J. Liehm and Peter Kussi); and Ludvík Vaculík (Antonín J. Liehm).

845 **The fiction of freedom, the development of the Czechoslovak literary reform movement: 1956-1968.**
Elizabeth Gray. Clayton, Victoria: Monash University, Department of History, 1991. 73p. bibliog. (Monash Publications in History, 11).

This was written originally as a thesis and as such has been painstakingly researched and is documented by numerous footnotes, quotations and a substantial bibliography. The appendix is a list of 'Banned books in Czechoslovakia', as taken from the *Index on Censorship*, vol. 2, no. 4 (winter 1973), p. 93-97. The thesis provides a reasonable account of events generally and of the activities of the Czech intelligentsia specifically during the eight years prior to the invasion of Czechoslovakia by the Warsaw Pact countries in 1968.

846 **Český Parnasus, literatura 1970-1990: interpretace vybraných děl 60 autorů.** (Czech Parnasus, literature 1970-90: interpretation of selected works of sixty authors.)
Text by Jiří Holý et al. Prague: Galaxie, 1993. 405p. bibliog.

During the period from which the authors and works were selected, Czech literature was divided into three segments: indigenous public literature and indigenous underground (samizdat) literature; samizdat publications; and Czech literature in exile. This anthology of critical essays covers all three subdivisions fairly comprehensively. For each of the sixty authors, one work was selected for appraisal; and the essays are by various contemporary literary critics.

847 **Assimilation, childhood and death: new Czech fiction-writers of the 1970's.**
Robert B. Pynsent. *Slavonic and East European Review*, vol. 59, no. 3 (July 1981), p. 370-84.

The article goes a long way to show how much of interest was being produced in Czechoslovakia in the 1970s, contradicting the claims that Czech fiction was dead or dormant. The 'assimilation' of the title is primarily concerned with that of the outsider, and this is seen as a common feature of much of the writing. Childhood is a state of pre-assimilation and many writers are concerned with the processes of physical and emotional development. Death is the great universal assimilation. Literary theoretical questions apart, the reader is given an insight into contemporary Czech society with some incidental comparison with society in Britain.

848 **Adolescence, ideology and society: the young hero in contemporary Czech fiction.**
Robert B. Pynsent. In: *The adolescent hero.* Edited by Ian Wallace. Dundee, Scotland: GDR Monitor, 1984, p. 65-86. (GDR Monitor Special Series, no. 3).

The protagonists of many serious and popular works of Czech literature of the 1970s and early 1980s were young people and Pynsent sees two main reasons for this: they are the future backbone of the state which must nurture them accordingly, and part of this process involves their indoctrination through literature about and for them; and they represent one group separate from the main body of society, marked out by specific characteristics, which gives authors some scope for imaginative writing. In the space available, an impressive number of writers and works of the 1970s and 1980s are discussed. The author shows that, within the general type of the *Bildungsroman* (psychological novel), which dominates the period, there is no shortage of variety, of either themes or treatment, and a fair number of genuinely interesting works offering more than just an insight into contemporary Czech society.

849 **A neglected generation.**
Václav Havel. In: *Czechoslovakia 1918-88: seventy years from independence.* Edited by Gordon H. Skilling. Basingstoke, England; London: Macmillan Academic and Professional Ltd in association with St Antony's College, Oxford, 1991, p. 211-14.

Havel was not allowed by the Czechoslovak authorities to attend the Toronto conference and his contribution was sent in written form and translated by Paul Wilson. It is a brief survey of the previous twenty years of Czech literature, dividing the authors into various categories and focusing on unofficial, 'samizdat' literature. With all respect to the editors of the contributions to the Toronto conference, Havel was not elected president of Czechoslovakia in 1939, at the tender age of three ('Notes on contributors', p. XIV.)

850 **Julius Zeyer: the path to Decadence.**
Robert B. Pynsent. The Hague: Mouton, 1973. 264p.

Zeyer (1841-1901) was a prolific poet, dramatist and novelist, some of whose works are still regularly re-published. Surprisingly little of his work is available in English – a few scattered poems and no prose. Pynsent provides not just an appraisal of a major writer in his Czech and European context, but includes a detailed analysis of six individual works. One of Pynsent's main academic interests is Decadence, and the book contains, among much else on Czech literature, an account of where and why Czech Decadence differs from that of Western Europe. Zeyer himself is discerned as standing on the path leading to Decadence from Romanticism.

851 **Sex under socialism: an essay on the work of Vladimír Páral.**
Robert B. Pynsent. London: School of Slavonic and East European Studies, University of London, 1994. 82p. (SEES Occasional Papers, no. 25).

The critics use epithets such as satirical, burlesque, picaresque when writing about Páral's novels, but they were sufficiently apolitical and opaque about sex to be published in puritanical Czechoslovakia in the 1960s. This critical study concentrates

263

on the use of sex in fourteen novels of Páral, with less attention to their considerable linguistic and literary qualities. The comic, even grotesque novel *Catapult*, which to many is Páral's best novel, was translated into English by William Harkins (Highland Park, New Jersey: Catbird Press, 1989, distributed by Independent Publishers Group). Páral's writing is noted for fluidity and the story has pace. It is considered to share Franz Kafka's feeling of alienation and absurdity, combined with Jaroslav Hašek's comic sardonic quality. Páral's work deserves further translations and further studies.

852 **Czech and Slovak literature in English: a bibliography.**
George J. Kovtun. Washington, DC: Library of Congress, 1988. 2nd ed. 152p.

A revised, expanded and updated version of the first edition, which was published in 1984. The work needs updating again since so much Czech writing has been translated since 1989. In this bibliography a total of 233 Czech authors are represented and the volume runs to 275 separate entries. The rules for inclusion and the arrangement follow the previous edition, being divided into anthologies of prose and poetry, folklore anthologies and works of history and criticism. Two further sections give additional titles, author by author and separately for Czech and Slovak, with cross-references to the first three sections, where relevant. This edition was dedicated to the memory of the poet Jaroslav Seifert, who died on 10 January 1986. Seifert was awarded the Nobel Prize for Literature in 1984.

The liberation of women and nation: Czech nationalism and women writers of the Fin de Siècle.
See item no. 18.

Translations and criticism of the works of individual writers

853 **May.**
Karel Hynek Mácha, translated by Hugh Hamilton McGoverne.
London: Phoenix Press, 1949. 177p.

It is widely agreed that Mácha's *Máj* (1836) is *the* verse classic of Czech literature, with a place in European Romanticism generally. Neither this, nor the translation which preceded it in English, is entirely satisfactory, but it is a notoriously difficult task anyway, chiefly on account of Mácha's exploitation of the acoustic side of Czech. The volume also includes translations of some of Mácha's occasional works, prose, letters and a biographical sketch. The reader with a knowledge of German may prefer the twin translations in *Máj: zweisprachige Ausgabe* (May: publication in two languages), by Otto F. Babler and Walther Schamschula (Cologne, Germany; Vienna: Böhlau, 1983. 132p. bibliog. Schriften des Komitees der Bundesrepublik Deutschland zur Förderung der slawischen Studien, no. 6). Though differently conceived, the translations are generally excellent.

854 **Prague tales.**
Jan Neruda, translated by Michael Henry Heim, with an introduction
by Ivan Klíma.   Budapest: Central European University Press, 1993,
reissued 1996. 368p.
The stories were also published as *Tales of Little Quarter* (Westport, Connecticut:
Greenwood Press, 1976. 296p.). Neruda was more prolific as a poet, but only a few of
his poems have been translated. As a prose-writer he was no less important and these
Tales are his best-known work – they are compulsory reading at Czech schools. The
tales are a set of observations, indulgent, ironic, humorous, on life among the people
of the Little Quarter, Malá Strana, that part of old Prague caught between the Castle
and the river. Neruda's style and method greatly influenced many Czech writers who
followed him, and he has been an inspiration to some non-Czechs as well (the Chilean
writer Neftali Ricardo Reyes is said to have chosen his pen-name, Pablo Neruda, out
of admiration for his Czech predecessor).

855 **Old Czech legends.**
Alois Jirásek, translated with an introduction and glossary by Marie K.
Holeček.   London; Boston, Massachusetts: Forest Books, 1992. 199p.
Alois Jirásek is considered the father of the Czech realistic historical novel. A
prodigious writer of the Romantic school, he was also a scholar in the Realist mould
and has been compared to Walter Scott and Henryk Sienkiewicz. This is a collection
of old legends, of which the first of many editions appeared in 1894; it became one of
the important literary works in national mythopoeia. The legends were written for
young people and are part of almost every Czech child's literary experience. The
translator has retained, with a few exceptions, the Czech names and their Czech
spelling, giving the phonetic pronunciation for each Czech name the first time it
appears. She also provides a sketch of Czech history, a brief biography of Jirásek, and
in the glossary (p. 179-99) explains the terms, places, persons and events, again with
the phonetic pronunciation of proper names. These legends had been translated
previously by Edith Pargeter and published, with illustrations by Jiří Trnka, under the
title *Legends of Old Bohemia* (London: Hamlyn, 1963. 337p.).

856 **Jaroslav Hašek, 1883-1983: proceedings of the International Hašek
Symposium, Bamberg, June 24-27, 1983.**
Frankfurt, Germany; New York: Verlag Peter Lang, 1989. 551p.
bibliog. (West Slavic Contributions – Westslavische Beitrage, vol. 1).
The Hašek symposium was held to celebrate the centenary of the birth of Jaroslav
Hašek, the Czech expressionist writer, and this volume was dedicated to Sir Cecil
Parrott, one of the translators of *The good soldier Švejk.* The introduction is in
English, the contributions are in Czech, German and English and the summaries are in
Czech. Inevitably, most of the contributions are concerned with Hašek's famous novel
on Švejk which, since its conception after the First World War, has been translated
into numerous languages. It was published for the first time in English in 1930.

857 **The good soldier Švejk and his fortunes in the world war.**
Jaroslav Hašek, translated and introduced by Cecil Parrott, illustrated by Josef Lada, bibliography and chronology by Robert Pynsent. London: Everyman, 1993. 800p. maps. bibliog. (Everyman's Library, vol. 151).

No list of Czech literature in translation would be complete without Hašek's *Švejk*, the classic about a Czech anti-hero in the First World War. This is a complete and unabridged translation, with the original, familiar illustrations by Josef Lada. *Švejk* was first published in translation by Paul Selver in 1930 (London: Heinemann; New York: Doubleday). This translation had numerous reprints and editions. Opinion on Hašek's writing and this book and its main character varies widely; not every Czech is at ease with this legacy. *Švejk* enriched the Czech language by the use of the word *švejkovina* (intentionally silly, subversive, anti-establishment behaviour). The book has been both dramatized and filmed and Berthold Brecht borrowed him for his *Schweik in the Second World War*, while the young Irish playwright Colin Teevan is the most recent and enthusiastic, imaginative interpreter of Hašek's original character. His *Švejk* was performed at the Gate Theatre in London in 1999.

858 **The Bachura scandal and other stories and sketches.**
Jaroslav Hašek, translated from the Czech with an introduction by Alan Menhennet. London: Angel Books, 1991. 160p. bibliog.

Hašek is undoubtedly best known for his semi-picaresque novel about the good soldier Švejk. He was, however, a prolific writer, especially of short (and shorter) stories, many of them scattered about the press of his day and based (or masquerading as based) on topical news items. They are typically marked by an unexpected twist in the tale, much admired and emulated by certain later writers (such as Bohumil Hrabal). The thirty-two stories selected for this collection are a good cross-section of two to ten pages in length. They are mostly set in the effervescent bureaucratic mini-universe of Prague before the First World War, at that time a provincial Austrian town and the Czech capital. Hašek's insight was described as of demonic quality and he writes with relish. The translator has produced a good, sizeable introduction on Hašek's work and on his turbulent life (p. 7-12) and provides bibliographical notes on p. 12. The stories were written well before the *Good soldier Švejk* (written 1921-23) and prove that Hašek was already a great humorist and satirist before the First World War.

859 **Karel Čapek: in pursuit of truth, tolerance and trust.**
Bohuslava R. Bradbrook. Brighton, England: Sussex Academic Press, 1998. 257p. bibliog.

Franz Kafka and Jaroslav Hašek stole the limelight as representatives of Czech literature in the English-speaking world after the Second World War from Karel Čapek, who had previously been the most widely translated Czech author. The only previous full-length study in English of Čapek, in the Czech Republic probably the most popular of 20th-century writers, was W. E. Harkins' *Karel Čapek* (New York: Columbia University Press, 1962). This biography seeks to expand the work of Harkins and includes Čapek as an essayist, a genre of which he was considered a pioneer in Czech literature, and his other lesser literary forms. The book is intended for an English audience and has a biographical chapter 'to show the English-speaking reader Čapek and his work in its cultural and political context and thus to understand better the critical analysis in this book'. The book is divided by genre, rather than

266

ordered chronologically. This was done, according to the author, to enhance the clarity. For evaluation Bradbrook refers to, or quotes from, the first or the most significant critical assessment of Čapek's individual works. The good reception Čapek received from the British critics testifies to his good relations with Britain. Although Čapek's work was published in the United States mostly parallel with the British editions, the opinions of American critics are not included here to any great extent. The book has a number of illustrations, pages of explanatory notes, a bibliography (p. 241-48) of Čapek's work and first editions of translations into English, as well as books and articles on Čapek and his work. These are mostly in Czech and the bibliography illustrates how little is available on Čapek in English. There is also an index.

860 **R.U.R. and The insect play.**
By the brothers Čapek, translated from the Czech by Paul Selver.
Oxford; New York: Oxford University Press, 1996. 177p.
This edition was first issued by Oxford University Press in 1961 and this, the 17th impression, makes *R.U.R*, a science fiction play, probably the most frequently published of any work of Czech literature. *The Insect play*, an allegory which introduces human and insect characters, has also been translated into English several times; the title has been changed four times. The two plays were first published in English in 1923 and won immediate international acclaim for the authors. There have been various versions and adaptations published since then. Josef Čapek collaborated on *The insect play* with his brother Karel; *R.U.R.* was written by Karel alone. Josef had a considerable reputation as a painter of the Cubist School and worked with his brother on the composition of sketches, stories and plays. *The insect play* was performed with great success in London and New York. *R.U.R.* was also hugely successful as a play in English and the word 'robot' was adopted from there. James D. Naughton gives an appraisal of symbolism and ideology of *R.U.R.* in 'Futorology and robots: Karel Čapek's R.U.R.' in *Renaissance and modern studies* (Nottingham, England: Nottingham University Press, 1984, p. 72-86). Darko Suvin wrote on science fiction in Čapek's writings in 'Karel Čapek or the aliens among us', which is part of *Metamorphosis of science fiction* (New Haven, Connecticut: Yale University Press, 1979, p. 270-83).

861 **War with the newts.**
Karel Čapek, introduced by Ivan Klíma, translated by M. and R.
Weatherall. Evanston, Illinois: Northwestern University Press, 1996.
348p. (European Classics).
Originally written in 1936, this novel was first published in the translation of M. and R. Weatherall in 1937 by George Allen & Unwin Ltd in London. Another translation, by Ewald Osers, was published in London by Picador in 1991. The edition above, with an excellent introduction by Ivan Klíma, was first published in 1985, the second printing was in 1990 and this is the first printing in the European Classics Series. Many critics consider *War with the newts* Čapek's greatest book. It is a satirical fantasy, a prophetic one, which was completed three years before the Nazi invasion of Czechoslovakia. The play was written in the tradition of Wells, Orwell and Vonnegut and is considered one of the great anti-utopian satires of the 20th century. Čapek satirizes science, runaway capitalism, fascism, journalism, militarism, even Hollywood. It is a 'bracing parody of totalitarianism and technological overkill, one of the most amusing and provocative books in its genre'.

862 **Three novels: Hordubal, Meteor, An ordinary life.**
Karel Čapek, translated from Czech by M. and R. Weatherall,
introduction by William Harkins. Highland Park, New Jersey:
Catbird Press, 1990. 464p. (A Garrigue Book).

A trilogy of philosophical novels, on three lives, which mark Čapek's transition from
relativism to absolutism. These novels are considered the culmination of Čapek's
literary output. The novels are markedly different but there are two common links.
The first is the theme of an individual's search for identity in the contemporary world.
The second link is Hegel's triad of thesis, antithesis and synthesis. In his excellent
introduction, Harkins concludes that while an individual life is necessarily tragic,
social life can sometimes transcend tragedy and become heroic and an occasion for
optimism. The three novels were first published in this translation in 1948, in London
by G. Allen & Unwin and in New York by A. A. Wyn, and reissued in 1949.

863 **Apocryphal tales: with a selection of Fables and Would be tales.**
Karel Čapek, translated from the Czech and with an introduction by
Norma Camrada. North Haven, Connecticut: Catbird Press, 1997.
188p. (A Garrigue Book).

A good read in a new translation, which uses updated language. Some stories, *Fables
and Would be tales*, have been added which have not before appeared in translation in
English. The tales show Čapek's humanistic outlook, his interest in human psychology and human experience, motivation and reaction. The author measures the
nature of truth and justice. The main section was published earlier as *Apocryphal
stories* (Harmondsworth, England: Penguin Books, 1975. Modern Classics), translated
by Dora Round.

864 **The tales from two pockets.**
Karel Čapek, translated from the Czech and with an introduction by
Norma Camrada. North Haven, Connecticut: Catbird Press, 1994.
365p. (A Garrigue Book).

These brilliant stories, about mysteries of all sorts, are, just like the *Apocryphal tales*,
about the nature of truth and justice. They remain very popular with Czech readers.
Milan Kundera, the contemporary Czech writer, considers the tales 'the most
agreeable reading' he knows. Others have described them as bleakly funny, prophetic,
clear and honourable. This edition brings to the English reader for the first time all
forty-eight tales in one book and all in a new translation. Arthur Miller tells the
prospective reader on the back cover that he reads Čapek 'for his insouciant laughter,
and the anguish of human blindness that lies beneath it . . . [Čapek] is a joy to read – a
wonderfully surprising teller of some fairly astonishing and unforgettable tales'.

865 **Towards the radical center: a Karel Čapek reader.**
Edited with an introduction by Peter Kussi, foreword by Arthur Miller.
Highland Park, New Jersey: Catbird Press, 1990. 408p. bibliog. (A
Garrigue Book).

A selection of Čapek's work by various translators, arranged loosely in chronological
order. Kussi provides a sizeable introduction on Karel, with some space devoted to his
brother Josef Čapek. The introduction is followed by notes on the translators of
Čapek's works, a short paragraph on each of them and a chronology of Čapek's life

and work. The work concludes with a chapter entitled 'At the cross-roads of Europe', an historical outline of the democratic idea in Czechoslovakia. This was published by the PEN Club of Prague in 1938, just prior to the German invasion of the country. The reader concludes with a list of English-language translations of Čapek's books.

866 **Nine fairy tales by Karel Čapek and one more thrown in for good measure.**
Karel Čapek, translated by Dagmar Hermann with illustrations by Josef Čapek. Evanston, Illinois: Northwestern University Press, 1990. 252p.

Presents satirical and original fairy-tales and more modern parables which should appeal to readers of all ages. The 'thrown in' story is by Josef Čapek, the illustrator brother of Karel. Dagmar Hermann undertook the difficult task of translating the verbal games and playfulness of the text of these modern versions of folk tales, of which the Czechs are so fond. The text reads well, the stories are spontaneous, and the people and situations are brought to life in a skilful way by the authors.

867 **The plague column.**
Jaroslav Seifert, translated by Ewald Osers, introduction by Cecil Parrott. London; Boston, Massachusetts: Terra Nova Editions, 1979. 106p.

Jaroslav Seifert was a very popular Czech poet, if not the most outstanding or original. Some indications of his popularity come in the appearances of translations of his work into English even before his nomination for the Nobel Prize, which he won in 1984. *The plague column* was first published in Cologne in 1977 and only later in Prague, in 1981, which indicates that he was out of favour with the Communist regime of the time and is not unconnected with the Nobel prize nomination. *The plague column* is also a rarity among Czech literature in that it produced not one, but two different translations, the other being by Lyn Coffin (Silver Spring, Maryland: SVU, 1980. 57p.), which also contains the Czech text.

868 **An umbrella from Piccadilly.**
Jaroslav Seifert, translated by Ewald Osers. London: London Magazine Editions, 1983. 80p.

The poems were published illicitly in Prague and then abroad, before seeing 'normal' publication in Communist Czechoslovakia. It is highly personal poetry, charged with melancholy. Another collection, *The wreath of sonnets – věnec sonetů* was published by the émigré publishing house Sixty-Eight Publishers and Larkwood Books, in Toronto, in 1987 (45p.). The delicate paperback gives the Czech text and a parallel English translation, complemented by sensitive illustrations. The translators, J. K. Klement and Eva Stucke, are also the authors of the parallel Czech and English introduction. Other translations of Seifert include: *The casting of bells*, translated by Paul Jagasich and Tom O'Grady (Iowa City, Iowa: The Spirit that Moves us Press, 1983. 61p.), an earlier work (1967) ill-served by the translation; *The selected poetry of Jaroslav Seifert,* translated by Ewald Osers, edited with additional translations by George Gibian (London: André Deutsch, 1986. 194p.); and the samples included in the *Exhibition notes* (London: British Library, 1985. 4p.) published to accompany the small display mounted at the British Library in response to the poet's award of the Nobel Prize for Literature.

869 **Mr Theodore Mundstock.**
Ladislav Fuks. New York: Four Walls and Eight Windows, 1991.
214p.
Fuks is considered by many the best Czech post-Second World War writer, a 'chronicler of absurdity and despair'. This novel, a classic about the most unbelievable phenomenon of modern history, is set in Prague in 1942, during the German occupation of the city. Mr Mundstock, a Jew, awaits his summons to a concentration camp. He decides to prepare himself and creates in his small flat a simulation of life in a camp. He resolves to learn to sleep on a wooden board, to be indifferent to insults and to toughen his body against hard labour. With stoic humour and economy of style, Fuks narrates the anticipation of, and the spiritual and psychological preparation for, adversity and evil.

870 **The cremator.**
Ladislav Fuks, translated by E. M. Kandler. London: Marion Boyars, 1984. 176p.
This is a bizarre, not to say horrifying, tale about a man who works in the crematorium in Prague at the time of the Nazi occupation. It is a powerful story of a mind gradually distorted by the 'hero's' belief that his family's existence is in jeopardy thanks to his wife's Jewish background. At the time this was no unique state of affairs, but set in the context of the crematorium it takes on a particularly gruesome aura. This was one of Fuks's earlier works (1967) and it enjoyed considerable success, as did the film based upon it.

871 **Mendelssohn is on the roof.**
Jiří Weil, translated by Marie Winn, with a preface by Philip Roth.
London: Flamingo; Harper Collins, 1992. 228p.
Set in the period of Nazi occupation, which Jiří Weil himself survived in hiding, this is a narration of the story of an SS officer in Prague in an anecdotal style. *Life with a star* (London: Collins, 1989), also by Jiří Weil, is a tragic book from the same period which sensitively captures the feelings of Czech Jews. It was translated by Rita Klímová with Roslyn Schloss, and Philip Roth again provided a preface. Both books have historical value as a record of the German occupation of Bohemia and Moravia.

872 **Living in truth.**
Edited by Jan Vladislav. London; Boston, Massachusetts: Faber & Faber, 1989. 315p. bibliog.
The subtitle is 'Twenty-two essays published on the occasion of the award of the Erasmus Prize to Václav Havel'. The collection was first published by Faber in Great Britain in 1987 and this is the first paperback edition. Six of the texts are by Havel, sixteen more are dedicated to Havel and there are testimonies by various fellow writers. Several translators are involved. The fellow writers are such distinguished literary names as Samuel Beckett, Heinrich Böll, Milan Kundera, Arthur Miller, Tom Stoppard (a friend of Havel), and Zdena Salivarová. Please note that 1986, the year when this book was assembled, was still in the age of darkness in Central Europe. The collection includes 'A short bio-bibliography of Václav Havel' (p. 295-315) and a good 'Introduction' for readers of Havel's essays, but there is no index.

873 **Open letters: selected prose 1965-1990.**
Václav Havel, selected and edited by Paul Wilson. London; Boston, Massachusetts: Faber & Faber, 1991. 415p.

This selection of Havel's non-dramatic writings is a companion volume to *Letters to Olga, Disturbing the peace* and *Selected plays* (qq.v.), all published by Faber. This book is thus intended to complete the picture of Havel as a dramatist, writer, thinker and future president. It is arranged chronologically by the date of origin of the piece and the time span is from the early 1960s to the late 1980s. The writings show vigour and depth of wisdom, lucidity and lack of pretence. Paul Wilson has, as always, carried out a very good job in the selection of material and he explains his selection criteria in his excellent preface (p. vii-xiv). There are also notes (p. 397-405), providing information on personalities, events and places, and a good index.

874 **Selected plays: 1963-83.**
Václav Havel. London; Boston, Massachusetts: Faber & Faber, 1992. 273p.

An anthology of Havel's plays by various translators. *The garden party, The memorandum, The increased difficulty of concentration* and *Protest* were translated by Vera Blackwell. Jan Novák translated *Unveiling*, also known as *Private view*, and George Theiner translated *Audience* (or *Conversation*) and *Mistake*. All of these plays made Havel's reputation as a playwright. Some of them have not appeared in book form in English before. They show the author's humour, wit and intellectual scope. The book contains just the texts of the plays and there are no introductions, explanations or indexes.

875 **Selected plays: 1984-1987.**
Václav Havel. London; Boston, Massachusetts: Faber & Faber, 1994. 207p.

The collection follows the same format as the previous anthology of selected plays but in this volume each play has a note on its production in England. *Largo Desolato* was translated by Havel's friend, the playwright Tom Stoppard, and was produced at the Bristol Old Vic in 1986. *Temptation* was translated by George Theiner and performed in Stratford-upon-Avon at The Other Place in 1987; it appeared separately under the Faber imprint in 1988 (71p.). *Redevelopment*, in this translation by James Saunders, was produced in Richmond in 1990 (see also separate entry below). The plays are written with Havel's typical irony and humour and their common theme is life in Central Europe under Communism.

876 **Redevelopment or slum clearance.**
Václav Havel, English version by James Saunders from a literal translation by Marie Winn. London; Boston, Massachusetts: Faber & Faber, 1990. 65p.

A play, written in 1987, set in the large hall of a mediaeval castle. Below the castle lies an old town which is going to be redeveloped. This project is being prepared by a team of architects and it is likely that it will be a high-rise development. The play, a condensed allegory of many depths, with political undertones, has a universal message. The architectural dilemma, the theme of the play, is universal. Being the work of Havel, it is both tragic and comic and functions as a political metaphor. The play has been performed in England.

877 **The rampage.**
Miroslav Holub, translated by David Young with Dana Hábová,
Rebekah Bloyd and the author. London: Faber & Faber, 1997. 84p.
Miroslav Holub is an internationally recognized poet who has been widely translated.
Ted Hughes considered him 'one of the half dozen most important poets writing
anywhere'. The cover of this slim paperback describes the poems in this collection as
poems of startling visionary intensity. They do not show any signs of Holub
mellowing with age, so the wit, irony and imagination of his earlier poems are still
powerfully represented. The translation was produced in consultation with the author
which renders it more than usually harmonious with the original. Miroslav Holub was
born in Pilsen in 1923 but spent most of his life in Prague. He was a medical man,
specializing in the field of immunology. David Young and Dana Hábová also
translated an earlier published book of Holub's poetry, *The vanishing lung syndrome*
(London: Faber & Faber, 1990). In 'Science, religion and myth: an interview with
Miroslav Holub', by Miroslav Holub and Ra Page, *New Humanist,* no. 110 (1
February 1995), p. 10-12, Holub is introduced as both poet and scientist. In this paper,
his humanism and religion and the political and mythical themes of his literary work
are discussed.

878 **The jingle bell principle.**
Miroslav Holub, translated by James Naughton. Newcastle upon
Tyne, England: Bloodaxe Books, 1992. 112p.
A selection from a very popular column in the Czech magazine *Vim,* subtitled 'Notes
and objections', containing contributions by Miroslav Holub. These contributions are
called 'essaylets', with a maximum length of forty-three lines and are brilliant
musings on ordinary daily events and happenings. The scientific mind of the author is
betrayed by sharp, precise observations. A well-known Czech cartoonist, Vladimír
Renčín, illustrated the essaylets and there are also photographs by Vojtěch Písařík. A
few examples of titles of these 'blackly funny' articles are: 'In defence of the
motorcar'; 'On aggression'; 'On natural respect'; 'The mythology of books'; 'Garden
gnomes'; 'Poetry in The Year 2000'; and 'Towards the physiology of joy'. Each
essaylet is introduced by a quotation from a thinker, writer, artist or scientist. In 1987
Bloodaxe Books also published Holub's poems in Ewald Osers' translation under the
title *The fly,* and in 1990 the collected English translations of Holub's poems by Ian
and Jarmila Milner, Ewald Osers and George Theiner as *Poems before and after.*
Holub wrote a number of books of poetry and of essays (fourteen books of poetry and
five collections of essays by 1990).

879 **Intensive care: selected and new poems.**
Miroslav Holub. [Ohio?]: Oberlin College Press, 1996. 205p. (FIELD
Translation Series, 22).
Nicely produced on quality paper, these new and previously published poems were
selected by Holub himself. The collection includes several prose-poems and a genre
which Holub calls 'stage poems' or short plays. Some of the work goes back as far as
the 1950s when Holub started publishing poems, as a newly qualified doctor. The
poems have several translators, who were guided in their work by Holub: George
Theiner; Dana Hábová; Stuart Friebert; David Young; Ewald Osers; and Ian and
Jarmila Milner.

880 **The dimension of the present moment.**
Essays by Miroslav Holub, edited by David Young. London; Boston, Massachusetts: Faber & Faber, 1990. 146p.

A number of translators worked on these essays, under the guidance of the author and the editor. The essays provide a fair representation of Holub's prose. The back cover of this slim paperback states: 'Readers attuned to the politics of Central Europe may discover here, and elsewhere in the book, a concealed allegory as well as a lucid scientific exposition . . . Miroslav Holub, a distinguished immunologist and a great poet, combines a scientific gift for accurate observation with a poetic impulse to imagine'. Holub died in Prague on 14 July 1998, aged seventy-four. *The Independent* had an obituary of the poet by J. Kirkup (16 July 1998, 'Review', p. 8) and *The Guardian* carried an obituary on Holub as a poet and scientist by E. Osers and T. Paulin under the title 'Two spheres, one domain' (16 July 1998, p. 22).

881 **Too loud a solitude.**
Bohumil Hrabal, translated from the Czech by Michael Henry Heim.
London: André Deutsch, 1991. 98p.

This book justifies Hrabal's renown as one of the best modern stylists. The tale was compiled in 1976, is set in a police state and the theme is the indestructibility of the written word. Some of Hrabal's work had numerous editions, such as the humorous *Closely observed trains* which was made into a film by Jiří Menzel. This work was published under various titles. Edith Pargeter's translation *Closely observed trains* was published by Abacus in London in 1990, another good edition was entitled *Closely watched trains* and has an introduction by Josef Škvorecký (New York: Penguin Books, 1981). In approximately the same period is set *I served the king of England* (latest edition, London: Pan Books [Picador], 1990). Michael Henry Heim has also translated fourteen short stories published in English under the title *The death of Mr Baltisberger* (London: Abacus, 1990) and *Dancing lessons for the advanced in age* (New York; San Diego, California; London: Harcourt Brace & Co., 1995). Hrabal was born in Brno but spent his later years in Prague.

882 **Total fears: letters to Dubenka.**
Bohumil Hrabal, translated from the Czech by James Naughton.
Prague: Twisted Spoon Press, 1998. 203p.

James Naughton, who lectures on Czech language and literature at Oxford, chose the texts, which, with the exception of the first one, 'The magic flute', are in a form of letters to a woman, Hrabal's muse, a woman called April (Dubenka is a free translation of this name, unusual in Czech). The time-span of the texts is 1989-92. Hrabal himself considered these letters a 'lyrical reportage' and, according to the blurb of the book, 'Hrabal provides something akin to memoir in a humorous and often moving tumult of free associations'. James Naughton also translated *Cutting it short and The little town where time stood still* which was published, with an introduction by Josef Škvorecký, in London by Abacus in 1993 and 1994 and in New York by Pantheon in 1993. Hrabal died in 1997, in Prague, at the age of eighty-two. There were obituaries in the English papers: in *The Guardian* by Igor Hájek and W. L. Webb on 5 February 1997 (p. 15) entitled 'Life closely observed'; and in *The Times* on 14 February (p. 23), under the title 'Bohumil Hrabal'.

883 **The spirit of Prague and other essays.**
Ivan Klíma, translated from the Czech by Paul Wilson. London:
Granta Books, in association with Penguin Books, 1994. 186p.
Comprises essays written over a period of fifteen years and selected by Klíma himself
for the English reader. He divided the essays into five sections. The first section
contains essays of a personal nature, that is on Klíma's life. Ivan Klíma was born in
Prague in 1931 and writes plays, novels and stories. Until 1989 his work was banned
in his own country, but during the Prague Spring he edited the journal of the Czech
Writer's Union. In 1969 Klíma was a visiting professor at the University of Michigan
but returned to Czechoslovakia the following year. The second section contains some
of his *feuilletons*, a literary genre popular with the Czechs. The third section contains
political essays and the fourth has two commentaries on literary dilemmas of the
modern age. The last section contains a paper written for a conference on Franz Kafka
at the University of British Columbia in Vancouver in 1983, entitled 'The spirit of
Prague'.

884 **The ultimate intimacy.**
Ivan Klíma, translated from the Czech by A. G. Brain. London:
Granta, 1997. 387p.
The theme of this latest novel by Klíma is the dilemma of faith and doubt – Klíma's
recurrent moral confusion. 'How should we live our lives? Which is strongest – a faith
without doubts, or a faith that contends with doubts?' It is not only a novel on faith
but also on love and change. The hero is Daniel Vedra, a Protestant pastor. The
background is the fast-changing post-1989 Czech society, which is undergoing total
social and economic upheaval. The love element is the relationship of Vedra, a
respectable clergyman and a public figure, and another man's wife. As always, Klíma
treats his hero with understanding. The translators are Gerald and Alice Turner, who
share the joint pen-name A. G. Brain and translated dissident literature of the 1970s
and 1980s.

885 **Waiting for the dark, waiting for the light.**
Ivan Klíma, translated from the Czech by Paul Wilson. London:
Granta Books, 1994. 234p.
The second printing of this book came out in 1995. The time-scale of this enjoyable
novel is before, during and after the Velvet Revolution of 1989. The hero is a middle-
aged television cameraman who was unhappy under the ideological constraints of the
Communist regime and felt artistically limited. Klíma describes, with his typical black
humour, but with sympathy, what happened to these artistic ambitions after 1989,
when freedom arrived – the cameraman is too busy with profitable small jobs which
he would have sneered at formerly, such as commercials, bits of porn films and
television spots. The novel, well translated by Paul Wilson from Toronto, has a touch
of surrealism but its message on moral confusion is universal. An interview with Ivan
Klíma, when he was in Britain to promote both this novel and *The spirit of Prague*,
was conducted by Mark Frankland and published in *The Observer*, 20 November
1994, 'Review', p. 18.

886 A summer affair.

Ivan Klíma, translated from Czech by Ewald Osers. London: Penguin Books, 1990. 263p.

First published in Czech as *Milostné léto* (Toronto: Sixty-Eight Publishers, 1979), with a revised edition by the same publisher in 1985. This English translation was first published by Chatto & Windus in 1987. It is considered by many to be the best of Klíma's novels, by some even as the best contemporary Czech novel. The setting is Prague and the hero is a middle-aged biologist who is researching the secrets of longevity. His conventional life loses control when he encounters a young, sensuous and frivolous girl. The novel is about getting old, about decomposition, the feeling of loss and being lost. Ewald Osers, who was himself born in Prague in 1917 but has lived in England since 1938, has translated this short and sharp novel very well, as befits a translator who has received many awards for his translations and is a Fellow of the Royal Society of Literature.

887 My golden trades.

Ivan Klíma, translated from the Czech by Paul Wilson. London: Granta Books, in association with Penguin, 1992. 284p.

The hero of this autobiographical, well-translated book tries being a smuggler, a painter, an archaeologist, an engine driver, a courier and a surveyor. The title draws from a Czech proverb, which like most proverbs is difficult to translate. It implies that one cannot go wrong being a tradesman-craftsman, because there is money in it. Klíma himself did most of the jobs in the stories. The hero does not become rich, but gains experience from every job. Klíma's other tales with autobiographical elements were published as *My merry mornings: stories from Prague*, translated by George Theiner (London; New York; Columbia, Louisiana: Readers International, 1993. 154p.). The stories provide a realistic picture of life in Czechoslovakia in the 1980s. The volume was first published in this English translation in 1985 (London; New York: Readers International). The latest collection of Klíma's stories, which span thirty years, is *Lovers for a day* (Cambridge, England: Granta, 1999. 229p.), translated by Gerald Turner. It was reviewed in *The Independent*, 28 August 1999, The Weekend Review, p. 11, by Dina Rabinovitch in an article entitled 'Czech mating game'.

888 Love and garbage.

Ivan Klíma, translated by Ewald Osers. London: Chatto & Windus, 1990. 222p.

This brilliant, compelling novel was written in 1986 and again, like most of Klíma's work, has autobiographical traits and is a political satire and love story, a 'meditation on the nature of freedom and guilt'. It is a forceful description of the fortunes of a creative artist living under a Communist regime. The hero is a writer who makes his living by sweeping the streets in Prague, an occupation which, however demeaning and tedious, has its rewards in providing a new viewpoint on life and society and in the company of his mates, other sweepers, who are both lively and eccentric. Ewald Osers also translated Klíma's *My first loves* (London: Chatto & Windus, 1986).

889 Judge on trial.

Ivan Klíma, translated from the Czech by A. G. Brown. London: Chatto & Windus, 1991. 547p.

This epic novel, which is reminiscent of the works of Dostoevsky and Kafka, and which is considered by some critics as Klíma's masterpiece, was first published in

275

1978 as an underground, samizdat publication. Klíma re-worked it in 1986. The setting is Prague and the time is after the invasion of Czechoslovakia in 1968. The hero is a judge, Adam Kindl, a 'flawed judge administering a flawed justice'. The personal and political are again interwoven in this portrait of the man and his times.

890 **The house of the tragic poet.**
Vladimír Janovic, translated by Ewald Osers.   Newcastle upon Tyne, England: Bloodaxe Books, 1988. 78p.

A lyrical epic poem which was first published in Czech in 1984 by Český spisovatel in Prague. It is an 'evocation of Pompeii a few days before its obliteration by volcanic ash'. Janovic was born in Czechoslovakia, where he still lives, in 1935. He is influenced by Italian culture, which is mirrored in his poetical works, and translates from Italian. In his introduction to the book Janovic relates how he was looking at the mosaic floor in a house in Pompeii and began to re-create in his mind the atmosphere and the persons represented in the mosaic, bringing them to life using his sensitive imagination; the accuracy of archaeological details is successful. Janovic is an admirer of the Czech poets Vítězslav Nezval and Josef Hora. The poem was published by Bloodaxe Books simultaneously with *The new Czech poetry* (q.v.), which was also translated by Ewald Osers.

891 **Selected poems.**
Josef Hanzlík, translated by Ewald Osers, Jarmila Milner, Ian Milner. Newcastle upon Tyne, England: Bloodaxe Books, 1993. 157p.

Hanzlík was born in 1938 and is considered to be one of the leading middle-generation poets. He has so far published ten books of poems. This selection of medium to long poems represents the work of the previous four years. In common with most of Hanzlík's poems, the subject is political violence. Most of the poems take the form of stirring monologues by imaginary, legendary or historical figures.

892 **Tremor of racehorses: selected poems.**
Sylva Fischerová, translated by Ian Milner, Jarmila Milner. Newcastle upon Tyne, England: Bloodaxe Books, 1990. 80p.

Ian Milner wrote the introduction to this first book of Fischerová's poetry to be published in English. Milner, a distinguished academic and translator, considers the poems a 'social comment and protest', reflecting 'the atmosphere and conditions of her homeland'. The poems were written in the early 1980s. The slim collection has biographical notes (p. 80) on Fischerová and on the translators. Sylva Fischerová is recognized as the most significant of the young Czech poets, perhaps taking over from Miroslav Holub as the leading light in Czech poetry.

893 **The sorrowful eyes of Hannah Karajich.**
Ivan Olbracht, translated by Iris Urwin Lewitová, with an introduction by Miroslav Holub.   Budapest: Central European University Press, 1999. 206p.

The author (1882-1952) was a novelist and Communist journalist. His writings which are set in the Sub-Carpathian region when it was part of Czechoslovakia between the wars represent his peak as an artist. This love story is set in the Czechoslovak Jewish community, a community which no longer exists.

894   **Bringing up girls in Bohemia.**
Michal Viewegh, translated from Czech by A. G. Brain.   London:
Readers International, 1997. 185p.
Published in Czech in 1994 under the title *Výchova dívek v Čechách* and made into a
film. It is a 'picaresque romp' which presents a sharp but amusing picture of the
Prague of today, with a mixed bag of characters including the so-called Mafiosi, their
ex-secret police bodyguards, some eccentric Czechs and expatriate Americans. The
novel also looks seriously into the role of the writer in a post-Communist society.

Anthologies

895   **Czech prose: an anthology.**
Translated and edited by William E. Harkins.   Ann Arbor, Michigan:
Michigan Slavic Publications, Department of Slavic Languages and
Literatures, University of Michigan, 1983. 321p. (Michigan Slavic
Translations, no. 6).
This volume contains some thirty-four excerpts dating from the 14th century to the
end of the First World War, together with a brief conventional history of the literature
and a cameo on each author or work. The 19th-century section is generally
conservative in its choice of authors, even if some of the passages selected are less so.
The real value lies in the fairly well-represented Old Czech and Baroque periods, with
meditational, hagiographic, allegorical and travel genres all included. The extracts are
supported by brief straightforward annotations and reproductions of some of the
manuscripts and portraits of some of the authors. Previously Harkins had edited an
Anthology of Czech literature (New York: King's Crown Press, 1953. 226p.) with
extracts, in the original, from twenty-two 19th- and 20th-century Czech authors, with
English commentaries. For breadth of choice and depth of commentary, the work
bears no comparison with Pynsent's *Czech prose and verse: a selection with
introductory essay* (q.v.).

896   **Czech prose and verse: a selection with an introductory essay.**
Robert B. Pynsent.   London: Athlone Press, 1979. 204p. (London East
European Series).
This is an anthology of extracts in the original, a far less conservative collection than
W. E. Harkin's *Czech prose: an anthology* (q.v.), and deliberately so. The selection
covers the period 1774-1939, beginning with Karel Thám and ending with Jan
Zahradníček, and as it is less conventional than many collections, translated or
otherwise, it gives a fairer representation of the modern literature. The work is
primarily intended for students of literature with a prior knowledge of the language,
though some language points and other vital annotations are given. The 'introductory
essay' takes up over a third of the book and is a useful alternative history of Czech
literature.

897   **Child of Europe: a new anthology of East European poetry.**
Edited by Michael March.   London: Penguin, 1990. 254p.
An older sister of the volume, *Description of a struggle: the Picador book of
contemporary East European prose* (see following entry). The title was this time

277

borrowed from the title of a poem by the Polish poet Czesław Miłosz. There were readings at the Royal Festival Hall, South Bank, London in February 1989 called 'Child of Europe', in which Sylva Fischerová took part. The majority of the poets included here were born during the First World War or immediately after and grew up in Communist states. Michael March selected poems from the contemporary Czech poets Sylva Fischerová, Ivo Šmoldas, Ewald Murrer and Jana Štroblová. The poems included here were all translated by Ian and Jarmila Milner. The anthology is again arranged by country. The editor provides 'Sources and acknowledgements' (p. 250-54), and brief notes on sources of the translation, but the reader will search in vain for helpful notes on the poets.

898 **Description of a struggle: the Picador book of contemporary East European prose.**
Edited by Michael March. London: Picador, 1994. 403p.

A follow-up to *Child of Europe: a new anthology of East European poetry* (see previous entry), also edited by Michael March. The Czech Lands are well represented in this anthology of short prose, on several levels: the title of the collection is borrowed from Franz Kafka; the introduction was written by Ivan Klíma; and the editor's preface starts with a quotation from the contemporary Czech philosopher Jan Patočka on morality: 'It is morality that defines man'. Forty-three writers were chosen from Eastern Europe, or, more accurately, from the former Soviet realm. The anthology is arranged by country. All the Czech entries (p. 111-44) and Klíma's introduction were translated by James Naughton. The Czech entries are: 'The pink scarf' by Bohumil Hrabal; 'The unborn' by Eda Kriseová; 'He wakes up' by Alexandra Berková; and 'Brownian motion' by Ondřej Neff. The editor provides 'Biographical notes' on individual authors (Czech authors are on p. 390) and 'Acknowledgements', which are bibliographical data on the first edition of each story (Czech stories are on p. 399-400).

899 **The poet's lamp: an anthology of Czech poetry.**
Alfred French. Canberra: The Leros Press, 1986. 145p.

With the exception of Karel Havlíček Borovský's satirical poem 'The baptism of St. Vladimír', this short anthology covers the modern period, the 20th century. Thus it covers Czech Expressionist poetry, Social Realism and Proletarian Art, Dada, Constructivism and Futurism and the style created by the Czechs, Poetism, as represented by Vítězslav Nezval and Jaroslav Seifert. The other poets are Fráňa Šrámek, S. K. Neumann, Josef Hora, Konstantin Biebl, Jakub Deml, František Halas, Jiřina Hauková, Vladimír Holan, Jiří Orten, Kamil Bednář, František Hrubín, Josef Kainar, Josef Hanzlík and Miroslav Holub. The texts are parallel, with the Czech on one page and the English translation on the opposite page. Most of the translations are by Alfred French, who also provides brief introductions to modern Czech poetry and the history of the country, 'Notes on the text' (p. 138-39), and a paragraph on each poet and on his work in 'Notes on the poets' (p. 140-45).

900 **The Czech avantgardists.**
Edited by Alfred French. Rockville, Maryland: Kabel Publishing, 1995. 104p.

A coffee-table book of almost A4 dimensions, with beautiful illustrations. The picture on the cover is by Alfons Mucha, the art nouveau artist. This collection of verse draws mainly from the wealth of Czech verse in the inter-war era, which was perhaps the most productive period. Czech poetry was closely involved and influenced by the current trends in European literature and art. The Czech poets came under the influence of Expressionism, Futurism, Cubo-Futurism, Dada, Surrealism and the modern Russian movements. The poems are followed by 'Notes on the poets' (p. 97-103). The poets included in this anthology are: Konstantin Biebl, Jakub Deml, Jaroslav Durych, František Halas, Jiřina Hauková, Vladimír Holan, Josef Hora, František Hrubín, Josef Kainar, Jiří Mahen, Stanislav Kostka Neumann, Vítězslav Nezval, Jiří Orten, Josef Palivec, Jaroslav Seifert, F. X. Šalda, Fráňa Šrámek, Otakar Theer, Richard Weiner, Jiří Wolker, Jan Zahradníček and Vilém Závada. There are also 'Notes on contributors' (p. 104), that is, René Wellek, Zdeněk Kalista, Zdeněk Pešat and Alfred French.

901 **The new Czech poetry.**
Jaroslav Čejka, Michal Černík, Karel Sýs, translated by Ewald Osers.
Newcastle upon Tyne, England: Bloodaxe Books, 1988. 62p.
A slender anthology of three modern Czech poets. Jaroslav Čejka (b. 1943) is an engineer by profession and an experimental dramatist. In the gently humorous 'Twelve laws of the heart', written in free verse, he applies the language of physical and other laws to human relationships (e.g. the Law of Gravitation, Pascal's Law, The Law of Inertia). The poems of Michal Černík (also b. 1943) 'show a strong sense of history, family and landscape'. The nucleus of this selection, which reflects his intimate relationship with landscape and is written in sparing language, is monologues – spoken by a stone, a jug, a rose, a mountain. The selection chosen from the playful poems of Karel Sýs (b. 1946), a poet who writes in 'sensuous language, direct and outspoken, full of enchantment with life and rejecting all hypocrisy and puritanism', includes 'The Time machine' (published in 1984), which was acclaimed by critics as his best work so far. Sýs was influenced by Rimbaud and Apollinaire and the Czech Vítězslav Nezval and is considered to be preoccupied with America as viewed through Raymond Chandler's novels. A companion volume to this book, *House of the tragic poet*, by Vladimír Janovic, was published by Bloodaxe Books at the same time.

902 **This side of reality: modern Czech writing.**
Edited by Alexandra Buchler. London; New York: Serpent's Tail, 1996. 230p.
An unassuming paperback published with the assistance of the Arts Council of Great Britain and dedicated to the memory of Ladislav Fuks (1921-94), one of the seventeen modern Czech writers included in this anthology. The contemporary stories have various translators, some having been translated by the editor, who was born in Prague and now lives in Glasgow. The selection of writers represents the 'fragmentation and dividedness' of Czech post-war literature, which was distorted by censorship and exile. Czech writers and the written word have, by tradition, a privileged status and infinite influence in Czech culture. The authors represented here follow in the tradition of humour and irony, the absurd and the surreal. What unites them is their rejection of formal ideological dogmatism and a genuine concern for the continuation of national culture, integrity and basic human values which were subdued in the aura of apathy and widespread complicity. The anthology also traces the history of the decades after the Second World War. The section 'About the authors' (p. 223-28) gives their short biographies and lists their published works. The authors are: Michal Ajvaz, Alexandra Berková, Zuzana Brabcová, Ota Filip, Ladislav Fuks, Jiří Gruša, Bohumil Hrabal, Ivan Klíma, Jiří Kratochvíl, Věra Linhartová, Arnošt Lustig, Ewald Murer, Sylvie Richterová, Josef Škvorecký, Jáchym Topol, Ludvík Vaculík and Michal Viewegh.

903 **Interference: the story of Czechoslovakia in the words of its writers.**
Compiled and edited by Peter Spafford, with a preface by Miroslav Holub. Cheltenham, England: New Clarion Press, 1992. 169p.

Presents extracts from short stories, novels, essays, plays and poetry by twenty-six Czech writers and poets: Konstantin Biebl, Karel Čapek, Jaroslav Hašek, Ivan Klíma, Jaroslav Seifert, Václav Havel, Bohumil Hrabal, Eva Kantůrková, Franz Kafka, Milan Kundera and Jiří Wolker. Each piece has its own translator, the names which appear most often being those of Jarmila and Ian Milner, Ewald Osers and Paul Wilson. This work started life as a theatre production, a 'collage of readings', which was performed by three actors and a saxophone player. The compiler of this anthology included 'Notes on authors' (p. 151-58) in short, one-paragraph biographies and of these the biographies of contemporary authors are particularly valuable. There is also a chronology of Czech history from 1900-89, an index of authors (p. 163-65), index of titles (p. 166-69) and an erroneously entitled 'Guide to Czechoslovak[?] pronunciation' (p. xxi-xxii).

904 **Czech plays: modern Czech drama.**
Selected and introduced by Barbara Day. London: Nick Hearn Books, 1994. 224p.

This anthology of 20th-century Czech drama provides in its introduction a fair historical outline of Czech cultural life, focusing on the theatre. The anthology in fact consists of only four modern plays in English translation: *Tomorrow!* by Václav Havel; *Games* by Ivan Klíma; *Cat on the rails* by Josef Topol; and *Dog and wolf* by Daniela Fischerová. Each play is preceded by a short biography of the author and a brief evaluation of his or her work.

905 **The Vanek plays: four authors, one character.**
Edited by Marketa Goetz-Stankiewicz. Vancouver: University of British Columbia Press, 1987. 258p. bibliog.

Four dissident authors of different artistic temperaments and intellect – Václav Havel, Pavel Kohout, Pavel Landovský and Jiří Dienstbier – used the same character, one Ferdinand Vaněk, in their plays, as a catalyst for problems. Vaněk is supposed to be a shy, unpretentious man, but is a formidable writer who appears to be manipulated by others while in fact he is in control of situations and nothing could make him change or do what he would consider wrong. This is the intellectual focus, as well as the spirit, of the eight plays, echoing Havel's famous essay, 'The power of the powerless'. The plays are as follows: *Audience, Unveiling* and *Protest* by Havel; *Permit, Morass* and *Safari* (the last one translated from the German) by Kohout; *Arrest* by Landovský and *Reception* by Dienstbier. There is an impressive 'reference list' of international performances of the Vaněk plays (p. 249) and of their premieres (p. 251). All of the premieres took place between 1976 and 1982.

906 **Prague: a traveller's literary companion.**
Edited by Paul Wilson. San Francisco: Whereabouts Press, 1995. 242p. map.

A good anthology of short stories. Wilson describes the gathering of material for this book as being like 'trying to pick the perfect bouquet from a field filled with beautiful flowers. There is only so much you can gather at once, and what you end up bringing home depends on the season, the climate, and even the time of day'. It is fortunate that Wilson was gathering the stories in the post-Communist era: the result is a selection with depth, reading which is a positive pleasure. The stories convey the history of the city, its traditional essence and its lively, dynamic present. The editor provides a background to literary Prague in the preface, and there is also a Prague chronology (p. 225-28), a brief glossary (p. 229-30), notes on contributors (p. 231-37) and notes on translators (p. 238-39). Paul Wilson himself translated a number of the stories.

907 **Prague: tales of the city.**
Václav Havel, Janet Malcolm, Milan Kundera, Bruce Chatwin, Josef Škvorecký, edited by John Miller, Kirsten Miller. San Francisco: Chronicle Books, 1994. 247p. (Chronicles Abroad).

A small-format gift book, enjoyable to read before visiting the city of Prague; it is an anthology of excerpts, essays and poems by eleven authors from different countries. The contributions are wide ranging and the idea is to portray Prague as a city outside time. Some of the entries are surprising, but they add to the richness of the pattern of this anthology. There is no bibliography or index.

908 **Literature and tolerance: views from Prague.**
Prague: Readers International (Prague), Czech Centre for International P.E.N., 1994. 239p.

A commemorative volume published on the anniversary of the last World Congress of International PEN (International Association of Poets, Playwrights, Editors, Essayists and Novelists) held in Prague in 1938. It is an anthology of essays, stories, poetry and drama, by mostly contemporary authors, all of which shed light on the historical role of Czech writers during the contest against fascism and Communism.

Czech and Slovak literature in English: a bibliography.
See item no. 852.

Émigré literature

909 **Knihy za ohradou: česká literatura v exilových nakladatelstvích.**
(Fenced-out books: Czech literature of exile publishing houses.)
Jan Čulík. Prague: Trizonia, 1991. 420p. bibliog.

A critical survey of the book production of Czech publishing houses in the West between 1971 and 1989. Čulík cites only publications in book form and concentrates on original Czech fiction and poetry. Only brief summaries are given for drama and non-fiction. Titles published in languages other than Czech and Czechoslovak samizdat publications are not included. Czech independent literature has its own distinctive culture, its own philosophy and its own system of values. One of the differences between the publishers of samizdat literature and exile publishing houses was that the latter had to survive commercially and thus, when publishing samizdat literature, had the function of a quality filter. To provide some background information on exile literature the book starts, as an introduction, with a summary of Czech literature from the beginning of the 1950s to the end of the 1960s and continues with independent Czech literature abroad, providing information on publishing houses, authors and individual works. Of interest is the entry for Ivan Blatný (1919-90), not because his fate was typical of writers in exile, but because to some he is one of the great poets of this century. Blatný came from Brno but from 1948 lived in England, finally spending a number of years in a mental home in Ipswich. Blatný published six books of poetry while still in Czechoslovakia, melodic poetry into which there later penetrated more raw, darker and metaphysical tones. *Stará bydliště* (q.v.) and *Pomocná škola Bixley*, a collection of poetry which is in fact a diary of Blatný, were published by Josef Škvorecký in Toronto. Čulík's survey continues with reference sections, 'Seznam publikací vydaných v hlavních exilových nakladatelstvích' (List of publications published in the main exile publishing houses) on p. 341-85 and concludes with a name index and index of titles. It is a very good reference book, well written and well organized.

910 **Česká a slovenská literatura y exilu a samizdatu: informatorium pro učitele, studenty i laiky.** (Czech and Slovak literature in exile: information for teachers, students and the layman.)
Václav Burian, Josef Galík, Lubomír Machala, Martin Podivínský, Jan Schneider, edited by Lubomír Machala. Olomouc, Czechoslovakia: Hanácké noviny, 1991. 166p.

This publication is a remake of a textbook for university students, the popularity of which indicated the widespread quest for information on émigré literature. The handbook, as the editor calls the booklet, starts with a survey of individual publishers, unofficial editions and literary magazines. This is followed by a section dedicated to poetry, fiction, drama and literary science. Then come cameos on selected major individuals in the field. Each is given approximately one page, with brief biographical details and an evaluation of his/her particular activities. This book contains probably the most comprehensive information on Czech literature in exile in the 1970s and 1980s; the authors provide a substantial name index.

911 **Katalog Sixty-Eight Publishers.**
Compiled and edited by Václav Krištof. Prague: Společnost Josefa Škvoreckého, 1991. 59p.

An annotated list of 212 publications of the most important Czech exile publishing house which was run by the writers Josef Škvorecký and his wife Zdena Salivarová in Toronto in the 1970s and 1980s. The annotations are good, mainly giving brief information on the given author, a description of the work, a note on the graphical design of the cover, the year and month of publication and the number of pages. The catalogue is a good indicator of the richness and quality of the world of émigré literature and of the legacy of Sixty-Eight Publishers.

912 **Samizdat and an independent society in Central and Eastern Europe.**
H. Gordon Skilling. Basingstoke, England: Macmillan in association with St Antony's College, Oxford, 1989. 293p. bibliog.

When Skilling was concluding this book the social and political scene in Czechoslovakia was changing and his study was becoming a history. The book was inspired by the Czech situation, and of the three various sections, part two is solely on: 'Independent tendencies in Czechoslovakia'; dissent and Charter 77; and independent historiography, religion, politics and philosophy. Parts one and three are generally on the origin of the modern samizdat in the Soviet Union, China and Central Europe, on independent communications in Central Europe and independent society in that region. Skilling traces the origin of the word *samizdat* (a Russian acronym of 1950, from the larger Samsebyaizdat, meaning publishing house for oneself), the first important book being Boris Pasternak's *Doctor Zhivago*, published abroad in 1958 after unsuccessful attempts to have the book published through normal channels in the Soviet Union. Where underground literature is concerned, the Czechs, according to this book (p. 11), 'perfected the system and made it an art'. Skilling provides pages of bibliographical 'Notes and references' (p. 239-83) and an index (p. 284-93).

913 **Czechoslovak samizdat: a catalogue of British Library holdings.**
Compiled by Peter Hellyer, Děvana Pavlík. London: British Library, Slavonic and East European Collections, 1990. 23p.

Czech samizdat publishing started in the early 1970s, originally publishing Czech writers whose works were banned after 1968, but gradually including translations of works of foreign authors which were undesirable and deemed not suitable for the public in Czechoslovakia. Incredible though it may seem today, such undesirable British authors included George Orwell and J. R. R. Tolkien, whose *Lord of the rings* was thought to be too religious. Several regular series were published and nearly 200 periodical titles. The techniques for producing material for underground dissemination were primitive to start with: multiple typed copies. Gradually mimeograph, xerox and other more efficient methods of reproduction were used. The British Library started collecting Czech samizdat publications in 1983 and this catalogue lists nearly 400 titles, available on interlibrary loans via the British Library Document Supply Center.

914 **Milan Kundera: an annotated bibliography.**
Glen Brand. New York; London: Garland Publishing, 1988. 133p.

Compiled in response to the rapid rise in interest in Kundera's novels, the bibliography offers a complete list of his work up to 1988 and a list of all significant works on Kundera and his writings up to that time. This time limitation now makes the lists dated, since Kundera has not been idle since 1988. The primary bibliography, of Kundera's own work, lists all his published work of poetry, drama, fiction, translations, critical essays, speeches, film scripts and art work, as well as all known translations of these works. Kundera's major essays and his comments in published interviews are annotated. The secondary bibliography starts with full-length studies and general secondary works, criticism of the plays and criticism of films based on Kundera's work. This is followed by sections on individual novels, written and published up to 1988. The English listings claim to be comprehensive and cover books, literary journals, general periodical articles and dissertations. The compiler also included important critical comments from French, Spanish, Italian, German and

Czech publications. Brand concentrates on French publications since Kundera was already living in France at the time and wrote critical essays in French. The introduction consists of Kundera's biography, notes on his literary career, assessment of political influences on Kundera's literature and two to four pages of comments on each of the novels published up to 1988: *Laughable loves, The joke, Life is elsewhere, The farewell party, The book of laughter and forgetting* and *The unbearable lightness of being*. The first monograph on Kundera was Robert C. Porter's *Milan Kundera: a voice from Central Europe* (Aarhus, Denmark: Arkona Publishers, 1981).

915 Milan Kundera and feminism: dangerous intersections.

John O'Brien. Basingstoke, England: Macmillan, 1995. 178p. bibliog.

Explores Kundera's work using the tool of feminism for the dissection of his writings. The book has two main sections, with self-explanatory headings. Chapter one, '(Mis)representing women', is on Kundera's work generally, and chapter two, 'Seeing through the opposition: Kundera, deconstruction and feminism', looks at the writer's individual novels. The 'Endnotes' (p. 145-65) and 'Works cited' (p. 168-70) offer an up-to-date, detailed and fairly comprehensive picture of the critical reception of Kundera's fiction. Different dimensions of Kundera's writing are looked into in *The political novels of Milan Kundera and O. V. Vijayan: a comparative study*, by C. Gopinathan Pillai (New Delhi: Prestige, 1996). This book also has a bibliography (p. 114-20) and an index.

916 Terminal paradox: the novels of Milan Kundera.

Marie Němcová Banerjee. Boston, Massachusetts: Faber & Faber, 1990; London: Faber & Faber, 1991. 294p.

Looks at six Kundera novels, which were all written in Czech, in the context of his time, his life and European culture generally. The novels considered are: *The joke* – Kundera's first novel; *The laughable loves*, which was the first of his novels to be published in the United States; *Life is elsewhere* – Kundera's second novel, which he started to write during the Russian invasion of Czechoslovakia and completed in 1969; the anti-realistic novel *The farewell party*; the discursive novel, *The book of laughter and forgetting*; and *The unbearable lightness of being*.

917 Milan Kundera and the art of fiction: critical essays.

Edited by Aron Aji. New York; London: Garland, 1992. 354p. bibliog.

Claims to be the first book-length critical work on Kundera published in the United States. It is a collection of essays, some of which had been published previously, on Kundera's contribution to world literature. There are comparative studies, e.g. the essay by R. B. Gill, 'The laughter of Vonnegut, Grass and Kundera', while some essays are concerned with linguistic analysis and are meditations on Kundera's verbal art. The majority are on specific works of the writer, such as: Michael Carroll's 'The cyclic form of Laughable loves' (p. 132-52); Jolanta W. Wawrzycka's 'Betrayal as a flight from kitsch in The unbearable lightness of being'; Nina Pelikan Straus' 'Erasing history and deconstructing the text: the book of laughter and forgetting' (p. 248-66); and Michael Richards' 'Tamina as alter ego: autobiography and history in The book of laughter and forgetting' (p. 221-30). *The joke* was also the subject of two essays, 'The abandonment of Lucie Sebetka in The joke' by Aron Aji (p. 170-82) and 'Homo Homini Lupus: Milan Kundera's The joke' by Frances L. Restuccia (p. 153-69).

918 **Understanding Milan Kundera: public events, private affairs.**
Fred Misurella. Columbia, South Carolina: University of South
Carolina Press, 1993. 216p. bibliog. (Understanding Modern European
and Latin American Literature).

An overview of both the literary and critical works of Milan Kundera in the context of
European culture. Kundera was influenced by German, Austrian and French literature
and the author analyses the debt Kundera owes to other contemporary writers. This,
and the comparative element of the critical study, makes it suitable to anyone with an
interest in literature generally. Misurella highlights Kundera as a major contemporary
theorist – see, for example, Milan Kundera's *Testaments betrayed* (London: Faber &
Faber, 1995), translated by Linda Asher. An essay, which was part of an introduction
to the new Czech edition of his own writings and in which Kundera evaluates and
discusses his own work, has been translated by Professor Misurella and is on p. 162-
64 of this book. More of Kundera's reflections, on the evolution of his work and on
the novel as a 'historical unity', a theory which Europe is finding impossible to
comprehend, can be found in 'Wisdom of being', *The Guardian*, 27 January 1994,
supplement, p. 8. In this article, Kundera also defends the French cultural supremacy
which can give rise to francophobia.

919 **The joke.**
Milan Kundera, translated from the Czech by Aaron Asher. London:
Faber & Faber, 1992. 317p.

The book has been translated several times. It appeared first in English in 1969
(London: Macdonald) and brought Kundera international fame, marking him as a
writer in a class of his own. This is already a fifth and fully revised version of this
tragi-comic novel, set in post-Second World War Czechoslovakia.

920 **Laughable loves.**
Milan Kundera, translated by Suzanne Rappaport. New York: Knopf,
distributed by Random House, 1974. 242p.

The first collection of Kundera's prose to be published and reach the American public,
while he was still living in Czechoslovakia. These short stories bear the hallmark of
Kundera's perceptive humour; the focus is, as usual with this author, the tragi-comic
paradoxes of love. It had several subsequent editions, the latest by Faber & Faber,
London, 1991. The bitterly funny *Life is elsewhere* was also published in 1974 by
Knopf in New York (distributed by Random House) in a translation by Peter Kussi.
The farewell party, translated by Peter Kussi, was published in 1976 (New York:
Knopf, distributed by Random House) and has several editions (London: Faber &
Faber, 1993). The latest edition, under the title *The farewell waltz* (London: Faber &
Faber, 1998), was translated by Aaron Asher. *The book of laughter and forgetting*
(New York: A. A. Knopf, 1980), a mixture of love, eroticism and fantasy is also a
sharp political satire. It was translated again by Michael Henry Heim and has had
several printings. Kundera emigrated from Czechoslovakia in 1975 and settled in
France. Initially he continued writing in Czech. *The unbearable lightness of being* was
translated from the Czech by Michael Henry Heim and published in 1984, in New
York by Harper & Row and in London by Faber. It has had several printings and is
described as dark and brilliant.

921 **Slowness.**
Milan Kundera, translated from the French by Linda Asher. London: Faber & Faber, 1996. 132p.

A fiction and fantasy novel published after five years of silence and the first of his novels which he wrote in French. It is more of a memoir and, as in most of Kundera's work, the autobiographical element is strong. Described as existential analysis, the main concepts are slowness and rapidity, discretion and exhibitionism. The philosophical *Immortality* is another of Kundera's paradoxical novels written in French. It was published in London and Boston, Massachusetts by Faber & Faber in 1991 and translated from the Czech by Peter Kussi.

922 **Identity.**
Milan Kundera, translated from the French by Linda Asher. London; Boston, Massachusetts: Faber & Faber, 1998. 153p.

A love story, the latest of Kundera's novels, is another intense narrative which bears witness to his art of switching from reality to fantasy. The story, just like *Slowness* (see previous entry), is set in France. The critics described *Identity* as one of Kundera's most profound, touching and illuminating books.

923 **Testaments betrayed.**
Milan Kundera, translated from the French by Linda Asher. London: Faber & Faber, 1995. 280p.

A fine collection of essays, comprising detailed studies on the translations and mistranslations of Franz Kafka, Thomas Mann, Robert Musil and other cosmopolitan writers. Kundera insists that translation is an example of the way in which an artist's testament may be betrayed. The model used is Leoš Janáček's German libretti in Max Brod's adaptation. The book was reviewed by Dan Gunn in *The Times Literary Supplement*, no. 4854 (12 April 1997), p. 21-22, in an article called 'The book of betrayals'.

924 **The fiction of Josef Škvorecký.**
Paul I. Trensky, assisted by Michaela Harnick. Basingstoke, England: Macmillan Academic and Professional Ltd, in association with the School of Slavonic and East European Studies, University of London, 1991. 134p. bibliog.

A critical guide which was written in the mid-1980s and completed only months before the Velvet Revolution in November 1989. Hence it was compiled while Škvorecký's work was still banned in his home country due to his early activities at home, his emigration and subsequent activities abroad; he emigrated to Canada in 1969 but in his writings he has never left the country of his youth. Now, after twenty years, his works are again published in his native country. Škvorecký pursues various genres and he has written poetry, a play, film scripts, literary and film criticism. His main medium is fiction and consists of novels, short stories and detective fiction. The organization of this monograph is a discussion on these genres, in chronological order. Trensky considers Škvorecký as one of the great Czech prose writers of this century. The bibliography lists Škvorecký's fiction in Czech and in English translation and his non-fiction and secondary literature (p. 128-31).

925 **Headed for the blues: a memoir with ten stories.**
Josef Škvorecký. London; Boston, Massachusetts: Faber & Faber, 1998. 280p.

Škvorecký's own story, told with irony and humour, in which he proves that the major forces and influences which shaped his life and work were 'jazz, politics, suspicion and desire'. Škvorecký and Kundera stand out among the Czech émigré writers, their work having been extensively translated and having received great attention from both critics and readers. Faber & Faber published a number of works by Škvorecký. *The bride of Texas* was published in 1996 in a translation by Kaca Polackova Henley. *The Independent* published an interview with Škvorecký about this book (5 October 1996, p. 3), with Jasper Rees talking to him about the experiences which helped to mould this Afro-Czech-American novel. The same translator also worked on *Sins for father Knox* (London; Boston, Massachusetts: Faber & Faber, 1990) from the detective series featuring Lieutenant Borůvka. Paul Wilson translated *The republic of whores* (London; Boston, Massachusetts: Faber & Faber, 1994) and *The miracle game*, which was also published by Faber, 1991.

926 **Miss Silver's past.**
Josef Škvorecký, translated from the Czech by Peter Kussi. London: Vintage, 1995. 296p.

This novel, written in 1969, is part love story and part detective story, set in a state publishing house in Prague. Being the work of Škvorecký, it is both amusing and sad.

927 **Dvořák in love: a light hearted dream.**
Josef Škvorecký, translated from the Czech by Paul Wilson. London: The Hogarth Press, 1989. 322p.

The novel was first published in Great Britain by Chatto & Windus in 1986. It is a tragicomedy set around the composer Antonín Dvořák during his sojourn in the United States, the New World of his famous symphony. It was Škvorecký's first attempt at a historical and biographical novel.

928 **Stará bydliště.** (Old dwellings.)
Ivan Blatný. Brno, Czech Republic: Petrov, 1992. 111p.

This small, unique book of poetry was first published by Sixty-Eight Publishers in Toronto, Canada, in 1979. Blatný was born in Brno in 1919 and died in Colchester, England in 1990. His very beautiful, lyrical poetry will bring a lump to the throat of many Czechs living in England. Blatný failed to cope with living in a different country and sought refuge in a mental hospital. The Czech critics described his existence there metaphorically as one of *trosečník*, a Czech term which is difficult to translate accurately – a shipwrecked person or a failure. His archives were moved to Brno.

929 **Pomocná škola Bixley.** (Bixley special school.)
Ivan Blatný. Prague: Torst, 1992. 111p.

This collection was also first published by Sixty-Eight Publishers in Toronto, in 1984. Some of the poems, written in physical and mental isolation, were written in English; some are half in Czech and half in English.

287

930 **Tento večer.** (This evening.)
Ivan Blatný. Prague: Československý spisovatel, 1991. 227p.

A selection of Blatný's poetry, covering his work from 1937, was prepared for publication in 1969, but could not be published for political reasons. This edition was enlarged by poetry written in exile and is supplemented by a biography of Blatný and a critical analysis of his poetry. The book contains some photographs, from Blatný's home town of Brno and from Ipswich in England.

931 **Stalin's shoe.**
Zdena Tomin. London; Melbourne: J. M. Dent & Sons Ltd, 1987.
157p.

This is a paperback edition, the first edition having been published in Great Britain by Century Hutchinson Ltd in 1986. Zdena Tomin, who was born in the Czech Lands in 1941, was a spokesperson for Charter 77. She and her family were consequently harassed by the police. When she went with her husband, the philosopher and academic Julius Tomin, and their children to Oxford in 1980, they were deprived of Czech citizenship as 'enemies of the state' and became refugees in Great Britain. At the time of writing this book, she was divorced and living in London with her two sons. This story is set in London and Wales. The heroine is a Czech exile and a large part of the novel consists of flashbacks to her childhood and adolescence in Prague. Both of Tomin's novels listed here (see also the following entry) have strong autobiographical traits. *Stalin's shoe* is a fine novel, which will be haunting to Tomin's generation, being a mixture of politics and private passions. Like many uprooted people Tomin has an outsider's (cosmic) view and where many would become overcritical, she is humorous and unsentimental. The style of her language is complimented by Fay Weldon on the back cover: 'Ms Tomin (as Conrad before her) writes with the ferocious and careful grace of someone to whom English is not a native tongue'.

932 **The coast of Bohemia: a winter's tale.**
Zdena Tomin. London; Melbourne: J. M. Dent & Sons Ltd, 1988.
201p.

First published in Great Britain by Century Hutchinson Ltd, in 1987. This is a paperback edition. Tomin was one of the vocal Czech refugees in the 1980s, writing articles, appearing on television and speaking on radio programmes. A graduate in philosophy and sociology, she wrote originally in Czech, and produced surrealistic poetry, short stories and essays. *The coast of Bohemia* is set in a city in Eastern Europe, at that time still under a totalitarian regime, and describes lives among the dissidents. Tomin is a strong and skilful writer on friendships between women, and the nucleus of the novel is a fragile and touching relationship between two women. She compares the force of state subjection with the strength of an individual and his/her private feelings.

288

Literature of other nationalities

German

General

933 **The relationship of the Prague German writers to the Czechoslovak Republic 1918-1939.**
Eve C. Bock. *Germano-Slavica*, vol. 2, no. 4 (fall 1977), p. 273-83.
Bock describes the political allegiances rather than the literary qualities of the major Prague writers. Two main groupings, the 'Prager Schule', which was pro-Masaryk and anti-Austrian, and a leftwing group with ties to like-minded Czech, Russian and German writers, produced a major contribution to German literature, quite distinct from their pro-Nazi Sudeten compatriots. Although the writers, who disappeared in exile or concentration camps after the occupation, had sought to be fully involved in the Czech cultural scene, they were, and are, largely ignored by, or unknown to, the Czech reading public. Many of the Prague German writers were Jews.

934 **Juden in der deutschen Literatur: ein deutsch-israelisches Symposion.** (The Jews in German literature: a German-Israeli symposium.)
Edited by Stéphane Moses, Albrecht Schone. Frankfurt, Germany: Suhrkamp Verlag, 1986. 394p. bibliog. (Suhrkamp Taschenbuch, 2063).
The eighth symposium in a series organized by The Hebrew University in Jerusalem and the University of Göttingen which took place from 23-30 October 1983. The Jews living in Bohemia were leading bearers of Jewish culture and several of the papers acknowledge this. Articles dealing specifically with the greatest of the writers, Franz Kafka, are: 'Brecht und Benjamin als Kafka-Interpreten' (Brecht and Benjamin as interpreters of Kafka) by Stéphane Moses; 'Milena, Kafka und das Judentum. Wie tief wirkt die intellektuelle Toleranz?' (Milena, Kafka and Judaism. How deep is the intellectual tolerance?) by Hana Arie-Gaifman; and 'Der unbekannte Bote. Zu einem neuentdeckten Widmunstext Kafkas' (The unknown messenger. A newly discovered dedicated text by Kafka) by Jost Schillemeit. Each paper has a separate bibliography but the book lacks an index.

935 **Die Prager deutsche Literatur und die tschechische Literatur in den ersten zwei Jahrzehnten des 20. Jahrhunderts.** (Prague-German literature and Czech literature in the first two decades of the 20th century.)
Antonín Měšťan. In: *Slavistische Studien zum IX. Internationalen Slavistenkongres in Kiev 1983* (Slavonic Studies. International Congress of Slavists in Kiev, 1983.) Edited by Reinhold Olesch et al. Cologne, Germany; Vienna: Bohlau, 1983, p. 339-46. (Slavistiche Forschungen, vol. 40).
Měšťan's central thesis is that, during the period in question, Prague literary life evinced a high degree of cooperation, friendship and even some joint publishing

289

ventures between the two linguistic and literary communities. The links worked to the advantage of Czech literature thanks to translations of their works by their German colleagues into the more widely known German language.

Franz Kafka

936 **Kafka: Judaism, politics and literature.**
Ritchie Robertson. Oxford: Clarendon Press, 1985. 256p.

Although traditionally assigned to German literature plain and simple, there is certainly sense in insisting that there is a distinctive Prague-German (or Prague-German-Jewish) literature, of which Kafka is the best known representative by far. This study is most concerned with Kafka's works as literature, relating them to his life and the historical background, and picking up the threads of the Jewish element. In addition to the literary and historical context, the social context – not merely Jewish – is also brought out. *The complete novels of Franz Kafka* (latest edition, London: Minerva, 1993) were translated from the German by Willa and Edwin Muir.

937 **Journal of the Kafka Society of America.**
Philadelphia: Kafka Society of America, 1977- . semi-annual.

A scholarly journal founded in 1977 as a newsletter to facilitate exchanges of research and ideas on Kafka in the United States and abroad. The Kafka Society of America is based at the department of Germanic and Slavic Languages and Literatures of the Temple University in Philadelphia.

938 **K: a biography of Kafka.**
Ronald Hayman. London: Phoenix Giant, 1996. 349p. bibliog.

The first edition of this work was published in Great Britain by Weidenfeld & Nicolson in 1981. This biography is often referred to in recent works on Kafka and is considered by some to be the best of the many biographies of Kafka which have been published in the last twenty or thirty years. The book has a detailed chronological table of Kafka's life from his birth in 1883 to his death of tuberculosis in 1924. It is a classic, skilful account of a 'tormented' man by a writer who has written many biographies of persons from the world of literature, drama and philosophy. Kafka's work is not analysed in such a depth as in Karl's biography, *Franz Kafka: representative man* (q.v.); Hayman concentrates on Kafka's life, including all forms of his relationships, giving prominence to Kafka's difficult relationship with his father, which was considered so influential to Kafka's development. The book is a biography of standard format, well documented by pages of notes, a selective bibliography, a glossary of German and Czech names, and an index and photographs of people and places. A curio in the bibliography is *A life study of Franz Kafka 1883-1924, using the intensive journal method of Ira Progoff*, by Ronald Gestwicki, with a foreword by Ira Progoff (Lewiston, New York: Edwin Mellen Press, 1992. 167p. bibliog.). It follows the procedure of keeping a journal for a person from history. This method of reconstructing a life brings a new dimension to the field of biographies.

939 **Franz Kafka.**
Ronald Speirs, Beatrice Sandberg. Basingstoke, England: Macmillan Press Ltd, 1997. 161p. bibliog. (Macmillan Modern Novelists).
The book is addressed to the general reader with an interest in modern literature and to students of German. The author starts with a chapter on Kafka's life and continues with 'Reading Kafka', a chapter on interpreting Kafka's writings. The religious, philosophical and psychological interpretations of various critics are compared. This is followed by three chapters on Kafka's individual works, on *The missing person, The trial* and *The castle*. The study is readable and comprehensible to a lay person. All quotations have been translated into English. The bibliography (p. 151-58) of works of Kafka, critical literature and background literature gives preference to items in English. The authors also provide substantial notes and a brief index (p. 159-61). Another work for the general reader is *Kafka*, by Pietro Citati, translated from Italian by Raymond Rosenthal (London: Secker & Warburg, 1990. 320p. bibliog.), a biography which describes Kafka's life in fair detail.

940 **Franz Kafka: representative man.**
Frederick R. Karl. New York: Ticknor & Fields, 1991. 810p. maps. bibliog.
This major, compendious critical biography of Kafka by a literary critic and literary scholar examines just about every aspect of Kafka's life and work. The combination of evaluation of both life and work makes the book valuable, since previous major studies have either been concerned with Kafka's life or they were analyses of his work alone. The author portrays Kafka as conqueror as much as victim, and views Kafka as a representative writer of his century. The setting of Prague as a cultural centre around the turn of the century is emphasized. The epigraphs to most chapters are from the works of the Prague-German poet Rainer Maria Rilke. The biography is accessible, and includes some photographs, a large index, notes and a short bibliography. *The nightmare of reason: a life of Franz Kafka* by Ernst Pawel (London: Harvill, 1984. 466p. map. bibliog.) is a well-researched and well-constructed detailed biography which pays tribute to Max Brod, Kafka's first biographer, but also incorporates some new material. The photographs of Kafka's family and of Prague help to capture the contemporary atmosphere. The book is concerned more with Kafka's life than with his writings, which are analysed in great detail and from a variety of perspectives in other critical treatises.

941 **The world of Franz Kafka.**
Edited with an introduction by J. P. Stern. London: Weidenfeld & Nicolson, 1980. 263p.
A collection of twenty-four essays divided into three sections: 'Local and biographic'; 'Summonses and interpretations'; and 'Fiction and semi-fiction'. The papers consider, from many angles, the life and times, works and ideas, and literary and social (Prague-Jewish) context of the best known non-Czech Prague writer. Another collection of essays is *Critical essays on Franz Kafka*, edited by Ruth V. Gross (Boston, Massachusetts: G. K. Hall, 1990. 281p. bibliog.). The essays are very readable and were written by, among others, Milan Kundera and Heinz Politzer. The well-produced volume divides the essays into the following sections: 'Kafka the writer from Prague'; 'Methods and other paradoxes'; 'Kafka and his metaphors'; 'Kafka and the psyche'; and 'Kafka and the reader'.

942 **Franz Kafka's loneliness.**
Marthe Robert, translated from French by Ralph Manheim. London: Faber & Faber, 1982. 251p. bibliog.

A translation of *Seul comme Franz Kafka*. This scholarly criticism and interpretation of Kafka's work is documented by numerous notes on Kafka's identity crisis, the result of his background, upbringing, education and the times in which he lived. Even heavier reading is *Kafka and language, in the stream of thoughts and life*, by Gabriele von Natzmer Cooper (Riverside, California: Ariadne Press, 1991. 208p. bibliog.). Ludwig Wittgenstein's insight into the nature of language is applied in this investigation of the relationship between Kafka and the spoken and written language. The linguistic environment of Prague at the turn of the century is examined, and with it Kafka's sense of cultural alienation and his relationship with Yiddish culture and German literature. The last two chapters are treatises on Kafka's aesthetics and on the limitations of language. Extensive notes, bibliographies and an index complete the book.

943 **Kafka's relatives: their lives and his writing.**
Anthony Northey. New Haven, Connecticut; London: Yale University Press, 1991. 115p. bibliog.

Traces the lives of members of Kafka's family or, to use the Yiddish word, *Mischpochen*. Kafka's mother and father came from a fairly humble background, from Southern Bohemia, yet most of their siblings, just like themselves, reached a prosperous middle-class level of society within one generation. This work is a curious and gripping illustration of life at the turn of the century and the first decades of the new century. The family spread into France, Spain, the United States, Panama, Paraguay and Africa. The photographs are numerous and illuminating and the text is accessible to a non-historian. There are substantial explanatory notes, an index and a short bibliography (p. 102), which is an acknowledgement of sources used.

944 **Kafka's clothes: ornament and aestheticism in the Habsburg Fin de Siècle.**
Mark M. Anderson. Oxford: Clarendon Press, 1992. 231p. bibliog.

An unconventional, yet subtle historical study by an expert on Franz Kafka. Kafka's father ran a haberdashery shop in Prague, which contributed to the young Franz's awareness of clothes: he came to be considered the best dressed man in Prague. The study, of course, goes deeper into various manifestations of Kafka's aestheticism and its importance for his writing. As the title suggests, this is also a study of the turn-of-the-century movements, decadent as well as reforming. Various aspects of Judaism and the issue of anti-Semitism are an inevitable part of any serious portrait of Kafka. Thirty illustrations provide an excellent supplement to the narrative. Another good study of Kafka was published by the same Oxford publisher in 1996 under the title *Kafka: gender, class and race in the letters and fictions*, by Elizabeth Boa (304p. bibliog.). Yet another, unusual, study is by Sander Gilman, *Franz Kafka, the Jewish patient* (New York; London: Routledge, 1995. 328p.). It is an analysis of Kafka's writing, of the *fin de siècle*, and Jewishness. The Dreyfus affair is discussed at length, as is the incidence of tuberculosis, the disease of which Kafka died in 1924. The official correspondence on this illness of Kafka's forms an appendix. The Jewish interest, Jewish culture and attitudes are prevalent; it is a book on Jews at the turn of the century. The author provides numerous photographs, illustrations, pages of explanatory notes and an index (p. 319-28).

945 **On Kafka: semi-centenary perspectives.**
Edited by Franz Kuna. London: Paul Elek, 1976. 195p. bibliog.
The papers in this volume were presented at the 'Kafka Symposium' which was held on the occasion of the fiftieth anniversary of Kafka's death, at the University of East Anglia, Norwich, 7-10 July 1974. The papers were revised for inclusion in this volume and they revolve around five major issues of Kafka's writings: the problem of the 'law', Kafka's central metaphor; the moral, social and political implications of his work; the wider context of the cultural and intellectual tradition within which Kafka wrote; the still highly enigmatic nature of his work; and, perhaps most importantly, Kafka's very status as a writer.

946 **The meaning of irony: a psychoanalytic investigation.**
Frank Stringfellow. Albany, New York: State University of New York Press, 1994. 177p. bibliog.
This volume seeks to define irony from the viewpoint of psychoanalysis. Stringfellow analyses Kafka's *Der Process* (*The trial*) and Jonathan Swift's *Gulliver's travels*, the two classic 'ironic' works. *Transgressive readings: the texts of Franz Kafka and Max Planck*, by Valerie D. Greenberg (Ann Arbor, Michigan: University of Michigan Press, 1990. 224p. bibliog.) is a scholarly study of literature and science which points out the affinities with science and mathematics in the texts of Kafka. The book has a substantial bibliography. *The call of the daimon*, by Aldo Carotenuto, translated by Charles Nobar (Wilmette, Illinois: Chiron Publications, 1994. 359p. bibliog.), focuses on the psychological aspects of Kafka's writings, particularly in *The trial* and *The castle*. The paperback has an extensive bibliography.

947 **Kafka's rhetoric: the passion of reading.**
Clayton Koelb. Ithaca, New York; London: Cornell University Press, 1989. 263p. bibliog.
An excellent, scholarly study, richly documented by footnotes, extracts, a fair-sized bibliography and an index. 'The author finds that Kafka proposes and illustrates in his texts two fundamentally different kinds of reading – one that exercises a painful, wounding power over the reader, and one that requires less engagement and provides more pleasure.' *Kafka and the contemporary critical performance: centenary readings*, edited by Alan Udoff (Bloomington, Indiana: Indiana University Press, 1987. 277p. bibliog.), is a collection of essays by American academics on the interpretation of Kafka's texts, which is richly documented by notes.

948 **Twentieth century interpretation of The trial: a collection of critical essays.**
Edited by James Rolleston. Englewood Cliffs, New Jersey; London: Prentice-Hall, 1977. 112p. bibliog.
This slim paperback examines in detail various aspects of this novel by Kafka. In addition to listing secondary literature on *The trial* in English (p. 108-12), it also contains a list of Kafka's principal works and his recorded private readings, an interesting pointer to Kafka's literary interests and influences. *The trial* has been translated and published several times. It is widely available in translations by Idris Parry (London: Penguin, 1994) and Willa and Edwin Muir, dating back to 1935 (London: Compact, 1994). Penguin also recently published *The man who disappeared (Amerika)* in a new translation by Michael Hofmann (London: Penguin, 1996).

293

949 **Kafka's narrators: a study of his stories and sketches.**
Roy Pascal. Cambridge, England: Cambridge University Press, 1982. 251p. (Anglica Germanica. Series 2).
The author died before completing this work on Kafka's narrative art, a contribution to reading and understanding difficult texts. The study is limited to the shorter stories with occasional references to the novels. Pascal clarifies the formal structures which Kafka invented, and his intentions. A selection of Kafka's short stories was published in Kevin Blahut's translation under the title *Contemplation and other stories* (Prague: Twisted Spoon Press, 1992), and in *Meditation*, in translation by Siegfried Mortkowitz (Prague: Vitalis, 1998).

950 **Meditations on Metamorphosis.**
Steven Berkoff. London: Faber & Faber, 1995. 142p.
A contribution to studies of Kafka's *Metamorphosis* by a modern interpreter. Steven Berkoff describes his own stage adaptation of this work in Tokyo in 1992 and several other productions, and contrasts the techniques and performance styles. *Metamorphosis and other stories* is available in translations by Stanley Appelbaum (New York; London: Constable, 1996) and Stanley Corngold (New York; London: W. W. Norton, 1996). The latter edition is entitled *The metamorphosis: translation, backgrounds and contexts, criticism.*

951 **The diaries of Franz Kafka: 1910-1923.**
Edited by Max Brod. Harmondsworth, England: Penguin, 1964. 519p.
The diaries are supplemented by notes, chronologies and lists of authors, artists, periodicals and works. This personal journal, originally thirteen notebooks, covers the years 1910-23. Kafka died in 1924 at the age of forty. He kept notes of his literary ideas and his dreams, as well as of the real everyday occurrences of the world around him. This edition kept the text of the notebooks as complete as possible and tried to preserve the stylistic whole formed by the diaries. The diaries reveal the depth of the relationship between Kafka and Milena Jesenská.

952 **Letters to Milena.**
Franz Kafka, edited by Willy Haas, translated by Tania Stern, James Stern. Harmondsworth, England: Penguin, 1983. 188p.; London: Minerva, 1992.
Translated from German, these letters were originally published by Secker & Warburg, 1953. Milena Jesenská translated some of Kafka's prose into Czech and was his mistress from 1920 to 1922. She was a descendant of an old Czech family and the fact that Kafka was in love with a woman who was not Jewish caused him grave complexes. Jesenská died in a concentration camp in 1944. The correspondence was edited with consideration to persons still alive at the time of publication. The letters are not dated and, as a result, this collection lacks chronology. *The language of nationality and the nationality of language*, by Derek Sayer, *Past and Present*, no. 153 (November 1996), p. 164-210. bibliog., examines how the correspondence of Franz Kafka and Milena Jesenská sheds light on the language of national identity and culture. Kafka and Jesenská were of historically diverse backgrounds, and of different ethnic origin and religion, all of which is revealed in their written words.

953 **Kafka, love and courage: the life of Milena Jesenská.**
Mary Hockaday. London: André Deutsch, 1995. 255p. bibliog.
Mary Hockaday lived in Prague for two years in the early 1990s, reporting for the BBC World Service and for *The Independent*. The warmth of her affection for Prague and for Jesenská radiates throughout this book. She was genuinely fond of the subject, the charismatic, flawed, artistic heroine of pre-war Czechoslovakia. The author, who was inspired by Kafka's *Letters to Milena* (q.v.), had the advantage of being able to draw on Milena's own written work, her many brilliant articles and letters from collections in Prague. Hockaday found the tone of Jesenská's own writing to be fresh, vivid and as relevant to today as ever, as classics are; this was the other inspiration for this book. The author looks at all dimensions of Jesenská's life: her childhood and education, love life, journalistic career, motherhood and involvement in politics. Milena Jesenská died in the Ravensbrück concentration camp at the age of forty-seven, in 1944. This is a sound, compassionate, objective yet loving and compelling account, which is both critical and admiring. The author provides bibliographical notes and an index, together with a fair number of photographs, some of which have not been published before.

954 **Milena.**
Margarete Buber-Neumann, translated by Ralph Manheim. London: Collins Harvill, 1990. 213p.
The story of the author of this biography is moving. Buber-Neumann was a German Communist, who, as an anti-fascist refugee in the Soviet Union, was handed over to Hitler and sent to Ravensbrück concentration camp as a political prisoner. Here she was ostracized by the Communists and other political prisoners but in 1940 met and befriended Milena Jesenská, who had the courage to speak to her. Jesenská, from an old, patriotic Czech family, was a journalist and a former friend of Franz Kafka. She had been sent to the concentration camp for her Communist and anti-German activities and for being friends with Jews. Buber-Neumann survived the camp and after the war lived in West Germany and wrote several books. Her book on Jesenská is the story of Milena's life and her last years in the concentration camp, a moving epitaph. The life story is based on what Milena told her and on information obtained from Milena's friends. Buber-Neumann describes their first meeting, when she was struck by the strong personality of 'Milena from Prague'. The author had never been to Prague and did not speak Czech. There are no photographs or illustrations in the book, which would have lightened the text, but there are annotated 'Biographical notes' (p. 207-13) on the personalities mentioned, just a few lines on each, thus supplementing the picture of political and cultural life in Central Europe in the first half of the 20th century. The first edition was published in London by Collins in 1989.

955 **Kafka's Milena.**
Jana Černá, translated from the Czech by G. Brain. London: Souvenir Press, 1988. 160p. map. Published again by Souvenir Press in 1992.
This biography of Milena Jesenská by her daughter was first published in Prague in 1969 under the title *Adresát Milena Jesenská*. It is a documentary of life in Prague, a vivid and touching account, rather then a literary work. It was written by an unsettled, disturbed woman who was deeply affected by her mother, whom she lost at the age of eleven. Jana Černá herself died in a car accident before the publication of the English edition. The translator treated the text as an authentic historical document and the

style of the English is not perfect. Milena had an intense brief relationship with Franz Kafka and was his inspiration for the character of Frieda in *The castle*. His beautiful *Letters to Milena* (q.v.) were translated into many languages. Milena's letters to Kafka have been lost. She was a complex and flawed woman, a journalist, a devoted Communist and a nationalist. This source, being the memoirs of a child, is not always accurate, yet it is a unique document and describes events which were not otherwise recorded. The book contains photographs of Milena, her lovers and husbands and her friends, and an index.

956 **Letters to Felice.**
Franz Kafka, edited by Erich Heller, Jurgen Born, translated from German by James Ster, Elizabeth Duckworth. Harmondsworth, England: Penguin, 1978. 697p.

This collection of letters incorporates correspondence between Kafka and the Bauer family, letters to friends, such as Grete Bloch, and letters from friends concerning the engagement of Kafka and Felice Bauer. The couple were friends between 1912 and 1917, having met through Kafka's great friend Max Brod, and became engaged twice. The letters are supplemented by notes, a chronology and an index, but the book lacks photographs of the characters involved, which would, together with scenes from the era, have made the reading of these letters even more enjoyable. This edition also includes 'Kafka's other trial' by Elias Canetti, a description of the relationship between Kafka and Felice Bauer, based on these letters. Letters from Felice to Kafka have not been traced.

Other

957 **Life of a poet: Rainer Maria Rilke.**
Ralph Freedman. New York: Farrar, Straus & Giroux, 1996. 639p. bibliog.

The earliest literary work of Rilke (1875-1926), who lived in Prague, shows links with Czech folk poetry. His main theme was the overcoming of deep feelings of isolation by love for other human beings and pantheistic assimilation with nature. The philosophical symbolism of Rilke is combined in his lyrical poetry with an exceptional feeling for the melodiousness of the verse and flexibility of refined expression. The verse in this book was translated by Helen Sword and by the author. Subject and name indexes and illustrations are included. Different dimensions of Rilke are studied in *The beginning of terror: a psychological study of Rainer Maria Rilke's life and work*, by David Kleinbard (New York: New York University Press, 1993. 275p. bibliog. Series: Literature and Psychoanalysis, 1). This paperback also has name and subject indexes. Rilke's poetry has been widely published recently in various translations: *Poems*, translated by Peter Washington (London: David Campbell, 1996); *New poems*, translated by Stephen Colin (Manchester, England: Carcanet, 1997); and *Uncollected poems*, selected and translated by Edward Snow (New York: North Point Press, 1996). *Two stories of Prague*, Rilke's short stories, were translated by Angela Esterhammer (Hanover, New Hampshire; London: University Press of New England, 1994), and there is also a cameo, *Looking is a marvellous thing: from Rainer Maria Rilke's letters to his wife Clara, on looking at Cezanne's pictures in the Salon d'Automme, Paris, October, 1907* (Hastings, England: Pickpockets, 1992).

958 **The Prague group of Ukrainian nationalist writers and their ideological origins.**
Roman Olynyk. In: *Czechoslovakia past and present.* Edited by
Miroslav Rechcígl, Jr. The Hague; Paris: Mouton, 1968, p. 1,022-31.
The Prague Ukrainian community was short-lived as a cohesive unit, their activities
being limited to the period of the 1920s and 1930s. They were numerically strong
enough to sustain more than twenty professional, scholarly and educational
institutions and included a number of writers. This article is a detailed account of the
pressures which gave rise to the ethnic and literary minority, with some details on
individual writers and works.

959 **Pits and pitfalls: the fate of Ondra Lysohorsky.**
David Gill. *Scottish Slavonic Review*, no. 3 (autumn 1984), p. 27-44.
bibliog.
A fairly detailed account of the life and literary career of Óndra Łysohorský (1905-
89), a poet who wrote in Lachian, to some a hybrid dialect of mixed Czech and Polish
features spoken in Silesia. His position from this aspect is comparable to that of Burns
or Hugh MacDiarmid, while his poems are in tune with works of another Silesian
poet, Petr Bezruč (1867-1958), who wrote in Czech. Łysohorský was a working-class
poet, with strong working-class passions and an almost fierce regional patriotism,
though he was free of xenophobia and accepted that Poles and Germans, the other
nations inhabiting the area, had a right to their existence. He was less happy about the
Czechs, whom he saw as oppressors. The article expands on political attitudes to the
poet, on relevant events in history and on the status of Lachian. It is illustrated by
quotations, in the original and in translation, and the bibliography contains three
studies in German or French, lists of editions of Łysohorský's Lachian and German
verse, and the main editions of translations, into German, French, English and Russian
inter alia.

960 **The white raven and other poems.**
Óndra Łysohorský, translated by David Gill. Grimsby, England: Big
Little Poem Books, 1989. 39p.
The poet has been widely translated, not just into English, German, French and
Russian, but, in the case of individual poems, into as many as sixty languages. Yet this
is contradictory from two aspects: Łysohorský writes in a language which is even less
known than Czech, and it is probably fair to say that he is not widely known to many
Czechs. Among the English editions of Łysohorský's poems, the most important is
Selected poems (London: Jonathan Cape, 1971. 116p.), which contains seventy-five
poems translated by Ewald Osers, Hugh McKinley, Isobel Leviten, W. H. Auden and
Lydia Pasternak-Slater.

The Arts

General

961 **Nová encyklopedie českého výtvarného umění.** (New encyclopaedia of Czech art.)
Edited by Anděla Horová.   Prague: Academia, 1995. 2 vols.

Covers the Czech Lands from earliest times up to, and including, the 1980s. It is limited by territory, not by nationality, and thus includes the work of artists of other nationalities active in the Czech Lands, but also artists of Czech origin active abroad. The fields are: architecture; painting; sculpture; graphic art; applied art; scenography; design; computer art and design; photography; cartoon and animated films; history of art; aesthetics; and art theory and criticism. The entries are names of artists, theorists, critics and historians; further entries are for trends in art, types of art, styles, groups, associations, actions, exhibitions, magazines, institutions, historical patrons of the arts and art schools. There are no illustrations. The entries follow the standard layout of encyclopaedic entries. The encyclopaedia does not exhaust the field since many good artist have been omitted, due to lack of space. It is not a definitive reference work and the editors intend to update it; volume two has a separate section of additions already. The arrangement is a simple, alphabetical one: volume one covers A-M; volume two N-Z. The name index for both volumes is in volume two. There is a permanent exhibition of 19th-century paintings, from the collections of the National Gallery in Prague, in the Convent of St Agnes of Bohemia in Prague. An illustrated catalogue of this exhibition, edited by Naděžda Blažíčkova-Horová, was published by the National Gallery in Prague in 1998 (343p. bibliog.) under the title, *Czech 19th century paintings*. The catalogue is divided into eight chapters; it gives an outline of each period, starting with Neo-Classicism and early Romanticism and ending with Neo-Romanticism, Symbolism and Naturalism at the close of the 19th century. The first work on Czech artists in exile was published in France, compiled by Genevieve Bénamou, *Sensibilités contemporaines 1970-1984* (Contemporary sensibilities, 1970-84) (Aubervilliers, France: G. Bénamou, 1985. 297p.), which has detailed medaillons and bibliographical details of seventy Czech and Slovak artists living abroad.

298

962 **Slavic and East European Arts.**
Stony Brook, New York: Slavic Cultural Centre Press, 1982- . twice-yearly. 182p.

Covers the literature, philosophy, music, painting, sculpture and architecture of the Slavic and East European Countries. Special issues are published occasionally.

963 **Court, cloister and city: the art and culture of Central Europe, 1450-1800.**
Thomas DaCosta Kaufmann. London: Weidenfeld & Nicolson, 1995. 576p. maps. bibliog.

A scholarly, weighty tome which covers a larger area than is today generally understood as Central Europe (if the area has ever been defined at all). The author is a specialist on visual art at the court of the Habsburg Emperor Rudolph II, who chose Prague as his seat in 1583. The book is rich in illustrations, all black-and-white, including a number of buildings from the Czech Lands. Although the title of the book indicates a general coverage of art and culture, architecture is the main field. There is a specific chapter on the Czech Lands: 'Early eighteenth-century art and architecture in the Bohemian lands' (p. 340-66). All chapters are painstakingly documented and the book has one, very detailed index (p. 553-76). A valuable introduction to the wealth of artistic activity at the court of Rudolph II is provided by an earlier work, by Jan Białostocki, *The art of Renaissance in Eastern Europe: Hungary, Bohemia, Poland* (Ithaca, New York: Cornell University Press, 1976. 256p. bibliog.).

964 **The self: destruction or synthesis, two problems of Czech art at the turn of the century.**
Petr Wittlich. In: *Decadence and innovation: Austro-Hungarian life and art at the turn of the century.* Edited by Robert B. Pynsent. London: Weidenfeld & Nicolson, 1989, p. 82-87.

A scholarly paper by a Prague academic, a specialist on Czech Art Nouveau, which was presented at an international conference in London. Wittlich examines the relationship between politics and culture and, by looking at a number of artists of various denominations, offers a brief but deep picture of the Czech cultural scene at the time. He selected a late Romantic painter Josef Mánes for special attention, because he successfully achieved the idea of 'national art'.

965 **Irreconcilable differences?**
Art Monthly, no. 178 (July-August 1994), p. 30-31.

A study of the polarization of Czech and Slovak artists in the years 1968-89, which reassesses Czech and Slovak art since their separation and reviews exhibitions of art from both nationalities.

Statistická ročenka České republiky. (Statistical Yearbook of the Czech Republic.)
See item no. 416.

299

Visual arts

966 **Magister Theodoricus, court painter to Emperor Charles IV: the pictorial decorations of the shrines at Karlštejn Castle.**
Edited by Jiří Fajt. Prague: National Gallery Prague, 1998. 549p. bibliog.

This large, beautifully produced and richly illustrated heavy tome was produced on the occasion of an exhibition in Prague in 1998 on the painter Theodoricus, or Dětřich in Czech. Theodoricus worked in Charles' favourite castle, Karlštejn in 1357-67 and produced panels, murals, encrustations of walls and vaulting, in particular in the Chapel of the Holy Cross. His work is characterized by monumental, soft form with light colours. This main section of the book, on Master Theodoricus, was written by Jiří Fajt, a director of the collections of Old Masters at the National Gallery in Prague and a specialist in mediaeval art. This book is not only on Theodoricus, but also on Karlštejn Castle; it is an erudite guide with an article by František Kafka on records from the reign of Charles IV, on the role and function of the Castle. The 'Selection of archival sources, materials on the history of Karlštejn Castle and its artistic decoration' (p. 29-33) was compiled by Libor Gottfried. The last section of the book is dedicated to restorers and their work at the Castle.

967 **Gothic mural painting in Bohemia and Moravia 1300-1378.**
Vlasta Dvořáková, Josef Krása, Anežka Merhautová, Karel Stejskal, translated by Roberta Finlayson-Samsour, Iris Unwin. London: Oxford University Press, 1964. 160p. maps. bibliog.

This collection of eleven essays provides the history and social background to mural painting and accounts of more specific topics such as: the development of the court under Charles IV; the castle at Karlštejn; Prague Cathedral; and paintings from outside the court circle. The 'Catalogue' lists and describes the twenty-seven main sites from which the photographic reproductions come, with an indication of sources from which the particular building's history is known, and sources for modern writings on them, cross-referenced to the 464-entry bibliography. One map is of the Bohemian Kingdom during the reign of the Luxembourgs, and the other indicates the location of the sites discussed. A useful asset to the work is its iconographic index.

968 **Wenceslaus Hollar: a Bohemian artist in England.**
Richard T. Godfrey. New Haven, Connecticut; London: Yale University Press, 1994. 168p. + 8 pages of plates. bibliog.

The catalogue of an exhibition held at the Yale Center of British Art between 16 November and 22 January 1995. The bibliography is on p. 163.

969 **Art Nouveau drawings.**
Petr Wittlich, translated by Till Gottheiner[ová]. London: Alpine Fine Art Collection (UK) Ltd, 1991. 198p. bibliog.

This important contribution to the study of Art Nouveau was first published in Czech (Prague: Aventinum, 1974). Wittlich, one of the leading scholars of the period, selected from the Czech artists Alfons Mucha, Jan Preisler, František Bílek, Alfred Kubín and František Kupka; the other artists included here are Aubrey Beardsley,

Odilon Redon, Edvard Munch, Auguste Rodin, Gustav Klimt and Egon Schiele. The book includes sixty-three quality full-page monochrome and colour plates. Wittlich provides a general introduction to the drawings of the period, which is followed by studies on the individual artists. The book has a bibliography and 'Biographical notes' on the artists (p. 195-96). Petr Wittlich also wrote the introduction to the catalogue for a Mucha exhibition held at the Imperial stables of the Prague Castle, from 1 June to 30 October 1994, *Alphonse Mucha: pastels, posters, drawings and photographs* (Prague: Mucha Foundation, in association with Malcolm Saunders Publishing, London, 1994), edited by Sarah Mucha.

970 **Mucha: the triumph of Art Nouveau.**
Francis Ellridge, illustrations by Alfons Mucha. Paris: Terrail, 1992. 223p.
A paperback monograph on the Czech painter and graphic artist, representative of Art Nouveau. Alfons Mucha (1860-1939) spent many years in Paris and his posters for the theatre performances of Sarah Bernhardt, decorative graphic cycles, illustrations and book graphic art are considered the ultimate representation of the Art Nouveau style. He was also the designer of the first Czechoslovak postage stamps. *Alphonse Mucha: the graphic works*, by Marina Henderson, Anna Dvořák, edited by Anne Bridges and with a foreword by the son of Alphonse, Jiří Mucha (London: Academy Editions, 1980. 152p. bibliog.) contains 163 beautiful colour plates and reproductions of his graphic art. Dover Publications in New York issued seventy-two lithographic plates of decorative and applied art, where possible in their original colours, under the title *The Art Nouveau style book of Alphonse Mucha: all 72 plates from 'Documents décoratifs' in original colour*, edited by David M. H. Kern (New York: Dover Publications, 1980). The same publisher also issued *Mucha's figures décoratives*, with an introduction by Anna Dvořák (New York: Dover Publications, 1981), a set of forty original monochrome plates, including drawings in pencil, pen, charcoal and chalk. A large-format hardback, entitled *Mucha* (Prague: BB/art, 1992. unpaginated), has excellent photographs, by Dalibor Kusák, of 135 illustrations in full colour, and text by Marta Kadlečíková; the short biography and the list of illustrations are in Czech, English, German, French and Italian.

971 **Alphonse Mucha: the spirit of Art Nouveau.**
Victor Arwas, Jana Brabcová-Orlíková, Anna Dvořák, with an introduction by Ronald Lipp, Suzanne Jackson, essays by Quentin Bajac, Jean-Marie Bruson, Geraldine Mucha, Jack Rennert.
Alexandria, Virginia: Art Services International, in association with Yale University Press, 1998. 344p. bibliog.
'A full scale treatment of Mucha's entire oeuvre, includes discussions and reproductions of paintings, posters. decorative panels, pastels, drawings, photographs, jewelry, and illustrations throughout his career' (cover text). This richly and lavishly illustrated A4 hardback is the catalogue for a Mucha exhibition which toured the United States in 1998. Mucha has merited many exhibitions and publications. In comparison, a leading personality of Czech painting, of the same period, Jakub Schikaneder, had achieved only a third exhibition by 1998. Tomáš Vlček published *Schikaneder: Jakub Schikaneder, Prague painter of the turn of the century. A thematic guide to retrospective exhibition National Gallery in Prague – Collection of Old Masters in the Wallenstein Riding School in Prague, 15th May 1998–10th January 1999* (Prague: National Gallery in Prague, 1998. 83p. bibliog.). The catalogue was translated into English by Barbara Day.

301

972 **Mucha.**
O. B. Duane. London: Brockhampton Press, 1996. 80p. (Discovering Art: The Life, Times and Work of the World's Greatest Artists).

Despite the occasional factual lapse (Ústí nad Orlicí is nowhere near Brno), this coffee-table publication is nonetheless a good introduction to the life and work of Alfons Mucha (1860-1939), the one Czech artist who is perhaps universally known, though this fact has probably much to do with the period of his career spent in Paris and his leading role in the Art Nouveau movement. The book is copiously illustrated *passim* and in the plates assembled at the back by not only the posters and other commercial works for which he is best known in the West, but also some of his neo-Revivalist patriotic works.

973 **Alphonse Mucha.**
Edited by John Hoole, Tomoko Sato, with an introductory essay by Victor Erwas. London: Lund Humphries, in association with Barbican Gallery, 1993. 120p. bibliog.

Published to accompany an exhibition at the Barbican Gallery, 30 September to 12 December 1993, the first full exhibition of Mucha's work in thirty years. This A4-format book/catalogue provides a biography of Mucha and an appreciation of the artist, who is known mainly for his posters, and presents over 140 reproductions of his works: paintings, drawings, posters, sculptures and jewellery. There are also photographs from Mucha's studios. This volume underlines two themes, representing the two sides of Mucha, the fashionable art world and the love of his country.

974 **Czechoslovak prints from 1900 to 1970.**
Irena Goldscheider. London: British Museum Publications Limited, 1986. 51p. + 102 plates of illustrations. bibliog.

This book is a result of successful collaboration between Czech and British institutions. The British Museum managed to acquire, by exchange with the National Gallery in Prague, over 100 prints. These prints were catalogued and exhibited in the British Museum, which made this 'the first historical survey of twentieth century Czech printmaking to have been shown outside Czechoslovakia', according to the preface by the then director of the British Museum, David M. Wilson (p. 7). This book accompanied the exhibition and included, on 102 plates, all the prints acquired by the British Museum. Irena Goldscheider supplied the introduction, biographical articles on the thirty-nine artists and the details and description of the plates. She divided the artists into six groups: '1. The founding generation' (such as Zdenka Braunerová, Józa Úprka, Max Švabinský, Arnost Hofbaur, Viktor Stretti and Vojtěch Preissig); '2. The Symbolists (František Bílek, František Kobliha, Jan Konůpek and Josef Váchal); '3. The Cubists and the *Tvrdošíjní* (The Stubborn)' (such as Josef Čapek, Emil Filla and Jan Zrzavý); '4. "The social trend" (Vojtěch Sedláček, Vladimír Silovský and others); '5. The Surrealists and Group 42' (for example, Josef Šíma and František Tichý); and '6. The 1960s' (Zdeněk Sklenář, Vladimír Tesař, Jiří John etc.).

975 Jan Konůpek: poutník k nekonečnu. A pilgrim to infinity.
Introduction and main text by Hana Larvová, translated into English by
Jan Valeška, Ivan Vomáčka. Prague: Galerie hlavního města Prahy &
Památník národního písemnictví v Praze, 1999. 178p. bibliog.

Published to accompany a retrospective exhibition of the Czech painter, graphic
designer and illustrator Jan Konůpek (1883-1950), a controversial artist who is best
known for Art Nouveau symbolism, but who embraced other styles, such as Cubism
and Surrealism. The text is in parallel columns, in Czech and English. The book
includes a bibliography of Konůpek's writings, of books, studies and catalogue essays
about the artist or containing references to him, a list of exhibitions and a list of
current exhibits. The exhibition was held in Prague, at Dům u Kamenného zvonu,
from 1 October 1998 to 3 January 1999. A book on another painter of the same period,
Painting the universe: František Kupka, pioneer in abstraction (Dallas, Texas: Dallas
Museum of Art; Prague: National Gallery in Prague, 1997. 220p. bibliog.), was
published on the occasion of an exhibition held at the Dallas Museum of Art in 1997.
The contributors were Jaroslav Anděl, Franziska Baetcke, Laurence Lyon Blum,
Pierre Brullé, Dorothy Kosinski, Benoit Mandelbrot, Marketa Theinhardt, and the
illustrated book has a checklist of exhibited works.

976 Styles, struggles and careers: an ethnography of the Czech art
world 1948-1992.
Maruška Svašek. Amsterdam: Amsterdam School for Social Science
Research, 1996. 336p. bibliog.

A doctoral thesis researching the complex relationship between Czechoslovak politics
and the visual arts. The work is much larger than the number of pages suggests – the
print is small, the page margins are narrow. The author did not have an easy task; with
the exception of a few exhibition catalogues there was little to go by. Svašek spent
more than a year in Prague, in 1992 and 1993, and her research was painstaking. Her
observations are very perceptive and intelligent. The work is academic, but it is
accessibly written and it will be of interest to the politician, historian, sociologist,
ethnographer, art historian, anthropologist, economist and teacher of art. The author
included a selection of illustrations of art styles but unfortunately the reproductions
are rather dull. The book has a number of appendices, tables, charts, maps, a huge
bibliography of general books on art, exhibition catalogues and a list of more than 100
recorded interviews, conducted by the author. The thesis has a summary in Dutch.
This is a good work, which does not leave much else in the field to be explored.

977 Three contemporary Czechoslovak artists.
Philip Vann. [Great Britain]: Peter Katt, [1990]. 11 leaves.

Three contemporary graphic artists with very different styles – Daisy Mrázková,
Vladimír Kokolia and Jaroslav Róna – are the subject of this short study, which is
supplemented by illustrations of their work. The author visited Czechoslovakia in 1988.

978 Současná grafika, Contemporary graphics, Zeitgenossische
Graphik.
Prague: SČUG Hollar, 1992. unpaginated.

This A4-format book was published on the occasion of seventy-five years of the
Hollar Gallery, Prague (1917-92). The text is in Czech, German and English. The
introduction sketches the history of Czech graphic art in fair detail. This is followed

by biographies and examples of the work of many graphic artists, such as: Jiří Anderle, Karel Beneš, Tomáš Bím, Ota Janeček, Věra Kotasová, Ladislav Kuklík, Pavel Sukdolák and many others. There is no index to this book, which consists chiefly of illustrations.

979 **Distant voices: Milena Dopitová, Petr Nikl, Václav Stratil, Ivan Kafka. Contemporary art from the Czech Republic.**
Selected by Susan Copping, translated by Karolinka Vočadlová.
London: South London Gallery, 1994. 32p.

Published to accompany an exhibition in the South London Gallery between 28 April and 20 May 1994. Four young Czech artists were selected, all representing very individual styles, dominant in Czech visual art, which have been influenced by political, social and cultural circumstances. Dopitová and Nikl are of the young generation and work with painting, sculpture and photography. Kafka and Stratil are of the older, young middle-aged generation, and they work with landscape, portraiture and documentary. The book has a chapter on each of the artists, a list of the artists' exhibitions and examples of their work.

980 **Ota Janeček.**
Jiří Kotalík, Luboš Hlaváček, Zdeněk Vaníček, edited by Peter Cannon-Brookes. Cardiff: Trefoil Books & the National Museum of Wales, 1984. 64p.

This volume serves two functions, being a catalogue to the Janeček exhibition held at the National Museum of Wales and a multi-authored monograph on one of 'Czechoslovakia's foremost living artists, whose paintings and sculptures derived their inspiration as much from the landscape and fauna of his native country as from the example of European art, classic and contemporary'. On his home ground, Janeček is also widely known as a book illustrator, especially of many modern children's classics. The book contains the author's biography and appreciation of his work, and a representative selection of both his representational and abstract works.

981 **Stanislav Kolíbal.**
Prague: Národní galerie v Praze, 1997. 248p.

Beautifully produced with black-and-white pictures of modern sculptures, this was published to accompany an exhibition at the Veletržní palác (Exhibition Palace) in Prague. Kolíbal's work is conceptual, while retaining the sculptural quality of the material. He uses the characteristics of materials, such as plaster, metal, wood and glass, to the full. The text is in Czech and English.

982 **Jiří Anderle: drawings, prints, paintings, objects 1954-1995.**
Preface by Jiří Machalický, translated by Anna Bryson. Prague: Slovart Publishing, National Gallery in Prague, 1996. 319p.

This large-format publication is dedicated to a leading contemporary Czech artist, Jiří Anderle (b. 1936), and is comprised chiefly of illustrations of his work. The preface traces his development and identifies influences of modern Czech and international art (Kandinsky, Picasso, Klee).

983 **Exiles.**
Photographs by Josef Koudelka, foreword by Robert Delpire.
London: Thames & Hudson, 1997. rev. and expanded ed. unpaginated.
65 plates. bibliog.
Reproduces beautiful photographs from various European countries by the world famous Czech photographer, who, according to the introduction, 'is one of those people who don't ask themselves questions about ethics or symbolism, but who have, deeply rooted in them, a sense of proportion, matter and light which unconsciously leads them to a perfect construction'. The book was originally published by Thames & Hudson in 1988.

984 **Pilgrims.**
Markéta Luskačová, with an introduction by Roy Strong. London: Victoria and Albert Museum, 1983. unpaginated.
Markéta Luskačová was born in Prague in 1944, emigrated to England in the early 1970s and is today recognized as one of the world's finest photographers. This is a visual record of an exhibition held at the Victoria and Albert Museum, London, in 1983-84 and presents forty-six sensitive photographs, the art of photography at its very best, set in rural Slovakia in the late 1960s and early 1970s.

Applied arts

985 **Prehistoric glass in Bohemia.**
Natalie Venclová. Prague: Archeologický ústav ČSAV, 1990. 415p. maps. bibliog.
The first and very specialized study of Pre-Roman glass from Bohemia, in which over 2,000 specimens of glass and faience are investigated, including early vitreous material but excluding enamels. The period covered is from the Early Bronze Age to the end of the La Tène period.

986 **Bohemian glass.**
Text by Helena Brožková, Olga Drahotová, Jan Mergl, designed by Pavel Hrach. Prague: Museum of Decorative Arts, 1992. 47p. bibliog.
It is unfortunate that this publication may not be easy to access for an English reader. The text is a history and appreciation of Czech glass of various periods and styles – Baroque, Rococo, Neoclassic, Empire, Biedermeier, Second Rococo, Historicism, Art Nouveau, Art Deco and Functionalism – and concludes with a chapter on contemporary glass. The text is followed by beautiful, well-reproduced pictures of the best examples of Czech glass from these periods. The modern examples are particularly striking in their beauty and contrast with those on offer in tourist shops. There is a short bibliography (p. 47) of books on the subject and of exhibition catalogues.

987 **Das Böhmische Glas: 1700-1950.** (Bohemian glass: 1700-1950.) Edited by Georg Höltl, photographs by Gabriel Urbánek. Passau, Germany: Passauer Glasmuseum, 1995. 6 vols. bibliog.

The museum of glass in the German town of Passau, on the border with the Czech Republic, published this hardback catalogue of Czech glass in six volumes. Each volume has different authors, specialists on the particular period, and all volumes have their own name, subject and place indexes, an index of companies, biographical data on the authors. All give both Czech and German place-names, since the majority of glass works were in the Sudeten areas of southern Bohemia and northern Bohemia, where the official language changed at various times in history from German to Czech and vice versa. Volume five is on the Jugendstil style as produced by glassworks in Bavaria and Silesia. Many of the contributions were translated from Czech. Details of the five volumes are as follows: volume one, *Barock – Rokoko – Klassizismus* (Baroque – Rococo – Classicism), by Helena Brožková et al (111p.); volume two, *Empire, Biedermeier, Zweites Rokoko* (Empire, Biedermeier, Second Rococo), by Jarmila Brožková, Margarete Gräfin von Buquoy, Walter Spiegl (223p.); volume three, *Historismus* (Historicism), by Helena Brožková et al (219p.); volume four, *Jugendstil in Böhmen* (Art Nouveau in Bohemia), by Alena Adlerová, Jan Mergl, Duňa Panenková (311p.); volume five, *Jugendstil in Bayern und Schlesien* (Art Nouveau in Bavaria and Silesia), by Jan Mergl, Helmut Ricke, Christiane Sellner (89p.); and volume six, *Art Deco, Moderne* (Art Deco, Modernism), by Alena Adlerová et al (138p.).

988 **České secesní sklo.** (Bohemian glass of the Art Nouveau period.) Edited by Tomáš Vlček, Helena Sekalová. Prague: Ústav teorie a dějin umění ČSAV, 1985. 256p. bibliog.

The proceedings of an international symposium held from 9-12 October 1984 in the Šumava hotel in Srní, Czechoslovakia. The papers, which are in English and German, are concerned with Bohemian glass from 1895 to 1914. Of particular interest are parallels between the Czech and French Art Nouveau schools and the new glass technology. Some of the papers deal with individual glass manufacturers of the period which were located in the Czech Lands.

989 **Marks on German, Bohemian and Austrian porcelain: 1710 to the present.** Robert E. Röntgen. Exton, Pennsylvania: Schiffer Publishing Limited, 1981. 636p. bibliog.

A bilingual publication, in English and in German, providing a classical, substantial reference book with a short introduction to ceramics and a definition of ceramic products. The directory is subsequently divided into three sections. Part one covers 'Marks'; part two is on 'Manufacturers according to location', arranged alphabetically by place-name, usually a town, with a brief history of the works; and part three deals with 'Marks that could be mistaken for those of other manufacturers'. These main sections are followed by an index of names – of manufacturers, historical names, designers and owners of the companies – a bibliography and a list of the motifs and symbols which appear in the marks.

306

990 **Hodiny a hodinky: ze sbírek Uměleckoprůmyslového muzea v Praze. Clocks and watches: from the collections of the Museum of Decorative Arts in Prague.**
Text by Libuše Urešová, catalogue compiled by Daniela Karasová.
Prague: Uměleckoprůmyslové museum, 1998. 124p. bibliog.

Published to accompany an exhibition held at the Museum of Decorative Arts in Prague between 25 June and 1 November 1998. The text is in Czech but the English summary is an only very slightly abridged version. The collection of clocks and watches in the Museum of Decorative Arts in Prague is the largest and, from an artistic point of view, the most valuable collection in the Czech Republic. The National Technical Museum has a collection which concentrates on mechanical clocks. The text sketches the history of watchmaking, starting with the first design for measuring time, the sundial, and continuing through table clocks (from the 15th to the 17th century), longcase clocks, bracket clocks, architectural and sculptural clocks, portico and wall clocks to decorative porcelain clocks and various wrist watches. After the text comes the catalogue of the exhibition, made up of fifty-four pages of full-colour photographs of the clocks which were exhibited. The book also has a list of watchmakers and artists (p. 121-24) who designed, shaped or manufactured clocks, and a short, multilingual bibliography on the general history of clocks and watchmaking (p. 124).

991 **Czech fashion 1918-1939: elegance of the Czechoslovak First Republic.**
Eva Uchalová.   Prague: Olympia Publishing House, in cooperation with the Museum of Decorative Arts in Prague, 1996. 120p.

The first study of the Czech fashion industry of the inter-war period. The modern form depended on first-class haute couture fashion houses, fashion design and shows, as well as the media: the fashion press, journalism and advertising. This large-format hardback has many photographs and illustrations, some in colour. At the time of writing, the publisher was intending to follow this publication with sister volumes, 'Czech fashion 1870-1918: from the waltz to the tango', 'Czech fashion: 10th-15th centuries', 'Czech fashion: 16th-18th centuries', Czech fashion: 1940-1990' and 'Children's fashion in the Czech Lands over the centuries'.

992 **Indigo country cloths and artefacts from Czechoslovakia.**
Catalogue written and compiled by Linda Brassington, introduction by Miroslava Ludvíková.   Farnham, England: West Surrey College of Art and Design, 1987. 72p. bibliog.

Indigo dyeing (*modrotisk*) is a craft – which has been lost in Western Europe – with a fairly long tradition (since the 16th century) and many modern practitioners in the Haná, Valašsko and Kyjov regions of Moravia (and the Liptov and Spiš regions of Slovakia), all of which are represented and illustrated in this catalogue. The exhibition draws on collections in Moravian and Silesian museums. The accompanying essays, and an interview with a modern practitioner, discuss the history, methods and use of resist printing and indigo dyeing, with generous illustrations of the techniques involved and some of the clothing and other textiles produced. A list of relevant museums etc. is appended.

Theatre

993 **Národní divadlo a jeho předchůdci.** (The National Theatre and its predecessors.)
Edited by Vladimír Procházka. Prague: Academia, 1988. 623p.

This represents a 'Who's who' of artists who were active in the Prague theatres Vlastenecké, Stavovské, Prozatimní and Národní (Patriotic, Estates, Provisional and National theatres). The directory was prepared on the occasion of the centenary of the National Theatre, which is widely considered the most important theatre in the Czech Republic. The entries on individual artists include biographical data and details of their roles in the Prague theatres. Over 600 photographs of artists in their roles and scenes from productions, together with sixteen colour plates of stage designs, illustrate the development of drama, opera and ballet in Prague.

994 **Czech nationalism: a study of the national theatre movement 1845-1883.**
Stanley Buchholz Kimball. Urbana, Illinois: Illinois University Press, 1964. 186p. (Illinois Studies in the Social Sciences, no. 54).

Theatre was a major vehicle in the National Revival's propagation of the Czech language, as well as a means to recreate persons and events from the nation's past and so aid the rediscovery of its history. This book's thesis is that the Czech National Theatre movement is one of the best examples.

995 **Le théâtre libéré de Prague. Voskovec & Werich.** (The Liberated Theatre of Prague. Voskovec & Werich.)
Daniele Monmartre, preface by Václav Havel, conclusion by Dena Bablet. Paris: Institut d'Études Slaves, 1991. 288p. bibliog.

The popular comic duo of Jiří Voskovec and Jan Werich, actors, clowns, singers and songwriters, authors of film scripts, plays and books, made an impact on the Czech theatre scene from 1927-38 and 1946-48. This is a scholarly, yet lively work on the birth of the avant-garde Prague stage, the Liberated Theatre (Osvobozené divadlo), and on cinema, comedy, poetry, satire, choreography, music and songs, illustrated with black-and-white photographs, cartoons and pictures.

996 **Czech drama since World War II.**
Paul I. Trensky, with an introduction by William E. Harkins. White Plains, New York: M. E. Sharpe, 1978. 250p. bibliog. (Columbia Slavic Studies).

A comprehensive survey, which needs updating, of Czech drama and dramatists up to the time of publication, addressed to Western theatre and television audiences. Relevant political background information and some comparisons with non-dramatic Czech literature and some non-Czech literature add meaning to the chapter divisions, which cover: the rise and fall of Socialist Realism; the drama of poets; political drama; drama of the absurd; other playwrights of the 1950s and 1970s; and an epilogue on the 1970s. The bibliography includes not only secondary literature, but also full personal bibliographies of the dramatists discussed, complete with details of first performances and English translations where relevant.

997 **A mirror of world theatre: the Prague Quadrennial 1967-1991.**
Věra Ptáčková, Vladimír Adamczyk (chapter on theatre architecture).
Prague: Divadelní ústav Praha, 1995. 382p.
The book was published by the Theatre Institute in Prague (Divadelní ústav Praha) and inevitably the Czech element is omnipresent. There is also a subchapter, 'A stage design of musical-dramatic works by Czech and Slovak authors' (p. 169-70), which is mostly on the production of Janáček's operas, and a major chapter entitled 'Czechoslovakia: a survey of Czech and Slovak stage design over the past thirty years' (p. 289-95). Since the book is written in the intellectual style which the Central Europeans are so fond of, the reader has to grope for the facts through a complicated narrative.

998 **The silenced theatre: Czech playwrights without a stage.**
Marketa Goetz-Stankiewicz. Toronto: University of Toronto Press, 1979. 319p. bibliog.
An account of the situation in the 1970s, when the works of many contemporary Czech playwrights were not allowed to be performed in their home country, although some were seen in the West. The author discusses the playwrights and plays but also describes some of the outstanding features of Czech theatre of the time – direction, production and stage design. She also introduces the English-speaking reader to as much of the cultural and political background as was needed for an understanding of the situation. The playwrights discussed include Václav Havel, Pavel Kohout, Ivan Klíma, Josef Topol, Milan Kundera and Vratislav Blažek. Recognition is given to the Czech dramatists' connections with, and/or debt to, writers in the West (such as Jarry, Brecht, Pirandello, Genet, Dürrenmatt, Beckett, Albee, and, among contemporary English dramatists, Harold Pinter and Tom Stoppard).

999 **Czech and Slovak theatre.**
Prague: Divadelní ústav Praha, 1991- . twice-yearly.
Contains entries in both French and English on various aspects of the theatre and items of theatrical interest. The issues are illustrated with black-and-white photographs of theatres, productions and characters from the world of theatre.

Film

1000 **Lexikon českého filmu: 2 000 filmů 1930-1997.** (Lexicon of Czech films: 2,000 films 1938-97.)
Václav Březina. Prague: Cinema, filmové nakladatelství, 1997. 546p.
The first truly comprehensive survey of all Czech sound and feature films in the history of Czech cinematography. The core of the lexicon, the films, is ordered alphabetically; the film entries are in encyclopaedic form and detail: title, year, production, length, colour/black-and-white, director's name, scriptwriter (or source the film is based on), cameraman, composer of music, filming location, the actors and

their roles, evaluation of the film on a scale of 0-100 per cent and attendance rate. This factual description is followed by a critical annotation on the film. The lexicon also has a separate summary of Czech film producers and directors and their work and concludes with a chronological index of the films and index of directors. The lexicon includes 250 monochrome photographs.

1001 **Barrandov: 1945-1970.**
Edited by Stanislav Brach. Prague: Barrandov Film Studio, 1971. 92p.

Published on the occasion of twenty-five years of the Barrandov Film Studios in the nationalized Czechoslovak film industry when these studios were the sole producers of feature films. Barrandov studios had in fact been in existence for forty years by then. The studios are described, as are their technical facilities and their cooperation with Czechoslovak television. The text is in English, Russian, German and French. Inevitably, the publication consists mostly of pictures of scenes from films shot at Barrandov.

1002 **The most important art: Eastern European film after 1945.**
Mira Liehm, Antonín J. Liehm. Berkeley, California; Los Angeles; London; University of California Press, 1977. 467p. map. bibliog.

Another excellent study which needs updating. The book consists of four parts. Part one is essentially introductory, summarizing developments up to 1945 and including references to Czech films during the period of the First Republic and even the first stirrings among Czech film-makers during the last years of Austria-Hungary. The last three chapters are subdivided on a country-by-country basis, each country's film history being roughly periodized as a reflection of general trends in current affairs and political development. For the Czech Lands the main turning points are, with some justification, 1955-56 and 1962-63. All major, and many minor, films are discussed and the careers of many directors and actors can be traced. The bibliography reveals that, with a few exceptions, items in French were at that time the major source of secondary literature.

1003 **The Czechoslovak New Wave.**
Peter Hames. Berkeley, California; Los Angeles; London: University of California Press, 1985. 322p. bibliog.

Czechoslovak cinema came into prominence in the 1960s and gained recognition as one of the most important movements in the world. The New Wave continued the tradition of Critical Realism, Neo-Realism and the experimental school and also drew on national cultural traditions. This excellent reference book, intended for the student of cinema history, consists of articles on directors, films and schools and is well documented by photographs from films and by notes. The last chapter describes the situation after the Warsaw Pact invasion of Czechoslovakia in 1968, which brought the movement to an end.

1004 **Closely watched films: the Czechoslovak experience.**
Antonín J. Liehm, translated by Káča Poláčková. White Plains,
New York: International Arts and Sciences Press, 1974. 485p.
bibliog.

An invaluable reference work, for the film scholar and layman alike, which, despite
being in need of updating, offers useful background on the Czech film industry. The
book includes short biographical sketches of, and interviews with, some thirty-two
directors. Wisely, it takes in more than just the New Wave of the 1960s, and looks
back, where relevant, to the First Republic and the war period. The emphasis is always
on the tensions between filmmaking and the social and political environment. Included
in the book are photographic portraits of each director and a complete filmography for
each, some sub-classified by leading stars, and an alphabetical index of films.

1005 **Jiří Menzel and the history of the Closely watched trains.**
Josef Škvorecký. Boulder, Colorado: East European Monographs,
distributed by Columbia University Press, New York, 1982. 100p.
(East European Monographs, no. 118).

A highly interpretive work which does not look just at the film of the title but at all
Menzel's work. It also examines in detail the genesis of the Hrabal works, on which
some Menzel films are based, and this section almost counts as an essay on the life
and work of Bohumil Hrabal as much as on Menzel. Much more up-to-date
information on Menzel can be gained from 'A checkpoint unlocked' by Andrew
Pulver, *The Guardian*, 26 October 1995, supplement, p. 12-13, an interview and
profile of his career as one of the leading figures of the Czech New Wave, who had
such a huge impact on world cinema. The Soviet tanks quickly extinguished the light
– after the invasion of 1968, in the era of re-inforcement of Communist ideology,
Menzel's artistic activity was subdued, but Pulver (and Menzel himself) believes that
Jiří Menzel is now back as an artist and still capable of making a great impact on the
world of cinema.

1006 **All the bright young men and women: a personal history of the
Czech cinema.**
Josef Škvorecký, translated by Michael Schonberg. Toronto: Peter
Martin Associates, 1975. 280p.

Although the book traces Czech film back to its earliest origins, it concentrates most
heavily on the generation with which Škvorecký is most acquainted, i.e. his own. He
knows many of the filmmakers personally and is able to fill out the relevant historical
detail with many reminiscences, not to say gossip, some bordering on the bitchy,
about several of the individuals mentioned. The 'personal' here descends into the
obtrusively intimate, the widespread use of first names being no contribution to a
serious study. Nevertheless, a wealth of information can be obtained from the book,
particularly on the 1969-70 period. The filmography lists the essential facts
concerning all the major films produced since 1898.

1007 **Turnaround, a memoir.**
Miloš Forman, Jan Novák. London; Boston, Massachusetts: Faber
& Faber, 1993. 295p.
Written in an amusing, lively and readable style by one of the best contemporary
Czech film directors who settled in the United States. Forman directed classics such as
Taking off, One flew over the cuckoo's nest and *Amadeus*. The autobiography
describes his childhood immediately before and during the war, his studies, and his
work in films in Czechoslovakia and in exile. It is an excellent documentary of the life
and work of a film director, of personalities from the world of film, and of the New
Wave of Czech cinema in the 1960s which came to international prominence. The
book is documented by photographs, but a more detailed contents page and an index
would have made the volume easier to use.

1008 **Dark alchemy: the films of Jan Švankmajer.**
Edited by Peter Hames. Trowbridge, England: Flick Books, 1995.
202p. bibliog. (Cinema Voice Series, vol. 246).
Brings together essays on the work of Jan Švankmajer and an extensive interview with
this artist, film director, animator and surrealist. The formative influences on
Švankmajer are identified as being pre-war Surrealism, echoes of the Prague of
Rudolph II, experimental theatre, folk puppetry (so popular in the Czech Lands), and,
above all, the political darkness of the last fifty years. The narrative is supported by a
filmography (p. 169-74) and a bibliography. *Švankmajer's Faust, the script: including
a preface by the author and excerpts from his diary kept during filming*, by Jan
Švankmajer, translated by Valerie Mason (Trowbridge, England: Flick Books, 1996.
65p.), is the screenplay of Švankmajer's acclaimed feature film *Lekce Faust* (The
lesson of Faust). The introduction and excerpts from the diary are fascinating and
disturbing. The film itself combines Faustiada by Goethe, Marlowe, Grabbe and
Gounod and is set in post-Stalinist Prague.

1009 **The art of laughter and survival. Permanent subversion.**
Judith Vidal-Hall, Peter Hames. *Index on Censorship*, vol. 24, no. 6
(November/December 1996), p. 95, 119-25.
These two articles on contemporary Czech cinema appeared in one issue of *Index on
Censorship*. One is an interview with Czech film director Jiří Menzel, the second a
study of the work of Jan Švankmajer. For political reasons, Švankmajer was not able
to work between 1973 and 1980, and Czech audiences had no opportunity to
appreciate his work until he was internationally acclaimed in the late 1980s.

1010 **Filmová Ročenka. Film Yearbook.**
Prague: Národní filmový archiv, 1992- . annual.
A bilingual (English and Czech) publication which summarizes data and information
on Czech cinema in the previous year: Czech film production (feature films,
documentaries, animated films and certain advertisements); Czech film distribution;
export of films; prize-winning Czech films and personalities; film events; a list of
publications and periodicals issued in the previous year; and a directory of the main
institutions, organizations and companies in Czech cinema, with addresses. There is
also a list of distinguished cinema personalities who died during the previous year and
information on special grants awarded by the state fund and others.

1011 Československé filmy 1977-1980: filmografie. (The Czechoslovak films 1977-80: a filmography.) Šárka Bartošková, Luboš Bartošek. Prague: Československý filmový ústav, 1983. 2 vols.

Presents documentary material on Czech and Slovak feature films produced in the Czech and Slovak film studios, with a filmography of the actors and artists involved. The filmography has three sections: a chronological list of films; an alphabetical list with a description of each film; and prizes and awards received at film fairs and film festivals.

1012 Bibliografie československé neperiodické filmové literatury: 1945-1985. (Bibliography of Czechoslovak non-periodical film literature: 1945-85.) Ivana Tibitanzlová, Alena Kahovcová, Alice Topolská. Prague: Československý filmový ústav, 1989. 466p.

This bibliography lacks a subject index. As such it is a straightforward compendious alphabetical list of film literature covering forty years and is based on the collections of the Czechoslovak Film Institute. It continues the work of Luboš Bartošek in his *Bibliografie československé filmové literatury: 1930-1945* (Bibliography of Czech film literature: 1930-45), published by Československý filmový ústav in 1971.

Architecture

1013 Baroko v Čechách a na Moravě. (Baroque in Bohemia and Moravia.) Text by Jan Burian, photographs by Dalibor Kusák, Vladimír Hyhlík, Miroslav Krob. Prague: BB/Art, 1993. 375p.

Leading Czech photographers have captured the dramatic development of society and culture in the 17th and 18th centuries in this beautiful, large-format book. There are parallel texts in Czech, English, French, German, Italian and Spanish. The English translator tried hard, but the text is stilted, which is unfortunate in a book of this quality. There is an introduction, a prologue, a chapter on the uprising of the Bohemian Estates in 1618-20 and on the Thirty Years' War, a chapter on the times after the Peace of Westphalia of 1648 and on the transition of the lands into a calmer Catholic period. The book also has a brief chronology (English text, p. 20-22), which combines history with art and starts with the first stirrings of the Baroque style during the reign of Rudolf II (1575-1611) and ends with the première of Mozart's *Don Giovanni* in Prague in 1787. The pictorial part of the book is divided into sections on ecclesiastical monuments; stately homes; urban environment; open spaces and sculpture (this being on gardens, bridges, both with statuary and other sculptures, and town square fountains); and village buildings. A jumble of copious information on Baroque can be found in *Baroque in Bohemia* by Milada Součková, with a postscript by Roman Jakobson (Ann Arbor, Michigan: Michigan Slavic Publications, 1980. 216p.). The book covers not only painting and architecture, but also literature, painting on glass, wayside crosses, gingerbread designs and much else.

1014   **Johann Blasius Santini-Aichel: a Gothic-Baroque architect in Bohemia, 1677-1723.**
S. Gold. *Transactions of the Ancient Monuments Society*, no. 42 (1998), p. 63-80. bibliog.

The name Johann Blasius Santini-Aichel was not well known in Britain until recently, and his work is not very well known even in his homeland. The author explains the reasons for this: some of the best buildings associated with this architect are in remote parts of rural Moravia and their attributions are not certain. The article presents a selection of the buildings, mostly ecclesiastical architecture outside Prague. Art historians are intrigued by the unusual mixture of Baroque and Gothic elements in Santini's buildings. The article has illustrations. A monograph on Santini was published in Czech as *Česká barokní gotika: dílo Jana Santiniho-Aichla* (The Czech Baroque Gothic: the work of Jan Santini-Aichl) by Viktor Kotrba (Prague: Academia, 1976. 197p.).

1015   **The castle of Prague and its treasures.**
Text by Charles, Prince of Schwarzenberg, Ivo Hlobil, Ladislav Kesner, Ivan Muchka, Tomáš Vlček, photographs by Miroslav Hucek, Barbara Hucková, translated into English by John Gilbert. London: Flint River Press, 1994. 272p. bibliog.

A beautifully produced, large-size book with numerous excellent colour photographs such as to make Prague totally irresistible to anyone with the mildest interest in history and art. Much of the book is on the city of Prague and on Bohemia. It includes a chronology of Czech history printed in columns parallel to the chronology of European history, and dozens of exquisite photographs of the Castle interiors, from the Romanesque barrel vaults of the mid-12th century, through the proud late Gothic of the Vladislav Hall (the most extensive enclosed space of the Castle), the decorative Spanish Room and Josip Plečnik's Hall of Columns, to the modern furnishing of the current president's office. A section of the book is devoted to St Vitus Cathedral; there is also a section on the collections of the National Gallery at St Georges's Convent; and there are small sections on the Castle gardens and 'Other secular buildings of the Castle'.

1016   **Prague Castle.**
Jiří Burian, Antonín Hartmann, photographs by Karel Neubert, translated by Jan Eisler. London; New York; Sydney; Toronto: Hamlyn, 1975. 175p.

There have been countless volumes of photographs of Prague Castle, but this is among the few early ones to carry a Western imprint. Although in the coffee-table mould, this large-format volume nevertheless has much to offer, providing a portrait of its subject, Hradčany castle, as an architectural monument of considerable size, complexity and beauty. It also depicts the Castle as a symbol of Czech history and identity, and the seat of the Bohemian, Czechoslovak and Czech head of state. It chooses just core events and periods from Czech history, with quotations from contemporary sources, 'to put flesh on the dry bones of history'. The 150 photographs range from the most ancient to the most recent elements of the architecture, and from panoramas to the easily overlooked detail; exteriors and interiors are included.

1017 **The palaces of Prague.**
Text by Zdeněk Hojda, Jiří Pešek, photographs by Lubomír Pořízka.
London: Tauris Parke Books, 1994. 216p. map.
Another of the beautiful and colourful coffee-table books which conspire to make
Prague irresistible to anyone with an interest in art and architecture. Forty-one palaces
are listed, including Prague Castle, all built between the Middle Ages and the 19th
century and of various architectural styles: Gothic, Rococo, Baroque and Neoclassical.
The book has 164 large colour photographs of exteriors and interiors of the
magnificent Prague palaces.

1018 **Palace palimpsest.**
Susan Dawson. *Architectural Review*, no. 199, 1187 (January
1996), p. 84-85.
The architects Jestico & Whiles were reconstructing the old Ericsson Palace in the Old
Town of Prague in 1996. This is a detailed study of a courtyard reception structure.

1019 **Prague: passageways and arcades.**
Michaela Brožová, Anne Hebler, Chantal Scaler, preface by Václav
Havel, presentation by Xavier Galmiche, contemporary photography
by Rudolf Duda, Petr Zhoř, Pavel Štecha. Prague: Euro Art Ltd &
Volvox Globator, 1997. 211p. bibliog.
This book was first published in French as *Prague: passages et galeries* (Paris: Norma
& Institut Français d'Architecture, 1993). A large-format, coffee-table book, it offers
historical, architectural and urbanistic studies of passageways and arcades; it is also 'a
reflection of the unique face of Prague, whose features are composed of poetry, magic,
spirituality, and metaphysical meaning' (Preface, p. 7). The passageways were
initially a part of mediaeval town planning, private and semi-public, and the authors
follow their development to the present day. More than half of the book consists of
photographs, mostly in colour, and plans and drawings.

1020 **Böhmen in 19. Jahrhundert: vom Klassizismus zum Moderne.**
(Bohemia in the 19th century: from Classicism to modernism.)
Edited by Ferdinand Seibt. Frankfurt, Germany: Propyläen, 1995.
485p. maps. bibliog.
Presents studies by twenty Czech, Austrian and German scholars. The focus is on
architecture but the essays also provide an insight into the culture of the period and
document the development of town planning in the Czech Lands.

1021 **Prague and Art Nouveau.**
Marie Vitochová, Jindřich Kejř, translated by Denis Rath, Mark
Prescott. Prague: Nakladatelství V ráji, 1995. 184p.
A glossy publication following fifteen walks through Prague, looking at hotels,
railway stations and house façades and examining their Art Nouveau features in great
detail. The colour photographs are by Jiří Všetečka.

315

1022 **Prague: fin de siècle.**
Petr Wittlich, translated into French by Sabina Skarbová, photographs by Jan Malý. Paris; New York: Flammarion; Abbeville, 1992. 280p. bibliog.
This large-format book focuses on the art-historical aspect of the period from 1890 to the pathétique style and Modernism. It contains stunning photographs by architectural photographer Jan Malý and some archival items, in black-and-white and in colour. The text is detailed and is supplemented by biographical notes and an index.

1023 **The architecture of new Prague: 1895-1945.**
Rostislav Švácha, translated by Alexandra Buchler, foreword by Kenneth Frampton, photographs by Jan Malý. London; Cambridge, Massachusetts: MIT Press, 1995. 573p. bibliog.
A study of architecture from the 1890s, when Modernism was taking over from the late historicism, to the 1940s, the end of the avant-garde movement in architecture. This was the third period in history when Czech architects were teaching Europe more than they themselves were learning from other countries. The previous two periods were the late Gothic in the 15th and 16th centuries and the High Baroque in the first half of the 18th century. The introduction assesses Prague's evolution as a city and its place in the context of international architectural movements. The author of this book walked all the streets which existed in 1920. The result is an index of 1,300 buildings (p. 501-50). Each entry in this alphabetical index gives the address, the name of the architect, the type of building and its date of construction. The accompanying narrative is an artistic interpretation of these accumulated facts and a pursuit of creative individuality. Modernism, Cubism, Purism, Neoclassicism, scientific and emotional Functionalism were the styles implemented in Prague by the architects Jan Kotěra, Pavel Janák, Josef Gočár and other major figures. There are more then 300 black-and-white and colour photographs of the buildings by the architectural photographer Jan Malý, some still showing the neglect and grimness of the Communist era. The book was published twice previously in Czech, first by Odeon in 1985 and again in 1994 by Victoria Publishing, both in Prague. The English edition was reviewed in *The Times Literary Supplement*, 4842 (12 January 1996), p. 16-17, by Joseph Rykwert, in an article entitled 'The city and the controversialist: Karel Teige, Czech functionalism and the reconstruction of Prague'. The book was described as an extensive catalogue of the buildings and of the alliances among the artists of the period. This is a book to be consulted rather than read from cover to cover.

1024 **Prague: a guide to 20th century architecture.**
Ivan Margolius, photographs by Keith Collie. London: Artemis, 1994. 320p.
This book offers a wealth of information on architecture and town planning. According to Margolius, there are 1,500 noteworthy buildings in Prague, built by distinguished architects such as Adolf Loos, Josip Plečnik, Bruno Paul and Mart Stam. This excellent study does not discriminate; it features ugly sites as well as beautiful ones. Individual items are analysed, each documented by a black-and-white photograph by Keith Collie, with a descriptive history, an address, transport links and access details.

1025 **Cubism in architecture and the applied arts: Bohemia and France 1910-1914.**

Ivan Margolius. Newton Abbot, England; London: North Pomfret, Vermont: David & Charles, 1979. 128p. bibliog.

Cubist architecture in Bohemia, inspired by Cubism in painting and born as a reaction to Art Nouveau, was an abrupt creation without a counterpart elsewhere, apart from a much smaller-scale flowering in France. This book introduces its main Czech exponents and many of their works (including some designs that never materialized), placing them in the general context of architectural history. Cubist furniture is mentioned, and there is also a useful 'Chronology 1900-1920'. The visitor to Prague with an eye for the city's great and varied architectural wealth will find this a handy introduction to a cross-section of the buildings from this short-lived but striking period.

1026 **Czech Cubism: architecture, furniture and decorative arts, 1910-1925.**

Milena B. Lamarová, Vladimír Šlapeta, Petr Wittlich, Jiří Šetlík, Josef Krontvor, Olga Herbenová, François Burkhardt, Alessandro Mendini, edited by Alexander von Vegesack, photographs by Jan Malý. Princeton, New Jersey: Princeton Architectural Press, 1992. 337p. bibliog.

This collection of essays on many aspects of Czech Cubism is an authoritative work on this style and its influence on architecture and town planning. The book contains black-and-white and colour photographs, drawings, biographies, a chronology, a list of exhibitions, an index of names, photographic credits and plans. A supplement to *T92 (Technical Magazine)* is a study by Zdeněk Lukeš, with translation by Kateřina Hilská, *Cubism in Czech architecture* (Prague: Panorama, 1993. 16p. maps). The text is in Czech and English. Another work in Czech and English is *Kubistická Praha – Cubist Prague: 1909-1925* by Michal Bregant, Lenka Bydžovská, Vojtěch Lahoda, Zdeněk Lukeš, Karel Srp, Rostislav Švácha (Prague[?]: Středoevropská galerie, 1995. 231p.). This publication was written by art historians from the Institute of Art History of the Czech Academy of Sciences in collaboration with other distinguished experts. The original photographs of Cubist buildings were taken by the leading Czech architecture photographer Jan Malý. After 1909, Prague became the second most important centre of European Cubism after Paris.

1027 **East European Modernism: architecture in Czechoslovakia, Hungary and Poland between the wars.**

Edited with an introduction and essays by Vojciech Lešnikowski, essays by Vladimír Šlapeta, John Macsai, János Bonta, Olgierd Czerner. London: Thames & Hudson, 1996. 304p. maps. bibliog.

Five architectural writers from the Czech Republic, Hungary and Poland cooperated on a period of architecture which had been, until recently, neglected and underrated, a poor relation to the popular Gothic and Baroque. The frontispiece of the book is a photograph of the most elegant arch that is part of the core of the Brno Exhibition Ground complex of buildings. The book gives great attention to Functionalism, a stimulating and rich style of great originality. It draws on recent publications from Central European countries and the authors fulfil the reader's expectations with the inclusion of many photographs of examples of the styles described: housing developments, private villas, sanatoriums, spas, sports complexes, schools and industrial buildings. Architects who worked in the Czech Lands, such as Adolf Loos, Bohuslav Fuchs, Jiří Kroha and others, are given due credit. The bibliography (p. 298-301) covers books, articles and catalogues in Czech and English. There is also an index (p. 302-04). A large critical study of almost the same period, richly illustrated and covering a variety of applied arts is *Das Bauhaus im Osten: Slowakische und Tschechische Avantgarde 1928-1939* (Bauhaus in the East: the Slovak and Czech avant-garde, 1928-39) (Ostfildern-Ruit, Germany: Verlag Gerd Hatje, 1997. 339p. bibliog.).

1028 Czech Functionalism: 1918-1938.
Foreword by Gustav Peichl, introductory essay by Vladimír Šlapeta.
London: Architectural Association, 1987. 175p. bibliog. map.

This publication accompanied an exhibition at the Architectural Association in London, organized in cooperation with the National Museum of Technology in Prague. It consists largely of black-and-white photographs, some contemporary, and is not limited to architecture only, but includes car design, aircraft, furniture and posters. The publication has brief biographies of major Czech architects. Czech architecture of this period occupies a special place in the history of modern art. The city of Brno took the initiative in the evolution of modern architecture. A similar exhibition catalogue was published under the title *Devětsil: Czech avant-garde art; architecture and design of the 1920s and 1930s* (Oxford: Museum of Modern Art; London: Design Museum, 1990. 115p. bibliog.), edited by Rostislav Švácha. This exhibition was conceived by František Šmejkal.

1029 Josip Plečnik – an architect of the Prague Castle.
Edited by Zdeněk Lukeš, Damjan Prelovšek, Tomáš Valena.
Prague: Správa Pražského hradu, 1997. 655p.

This beautifully produced, huge book (weighing nearly 5 kilograms) with high-quality colour and monochrome illustrations, offers plenty of material for the study of Modernism and the architecture of the first decades of the 20th century. An exhibition entitled, 'Josip Plečnik – Architecture for the new democracy', was held in Prague in 1996. This superb book, a sort of delayed catalogue to the exhibition (the Czech version also appeared only in 1997), has three sections. The first section consists of twenty-five essays by specialists on Plečnik's architecture and urban design. They are not confined to the Castle, but appraise other buildings in Prague, the presidential country seat in Lány and buildings elsewhere in Bohemia. Nor are they limited to the work of Plečnik (1872-1957); they also look at other architecture of his time. The second section consists of thirteen portfolios of illustrations and the third section is an appendix of more than fifty pages, containing a chronology of Plečnik's work at Prague Castle and in Lány, and plans.

1030 Architect Bohuslav Fuchs: the lifework.
Iloš Crhonek. Brno, Czech Republic: Petrov, 1995. 197p. bibliog.

Fuchs (1895-1972) was a leading personality in Czech architecture between the wars and his work had a significant impact on the townscape of Brno; he was one of the pioneers of modern town planning. Fuchs studied in Prague under Jan Kotěra and his development as an architect and designer took him, via Dutch architecture, to Constructivism with the purists ethics of Le Corbusier. Some of Fuchs' buildings

318

represent the high point of Czech functional architecture. Examples are the Brno hotel Avion or the thermal spa complex Green Frog (Zelená Žába) in Trenčianske Teplice (Slovakia), which is a specimem of 'organic architecture' and which, thanks to the remarkable symbiosis of the building with the landscape, won world-wide acclaim. The range of Fuchs' work was remarkable, from regional town planning and design, and public buildings, to private dwellings, monuments, interior and furniture designs and other applied arts. The last three are underrepresented in this book. The arrangement of the book is chronological: under each year are listed projects, about 600 altogether, starting with Fuchs' architecture school projects of 1914 and ending with his designs for memorial plaques in 1972. Wherever possible, drawings and photographs are given, of which there are many hundreds. The book concludes with bibliographies, a list of 'The theoretical works of Bohuslav Fuchs' (p. 193-96) and 'Sources and literature used' (p. 197).

1031 **Trade Fair Palace in Prague.**
Miroslav Masák, Rostislav Švácha, Jindřich Vybíral. Prague: National Gallery in Prague, 1995. 79p. bibliog.

A collection of articles, some contemporary, some taken from journals in the 1920s on the project for constructing a trade fair complex in the Holešovice part of Prague. The collection lacks a framework and there is no introduction or conclusion to help the reader. The contributions are on: the events leading up to, and including, the founding of the Prague Trade Fair in 1924; the architectural competition; the final winning design of architects Josef Fuchs and Oldřich Tyl; urban development generally; Constructivism and Functionalism of the 1920s; Le Corbusier's visits to Prague; and the reconstruction of the Prague Trade Fair Palace in the 1970s and 1980s. There is also an article on Václav Boháč (1874-1935), the founder and first president of the Prague Trade Fair, and on the architects Josef Fuchs (1894-1979) and Oldřich Tyl (1884-1939). The book has photographs, plans of the construction, and a 'Select bibliography' (p. 78-79) of articles, the majority of which are in Czech, on both the construction and recent reconstruction of the Trade Fair Palace.

1032 **Public monuments: art in political bondage 1870-1997.**
Sergiusz Michalski. London: Reaktion Books, 1998. 256p. bibliog.

One chapter of this volume concerns the monumental architecture of Soviet Communism, including its impact on Prague. This relates in particular to the monstrous, and alarmingly prominent, statue of Stalin in Prague and the new quarter of Stalinist architecture in the city. The book is accorded an illustrated review by Alex Mayhew in *BCSA Newsletter*, 48 (April/May 1999), p. 9. The book contains 130 illustrations of various monuments and a selective bibliography (p. 236).

1033 **Dancing house.**
Helga Miklosko. *Architectural Review*, no. 201, 1202 (April 1997), p. 38-44.

The building in Prague by the river Vltava, the work of architect Frank Gehry which caused a stir in architectural circles when it was built in the mid-1990s, has also been called the 'Fred and Ginger' house. The article calls the building exuberantly gestural, a bold symbol of Prague's architectural, economic and political revival.

319

1034 **Prague competition.**
Architectural Review, no. 202, 1211 (January 1998), p. 49-53.
A report on an international competition to build a completely new urban park within the complex and grounds of Prague Castle. The condition was to preserve historic elements. This article presents the first, second and third joint awards together with the comments of the jury.

1035 **Eva Jiřičná: design in exile.**
Martin Pawley. London: Fourth Estate, 1990. 112p. (A Blueprint Monograph).
A portrait of a Czech architect and designer. Jiřičná was born in Zlín, a town with remarkable modern architecture; her father was an architect, an adherent of Functionalism. Jiřičná emigrated to England in 1968 and worked for several architectural institutions before setting up her own company, building and re-designing shops and restaurants in London, Paris and New York. Some of her interior designs, e.g., in Harrods, have been widely written about; in 1999 she was asked to plan an additional new Friends' room in the Royal Academy's 18th-century building in London, to update the Royal Academy's image. She is also involved with the Millennium Dome. Her designs are modern, using steel and glass, and in this monograph Pawley traces the elements of 20th-century Czech design and architecture in her work. The publication has many photographs of Jiřičná's designs and of projects she worked on. A pictorial book on the architecture of Jiřičná's birthplace has been published in Czech, with summaries in English, German and French: Pavel Novák's *Zlínská architektura, 1900-1950* (The architecture of Zlín, 1900-50) (Zlín, Czech Republic: Čas, in cooperation with Nadace studijního ústavu Tomáše Bati, 1993. 320p. bibliog.). Two other publications on Jiřičná's work, mostly on her interior designs, are available in English: *Eva Jiřičná designs* (London: Architectural Association, 1987. 43p.); and, *Joseph shops: Eva Jiřičná, Jose Manser* (London: Architecture Design and Technology Press, 1991), by Jose Manser, with photographs by Richard Bryant and Alastair Hunter.

1036 **Future Systems: the story of tomorrow.**
Martin Pawley. London: Phaidon Press, 1993. 156p. bibliog.
The story of an architectural practice, of which Jan Kaplický is a founder and partner. Kaplický, an architect and designer, was born in Czechoslovakia in 1937 and, like Jiřičná, came to England in 1968. Over the following twenty-five years he worked with Richard Rogers, Norman Foster and other modern architects. Pawley traces the influences on, and development of, Kaplický's work and provides examples in the form of monochrome and colour illustrations and drawings.

1037 **Hauer-King House: Future Systems.**
Martin Pawley. London: Phaidon Press, 1997. 60p. bibliog.
(Architecture in Detail).
Hauer-King House, also known as the glass house, was completed in London in 1994 and is considered a landmark in the history of modern architecture: 'the house exemplifies the architects' space-age aesthetics' while providing a carefully designed modern living environment. Pawley gives a profile of Jan Kaplický and his partner Amanda Levete, the two architects of the glass house. Like Jiřičná, Kaplický carried over the principles of modern Czech architecture, particularly Functionalism. This large landscape-format book, a sister volume to that mentioned in the previous entry, includes many photographs and drawings of the glass house.

Music

General

1038 **Czech opera.**
John Tyrrell. Cambridge, England: Cambridge University Press, 1988. 352p. bibliog. (National Traditions in Opera).
The first publication in the 'National Traditions in Opera' series, which aims to study the development of the genre in individual European countries. Opera had its own unique place in the Czech national movement, which culminated in the founding of the Czechoslovak Republic in 1918. This book, written by *the* authority on Czech music, discusses operas written in Czech, but is also concerned with the circumstances which influenced these operas. These include the historical and political background to the period, the theatres in which Czech plays and operas were first performed, and the composers and performers who worked in them. The role of the librettist is given particular prominence. Special attention is paid to two further factors which helped to establish a Czech style in opera: the role of folksongs; and the metrical implications of the Czech language for musical settings. The history of opera is covered from its beginnings, but the book concentrates on the period from 1862 to 1928, the year in which Janáček died. As in all Tyrrell's work on Czech music, the text is accompanied by footnotes, indexes, illustrations and a bibliography.

1039 **Dějiny české hudby v obrazech, od nejstarších památek do vybudování Národního divadla.** (The history of Czech music in pictures.)
Prague: Supraphon, 1977. 457p. bibliog.
Published in Czech, German and English; the English translation, however, is awkward. The pictures present major figures from the world of music, stage design, concert halls and opera buildings. At the end of this substantial volume the researcher will find a commentary on each of the 371 pictures, with information on the type of document, its location, age, in some cases physical dimensions, and its significance from the point of view of history or musical iconography.

1040 **Czechoslovak music: Bohemia and Moravia.**
Prague: Orbis, 1948. 112p. bibliog.

A brief summary of the Czech musical scene, which traces the history of music from the Middle Ages to modern times. This slim volume is of value because it offers information in English, however concise, on old Czech music, musical institutions and on lesser-known figures from Czech musical life, such as J. L. Dusík, Josef Suk, J. B. Foerster and Vítězslav Novák. Thirty-two plates supplement the text.

1041 **Rafael Kubelík v Praze, in Prague, in Prag: 1990-1996.**
Zdeněk Chrapek. Prague: nakladatelství Jalna, 1997. 145p.

A brief trilingual text (Czech, English and German) accompanies black-and-white photographs in this pictorial publication which was issued in homage to the conductor Rafael Kubelík, son of the violinist Jan Kubelík. Rafael Kubelík was born in Býchory near Prague and studied at the Prague Conservatory. In 1945 he founded the Prague Spring International Music Festival. Kubelík emigrated from Czechoslovakia in 1948. In the West he held prominent positions in the world of music, for example, between 1955 and 1958 he was Musical Director of the Royal Opera House, Covent Garden, London. The photographs here are from his last years, when he could freely visit Prague, that is from 1990 to his death in 1996. A concert in Prague, after the Velvet Revolution, in which Kubelík conducted Smetana's symphony *Má vlast* (My country), is considered one of the greatest musical experiences of the century. Rafael Kubelík is buried next to his father in the part of the Vyšehrad cemetery in Prague which is reserved for leading figures in Czech culture. The book consists almost exclusively of photographs, with short lyrical texts. There is also a chronology of Rafael Kubelík's life (unpaginated). A brief review of the Prague Spring festival, founded by Kubelík, is *Pražské jaro. Prague Spring* (Prague: Sekretariát mezinárodního hudebního festivalu Pražské jaro, 1988), by author Zdeněk Vokurka. Information on the festival can be obtained from *The Prague Spring* site, http://www.festival.cz/.

1042 **Český hudební adresář.** (Czech musical directory.)
Edited by Mojmír Sobotka. Prague: Music Information Centre of the Czech Music Fund, 1991. 256p.

A comprehensive reference work on the state of the contemporary Czech musical scene. The directory provides information on composers, writers on music and writers of texts set to music, concert artists, singers, instrumental chamber ensembles, vocal and instrumental chamber ensembles, chamber orchestras, symphonic orchestras, wind orchestras, folk instruments, jazz, dance and string orchestras, choirs and stage music ensembles. Educational establishments, universities and secondary-level music schools are listed, as well as the production, servicing and sales of musical instruments, ministries, various organizations, museums, archives and libraries and art agencies. The publication also lists Czech musicians and music writers abroad and Czech musical organizations abroad. In addition, the directory covers the media: music and cultural journals, radio and television, publishing houses and studios.

1043 **Czech Music.**
Prague: Czech Music Information Centre, 1964- . bimonthly.

Provides information on opera productions, concerts in the Czech Republic and abroad and other musical events in the Czech Republic. The periodical started in 1964 under the name, *Music News From Prague*, and is published with the support of the

Bohuslav Martinů Foundation and the Leoš Janáček Foundation. Originally it was printed in English, French, German, Spanish, Italian and Russian; from 1990 it was published in English, French and German only; later it appeared only in English. From 1995 it appeared under a new name, *Czech Music*, still in English only but with a new graphical design. The publisher's name also changed, in 1997, from 'Music Information Centre of the Czech Music Fund' to its present name.

1044 Czech Music.
London: Dvořák Society, 1975- . quarterly.

The Dvořák Society for Czech and Slovak music is 'devoted to musical arts of all Czech and Slovak performers and composers, past and present'. Its president is Sir Charles Mackerras and patrons are John Clapham and Josef Suk. This quarterly offers reviews, information on concerts and on the events of the Dvořák Society. In addition, the Society publishes a *Newsletter* and a *Year-Book*.

1045 Czech music in the web of life.
Jana Marhounová, translated by Deryck Viney. Prague: EMPATIE, 1993. 237p.

The foreword to the English edition of this work, a collection of interviews with leading figures in contemporary Czech music, comments: '. . . it is an attempt to picture the Czech musical world of the past few decades in terms of personal interrelations with their political, academic and spiritual backgrounds, explored in a series of relaxed but probing interviews'. To appreciate these interviews the reader needs some familiarity not only with the contemporary Czech musical scene and the recent history of the country, but also with the intellectual style of Czech thought and writing. The translator, Deryck Viney, has translated many opera libretti from Czech, as well as books.

1046 Contemporary Czechoslovak composers.
Edited by Čeněk Gardovský. Prague, Bratislava: Panton, 1965. 564p.

Contains biographies and musicographies of 360 Czech and Slovak composers of serious and light music, who were living at the time of publication. Many features of the book are now outdated, such as the appendices describing various Czech institutions and organizations (specialist schools, societies and publishers) and the list of gramophone recordings.

1047 Eva Urbanová: soprano.
Petr Čantovský, Jiří Kováč. Prague: Votobia, 1997. 220p.

A biography, in Czech, German and English, of a well-known contemporary Czech opera singer. The core of the book is an interview with Urbanová in which she talks about her childhood, youth, the beginning of her career and her experiences 'of the highest spheres of musical art – and the music business'. The book includes a discography of her recordings (p. 199), a list of her concert and opera premières and a number of photographs. Votobia published simultaneously, as an accompaniment to the book, a compact disc with Dvořák's 'Biblical songs' and 'Gypsy melodies', sung by Eva Urbanová. *Ema Destinová a její jihočeské sídlo. Emmy Destinn und ihr sudbömischer Sitz. Emmy Destinn and her South Bohemian seat* (Třeboň, Czech Republic: Carpio, 1999) is a trilingual (Czech, German and English) publication on

323

the most famous of Czech female opera singers, Ema Destinová (1878-1930), and her beloved country retreat, the castle Stráž nad Nežárkou. The text is by František Furbach and the book has photographs of the beautiful South Bohemian countryside and excerpts from Destinnová's own writings.

1048 **Opera v Praze. Opera in Prague.**
Alexander Buchner, translated from the Czech by Joyce Páleníčková.
Prague: Panton, 1987. 2nd ed. 237p.

A history of the Prague opera from the baroque epoch to the present day, in Czech, German, Russian and English. The book offers information on famous singers, photographs of libretti, stage designs, extracts from arias, and copious quotations from composers and their correspondence. One appendix is a list of Czech opera produced in Prague from 1763 to 1982, giving the director, choreographer, libretto and other details. On a very specific theme is the lavishly illustrated *Mozart's Don Giovanni in Prague* (Prague: Theatre Institute, 1987. 191p.), by Jiří Hilmera, Tomislav Volek, Věra Ptáčková, edited by Jan Křístek, which contains several very different articles on this famous opera, first produced at the Stavovské divadlo (Estates Theatre) in Prague in 1787. What remains today of Prague's operatic legacy is examined in an article, 'The thin lady sings', *The Economist*, no. 336, 7927 (12 August 1995), p. 81.

1049 **Rocking the state: rock music and politics in Eastern Europe and Russia.**
Edited by Sabrina Petra Ramet. Boulder, Colorado; San Francisco; Oxford: Westview Press, 1994. 317p.

There is a scarcity of information in written form on popular music in Eastern Europe. This book brings together some of the world's leading authorities on rock music under Communism and analyses the rise of specific rock groups. 'Rock music in Czechoslovakia' (p. 55-72) is by Sabrina Petra Ramet and is probably the best comprehensive survey in English of the Czech rock scene from the 1960s to the 1990s. The only Czech group to have achieved worldwide acclaim is the psychedelic Plastic People of the Universe.

Bedřich Smetana

1050 **Smetana.**
John Clapham. London: Dent; New York: Octagon Books, 1972. 161p. bibliog.

A full, readable biography and analysis of the work of the first Czech composer to achieve worldwide recognition. Bedřich Smetana is esteemed by the Czechs as the father of modern Czech music and the most national of their great composers. Clapham also includes a summary history of music in the Czech Lands before Smetana's time and gives recognition to earlier composers who ought to be better known. The book has a chronology, a complete list of Smetana's works and a sizeable bibliography. The latest performance in England of the most national of Smetana's operas, *The bartered bride*, has been, at the time of writing, by The Royal Opera in London in December 1998. The programme for this production has articles on Smetana's music by Jan Smaczny and John Tyrrell and a background article on the 19th-century Bohemian village by David Short. The Glyndbourne Opera in Sussex is producing this opera in late summer 1999.

1051 **Smetana.**
Brian Large. London: Duckworth, 1970. 473p. bibliog.
Another detailed biography and musicography of Smetana, which also covers other topics, such as mediaeval Czech history and literature, 19th-century music and the history of some Prague theatres. The text is supplemented by generous illustrations, photographs of people, places and manuscripts and passages from the scores discussed. The biography includes a chronology of works, a classified list of works and synopses of the operas.

1052 **The Smetana centennial, an International Conference and Festival of Czechoslovak Music, March 29-April 8, 1984.**
San Diego, California: San Diego State University, [1984]. unpaginated.
During this festival of music, Smetana's orchestral and operatic works were performed and numerous recitals given. Some of the world's most important authorities on Smetana and Czech music took part in the conference. This large volume covers documentation connected with the organization of the event and publishes the papers presented. The majority of the papers were given in English, with some in Czech.

Antonín Dvořák

1053 **Dvořák and his world.**
Edited by Michael Beckerman. Princeton, New Jersey: Princeton University Press, 1993. 284p.
Published 100 years after the première of the symphony *From the New World*, this scholarly work consists of two parts, 'Essays' and 'Documents and criticism'. The first section includes: an article on Dvořák's innovation, modernity and ideology, by Leon Botstein; a discourse on Dvořák and Brahms, by David Beveridge; a treatise on Dvořák's operas, by Jan Smaczny; and a description of the genesis and première of the New World symphony, by Michael Beckerman. The latter article also discusses the influence of Dvořák's nationality on his work. The second part includes: reviews and criticisms from the American and Czech press; letters to Dvořák; a biographical sketch by Hermann Krigar; and notes by Dvořák's great champion Leoš Janáček on his musical interpretation of the poems 'The wood dove'(or Turtle dove) and 'The golden spinning wheel'. The majority of the articles from Czech were translated by Tatiana Firkušný.

Music. Antonín Dvořák

1054 **Dvořák.**
John Clapham. Newton Abbot, England; London: David & Charles, 1979. 235p. bibliog.
Another full biography by John Clapham, this time of the Czech composer who enjoys the greatest popularity abroad. Clapham discusses Dvořák's principal compositions, provides a number of photographs and quotations from scores, a chronology, a list of compositions and a select bibliography, which covers many other biographies and critical works. John Clapham is also the author of *Dvořák's first cello concerto* (Leiden, the Netherlands: Clipers Press, 1985. 10p.), originally an article in *Music and Letters* (London), vol. 37, no. 4 (1995), p. 350-55, which analyses the work in fair detail. The text is supplemented by examples of the score of this concerto for violoncello with piano accompaniment. Clapham also wrote a short biography of Dvořák in *Late romantic masters: Bruckner, Brahms, Dvořák, Wolf, Deryck Cooke* (London: Macmillan, 1986. 401p. bibliog. The Composer Biography Series, The New Grove Dictionary of Music and Musicians). The description of Dvořák's life and work is on p. 205-99 and is supplemented by a substantial bibliography.

1055 **Dvořák in America: 1892-1895.**
Edited by John C. Tibbetts. Portland, Oregon: Amadeus Press, 1993. 447p. bibliog.
An anthology of articles by world authorities on Dvořák, who write about the composer from the viewpoint of a biographer, a musicologist, an educator, a historian, an archivist, a musician, a novelist, a media reporter and a psychoanalyst. The editor describes it as not a biography of Dvořák, but rather 'a portrait of a figure in a landscape'. The introduction is by Rudolf Firkušný. Several essays discuss and analyse Dvořák's 'American works'. Dvořák was the only great composer active as a pedagogue in the United States. The anthology demonstrates the impact Dvořák's visit had on the development of American music and the long-lasting impression and influence of his music on the United States.

1056 **Dvořák.**
Alec Robertson. London: Dent, 1945. 234p. bibliog.
Probably the best biography of Dvořák in English in its time, this was also translated into German. The biographical information provided is well balanced, and includes analysis of the composer's music. The book is well documented by extracts from musical scores and by photographs. Appendixes cover Dvořák's life and include a catalogue of his works.

1057 **Dvořák, his life and time.**
Neil Butterworth. Tunbridge Wells, England: Midas Books, 1980. 135p. bibliog.
Beautifully produced and richly documented by numerous interesting photographs, the book starts with Czech musical history and goes on to describe Dvořák's life, music and travels. The work is well researched but is intended for the general reader rather than the scholar.

1058 **Rethinking Dvořák: view from five countries.**
Edited by David R. Beveridge. Oxford: Clarendon Press, 1996.
305p.

This collection of studies, contributions to the Dvořák Sesquicentennial Conference and Festival in America (New Orleans, 1991), 'presents views on a panoply of topics that concern all phases of his career, his compositional process, his personality, the reception history of his music, and the musical content of his work in most major genres' ('Introduction', p. 10). The book is also a tribute to the dedicated Dvořák scholar Jarmil Burghauser. There are interesting appendices, including 'Dvořák's interviews with British newspapers', with critical commentary by David R. Beveridge (p. 281-93), contributors' profiles, and an index.

1059 **The chamber music of Antonín Dvořák.**
Otakar Šourek, English version by Roberta Finlayson Samsour.
Prague: Artia, [n.d.]. 177p.

An important work of reference which offers a detailed and systematic analysis of the sextet, quintets, quartets, trios, sonatas and other chamber music by Dvořák, richly documented by extracts from scores. Their melodic and rhythmical structure is also evaluated. Dvořák's chamber music is of considerable artistic value and has been, for both its content and form, a base for the development of this form of art worldwide. Dvořák's chamber music was, just like his other music, influenced by Czech folksongs and folkdance music. Šourek has been described as the founder of Dvořák research. The sister volume to this work is *The orchestral works of Antonín Dvořák* (Prague: Artia [1956]. 351p.) and *Antonín Dvořák: letters and reminiscences* (Prague: Artia, 1954. 234p.) both by Otakar Šourek and translated by Roberta Finlayson Samsour. The works listed here are just three of Šourek's many Dvořák titles. For others the reader is referred to the bibliography in John Clapham's *Dvořák* (q.v.).

1060 **Antonín Dvořák (8.9.1841-1.5.1904): bibliographical catalogue.**
Compiled by Blanka Červinková et al. Prague: Městská knihovna,
1991. 188p. bibliog.

This catalogue in Czech and English covers the published works of Dvořák, sound recordings of his works and books about the composer which can be found in the Town Library (Městská knihovna) of Prague and in the National Library (Národní knihovna) in Prague. The catalogue provides details of the editions of original versions, piano scores of concertos and vocal compositions, including arrangements by other composers. The substantial bibliography of 'Book literature on the life and work of Antonín Dvořák' (p. 133-74) will be of value to any student of Dvořák.

1061 **Antonín Dvořák, complete catalogue of works.**
Compiled by Ian T. Trufitt. London: Dvořák Society of Great
Britain and The Author, 1974. 31p.

Based on the thematic catalogue of Dvořák's work by Jarmil Burghauser, which was published in Prague in 1960. This simply produced volume provides the number in Burghauser's catalogue, opus number, the year of composition, the title of the work, and, in the majority of entries, some brief information which will be of interest to researchers. The compiler was the founder of the Dvořák Society. Jarmil Burghauser's *Antonín Dvořák: thematic catalogue, bibliography, survey of life and work*, referred to above, was published in a second, revised and supplemented edition in Prague by Supraphon in 1996. The text is in Czech, German and English.

1062 **Antonín Dvořák on records.**
    Compiled by John H. Yoell.   New York; London: Greenwood Press, 1991. 152p.

This selective discography '... aims to bring home the diversity and overall excellence of Dvořák's art as documented on a host of recordings from many nations'. This reference work is intended for collectors, musicians, teachers and librarians and is well organized and indexed. The introduction provides an overview of historical recordings.

Leoš Janáček

1063 **Turn of the century masters: Janáček, Mahler, Strauss, Sibelius.**
    John Tyrrell et al.   London: Macmillan, 1985. 324p. bibliog. (The Composers Biography Series, The New Grove Dictionary of Music and Musicians).

This includes, on page 1-77, a short biography of Leoš Janáček by John Tyrrell, with an extensive bibliography. The contribution on Gustav Mahler, on p. 81-181, is by Paul Banks and Donald Mitchell. Gustav Mahler was born in Kaliště, near Jihlava, the family later moving to Jihlava where Mahler spent his childhood and first attempted musical compositions. The coaching inn in Kaliště, where Mahler was born, is being turned into an arts complex. A report on the project has been written by J. Hendershott and published under the title 'Grand restoration of a humble birth place' (q.v.). There are many biographies of Gustav Mahler, but he has always been considered an Austrian musician; for that reason they fall outside the framework of the present bibliography. However, among the recent publications the reader should note *Gustav Mahler, an essential guide to his life and works*, by Julius Haylock (London: Pavillion, 1996), *The life of Mahler*, by Peter Franklin (Cambridge, England: Cambridge University Press, 1997), and *The real Mahler* by Jonathan Carr (London: Constable, 1997).

1064 **Dvořák, Janáček and their time.**
    Edited by Rudolf Pečman.   Brno, Czech Republic: Česká hudební společnost, 1985. 318p. bibliog. (Colloquia on the History and Theory of Music at the International Musical Festival Brno, vol. 19).

History, criticism and interpretation were the themes of the colloquium which took place in Brno in 1984. The articles in English were contributed by the chairman of the colloquium, Jiří Vysloužil, by Jarmil Burghauser and by British and American authorities on Czech music: John Clapham, Michael Beckerman and Hugh Macdonald. Dvořák and Janáček were contemporaries and shared a deep friendship although the differences in their musical styles were great, in particular in their vocal works. Dvořák's music is rooted in the 19th-century tradition, in the classical-romantic national movement, whereas Janáček is very much a 20th-century composer, a realist. His contribution to music was unique at the time. The 'Czechness' of the work of the two composers and the influence of Slavonic music on their work are given special attention. The articles are in English, German, Czech and French. An article by Michael Beckerman, 'In search of Czechness in music', was published in *19th Century Music*, vol. X, no. 1 (summer 1986).

1065 Leoš Janáček: the field that prospered.
Ian Horsbrugh. Newton Abbot, England; London: David & Charles; New York: Charles Scribner's, 1981. 327p. bibliog.
The authoritative work on Janáček in English, this is an illustrated biography written with the English reader in mind. Janáček himself visited England in 1926 and the appendices (p. 241-316) contain items relevant to England (his diary from 1926 and a list compiled from early BBC broadcasts of his work). The study examines all his works in detail, introducing related features of other contemporary music and elements from the Czech literary scene. The remaining appendices provide synopses of the operas and a classified, annotated list of the other compositions.

1066 Leoš Janáček: a biography.
Jaroslav Vogel, foreword by Charles Mackeras, translated by Geraldine Thomsen Muchová, new edition revised by Karel Janovický. London: Orbis Publishing, 1981. 439p. maps. bibliog.
The Moravian Janáček (1854-1928) is probably the Czech composer whose work is most performed in Britain today, largely due to the activities of Charles Mackerras, who studied music in Prague. The biography was re-published in 1997 in Czech (Prague: Academia, 1997. 2nd ed.), which is an indication that it has perhaps not been superseded by any superior work. Individual periods of Janáček's life are followed by detailed musicological analysis of the work from that period. The works are brought together in the appendix as a catalogue. The book contains a bibliography, which lists books, articles and Janáček's correspondence.

1067 Intimate letters: Leoš Janáček to Kamila Stösslová.
Edited and translated by John Tyrrell. London; Boston, Massachusetts: Faber & Faber, 1994. 397p. bibliog.
Several books of Janáček's correspondence have been published in Czech, for example his correspondence with Max Brod. Kamila Stösslová was the inspiration for many of Janáček's works and was supposed to have been the model for the heroine of *Káťa Kabanová*, although the story is taken from Ostrovskij's *The thunderstorm*, yet the relationship between Janáček and Stösslová has been taboo for many years. The history of Janáček's letters is described by Svatava Přibáňová in Appendix I, p. 371-73; Přibáňová published these letters in Czech in 1990. Janáček and Stösslová met at the Moravian spa town of Luhačovice when Janáček was sixty-three and Mrs Stösslová twenty-six. After the holiday Janáček started writing to Kamila. This is a comprehensive selection which concentrates on the almost daily letters of the final eighteen months of his life. The letters reveal a lonely man, 'an artist at the height of his creative powers and the beginning of his fame . . . and illuminate the inner life of a great operatic composer and provide vital clues to the nature of his creative genius'. The letters have been painstakingly researched and have numerous footnotes and explanations and the book includes some previously unknown photographs. John Tyrrell is the best authority in England on the life and works of Leoš Janáček.

1068 **My life with Janáček: the memoirs of Zdenka Janáčková.**
Edited and translated by John Tyrrell. London: Faber & Faber, 1998. 278p.

Michael Kennedy reviewed this book in the *Sunday Telegraph*, 27 December 1998, and found the composer's widow's memoirs painful but rewarding reading. John Tyrrell described how he traced the reminiscences of Janáček's widow in 'He was one of the great composers – and also the cruellest', *The Guardian*, 5 February 1999, Music feature p. 4-5. Mrs Janáček died in 1937; she dictated the memoirs to her secretary between 1933 and 1935, but the manuscript had been considered, until recently, too intimate for publication. John Tyrrell has authenticated, translated and edited the work, with the English reader in mind.

1069 **Leoš Janáček: leaves from his life.**
Edited and translated by Vilém Tausky, Margaret Tausky. London: Kahn & Averill, 1982. 159p.

The conductor Vilém Tauský was a pupil of Janáček. In this book he has gathered thirty of Janáček's newspaper articles, which were written in his capacity as a music critic and journalist and reveal the composer's personality and his responses to people, places and events. The editor added some of his own recollections of the great Moravian composer. Tauský's own biography has been published under the title *Vilem Tausky tells his story: a two part setting, recounted by Margaret Tausky* (London: Stainer & Bell, 1979).

1070 **Janáček's operas: a documentary account.**
John Tyrrell. Princeton, New Jersey: Princeton University Press, 1992. 405p. bibliog.

Drawing on Tyrrell's twenty-five years of work at the Janáček archives in Brno, this volume consists mostly of letters. Janáček was a prolific letter-writer and kept most of the correspondence he received. Thus a large quantity of material survived, 'rich and fascinating which provides unique insight into Janáček's working methods'. The material is well documented and annotated and is of great scholarly value. The volume includes a chronology of Janáček's life and works, chronologies of the operas, glossaries of names and terms, a list of sources and a bibliography. Most of the entries on individual operas are divided into: the genesis of the work; the chronology of composition; production; publication; performances abroad; translations; and dedications. John Tyrrell, a leading Janáček scholar, currently lectures in music at the University of Nottingham.

1071 **Janáček's tragic operas.**
Michael Evans. London: Faber & Faber, 1977. 284p. bibliog.

Contains essays on six of Janáček's operas: *Jenůfa*; *Destiny*; *Káťa Kabanová*, *Adventures of the vixen Bystrouška* (elsewhere known as *The cunning little vixen*); *From the house of the dead*; and *Makropulos* (also known as *The Makropulos affair*). Janáček's music was very different from that of his contemporaries. This work, like others, stresses the importance of Moravian, particularly east Moravian, folksongs on his music. The volume includes a synopsis of each opera and a description of the scores, and is documented by illustrations of the scores. Only Janáček's own final versions of the musical texts are discussed.

1072 **Svět Janáčkových oper. The world of Janáček's operas.**
Svatava Přibáňová, Zuzana Ledererová-Protivová, with an
introduction by Alena Němcová, translated into English by Vanda
Oakland, Oswald Oakland. Brno, Czech Republic: Moravské
zemské muzeum – Nadace Leoše Janáčka, 1998. 30p. + supplements
(63p. + 29p. + 290 plates).

The leading Czech expert on Janáček, musicologist Svatava Přibáňová from Brno,
lists all stage productions of Janáček's operas from 1894, when *Počátek románu* (The
beginning of a novel) was performed at the National Theatre in Brno, up to the most
recent productions from around the world. She also includes the critical reception of
Janáček's works. The second author, Zuzana Ledererová-Protivová, contemplates the
stage settings and the visual artistic appearance of each *mise-en-scène*. The book has
parallel Czech and English texts and its value is enhanced by 290 black-and-white and
colour photographs and a chronological summary of productions up to 1998. Another
volume on Janáček, published in Brno, is *Leoš Janáček: born in Hukvaldy* by Jarmila
Procházková and Bohumír Volný, translated by Timothy Stejskall (Brno: Moravian
Museum, 1995. 115p. bibliog.). Janáček acquired a house in Hukvaldy, his birthplace
in Northern Moravia, and spent his last days there.

1073 **Leoš Janáček: *Katya Kabanová.***
Compiled by John Tyrrell. Cambridge, England; London; New
York; New Rochelle, New York; Melbourne; Sydney: Cambridge
University Press, 1982. 234p. bibliog. (Cambridge Opera
Handbooks).

This opera assured Janáček's popularity in England after its production at Sadler's
Wells in 1951 and it is perhaps the most frequently performed of Janáček's operas in
Britain. It was based on the play, *The thunderstorm*, by Ostrovskij. The book contains
letters, reviews and other documents, analyses the various interpretations of the work,
and gives the history of some of the performances with supporting illustrations.

1074 **Janáček: Glagolitic Mass.**
Paul Wingfield. Cambridge, England: Cambridge University Press,
1992. 135p. bibliog.

Janáček started composing the *Glagolitic Mass* when he was seventy-two, at the peak
of his creativity. Although he was educated at a monastic school, he neglected sacred
music; this is, however, the best known of his non-operatic works and is considered a
'masterpiece of 20th century choral repertoire'. The author describes the genesis of
the Mass and its reception, and analyses the score and the Old Church Slavonic text.
The importance of Kamila Stösslová, the young woman he loved in the last,
artistically most vigorous and successful years of his life, is also noted.

1075 **Janáček as theorist.**
Michael Beckerman. Stuyvesant, New York: Pendragon Press,
1994. 141p. bibliog. (Studies in Czech Music, no. 3).

Offers an alternative view of Janáček's intellectual and creative personality, on the
abstract level. Janáček's musical works are enjoying enormous esteem and popularity,
yet his works as a theorist are hard to trace. Janáček's writings in music theory are

listed chronologically on p. 119-20, with a glossary of his terms on p. 133-36. The 'General bibliography' on p. 120-31 is good. As well as a composer and, to some, a controversial music teacher, Janáček was also a philosopher and prolific literary figure. It is a pity that the book was not proofread by a Czech speaker, since there are many Czech accents missing in the text. A further reading on the subject is *Janáček's uncollected essays on music*, selected, edited and translated by Mirka Zemanová, with a preface by John Tyrrell (London: Boyars, 1989).

1076 **Leoš Janáček's aesthetic thinking.**
       Jiří Kulka. Prague: Academia, 1990. 75p. bibliog. (Rozpravy
       Československé akademie věd. Řada společenských věd, vol. 100,
       no. 1).

Evaluates Janáček's work in music theory from the aesthetic viewpoint and attempts to solve some fundamental issues in the aesthetics of music. Janáček studied general aesthetics and was intensely interested in science and psychology; however, his musical art overshadowed his scholarly musico-aesthetic legacy.

1077 **Janáček-Newmarch correspondence.**
       Edited by Zdenka E. Fischmann. Rockville, Maryland: Kabel
       Publishers, 1986. 184p. bibliog.

Rosa Newmarch was an Englishwoman who visited Janáček in Brno and was instrumental in organizing his stay in England and in gaining recognition for his then modern music, previously unknown in England. This work reproduces letters written between 1922 and 1928; the letters in Czech were translated by the editor, who also added copious and extensive footnotes. However, a summary of the relationship between Janáček and Newmarch and of their joint activities is lacking. The letters disclose the diverse personalities of the two correspondents. The collection also includes letters by other persons, newspaper articles and photostats of the letters. Rosa Newmarch was the author of *The music of Czechoslovakia* (Oxford: Oxford University Press, 1942. 244p.), a book which has been described as enlightened but sometimes inaccurate and is widely referred to as the only book covering the totality of Czech music.

1078 **Janáček and Brod.**
       Charles Susskind, foreword by Sir Charles Mackerras. New Haven,
       Connecticut; London: Yale University Press, 1985. 169p. bibliog.

Leoš Janáček and Max Brod, a German-speaking Jewish literary figure, were friends and associates. Brod was an enthusiastic supporter and zealous promoter of Janáček's music, who translated Janáček's operas into German and was Janáček's first biographer. Among his translations of the operas, the most noteworthy was *Jenůfa*, which was prepared for its Viennese production. The author is concerned with the relationship between the two men and 'captures exactly the contrast between the artistic milieu of the Jewish intelligentsia in Prague, as represented by Brod, and the passionate Slavism of the nature-loving pantheist Janáček'.

1079 **The first editions of Leoš Janáček: a bibliographical catalogue with reproductions of title pages.**
Nigel Simeone. Tutzing, Germany: Hans Schneider, 1991. 316p. (Musikbibliographische Arbeiten, Bd. 11).

A well-presented, comprehensive and perfectionist's catalogue of all Janáček's printed works which follows the order of John Tyrrell's work in the Janáček section of *Turn of the century masters: Janáček, Mahler, Strauss, Sibelius* (q.v.). The works are arranged in chronological order of composition by genre. The Czech titles are used throughout, followed by the English translation. Each entry further includes the date of composition, number, date of publication, format, printing method and additional information such as any dedication, language, graphics or subsequent editions. Numerous appendices supplement this bibliography.

1080 **Janáček's works: a catalogue of the music and writings of Leoš Janáček.**
Nigel Simeone, John Tyrrell, Alena Němcová, catalogue of writings by Theodora Straková. Oxford: Clarendon Press, 1997. 522p. maps. bibliog.

Aimed at lovers of Janáček's music, this volume was written by leading Janáček scholars, and published in celebration of the seventieth birthday of Charles Mackerras, the great enthusiast for Janáček's work and his leading promoter in England, and of the eightieth birthday of Theodora Straková, who compiled the annotated list of articles, studies and essays in this volume. The general organization of the catalogue is explained in the introduction. The book also includes maps of Bohemia and Moravia in 1918 and of Brno, the city where Janáček spent most of his life, showing buildings associated with him. The catalogue proper has fifteen sections: 'Stage'; 'Liturgical'; 'Choral-orchestral'; 'Choral'; 'Vocal'; 'Orchestral'; 'Chamber'; 'Keyboard'; 'Unfinished'; 'Lost'; 'Planned'; 'Arrangements and transcriptions'; 'Folk music editions'; and 'Spurious'. The last and fifteenth chapter is Straková's compilation. The catalogue concludes with glossaries, an index of compositions, a general index and index of writings and a large bibliography (p. 467-82), which supports the author-date references in the catalogue entries. This perfectly compiled catalogue is enlivened by nine illustrations, which are facsimiles of autographs, title pages of operas, programmes and frontispieces. Rudolf Pečman, in *Hudební věda*, no. 2, (1998), recenze, acclaimed the work as a highly important reference book for the scholar and ordinary concert and opera lover alike, and recommends the adoption of the catalogue's numbering of Janáček's work to the Czech and international musical community, with designation *JW* (=Janáček's Works).

Bohuslav Martinů

1081 **Martinů.**
Brian Large. London: Duckworth, 1975. 198p. bibliog.
A detailed biography and musicography of a Moravian composer, and elusive artist, whose life and friendship with Vítka Kaprálová was the theme of Ken Russell's

333

televison film *The mystery of Dr. Martinů*. The book is rich in detail, illustrations and indexes. An informed biography of Martinů, by his long-standing friend Miloš Šafránek, *Bohuslav Martinů – the man and his music*, was translated from Czech into English (London: Dennis Dobson, 1946. 135p. bibliog.). It provides a description of Martinů's compositions prior to 1945. Further information on the life of the composer and the genesis of his major work is to be found in the intimate biography by his wife Charlotte Martinů, *My life with Martinů* (Prague: Orbis Press Agency, 1978. 176p.).

1082 **Martinů: out of exile.**
Programme editor Margaret Rand.   London: BBC Radio 3, 1998. 85p.

A programme to accompany a weekend of music, talks and films about the Czech composer at the London Barbican Centre, 16-18 January 1998. This excellent programme, with many photographs from Martinů's life, has a detailed chronology of the composer's life and work, a well-informed, long essay on each of the works performed, and translations of his first important work, the songs *Nipponari* (1912) which, it is believed, had not been translated previously. A slimmer sibling of the programme, yet equal in quality and depth, is another *Martinů: out of exile* (London: Guildhall School of Music and Drama in association with the BBC Symphony Orchestra, 1998. 29p.). This programme accompanied the BBC Symphony Orchestra's Martinů Festival at the London Barbican from 12-16 January 1998.

1083 **Bohuslav Martinů (8.12.1890-28.8.1959): bibliographical catalogue.**
Compiled by Blanka Červinková et al.   Prague: Panton, 1990. 206p. bibliog.

This publication in Czech and English comprises a catalogue of Martinů's compositions, including information on different editions of his musical works, a bibliography of his own musical writings and a substantial bibliographical survey of books, articles, reviews and studies on Martinů as found in specialized Czech libraries, archives and museums. The catalogue covers information in printed form as well as sound recordings.

1084 **Bohuslav Martinů anno 1981.** (Bohuslav Martinů in the year 1981.)
Edited by Jana Brabcová.   Prague: Česká hudební společnost, 1990. 339p. (Conferences on the History and Theory of Music at the International Musical Festival Prague Spring, vol. 1.)

Brings together papers from the International Musicological Conference, Prague, 26-28 May 1981. Most of the papers were presented in German but some were in English. The talks covered the following topics: 'Bohuslav Martinů in the development of music – the followers and the parallels'; 'Bohuslav Martinů's creative system'; 'Bohuslav Martinů – the value of contemporary cultural practice'; and 'Personal declarations by his interpreters'. 'Colloquium Bohuslav Martinů, his pupils, friends and contemporaries, Brno. 1990' was chaired by Jiří Vysloužil (proceedings published in Brno, Czech Republic: Masarykova univerzita, 1993).

1085 **Catalogue of autographs, manuscripts, facsimiles and other printed versions of Bohuslav Martinů compositions at the Bohuslav Martinů Museum. Soupis autografů, manuskriptů, faksimile a přidružených tisků skladeb Bohuslava Martinů ve fondech Památníku Bohuslava Martinů.**
Polička, Czech Republic: Městské Muzeum, 1997. 119p.

The Moravian town of Polička, the birthplace of Martinů, has a museum dedicated to him. This catalogue, published by the Museum, is similar to the previous entry and is also in Czech and English.

Food and Drink

1086 **Czech national cookbook.**
Hana Gajdošíková, translated by Jana Jennings. Prague: Jan Kanzelsberger Publishing House, 1998. 2nd ed. 165p.
A hardback with colour illustrations, which claims to include the typical dishes of Czech cuisine which Czech grandmothers used to cook and which a beginner will have no problem in preparing. The recipes for soups, sauces, cold dishes, meat dishes (a larger section, as the Czechs are great meat-eaters), fish, meatless dishes, assorted dumplings (the Czech national dish), fancy desserts, cakes (another large section) and festive dishes appear easy to follow and the ingredients should not be difficult to obtain in Britain or the United States. Many international cookery books include Czech dishes, some traditional (such as roast goose with sauerkraut and dumplings), and some which would surprise most Czech housewives.

1087 **Encyclopedia of Czech and Moravian wine.**
Vilém Kraus, Zdeněk Kuttelvašer, Robert B. Vurm, translated into English by Helena Baker. Prague: Published by Robert V. Vurm and Zuzana Foffová, 1997. 167p. bibliog.
This encyclopaedia is intended for the general public as well as for wine enthusiasts, and offers information on the following topics: how to understand wine; how to select and appreciate wine; vines and wines of the Bohemian and Moravian regions; information on the origin and symbolism of wine; and the history of Bohemian and Moravian viticulture and winemaking. The reader will also find advice on: wine buying, storing and tasting; how to match wine with food; a list of vine-growing districts of the Czech Republic; and the names of the most important wine-producers in the country. Some Bohemian and Moravian wines are exported, but most of the production, which is of not inconsiderable volume, is absorbed by the domestic market. Most general reference books on wine give space to Bohemian and Moravian wines, for example Hugh Jonson's very popular *Pocket guide to wines* (latest ed., London: Mitchell Beazley, 1999) has a section on the 'Wines of former Czechoslovakia'.

336

1088 **Good beer guide to Prague and to the Czech Republic.**
Graham Lees. St. Albans, England: CAMRA, 1996. 156p. maps.
This paperback, published by the Campaign for Real Ale, took a long time to
germinate. Graham Lees lived in Bavaria and used to visit the Czech Lands, whence
hops were exported long before William the Conqueror came to England. The country
enriched the vocabulary of most languages with the word 'pilsener', and holds the
world record for the highest number of pints consumed per capita per year. The author
conscientiously tasted all the famous brands as well as just about every product of
smaller local breweries, and made a brave effort to visit many pubs in Prague and in
the rest of Bohemia and in Moravia. He takes the reader on a tour of twenty-five
Czech breweries, gives sound advice on how to get to a good pint quickly, and
includes a few useful phrases, albeit not very grammatically expressed, in Czech. His
forecast for the traditional Czech brewing industry is not very optimistic: in the near
future, market forces may reduce the number of breweries and thus limit the wide
selection of beers which is available today. A more substantial book on Czech
drinking customs, so far available in Czech only, is *Hospody a pivo v české
společnosti* (Pubs and beer in Czech society), edited by Vladimír Novotný (Prague:
Academia, 1997. 259p.).

1089 **A good guide to beer-halls of Prague.**
László Polgár, Gyorgy Simko, translated by Babel services,
illustrated by Haba Davidová. Prague: Mladá Fronta, 1992. 136p.
map.
A pocket guide with a map which indicates thirty-two beer-halls in the centre of
Prague. There are a few comments on each of the pubs listed as to the type of beer
served and each of the entries gives the telephone number and address, opening times,
accessibility by public transport (including the nearest tram and bus stop), the type of
any food served, the seating and pub category. There is a physical description of each
building, and quotations describing Prague, from various authors, are given.

1090 **The world guide to beer.**
Edited by Michael Jackson. London: New Burlington Books, 1982.
255p. maps.
Michael Jackson is a leading specialist on beer, wine and whisky. His history of beer
and brewing, *World guide to beer*, was first published in London in 1977 by Mitchell
Beazley, and again published as *New world guide to beer* by Bloomsbury in 1988 and
under the same title also in 1988 in Philadelphia, by Running Press. The edition given
here has a separate chapter on Czechoslovakia (p. 25-35), which includes many
photographs and a map. The history of beer in the Czech Lands is given in outline and
Jackson also provides a guide to all major, and many minor, beers and breweries.
Many types of Czech beers are widely available in Britain and in other Western
countries in supermarkets and other stores.

The Media and Publishing

1091 **The post-socialist media: what power the West? The changing landscape in Poland, Hungary and the Czech Republic.**
Liana Giorgi, with a foreword by Philip Schlesinger, and with the collaboration of Ronald J. Pohoryles. Aldershot, England: Avebury; Brookfield, Vermont: Ashgate Publishing Company, 1995. 151p. bibliog.

A collection of papers on the restructuring of the media sector after 1989. Section four, 'The old days are gone: the case of the media in the Czech Republic' (p. 104-23), is by Barbara Köpplová and Jan Jirák. The other, general chapters also allude to the Czech Republic. They analyse the impact of the transition to a market economy on the media, the effect of the political changes, the legislation and regulations relating to the press and the audio-visual sector, freedom of the press and the advent of plurality of opinion, and the economic transformation of the Czech media scene. The contribution of Köpplová and Jirák expands on the political and economic transformation and re-definition, supplies background by describing the situation prior to 1989 and discusses trends within the Czech media after 1989. The book concludes with a few statistical tables on ownership structure, readership and circulation.

1092 **Media beyond socialism: theory and practice in East-Central Europe.**
Slavko Splichal. Boulder, Colorado; San Francisco; Oxford: Westview Press, 1994. 177p. bibliog.

A first book to analyse 'the changing relationship among the media, state, economy and civil society' in the period of transition from socialism to Western-type democracies. Splichal, a Professor of communication science and sociology of information processes at the University of Ljubljana, examines the role of media and the relevance of mass communications in the democratization process. The book has a sizeable bibliography (p. 153-62). Splichal is a co-editor, with Janet Wasko, of a complimentary book on political aspects of communication, *Communication and democracy* (Norwood, New Jersey: Ablex Pub. Corp., 1993).

338

1093 **Le marketing en Europe centrale.** (Marketing in Central Europe.) Čedomir Nestorovič. Paris: Vuibert, 1995. 139p. (Gestion internationale).

An illustrated paperback which supports its findings by graphs and tables. The topics are the mass media, marketing and advertising in Central Europe. The book has a subject index.

1094 **Die Massenmedien der sozialistischen Tschechoslowakei.** (Mass media in socialist Czechoslovakia.) Peter Löbl. Munich: Tuduv-Verlagsgesellschaft, 1986. 383p. bibliog.

A detailed study of the Czech press, radio and television from 1945 to 1985. Löbl first examines chronologically the role of the mass media in the recent history of Czechoslovakia: the struggle for the victory of socialism, censorship, media activities surrounding the Prague Spring of 1968, the period of normalization, and the contemporary situation. Subsequently, he devotes a substantial chapter to the press in Czechoslovakia and another larger section to radio and television broadcasting. The author incorporates statistical data into the study and adds a substantial bibliography, of mostly German and Czech books and articles.

1095 **The development of the Czech media since the fall of Communism.** Steve Kettle. *Journal of Communist Studies and Transition Politics*, vol. 12, no. 4 (December 1996), p. 42-60.

The author feels that, despite considerable progress, the Czech media could not yet be considered independent and free. The working methods of journalists are still influenced by the old attitudes and this applies no less to their own perception of their role. Media outlets multiplied in the early 1990s but later there were many amalgamations and closures, which were the result of such commercial pressures as foreign investment. Old staff were dismissed and new people were recruited by the commercial media and this had an effect on quality. The pursuit of popularity and the poor professional standards lead the author to question the role of the media in the political life of the country.

1096 **Almanach Labyrint 1994.** Edited by Joachim Dvořák. Prague: Labyrint, 1994. 440p.

This is an annual venture, listing not only 350 alphabetically ordered Czech (and some Slovak) publishing houses (the majority in Prague), but also their publishing plans and books in print. In addition it contains a directory of 530 bookshops (Prague shops on p. 377-85) and specialist second-hand bookshops (those in Prague are on p. 421-22). The publisher provided similar information, in English, in *Books from the Czech Republic (an official publication of the Ministry of Culture of the Czech Republic)* (1995. 176p.).

339

1097 **Boom-time for Bonton.**
Andrew Clark. *Financial Times*, 19 August 1996, p. 13.
A profile of Bonton, a company which started as a four-men band and developed into a conglomerate of fifteen companies comprising radio, film and music interests. This successful company benefited from a gap in the market for home-grown music and entertainment after the Velvet Revolution, which had occurred six-and-a-half years previously.

1098 **Boxed in: East European television.**
The Economist, vol. 351, no. 8117 (1-7 May 1999), p. 94.
Most of this report from Prague is on the Czech Republic's leading television station Nova, the most profitable operation of Bermuda-based Central European Media Enterprises (CME), which has commercial television channels in seven East and Central European countries. Some strange deals had been going on within Nova, initiated by the local management.

1099 **Hate speech.**
Index on Censorship, vol. 27, no. 1 (January/February 1998),
p. 30-59, 61-71.
This article questions who is in fact paying the price for freedom of speech and how high this price should be allowed to be. It suggests that there are circumstances which justify censorship, or even criminalization of speech, to protect vulnerable citizens. One of the examples given of hate language and media influence is the role the media had in inciting the departure of Roma from the Czech Republic and Slovakia to Great Britain.

Newspapers and Periodicals

Czech-language newspapers and periodicals

1100 **Lidové noviny.** (The People's Paper.)
Prague: Lidové noviny a.s., 1988- . daily. (Refounded in 1988; originally Brno, 1893- .)

Widely, but not entirely accurately, perceived as the newspaper of the government, this is nevertheless usually fairly pro-government. It has changed character considerably since the years 1948-88 when the same title was a fringe paper, nominally the organ of the Czechoslovak People's Party (one of the parties which enjoyed a nominal existence side by side with the Communist Party, but which lacked any real political power), and is now more like its inter-war antecedent. It appears in both Prague (for Bohemia) and Brno (for Moravia) editions, and is one of the few newspapers to take over occasional untranslated items from the Slovak press. It has a good weekend supplement. The Czech-language website 'Trafika' (http://www.trafika.cz) contains articles from this newspaper, among articles from other daily newspapers which are listed as entries below, such as *Mladá fronta DNES* (q.v.).

1101 **Mladá fronta DNES.** (Young Front Today.)
Prague: Mladá fronta, 1945- . daily.

One of the most popular serious dailies, as it also was in the days when it was called *Mladá fronta* and served, nominally, the 'youth' wing of the Communist Party (the Socialist Union of Youth). It has a good weekend colour supplement.

1102 **České noviny.** (Czech News.)
http://ctk.ceskenoviny.cz

ČTK, the official and original Czech press agency, brings full daily coverage. *Neviditelný pes* (The Invisible Dog) is a daily newspaper available only on the

Internet. It combines the normal functions of a newspaper, but with a highly informal and occasionally viciously critical or satirical bent as regards Czech affairs, with shades of tabloid journalism.

1103 **Večerník Praha.** (Evening Paper Prague.)
Prague: Večerník Praha, 1955- . daily.

This is the descendant of *Večerní Praha* (Evening Prague), which used to be published by the Prague City Committee of the Communist Party of Czechoslovakia. For many Praguers it is their staple news source, with television listings and good sports coverage.

1104 **Český dialog. Měsíčník pro Čechy doma i ve světě.** (Czech Dialogue. A Monthly for Czechs at Home and Abroad.)
Prague: Martin Jan Stránský Foundation, 1991- . monthly.

This magazine is addressed pre-eminently to people in the Czech diaspora and accordingly carries items – of a historical, cultural or current-affairs nature – about, or of interest to, their communities. It enjoys the blessing of the foreign ministry, which is one of the distributors; it is regularly available at Czech embassies and cultural centres. It has a website: www.cesky-dialog.cz. Of a similar nature is *Nová přítomnost. New Presence* (Prague: Martin Stránský Foundation, 1996-), published in Czech and English. The website is at www.enp.cz.

English-language newspapers and periodicals

1105 **Prague Post.**
Prague: 1991- . weekly.

This began as an amateur paper for the huge floating American population that drifted into Prague after 1989. It is still heavily focused on that readership, for which it seeks to interpret current Prague and Czech affairs, as well as serving as a listings paper, cultural review, travel and tourism guide and local gossip sheet. *Prague Post Newspaper* is on the Internet at www.centraleurope.com/media/praguepost/ppmiss.html.

1106 **Daily News.**
Prague: Czech News Agency, ČTK, 1918- . daily (weekdays).

Provides political, economic, social, cultural, religious and sports news, as well as a review of the morning's Czech and Slovak press, although the bias is towards Czech news, since there is an independent Slovak news agency (TK SR), and extracts from speeches by statesmen politicians. ČTK was originally established as an independent news agency on 28 October 1918 when Czechoslovakia came into being. The 'In focus' section analyses topical aspects of Czech life. A sister publication is *Business News* (q.v.).

1107 The Fleet Sheet.
Prague: E.S. Best, 1992- . daily.
A one-page English-language news sheet which is very popular with the expatriate business community. It offers concise summaries of daily business and political news in the Czech press. Rates descend from the early daily fax (9 am) to a Friday mailing of the week's issue.

1108 Golem: Prague Cultural Review.
Edited by Jan Dvořák, Miloš Petana. Prague: Scéna, 1990- . twice-yearly.
This seasonal review in English and German, which appears sporadically and is aimed at English and German tourists, includes essays and articles on all aspects of Prague cultural life. Examples of sections are: 'What's on', 'Theatre', 'Cinema', 'Comments', 'Museums, galleries and exhibitions', 'Entertainment', 'Children', and 'Divine services'.

1109 Resources.
Prague: Resources, 1992- . quarterly.
An important and, due to its quarterly update, indispensable register of addresses and telephone numbers of businesses, ministries and hotels – among many other categories – which is designed specifically for English and German speakers, but is also useful to the locals. The coverage is the Czech Republic and Slovakia and it contains a complete and updated list of foreign companies operating there, services, such as schools, both international and Czech, shops, ticket agencies and clubs.

1110 Welcome to the Heart of Europe.
Prague: Theo Publishing, in cooperation with the Czech Foreign Ministry. 1994- . bimonthly.
A glossy general-interest publication, palatably propagandistic, with well-written articles on arts and crafts, folklore, politics, industry, history, personalities, etc. In short, it covers 'culture' in the broadest sense of the word.

1111 Český klub – Czech Club.
Prague: Made in . . . (Publicity), 1995- . quarterly.
This glossy periodical's mission statement says: 'The primary intention of this representative revue with its rich pictorial material is to promote the Czech Republic abroad. We would like not only to present the natural and cultural beauty of our country, but also its economic and entrepreneurial potential, as well as devoting some space to individual firms and personalities'. It also pays attention to fashion, sport and leisure and carries numerous advertisements. The publisher is a leading advertising agency. The entire magazine is published with parallel Czech and English texts.

1112 BCSA Newsletter.
London: British Czech and Slovak Association, 1990- . bimonthly.
Available only through membership of the British Czech and Slovak Association, which came into being as a new type of friendship association linking interested Britons with post-revolutionary Czechoslovakia, and then the two daughter states, the Newsletter carries regular items about cultural, political, economic and media affairs,

343

and some relevant advertising, concerning the two countries in general, but often with a strong Prague-centred content.

1113 SWB BBC Monitoring: Summary of World Broadcasts. Part 2: Central Europe, The Balkans.
Reading, England: BBC Monitoring, 1996- . daily.
SWB publishes material from foreign media, including verbatim texts and excerpts, BBC Monitoring editorial accounts of original pieces, compilations of reports and other supplementary material. All items have an indication of their origin, with comments in parenthesis where meanings of passages are unclear or indistinct. The *Summary* includes items on events in the Czech Republic. The number of pages varies from day to day.

Scholarly journals

1114 BASEES Newsletter.
London: British Association for Slavonic and East European Studies, 1992- . twice-yearly. bibliog.
This newsletter provides information on studies, prizes and reviews, as well as congresses, business, study and research trips, announcements and information.

1115 Bohemia: Zeitschrift für Geschichte und Kultur der Böhmischen Länder. (A Journal of History and Civilization in East Central Europe.)
Munich: Collegium Carolinum, R. Oldenburg Verlag, 1960- . biannual.
The contributions in this periodical are mostly by Germans and the content covers all periods of Czech history and civilization, and especially, but not solely, events and affairs with a Jewish or German connection. It was originally published by the Verein für Geschichte der Deutschen in den Sudenten Ländern (Society for the History of Germans in the Sudetenland). The journal contains an extensive review section with the emphasis being on titles in German. The text is in German, and summaries are in Czech, English and French.

1116 Canadian American Slavic Studies – Revue Canadienne Americaine d'Etudes Slaves.
Los Angeles: University of California, 1967- . quarterly.
This periodical originally had the title 'Canadian Slavic Studies – Revue Canadienne d'Études Slaves' and occasionally appears as an annual – the 1998 issue contained the spring, summer, autumn and winter issues. It is one of the main North American Slavonic Studies periodicals from countries which have a sizeable Slav immigration population. It occasionally carries items with a Czech interest, as well as being a source for reviews and bibliographical information. The text is in English, French, German and Russian.

1117 **Czech Language News.**
Philadelphia: North American Association of Teachers of Czech,
1993- . biannual.
Available to members of the Association, which has a growing membership outside North America, particularly in Europe, the newsletter carries articles on the state of Czech, reviews of new textbooks – often the sole source of commentary on the many new textbooks for foreigners emanating from Prague (and elsewhere in the Czech Republic) – and details of some of the language summer schools held in Prague.

1118 **East European Quarterly.**
Boulder, Colorado: East European Quarterly, University of Colorado,
1967- . quarterly.
Czech topics are included in this periodical fairly regularly. The contributors and editors are distinguished Slavic scholars. The text is in English, French and German and the quarterly is also available on-line.

1119 **Europe-Asia Studies.**
Abingdon, England: Carfax Publishing for University of Glasgow,
1993- . quarterly.
This periodical used to be called *Soviet Studies* (1949-93) and it remains one of the main outlets for Scottish academics working in the field. The coverage of the subjects is broad, with the emphasis being on the socio-political and economic sphere. It is also available on-line at http://www.carfax.co.uk/eas-ad.htm.

1120 **ICEES International Newsletter.**
[s.n.]: The International Council for Central and East European
Studies, 1992- . irregular.
The place of publication of this newsletter varies. It includes coverage of the Czech Republic and offers details of international news and views, research, new titles, publications and conferences.

1121 **Slavic Review: American Quarterly of Russian, Eurasian and East European Studies.**
Cambridge, Massachusetts: American Association for the
Advancement of Slavic Studies, 1942- . quarterly.
The emphasis in this, one of the main US periodicals on Slavic studies, is on literature, history and politics, the Czech Republic being just one of the countries covered quite regularly. Of great value is the extensive review section.

1122 **Slavonica.**
Manchester, England: University of Manchester, 1993- . twice-yearly.
Formerly entitled *Scottish Slavonic Review*, this covers the languages, literatures, history and culture of Russia and Central and Eastern Europe. It includes an editorial and index of contents, as well as book reviews, scholarly articles, original documents, translations of poetry and short stories, mostly in English.

1123　**Slavonic and East European Review.**
　　　Leeds, England: W. S. Maney & Son, 1922- . quarterly.
A serious scholarly periodical covering all aspects of the languages, literatures and history of all of Eastern Europe, although the emphasis tends to be historical. Czechoslovakia, and now the Czech Republic, have always been fairly well represented among the contributions. The long review section provides a valuable guide to recent relevant publications. The periodical was formerly published in London by the Modern Humanities Research Association.

Business periodicals

1124　**Business Central Europe.**
　　　Edited by Béla Papp.　Vienna: Economist Group, 1992- .
　　　bimonthly.
A sister magazine to *The Economist*, which is an excellent source of business information. The coverage is wide: politics and economics, business and feature, including editorial, letters, statistics, city focus, cover story and survey. This is a glossy publication, averaging seventy-four pages, written by an editorial board drawn from across Central Europe.

1125　**Central European Business Weekly.**
　　　Prague: Central European Business Weekly, 1993- . weekly.
A small tabloid which includes English-language news features, market reports and results, regional market news, currencies, regional banking reviews, a leader and advertisements. The weekly usually has sixteen pages and two pages of news are dedicated to the Czech Republic.

1126　**Business Update C & S.**
　　　Switzerland: Business Update Series, 1992- . twice-weekly.
This periodical publication is also distributed to subscribers by fax, twice-weekly, and is similar to the previous item in that it provides English-language summaries of features from Slovak and (mostly) Czech newspapers and other media, focusing on business, legal, political and statistical items. Daily Czech exchange rates as given by the Czech National Bank are included, as well as news of selected shares from the Prague Stock Exchange.

1127　**Eastern European Business Quarterly: Business Opportunities in
　　　the Czech Republic, Poland, CIS, Slovakia, Hungary, Romania.**
　　　Chester, England: VP International, 1995- . quarterly.
An information sheet on business in Central and Eastern Europe.

1128 **Journal of Russian and East European Economic Affairs.**
London: ABREES, 1993- . annual.
Contains English-language summaries and abstracts of articles, notes, reports from newspapers and periodicals and English translations of the titles of articles on the region's countries, including the Czech Republic. The main Czech source is the daily *Hospodářské noviny*, the lighter Czech equivalent to Britain's *Financial Times*.

1129 **Revue L'Est: Économie et Techniques de Planification, Droit et Sciences Sociales.** (Eastern Journal: Planning Economy and Techniques, Law and Social Sciences.)
Paris: Centre National de la Recherche Scientifique, 1970- . quarterly.
A major periodical on the subject of its subtitle, which actually gives the publication more breadth than at first sight. The articles are in French, but there are summaries in English and the contents page is also reproduced in English.

1130 **Business News.**
Prague: Czech News Agency, ČTK, 1918- . daily (weekdays).
Provides a daily economic news service from the republic. The information offered here is detailed and covers economic development, legislation, statistics, analyses and reforms, exchange rates and advertises possible business ventures for foreign companies.

1131 **The Prague Business Journal.**
Prague: New World Publishing, 1996- . weekly.
The content of this Prague-orientated weekly is business news, question-and-answer interviews, features and articles, details of capital markets and a company index. It includes items on property and development, a regional round-up and an opinion page.

Archives, Libraries, Museums and Galleries

Archives and libraries

1132 **Guide to libraries in Central and Eastern Europe.**
Compiled by Maria Hughes, with the assistance of Paul Wilson.
London: British Library, Science Reference and Information
Services, 1992. 82p. maps.

A guide to libraries which have major collections of national importance or of relevance to Western information needs. The then Czechoslovakia is given thirty-four entries; the section on the United Kingdom includes collections that are 'centres of excellence' for Central and Eastern European studies. Each entry in the guide includes, where available, the library's title in English and Czech, its address, telephone and fax numbers, name of head librarian or director, stock, hours, services and publications. Each country chapter includes a simple map and the guide has a subject index and a geographical index.

1133 **Libraries of the Czech Republic. Bibliotheken der Tschechischen Republik.**
Prague: Ministry of Culture of the Czech Republic, 1996. 125p. maps.

This official publication of the Ministry of Culture provides brief and comprehensive information about the public libraries on the territory of the Czech Republic. The bilingual work, the first of its kind, offers a historical survey of the development of libraries in the Czech Lands, a summary of the present Czech library system, the standing of libraries from the legislative viewpoint, and the role of the Ministry of Culture. The core of the publication is the 'Library address list', which is divided into two sections. The first section deals with the National Library of the Czech Republic, the state research libraries and the largest departmental libraries. The address and contact person are given and a brief description of the stocks and activities. The second section covers district and municipal libraries. Here the address list contains

348

only one library from each administrative area. The book also gives a survey of professional library organizations, regular library events and specialist publications emanating from the Czech Republic.

1134 **Czechoslovakia.**
Herbert Schur. London: British Library, 1990. 87p. map. bibliog. (The Research and Development Department of the British Library: National Surveys of Library and Information Services, no. 3).
This survey (intended for the use of professional librarians and information scientists) of the library and information services in the republic covers national, public, academic and technical libraries, collections of literature and libraries for the physically handicapped. The various information systems are also examined: the scientific, technological and economic system and the educational sector support system. Schur also includes sections on professional manpower, professional associations and educational cooperation. The survey has a number of tables, some illustrations and the author's notes on sources of information.

1135 **Sdružení knihoven České republiky – The Czech Republic Library Association – Bibliotheksverbant der Tschechischen Republik. Rok 1998. (Year 1998.)**
Edited by Jaromír Kubíček. Brno, Czech Republic: Sdružení knihoven ČR, 1998. 53p.
The annual report of the Czech Library Association. Despite the multilingual title, the contents are solely in Czech. The articles' emphasis, in the year in question, is the use of statistics in librarianship. It also reports on recent projects and publications, but it is included herein chiefly for the directory of member-libraries of the Association (p. 46-51), which includes contact names, telephone numbers and contact addresses.

1136 **Historical account of the development of scholarly libraries in Bohemia up to the establishment of the State Library in Prague.**
Děvana Pavlík. Fellowship thesis, Library Association, London, 1976. 333p. bibliog.
As the title indicates, this thesis is concerned with the development of learned libraries, i.e. libraries which collect, preserve and make available to readers literature for study and research. Their history is traced back to the first collections formed by the monasteries and the scholarly elite and is described against the background of historical and social events. Library development is divided into several distinct periods with general characteristics that influenced the founding, function and organization of libraries. Besides the growth of the country's largest libraries attention is paid to the development of smaller specialized collections and of libraries of various professional institutions. The last chapters deal with the progress made after the founding of Czechoslovakia in 1918, and the fundamental changes within Czech librarianship after 1948, characterized by the re-orientation of librarianship towards the Marxist-Leninist conception. The thesis ends with the establishment of the State Library and the passing of the Library Act for the Unified System of Libraries in 1959. A chronology of book- and library-orientated events from 1863-1959 is appended.

1137 Národní knihovna ČR: průvodce historií. **National Library of the
Czech Republic: guide to the history.**
Edited by Eva Novotná. Prague: National Library of the Czech
Republic, 1997. 48p.

The Klementinum, one of the largest and most beautiful complexes of baroque
buildings in the centre of Prague, houses the core collections of the Czech National
Library. This short history, in Czech and in English, starts with the 11th century, when
a chapel dedicated to St Clement stood on the site, and continues through to the 16th
century when the Jesuits founded a Latin school there, St Clement's College, which
later became the main library of the Czech Lands. The slim paperback has good,
colour photographs of this seat of learning. The picture of the Baroque Library,
completed in 1727 by the great Kilián Ignác Dienzenhofer (1689-1751), is an example
of the beautiful interiors in this old building. The 'Historical summary' (p. 45-47) is a
chronology in English. The book was published on the occasion of the 220th
anniversary of the opening of the library to the public.

1138 **Klementinská knihovna. The Clementinum Library. Bibliotheca
semper viva.**
Kateřina Hekrdlová, Zdeněk Franc. Prague: National Library of the
Czech Republic, 1997. 57p.

Another publication on the occasion of the library's 220th year of service to the
public. The content of this illustrated bilingual paperback is the history of the library
and biographies of its prominent librarians.

1139 **Knihovna národního muzea: zámecká knihovna Český Krumlov.
The National Museum Library: Castle Library of the Český
Krumlov.**
Compiled by Jitka Šimáková. Prague: Mezinárodní asociace
bibliofilů, 1995. 235p. bibliog.

The mediaeval town of Český Krumlov, a jewel of Southern Bohemia, is dominated
by its castle. This introduction to the castle library, published on the occasion of the
nineteenth Congress of Bibliophiles in Prague in 1995, also includes an annotated list
of the most precious books held there.

1140 **Retrospective conversion in Czech libraries.**
Bohdana Stoklasová, Miroslav Bareš. Prague: Národní knihovna,
1995. 39p.

This publication, intended for librarians and cataloguers, identifies the problems of
retrospective conversion of large catalogues, some several hundred years old. The
main problems of computerization are: shortage of funds; shortage of technological
equipment; lack of know-how; lack of knowledge of international standards; and the
size and content of the catalogues, the problem with content being old material and
old catalogue cards and cards of non-roman script.

Museums and galleries

1141 The Museum of Czech Literature: Prague.
Translated by Karel Kovanda, photographs by Jaromír Kuchař, Miloš
Novotný. Prague: The Museum of Czech Literature, 1969. 87p.
This guide is rather outdated now. The Museum of Czech Literature (Památník
národního písemnictví) was founded in 1953, the objective being to document the
development of Czech literature from the very beginnings of Slavonic writings to the
present. Also part of the Museum are the Strahov Library, which goes back to the 12th
century (originally a Romanesque building and a part of the Prague Castle complex),
and a large literary archive. The Museum houses some 900,000 volumes, of which
4,000 are manuscripts. It still awaits a new permanent home.

1142 200 years, National Gallery in Prague: 1796-1996.
Edited by Vít Vlnas, photography by Milan Posselt et al, translation
by Joanne P. Domin. Prague: Gallery, in cooperation with the
National Gallery of Prague, 1995. [unpaginated].
In 1796, the Society of Patriotic Friends of Art founded, from gifts from private
collections, a Picture Gallery which was accessible to public. The National Gallery
was an heir to this collection, which over the two centuries grew into a notable
collection of art and today comprises hundreds of thousands of paintings, sculptures
and graphic sheets. This publication is beautifully produced and balances well the
amount of text on the history of the Gallery and beautiful colour and monochrome
illustrations. The slim, large-format book has several supplements: a historical-
chronological survey of the history of the National Gallery; and lists of past
presidents, inspectors, chairmen of the curatorium and directors of the Gallery.

1143 Bulletin of the National Gallery in Prague.
Prague: Národní galerie v Praze, 1991- .
Published in Czech, English and German and addressed to the art enthusiast and art
historian, the bulletin features articles on items in the Prague's National Gallery, on
paintings and painters, art history, analyses of drawings and three-dimensional
objects, from various periods and styles, from altarpieces to Cubism. The issues are
illustrated throughout with black-and-white and colour plates.

1144 The National Museum of Prague.
http://www.nm.cz
This site offers information on the history of the museum, its main building, its
collections, concerts and lectures given within the complex, on periodicals and other
publications. The National Museum celebrated its 180th anniversary in 1999.

**1145 Historický ústav armády České republiky. The History Institute
of the Army of the Czech Republic.**
Prague: Ministerstvo obrany České republiky, 1997. 76p. bibliog.
A bilingual, paperback publication in A4 format with dozens of beautiful colour
photographs. This Prague institute is a research museum, library and archive

establishment. It is a body of the Czech Academy and is subordinate to the Ministry of Defence. This is a guide to the institution and its branches, providing its history and explaining the evolution of the institute and mergers of various organizations (e.g. Memorial of Resistance, Archives of the Legions, Memorial of Liberation). The institute was given its present name in 1993. The book has sections on 'Military history', 'The Army Museum', 'The Aviation Museum', 'The Military Technical Museum', 'The Military History Library' and 'The Military History Archives'. There is also a list of publications of the History Institute of the Army (p. 64-67).

1146 **European fajáns: from the collections of the Museum of Decorative Arts in Prague: Troja Castle, 1992-1993.**
Jana Kybalová. Prague: MDA. Prague Gallery, 1992. 80p. bibliog.

This catalogue of the museum's exhibits is introduced by the history of the faience, or delftware, in Europe. Deserved attention is given to cultural phenomenon of the 'Habener faience' from Southeast Moravia. The Habener were religious and social reformists who settled in that region and excelled in tin-glazed pottery with floral patterns. The museum houses, in addition to faiences from the Czech Lands and Slovakia, objects representative of Italian maiolica and faiences from Switzerland, Spain, Austria, France, Germany and Russian.

1147 **The State Jewish Museum in Prague.**
Text prepared by a team of employees of the State Jewish Museum in Prague, translated by Joy Turner-Kadečková. Prague: Olympia, 1978. 40p.

This slim introductory guide to the museum also serves as a historical background to Prague's one-time quite large Jewish community. It describes not only the six synagogues and the famous old cemetery, but also the various collections – textiles, artefacts, paintings, and exhibits connected with the Second World War, during which many thousands of Czech Jews perished – and the library, which contains many valuable prints dating from the 16th to the 18th century. *Jewish art treasures from Prague. The State Jewish Museum in Prague and its collections*, edited and with a foreword by Professor C. R. Dodwell (London: Whitworth Art Gallery/Lund Humphries, 1980. 151p.), is a catalogue of an exhibition held in 1980 at the Whitworth Art Gallery in Manchester, England. It includes 300 examples of Judaica from the State Jewish Museum in Prague, ranging from the late Renaissance to the mid-20th century, and the colour plates provide examples of textiles, books, monuments and paintings. An older publication, a catalogue of the collection of Jewish textiles, is *The synagogue treasures of Bohemia and Moravia*, by Hana Volavková, translated by G. Hort and Roberta Finlayson Samsour (Prague: Sfinx, 1949. 39p.).

1148 **The encyclopedia of European historical weapons.**
Vladimír Dolínek, Jan Durdík, translated by Petr Nykrýn, photographs by Pavel Vácha, Dagmar Landová, line-drawings by Petr Moudrý. London: Hamlyn, 1993. 351p. bibliog.

The encyclopaedia is based mostly on the collections in Czech museums and Czech country houses. The museums are: the Museum of Capital City of Prague (Museum hlavního města Prahy); the National Museum (Národní museum); the Museum of Decorative Arts (Umělecko-průmyslové museum); the Military Museum (Vojenské museum); and the Museum of the Hussite Revolutionary Movement (Museum husitského revolučního hnutí) in Tábor. Among the country houses, the collections which were studied are in Žleby, Orlík, Frýdlant v Čechách, Hluboká nad Vltavou, Konopiště and Mnichovo Hradiště. The scope of the encyclopaedia is weapons in the 'proper sense of the word', meaning arms, so no armour is included. The content is divided into edged weapons, mechanical shooting weapons, firearms, combined weapons and air-operated weapons. Each of these sections includes a definition of the type of weapon and a chronological survey of its evolution. The sections are further subdivided into categories of weapons. There are 420 illustrations within the text, mostly photographs; the 'Bibliography' (p. 347-48) is necessarily a selection of the most significant books and periodicals on arms generally since the volume of books on the topic is vast. The books and periodicals listed here are mostly in English and German. There is also an 'Index of arms manufacturers and designers' (p. 349-50) and an 'Index of monogramists' (p. 351).

1149 **Lapidarium of the National Museum, Prague. Guide to the permanent exhibition of Czech sculpture in stone of the 11th to 19th centuries in the pavilion of the lapidarium in the exhibition grounds in Prague.**
Jiří Fajt, Lubomír Sršeň, translated from the Czech by Joanne Dominová. Prague: Asco, 1993. 112p.

A readable, lucid description of the exhibition, its characteristics, history and technology. The Museum houses a collection of about 2,000 statues and architectural fragments.

1150 **Stálá expozice českého umění 20. století. Permanent exhibition of 20th century Czech art: Moravská galerie, Brno.**
Compiled by Jitka Sedlářová, Hana Karkanová, Kateřina Svobodová, Vilém Levínský, Jiří Šimáček, Lada H. Vacková. Brno: Moravská galerie, 1994. [unpaginated].

This illustrated spiral-bound landscape-format catalogue has Czech and English text in parallel columns, although unfortunately on some of the pages the English column has been set in elegant silver italic font which is nearly illegible in normal light. The exhibition, which opened on 17 November 1994 in Pražákův Palace in Brno, houses 231 paintings and sculptures. The timespan of the works is declared to be from the 1890s to the present, yet there are only a very few exhibits from the post-Second World War period. The majority of the works were created between the wars.

1151 **Olomouc Picture Gallery (I): Italian paintings of the 14th-18th centuries from Olomouc collections.**
Ladislav Daniel, Olga Pujmanová, Milan Togner, edited by Michal Soukup, translated from the Czech by Jaroslav Peprník. Olomouc, Czech Republic: Muzeum umění Olomouc, 1996. 192p. 100 plates.

A Czech edition was published simultaneously under the title *Olomoucká obrazárna (I): italské malířství 14. – 18. století z olomouckých sbírek.* It is a high-quality, elegant catalogue of a permanent exhibition, which was opened in 1994 and is intended to run until the end of 1999, which is made up from: the collections of Olomouc archbishops; the collection of the city of Olomouc (the former capital of Moravia); the collections of the Museum of Art, which published this book; and from private collections. The reproductions are of high quality, as is the text. Pavel Zatloukal introduces the text with a narrative on Italians, Italy and Olomouc (p. 13-15) and Milan Togner continues the introduction with an essay on Italian paintings in Olomouc collections (p. 16-21). Both articles offer a brief insight into the cultural history of Olomouc. The catalogue has an iconographic index and indexes of names and places.

Bibliographies

1152 **European bibliography of Slavic and East European Studies (EBSEES). Bibliographie européenne des travaux sur l'ex-USSR et l'Europe de l'Est.**
Edited by M. Armand, W. Gaignebet, P. Kornbaum. Paris: École des hautes études en Sciences Sociales, 1990- . annual.

Formerly (from 1980-89) published as *European Bibliography of Soviet, East European and Slavonic Studies*, this covers works (books, journal articles, reviews and theses) in social sciences, language, literature and the arts published in Austria, Belgium, Finland, France, Germany, Great Britain and the Netherlands and some from Switzerland. It is one of the largest general bibliographies – the 1992 volume had 9,981 references – but unfortunately it tends to be in arrears. For example, vol. 16 (1990) was published in 1994. The Czech Republic is among the countries covered. The introduction to this bibliography is in French, English and German, and there is a name and subject index and a list of periodicals searched. The bibliography should be shortly available on-line.

1153 **The American bibliography of Slavic and East European Studies (ABSEES).**
Urbana, Illinois: University of Illinois Library, 1956- .

A cousin to *EBSEES* (see previous entry), this publication used to be available in hard copy only; from 1977 it was published in hard copy and microfiche. Now it can also be searched on the on-line version, at http://www.library.uiuc.edu/absees/. The bibliography contains records for journals, articles, books, book reviews, theses and selected government publications. The aim of *ABSEES* is to cover North American scholarship on Central and Eastern Europe, Russia and the countries of the former Soviet Union. The coverage of the Czech Republic is consistent.

355

1154 **Česká národní bibliografie: knihy.** (Czech National Bibliography: Books.)

Prague: Národní knihovna České republiky, 1994- . monthly.

Published previously, from 1922, under the title *Bibliografický katalog. České knihy* (Bibliographical Catalogue. Czech Books). In 1993 this major national series was published as *Národní bibliografie ČR – Knihy* (National Bibliography of ČR – Books), and the current title has been used since 1994. Since that year the bibliography has also been published on CD-ROM, which is published four times a year, with updates on floppy disc every month. The bibliography is now also accessible on the Internet at http://www.nkp.cz. The printed form has the title page and contents in Czech, English, German, French and Russian. The National Library of the Czech Republic has a right to a copy of non-periodical works published in the Czech Republic and the bibliographical entries are based on this. The Anglo-American Cataloguing rules (AACR2R) and the UDC classification are followed. An annual index, no. 13, is produced. Since 1954 the Czech National Library in Prague has also produced *Články v českých časopisech* (Articles in Czech periodicals).

1155 **Česká národní bibliografie: zahraniční bohemika.** (Czech National Bibliography: Foreign Bohemica.)

Prague: Národní knihovna České republiky, 1994- . annual.

The bibliography has changed its name slightly over the last few years. In 1993 it carried the title *Národní bibliografie České republiky: zahraniční bohemika* (The National Bibliography of the Czech Republic: Foreign Czech Studies); between 1990-1992 the annual publication bore the title *Bibliografický katalog ČSFR: zahraniční bohemika* (Bibliographical Catalogue of the CSFR: Foreign Czech Studies). It lists publications acquired by The National Library of the Czech Republic usually two years earlier (e.g. the latest catalogue, at the time of writing, was for the year 1994, published in 1996). The term 'Foreign Bohemica' refers to publications relating to the Czech Republic published abroad. The criteria for inclusion are: language (publications written in Czech); nationality (publications in any language, written by authors of Czech origin); territory (publications dealing with the Czech lands, in any language); and subject matter (publications dealing with Czech matters). The entries are arranged according to the Universal Decimal Classification and the description follows the International Standard Bibliographic Description. The publications listed from 1992 are accessible in the database located in the National Library of the Czech Republic in Prague.

1156 **Česká národní bibliografie: soupis bibliografií, 1994- .** (Czech National Bibliography: A List of Bibliographies, 1994- .)

Prague: Národní knihovna České republiky, 1995- . annual.

This annual has also changed name recently, in line with the main Czech national bibliography. The predecessor of the current title was *Národní bibliografie České republiky: soupis českých bibliografií, 1993* (National Bibliography of the Czech Republic: A List of Czech Bibliographies). The title page and contents are again in Czech, English, German, French and Russian. From 1996 this list is available on CD-ROM only. The majority of entries are Czech-language publications, a few are foreign. The coverage is generally monographs, but the list also includes important 'hidden' bibliographies, from inside or the end of books, or bibliographies accompanying articles.

1157 **Čeština jako cizí jazyk II. Výběrová bibliografie příruček češtiny jako cizího jazyka.** (Czech as a foreign language II. Selective bibliography of handbooks of Czech as a foreign language.) Ludmila Nováková. Prague: Univerzita Karlova, 1992. 2nd rev. ed. 158p.

Although this bibliography of language-learning aids for Czech as a foreign language has to have the word 'selective' in the title (the postscript describes the particular sources of limitations to the coverage), it is nonetheless a goldmine consisting of 1,395 titles going as far back as 1540. Separate sections deal with books that appeared 'on the territory of the Czech and Slovak Federal Republic' pre-1918, pre-1945 and post-1945, books that appeared abroad pre- and post-1945, post-war college textbooks (usually short-life publications published for crash courses for third-world students), and textbooks for primary and secondary schools serving sundry Czech minorities abroad. Regrettably, a further updated edition seems unlikely to appear, though there is no shortage of new titles, triggered by interest in events since 1989 (fall of Communism) and 1993 (independence).

1158 **Český biografický archiv a Slovenský biografický archiv. Czech and Slovakian biographical archive.** Compiled by Ulrike Kramme, Čelmíra Urra Muena. London: Bowker-Saur, 1993- . microfiches. Distributed by Butterworth Services, Borough Green, England. Reader factor 24X.

At the time of writing the archive was not far from completion. In 1996 the number of fiches issued was 550, the final number should be around 1,000. It is an alphabetical cumulation of 213 of the most authoritative biographical multilingual reference works published between 1559 and 1992. The researcher will find in CSBA people who influenced the history and culture of the two lands, c. 110,000 individuals from all classes and professions, including Czechs and Slovaks who lived in exile. It is planned that a 'Czech and Slovak Biographical Index' will be published upon completion of the CSBA.

1159 **Czechoslovakia.** David Short. Oxford; Santa Barbara, California: Clio Press, 1986. 411p. map. (World Bibliographic Series, vol. 68).

The predecessor to the present volume, this focuses mostly on English publications and contains 1,000 selected, critically annotated and informative entries on a broad spectrum of subjects: history, with an accent on the Prague Spring 1968; literature; language; music and the arts; politics; economy; education; religion; minorities; natural sciences; sports and recreation. The source material is books, articles, periodicals, and some reports and theses.

1160 **Czechoslovakia: a guide to literature in English, covering the historical and cultural development of Czech and Slovak nations up to 1939.**
V. Edmondson. Fellowship thesis, Library Association, London, 1978. 741p. (Available from the Library Association, London, and from the British Library).

Covers material in book form written in English or translated into English. The objective of the thesis was to survey and assess material published in the English language from the 16th century to the beginning of the Second World War and thus present a general picture of printed information available on the subject to the English-speaking reader.

1161 **Czechoslovakia: a bibliographic guide.**
Rudolf Sturm. Washington, DC: Library of Congress, 1967. 157p.

Inevitably outdated, it still gives useful information on material which is available from many libraries.

1162 **Bohemian (Čech) bibliography: a finding list of writings in English relating to Bohemia and the Czechs.**
Thomas Čapek, Anna Vostrovský Čapek. New York; Chicago; London; Edinburgh: Fleming H. Revell, 1918. 256p.

This remained the main, authoritative list for a long time, practically until the appearance of David Short's *Czechoslovakia* (q.v.), which has the added bonus of critical annotations. Čapek (1861-1950) was a practising lawyer who became president of a bank in New York. His collection relating to American Czechs is housed in the Library of Congress. It is certainly outdated, yet still useful in the section on early English publications, or on Bohemia in British State Papers (with the earliest entry at 1302).

1163 **Prague.**
Susie Lunt. Oxford; Santa Barbara, California; Denver, Colorado: Clio Press, 1997. 182p. (World Bibliographical Series, vol. 195).

Covers all aspects of the culture, history, politics, population and economy of the Czech capital. Susie Lunt selected over 500 entries, principally in English, and provides evaluative annotations. The bibliography is intended for students, librarians, tourists, business people, journalists and general readers.

1164 **Russia, the USSR, and Eastern Europe: a bibliographic guide to English language publications. 1964-1980.**
Stephen M. Horak. Littleton, Colorado: Libraries Unlimited, 1978-87. 3 vols.

A large bibliography, all three volumes had nearly 300 pages each and included over 1,000 annotated entries of American, British and Canadian material. However, the sections on Czechoslovakia are small. In the third volume (p. 199-205) only twenty-five works were listed.

1165 Bohemica 1500-1800.
Petr Voit. Prague: Charles Bridge Bookstore and Gallery, 1996.
3 vols.

A catalogue of books available from this bookseller, which comprises 1,500 pages in its three volumes. It is intended for antiquarian booksellers, libraries, museums, archives and collectors and the content of the entries, and the number of indexes, reflect the interests of that audience. The largest section consists of religious literature. The catalogue has a preface in English and Czech, an English-Czech glossary, English summaries of the entries and English translations of the subject and iconographic indexes.

1166 Index to articles on Czechoslovak philately: 1950-1979.
James Negus. Dartford, England: Czechoslovak Philatelic Society of Great Britain, 1989. 15p. (Publications, no. 7).

The index is divided by regions: Czechoslovakia, Bohemia and Moravia, Carpatho-Ukraine, East Silesia, Slovakia, Sudetenland and Hungary.

Indexes

There follow three separate indexes: authors (personal or corporate); titles; and subjects. Title entries are italicized and refer either to the main titles, or to other works cited in the annotations. The numbers refer to bibliographical entry rather than page number. Individual index entries are arranged in alphabetical sequence.

Index of Authors

A

Aarebrot, F. 424
Abbott, A. 695
Absolon, K. 313
Academy of Sciences 328
Adam, J. 363, 458
Adam, J. H. 784
Adamczyk, V. 997
Adler, M. 278
Adlerová, A. 987
Adovasio, J. M. 91
Aji, Aron 917
Ajvaz, M. 902
Aldis, A. 240
Aleš, M. 29
Altvater, E. 510
Anděl, J. 975
Anderson, M. 23
Anderson, M. M. 944
Anderson, M. R. 117
Anderson, Robert 576, 651
Anderson, Ronald 603
Anselmi, A. 714
Anthony, I. 647
Antohi, S. 235
Appelbaum, S. 950
Archives of the Jewish
  Museum in Prague 279
Ardura, B. 347
Arie-Gaifman, H. 934
Armand, M. 1152
Arnold, J. 649

Arnst, H.-W. 518
Arthur, W. 702
Arwas, V. 971
Asher, A. 919-20
Asher, L. 918, 921-23
Asselain, J.-C. 361
Attwater, D. 326
Auden, W. H. 960

B

Babiuch, J. 322
Babler, O. F. 853
Bablet, D. 995
Baetcke, F. 975
Baker, H. 1087
Banks, P. 1063
Bareš, M. 1140
Barnard, F. M. 427
Barnes, S. 751
Bartoš, F. M. 136
Bartošek, L. 1011-12
Bartošková, Š. 1011
Baše, M. 714
Bašeová, O. 64
Batt, J. 452
Bauer, Z. 686
Baumgartner, C. 518
Bečka, J. V. 769
Beckerman, M. 1053,
  1064, 1075
Beckett, S. 872

Bednář, K. 899
Bednář, M. 284
Beeson, T. 320
Bělič, J. 761, 763
Beloff, Max 272
Beňáček, V. 543
Bénamou, G. 961
Benčík, A. 225
Beneš, E. 290
Bennett, R. J. 522
Beran, J. 694
Beránek, J. 342
Berglund, S. 424
Berkley, G. E. 206
Berkoff, S. 950
Berková, A. 898, 902
Berry, J. 705
Bettauer Dembo, M. 309
Betts, R. R. 115, 128
Beveridge, D. R. 315,
  1053, 1058
Białostocki, J. 963
Bicha, K. D. 304
Bičík, I. 630
Bickerton, D. 805
Biebl, K. 899-900, 903
Bielik, M. 110
Billington, E. 798
Bína, A. 335
Binns, D. 256
Birnie, J. E. 640
Bisi, R. 480
Bittnerová, D. 316

Blackwell, V. 831, 874
Bláha, K. 790
Blahut, K. 949
Blatný, I. 928-30
Blažek, M. 25
Blažíčová-Horová, N. 961
Blodig, V. 193
Bloed, A. 535
Bloyd, R. 877
Blum, L. L. 975
Boa, E. 944
Bociurkiw, B. 332
Bock, E. C. 933
Bock, P. 337
Boguszak, M. 359
Bohatá, M. 646
Bohigas, O. 714
Bolan, V. 573, 615
Böll, H. 872
Bonin, J. 600-01
Bonta, J. 1027
Borish, M. 547, 604
Born, J. 956
Borowiecki, B. 304
Bort, E. 23
Bosák, E. 449
Botstein, L. 1053
Bouché, N. 714
Bouda, J. 686
Boudre, A. 350
Bowe, P. 78
Bowler, P. J. 701
Bowlus, C. R. 96, 102
van Brabant, J. M. 534,
  537-38
Brabcová, J. 1084
Brabcová, Z. 902
Brabcová-Orlíková, J. 971
Brabec, J. 843
Brach, S. 1001
Brada, J. C. 641
Bradbrook, B. R. 859
Bradburne, J. M. 154
Bradley, J. F. N. 160, 169,
  439, 448
Brain, A. G. 884, 894
Brain, G. 955
Braley, A. 324
Brand, G. 914
Brassington, L. 992
de Bray, R. G. A. 757
Brazda, J. 551
Bregant, M. 1026

Breidenbach, S. 518
Brenner, C. 193
Březina, V. 1000
Brezinski, H. 550
Bridges, A. 970
Bright, W. 757
Brisch, H. 14
Brock, M. 167
Brock, P. 143, 158
Brod, M. 951
Brokl, L. 469
Broklová, E. 284
Broun, J. 320
Brown, A. G. 889
Brown, Alan 201
Brown, Archie 441
Brown, J. F. 466
Brown, M. 223, 450
Brown, R. 756
Brožek, J. 703
Brožková, H. 986-87
Brožková, J. 987
Brožová, M. 1019
Brullé, P. 975
Brušák, K. 148, 352
Bruson, J.-M. 971
Bryant, R. 1035
Bryson, A. 982
Buber-Neumann, M. 954
Buchholz Kimball, S. 160,
  994
Buchler, A. 902, 1023
Buchner, A. 1048
Budina, N. 619
Bukovinská, B. 154
Bulínová, M. 495
Bull, M. J. 457
von Buquoy, M. 987
Burghauser, J. 1061, 1064
Burian, Jan 1013
Burian, Jiří 1016
Burian, V. 910
Burke, M. J. 5
Burkhardt, F. 1026
Butterworth, N. 1057
Bůžek, V. 153
Bydžovská, L. 1026

C

Cabanová, D. 279
Cach, J. 409

Caforio, A. 783
Caha, J. 778
le Caine Agnew, H. 159
Calzolari, V. 714
Campbell, D. 269, 384
Campbell, F. G. 607
Camrada, N. 863-64
Canetti, E. 956
Cannon-Brookes, P. 980
Čapek, A. V. see
  Vostrovský Čapek, A.
Čapek, J. 860, 866
Čapek, K, 188, 810, 828,
  860-64, 866, 903
Čapek, T. 300, 1162
Čapek-Chod, K. M. 810
Čaplovič, D. 95
Čarek, J. 100
Carotenuto, A. 946
Carr, J. 1063
Carroll, M. 917
Carruth, J. 312
Carter, F. W. 22, 30, 35,
  44, 715-18, 721-22
Casper, M. 534
Catchpole, P. 698
Cattan, N. 22
Cauly, O. 407
Čech, Z. 335
Čejka, E. 201
Čejka, J. 901
Čelakovský, F. L. 316
Čermák, F. 767, 799
Černá, A. 731
Černá, J. 955
Černík, M. 901
Černý, B. 291
Cervenka, Z. 557
Červinková, B. 1060,
  1083
Cetkovský, P. 731
Chaloupka, O. 843
Chalupský, Z. 533
Chamberlain, L. 822
Chandler, D. G. 161
Charlton, S. E. M. 374
Charvát, P. 87
Chatwin, B. 907
Chernyshev, I. 413
Chirot, D. 237
Chloupek, J. 812
Choay, F. 714
Chowdhury, N. 372

362

Chrapek, Z. 1041
Chromá, M. 787
Chvalný, J. 742
Citati, P. 939
Cizkovský, M. 546
Clapham, J, 1050, 1054, 1064
Clark, A. 1097
Clark, E. 371, 574
Clayton, J. D. 834
Čmejrková, S. 813
Cobb, R. 167
Coffin, L. 867
Cohen, G. B. 281
Colin, S. 957
Collie, K. 1024
Comenius 405, 828
Comrie, B. 757
Confederation of British Industry 583
Connelly, J. 211, 398
Connelly, K. 269, 384
Cook, J. 34
Coombes, D. 464
Copping, S. 979
Corbett, G. G. 757
Čornej, P. 123-24
Čornejová, I. 348
Corngold, S. 950
Cornwall, M. 285-86, 485
Cosman, C. 280
Cotic, M. 220
Cottrell, P. L. 605
Coulson, A. 521
Coulter, F. 580
Cox, H. E. 40
Coxon, D. 85
Crampton, B. 38
Crampton, R. 38
Crane, J. O. 215
Crane, S. 215
Crawford, B. 540
Crawford Mitchell, R. 191
Crhonek, I. 1030
Crowe, D. M. 252, 258-59
Csaki, C. 626
Cubberley, P. 757
Čulík, J. 909
Cumberpatch, C. G. 94
Czech Fishing Association 755

Czech Tourist Authority 56
Czechoslovak Helsinki Committee, Prague 445
Czerner, O. 1027

D

DaCosta Kaufmann, T. 963
Daems, C. 244
Dalimil 828
Daly, J. C. K. 107
Daněk, M. 661
Daneš, F. 762, 813
Daniel, B. 262
Daniel, L. 1151
Daniels, P. T. 757
Davey, K. 521
Davidová, E. 260
Davidová, H. 1089
Davies, K. 389
Davies, M. M. 614
Dawson, S. 1018
Dawson, W. A. 203
Day, B. 9, 423, 904, 971
Dědek, O. 554
Dědič, J. 518
Dekan, J. 96
DeKuiper, K. 509
Deletant, D. 107
Delpire, R. 983
Demek, J. 25
Demetz, P. 61, 833
Deml, J. 899-900
Denešová, A. 312
Dermek, A. 80
Derrida, J. 714
Dick, C. 240
Dick Howard, A. E. 504
Dickins, T. 804
Dienstbier, P. J. 905
Dillon, K. J. 151
Ding, W. 604
Dobbie, A. M. O. 405
Dobrovodský, V. 747
Dodwell, C. R. 1147
Doherty, M. 658
Dohnal, M. 603
Dolejšová, I. 345
Doležal, M. 548
Doležel, L. 834

Doleželová, J. 279
Dolínek, V. 669, 1148
Dolista, K. 347
Domin, J. P. 1142
Dominová, J. 1149
Done, K. 573, 576, 653
Dopita, R. 670
Dornberg, J. 101
Dostál, J. 75
Doucha, T. 625
Doyle, H. L. 698
Drabble, M. 818
Drábek, Z. 602
Drahotová, O. 986
Drews, P. 485
Drtina, T. 648
Duane, O. B. 972
Dubček, A. 231
Ducke, L. 88
Duckworth, E. 956
Duda, R. 1019
Dufek, J. 495-96
Dunay, P. 498
Duncan-Jones, A. S. 330
Durdík, J. 1148
Durrant, A. E. 685
Durych, J. 900
Dušková, L. 811
Dutkova, L. 813
Dvořák, A. 970-71
Dvořák, I. 317
Dvořák, Jan 1108
Dvořák, Joachim 1096
Dvořáková, V. 967
Dvornik, F. 103

E

Earle, J. S. 650
East 8 710
Eckert, E. 813
Economist Intelligence Unit 593
Edmondson, V. 412, 1160
Edwards Harrison, M. 548
Eidlin, F. 444
Einhorn, B. 460
Eisen, A. 551
Eisler, J. 1016
Elias, R. 309
Ellridge, F. 970

363

Elman, J. 785, 788
Encyklopedický dům 764
Erben, K. J. 310
Erikson, R. 360
Erven Andic, V. 299
Erwas, V. 973
Essinger, J. 597
Esterhammer, A. 957
European Bank for
  Reconstruction &
  Development 725
European Communities
  PHARE Programme 725
Evans, A. 541
Evans, G. 454
Evans, M. 1071
Evans, R. J. W. 150, 152,
  155, 157, 167, 412
Everett, J. 374

F

Fajt, J. 966, 1149
Falk, W. 634
Farmer, K. V. 305
Farr, M. 43
Farrell, B. 148
Fassmann, M. 368
Faulkner, S. 749
Feierabend, L. 429
Fernández-Armesto, F. 1
Fiala, P. 344
Fialová, L. 2
Fic, V. M. 170
Fiedler, J. 276
Filip, O. 902
Filipec, J. 762
Filla, P. 62
Filler, R. K. 386
Finlayson Samsour, R.
  967, 1059, 1147
Finn, S. 699
Firbas, K. 714
Firkušný, R. 1055
Firkušný, T. 1053
Fischer, M. 646
Fischerová, D. 904
Fischerová, S. 892, 897
Fischmann, Z. E. 1077
Fleischer, F. 566
Flennes, M. 67
Fogel, D. S. 548-49, 558

Forbelský, J. 353
Foret, M. 548
Forman, M. 1007
Forrest Keen, M. 358
Forst, V. 843
Foulds, D. E. 675
Fowkes, B. 212
Frampton, K. 1023
Franc, Z. 1138
Francis, A. B. 697
Francis, P. 727
Frankland, M. 885
Franklin, P. 1063
Fraser, A. M. 257
Freed Taylor, M. 414
Freedman, R. 957
Freeland, D. 806
Frejka, T. 480
French, A. 842, 899-900
French, R. A. 716
Freudenberger, H. 633
Friebert, S. 879
Frištenská, H. 250
Fritsch, M. 550
Fronek, J. 774, 805
Frydman, R. 540, 650
Fučíková, E. 154
Fudge, Thomas A. 135
Fuks, L. 869, 870, 902
Furbach, F. J. 1047

G

Gabriel, J. 422
Gaignebet, W. 1152
Gaisford, J. 389
Gajan, K. 284
Gajdošíková, H. 1086
Galík, J. 910
Galligan, D. J. 506
Galmiche, X. 1019
Gammelgaard, K. 814
Gardovský, Č. 1046
Gargett, R. H. 92
Garner, T. 370
Garrison Walters, E. 104
Garton Ash, T. 234-35,
  476
Garver, B. M. 14, 166,
  435
von Gehlen, K. 33
Gellner, E. 440

Georgeoff, P. J. 305
Gestwicki, R. 938
Gibian, G. E. 844, 868
Gibianskii, L. 211, 398
Giele, J. Z. 373
Gilbert, J. 1015
Gill, A. 43
Gill, D. 959-60
Gill, R. B. 917
Gioia, I. 43
Giorgi, L. 709, 1091
Girardin, E. 606
Gissing, V. 310
Gleeds International
  Property and
  Construction
  Consultants 587
Glenny, M. 236
Glettler, M. 308
Godfrey, R. T. 968
Goetz-Stankiewicz, M.
  905, 998
Gojda, M. 89
Gold, S. 1014
Goldberg, S.-A. 280
Goldman, M. F. 447
Goldscheider, I. 974
Goldstücker, E. 15
Goldthorpe, J. H. 360
Gopinathan Pillai, C. 915
Gordon, C. E. 546
Gorys, E. 46
Gossmann, K. 408
Gottfried, L. 966
Gottheinerová, T. 137,
  279, 969
Götz, A. 26, 630
Gourvish, T. 596
Government Committee
  for Tourism of the
  Czech Socialist
  Republic 755
Grant, L. 267
Grasland, C. 22
Gray, E. 845
Green, C. J. 606
Greenberg, V. D. 946
Gribbin, J. 700
Gribbin, M. 700
Griffin, A. 588
Griffith-Jones, S. 602
Gros, D. 540
Gross, R. V. 941

Grumbach, A. 714
Grund, A. 832
Grunell, M. 380
Gruša, J. 9, 65, 244, 843, 902
Grygar, M. 7
Gunn, D. 923
Gut, K. 746
Guy, W. 265
Gwynne, J. 9

H

Haas, W. 952
Habenicht, J. 299
Haberštát, L. 397
Hábová, D. 877, 879
Hagedorn, K. 551
Haglund, D. G. 500
Hahn, F. 287, 485
Hahnová, E. 282-83
Hais, K. 775
Hájek, I. 824, 843, 882
Hájek, J. 596
Halas, F. 19, 899-900
Halásek, S. 747
Hall, D. R. 44
Haller, J. 773
Haller, M. 359
Hamar, J. 640
Hames, P. 1003, 1008-09
Hamilton, F. E. I. 716
Hanáček, J. 99
Hanak, H. 107, 181, 485
Hancock, I. 259
Hanel, P. 646
Hannan, K. 809
Hanousek, J. 619
Hanuš, J. 344
Hanzlík, J. 891, 899
Harák, M. 687
Harkins, W. E. 800, 832, 844, 851, 859, 862, 895, 996
Harna, J. 284
Harnick, M. 924
Hartmann, A. 1016
Hartmann, J. 350
Hasalová, V. 317
Hašek, J. 857-58, 903
Haubner, W. 65

Hauková, J. 899-900
Hauner, M. 283
Hausenblasová, J. 154
Havel, V. 225, 242, 245, 350, 472-73, 828, 831, 849, 872-76, 903, 905, 907, 995, 1019
Havelková, H. 376
Havlíček Borovský, K. 831, 899
Havlík, P. 714
Havlová, E. 813
Havránek, B. 761, 763
Hayes, K. 836
Hayman, R. 938
Heady, C. 579
Hebler, A. 1019
Hecht, M. 53
Heftrich, U. 841
Hegedus, J. 706
Heim, M. H. 188, 794, 837, 854, 881, 920
Heinl, O. 65
Heitlinger, A. 382, 390
Hejný, S. 74, 77
Hekrdlová, K. 1138
Helcl, M. 761, 763
Held, J. 108, 208
Heller, E. 956
Hellyer, P. 913
Helweg, A. W. 470
Hendershott, J. 72, 1063
Henderson, M. 970
Herbenová, O. 1026
Hermann, A. H. 116
Hermann, D. 866
Herold, L. C. 753
Herrity, P. 759
Heymann, F. G. 138, 142
Higley, J. 469
Hill, J. D. 588
Hilmera, J. 1048
Hilská, K. 353, 1026
Hingorani, A. N. 549
Hitchens, D. M. W. 640
Hitchins, K. 281
Hladký, J. 80
Hlaváček, L. 980
Hlavsa, Z. 768
Hlobil, I. 714, 1015
Hník, F. M. 331, 339
Hobér, K. 506
Hobland, W. 840

Hočevar, T. 305
Hochman, J. 112, 222, 230
Hockaday, M. 953
Hodek, B. 775
Hoen, H. W. 539
Hoensch, J. K. 119
Hofmann, M. 948
Hofmeyer, U. 389
Hohmann, J. S. 262
Hojda, Z. 1017
Holan, O. 8
Holan, V. 831, 899-900
Holeček, M. 26
Holeček, M. K. 855
Holt, J. 748
Höltl, G. 987
Holtsmark, S. 489
Holub, Jan 799
Holub, Josef 771
Holub, M. 877-80, 893, 899, 903
Holý, J. 846
Holý, L. 3
Hoole, J. 973
Hora, J. 899-900
Horáček, M. 399
Hora-Hořejš, P. 120
Horák, J. 312
Horak, S. M. 252, 1164
Horálek, K. 759
Hornschild, K. 566
Horová, A. 961
Horsbrugh, I. 1065
Hort, G. 1147
Horyna, M. 353
Hoskovec, J. 703
Hošťálek, A. 443
van Houwelingen, A. 569
Howard, M. 167
Hoy, F. 548
Hrabal, B. 881-82, 898, 902-03
Hrabinská, M. 397
Hrabová, A. see Hrabová, L.
Hrabová, L. 7
Hrach, P. 986
Hrala, J. 87
Hrdlička, J. 100
Hrnčíř, M. 601, 606
Hromada, J. 391
Hromádka, J. 351

Hronek, J. 767, 799
Hronková, N. 327
Hronová, K. 803
Hrubín, F. 899-900
Hrubý, P. 838
Hružík, L. 79
Hübschmannová, M. 262
Hucek, M. 1015
Hucková, B. 1015
Hudec, K. 82
Hudson, A. 134
Hufner, K. 394
Hughes, M. 1132
Humphreys, R. 47
Hunter, A. 1035
Hupchick, D. P. 40
Hus, J. 810
Husák, G. 233
Husáková, V. 510
Hutchins, K. 607
Hvížďala, K. 242
Hyde-Price, A. 479
Hyhlík, V. 1013

I

Ibrmajer, J. 27
Iggers, W. A. 381
Illman, Z. 739
Illyés, E. 305
Ingham, M. 457
Innes, R. 668
Institute for the Czech
  Language of the
  Czechoslovak Academy
  of Sciences 761
Interdisciplinary Centre
  for Comparative
  Research in the Social
  Sciences, Vienna 709
Ivory, M. 51, 59

J

Jackson, M. 1090
Jackson, S. 971
Jagasich, P. 868
Jäger, P. 518
Jakobson, R. 1013
Jakubec, I. 692
Janáček, L. 1053

Jandová, L. 207
Janisová, M. 329
Jankovič, M. 7
Janouch, F. 222, 443
Janovic, V. 890, 901
Janovický, K. 1066
Jaromír Erben, K. 831
Jechová, K. 443
Jedlička, A. 761, 763
Jelinek, Y. 485
Jennings, J. 1086
Jenšík, M. 744
Jerabek, E. 297
Jewish Publication Society
  of America 273
Jílek, J. 415
Jirák, J. 1091
Jirásek, A. 855
Jirásko, L. 346
Jirsák, V. 662
Jist, A. 312
John, C. R. 326
Johnston, R. J. 24
Jolly, A. 581
Jonson, H. 1087
Jordan, P. 22
Judah, H. 268
Justová, H. 403

K

Kabeš, P. 843
Kadečková, J. 482
Kafka, František 966
Kafka, Franz 903, 936,
  948-52, 956
Kafka Society of America
  937
Kahne, H. 373
Kahovcová, A. 1012
Kainar, J. 899-900
Kaldor, M. 460
Kalista, Z. 900
Kalvoda, J. 174, 252
Kamarýt, S. 817
Kandler, E. M. 870
Kanikova, S. I. 819
Kann, R. A. 253
Kantor, M. 325
Kantůrková, E. 131, 222,
  443, 903
Kaplan, J. 205

Kaplan, K. 216, 218-19,
  328-29, 444, 495-96
Karásek ze Lvovic, J. 828
Karasová, D. 990
Karbusický, V. 315
Kardos, G. 498
Karel, J. 130
Karel, R. 130
Karkanová, H. 1150
Karl, F. R. 940
Karlický, V. 669
Kárník, Z. 284
Karný, M. 206
Kaser, M. C. 393, 529
Kavan, J. 222
Kaván, Z. 239, 460
Kavka, F. 142
Kavka, S. 793
Keane, J. 478
Keating, P. 271
Kegels, C. 603
Kejř, Jindřich 1021
Kejř, Jiří 137, 142
Kelly, D. 432
Kelly, Michael 493
Kelly, Milena 801
Kemme, D. M. 546
Kende, P. 361
Kenny, B. 614
Kenrick, D. 255, 264
Kenway, P. 612
Kepl, J. 781
Kern, D. M. H. 970
Kerner, R. J. 114
Kesner, L. 1015
Kettle, S. 466, 1095
Kieval, H. J. 274
Kindlová, E. 754
King, J. 48
Kingsley, G. T. 707
Kirkup, J. 880
Kirschbaum, S. J.
  105-06
Klacek, J. 606
Klassen, J. M. 136, 139
Klaus, V. 563-64
Klein, G. 251
Klein, P. W. 470
Kleinbard, D. 957
Klement, J. K. 868
Klemm, D. D. 33
Klenovský, J. 277
Klíma, B. 91

Klíma, I. 854, 861, 883-89, 898, 902-04
Klímek, A. 175, 198
Kliment, C. K. 698
Klimeš, L. 764
Klímová, R. 871
Klvačová, E. 612
Kocmannová, J. 486
Kocourek, J. 686
Koelb, C. 947
Kohout, P. 905
Kolářová, J. 806
Kolíbal, S. 981
Kollár, J. 18
Kolmačka, P. 348
Kolosi, T. 359
Kolsti, J. 259
Konečný, L. 154
Kopecká, A. 778
Kopecký, K. 77
Köpplová, B. 1091
Kopřivová, A. 293
Korbel, J. 109
Kornbaum, P. 1152
Kosinski, D. 975
Kossl, J. 739
Kostelecký, T. 467
Kostka Neumann, S. 900
Kotalík, J. 980
Kotišová, M. 263
Kotrba, J. 739
Kotrba, V. 1014
Kotrba-Novotná, L. 10
Kotyk, P. 843
Kouba, K. 552
Koudelka, J. 225, 265, 983
Koudelka, M. 299
Kováč, D. 217
Kováč, J. 1047
Kovacs, M. L. 305
Kovanda, K. 1141
Kovář, F. 339
Kovařík, J. 383
Kovtun, G. J. 177, 184-85, 852
Kowarik, I. 77
Kozera, N. 378
KPMG Peat Marwick McLintock 583
Král, P. 225
Král, R. 786
Kramer, M. 225
Kramme, U. 1158

Krámský, J. 778
Krása, J. 967
Kraszewski, C. S. 831
Krátký, K. 489
Kratochvíl, J. 902
Kratochvíl, P. 714
Kraus, Jiří 763
Kraus, Josef 625
Kraus, V. 1087
Krejčí, J. 118, 140, 354, 536
Krejčí, O. 431
Krejčíř, J. 122
Krejčír, M. 335
Křen, J. 291
Krigar, H. 1053
Krikovszki, P. 714
Kriseová, E. 244, 898
Křístek, J. 1048
Křístek, V. 761, 763
Krištof, V. 911
Křivánek, J. 690
Kříž, J. 392
Krob, J. 422
Krob, M. 1013
Krofta, K. 114
Krontvor, J. 1026
Kroulík, B. 782
Kroulíková, B. 782
Kubíček, J. 125, 1135
Kubíková, J. 77
Kubíková, P. 843
Kučera, H. 304
Kučera, M. 284
Kuchař, J. 1141
Kudrnáč, J. 835
Kukral, M. A. 31
Kulka, E. 13, 204
Kulka, J. 1076
Kuna, F. 945
Kundera, L. 19
Kundera, M. 19, 828, 872, 903, 907, 918-23, 941
Kundrata, M. 732
Kural, V. 225, 291
Kuras, B. 17, 806
Kusák, D. 70, 970, 1013
Kussi, P. 832, 844, 865, 920-21, 926
Kuttelvašer, Z. V. 1087
Kutschera, P. 518
Kux, J. 413
Kvaček, R. 179, 284

Kybal, M. 299
Kybalová, J. 1146
Kyralová, M. 411

L

Lacina, V. 596, 605
Lada, J. 857
Lahoda, V. 1026
Lamarová, M. B. 1026
Lamont, C. 215
Lampe, J. R. 497, 542
Land, T. 660
Land Survey Office (Zeměměřický ústav), Prague 41
Landová, D. 1148
Landovský, P. 905
Large, B. 1051, 1081
Larvová, H. 975
Lášek, J. B. 68
Lasťovka, M. 62
Laštůvka, Z. 86
Latawski, P. 248
Lavenex, S. 480
Lavigne, M. 534
Ledbetter, E. E. 302
Ledererová-Protivová, Z. 1072
Ledvinka, V. 62
Lees, G. 1088
Leff, C. S. see Skalnik Leff, C.
Lehrskov, C. 712
Leoncini, F. 106
Leopold, N. 65
Lešnikowski, V. 1027
Leviathin, D. 362
Levínský, V. 1150
Leviten, I. 960
Levitsky, A. 813
Lewis, P. G. 209
Líbal, D. 714
Liehm, A. 222, 844, 1002, 1004
Liehm, M. 1002
Lijphart, A. 465
Linek, J. 688-89
Linhart, Z. 551
Linhartová, V. 902
Lipp, R. 971
Lipský, Z. 742

Lobkowicz, J. 520
Löbl, P. 1094
Locatelli, C. 724
Lochman, J. M. 340-41
Lockerová, J. 124
Lockhart, B. 190
Lockwood, C. 477
Loewy, J. 222
Longworth, P. 102
Lopatka, J. 843
Loua, M. S. 712
Louda, J. 97-98
Löw, J. 732
Lowensteinová, Š. 284
Lubínová, M. 318
Lubyová, M. 370
Ludvíková, M. 992
Luelsdorff, P. A. 811
Lukeš, I. 192, 196, 211
Lukeš, Z. 714, 1026, 1029
Lunt, S. 20, 353, 1163
Lusk, S. 754
Luskačová, M. 984
Lustig, A. 902
von Lützow, F. 113, 827
Luxmoore, J. 322
Luža, R. 179, 291
Lyer, S. 771
Lynes, R. 401
Łysohorský, Ó. 960
Lytle, D. 21

M

Maag, K. 338
Macartney, C. A. 145
McCarthy, T. 389
McCrea, B. P. 470
McDermott, K. 105, 433
MacDonald, C. 205
Macdonald, H. 1064
Macdonald, M. 752
MacFarlane, S. N. 500
McGoverne, H. H. 853
McGreal, S. 705
Mácha, K. H. 828, 831, 853
Machač, J. 762
Macháčková, J. 667
Machala, L. 910
Machalický, J. 982
Machek, V. 770
Machonin, P. 354

McKenna, C. 513
Mackeras, C. 1066, 1078
McKinley, H. 960
Macků, J. 744
Maclagan, M. 97
McNeely, S. 48
Macsai, J. 1027
Madariaga, J. S. 502
Magocsi, P. R. 39, 426
Mahen, J. 900
Major, P. 124
Makhija, A. K. 549
Makovsky, P. M. 299
Malcolm, J. 907
Malý, Jakub 85
Malý, Jan 1022-23, 1026
Malý, V. 349
Mamatey, V. S. 179, 485
Mandelbrot, B. 975
Manheim, R. 942, 954
Mann, S. E. 760
Manser, J. 1035
Mansfeldová, Z. 106, 469
Mantin, P. 194
March, M. 897-98
Mareš, P. 367
Marešová, J. 480
Margolius, I. 67, 1024-25
Marhounová, J. 1045
Marsh, P. 642
Martincová, O. 765
Martinů, C. 1081
Marzik, T. D. 110
Masák, M. 1031
Masaryk, T. G. 188
Maslan, F. 342
Mason, V. 1008
Mastny, V. 494
Matějček, J. 667
Matějů, P. 359, 414
Mathernová, K. 504
Matthews, D. 9
Matthews, G. J. 39
Matuštík, M. J. 471
Maurel, M.-C. 631
Maxwell, R. 233
Mayhew, A. 1032
Mazon, A. 792
Mazurkiewicz, L. 24
Mejstřík, B. 413
Mejstřík, M. 568
Mejstřík, V. 762
Melissinos, A. 714

Mendini, A. 1026
Menhennet, A. 858
Mergl, J. 986-87
Merhautová, A. 967
Meřtlík, P. 545
Mesik, J. 723
Měšťan, A. 935
Meth-Cohn, D. 32
Michálek, V. 788
Michálková, M. 225
Michalski, S. 1032
Michel, P. 324
Miesel, V. 19
Mihalovic, P. 706
Mikelsons, M. 707
Miklaszewska, E. 603
Miklosko, H. 1033
Miková, K. 400
Miková, M. 296
Millar, J. R. 366
Miller, A. 865, 872
Miller, D. E. 436
Miller, J. 907
Miller, K. 907
Mills, J. 517
Milner, I. 831, 878-79,
   891-92, 897, 903
Milunič, V. 714
Minihofer, O. 791
Ministry for the
   Environment 734
Misurella, F. 918
Mitchell, D. 1063
Mizsei, K. 600
Mlčoch, L. 545
Moldan, B. 733
Monmartre, D. 995
Moody, S. 682
Morath, T. 123
Moravčíková, I. 369
Morison, J. 180, 186, 248,
   275, 285, 287, 428, 430,
   435-36
Mortkowitz, S. 949
Moses, S. 934
Moss, J. 225
Moudrý, P. 1148
Možný, I. 355, 367
Mucha, A. 900, 970
Mucha, G. 482, 971
Mucha, Janusz 358
Mucha, Jiří 970
Mucha, S. 969

Muchka, I. 154, 1015
Muchlinski, P. T. 652
Muchová, G. see Thomsen Muchová, G.
Muhr, R. 400
Muir, E. 936
Muir, W. 936
Muller, P. P. 823
Müller, V. 839
Muller-Graff, P. C. 508
Mullineux, A. W. 606
Munich, D. 365
Murer, E. 902
Murphy, D. 405
Murray, J. P. 789
Murrer, E. 897
Muschka, W. 172
Museum, Old Salem 10
Musil, J. 450, 706, 709, 711
Musil, L. 367
Myant, M. 531, 566
Mynařík, J. 122
Mysliveček, M. 99

N

Nagel, S. S. 463
Naimark, N. 211, 398
Národní museum see National Museum, Prague
Nash, J. 626
National Museum, Prague 10
National Westminster Bank 583
Natmessnig, C. 596
von Natzmer Cooper, G. 942
Naughton, J. D. 485, 797, 816, 818, 860, 878, 882
Navrátil, J. 225
Navrátilová, M. 749
Nebeský, R. 48
Nečas, C. 263-64
Neff, O. 898
Negus, J. 1166
Nejezchleb, L. 603
Nekvapil, J. 812
Nelson, B. J. 372
Nelson, D. N. 497

Nelson, J. 749
Němcová, A. 1072, 1080
Němcová, B. 311, 831
Němcová Banerjee, M. 916
Němec, L. 321, 339, 353
Ners, K. J. 550, 569
Neruda, J. 854
Nestorovič, Č. 1093
Neubert, K. 53, 353, 1016
Neubert, L. 64, 353
Neudorfl, M. L. 106
Neumann, I. B. 489
Neumann, J. 203
Neumann, S. K. 899
Neumeister, W. 334
Neustadt, A. 552
Neústupný, E. 88
Neústupný, J. 88
Neuwirth, W. 678
Newall, V. 319
Newman, K. L. 549
Newmarch, R. 1077
Newton, J. 806
Newton-Marinelli, D. 837
Nezval, V. 899-900
Nobar, C. 946
Noble, T. 349
Noel, M. 547, 604
Noll, T. 47
Nollen, S. D. 549
Nollen, T. 52
Nolte, C. E. 303, 741
Northey, A. 943
Nosek, V. 114
Novák, A. 832
Novák, Jan 874, 1007
Novák, Josef 187
Novák, P. 662, 1035
Nováková, J. 802
Nováková, L. 1157
Novotná, E. 1137
Novotný, J. 714
Novotný, M. 1141
Novotný, V. 1088
Nowak, C. M. 492
Nykrýn, P. 1148

O

Oakland, O. 1072
Oakland, V. 1072

Obenausová, S. 805
Obermeier, O. 671
Oberstein, I. 714
O'Brien, J. 915
Obrusníková, L. Z-. see Zorin-Obrusníková, L.
Odložilík, O. 141
O'Grady, T. 868
Olbracht, I. 893
Oldfield, H. 750
Olesch, R. 935
Olivová, V. 284, 290, 430
Olson, D. M. 505
Olynyk, R. 958
Ončák, O. 364
Ondrůjová, L. 311
Opat, J. 176
Ordnung, M. 546
Orel, V. 699
Orten, J. 899-900
Orton, L. D. 163
Osers, E. 867-68, 878-80, 886, 888, 890-91, 901, 903, 960
Otáhal, M. 217, 291
Otčenášek, P. 659
Outrata, K. 29
Outrata, V. 142

P

Pachman, L. 756
Pacina, V. 737, 747
Page, B. 351
Page, M. 351
Page, W. A. 169, 202-03
Pakulski, J. 469
Pala, K. 769
Páleníčková, J. 1048
Palivec, J. 900
Palmer, M. 569
Pánek, J. 125
Panenková, D. 987
Papeš, Z. 386
Papp, B. 1124
Páral, V. 851
Parent, M. 714
Pargeter, E. 855, 881
Pařík, A. 276
Pařízek, V. 393
Parolková, O. 802
Parrott, C. 857, 867

Parry, I. 948
Parry, P. 642
Pascal, R. 949
Pasternak-Slater, L. 960
Paul, D. W. 441
Paulin, T. 880
Pavel, J. 312
Pavlík, D. 913, 1136
Pavlík, J. 348
Pavlincová, H 422
Pavlů, I. 93
Pawel, E. 19, 940
Pawley, M. 1035-37
Pearson, M. 579
Pearson, R. 254
Pech, S. Z. 163
Pechota, V. 507, 509
Pečírková, J. 325
Pečman, R. 1064, 1080
Pehe, J. 222, 466
Peichl, G. 1028
Pejchar, J. 743
Pelikán, J. 144
Pelikan Straus, N. 917
Pelíšek, J. 28
Peprník, J. 483, 779, 1151
Pešat, Z. 900
Peschar, J. L. 359
Pešek, J. 338, 1017
Pešková, J. 409
Petana, M. 1108
Péter, L. 148
Petiška, E. 129, 314, 327
Petr, M. 686
Petráčková, V. 763
Petrov, A. 543
Pfaff, I. 488
Phillips, D. 393
Phillips, P. 475
Pichlík, K. 284
Piehler, H. A. 113
Pienkos, D. E. 304
Písařík, V. 878
Pistorius, G. 821
Pithart, P. 509
Plečnik, J. 67
Pleiner, R. 87
Plichtová, J. 249
Plicka, I. 719
Podivínský, M. 910
Pogány, A. 596
Pohoryles, R. J. 709, 1091

Pokorný, P. R. 99
Poláčková, K. 925, 1004
Polackova Henley, K. see Poláčková, K.
Polanský, P. 263
Poldauf, I. 777-78
Polgár, L. 1089
Polišenský, J. V. 115, 142, 156-57, 284, 484, 486, 714
Politzer, H. 941
Pondělík, J. 743
Pořízka, L. 1017
Porket, J. L. 363
Porter, R. C. 914
Posselt, M. 1142
Postolková, B. 766
Potůček, M. 355, 357, 537
Poulík, J. 96
Prague Institute of Health Information Statistics 420
Prchal, J. 746
Prečan, V. 485
Prelovšek, D. 1029
Prescott, M. 1021
Pressouyre, L. 714
Přibáňová, S. 1067, 1072
Přibyl, J. 36
Price Waterhouse 583
Přívratská, J. 411
Procházka, I. 391
Procházka, V. 993
Procházková, J. 1072
Progoff, I. 938
Prouza, B. 625
Průcha, V. 529, 634
Prunskiené, K. 510
Ptáčková, V. 997, 1048
Pujmanová, O. 1151
Pulver, A. 1005
Purš, J. 704
Pursey, H. L. 76
Putík, A. 279
Puxton, G. 264
Pynsent, R. B. 6-7, 18, 107, 148-49, 181, 246, 308, 474, 777, 819, 835, 840, 847-48, 850-51, 857, 896, 964
Pysek, A. 77
Pysek, P. 77

Q

Quentin Bajac, S. 971

R

Rabb, T. K. 154
Rabinovitch, D. 887
Rajah, N. 579
Rajmš, Z. 714
Rakusan, J. 813
Ramet, P. 321
    see also Ramet, S. P.
Ramet, S. P. 337, 1049
    see also Ramet, P.
Rand, M. 1082
Rapaczynski, A. 540, 650
Rappaport, S. 920
Rath, D. 1021
Read, F. 361
Reader, R. E. 202
Reban, M. J. 251, 321-32
Rebstöck, R. 73
Rechcígl, Jr., M. 11-12, 299, 696, 821, 958
Rees, H. L. 168
Rees, J. 925
Reguliová, D. 80
Řehák, S. 22
Reinfeld, B. K. 165
Rejchrtová, A. 742
Rejzl, J. 127
Remington, T. F. 505
Renčín, V. 878
Renner, H. 214
Rennert, J. 971
Řepka, O. 686
Restuccia, F. L. 917
Rey, V. 22, 453
Řezníček, I. 367
Richards, M. 917
Richterová, S. 902
Ricke, H. 987
Rilke, R. M. 940, 957
Ringen, S. 355, 357
Riordan, J. 738
Ripellino, A. M. 837
Roach, D. 517
Robert, M. 942
Róbert, P. 359
Robertson, A. 1056
Robertson, R. 936

Robinson, A. 615
Rolleston, J. 948
Röntgen, R. E. 989
Rosenthal, R. 939
Roth, M. 73
Roth, P. 871
Rothschild, J. 178, 212, 438
Roubalová, E. 798
Roucek, J. S. 301
Roullier, J.-E. 714
Round, D. 863
Rowbotham, I. 517
Royt, J. 53, 353
Rubeš, J. 244
Rubín, J. 26
Rubin, P. H. 511
Rueschemeyer, M. 375
Rukavishnikov, V. 463
Rupnik, J. 450
Rusnok, J. 368
Russell, J. 724
Růžička, R. 550
Ryavec, K. W. 447
Rybár, C. 63
Rychlík, J. 110, 487
Rykwert, J. 1023

S

S. J. Berwin & Co. 583
Sacker, R. 493
Sacks, J. 272
Sadler, J. E. 406
Sahai, V. 720
Šalda, F. X. 900
Salfellner, H. 66
Salivarová, Z. 872
Salzmann, Z. 306
Sandberg, B. 939
Sapieha, N. 78
Šára, M. 799
Satava, L. 307
Sato, T. 973
Saunders, C. T. 552
Saunders, J. 875-76
Saunders, N. 388
Savin, J. 106
Saxon-Ford, S. 298
Sayer, A. 4
Sayer, D. 4, 951
Scaler, C. 1019

Schaarschmidt, G. 834
Schamschula, W. 853
Scheilke, C. Th. 408
Scheiner, A. 310
Schenker, A. M. 758
Schillemeit, J. 934
Schindler, F. 316
Schlegel, H. 147
Schlesinger, P. 1091
Schloss, R. 871
Schmidt, G. 520
Schmidt-Hartmann, E. 105, 485
Schneider, J. 910
Schneider, J. Z. 696
Schonberg, M. 60, 1006
Schone, A. 934
Schonfeld, R. 497
Schrettl, W. 534
Schur, H. 1134
Schwartz, J. 797
Schwarzenburg, Charles, Prince of 1015
Scruton, R. 9
Šebek, J. 284
Šedinová, J. 279
Sedlák, J. 655, 714
Sedláková, R. 60
Sedlar, J. W. 126
Sedlářová, J. 1150
Seibt, F. 334, 1020
Seifert, J. 867-68, 899-900, 903
Sekalová, H. 988
Sellner, C. 987
Selucký, R. 222, 226, 532
Selver, P. 857, 860
Šembera, J. 723
Šemberová, K. 785
Šetlík, J. 1026
Seton-Watson, C. 111, 485
Seton-Watson, H. 111, 178, 210
Seton-Watson, R. W. 114
Sgall, P. 815
Sharma, S. 543
Shashko, P. 304
Shawcross, W. 229
Shemetilo, D. 543
Short, D. 7, 16, 133, 485, 757, 793, 796, 799, 808, 810, 1050, 1159
Sibley, K. A. S. 213

Sikorska, G. 320
Siksö, O. 706
Šilar, J. 37
Šimáček, J. 1150
Šimáková, J. 1139
Šimečka, M. 440
Simeone, N. 1079-80
Simko, G. 1089
Simmons, M. 243
Singh, I. 641
Sirovátka, T. 367
Skála, B. 686
Skalický, K. 13
Skalnik Leff, C. 425, 461, 470
Skarbová, S. 1022
Sked, A. 146
Skilling, H. G. 19, 158, 176, 183, 185-86, 197, 227, 282, 426-27, 434, 441-42, 532, 824, 849, 912
Skran, C. M. 481
Skřivánek, J. M. 299
Škutina, V. 222
Škvorecký, J. 19, 222, 304, 882, 902, 907, 909, 925-27, 1005-06
Sládek, Z. 294
Šlapeta, V. 1026-28
Slavíčková, E. 772
Slavík, B. 74
Slay, B. 466
Sljivic, N. 388
Šlosar, V. 495-96
Smaczny, J. 1050, 1053
Smejkalová-Strickland, J. 377
Smelser, R. M. 282
Šmída, V. 71
Smilov, D. M. 506
Smit, H. 509
Smith, G. B. 318
Smith, S. 579
Smith, T. 654
Šmoldas, I. 897
Snow, E. 957
Sobotka, M. 1042
Sochová, Z. 766
Soffen, O. 91
Soják, S. 122
Sojka, M. 545
Sokol, Z. 625

Sokolsky, J. J. 500
Šolle, Z. 284
Souček, Z. 566
Součková, E. 714
Součková, M. 1013
Soukup, K. 686
Soukup, M. 1151
Soulsby, A. 371, 574
Šourek, O. 1059
Spafford, P. 903
Speirs, R. 939
Spiegl, W. 987
Spindler-Brown, A. 455
Spinka, M. 132
Spisar, A. 339
Splichal, S. 1092
Spring, D. W. 167
Šrámek, F. 899-900
Šroněk, M. 154
Srp, K. 1026
Sršeň, L. 1149
Staff of the Commission
  on Security and
  Cooperation in Europe,
  Washington, DC 515
Staněk, T. 289
Stanford, P. 343
Stankiewicz, Edward 758
Stankovsky, Jan 555
Šťastný, K. 84
State Jewish Museum,
  Prague 1147
Staudt, K. 374
Štecha, P. 1019
Steedman, J. 543
Stehlíková, D. 391
Steiner, P. 811
Steinherr, A. 540
Stejskal, K. 130, 967
Stejskall, T. 1072
Stephens, P. 68
Ster, J. 956
Sterling, C. 190
Stern, J. 952
Stern, J. P. 820, 941
Stern, T. 952
Stevenson, G. 55
Stíbal, J. 644
Stoklasa, J. 723
Stoklasová, B. 1140
Stolze, F. 639
Stone, N. 13, 278
Stoppard, T. 831, 872,

875
Storm Steel, K. 569
Štouračová, J. 552
Šťovíček, I. 199
Straková, T. 1080
Strandmann, H. P. von
  167
Stránský, F. 533
Straussman, J. D. 549
Střída, M. 25-26
Stringfellow, F. 946
Strmiska, Z. 361
Štroblová, J. 897
Strong, J. W. 332
Strong, R. 984
Strouhal, E. 13
Struben, H. W. 714
Struyk, R. J. 707-08
Stryjan, Y. 551
Stuchlý, V. 810
Stucke, E. 868
Studnička, L. 65
Štulíková, M. 725
Sturm, R. 1161
Sugar, A. 231
Suk, M. 27
Sukopp, H. 77
Sulitka, A. 250
Šupich, Z. 739, 742
Susskind, C. 1078
Suvin, D. 860
Švábová, J. 314
Švábová, M. 714
Švácha, R. 1023, 1026,
  1028, 1031
Švankmajer, J. 1008
Svašek, M. 976
Svatoš, M. 409
Svejda, M. N. 299
Švejnar, J. 365, 369-70,
  386, 415, 556, 619, 644,
  646, 731
Sviták, I. 217, 222
Svoboda, G. 180
Svoboda, P. 786
Svobodová, K. 1150
Swatos, Jr., W. H. 323
Swinnen, J. F. M. 625
Sword, H. 957
Sýkora, L. 705, 713
Symynkywicz, J. 247
Synek, M. 677
Sýs, K. 901

Szczepanski, M. S. 35
Székely, I. P. 600-01

T

Taborsky, E. 198
Tauer, J. 694
Tausky, M. 1069
Tausky, V. 1069
Taylor, G. 255
Taylor, J. 780
Teich, M. 179, 217
Teichova, A. 529-30, 542,
  596
Tejchman, M. 284
Tejerizo, M. 774
Telgarsky, J. P. 708
Terrell, K. 365, 370
Theer, O. 900
Theiner, G. 874-75,
  878-79, 887
Theinhardt, M. 975
Thomas, A. 826, 828-29
Thomas, T. V. 150
Thomsen Muchová, G.
  1066
Thurlow, C. 43
Tibbetts, J. C. 1055
Tibitanzlová, I. 1012
Tichý, L. 786
Tielsch, I. 292
Tigrid, P. 222
Tismaneanu, V. 235
Togner, M. 1151
Tollingerová, D. 397
Toma, P. A. 332
Tomášková, S. 90
Tomeš, I. 355, 357
Tomin, Z. 931-32
Tong, D. 256
Topol, J. 902
Topolská, A. 1012
Tosek, R. 225
Tosics, I. 706
Tošovská, E. 731
Toufar, F. A. 740
Townsend, C. E. 795, 808
Trade Links 455, 516,
  560, 567
Trávníček, F. 761-63
Traynor, I. 336
Trebatická, H. 96

Trejdl, L. 739
Trensky, P. I. 844, 924, 996
Trhlík, Z. 195
Trick, R. R. 614
Tříska, J. 76
Triska, J. F. 171
Trnka, J. 312, 855
Trnka, S. 382
Trufitt, I. T. 1061
Tuck, K. P. 318
Tucker, A. 414
Tůma, O. 228
Tůma, Z. 619
Turkewitz, J. 650
Turner, A. 884
Turner, B. 706
Turner, G. 884, 887
Turner-Kadečková, J. 1147
Turnock, D. 630, 722
Turzíková, M. 803
Tusa, J. 482
Tyl, J. K. 831
Tyrrell, J. 1038, 1050, 1063, 1067-68, 1070, 1073, 1075, 1080

U

Uchalová, E. 991
Udoff, A. 947
Ueda, M. 813
Uher, J. 70
Uhlíř, D. 71, 162
Ulam, A. B. 190
Ulč, O. 222
Ullmann, W. 197
Ungerman, J. 732
Unterberger, B. M. 173
Unwin, I. 967
Urban, O. 147
Urbánek, E. 358
Urbánek, G. 987
Urešová, L. 990
Urra Muena, Č. 1158
Urwin Lewitová, I. 893
Uttitz, F. 15

V

Vacek, J. 294
Vacek, V. 725

Vácha, P. 669, 1148
Vachek, J. 811
Vacic, A. M. 534
Vacková, L. H. 1150
Vaculík, L. 844, 902
Vajdiš, J. 317
Válek, V. 534
Valena, T. 1029
Valenta, Jaroslav 199
Valenta, Jiří 224
Valeška, J. 975
Vanderjagt, J. A. 410
Vaníček, Z. 980
Vann, P. 977
Váša, P. 762
Vaughan-Whitehead, D. 368
Vavrejnová, M. 369
Vavřík, I. 714
Večerník, J. 355-56
Vecsey, G. 749
von Vegesack, A. 1026
Veiter, T. 305
Veltruský, J. F. 830
Venclová, N. 985
Vepřek, J. 386
Vepřek, P. 386
Verheijen, T. 464
Viard, J. 714
Vidal-Hall, J. 1009
Viewegh, M. 894, 902
Vinaver, K. 723
Viney, D. 1045
Vintrová, R. 566
Vítek, J. 690
Vitochová, M. 1021
Vladislav, J. 222, 872
Vlasak, L. 191
Vlček, T. 148, 971, 998, 1015
van Vliet, P. 410
Vlnas, V. 1142
Vočadlová, K. 979
Vogel, J. 1066
Voit, P. 1165
Volavková, H. 1147
Volek, T. 1048
Volf, J. 412
Volgyes, I. 14
Volný, B. 1072
Vomáčka, I. 975
Vondracek, Th. J. 514
Vondrová, J. 225

Vosahlík, A. 714
Vostrá, A. 810
Vostradovský, J. 754
Vostradovský, K. 85
Vostrovský Čapek, A. 1162
Všetečka, J. 68, 315, 1021
Všianský, J. 769
Vurm, R. B. 1087
Vybíral, J. 1031
Výborná, O. 386
Vysloužil, J. 1084

W

Wachtel, P. 600
Wagner, K. 640
Wagstyl, S. 611
Waisman, C. H. 465
Walker, M. 745
Walker, R. 414
Wallace, C. 355, 357
Wallace, D. 826
Wallace, I. 848
Wallace, W. V. 109
Ward, C. A. 304
Washington, P. 957
Wasko, J. 1092
Wawrzycka, J. W. 917
Weatherall, M. 331, 861-62
Weatherall, R. 331, 861-62
Webb, W. L. 882
Webber, J. 272
Wehrle, F. 451
Weil, J. 871
Weiner, R. 900
Weisberger, R. W. 342
Wellek, R. 184, 191, 833, 900
Wesolowski, W. 469
Westad, O. A. 489
Wheaton, B. 239
Whipple, T. D. 241
White, L. M. 200
Whitefield, S. 454
Wightman, G. 467
Williams, A. J. 498
Williams, K. 223
Wilson, D. M. 974

Wilson, P. 19, 242, 245, 442, 472-73, 873, 883, 885, 887, 903, 906, 925, 927, 1132
Wingfield, N. M. 275, 288, 485
Wingfield, P. 1074
Winn, M. 871, 876
Winner, T. G. 844
Winter, K. 226
Winters, S. B. 181, 485
Wiskemann, E. 491
Wittlich, P. 964, 969, 1022, 1026
Wolchik, S. L. 108, 366, 372-73, 375, 379, 450, 459
Wolker, J. 900, 903
Woodhead, M. 385
Wormell, S. 46
Wratislaw, A. H. 825

Y

Yeadon, R. 642
Yee, C. 528
Yoell, J. H. 1062
Young, D. 877, 879-80
Young, J. W. 437

Z

Zacek, J. F. 164
Zahradníček, J. 831, 900
Zamagni, S. 545
Žantovský, P. 1047
Zápotocká, M. 93
Zarecký, P. 522
Zatloukal, P. 1151
Závada, V. 900

Zbořil, Z. 467
Žegklitz, J. 329
Zeithammer, K. 686
Zeman, J. K. 144
Zeman, K. 566
Zeman, Z. A. B. 167, 189, 198, 428, 446
Zemánek, J. 786
Zemanová, M. 1075
Zemplinerová, A. 640, 644
Zhoř, P. 1019
Zímová, I. 305
van Zon, H. 636
Zorin-Obrusníková, L. 781
Zouhar, J. 422
Zřídkaveselý, F. 71
Zrůstová, Z. 806
Zuzowski, R. 462

Index of Titles

A

Acts of faith 336
Adapting to a free market: the task faced by a Czech pump manufacturer 670
Administrative law in Central and Eastern Europe 480
Adolescence, ideology and society: the young hero in contemporary Czech fiction 848
Adresář českých a československých krajanských organizací, společností přátel České republiky, dalších organizací se vztahem k Čechům v zahraničí, krajanského tisku k 1.1.1997 296
Adresát Milena Jesenská 955
After the Velvet Revolution: Václav Havel and the new leaders of Czechoslovakia speak out 241
Agrarian economies of Central and Eastern Europe and the Commonwealth of Independent States: situation and perspectives, 1997 626
Agriculture of the Czech Republic 628
Akademický slovník cizích slov 763
Alice Garrigue Masaryk, 1879-1966: her life as recorded in her own words and by her friends 191

All the bright young men and women: a personal history of the Czech cinema 1006
Alma Mater Carolina Pragensis: výbor svědectví cizích návštěvníků. Charles University and foreign visitors 404
Almanach Labyrint 1994 1096
Alphonse Mucha 973
Alphonse Mucha: the graphic works 970
Alphonse Mucha: pastels, posters, drawings and photographs 969
Alphonse Mucha: the spirit of Art Nouveau 971
American bibliography of Slavic and East European Studies (ABSEES) 1153
Anabaptists and the Czech Brethren in Moravia 1526-1628: a study of origins and contacts 144
Analysis of Czech Neolithic pottery: morphological and chronological structure of projections 93
Anglicko-český – českoanglický slovník 774, 778
Anglicko-český chemický slovník – English-Czech chemical dictionary 790
Anglicko-český ekonomický slovník 785
Anglicko-český ekonomický slovník s výkladem a výslovností 784

Anglicko-český lékařský terminologický slovník 789
Anglicko-český právnický slovník – English-Czech law dictionary 787
Anglicko-český slovník s nejnovějšími výrazy 774
Anglicko-český výkladový slovník 776
Anglicko-český výkladový slovník výpočetní techniky 791
Anne's Bohemia: Czech literature and society 1310-1420 826
Anthology of Czech literature 895
Antonín Dvořák: complete catalogue of works 1061
Antonín Dvořák (8.9.1841-1.5.1904): bibliographical catalogue 1060
Antonín Dvořák: letters and reminiscences 1059
Antonín Dvořák on records 1062
Antonín Dvořák: thematic catalogue, bibliography, survey of life and work 1061
Antonín Švehla: master of compromise 436
Antonín Vondrejc 840
Apocryphal stories 863
Apocryphal tales: with a selection of Fables and Would be tales 863
Appeasement and the Munich crisis 194
Archaeology in Bohemia: 1981-1985 87
Architect Bohuslav Fuchs: the lifework 1030

375

Architecture of new Prague: 1895-1945 1023
Arrest 905
Art Nouveau drawings 969
Art Nouveau style book of Alphonse Mucha: all 72 plates from 'Documents Décoratifs' in original colour 970
Art of the impossible: politics and morality in practice. Speeches and writings, 1990-1996 472
Art of laughter and survival. Permanent subversion 1009
Art of Renaissance in Eastern Europe: Hungary, Bohemia, Poland 963
Assimilation, childhood and death: a new Czech fiction-writers of the 1970's 847
Atlas of Eastern Europe in the twentieth century 38
Audience 905
Augustine Heřman of Bohemia Manor 299
Auroro 817
Austerlitz 1805: battle of three emperors 161

B

Babel: the Roma 270
Babička 831
Bachura scandal and other stories and sketches 858
Banking and financing 609
Banking and nationality conflict in the modernization of the Bohemian Crown Lands 697
Banking in transition economies: developing market oriented banking sectors in Eastern Europe 600

Baroko v Čechách a na Moravě 1013
Baroque in Bohemia 1013
Baroque theatre of Český Krumlov 72
Barrandov: 1945-1970 1001
BASEES Newsletter 1114
Das Bauhaus im Osten: Slowakische und Tschechische Avantgarde 1928-1939 1027
BCSA Newsletter 1112
Beginning of terror: a psychological study of Rainer Maria Rilke's life and work 957
Beneš between East and West 197
Berlin to Bucharest: travels in Eastern Europe 43
Between past and future: the revolutions of 1989 and their aftermath 235
Bibliografický katalog. České knihy 1154
Bibliografický katalog ČSFR: zahraniční Bohemika 1155
Bibliografie československé filmové literatury: 1930-1945 1012
Bibliografie československé neperiodické filmové literatury: 1945-1985 1012
Bibliografie k dějinám měst České republiky 125
Bibliography of sources concerning the Czechs and Slovaks in Romania 306
Birds of Britain and Europe: a comprehensive illustrated guide to over 360 species 84

Birds of sea and fresh water 84
Biskupové Čech, Moravy a Slezska po roce 1918 a jejich znaky 99
Bitva tří císařů: Slavkov/Austerlitz 162
Bohemia from the air: seven decades after Crawford 89
Bohemia: an historical sketch 113
Bohemia in history 179, 217
Bohemia sacra: das Christentum in Böhmen 973-1973. Ecclesia universalis, ecclesia magistra, ecclesia 334
Bohemia. Zeitschrift für Geschichte und Kultur der Böhmischen Länder 1115
Bohemian (Čech) bibliography: a finding list of writings in English relating to Bohemia and the Czechs 1162
Bohemian glass 986
Bohemia's fading rhapsody 589
Bohemica 1500-1800 1165
Böhmen in 19. Jahrhundert: vom Klassizismus zum Moderne 1020
Das Böhmisch Glas: 1 700-1950 987
Bohumil Hrabal 882
Bohuslav Martinů anno 1981 1084
Bohuslav Martinů (8.12.1890-28.8.1959): bibliographical catalogue 1083
Bohuslav Martinů – the man and his music 1081
Bolsheviks and the Czechoslovak legion: the origin of their armed conflict March-May 1918 170

Book of betrayals 923
Books from the Czech
  Republic (an official
  publication of the
  Ministry of Culture of the
  Czech Republic) 1096
Boom-time for Bonton 1097
Borders of language and
  identity in Teschen
  Silesia 809
Boundaries and identities:
  the eastern frontier of
  the European Union 23
Boxed in: East European
  television 1098
Brave new world for
  Czech glassmakers 677
Breaking out of fortress
  church 349
Break-up of
  Czechoslovakia:
  an in-depth economic
  analysis 554
Brewing row puts Czech
  regulators in spotlight:
  Bass and IPB are each
  hoping that the
  competition authorities
  will back their plan for
  the republic's second
  biggest brewer 651
Bride of Texas 925
Brief spring: a journey
  through Eastern Europe
  43
Bringing up girls in
  Bohemia 894
Britain and
  Czechoslovakia: a study
  in contacts 484
Británie a Česká
  republika. Britain & the
  Czech Republic 482
British attitudes towards
  Czechoslovakia. 1944-
  454, 483
Brno 34
Brno a okolí 70
Brno – fair trading 34
Brno, Výstaviště, Bitva u
  Slavkova 71
Brown Slavic
  contributions 813

Bulletin of the National
  Gallery in Prague 1143
Business Central Europe
  1124
Business law guide to the
  Czech Republic 517
Business News 1130
Business Newsletters 593
Business Update C & S 1126

C

Cafés in Prague: the 50
  most interesting cafés 65
Calendar of tourist events
  – Czech Republic 57
Call of the daimon 946
Camping CZ 56
Canada and
  Czechoslovakia 486
Canadian American Slavic
  Studies – Revue
  Canadienne Americaine
  d'Etudes Slaves 1116
Canadian Slavic Studies –
  Revue Canadienne
  d'Études Slaves 1116
Case of Czech beer:
  competition and
  competitiveness in the
  transitional economies 652
Casting of bells 868
Castle 955
Castle of Prague and its
  treasures 1015
Castles on the landscape:
  Czech-German relations
  282
Cat on the rails 904
Catalogue of autographs,
  manuscripts, facsimiles
  and other printed
  versions of Bohuslav
  Martinů compositions at
  the Bohuslav Martinů
  Museum. Soupis
  autografů, manuskriptů,
  faksimile a přidružených
  tisků skladeb Bohuslava
  Martinů ve fondech
  Památníku Bohuslava
  Martinů 1085

Catapult 851
Catholic church in the
  Czech Republic 335
Catholic clergy in the
  Czech Republic:
  progress or regress 320
Catholicism and politics in
  Communist societies
  321
Cave bears and modern
  human origins: the
  spatial taphonomy of
  Pod Hradem Cave,
  Czech Republic 92
Čechs (Bohemians) in
  America: a study of the
  national, cultural,
  political, social,
  economic and religious
  life 300
Centenary of Czech
  Academy of Sciences
  and Arts 694
Central and East
  European legal
  materials 507
Central and Eastern
  Europe 101
Central and Eastern
  Europe: problems and
  prospects 240
Central Europe after the
  fall of Iron Curtain:
  geopolitical
  perspectives, spatial
  patterns and trends 22
Central Europe in
  8th-10th centuries.
  Mitteleuropa in 8-10
  Jahrhundert 95
Central Europe in the
  twentieth century:
  an economic history
  perspective 529
Central Europe since 1945
  209
Central European
  Business Weekly 1125
Central European
  handbook: a guide to
  financial markets in
  Central and Eastern
  Europe 598

Češi a Němci: ztracené dějiny? Tschechen und Deutsche: verlorene Geschichte? 490
Češi a Slováci ve 20. Století 487
Češi na vlásku 17
Češi, Němci a odsun: diskuze nezávislých historiků 291
Česká a slovenská literatura v exilu a samizdatu: informatorium pro učitele, studenty i laiky 910
Česká barokní gotika: dílo Jana Santiniho-Aichla 1014
Česká národní bibliografie: knihy 1154
Česká národní bibliografie: soupis bibliografií 1156
Česká národní bibliografie: zahraniční bohemika 1155
Česká přísloví: soudobý stav konce 20. století 316
Česká republika a ekonomická transformace ve střední a východní Evropě 556
Česká zahraniční politika: Česká republika v Radě bezpečnosti OSN: 1994-1995 501
České noviny 1102
České secesní sklo 988
Česko-anglický ekonomický slovník 783
Česko-anglický slovník 774
Československá obchodní banka, a.s.: annual report 1996 613
Československá spartakiáda 1980 742
Československé dějiny v datech 121

Československé filmy 1977-1980: filmografie 1011
Československo a Izrael, 1945-1956: dokumenty 495
Československo a Izrael, 1947-1953: studie 496
Československý odboj na Západě (1939-1945) 201
Českoslovenští Romové v letech 1938-1945 263
Český biografický archiv a Slovenský biografický archiv. Czech and Slovakian biographical archive 1158
Český dialog. Měsíčník pro Čechy doma i ve světě 1104
Český hokej 746
Český hudební adresář 1042
Český klub – Czech Club 1111
Český Parnasus, literature 1970-1990: interpretace vybraných děl 60 autorů 846
Český slovník věcný a synonymický 773
Čeští spisovatelé – Czech writers 843
Čeští spisovatelé literatury pro děti a mládež 843
Čeština jako cizí jazyk II. Výběrová bibliografie příruček češtiny jako cizího jazyka 1157
Čeština pro cizince 803
Chamber music of Antonín Dvořák 1059
Changes in Czech 671
Changes in expenditure and household inequality in the Czech and Slovak Republic 370
Changing foreign trade patterns in post-reform Czech industry (1989-1995): empirical evidence 639

Charles IV., the king from golden cradle 129
Charles University 403
Charta 77 Foundation: twenty years 443
Chata and chalupa: recreational houses in the Czech Socialist Republic 753
Checkmate in Prague: memoirs of Luděk Pachman 756
Chemicals, pharmaceuticals and rubber: December 1996 664
Child of Europe: a new anthology of East European poetry 897
Childhood as a social phenomenon: national report – Czechoslovakia 383
Children's fashion in the Czech Lands over the centuries 991
Church and state in Czechoslovakia, historically, juridically and theologically documented 321
Church in a Marxist Society: a Czechoslovak view 341
Church of the Sacred Heart 67
Church of St. Nicholas 68
Církev a majetek: k restituci majetku církví a náboženských organizací 329
Církevní řády a kongregace v zemích českých 346
Citizenship and democratic control in contemporary Europe 460
City and the controversialist: Karel Teige, Czech functionalism and the reconstruction of Prague 1023

Civic freedom in Central Europe: voices from Czechoslovakia 442
Články v českých časopisech 1154
Class structure in Europe: new findings from East-West comparisons of social structure and mobility 359
Closely observed trains 881
Closely watched films: the Czechoslovak experience 1004
Closely watched trains 881
Co v slovnících nenajdete 766
Coast of Bohemia: a winter's tale 932
Coasts of Bohemia 4
Cold War 213
Cold War Europe, 1945-1991: a political history 437
Colloquial Czech 797
Colloquium Bohuslav Martinů, his pupils, friends and contemporaries, Brno 1990 1084
Columbia history of Eastern Europe in the twentieth century 108
Comenius 407
Comenius: a critical reassessment of his life and work 405
Comenius 1592-1670: European reformer and Czech patriot, an exhibition 412
Coming of the First World War 167
Commentary on the Czechoslovak Civil Code 514
Communication and democracy 1092
Communist higher education policies in Czechoslovakia, Poland and East Germany 398
Communist party in power: a profile of party politics in Czechoslovakia 444
Competitiveness of industry in the Czech Republic and Hungary 640
Complete novels of Franz Kafka 937
Concentrated Prague 715
Concise historical atlas of Eastern Europe 40
Conditions for business activities of foreign investors in the Czech Republic 559
Conscience and captivity: religion in Eastern Europe 320
Conservation problems of historic cities in Eastern Europe 717
Constant flux: a study of class mobility in industrial societies 360
Constitution making in Eastern Europe 504
Construction and property in the Czech Republic: 1994-2000 712
Construction I: October 1997 666
Consumer Eastern Europe 594
Contemplation and other stories 945
Contemporary Czech 794
Contemporary Czechoslovak composers 1046
Contemporary nationalism in East Central Europe 248
Co-operatives in Central and Eastern Europe: self-help in structural change 551
Corporate governance in Central Eastern Europe: case studies of firms in transition 641
Council for Mutual Economic Assistance – the new tasks 533
Country forecasts 593
Country profiles 593
Country reports 593
Country risk services 593
Court, cloister and the city: the art and culture in Central Europe, 1450-1800 963
Creating capital markets in Eastern Europe 542
Cremator 870
Criminal law reform in the Czech Republic in the interdisciplinary perspective 513
La crise de l'environnement à l'Est 723
Crisis of Leninism and the decline of the Left: the revolutions of 1989 237
Critical essays on Franz Kafka 941
Cross currents: a yearbook of Central European culture 19
Crossing the Yabbok: illness and death in Ashkenazi Judaism in the sixteenth- through nineteenth-century Prague 280
Crown, church and estates: Central European politics in the sixteenth and seventeenth centuries 150
Čtyřjazyčný slovník práva Evropských společenství 786
Cubism in architecture and the applied arts: Bohemia and France 1910-1914 1025
Cubism in Czech architecture 1026
Culture, identity and politics 440

Culture shock: a guide to customs and etiquette 52
Cutting it short and The little town where time stood still 882
Czech Americans 298
Czech and English names of mushrooms 80
Czech and Slovak Construction Journal 666
Czech and Slovak experience: selected papers from the Fourth World Congress for Soviet and East European Studies, Harrogate 1990 180, 186, 275, 285, 287
Czech and Slovak literature in English: a bibliography 852
Czech and Slovak republics 48, 710
Czech and Slovak republics at a glance 560
Czech and Slovak republics: nation versus state 461
Czech and Slovak republics: the Rough Guide 47
Czech and Slovak steel industries 654
Czech and Slovak theatre 999
Czech and Slovak trolleybus and tram guide 687
Czech and Slovak women and political leadership 379
Czech avantgardists 900
Czech business and foreign trade 595
Czech chivalric romances Vévoda Arnošt and Lavryn in their literary context 829
Czech: a complete course for beginners 796

Czech Cubism: architecture, furniture and decorative arts, 1910-1925 1026
Czech drama since World War II 996
Czech exporters and importers 98 525
Czech fascist movement: 1922-1942 432
Czech fashion 1870-1918: from waltz to the tango 991
Czech fashion 1918-1939: elegance of the Czechoslovak First Republic 991
Czech fashion: 10th-15th centuries 991
Czech fashion: 16th-18th centuries 991
Czech finance and investment 617
Czech firearms and ammunition: history and present 669
Czech for foreigners 802
Czech for you 801
Czech Functionalism: 1918-1938 1028
Czech historical grammar 760
Czech history: chronological survey 122
Czech household sector in transition 369
Czech housing system in the middle of transition 711
Czech in three months 798
Czech industry and investment: Financial Times survey 573
Czech industry growth despite heavy debts 676
Czech Language News 1117
Czech literature 832
Czech literature since 1956: a symposium 844
Czech mating game 887

Czech: a multi-level course for advanced learners 799
Czech music 1043-44
Czech music in the web of life 1045
Czech national cookbook 1086
Czech nationalism in the nineteenth century 160
Czech nationalism: a study of the national theatre movement 1845-1883 994
Czech 19th century paintings 961
Czech opera 1038
Czech phrase book travel pack 806
Czech plays: modern Czech drama 904
Czech prose and verse: a selection with an introductory essay 896
Czech prose: an anthology 895
Czech red unions, 1918-1929: a study of their relations with the Communist Party and the Moscow International 433
Czech renascence of the nineteenth century: essays in honour of Otakar Odložilík 158
Czech Republic 401, 577-78, 611, 618, 643, 682, 697
Czech Republic and economic transition in Eastern Europe 556
Czech Republic: Berlitz pocket guides 50
Czech Republic: a business and investment guide 562
Czech Republic: businessman's guide to Czech legislation in 1995-96 516
Czech Republic: country profile 565

380

Czech Republic country report 674
Czech Republic: Financial Times survey 576, 611, 615
Czech Republic in brief 26
Czech Republic – industry and investment 573
Czech Republic: presented on the occasion of the EBRD Annual Meeting Business Forum, London, 12-15 April 610
Czech Republic: the property, construction and building material markets 587
Czech Republic: the quest for integration with the West 557
Czech Republic's strengthened academy 695
Czech revolution of 1848 163
Czech stockmarket guide: October 1997 – September 1998 622
Czech studies: literature, language, culture. České studie: literatura, jazyk, kultura 7
Czech textile industry 668
Czech through Russian 795
Czech translation of the Bible 325
Czech women in the labour market: work and family in the transition economy 378
Czech writers and politics, 1945-1969 842
Czech-English dictionary 777
Czech-English idioms and figurative expressions 781
Czechoslovak Air Force in Britain, 1940-1945 201

Czechoslovak armoured fighting vehicles: 1918-1945. Development for Czechoslovakia. Exploitation by Germany 698
Czechoslovak army in France: 1939-1945 202
Czechoslovak church 339
Czechoslovak contribution to world culture 11
Czechoslovak Declaration of Independence: a history of the document 177
Czechoslovak economy: 1918-1980 530
Czechoslovak economy 1948-1988: the battle for economic reform 531
Czechoslovak engineering until the Second World War 696
Czechoslovak foundry industry – past, present and future 655
Czechoslovak government and its disloyal opposition: 1918-1938 430
Czechoslovak heresy and schism: the emergence of a national Czechoslovak Church 339
Czechoslovak legions in Russia: 1914-1920 169
Czechoslovak mineral springs 37
Czechoslovak music: Bohemia and Moravia 1040
Czechoslovak new wave 1003
Czechoslovak partial mobilization in May 1938: a mystery (almost) solved 196
Czechoslovak prints from 1900-1970 974
Czechoslovak samizdat: a catalogue of British Library holdings 913

Czechoslovak Spartakiad 1985 742
Czechoslovakia 5, 46, 109, 114, 673, 1134, 1159
Czechoslovakia and Olympic Games 739
Czechoslovakia: anvil of the Cold War 215
Czechoslovakia at the crossroads of European history 118
Czechoslovakia before the Slavs 88
Czechoslovakia behind the Iron Curtain (1945-1989) 217
Czechoslovakia between Stalin and Hitler: the diplomacy of Edvard Beneš in the 1930s 192
Czechoslovakia between the wars: democracy on trial 428
Czechoslovakia: a bibliographical guide 1161
Czechoslovakia: crossroads and crisis, 1918-1988 13
Czechoslovakia: difficult times after divorce 672
Czechoslovakia. Exploitation by Germany 698
Czechoslovakia: a guide to literature in English, covering the historical and cultural development of Czech and Slovak nations up to 1939 1160
Czechoslovakia in transition 557
Czecho-Slovakia in transition: from federation to separation 452
Czechoslovakia in transition: politics, economics and society 459
Czechoslovakia 1918-88: seventy years from independence 185, 197, 282, 426

Czechoslovakia, 1918-92: a laboratory for social change 354
Czechoslovakia past and present 12
Czechoslovakia: the plan that failed 226
Czechoslovakia: the unofficial culture 9
Czechoslovakian glassmakers 676
Czechoslovakia's agriculture, situation, trends and prospects: document 629
Czechoslovakia's interrupted revolution 227
Czechoslovakia's North-Moravian region: a geographical appraisal 35
Czechoslovakia's Velvet Revolution: a political analysis 448
Czechoslovak-Polish negotiations on the establishment of confederation and alliance: 1939-1944 199
Czechoslovak-Polish relations,1918-1939: a selected and annotated bibliography 492
Czechs and balances 17
Czechs and Germans: a study of the struggle in the historic provinces of Bohemia and Moravia 491
Czechs and Germans: yesterday and today 283
Czechs and Slovaks in America 301
Czechs and Slovaks in Latin America 299
Czechs and Slovaks in modern history 217
Czechs and Slovaks in North America: a bibliography 297
Czechs during World War I: the path to independence 168

Czechs in Texas 299
Czechs of Cleveland 302

D

Daily News 1106
Dances of Czechoslovakia 318
Dancing house 1033
Dancing lessons for the advanced in age 881
Dark alchemy: the films of Jan Švankmajer 1008
Daydreams and nightmares: Czech Communist and ex-Communist literature 1917-1987 838
Death of Mr Baltisberger 881
Decadence and innovation: Austro-Hungarian life and art at the turn of the century 149
Decline and fall of the Habsburg Empire: 1815-1918 146
Dějiny české hudby v obrazech, od nejstarších památek do vybudování Národního divadla 1039
Dějiny obyvatelstva českých zemí 2
Dějiny svobodného zednářství v Čechách 342
Description of spoken Prague Czech 808
Description of a struggle: the Picador book of contemporary East European prose 898
Deset pražských dnů, 17.–27. listopadu 1989: dokumentace 238
Destiny of Europe's Gypsies 264
Development and reform of the financial system in Central and Eastern Europe 601

Development of the Czech media since the fall of Communism 1095
Devětsil: Czech avant-garde art; architecture and design of the 1920s and 1930s 1028
Diaries of Franz Kafka: 1910-1923 951
Dictionary of East European history since 1945 208
Dilemmas of regionalism and the region of dilemmas: the case of Upper Silesia 36
Dimensions of the present moment 880
Discretion and valour: religious conditions in Russia and Eastern Europe 320
Distant voices: Milena Dopitová, Petr Nikl, Václav Stratil, Ivan Kafka. Contemporary art from the Czech Republic 979
Distribution and retailing in Eastern Europe: supplying the new consumers 649
Disturbing the peace: a conversation with Karel Hvížďala 242
Le divorce Tchéco-Slovaque: vie et mort de la Tchécoslovaquie 1918-1992 451
Do Czech women need feminism? Perspectives of feminist theories and practices in Czechoslovakia 377
Dog and wolf 904
Doing business in the Czech Republic 581-82, 584
Doing business in the Czech Republic: 1997/1998 585

Doing business in Czechoslovakia 583
Doing business with the Czech Republic 586
Dopisy Olze 245
Dr Edvard Beneš and Czechoslovakia's German minority: 1918-1943 285
Dubček: Dubček and Czechoslovakia 1968-1990 229
Dubček: profily vzdoru. Profiles of defiance. Profile des Trotzes. Les portraits de l'obstination 232
Dubček speaks: Alexander Dubček with Andras Sugar 231
Dvořák 1054, 1056
Dvořák and his world 1053
Dvořák, his life and time 1057
Dvořák in America: 1892-1895 1055
Dvořák in love: a light hearted dream 927
Dvořák, Janáček and their time 1064
Dvořák's first cello concerto 1054

E

East Central Europe between the two world wars 178
East European Constitutional Review 504
East European history: selected papers of the Third World Congress for Soviet and East European Studies 105
East European modernism: architecture in Czechoslovakia, Hungary and Poland between the wars 1027

East European national minorities: 1918-1980. A handbook 305
East European Quarterly 1118
East European revolution 210
East European security reconsidered 497
East-Central Europe in the Middle Ages: 1000-1500 126
East-Central European states and the European communities: legal adaptations to the market economy 508
Eastern Europe and the Commonwealth of Independent States, 1999 528
Eastern Europe between the wars, 1918-1941 178
Eastern Europe in crisis and the way out 552
Eastern Europe in transformation: the impact on sociology 358
Eastern Europe market atlas 528
Eastern European banking 597
Eastern European Business Quarterly: Business Opportunities in the Czech Republic, Poland, CIS, Slovakia, Hungary, Romania 1127
Eastern European development and public policy 463
Eastern European national minorities, 1919-1980: a handbook 252
Eastern Europe's emerging cities: operating outside the region's capitals 553

Economic development and reforms in cooperation partner countries: the role of the state with particular focus on security and defence issues: Colloquium 17-19 June 1998, Ljubljana, Slovenia 499
Economic impact of new firms in post-socialist countries: bottom-up transformation in Eastern Europe 550
Economic performance and financial sector reform in Central and Eastern Europe: capital flows, bank and enterprise restructuring 606
Economic restructuring of the former Soviet Union: the case of housing 707
Economic transformation and the environment 731
Economist Intelligence Unit Business Report Czech Republic and Slovakia 593
Education and economic change in Eastern Europe and the former Soviet Union 393
Egg at Easter: a folkore study 319
Ekonomika a cudzie jazyky. Economy and foreign languages. Ökonomie und Fremdsprache 400
Ema Destinová a její jihočeské sídlo. Emmy Destin und ihr sudbömischer Sitz. Emmy Destin and her South Bohemian seat 1047
L'Empéreur Charles IV: l'art en Europe au XIVe siècle 130

383

Employment policies in the Soviet Union and Eastern Europe 362
Empty victory for conqueror of tyranny 477
Encyclopedia of Czech and Moravian wine 1087
Encyclopedia of European historical weapons 1148
End of central planning? Socialist economies in transition: the cases of Czechoslovakia, Hungary, China and the Soviet Union 546
End of Czechoslovakia 450
Energy and environmental conflicts in East/Central Europe: the case of power generation 724
Energy, water and the environment in the Czech Republic: an overview 661
English-Czech dictionary of idioms 782
English-Czech technical dictionary – Anglisko-český technický slovník 788
Environmental impact legislation: Czech Republic, Estonia, Hungary, Latvia, Lithuania, Poland, Slovak Republic, Slovenia 725
Environmental laws in the Czech Republic 725
Environmental problems in Eastern Europe 72
Environmental Yearbook of the Czech Republic 729
Equality and inequality in Eastern Europe 361
Erbovník, aneb Kniha o znacích i osudech rodů žijících v Čechách a na

Moravě podle starých pramenů a dávných ne vždy věrných svědectví 99
Essays in Czech and Slovak language and literature 810
Essays in Czech history 128
Essays on Czech literature 833
Essential Czech Republic: (with excursions into Slovakia) 51
Establishment of Communist regimes in Eastern Europe, 1944-1949 211
Ethnic national minorities in Eastern Europe 1848-1945 254
Etymologický slovník jazyka českého 770
Euromoney: Central and Eastern European financial resources book 599
European bibliography of Slavic and East European Studies (EBSEES). Bibliographie européenne des travaux sur l'ex-USSR et l'Europe de l'Est 1152
European cities, planning systems and property markets 705
European fajáns: from the collections of the Museum of Decorative Arts in Prague: Troja Castle, 1992-1993 1146
Europe-Asia Studies 1119
Europe's sex supermarket 384
Eva Jiřičná 1035
Eva Jiřičná: design in exile 1035
Eva Urbanová: soprano 1047

'Every Czech a Sokol': feminism and nationalism in the Czech Sokol movement 741
Everyman companion to East European literature 819
Evolution and efficiency of concentration in manufacturing 644
Evolution of the state-owned banking sector during transition in Central Europe 604
Ex-Communists in post-Communist societies 822
Exhibition notes 868
Exiles 983
Export promotion in the Czech Republic 571
External relations of the Council for Mutual Economic Assistance 535

F

Fables 863
Facts on foreign trade of the Czech Republic 570
Fairy tales from Czechoslovakia 311
Fakta o sociální situaci v České republice 418
Family in the mother of towns. Today's Prague portrayed in statistical data 421
Fauna ČR a SR 81
Feminism meets socialism: women's studies in the Czech Republic 380
Fiction of freedom, the development of the Czechoslovak literary reform movement: 1956-1968 845
Fiction of Josef Škvorecký 924

384

Field post of the Czechoslovak and Allied Forces in Russia, 1918-1920: an anthology 169
Filmová ročenka. Film Yearbook 1010
Finance, investment and trade with Czechoslovakia: Prague 7th & 8th November 1991 572
Financial reform in Central and Eastern Europe 602
Financing foreign operations 593
Financing operations in the Czech Republic, 1997: a guide to finding, managing and moving money 608
Firm behavior in emerging market economies: cases from the private and public sectors in Central and Eastern Europe 549
First editions of Leoš Janáček: a bibliographical catalogue with reproductions of title pages 1079
Fiscal system in transition: the case of the Czech income tax 580
Fish and fisherman 754
Fishing in the Czech Socialist Republic 755
Fleet Sheet 1107
Fly 878
Focus 621
Fodor's new Czech Republic and Slovakia: the complete guide with great city walks and country drives 49
Folk and fairy tales from Bohemia 312
Folk art of Czechoslovakia 317

For better or for worse 20
Forests of Czechoslovakia 79
Forging ahead, falling behind 466
Forgotten Czechs of the Banat. Zapomenutí Češi v Banátu 305
Foundry engineering in the Czech Republic 399
Four years on 588
Franks, Moravians and Magyars: the struggle for the Middle Danube, 788-907 96, 102
Franz Kafka 939
Franz Kafka, the Jewish patient 944
Franz Kafka: representative man 940
Franz Kafka's loneliness 942
Freshwater fishes 85
From capitalism to socialism 532
From Oxford to Prague: the writings of John Wycliffe and his English followers in Bohemia 134
Fundamentals of Czech history 123
Future of the defence industries in Central and Eastern Europe 647
Future of industry in Central and Eastern Europe 636
Future systems: the story of tomorrow 1036
Futurology and robots: Karel Čapek's R.U.R. 860

G

Games 904
Gardens in Central Europe 78
Gender agenda 345
Genesis of Czechoslovakia 174

Geofyzikální obraz ČSSR 27
Geography of Czechoslovakia 25
George of Poděbrady: king of heretics 142
German occupation of Sudetenland: 1938 203
German Social Democratic Party of Czechoslovakia: 1918-1926 287
Geschichte Böhmens: von der slavischen Landnahme bis zur Gegenwart 119
Geschichte der Roma in Böhmen, Mähren und Slowakei 262
Glassmaking trends in Czechoslovakia 676
Global trends and changes in East European banking 603
Golden Lane 66
Golem 314
Golem: Prague Cultural Review 1108
Good beer guide to Prague and to the Czech Republic 1088
Good guide to beer-halls of Prague 1089
Good King Wenceslas: the real story 127
Good soldier Švejk and his fortunes in the World War 857
Gothic mural painting in Bohemia and Moravia 1300-1378 967
Government cautious over future of gas 660
Grammaire de la langue tchèque 792
Grammar of the Bohemian or Čech language 816
Grand restoration of a humble birth place 72
Great revolutions compared: the outline of a theory 140

Great War's forgotten front: a soldier's diary and a son's reflections 171
Greater integration is the solution 533
Gregor Mendel: the first geneticist 699
Grossbritannien, die USA und die böhmische Länder 1848-1938: Vorträge der tagung des Collegium Carolinum in Bad Wiessee, vom 2. Bis 6. November 1988. Great Britain, the United Sates and the Bohemian lands 1848-1938 485
Grosse und mittelständische Unternehmen in der Tschechischen Republik 1996 527
Grove dictionary of music and musicians 1054
Growing the alliance 502
Guide to birds 82
Guide to Bohemian Forest-Šumava 73
Guide to Czech and Slovak glass 675
Guide to guides 59
Guide to libraries in Central and Eastern Europe 1132
Guide to Slavonic languages 757
Gustáv Husák, president of Czechoslovakia: speeches and writings 233
Gustav Mahler, an essential guide to his life and works 1063
Gypsies 257, 265
Gypsies in Czechoslovakia 260
Gypsies: a multidisciplinary annotated bibliography 256

Gypsies of Eastern Europe 259
Gypsy bibliography 256
Gypsy malady 269

H

Habsburg Empire 1760-1918 145
Hamlyn encyclopedia of plants 76
Hana Mandlíková 749
Handbuch Wirtschaft und Recht in Osteuropa 518
Harmony under the bonnet 653
Hate speech 1099
Hauer-King House: Future Systems 1037
He was one of the great composers – and also the cruellest 1068
Headed for the blues: a memoir with ten stories 925
Health care and the pharmaceutical industries of the Czech Republic and Slovakia 388
Health care reform in the Czech Republic 386
Health care system in the Czech Republic 387
Heart of Europe: essays on literature and ideology 820
Heart of Kunstkammer: Prague's Golden Age and the eclecticism of Rudolfine aesthetics 154
Higher education in the Czech and Slovak Federal Republic: guide for foreign students 397
Higher education in the Czech Republic: guide for foreign students 397
Higher education in the Czech Republic, 1998 396

Higher education reform process in Central and Eastern Europe 394
Hints to exporters visiting Central Europe: Czech Republic, Hungary, Poland, Slovak Republic, Slovenia 638
Historians as nation builders: Central and South-East Europe 107
Historical account of the development of scholarly libraries in Bohemia up to the establishment of the State Library in Prague 1136
Historical atlas of East Central Europe 39
Historical dictionary of the Czech state 112
Historical dictionary of the Gypsies (Romanies) 255
Historical reflections on Central Europe: selected papers from the Fifth World Congress of Central and East European Studies, Warsaw, 1995 106
Historický ústav armády České republiky. The History Institute of the Army of the Czech Republic 1145
Historio de la Esperanto-movado en Ĉehoslovakio: iom da historio kaj iom da rememoroj 817
History of Bohemian literature 827
History of British-Czech relations 483
History of Czechoslovak nuclear energy and the future of nuclear power in the Czech Republic 659

*History of the
  Czechoslovak Republic
  1918-1948* 179
*History of Czechoslovakia
  in outline* 115
*History of Czechoslovakia
  since 1945* 214
History of the Czechs 116
*History of the Czechs and
  Slovaks* 114
*History of Czechs in
  America* 299
*History of elections in
  Bohemia and Moravia*
  431
*History of the Gypsies of
  Eastern Europe and
  Russia* 258
*History of the present:
  essays, sketches and
  despatches from Europe
  in 1990s* 234
*Hitler's gift: the story of
  Theresienstadt* 206
*Hlasové o potřebě jednoty
  spisovného jazky pro
  Čechy, Moravany a
  Slováky* 18
*Hodiny a hodinky: ze
  sbírek Umělecko-
  průmyslového muzea v
  Praze. Clocks and
  watches: from the
  collections of the
  Museum of Decorative
  Arts in Prague* 990
Holy infant of Prague
  353
Homage to J. A. Comenius
  409
*Homosexuality, society
  and AIDS in the Czech
  Republic* 391
*Hope dies last: the
  autobiography of
  Alexander Dubcek* 230
Hordubal 862
Hospodářské noviny
  1128
*Hospody a pivo v české
  společnosti* 1088
House of the tragic poet
  890

Hradec Králové 69
*Hugo's Czech cassette
  course* 798
*Human geography in
  Eastern Europe and
  the former Soviet Union*
  24
*Human rights and
  democratization in the
  Czech Republic* 515
*Human rights in
  Czechoslovakia* 445
100 pearls of Moravia 8
*100 perel Čech – 100
  Perlen Böhmens – 100
  pearls of Bohemia* 8
*Hussite king: Bohemia in
  European affairs
  1440-1471* 141
Hussite revolution 137

I

*I served the king of
  England* 881
*ICEES International
  Newsletter* 1120
Identity 922
*Images of the prostitutes
  in Czech fin de siècle
  literature* 836
*Immobilienerwerb in der
  Tschechischen Republik*
  520
In the ghetto 267
*In search of Czechness in
  music* 1064
*Index to articles on
  Czechoslovak philately:
  1950-1979* 1166
*Indigo country cloths and
  artefacts from
  Czechoslovakia* 992
*Industrial geography of
  Prague: 1848-1921* 30
*Industrialisation of a
  Central European city:
  Brno and the fine
  woollen industry in the
  18th century* 633
*Industry in the Czech and
  Slovak Republics* 635

*Infant of Prague: the story
  of the Holy Image and
  the history of the
  devotion* 353
*Inform katalog 93/94:
  katalog českých
  podniků: Directory of
  Czech companies* 524
*Inform, Katalog, Export
  1995: Czech trade and
  investment promotion*
  525
*Information dissemination
  and access in Russian
  and Eastern Europe:
  problems and solutions
  in East and West* 414
*Innovations in public
  management:
  perspectives from East
  and West Europe* 464
Insect play 860
*Institutional design in new
  democracies: Eastern
  Europe and Latin
  America* 465
*Integration of the
  European Community
  and third states in
  Europe: a legal analysis*
  541
*Intellectual property
  rights in Central and
  Eastern Europe: the
  creation of favourable
  legal and market
  preconditions* 310
*Intellectuals and the future
  in the Habsburg
  monarchy, 1890-1914*
  148
*Intensive care: selected
  and new poems* 879
*Interaction between
  agriculture and nature
  conservation in the
  Czech and Slovak
  Republics. IUCN
  European Programme*
  732
*Interference: the story of
  Czechoslovakia in the
  words of its writers* 903

387

Internalization of retailing in Czech and Slovak Republics 648
International migration in Central and Eastern Europe and the Commonwealth of Independent States 480
International politics of East Central Europe 479
Interpretation of the Bible. Interpretation der Bibel. Interprétation de la Bible. Interpretacija svetega pisma 325
Intimate letters: Leoš Janáček to Kamila Stösslová 1067
Introduction to the study of the Slavonic languages 759
Investing 593
Investing, licencing and trading in the Czech Republic: 1997 561
Investment engineering: February 1998 65
Investor's environmental guidelines: Bulgaria, Czech Republic and Slovak Republic, Estonia, Hungary, Latvia, Lithuania, Poland, Romania 725
Irreconcilable differences? 965
Is a Czech era ending? 590
Italy and East-Central Europe: dimensions of the regional relationship 494

J

J. A. Comenius and the concept of universal education 406
J. E. Purkyně and psychology: with a focus on unpublished manuscripts 703

Jan Amos Comenius 1592-1992: theologische und pädagogische Deutungen 408
Jan Evangelista Purkyně in science and culture: scientific conference, Prague, August 26.-30. 1987 704
Jan Hus 131, 831
Jan Hus as a general linguist, with special reference to Česká nedělní postila 133
Jan Konůpek: poutník k nekonečnu. A pilgrim to infinity 975
Jan Masaryk: personal memoir 190
Jan Žižka and the Hussite revolution 138
Janáček and Brod 1078
Janáček as theorist 1075
Janáček: Glagolitic Mass 1074
Janáček-Newmarch correspondence 1077
Janáček's operas: a documentary account 1070
Janáček's tragic operas 1071
Janáček's uncollected essays on music 1075
Janáček's works: a catalogue of the music and writings of Leoš Janáček 1080
Jaroslav Hašek, 1883-1983: proceedings of the International Hašek symposium, Bamberg, June 24-27, 1983 856
Jawaharlal Nehru and the Munich betrayal of Czechoslovakia 195
Jewish anecdotes from Prague 315
Jewish art treasures from Prague. The State Jewish Museum in

Prague and its collections 1147
Jewish community in Prague during the inter-war period 275
Jewish customs and traditions 279
Jewish identities in the new Europe 272
Jewish sights of Bohemia and Moravia 276
Jews in Svoboda's army in the Soviet Union: Czechoslovak Jewry's fight against the Nazis during World War II 204
Jews of Czechoslovakia: historical studies and surveys 273
Jingle bell principle 878
Jiří Anderle: drawings, prints, paintings, objects 1954-1996 982
Jiří Menzel and the history of the Closely watched trains 1005
Johan Blasius Santini-Aichel: a Gothic-Baroque architect in Bohemia, 1677-1723 1014
Johannes Amos Comenius (1592-1670): exponent of European culture? 410
John Hus: a biography 132
Joke 919
Joseph shops: Eva Jiřičná, Jose Manser 1035
Josip Plečnik – an architect of Prague castle 1029
Journal of the Kafka Society of America 937
Journal of Russian and East European Economic Affairs 1128
Juden in der deutschen Literatur: ein deutsch-israelisches symposion 934

388

Judge on trial 889
Julius Zeyer: the path to decadence 850

K

K: a biography of Kafka 938
Kafka 939
Kafka and the contemporary critical performance: centenary readings 947
Kafka and language, in the stream of thoughts and life 942
Kafka: gender, class and race in the letters and fictions 944
Kafka: Judaism, politics and literature 936
Kafka, love and courage: the life of Milena Jesenská 953
Kafka's clothes: ornament and aestheticism in the Habsburg Fin de Siècle 944
Kafka's Milena 955
Kafka's narrators: a study of his stories and sketches 949
Kafka's relatives: their lives and his writing 943
Kafka's rhetoric: the passion of reading 947
Kardinál Tomášek 350
Karel Čapek 859
Karel Čapek: in pursuit of truth, tolerance and trust 859
Karel Havlíček (1821-1856): a national liberation leader of the Czech renascence 165
Karel Matěj Čapek-Chod: proceedings of a symposium held at the School of Slavonic and East European Studies 840
Kašpar Lén mstitel 840

Katalog Sixty-Eight Publishers 911
Katolická církev a pozemková reforma 1945-1948: dokumentace 329
Kdo je kdo v České republice na přelomu 20. století 455
King and estates in Bohemian lands, 526-1564 151
Klementinská knihovna. The Clementinum Library. Bibliotheca semper viva 1138
Kniha apokryfů 828
Kniha smíchu a zapomění 828
Knihovna národního muzea: zámecká knihovna Český Krumlov. The National Museum Library: Castle Library of the Český Krumlov 1139
Knihy za ohradou: česká literatura v exilových nakladatelstvích 909
Kompass: Czech Republic 1997, company information, products and services: directory of industry and commerce of Czech Republic 523
Království české: erby a rodokmeny vládnoucích rodů. Kingdom of Bohemia: arms and pedigrees of reigning houses. Königreich Böhmen: Wappen und Genealogie der regierenden Häuser. Royaume de Bohême: armoiries et généalogie des maisons souveraines 98
Kronika českého fotbalu do roku 1945. Kronika českého fotbalu od roku 1945 744

Kubistická Praha – Cubist Prague: 1090-1925 1026
Květena České republiky 74
Květena České socialistické republiky 74
Kytice 831

L

Labour statistics for a market economy: challenges and solutions in the transition countries of Central and Eastern Europe and the former Soviet Union 413
Labyrint světa a ráj srdce 828
Labyrinth of the word: truth and representation in Czech literature 828
Language of nationality and the nationality of language 952
Lapidarium of the National Museum, Prague. Guide to the permanent exhibition of Czech sculpture in stone of the 11th to 18th centuries in the pavilion of the lapidarium in the exhibition grounds in Prague 1149
Largest cave system of the Czech Socialist Republic in the Moravský kras (Moravian Karst) 36
Largo desolato 828, 875
Laughable loves 920
Laveur des vitres et archevêque. Biographie de Mgr Miloslav Vlk (Prague) 350
Legal guide, Czech Republic: general report 513
Legenda o Sodomovi 828

389

Legends of Old Bohemia 855
Der Legionär: ein deutsch-tschechischer Konflikt von Masaryk bis Havel 172
Lékařský slovník anglicko-český česko-anglický 789
Lekce Faust 1008
Leoš Janáček: a biography 1066
Leoš Janáček: born in Hukvaldy 1072
Leoš Janáček: the field that prospered 1065
Leoš Janáček: Katya Kabanová 1073
Leoš Janáček: leaves from his life 1069
Leoš Janáček's aesthetic thinking 1076
Letní přemítání 473
Letters to Felice 956
Letters to Milena 952
Letters to Olga: June 1979-September 1982 245
Lexikon českého filmu: 2 000 filmů 1930-1997 1000
Liberation of women and nation: Czech nationalism and women writers in the Fin de Siècle 18
Libraries of the Czech Republic. Bibliotheken der Tschechischen Republik 1133
Licencing and trading conditions abroad 593
Lidové noviny 1100
Lidská práva, ženy a společnost 376
Life closely observed 882
Life of Edvard Beneš, 1884-1948: Czechoslovakia in peace and war 198
Life of Mahler 1063
Life of a poet: Rainer Maria Rilke 957

Life study of Franz Kafka 1883-1924, using the intensive journal method of Ira Progoff 938
Life with a star 871
Lines of succession: heraldry of the royal families of Europe 97
Linky městské hromadné dopravy v Praze: 829-1990 691
Lions or foxes: heroes or lackeys? 434
Literature and tolerance: views from Prague 908
Literature of nationalism: essays on West European identity 821
Little Czech and the great Czech nation 3
Little town where time stood still 882
Lives of St. Wenceslas, St. Ludmila and St. Adalbert 327
Living Czech: the language of the he(a)rd 808
Living in truth 872
Living standards and social conditions in Czechoslovakia 364
Living through it twice: poems of the Romany holocaust (1940-1997). Dvakrát tím samým: básně o romském holocaustu (1940-1997) 264
Living within the truth 475
Local government and market decentralization: experiences in industrialized, developing and former Eastern Block countries 522
Local government in Eastern Europe: establishing democracy at the grass roots 521

Local urban restructuring as a mirror of global processes: Prague in the 1990s 713
Looking is a marvellous thing: from Rainer Maria Rilke's letters to his wife Clara, on looking at Cezanne's pictures in the Salon d'Automme, Paris, October, 1907 957
Love and garbage 888
Love match: Nelson vs. Navrátilová 749
Lovers for a day 887

M

Magic Prague 837
Magister Theodoricus, court painter to Emperor Charles IV: the pictorial decorations of the shrines at Karlštejn Castle 966
Magnificent ride: the first Reformation in Hussite Bohemia 135
Máj 828, 831
Máj: zweischprachige Ausgabe 853
Making and breaking of Communist Europe 446
Making of Czech Jewry. National conflict and Jewish society in Bohemia, 1870-1918 274
Making of Eastern Europe 102
Making of the Habsburg Monarchy, 1550-1700: an interpretation 152
Making of new Europe: R. W. Seton-Watson and the last years of Austria-Hungary 111
Man for all seasons 665
Man who disappeared (Amerika) 948

Managing in emerging market economies: cases from the Czech and Slovak republics 558

Market opportunities brief: Czech Republic 726

Le marketing en Europe centrale 1093

Markets and people: the Czech reform experience in a comparative perspective 356

Markets, states and democracy: the political economy of postcommunist transformation 540

Marks on German, Bohemian and Austrian porcelain: 1710 to the present 989

Martina: an ace of an autobiography from the greatest women's tennis player the world has ever known 749

Martina Navrátilová 748, 752

Martinů 1081

Martinů: out of exile 1082

Masaryk case: the murder of democracy in Czechoslovakia 190

Masaryk: religious heretic 186

Masaryks: the making of Czechoslovakia 189

Die Massenmedien der sozialistischen Tschechoslowakei 1094

Mastičkář 830

May 853

Meaning of irony: a psychoanalytic investigation 946

Media beyond socialism: theory and practice in East-Central Europe 1092

Meditation 949

Meditations on Metamorphosis 950

Mendel (1822-1884) in 90 minutes 700

Mendelian revolution: the emergence of hereditarian concepts in modern science and society 701

Mendelssohn is on the roof 871

Městské znaky v českých zemích 100

Metamorphosis 950

Metamorphosis in the Czechoslovak economy: the Stamp memorial lecture 26. November 1991 563

Metamorphosis of science fiction 860

Metamorphosis: translation, backgrounds and contexts, criticism 950

Meteor 862

Milan Kundera and the art of fiction: critical essays 917

Milan Kundera and feminism: dangerous intersections 915

Milan Kundera: an annotated bibliography 914

Milan Kundera: a voice from Central Europe 914

Milena 954

Milostné léto 886

Mineral deposits of the Erzgebirge/Krušné hory (Germany, Czech Republic): reviews and results of recent investigations 33

Minorities in politics: cultural and language rights 249

Minority culture in a capital city: the Czechs in Vienna at the turn of the century 308

Minority politics in a multinational state: the German Social Democrats in Czechoslovakia: 1928-1938 288

Miracle game 925

Mirror of world theatre: the Prague Quadrennial 1967-1991 997

Miss Silver's past 926

Mladá fronta DNES 1101

Mluvte s námi česky! Audovizuální kurs 805

Mnichov 1938 193

Modern Czech grammar 800

Money demand and seignorage in transition 619

Monthly Statistics of Czech Republic 417

Moral leader of Europe 476

Morass 905

Moravia Magna: the Great Moravian Empire, its art and times 96

Moravian tales, legends, myth 313

Morfill and the Czechs 816

Most important art: Eastern European film after 1945 1002

Mountains of Central and Eastern Europe 732

Moving beyond assistance: final report of the IEWS Task Force on Western assistance to transition in the Czech and Slovak Federal Republic, Hungary and Poland 569

Moving to sustainability: how to keep small business development centres alive. Studies on centres in Poland, Hungary and the Czech Republic 548

391

Mozart's Don Giovanni in Prague 1048
Mr Theodore Mundstock 869
Mucha 970, 972
Mucha: the triumph of Art Nouveau 970
Mucha's figures décoratives 970
Multinational empire: nationalism and national reform in the Habsburg Monarchy 1848-1918 253
Museum of Czech literature: Prague 1141
Mushrooms and other fungi 80
Music news from Prague 1043
Music of Czechoslovakia 1077
My first loves 888
My golden trades 887
My life with Janáček: the memoirs of Zdenka Janáčková 1068
My life with Martinů 1081
My merry mornings: stories from Prague 887
Mystery of Dr. Martinů 1081
Le mythe de Munich. Mythos München. The myth of Munich 193

N

Národní bibliografie České republiky: soupis českých bibliografií 1156
Národní bibliografie České republiky: zahraniční bohemika 1155
Národní bibliografie ČR – Knihy 1154
Národní divadlo a jeho předchůdci 993
Národní knihovna ČR: průvodce historií.

National Library of the Czech Republic: guide to the history 1137
Narrative modes in Czech literature 834
Náš hokej 747
Naše řeč 770
Nástin vývoje textilní výroby v českých zemích v období 1781-1848. Abriss der Geschichte der Textilindustrie in den Böhmishe Landern 667
National conflict in Czechoslovakia: the making and remaking of a state, 1918-1987 425
National environmental protection funds in Central and Eastern Europe: case studies of Bulgaria, the Czech Republic, Hungary, Poland, and the Slovak Republic 727
National income and outlay in Czechoslovakia, Poland and Yugoslavia 536
National Institute of Public Health, Prague, Czech Republic, in 1995-2000 392
National minorities in Romania: change in Transylvania 305
'National reparation'? The Czech land reform and the Sudeten Germans 1918-38 286
National report on the Czech and Slovak Federal Republic: United Nations Conference on Environment and Development, Brazil June 1992 733
Native literature of Bohemia in the fourteenth century 825

NATO handbook: a companion volume to the 50th anniversary edition of the NATO handbook, 1998 503
NATO handbook: 50 anniversary edition 503
NATO's eastern dilemmas 500
Der Naturalismus in der tschechischen Literatur 840
Nature of urbanism 720
Neglected generation 849
Net result 750
Netečný divák 828
Neviditelný pes 1102
New Czech poetry 901
New forms of security: views from Central, Eastern and Western Europe 498
New Glass Review 679
New poems 957
New sources on Soviet decision making during the 1968 Czechoslovak crisis 223
Newsletter, Dvořák Society 1044
Nightmare of reason: a life of Franz Kafka 940
Nine fairy tales by Karel Čapek and one more thrown in for good measure 866
Nobility and the making of the Hussite revolution 139
Noc s Hamletem 831
Notes zur destin des Tsiganes tchèques 264
Nová encyklopedie českého výtvarného umění 961
Nová květena ČSSR 75
Nová přítomnost. New Presence 1104
Nová slova v češtině: slovník neologismů 765

392

O

Obchod se ženami v postkomunistických zemích střední a východní Evropy – Traffic in women in Postcommunist countries of Central and Eastern Europe 376
Obnovení pořádku 440
Occupation of Czechoslovak frontier territories by Beck's Poland from the postal history view-point 203
Odkaz T. G. Masaryka 182
Odsun Němců: výbor z paměti a projevů doplněný edičními přílohami 290
Odsun Němců z Československa: 1945-1947 289
Old Czech legends 855
Olomouc Picture Gallery (I): Italian paintings of the 14th-18th centuries from Olomouc collections 1151
On all fronts: Czechs and Slovaks in World War II 200
On the emergence of Czechoslovakia 176
On Kafka: semi-centenary perspectives 945
On Masaryk: texts in English and German 187
On the way to Jesus: Czech Jesuits during the Communist oppression 348
Open letters: selected prose 1965-1990 873
Opera v Praze. Opera in Prague 1048
Opportunities and incentives in a newly emerging market 658
Orchestral works of Antonín Dvořák 1059

Ordinary life 862
Organizational changes in post-Communist Europe: management and transformation in the Czech Republic 574
Origins of Christianity in Bohemia: sources and documents 325
Origins of the Czech national renascence 159
Other Europe: Eastern Europe to 1945 104
Otokar Březina: zur Rezeption Schopenhauers und Nietzsches im tschechischen Symbolismus 841
Otta Janeček 980
Our brothers across the ocean: the Czech Sokol in America to 1914 303
Outline of the history of the Czech nation from 1879 to 1939 113
Outline of modern Czech grammar 793
Overcoming of the regime crisis after Stalin's death in Czechoslovakia, Poland and Hungary 221
Oxford photo dictionary anglicko-český 780

P

Painting the universe: František Kupka, pioneer in abstraction 975
Palace palimpsest 1018
Palaces of Prague 1017
Palacký: the historian as scholar and nationalist 164
Paleohydrography of the caves in the Moravský Kras 36

Panorama: a historical review of Czechs and Slovaks in the United States of America 302
Panorthosia or Universal Reform 405
Parliaments in transition: the new legislative politics in the former USSR and Eastern Europe 505
Parní symfonie 686
Party formation in East-Central Europe: post-Communist politics in Czechoslovakia, Hungary, Poland and Bulgaria 467
Past glory, shaky future 645
Paying the price: the wage crisis in Central and Eastern Europe 368
Payment systems in the Czech Republic 620
Penguin dictionary of saints 326
Performance of manufacturing 646
Perlen aus Gablonz: Historismus. Jugendstil. Beads from Gablonz: historicism, art nouveau 678
Permanent subversion 1009
Permit 905
Pharmaceuticals in Central and Eastern Europe 663
Philanthropic motive in Christianity: an analogy of the relations between theology and social services 331
Pilgrims 984
Pillars of Central Europe: the roles of cities in the process of transformation 709
Pink tanks and velvet hangovers: an American in Prague 21

Pits and pitfalls: the fate of Ondra Lysohorsky 959
Plague column 867
Plzeň 32
Pobyt americké armády v Plzni v roce 1945: (dobové fotografie a dokumenty); The story of the American army in Pilsen in the year 1945: (period photos and documents) 207
Pocket guide to wines 1087
Poems before and after 878
Poetica Slavica: Studies in honour of Zbigniew Folejewski 834
Der Poetismus: das Programm und die Hauptverfahren der tschechischen literarischen Avantgarde der zwanziger Jahre 839
Poet's lamp: an anthology of Czech poetry 899
Policy and institutional reform in Central European agriculture 625
Political and social doctrines of the Unity of Czech Brethren in the fifteenth and early sixteenth centuries 143
Political changes in Eastern Europe since 1989: prospects for liberal democracy and a market economy 462
Political culture and Communist studies 441
Political culture – continuity and discontinuity 427
Political economy of transition: coming to grips with history and methodology 537

Political history of Eastern Europe in the 20th century: the struggle between democracy and dictatorship 424
Political novels of Milan Kundera and O. V. Vijayan: a comparative study 915
Political persecution in Czechoslovakia: 1948-1972 218
Politické vzpomínky 429
Politics and religion in Central and Eastern Europe: traditions and transitions 323
Politics and religion in Eastern Europe: Catholicism in Hungary, Poland and Czechoslovakia 324
Politics in Czechoslovakia: 1945-1990 439
Politics of ethnic survival: the Germans in Prague, 1861-1914 281
Politics of ethnicity in Eastern Europe 251
Pollution in Prague: environmental control in a centrally planned socialist country 718
Pomocná škola Bixley 909, 929
Post Stalinist Central European drama on the British stage 823
Post-Communist elites and democracy in East Europe 469
Postnational identity: critical theory and existential philosophy in Habermas, Kierkegaard and Havel 471
Post-socialist media: what power the West? The changing landscape in Poland, Hungary and the Czech Republic 1091

Pověsti českých hradů a zámků 312
Die Prager deutsche Literatur und die tschechische Literatur in den ersten zwei Jahrzehnten des 20. Jahrhunderts 935
Prager wirtschafts- und sozial- historische Mitteilungen. Prague economic and social history papers 592
Prague 1163
Prague and Art Nouveau 1021
Prague and Sophia: an analysis of their changing internal city structure 716
Prague and Viennese Freemasonry, the Enlightenment, and the operations of the Harmony Lodge in Vienna 342
Prague: an architectural guide 60
Prague. Avenir d'une ville historique capitale 714
Prague Business Journal 1131
Prague castle 1016
Prague competition 1034
Prague Economic Papers. Quarterly Journal of Economic Theory and Policy 591
Prague et la Bohême centrale: quelques problèmes de croissance 721
Prague: fin de siècle 1022
Prague group of Ukrainian nationalist writers and their ideological origins 958
Prague: a guide to 20th century architecture 1024
Prague 100+100 63
Prague in black and gold: the history of a city 61

Prague in the shadow of the swastika: a history of the German occupation 1939-1945 205

Prague 1989, theatre of revolution: a study in humanistic political geography 31

Prague, 1968 225

Prague '93: metropolitan area report; urbanistic development of the town 719

Prague: passageways and arcades 1019

Prague Post 1105

Prague Post 1998 book of business list: key business and financial data on more than 1,500 top Czech companies 526

Prague School: selected writings, 1929-1946 811

Prague Slav Congress of 1848 163

Prague: some contemporary growth problems 721

Prague Spring and its aftermath: Czechoslovak politics, 1968-1970 223

Prague Spring: a mixed legacy 222

Prague Spring '68: a national security archives documents reader 225

Prague sprung: notes and voices from the New World 362

Prague tales 854

Prague: tales of the city 907

Prague: a traveller's literary companion 906

Prague trial: the first anti-Zionist show trial in the Communist Bloc 220

Prague Winter: restrictions on religious freedom in Czechoslovakia twenty years after the invasion 333

Praguiana: some basic and less known aspects of the Prague linguistic school 811

Pravidla českého pravopisu 768

Pražská heraldika 100

Pražské jaro. Prague Spring 1041

Pražské metro 690

Pražské zahrady 65

Pražský uličník: Encyklopedie názvů pražských veřejných prostranství 62

Prehistoric glass in Bohemia 985

Prémonstrés en Bohème, Moravie et Slovaquie. Premonstráti v Čechách, na Moravě a na Slovensku. Premonstratenser in Böhmen, Mähren und der Slowakei. Premonstratensians in Bohemia, Moravia and Silesia 347

Present-day Czech geography 25

President Edvard Beneš between East and West 1938-1948 198

Priest Rome can't embrace 343

Příruční slovník jazyka českého 761

Privatization in the Czech and Slovak republics 567

Privatization in Eastern Europe: is the state withering away? 540

Privatization in Eastern Europe: legal, economic and social aspects 509

Privatization in rural Eastern Europe: the process of restitution and restructuring 630

Privatization in the Visegrad countries: a comparative assessment 547

Privatization process in East-Central Europe: evolutionary process of Czech privatization 568

Programme 57

Promises, promises: contracts in Russia and other post-Communist economies 511

Promoting cleaner and safer industrial production in Central and Eastern Europe 637

Prospect for East-West European transport 680

Protest 905

Protestantism and politics in Eastern Europe and Russia: the Communist and post Communist eras 337

Průvodce právy příslušníků národnostních menšin v České republice 250

Ptáci-aves 82

Public monuments: art in historical bondage 1870-1887 1032

Q

Quality and availability of statistical data 415

La question énergétique en Europe de l'Est 724

Questions of identity and responsibility in Václav Havel 246

Questions of identity: Czech and Slovak ideas of nationality and personality 6, 246

Quiet Karel amid the clamour 745

R

R. W. Seton-Watson and his relations with the Czechs and Slovaks: documents 1906-1951 110
Radiant future: the French Communist party and Eastern Europe: 1944-1956 493
Rafael Kubelík v Praze, in Prague, in Prag: 1990-1996 1041
Rampage 877
Reader in Czech socio-linguistics 812
Real Mahler 1063
Rebirth of history: Eastern Europe in the age of democracy 236
Rebuilding the financial systems in Central and Eastern Europe 605
Reception 905
Redevelopment or slum clearance 875-76
Reflections of heresy in Czech fourteenth- and fifteenth-century rhymed composition 352
Reform of housing in Eastern Europe and the Soviet Union 706
Reform of the socialist system in Central and Eastern Europe 457
Reformation in Eastern and Central Europe 338
Re-formation of the managerial elite in the Czech Republic 371
Reforms in the foreign economic relations of Eastern Europe and the Soviet Union: proceedings of a Symposium conducted in association with

Osteuropa-Institut Munich and Sudost-Institut, Munich 534
Refugees in inter-war Europe: the emergence of regime 481
Relationship of the Prague German writers to the Czechoslovak Republic 1918-1939 933
Religion and atheism in the USSR and Eastern Europe 332
Reluctant president: a political life of Václav Havel 243
Remaking Eastern Europe – on the political economy of transition 538
Renaissance and Modern Studies 860
Report on the environment of the Czech Republic in 1996 734
Report on the murder of the General Secretary 219
Reproduction, medicine and the social state 390
Republic of whores 925
Resources 1109
Responding to changing conditions 655
Restructuring Eastern Europe: the microeconomics of the transition process 543
Rethinking Dvořák: view from five countries 1058
Retrográdní morfematický slovník češtiny 772
Retrospective conversion in Czech libraries 1140
Return to diversity: a political history of East Central Europe since World War II 438
Review of agricultural policies: Czech Republic 627

Review of the labour market in the Czech Republic 575
Reviews of national policies for education: Czech Republic 395
Revolution and change in Central and Eastern Europe: political, economic and social challenges 447
Revolutionary war for independence and the Russian question: Czechoslovak army in Russia 1914-1918 170
Revue L'Est: Économie et Techniques de Planification, Droit et Sciences Sociales 1129
Rise and fall of Communism in Eastern Europe 212
Risk-adjustment and its implications for efficiency and equity in health care systems. Examples from the Czech Republic, England, Germany, the Netherlands, Switzerland, the United States of America 389
Road strengthening in Central and Eastern European countries 681
Rocking the state: rock music and politics in Eastern Europe and Russia 1049
Role of the market, government and civic sector in the development of postcommunist societies 537
Romantic hero and contemporary anti-hero in Polish and Czech literature: great souls and grey men 831
Romany Holocaust and Romany present 266

*Rudolf II and his world:
a study in intellectual
history 1576-1612*
155
*Rudolf II and Prague:
the court and the city*
154
*Rudolf II and Prague: the
Imperial Court and
residential city as the
cultural and spiritual
heart of Central Europe*
154
Rulers of the Czech Lands
124
R.U.R. and The insect play
860
*Ruská, ukrajinská a
běloruská emigrace v
Praze: Adresář.
Russian, Ukrainian and
Belorussian emigration
in Prague: directory*
293
*Ruská, ukrajinská a
běloruská emigrace v
Praze: Katalog výstavy*
294
*Russia, the USSR, and
Eastern Europe:
a bibliographic guide to
English language
publications. 1964-1980*
1164
Rytíři renesančních Čech
153

S

*Sacred farce from
medieval Bohemia.
Mastičkář* 830
Safari 905
*Safe Third Countries:
Extending the EU
Asylum and immigration
policies to Central and
Eastern Europe* 480
*Samizdat and an
independent society in
Central and Eastern
Europe* 912

*Schikaneder: Jakub
Schikaneder, Prague
painter of the turn of the
century. A thematic
guide to retrospective
exhibition National
Gallery in Prague –
Collection of Old
Masters in the
Wallenstein Riding
School in Prague,
15th May 1998 –
10th January 1999* 971
*Schweik in the Second
World War* 857
*Science, religion and
myth: an interview with
Miroslav Holub* 877
Scottish Slavonic Review
1122
*Sdružení knihoven České
republiky – The Czech
Republic Library
Association –
Bibliotheksverbant der
Tschechischen Republik.
Rok 1998* 1135
*Sectoral changes in
industry after WW1* 634
*Securities and the stock
exchange* 624
*Security policy of the
Czech Republic* 468
Selected plays: 1984-1987
875
Selected plays: 1963-83
874
Selected poems 891, 960
*Selected poetry of
Jaroslav Seifert* 868
*Self: destruction or
synthesis, two problems
of Czech art at the turn
of the century* 964
*Sensibilités
contemporaines
1970-1984* 961
*Serenity greets the
ultimate athlete reborn*
751
*Sex under socialism: an
essay on the work of
Vladimír Páral* 851

Sexual abandon 385
*Seznam motýlů České a
Slovenské republiky.
Checklist of lepidoptera
of the Czech and Slovak
Republics* 86
*She-Pope: a quest for the
truth behind the mystery
of Pope Joan* 343
*Short history of
Czechoslovakia* 114
*Short march: the
Communist takeover in
Czechoslovakia:
1945-1948* 216
*Significance of Czech
Fin-de-Siècle criticism*
835
*Silenced theatre: Czech
playwrights without a
stage* 998
Sins for father Knox 925
*Site in history:
archaeology in Dolní
Věstonice/
Unterwisternitz* 90
*Skoda overtakes Fiat in
Eastern Europe: VW
investment has helped
the Czech carmaker
become biggest
producer in the region*
653
*Slavic and East European
arts* 962
*Slavic Review: American
Quarterly of Russian,
Eurasian, and East
European Studies* 1121
*Slavonic and East
European Review* 1123
Slavonic languages 757
*Slavonic literary
languages* 758
Slavonica 1122
*Slavs in European history
and civilisation* 103
*Slovaks and Czechs: an
uneasy coexistence* 449
Slovník amerikanismů 779
*Slovník české frazeologie
a idiomatiky: přirovnání*
767

Slovník české literatury 1970-1981 843
Slovník českých filozofů 422
Slovník českých spisovatelů 843
Slovník českých spisovatelů: pokus o rekonstrukci dějin české literatury 1948-1979 843
Slovník českých synonym 769
Slovník cizích slov 764
Slovník spisovné češtiny pro školu a veřejnost 762
Slovník spisovného jazyka českého 761
Slovník synonym a frazeologismů 769
Slowness 921
Small privatization: the transformation of retail trade and consumer services in the Czech Republic, Hungary and Poland 650
Smetana 1050-51
Smetana centennial, an International Conference and Festival of Czechoslovak Music, March 29-April 8, 1984 1052
Social consequences of a change in ownership: two case studies in industrial enterprises in the Czech Republic, Spring 1993 367
Social legacy of Communism 366
Social reform in the Czech Republic 355
Socialist remembers 278
Societies in transition: East Central Europe today. Prague papers on social responses to transformation 357
Soils of Czechoslovakia 28

Sokol: the Czechoslovak national gymnastic organisation 740
Something clunky out east 657
Songbirds 84
Sorrowful eyes of Hannah Karajich 893
Současná grafika, Contemporary graphics, Zeitgenossische Graphik 978
Soul of Czechoslovakia: the Czechoslovak nation's contribution to Christian civilization 330
Sourcing czech-up 642
Soviet intervention in Czechoslovakia, 1968: anatomy of a decision 224
Soviet Studies 1119
Soviet Union in Eastern Europe: 1945-89 489
Die Sowjetunion und die Verteidigung der Tschechoslowakei 1934-1938: Versuch der Revision einer Legende 488
Spirit of Bohemia: a survey of Czechoslovak history, music and literature 114
Spirit of Prague and other essays 883
Spirit of Thomas G. Masaryk (1850-1937): an anthology 184
Spoken Czech in literature. The case of Bondy, Hrabal, Placák and Topol 814
Spoken Czech. Situational dialogues for intermediate level students 804
Sport under Communism: the USSR, Czechoslovakia, the GDR, China, Cuba 738

Sport v království českém 737
Spuren des "Realsozialismus" in Böhmen und der Slowakei: Monumente, Museen, Gedenktage 54
Srpen '69: edice dokumentů 228
Staat und Kirche in der Tschechoslowakei: die kommunistische Kirchenpolitik in den Jahren 1948-1952 328
Stability through monetary integration in Eastern Europe: a scenario for the Czech Republic 616
Stálá expozice českého umění 20. století. Permanent exhibition of the 20th century Czech art: Moravská galerie, Brno 1150
Stalin's shoe 931
Standard approach in Eastern Europe 689
Stanislav Kolíbal 981
Stará bydliště 928
Stát a církev v Československu v letech 1948-1953 328
State Jewish Museum in Prague 1147
State Map Series 41
State of the environment in Czechoslovakia 730
Statistická ročenka České republiky 416
Statistický lexikon obcí České republiky 419
Steam and rail in Slovakia 698
Steam locomotives of Eastern Europe 685
Stock exchanges 623
Století fotbalu: z dějin československé kopané 743
Stones of Prague 117
Strangers in their own land 268

398

Stručný etymologický slovník se zvláštním zřetelem k slovům kulturním a cizím 771

Structuring of political cleavages in post-Communist societies: the case of the Czech Republic and Slovakia 454

Struggling for ethnic identity: Czechoslovakia's endangered Gypsies 261

Struggling with the Communist legacy: studies of Yugoslavia, Romania, Poland and Czechoslovakia 470

Studies in ethnicity: the East European experience in America 304

Styles, struggles and careers: an ethnography of the Czech art world 1948-1992 976

Successful transformation? The creation of market economies in Eastern Germany and the Czech Republic 566

Die "Sudetendeutsche Frage" und die Historiker in den USA 282

Sudetoněmecký problém: obtížné loučení s minulostí 283

Summer affair 886

Summer mediations: on politics, morality and civility in a time of transition 473

Švankmajer's Faust, the script: including a preface by the author and excerpts from his diary kept during filming 1008

Svejk 857

Svět Janáčkových oper. The world of Janáček's operas 1072

SWB BBC Monitoring: Summary of World Broadcasts. Part 2: Central Europe, The Balkans 1113

Symposium Comenianum 1986: J. A. Comenius' contribution to world science and culture 411

Synagogue treasures of Bohemia and Moravia 1147

T

T. G. Masaryk against the current: 1882-1914 183

T. G. Masaryk and vztahy Čechů a Němců: sborník příspěvků přednesených od listopadu 1993 do června 1995 v rámci Masarykovy společnosti na FFUK v Praze 284

T. G. Masaryk (1850-1937) 181

T. G. Masaryk: the problem of small nations 185

Tajemství lóží: svobodné zednářství bez legend a mýtu 342

Tales from Bohemia 310

Tales from Karlštejn 129

Tales from two pockets 864

Tales of Little Quarter 854

Talks with T. G. Masaryk by Karel Čapek 188

Tanks and thyme: biodiversity in former Soviet military areas of Central Europe 732

Tax reform in Czechoslovakia 579

Teach yourself Czech 797

Die Teilung der ČSFR: eine österreichische Perspective 555

Temptation 875

Tento večer 930

Terezín memorial book: Jewish victims of Nazi deportations from Bohemia and Moravia 1941-1945 206

Terminal paradox: the novels of Milan Kundera 916

Testaments betrayed 923

Le théâtre libéré de Prague. Voskovec a Werich 995

Theories of life: Darwin, Mendel and beyond 702

Thin lady sings 1048

Thinking small: mountain streams power micro-hydro plants 662

Thirty Years War 157

This side of reality: modern Czech writing 902

Thomas Cook airports guide to Europe 684

Thoughts of a Czech pastor 351

Thousand years of Czech culture 10

Three contemporary Czechoslovak artists 977

Three novels: Hordubal, Meteor, An ordinary life 862

Times 578

Times guide to the peoples of Europe 1

Tkadleček 828

Tomorrow 904

Too loud a solitude 881

Total fears: letters to Dubenka 882

Toulky českou minulostí 120

Tourism and economic development in Eastern Europe and the Soviet Union 44

Tourrets and tourists in Bohemia 55

Tovaryšstvo Ježíšovo: Jesuité v Čechách 348
Toward a market-oriented housing sector in Eastern Europe: developments in Bulgaria, Czechoslovakia, Hungary, Poland, Romania and Yugoslavia 708
Towards better reproductive health in Eastern Europe: concern, commitment and change 390
Towards the radical center: a Karel Čapek reader 865
Trade Fair Palace in Prague 1031
Traditions of Czech literature: curses and blessings 824
Tragedy of king Havel 478
Tragic triangle: the Netherlands, Spain and Bohemia 1617-1621 156
Tramways of Czechoslovakia. Pt. 1 688
Tramways of Czechoslovakia. Pt. 2. Brno, Opava, Teplice and Praha 688
Transfer of the Sudeten-Germans 291
Transformation of Czech society, retrospect and perspect 564
Transformation of economic systems in Central Europe 539
Transforming East European law: selected essays on Russian, Soviet and East European law 506
Transgressive readings: the texts of Franz Kafka and Max Planck 946

Transition, fragmentation, recomposition: la Tchéco-Slovaqui en 1992 453
La transition post-collective: mutations agraires en Europe central 631
Transition report 1998: financial sector in transition 655
Transition report update 544
Transport problems of a new state: Czechoslovak rivers, 1918-38 692
Traveller's literary companion to Eastern and Central Europe 818
Treasures from the past: the Czechoslovak cultural heritage 53
Tremor of racehorses: selected poems 892
Trends in Czech and Slovak economic enterprise in the New World 299
Triumph of hope: from Theresienstadt and Auschwitz to Israel 309
Die tschechische Gesselschaft 1848 bis 1918 147
Tschechisches und slowakisches Wirtschaftsrecht: ausgewahlte Gebiete 518
Turbína 840
Turn of the century masters: Janáček, Mahler, Strauss, Sibelius 1063
Turnaround: a memoir 1007
Twentieth century Czechoslovakia: the meaning of its history 109

Twentieth century interpretation of The trial: a collection of critical essays 948
200 Years, National Gallery in Prague: 1796-1996 1142
Two spheres, one domain 880
Two stories of Prague 957
Two studies on written language 814
Tyrolské elegie 831

U

UK joint venture activity in the Czech Republic: motives and uses 614
Ultimate intimacy 884
Umbrella from Piccadilly 868
Unbearable burden of history: the Sovietization of Czechoslovakia 217
Uncollected poems 957
Understanding Milan Kundera: public events, private affairs 918
Unemployment in capitalist, communist and postcommunist countries 363
Unemployment in the Czech and Slovak republics 365
United States, revolutionary Russia, and the rise of Czechoslovakia 173
Universal banking in the twentieth century: finance, industry and state in north and Central Europe 596
Universal peace organization of King George of Bohemia: a fifteenth century plan for world peace 1461-1464 142

Unveiling 905
Upper Palaeolithic fibre
  technology: interlaced
  woven finds from Pavlov
  I, Czech Republic,
  c. 26,000 years ago
  91
Urban ecology: plants and
  plant communities in
  urban environment 77
Uses of adversity. Essays
  on the fate of Central
  Europe 234

V

Václav Havel and the
  Velvet Revolution 247
Václav Havel:
  la biographie 244
Václav Klofáč and the
  Czechoslovak National
  Socialist Party 435
Vanek plays: four authors,
  one character 905
Vanishing borders:
  the rediscovery of
  Eastern Germany,
  Poland and Bohemia
  43
Vanishing lung syndrome
  877
Variation in language:
  code switching in Czech
  as a challenge for
  sociolinguistics 815
Varieties of Czech.
  Studies in Czech
  sociolinguistics 813
Vatican and the red flag:
  the struggle for the soul
  of Eastern Europe 322
Večerní Praha 1103
Večerník Praha 1103
Velký americko-český
  slovník 777
Velký anglicko-český
  slovník 775
Velký auto atlas. Česká
  republika. Slovenská
  republika 42
Velvet philosophers 423

Velvet Revolution:
  Czechoslovakia
  1988-1991 239
Viereckschanzen in
  Czechoslovakia 94
Vilem Tausky tells his
  story: a two part setting,
  recounted by Margaret
  Tausky 1069
Volhynian Czechs 307
Výchova dívek v Čechách
  894
Výrazy neslovesné 767
Výrazy slovesné 767
Vyrozumění 831
Vznik Československa:
  1918 175

W

Waiting for the dark,
  waiting for the light
  885
War with the newts 861
We the people:
  the revolution of '89
  witnessed in Warsaw,
  Budapest, Berlin and
  Prague 235
Web of cross-ownership
  among Czech financial
  intermediaries:
  an assessment 612
Welcome to the Czech
  Republic 45
Welcome to the Heart of
  Europe 1110
Wenceslaus Hollar:
  a Bohemian artist in
  England 968
What markets can and
  cannot do: the problem
  of economic transition
  in Central-Eastern
  European countries
  545
Where to watch birds in
  Eastern Europe 83
White raven and other
  poems 960
Who's who of Czech
  politicians 455

Why did the socialist
  system collapse in
  Central and Eastern
  European countries?
  The case of Poland, the
  former Czechoslovakia
  and Hungary 458
Die Wiener Tschechen um
  1990 308
Winds of change:
  economic transition in
  Central and Eastern
  Europe 540
Wirtschaftspartner
  Tschechische Republik
  518
Wisdom of being 918
Wolf in sheep clothing:
  the 1996 Amendments to
  the Czech Commercial
  Code 519
Women and politics
  worldwide 372
Women in the politics of
  postcommunist Eastern
  Europe 375
Women of Prague. Ethnic
  diversity and social
  change from the
  eighteenth century to the
  present 381
Women, the state and
  development 374
Women's ordination in the
  Czech silent church 344
Women's work and
  women's lives:
  the continuing struggle
  worldwide 373
Work of Václav Havel
  474
World guide to beer 1090
World of Franz Kafka
  941
World's writing systems
  757
Would be tales 863
Wreath of sonnets – věnec
  sonetů 868
Writing vs. speaking.
  Language. Text.
  Discourse.
  Communication 813

Y

Year Book, Dvořák Society
1044
*Young Czech Party
1874-1901 and the
emergence of a
multiparty system* 166
Young women of Prague
382

Z

*Zátopek a ti druzí: galerie
čs, olympijských vítězů*
739

*Zdravotnická ročenka
České republiky*
420
*Zeal for truth and
tolerance:
the ecumenical
challenge of the Czech
reformation* 340
*Zemědělská technika:
katalog výstavy výrobců,
dovozců, a prodejců
zemědělské techniky*
632
*Die Zerstörung der Bilder:
unsentimentale Reisen
durch Mähren und
Böhmen* 292

*Židé v československé
Svobodově armádě*
204
*Židovské památky města
Brna: stručná historie
židovského osídlení
Brna* 277
*Zigeneur in Osteuropa:
Eine Bibliographie zu
den Ländern Polen,
Tschechoslowakei und
Ungarn* 256
*Zlínská architektura,
1900-1950*
1035
Znamení noci
831

Index of Subjects

A

Abortion rate statistics 421
Absolutism see History
Academia, purges of see History
Academy of Science of the Czech Republic (ASCR) 693
Accident statistics 416
Accounting 516, 526, 579-86
'Act on Economic Relations with Foreign Countries, 19. April 1990' 507
Administrative divisions, maps 41
Adventures of the vixen Bystrouška (Leoš Janáček) 1071
Advertising 594, 1093
Aesthetics 961
Afforestation 79
Age rate statistics 421
Agency distribution and franchise agreements 513
Agricultural trade relations 627
Agriculture 528, 625-32
  and environment 627-28
  and brewing industry 630
  collectivism 631
  cooperatives 630
  effects of privatization 627
  farm structure 625
  food consumption 625
  foreign trade in agricultural commodities 628
  forestry 79, 628
  machinery 632
  price development 625
  privatization 627-28, 630
  reform 628
  statistics 416, 626
  subsidies 628
  taxation policies 627
  transformation of collective farms 627
  transition 630
  water 628
  see also History
AIDS 391
Air transport 680, 683-84, 710
Aircraft design 1028
Ajvaz, Michal 902
Albee, Edward 998
Americans 21
Ammunition production 669
Anabaptists see History
Anderle, Jiří 978, 982
Angling see Fishing
Anglo-Czechoslovak Bank 596
Anheuser-Busch 652
Anne of Bohemia 826
Anti-Semitism 272, 278, 432, 944
Anti-trust legislation 516
Antonín Vondrejc (Karel Matěj Čapek-Chod) 840
Apocryphal stories (Karel Čapek) 828
Appeasement see History
Applied art 961, 985-92
Arbitration 513
Archaeology see Prehistory and archaeology
Architects 67, 705-21, 1014, 1018, 1027-37
  see also individual architects by name
Architecture 63, 67-68, 317, 705-21, 961-62, 1013-37
  and Soviet Communism 1032
  Baroque 60, 68, 72, 78, 1013-14, 1023, 1137
  Constructivism 1031
  Cubism 1025-26
  Functionalism 1027-28, 1031, 1037
  Gothic 1014
  inter-war period 1026-28, 1030
  landscape 64, 78
  Prague 1015-25, 1029, 1031-33
    guides 60, 63
  rural 53
  vernacular 53
Archives and libraries 1132-40
Archives of the Legions 1145
Armaments industry 669
Armed forces 459
  see also International security; NATO
Arms 669, 1148
Arms exports 647
Army Museum 1145
Art Glass Studio Svoboda 677
Art Nouveau 969-73, 986-88, 1021
Art sector 549
Artcristal Bohemia 677
Artists in exile 961
Arts 9-10, 12, 317, 961-65, 976
  applied arts 985, 1027-30
  Art Nouveau 969-71, 1021
  Bauhaus 1027
  bibliography 1152
  ceramics 989
  clocks and watches 990
  encyclopaedia 961
  criticism 19, 961
  faience 985

Arts contd
  glass 675, 985-88
  graphic art 978
  indigo dyeing 992
  Jugendstil 987
  painting 979
  photography 256-66,
    961, 979, 983-84
  porcelain 989
  Prague 1015, 1021
  sculpture 979, 981
  since separation of
    Czechoslovakia 965
  theory 19, 961
  visual art 966-84
  see also History; and
    individual genres of
    art, e.g. Architecture;
    Film; Painting, etc.
Association for Foreign
  Direct Investment 610
Association for Physical
  Education 735
Auschwitz concentration
  camp see History
Austerlitz, Battle of
  (1805) see History
Austria-Hungary / Austro-
  Hungarian Empire see
  History
Aviation Museum 1145
Avion hotel, Brno 1030

B

Babička (Božena
  Němcová) 831
Ballet 993, 997
Banat region, southern
  Romania 305
Banking and finance 528,
  595-624, 645, 712
  and transition economy
    597, 600, 603-04, 606
  privatization 598-600,
    604
  reform 601-02
  currency 610
  directory 599
  EMU (European Monetary
    Unit) 599, 603
  exchange rate 609

foreign debt 618
foreign trade 618
insurance 610
investment 528, 598, 610
monetary and fiscal
  policies 618
Prague stock exchange
  567, 617, 622-24
privatization 598-600, 604
Soviet Communist era 607
  state-owned banks 604
stock exchange 567,
  610, 617, 622-24
stock market 576-77
taxation 610, 621-22
trade deficit 615
transition economies
  600, 604-06
see also History
Bankruptcy and
  composition act 516
Baroque
  architecture 1013-14
  glass 986-87
  literature 1013
  theatre 72
Barrandov Film Studios
  1001
BASEES see British
  Association for Slavonic
  and East European Studies
Bass 651
Beardsley, Aubrey 969
Beckett, Samuel 998
Bednář, Kamil 899
Beer 1088
  guides 1088-90
  Prague 1088-89
Beer and brewing 630,
  651-52
Beer-halls, Prague 1089
Beneš, Edvard 174, 197,
  290
  and Czechoslovakia's
    German minority
    1918-43 285
  biography 198
  diplomacy of 192, 197
  political activities 285
  resentment towards 432
Beneš, Karel 978
Benešová, Božena 18
Beránek Glassworks 677

Berková, Alexandra 902
Bezruč, Petr 959
Bible translations 819
Bibliographies 1152-56,
  1159-62, 1164-65
  bibliographies of 1156
  Czech national 1154-56
  items relating to Czech
    Republic published
    abroad 1155
  language-learning aids
    (for learning Czech as
    a foreign language)
    1157
  literary bibliographies
    852, 914
  émigré 911
  samizdat 913
  film 1012
  philately 1166
  Prague 1163
  town history
    bibliography 125
Biebl, Konstantin 839,
  899-900, 903
Bílek, František 148, 969,
  974
Bilianová, Popelka 18
Bím, Tomáš 978
Biographical archive 1158
Birdlife 82-84
Birdwatching 83
Birth rate statistics 421
Blansko, caves 36, 313
Blatný, Ivan 909, 928-30
Blažek, Vratislav 998
Boháč, Václav 1031
Bohemia see History
Bohemia-Moravia
  Commodity Exchange
  Kladno 623
Bohemian Academy of
  Sciences, Literature and
  Arts see History
Bohemian Crown Lands
  see History: Bohemia
Bohemian Forest 73
Bohemian glass 675-79,
  985-88
Bohemian Kingdom see
  History: Bohemia
Bohemian-Bavarian
  border 73

Bolshevik Revolution *see*
  History
Bolzano, Bernard 820
Bonton 1097
*Book of laughter and
  forgetting, The* (Milan
  Kundera) 828, 914,
  916-17
Bookshops 1096
Borovský, K. H. 165, 330,
  831, 899
  and National Revival
  165
Botany 74-80
Boundaries 23
Brabcová, Zuzana 902
Brahe, Tycho de 155
Brahms, Johannes 1053
Brandejs, Bedřich 669
Bratislava 53, 689
Braunerová, Zdenka 974
Break-up of Austria-
  Hungary *see* History
Break-up of
  Czechoslovakia *see*
  History
Break-up of Yugoslavia
  see History
Brecht, Berthold 998
Břetislav I, ruler of
  Bohemia 97
Brewing and breweries
  630, 651-52, 1088
  see also History
Březina, Otokar 841
Bride of Texas, The (Josef
  Škvorecký) 925
British academics 423
British Association for
  Slavonic and East
  European Studies
  (BASEES) 1114
British Czech and Slovak
  Association 1112
British Embassy and
  Ambassador's
  Residence, Prague *see*
  History
Brno 34, 553
  architecture 70, 1028,
  1030
  guide 70
  city transport 687

commercial success,
  reflection in its
  architecture 71
guides 70-71
industry 643
infrastructure, business,
  finance, politics 34
Jews 177
map 1080
museum collections of
  trolleybuses and trams
  687
  see also History
Brno commodity exchange
  623
Brno exhibition centre 71,
  1027
Brno Grand Prix 42
Brod, Max 1078
Budapest 709
Budějovické pivovary 652
Budweiser Budvar 652
Building materials
  industry 708
Bulgaria
  Czech émigrés 305
  economy 619
  environment 725, 727
  housing 708
  politics 467
Burghauser, Jarmil 1061
Business 581-86, 590, 593
  guides 16, 52
  law 516-20, 559
  periodicals 1124-31
Butterflies 86
Buzková, Pavla 18

C

Cafés 65
Camping 56
Canada 304, 481, 486
Čapek, Josef 865, 974
Čapek, Karel 810, 828,
  833-34, 858-60, 865,
  903
Car design 1028
Car manufacturing 653
Carmelite Church of Our
  Lady Victorious in
  Prague 353

Carpathian region 1
Cartoons and animated
  films 961
Castle Library of Český
  Krumlov 1139
Castle, The (Franz Kafka)
  939, 946
Castles 53, 55
Catapult (Vladimír Páral)
  851
Catholic Church 320-24,
  326, 328-29, 335-36,
  343-44, 346-48
  see also History
Catholicism 324, 351
Caves 36, 92, 313
Censorship 845, 849, 909,
  912, 1091-92, 1094,
  1099
Central European Small
  Business Enterprise
  Development
  Commission 548
Cereals 628
Červinková-Riegrová,
  Marie 18
Česká nedělni postila (Jan
  Hus) 133
Česká Zbrojovka Uherský
  Brod, a.s. 669
České Budějovice 553,
  687
Československá obchodní
  banka (ČSOB) 613
Český Krumlov
  Baroque theatre 72
  Castle Library 1139
Chalupa 753
Charles I, last Emperor of
  Austria-Hungary
  genealogies and coats of
  arms 97
Charles IV (1316-78) 129-
  30, 132, 966-67
Charles University, Prague
  396, 402-04
Charles University Press
  402
Charter 77 *see* History
Chata 753
Chelčický, Petr 143
Chemapol 665
Chemical industry 664-65

405

Chess 756
Children's issues 383-85
China 237, 546, 738, 912
Chlum battlefield 69
Chlumčany Ceramics
    Works 577
Chomutov-Jirkov 687
Choreography 995
Christianity 10
    see also History
Chronicle (Dalimil) 828
Chronological surveys see
    History
Church see History
Church of the Sacred
    Heart 67
Church of St Nicholas,
    Old Town, Prague 68
Cinema 19, 995
    see also Film
CIS see Commonwealth of
    Independent States
Cities 705, 709, 716-17, 720
City transport see
    Transport
Civic Forum see History
Civil code and commercial
    code 511
Civil Code of
    Czechoslovakia 514
Civil engineering 587,
    666, 712
Civil law 514
Civil parishes statistics
    419
Civil-military relations
    500
ČKD Praha 698
ČKD Praha Holding 573
ČKD-Tatra 687
Class structure 359-61
Clementinum Library,
    Prague 1137-38
Cleveland 302
Climate 25, 416
Clocks 990
Closely Watched Trains
    1005
CMEA see Council for
    Mutual Economic
    Assistance
Coats of arms 97-100
Cold War see History

Comedy 995
Comenius 405-12, 834
    and culture 411
    and education 405-12
    and language 405-06
    and science 411
    and theology 408
    idea of universal
        education 405-06
    'Map of Moravia' 412
Comintern sources 433
Commercial Code,
    amendments to, 1996
    519
Commercial law 516, 518
Committee for Agriculture
    of OECD 627
Commonwealth of
    Independent States 497
Communications 112, 460
Communism see History:
    Soviet Communism
Communist Party see
    History
Communities 419
Companies 525-27
    and transition 558
    directories 523-24
Company law 710
Computer art and design
    961
Computers 697
Concerts 1043-44
Constitution and law 504-15
Constitutional Court of the
    Czech Republic 512
Construction industry 666,
    681, 710, 712
    privatization 712
Constructivism 899
Consumers 528, 648-50
Contracts 511, 559
Convents 18, 53
Le Corbusier 1031
Corporate law 519
Cost of living 370, 528
Costume jewellery 678
Council for Mutual
    Economic Assistance
    (CMEA) 533, 538
Country houses 53
Crécy, Battle of see
    History

Crests see Coats of arms
Crime statistics 416, 418,
    468
Criminal law reform 513
Criminality see Crime
    statistics
Crystal 49, 675
    see also Bohemian
    glass; Glass
CSAO Teplice a.s. 641
Cuba 738
Cubo-Futurism 900
Cuisine 1086
Cultural and sporting
    events 736
    websites 57-58
Culture 3-4, 7, 9-10, 12,
    16, 549, 560
    statistics 416
    see also History
Cunning little vixen, The
    (Leoš Janáček) 1071
Customs 16, 52
Customs and import duties
    55
Czech Academy 1145
Czech Academy of
    Sciences and Arts 694
Czech Agrarian Party see
    History
Czech Association for
    Physical Education 735
Czech Brethren see
    History
Czech Lands see History
Czech language see
    Language
Czech Massif 27
Czech National Corpus
    807
Czech National Revival,
    19th century see History
Czech National Socialist
    Party see History
Czech National Theatre
    see History
Czech people 1-2, 11, 16,
    52
    contribution to world
    culture 11
Czech renaissance see
    History: National
    Revival, 19th century

Czech Republic Library Association 1135
Czech studies *see* History
Czech Tourist Authority 57
Czech Writer's Union 883
Czech-British relations 476, 482
see also History
Czech-German frontiers 23
Czech-German relations 290, 490
see also History
CzechInvest 610
Czechoslovak Academy of Arts and Sciences in America *see* History
Czechoslovak Airlines 558
Czechoslovak Church *see* History
Czechoslovak Communist Party *see* History
Czechoslovak Helsinki Committee *see* History
Czechoslovak Hussite Church 345
Czechoslovak National Council *see* History
Czechoslovak Red Cross *see* History
'Czechoslovakianism' *see* History
'Czechoslovakia-USA: Agreement on Trade Relations between Czechoslovakia and the United States of April 12, 1990' 507
Czechoslovak-Israeli relations *see* History
Czechoslovak-Polish negotiations 1939-44 *see* History
Czechs abroad 12, 295-96, 909-32
Banat region, southern Romania 305
Israel 309
North America 297-98, 304
Romania 305-06
see also History
Czech-Slovak relations 18, 487

D

Dada 899-900
Daewoo Avia 573
Dairy industry 628, 671
Dalimil chronicle 352
Dancing House, Prague 60, 1033
Davídek, Felix 343-44
Davidová, Eva 259
Decadence *see* History
Declaration of Independence, 18 October 1918 *see* History
Decree of Adolf Hitler on occupation of Czech Lands *see* History
Defence 468, 528
Defence and military policy 468
see also NATO
Deml, Jakub 899-900
Demography statistics 29, 420
see also History
Design 961
see also Architecture; Fashion; Stage design
Destinová, Ema 1047
Destiny (Leoš Janáček) 1071
Dětřich 966
Development control 710
Devotional objects 317
Dictionaries 761-67, 769-71, 773-91
Diplomacy *see* History
Diplomatic archives *see* History
Disease prevention 392
Dispute settlement 513
Distribution of goods and services 649
Domestic appliances 697
Domus Factory 367
Don Giovanni (Mozart) première in Prague, 1787 1013, 1048
Dopitová, Milena 979
Drama 993, 996-98
Drda, Jan 838
Dreyfus affair *see* History

Drug abuse 366
Dubček, Alexander 225, 229-32
and 1989 revolution 230
and Slovak Uprising 1944 230
conversations with Brezhnev, Leonid 225
Prague Spring 1968 229-31
Dubno, Ukraine *see* History
Dürrenmatt, Friedrich 998
Durych, Jaroslav 900
Dusík, J. L. 1040
Dvořák, Antonín 1053-62, 1064
and United States 1055
bibliographies and catalogues 1060-62
chamber music 1058
operas 1053
Dvořák, Jan *see* St Clement Hofbauer
Dvořák Society for Czech and Slovak music, London 1044

E

Earnings 356
East Germany (GDR) 43, 398, 566
Easter eggs 319
Eastern Europe, journals 1118, 1123
EBRD *see* European Bank for Reconstruction and Development
Ecology 77
see also Environment
Economic Community 541
Economy 12, 101, 418, 460, 463, 523-28, 538, 557, 560-62, 564-66, 587, 589, 591-95, 597, 710
agriculture 586, 626
and environment 726
and Klaus, Václav 563-64

Economy *contd*
and law 514
and political events of 1989 554
and world economy 537
banking *see* Banking and finance
break-up of ČSFR (Czechoslovak Federal Republic) 554-55
British investors 614
business *see* Business
capital gains tax 579
capital markets 542, 573, 617
centrally planned 708
communications 586
companies 549-50
consumer expenditure 594
corporate governance 556
defence industry 647
demography 594
economic indicators 594
economic miracle, sustainability of 553, 557
economic progress 370, 617
engineering sector 611
entry of Czech Republic into world trade 644
European transport networks 617
exchange rate policy 617
export customs procedures and Czech customs tariff systems 525
exports 571
foreign business 578
foreign investment 525, 543, 559, 561-62, 565, 567, 570, 586, 588, 617
fraud 573
fund managers 577
government budgets 578
harmonization of import and export legislature 525

health care reforms 556
hidden 415
household characteristics 594
human resources 561
import information 593
income tax 579
industry 543, 573, 566, 578, 586, 589, 611
infrastructure and key sectors 593
insurance company act provisions 559
international assistance 537
investment 561, 567, 590, 593, 610
see also Economy: foreign investment
labour 575, 593
land 593
liberalization 537
licensing 525, 561
macroeconomy 556, 610
management and enterprise 574
market economy 537
military expenditure 647
money demand 556
National Property Fund 617
organizational transformation and institutional change 574
periodicals 591-95, 1124, 1128, 1130
personal income tax 580
personal taxes 561-62
PETs *see* Economy: Planned Economies in Transition
Planned Economies in Transition 538
Prague stock exchange 567, 617, 622-24
privatization 367, 460, 509, 513, 547, 556, 567-68, 602
bibliography 509
problem loans for banks 617
property market 587
quality guarantees 525

recession 611
reform 464, 516, 572-73, 590
and Klaus, Václav 590
post-Communist European countries 464
Western Europe 464
retail distribution 594
Roma 611
sales distribution and marketing 593
services 586, 594
small businesses 548
social and environmental issues 556
standard of living 594
statistics 416, 556, 560, 566
stock exchange 559, 567
tax 561-62
reform 579-80, 587
theory and policy 591
tourism 577-78, 588
trade 588
trade deficit 589
transition, 1989- 38, 357, 459-60, 462-63, 508, 537-53, 556, 616
and the environment 731
banking and finance 600
relationship between inflation and money growth 619
stabilization 569
state-owned banking sector 604
structural transformation 569
Western assistance 569
UK joint venture activity 614
unemployment 556
VAT 525, 562
voucher privatization 509, 556, 567
see also Banking and finance; Business; History; Industrial sectors

Edice Petlice 9
Education 393-404, 416, 418
and information 528
and transition 459
attitudes towards 361
convent 18
higher 394, 396-97
institutions of higher education 396-97
policies 395
primary 393, 395
reform 393-94
secondary 393, 395
statistics 416, 418
teaching of foreign languages 400
university 393
vocational 395
Elections 431, 505
statistics 452
Electricity generation 658-62
Electronics 697
Emigration 480-81
Émigrés 3, 11-13, 17, 297-309, 909-32
Emperor Charles IV 129-30, 132, 966-67
Emperor Francis Joseph 694
Employment 357, 363, 513, 540
EMU (European Monetary Unit) 599, 603
Energy 528, 661, 712, 724
and environment 658, 661
electricity 658, 661
gas 660-61
privatization 660
hydroelectric potential 661-62
independent power sector 658
natural gas 658
nuclear energy 661
oil 658
statistics 416, 724
Engineering Fair, Brno 71
England 389
English language, teaching of 400-01
Enterprise ownership 557

'Enterprise with Foreign Property participation Act of April 19, 1990' 507
Environment 22, 416, 418, 463, 528, 722-34
air 722, 725-26, 730
and construction industry 712
and energy 724, 726, 731
and health 722, 729-30
and transition 459, 556, 722
atmospheric pollution 661
attitudes of governments 722
audits 725
chemicals 725
conservation 732
contacts in the Czech Republic 726
contaminated land remediation 726
decrease in emissions 731
economic factors 722
environmental companies / services 726
green politics 722
international 722, 734
investment 725, 731
land-use planning 725
legislation and regulations 725-26
Ministry of Environment of the Czech Republic 728
mountains 732
National Environmental Policy 729
natural resources and commercial activities 733
noise 725-26
non-governmental organizations 722
nuclear power 722
planning for sustainable development 733
policy 726, 729-30, 734

pollution 722, 725-26, 731
problems 722
protected areas 416
protection 727
renewables / cleaner technology 726
soil and vegetation pollution 722
statistics 416, 418
UK environmental companies 726
waste management 725-26
water 725-26, 730-31
Environmental Institute 729
Erben, Karel Jaromír 831
Ericsson Palace, Old Town, Prague 1018
Eroticism 18
Estonia 725
Ethnic and religious groups 38, 809
Ethnicity and ethnic structure 248-49, 251, 366
Etiquette 52
EU see European Union
European Bank for Reconstruction and Development (EBRD) 610
European Championship football tournament 1996 745
European Community 541
European integration 541
European Monetary Unit 599, 603
European Union 240, 460, 494
and agriculture 627
asylum and immigration policies 480
harmonization 513
preparations for the membership of 576-77
Exchange rates 617
Expatriate organizations 296
Exporters 525
Expressionism 899-900

409

F

Faience 1146
Fairy-tales 310-12
Families 18, 52, 355, 418
  effect on educational
    attainment 359
  Prague 421
  statistics 418, 421
Farewell party, The
  (Milan Kundera) 914,
  916
Farms see Agriculture
Fashion 991
Fastrová, Olga 18
Faulfis, Mikuláš 134
Fauna 81-86, 416
Federal Assembly 505
Federal states 251
Federalism 505
Federation 251
Feierabend, Ladislav 429
Female employment 373
Feminism 377, 380
Ferdinand of Habsburg
  151
Filip, Ota 902
Filla, Emil 974
Film 1000-12
  bibliography 1012
  New Wave 1960s-1968
    1003-05, 1007
  producers and directors
    1000, 1003-04
  tensions between
    filmmaking and social
    and political
    environment 1004
Finance see Banking and
  finance
Fine arts 12
  see also Arts
Firearms 669, 1148
Fischerová, Daniela 904
Fischerová, Sylva 892
Fish 81, 85, 754-55
Fishing 628, 754-55
Floods 576
Flora 74-80, 416
Foerster, J. B. 1040
Folk art 10, 49, 317
Folk costumes 317-18
Folk customs 319

Folk dance 318
Folktales 312-13
Food and agriculture 626
Food and drink 1086-90
Food policy 627
Football 743-44
Foreign debt 618
Foreign direct investment
  516
Foreign Direct Investment
  (FDI) 610
Foreign exchange act and
  financial legislation 516
Foreign investment 513
Foreign policy 468, 557
Foreign relations see
  International relations
'Foreign Stock Companies
  Act' 507
Foreign trade and the
  customs code 516
Forests and forestry 79,
  628
  statistics 416
Forman, Miloš 1007
Foundry engineering 399
Foundry industry 399, 655
Four Power Agreement
  1938 see History:
  Munich Agreement
  1938
Fourth World Congress for
  Soviet and East
  European Studies,
  Harrogate, 1990 see
  History
'Fred and Ginger' house,
  Prague 60, 1033
Frederick, Elector
  Palatine, King of
  Bohemia (Winter King)
  97
Freemasonry see History
French, Alfred 900
French Communist Party
  see History
From the house of the
  dead (Leoš Janáček)
  1071
From the New World
  (Antonín Dvořák) 1053
Fruit growing 628
Frýdlant v Čechách 1148

Fuchs, Bohuslav 1027, 1030
Fuchs, Josef 1031
Fučik, Julius 6
Fuks, Ladislav 902
Fungi 79
Furniture 640, 1026, 1028,
  1030
Future Systems 1036-37
Futurism 899-900

G

Gablonz 678
Gardens 78
Gas 660
Gay community 391
GDR see East Germany
Gehry, Frank O. 60, 1033
Gender issues 3, 372, 374,
  376, 459
Gender studies 382
Gender Studies Centre 380
Genet, Jean 998
Genetics 699-702
Geography 5, 22, 25-27,
  560
  Blansko, caves 36
  climate 25
  demography 29
  human 24
  hydrology 25
  Krušné hory mountain
    range 33
  Macocha chasm and
    caves 36
  migration 22
  mineral springs 37
  Moravia 36
  Moravian Karst 36
  Moravský Kras see
    Geography: Moravian
    Karst
  North-Moravian region
    35
  population and
    settlements 25
  Prague 31
  Punkva (underground
    river) 36
  Slovak Republic 560
  social and economic
    conditions 26

Geography *contd*
  soils 25, 28
  structure and relief 25
  see also History
Geological Institute 729
Geology 27-28
George of Poděbrady
  141-42
German minority *see* History
German Roma *see History*
German Social
  Democratic Party *see*
  History
Germany 252, 389, 497
Glagolitic Mass (Leoš
  Janáček) 1074
Glass 675, 678-79
  see also Bohemian glass
Glass industry 558
Glass production 675-79
Glassmaking 676-79
  beads 678
Glassworks 675, 987-88
Glavunion 641
Glazarová, Jarmila 838
Gočár, Josef 1023
Golden Lane, Prague
  Castle 66
'Golden spinning wheel,
  The' (poem) 1053
Goldstücker, Eduard,
  memoirs 15
Good Soldier Švejk, The
  (Jaroslav Hašek) 834, 856
Gottwald, Klement 198
Government 362, 528
  structure 459
  transformation into
  democratic systems
  505
Grandmother (Božena
  Němcová) 831
Graphic art 961
Great Bear Cave, near
  Brno 70
Great Moravian Empire
  see History
Green Frog, Trenčianske
  Teplice, Slovakia 1030
Gruša, Jiří 902
Gulliver's Travels
  (Jonathan Swift) 946
Guth, Jiří 739

Gymnastics *see* History:
  Sokol; History:
  Spartakiad
Gypsies *see* Roma

H

Habener 1146
Habermas, J. 471
Habsburg Empire
  1848-1918 *see* History
Halas, František 899-900
Hall of Columns, Prague
  Castle 1015
Hanzlík, Josef 899
Harvard Group 558
Hašek, Jaroslav 7, 148,
  820, 834, 838, 858, 903
Hate language 1099
Hauer-King House 1037
Hauková, Jiřina 899-900
Havel, Olga 245
Havel, Václav 106, 124,
  239, 241-47, 405, 434,
  471, 475-78, 820, 823,
  828, 872, 903-04, 998
  and Charter 77 242, 245
  and Velvet Revolution
  1989 247
  essays 474
  in prison 1979-82 245
  letters 245
  literary work 246, 474
  philosophy 246, 471
  plays 474
  speeches and writings
  472-74
  visit to the United
  Kingdom 1998 476-77
Havlíček, Karel *see*
  Borovský
Hayek, Friedrich von 564
Health and health care
  355, 386-89, 418, 528, 663
  and economic transition
  556
  and pollution 722
  insurance 516
  privatization 386
  reform 386-87
  statistics 416, 418, 420
Heraldry 97-100

Herbaria 76
Herbs 76
Heřman, Augustin 299
Historiography 13, 107
History 5, 9-10, 12, 101-
  02, 104-06, 114-15, 123,
  178-79, 247, 560
  15th century 138, 140
  15th and early 16th
  centuries 141-43
  16th century 151
  16th and 17th centuries
  150, 152-53
  17th century 156
  18th century 180
  19th century 109, 120,
  158-59, 164-65, 281,
  330, 994
  20th century 13, 101,
  108-09, 116, 189, 208-
  09, 903, 426, 446, 459
  absolutism 150
  academia, purges of 398
  agriculture 14, 629-31
  Alfred the Great's *Anglo-
  Saxon Chronicle* 484
  anabaptists 144
  Anglo-Czechoslovak
  relations 110, 482-85
  anti-Hitler emigrants 106
  anti-masonry 342
  anti-Semitism 272, 278,
  432, 944
  appeasement 194
  architecture 963
  armaments industry 669
  armoured fighting
  vehicles 698
  Art Nouveau 969-71
  arts 14, 961, 963, 974, 976
  and Court of Habsburg
  Emperor Rudolph II
  963
  Art Nouveau 964,
  969-71
  Communist period 965
  18th century 963
  fin-de-siècle 964
  Gothic mural painting
  967
  mediaeval 130
  Association for Physical
  Education 735

History *contd*
  atheism 332
  Auschwitz concentration
    camp 309
  Austerlitz, Battle of
    (1805) 71, 161-62
  Austria-Hungary /
    Austro-Hungarian
    Empire 152
    collapse of 168, 173
    maps and atlases 38
  banking and finance 596,
    605, 607
  Baroque 60, 1013-14,
    1023, 1137
  Battle of Austerlitz
    (1805) 71, 161-62
  Battle of Crécy 1346 483
  beer 1090
  bishops 99
  Bohemia 8, 97, 113-14,
    119, 128-31, 138,
    140-42, 151-53, 156,
    276, 334, 338, 342,
    347, 607 828, 830,
    967, 1050
    architecture 1013-14
    Christianity 325, 337
    coats of arms 98-99
    elections 431
    folk customs 319
    journal 1115
    knights 153
    landownership 152
    literature 825-27, 830
    map 967, 1080
    serfdom 180
    traveller's account 43
  Bohemian Academy of
    Sciences, Literature
    and Arts 694
  Bohemian Crown Lands
    see History: Bohemia
  Bohemian Kingdom *see*
    History: Bohemia
  Bolshevik Revolution
    168, 170, 173, 176
  break-up of Austria-
    Hungary 176
  break-up of
    Czechoslovakia 101
  break-up of Yugoslavia
    101

  brewing 1090
  British, concept of
    Bohemia and Czechs
    485
  British Embassy and
    Ambassador's
    Residence, Prague 482
  Brno 34, 70-71, 633
  Budapest 709
  Canada 481
  Canadian-Czech
    relations 486
  Catholic Church 13, 329
    and land reform 329
    and relationship with
      state 329
    ordination of women
      and married men
      343-44
    priests, secret
      ordination during
      Communist rule 336
  census 1754 2
  charity 331
  Charles University,
    Prague 402-04
  Charta 77 Foundation *see*
    History: Charter 77
    Foundation
  Charter of fundamental
    rights and freedoms 112
  Charter 77 112, 234, 242,
    349, 442-43, 912-31
  Charter 77 Foundation
    443
  children, rights of 383
  China 237
  Christianity 325, 327, 332
  chronological surveys
    46, 49, 112, 121-22
  Church 121, 331, 334
    relations with state in
      Communist period
      332
  Church of the Sacred
    Heart 67
  Church of St Nicholas,
    Old Town, Prague 68
  Church Slavonic works
    325
  Civic Forum 235
  clergy, persecution of
    328, 333

  Cold War, 1945-91 213,
    215, 217-18
  Comenius' *Panorthosia*
    739
  Committee for
    Agriculture of OECD
    627
  Communism *see* History:
    Soviet Communism
  Communist Party 105,
    444
  Communist Party and
    Moscow International
    433
  Communist period *see*
    Soviet Communist
    period
  Communist unions 433
  Crécy, Battle of, 1346 483
  cultural nationalism 160
  culture 14, 39, 116, 126,
    147, 844
  cycling 737
  Czech Agrarian Party 436
  Czech Brethren 143-44
  Czech Lands 5, 14, 100,
    108-09, 112, 117, 120,
    124, 148, 272, 274-75,
    317
  Czech National Revival
    see History: National
    Revival, 19th century
  Czech National Socialist
    Party 435
  Czech National Theatre
    160, 993-94
  Czech renaissance *see*
    History: National
    Revival, 19th century
  Czech studies 816
  Czech-Austrian relations
    12, 116
  Czech-British relations
    476, 482-84
  Czech-German relations
    283, 354, 426, 490-91
  Czech-Hungarian
    relations 12
  Czech-Jewish movement
    274
  Czechoslovak Academy
    of Arts and Sciences in
    America 301

412

History *contd*
Czechoslovak Church 339
Czechoslovak
  Communist Party 223
Czechoslovak Helsinki
  Committee 445
Czechoslovak minority
  treaty, 10 September
  1919 285
Czechoslovak National
  Council 175
Czechoslovak Red Cross
  191
Czechoslovak-Israeli
  relations 495-96
Czechoslovak-Polish
  negotiations 1939-44
  199
'Czechoslovakianism' 18
Czech-Polish relations
  12, 492
Czech-Romanian
  relations 12
Czech-Slovak relations
  12, 14, 114, 354, 379,
  426, 450, 487
Czech-Yugoslav
  relations 12
Czechs abroad 298-302,
  304-05, 307
decadence 148
Declaration of
  Independence 18
  October 1918 174-75,
  177
decree of Adolf Hitler on
  occupation of Czech
  Lands 290
demography 2, 39, 109,
  121
diplomacy 485
diplomatic archives 192
discrimination against
  German minority 428
drama 996
Dreyfus affair 944
Dubno, Ukraine 307
Eastern and Western
  Europe, separation of
  in 20th century 446
ecclesiastical structures 39
economy 14, 109, 147,
  485, 529-36

CMEA *see* History:
  economy: Council
  for Mutual
  Economic
  Assistance
Communism 364
Council for Mutual
  Economic
  Assistance (CMEA)
  533
economic relations
  CMEA countries
  534
  Czechs and Slovaks
  554
  Eastern Europe and
  Soviet Union 534
  foreign investment
  542
  GNP statistics 536
  inter-war capital
  markets 542
  maps 39
  property rights and
  debt in East-West
  European relations
  529
  reforms 531
education 14, 39, 126,
  393, 396
elderly 364
elections 121, 178, 431,
  469
emigration 480
  Czech Jews to Israel 496
  North America 297-301
engineering 696
enterprise and
  management 574
environment 731
Esperanto movement 817
ethnic and cultural
  diversity 40
ethnic conflicts 426
ethnic national minorities
  254
ethnicity 126
  maps and atlases 39
extreme Right, rise of 432
Fascism 425, 432
fashion 991
federal solution, 1969
  425

film 1006
fin-de-siècle 148-49, 944,
  964
firearms 669, 1148
First Czechoslovak
  Republic (1918-38)
  12, 14, 179, 215, 451
First World War 167-68,
  171, 173
  activities of Czech
  leaders abroad 174
  activities of political
  leaders in Prague
  and Vienna 168
  army 174
  domestic situation
  167-68
  Czech legions in Italy
  171
  Czech legions in
  Russia 169-70, 172
  Czech political
  resistance abroad 175
  government in exile 198
  maps and atlases 38
fishing 755
football 743-44
foreign relations *see*
  History: international
  relations
Four Power Agreement
  1938 *see* History:
  Munich Agreement
  1938
Fourth World Congress
  for Soviet and East
  European Studies,
  Harrogate, 1990 180
freemasonry 342
French Communist Party
  493
genetics 699-702
geography 30
German minority 285-86,
  289
  expulsion of after
  Second World War
  285, 289-92
  Prague 281
German Roma 263
German Social
  Democratic Party
  287-88

History contd
  governments 121, 126
  Great Moravian Empire
    96
  gymnastics see History:
    Sokol movement;
    History: Spartakiad
  Habsburg Empire 1848-
    1918 253
  Habsburgs 150
  historiography 13, 107
  Hungarians 426
  Hussite revolution 118,
    135-38, 140
  independence movement
    168-77, 486
  intelligentsia 845
  international relations 12,
    479
    between Britain,
      United States and
      Bohemia 1848-1938
      485
    between Czechs and
      Austrians 12, 116
    between Czechs and
      British 476, 482-84
    between Czechs and
      Germans 283, 354,
      426, 490-91
    between Czechs and
      Hungarians 12
    between Czechs and
      Jews 274
    between Czechs and
      Romania 12
    between Czechs and
      Slovaks 12, 14, 114,
      354, 379, 426, 450,
      487
    between estates of
      Habsburg Crown 150
    with Great Powers 12
    with neighbours 12
  inter-war years 38, 178,
    180
  invasion by Warsaw Pact
    armies, 1968 222-23,
    229
  Jesuit order 348
  Jewish immigrants 309
  Jewish organizations 495
  Jews 10, 272-73, 944

  Brno 177
  concentration camps
    and labour camps
    276
  German-speaking
    275
  mass graves 276
  Prague 275, 281
  Second World War
    206
  synagogues and
    cemeteries
    destroyed during the
    Holocaust 276
journals 1115
justice 14, 126
Karlštejn Castle 129,
  966-67
KGB records 225
kings and rulers 122, 124
Korea 237
Krakow 709
land fund 628
land reform 286, 428
landownership 152
Lands of Bohemian
  Crown 97, 122
language 158-59
  Czech 757, 759-60,
    804, 806
  Prague School 811
  regulations 428
League of Nations 481
Liberated Theatre,
  Prague 995
libraries 1133, 1136-39,
  1141
literature 114, 148, 818-
  19, 824, 827, 832, 840,
  844, 896
  and politics 824
  and religious history
    827
  avant-garde 839
  Baroque 828, 895
  Communist period 842
  Czech-German literary
    contacts 833
  decadence 850
  dictionary of writers 843
  fin-de-siècle criticism
    835-36
  folk literature 832

  14th century 825, 829
  in Britain 485
  Lavryn 829
  literary reform
    movement 845
  Mastičkár 830
  mediaeval 826, 830
  Naturalism 840
  novel 844
  Old Czech 825
  playwrights of the
    Krejča Circle 844
  Poetism 839, 899
  Poetismus 839, 899
  poetry 844
  Prague 837
  Prague German writers
    933
  Romanticism 831
  samizdat 849
  Vévoda Arnošt 829
  writers and
    Communism/
    Bolshevism 838
living standards 364
local government 521
Luck, Ukraine 307
Magyars 354
manufacturing industry
  634
maps and atlases 39-40,
  121, 1080
Marshall Plan 489
Masaryk's philosophy of
  history 128
masonic lodges 342
media statistics 1094
mediaeval 7, 103, 126,
  128, 130-32, 830, 1051
  chronologies 126, 130
medicine 390
migration 126
military 1145
military affairs, maps and
  atlases 39
minorities 253-54
Moderní Revue 148
monarchies 126
Moravia 276
  architecture 1013-14
  coats of arms 99
  elections 431
  folk customs 313, 319

414

History *contd*
    intellectual life 841
    map 1080
    Premonstratensians
        347
    religious history 144
Munich Agreement,
    1938 192-95
Munich crisis, 1930s 13,
    179, 192-96, 215, 290
Munich Diktat *see*
    History: Munich
    Agreement, 1938
music 114, 1038, 1040,
    1051-52
National Gallery, Prague
    1142
national group 253
National Library, Prague
    1137-38
National Museum,
    Prague 694, 1144
national question 13
National Revival, 19th
    century 120, 158-59,
    164-65, 281, 330, 994
National Theatre
    Movement, 1845-83
    160, 994
Nationalism 18, 104,
    160, 253, 286, 425,
    430, 440
NATO 503
Netherlands 156
nobility 153
non-Czech minorities 254
'normalization', 1968- 451
October Revolution *see*
    History: Bolshevik
    Revolution
Office for Religious
    Affairs 320
Olomouc 1151
Olympic games 739
opera 1038
Operation Danube, 1968
    225
Ottoman Empire 38
Panorthosia 739
Pan-Slavism 6, 838
Paris conference, 1918 174
parliamentary democracy
    425

Peace of Westphalia,
    1648 1013
Pilsen 207
Poland 446, 536
Poles 354
political nationalism 160
political parties 281, 288
politics 14, 105, 147, 166,
    233, 424-36, 440, 844
    after Second World
        War 208, 212
    Cold War 1945-91 437
    Czechoslovak
        language idea 449
    Czech-Slovak relations
        449
    First Republic
        (1918-38) 425, 430
    government in exile
        429
    inter-war years 428,
        438
    maps and atlases 40
    mediaeval 131
    party politics 444
    pluralism 441
    Prague 62
    separation of Czechs
        and Slovaks 450,
        452
    Slovak quest for
        recognition 425
    Soviet Communist era
        425, 437-46, 448,
        844
        central government
            439
        constitutions 439
        party politics 444
        transition period 450,
            452
popes 122
Prague 30, 61, 66, 691,
    705, 714, 716, 719,
    721, 1015, 1022-23
    ancient 714
    architecture 715-16
    Ashkenazi Judaism
        280
    battlefields 61
    cafés 65
    Belorussian minority
        293-94

    cultural scene 244
    geopolitical situation
        709
    Germans 281
    historical sites 61
    Hussite 61
    industry 30
    Jewish community
        1147
    Judaism 280
    literary 906
    mediaeval 130
    19th century 30, 1020
    opera 1048
    patrimony 714
    Russian minority
        293-94
    Swedish siege of, 1648
        157
    transport 690-91
    Ukrainian minority
        293-94
    urban areas 30
    urban planning 705
Prague Esperanto Club
    817
Prague Golden Lane 66
Prague Lodge of the
    Three Stars 342
Prague opera 1048
Prague School 793, 799,
    811
Prague Slav Congress,
    1848 163
Prague Spring, 1968
    13-14, 212, 214,
    222-27, 234, 451
    and cultural and
        literary movement
        222
    economic reforms
        behind it 226
    Soviet invasion
        223-24, 234
Prague Zionism 274
Premonstratensian order
    347
Přemyslide dynasty 61,
    130
presidents 112
    see also individual
    presidents by name
press 1094

History *contd*
  princes, kings and
    presidents 112
    see also individual
    princes, kings and
    presidents by name
  Program of the
    Communist Party of
    Czechoslovakia, April
    1968 230
  Protestant Church and
    Protestantism 337, 341
  psychology 703
  public transport 687-88,
    690-91
  purges of academia, 1948
    398
  radio 1094
  recognition of the state of
    Israel 1948 495
  recreational homes 753
  Red trade unions 29
  refugees 481
  religion 14, 334, 830
    and Czech language
      758
    and state restrictions
      333
    Christianization of
      Moravia and
      Bohemia 325
    Communist policy
      towards the Church
      1948-56 328
    Hussitism 330
    Reformation 338, 340
    Soviet Communist
      period 324, 445
  religion-based
    controversies 114
  religious groups 333
  religious orders 346
  renaissance *see* History:
    National Revival, 19th
    century
  reproduction 390
  Republican Party 436
  republicanism 430
  retailing 650
  revolution, 1848 163
  revolutions of 1989 *see*
    History: Velvet
    Revolution, 1989

rivers 692
Roma 255, 258, 260-65
  sterilization of women
    during Soviet
    Communist era 261
Roman Catholic Church
  320-22
  and Soviet
    Communism 321-22
Romania 481
Romany *see* History:
  Roma
Rovno, Ukraine 307
Russia 446
  civil war 169-70,
    172-73
  Russian Empire 38
  Russian minority 252,
    293-94
Ruthenia 278, 354
Ruthenians 426
samizdat literature 442-
  43
Samo 124
scholarship 14
science and technology
  14, 700
sculpture 148
Second Republic (1938-
  39) 451
Second World War 12,
  14, 179, 200-02, 207,
  331, 438, 451, 485,
  488
  army 698
  Czech National
    Council
    (Československý
    národní výbor) 201
  government in exile
    198, 201
  Jews 206
  maps and atlases 38
  Prague, German
    occupation of 1939-
    45 205
  Protectorate of
    Bohemia and
    Moravia 290
  relationship between
    Jews, Czechs and
    Slovaks 204
  resistance 175, 201

Roma, extermination
  in concentration
  camps 263-64, 267
Sudetenland 203
show trials 219-20, 493
Sixty-Eight Publishers,
  Toronto, establishment
  of 1968 222
Slánský trial, 1952
  219-20, 493
Slav Congress, 1848 103
Slavkov 162
Slavkov, Battle of *see*
  History: Austerlitz,
  Battle of
Slavonic hagiography 325
Slavs 103
Slovak National Uprising
  1944 698
Slovakia / Slovak
  Republic 560
  economic migrants 481
  glassmaking 675, 679
  hostilities with
    Hungary, 1919 698
  politics 487
  Premonstratensians 347
  Roma 267
Slovaks abroad 299,
  301-02, 306, 308
social change *see*
  History: society and
  social change
social democratic unions
  433
social partnership 106
social security 364
socialism 425, 838
society and social change
  109, 128, 147, 212,
  354, 383, 451, 847
Sofia 716
Sokol movement 281,
  303, 330, 737, 740-41
Soviet bloc – crisis after
  death of Stalin
  1953-57 221
Soviet Communism
  12-13, 430
  collapse of 235, 237,
    446
  economic and social
    inequality 361

History, Soviet
Communism *contd*
fear of 432
rise of 446
Soviet Communist period
209, 212, 243, 439
advent of 13
and link to Soviet bloc
216
attitude of the West
towards 215
Central European
democratic
revolutions 217
crisis after death of
Stalin, 1953-57 221
crisis of 1968 *see*
History: Prague
Spring 1968
education 211, 398
establishment of
Communist regimes
1944-49 210-11
maps and atlases 38
'normalization'
1969- 228
police surveillance 218
political persecution
1948-72 218
Prague Spring 1968
217
show trials, 1952 219-20
Slánsky affair 220
Soviet socialism 1968-
88 217
Sovietization 216
takeover 1948 215-16
Soviet Jewry 220
Soviet supremacy in
Eastern Europe, end of
223
Soviet Union 197, 237,
488-89
Spain 156
Spartakiad 742
sport 737-38
St Vitus' cathedral,
Prague 130
statistics 101
steam locomotives 685-86
Sudeten Germans *see*
History: German
minority

Sudeten question, 1918-
283
Sudetendeutsche Party
194
Sudetenland 288
Taborites 137
Talmud school of Prague
314
technical colleges 696
television 1094
Terezín, northern
Bohemia 206
Teschen 492, 809
textiles industry 667
theatre 106
theology 351
Theresienstadt *see*
History: Terezín
Theresienstadt
concentration camp
309
Third Republic 1945-48
451
Thirty Years War 118,
156-57, 1013
Thun Palace 482
tourism 44
town planning 1020,
1024, 1026, 1030
towns 125
trams 687
transport 687, 691-92
travel guides 46-47
Prague 46, 49
trolleybuses 687
tuberculosis 944
Turkish wars 151
turn of century *see*
History: *fin-de-siècle*
movements
United States 481, 485
Unity of Czech Brethren
143-44
universities 485
University of Prague
128, 281
Uprising of Bohemian
Estates, 1618-20 1013
Uprisings, 1953 493
urban planning 705
USSR *see* History:
Soviet Union
Vatican 320-22

Velvet Revolution, 1989
223, 235-39, 241, 349
Vienna 342, 709
Viennese Czechs 308
Volhynian Czechs 307
Warsaw Pact 223, 225
invasion of
Czechoslovakia
1968 225
watchmaking 990
weapons 669, 1148
Western European
powers, 1939-48 197
White Mountain, Battle
of, 1621 157
women 372, 376, 379,
381, 741
wool industry 633
World War I *see* History:
First World War
World War II *see*
History: Second World
War
Young Czech Party 166
Yugoslavia 481, 536
Žalud-Vysokomýtský
107
Žatec 307
Žďárec 244
Zionism 273, 495
see also Prehistory and
archaeology; and
individual historical
figures by name
History Institute of the
Army of the Czech
Republic 1145
Hitler 290
Hluboká nad Vltavou 1148
Hockey 746
Hofbaur, Arnost 974
Holan, Vladimír 899-900
Holek, Emanuel 669
Hollar, Wenceslaus 968
Holub, Miroslav 877, 880,
899
Holy Infant of Prague wax
effigy 353
Homosexuality 391
Honey 628
Hora, Josef 838, 899-900
Horáková, Milada 381
Hotels 45, 710

417

Household incomes 356, 369
Households 418
  statistics 418
Housing 361, 418, 706-08,
  712
  policy 615, 708
  privatization 707
  reform 706-07
  statistics 418
Hrabal, Bohumil 7, 844,
  882, 902-03, 1005
Hrabová, Libuše 7
Hradčany castle 66, 963,
  1015-17, 1029, 1034
Hradec Králové 69, 687
HRH Queen Elizabeth II,
  visit to Czech Republic,
  1996 482-83
HRH The Duke of
  Edinburgh, visit to Czech
  Republic, 1996 482
Hromádka, Josef 351
Hrubín, František 899-900
Hübschmannová, Milena
  259
Hukvaldy, Northern
  Moravia 1072
Human rights 515
Hungary
  and NATO 502
  architecture 1027
  banking and finance 602
  Catholic Church 324
  contracts 511
  Czech émigrés 305
  economy 508, 546-48,
    569
  environment 725, 727
  housing 708
  industry 638
  international relations
    479
  media 1091
  minority in former
    Czechoslovakia 252
  politics 467
  privatization 650
  retail trade and consumer
    services 650
  Soviet Communism,
    collapse of 458
Hus, Jan (1371-1415) 4,
  14, 18, 128, 131-33

Hussite revolution see
  History
Husák, Gustáv 233
Hydroelectric potential
  661-62
Hydrometeorological
  Institute 729
Hymns 325

I

Ice hockey 746-47
ICEES see International
  Council for Central and
  East European Studies
Identity 23, 249
IFTU (International
  Federation of Trade
  Unions) sources 433
Income distribution 361,
  369-70
Income policy 357
Income support system 355
Incomes and expenditures
  418
Independence movement
  see History
Independent power sector
  – Czech Republic 658
Indifferent observer, The
  (Richard Weiner) 828
Industrial enterprises 367,
  633-79
Industrial offices 710
Industrial property and
  technology 510
Industrial research 695
Industrial sectors 651-79
  armaments 647, 669
  brewing 651-52, 1088
  canning 636
  car manufacturing 653
  chemical industry 637,
    664-65
  coal-fired power stations
    643
  communications 112, 643
  construction 666
  dairy 628, 671
  drugs see Industrial
    sectors:
    pharmaceuticals

  energy 658-59, 661, 665
  engineering 640, 645, 657
  foundry industry 655
  gas 660
  glass 645, 675-79
  information technology
    697
  investment banking 645
  investment engineering
    656
  IT 697
  jet trainer 647
  manufacturing 639-40,
    643
  papermaking 673
  pharmaceutical industry
    636, 663-64
  plastics 674
  pump manufacturing 670
  rubber industry 664
  steel industry 645, 654
  sugar 672
  textiles 636, 640, 668
  water 661
Industrialization 359
  effects on society 359
Industry 528, 615, 633-47
  and environment 637
  and transition 640-41,
    646
  attracting foreign
    investment 642-43
  British commercial
    representatives 638
  defence 647
  labour 640
  privatization of 635
  reform of 635-36, 645
  statistics 416
  see also Industrial sectors
Information technology
  697
Infrastructure 528
Institute for Nature
  Conservation 729
Insurance, health 386,
  388-89
Intellectual life 362, 380
Intellectual property rights
  510
Intelligentsia see History
Internal security and
  public order 468

International Conference and Festival of Czechoslovak Music, 1984 1052
International Council for Central and East European Studies (ICEES), journal 1121
International migration 480
see also Migration; Refugees
International relations 179, 479-97
refugees 480
with British 476, 482
with Germans 23, 290, 476, 482, 490
see also History
International security 497-503
Interpersonal relations 391
Inter-war years *see* History
Invasion by Warsaw Pact armies *see* History
Investiční a Poštovní banka 573
Investment *see* Banking and finance
Investment engineering 656
IPB 651
IPS Praha 615
Israel, and Slánský affair 220
IT *see* Information technology 697

J

Jablonec nad Nisou 678
Jakobson, Roman 811
Jan Hus (Josef Kajetán Tyl) 831
Jan Žižka 138
Janáček, Leoš 1063-80
and Brod, Max 1078
and Janáčková, Zdenka 1068
and Moravian folksongs 1071
and Newmarch, Rosa 1077
and Stösslová, Kamila 1067
bibliographies and catalogues 1063, 1066, 1079-80
letters 1067, 1070, 1073
music theory 1075-76
newspaper articles 1069
operas 997, 1070-73
Janáčková, Zdenka 1068
Janák, Pavel 1023
Janeček, Ota 978, 980
Janouch, František 443
Jarry, Alfred 998
Jasov abbey, Slovakia 347
Javarová, Ludmila 343
Jenůfa (Leoš Janáček) 1071
Jerome of Prague 128
Jesenská, Milena 951-55
and Kafka, Franz 951-53
Jesenská, Růžena 18, 836
Jesuit order *see* History
Jet trainer 647
Jews 1, 10, 18, 249, 251, 272
anecdotes 315
customs 279
Czech attitudes towards 283
German attitudes towards 283
legends 314
minority in former Czechoslovakia 252
women 18
see also Anti-Semitism; History
Jihlava 687
Jirásek, Alois 855
Jiřičná, Eva 1035
John of Luxembourg, King of Bohemia 483
John, Zdeněk 974
Joke, The (Milan Kundera) 914, 916-17
Journals 1114-23
Judaism 279
Justice statistics 416

K

Kadečková, Joy 482
Kafka, Franz 883, 903, 934, 941-42, 944-45
and anti-Semitism issue 944
and Bauer, Felice 156
and Jesenská, Milena 951
and Judaism 944
and Prague 940-41
and Yiddish culture and German literature 942
biography 938-41
Bloch, Greta 956
critical essays on 941
diaries 951
letters 952, 956
relatives 943
work of 936, 939-40, 942, 945-46, 948-49
bibliography 939, 946
criticism / studies of 947
Kafka, Ivan 979
Kainar, Josef 899-900
Kalista, Zdeněk 900
Kaliště 72
Kantůrková, Eva 903
Kaplický, Jan 1036-37
Karásek ze Lvovic, Jiří 148
Karlštejn Castle 129, 966-67
see also History
Kašpar Lén mstitel (Karel Matěj Čapek-Chod) 840
Káťa Kabanová (Leoš Janáček) 1067, 1071, 1073
Kepler, Johann 155
KGB records *see* History
Kierkegaard 471
Kings and rulers *see* History; and individuals by name
Klaus, Václav 563-64, 590
Klementinum, Prague 1137-38
Kles, Petr 836
Klíma, Ivan 405, 822, 838, 885, 902-04, 998
Klimt, Gustav 969
Klofáč, Václav Jaroslav 435
Kněhnic, Jiří 134
Kniha apokryfů (Karel Čapek) 828
Kniha smíchu a zapomění (Milan Kundera) 828

Kobliha, František 974
Kohout, Pavel 998
Kokolia, Vladimír 977
Kolíbal, Stanislav 981
Kollár, Jan 6
Komenský, Jan Amos see
  Comenius
Koniáš, Antonín 348
Konopiště 1148
Konůpek, Jan 974-75
Korbel, Josef 14
Korea see History
Košice, Slovakia 261, 654
Kotasová, Věra 978
Kotěra, Jan 1023
Koucký, František 669
Koucký, Josef 669
Koudelka, Josef 983
Kožený, Viktor 558
Krakow 709
Kramář, K. 174
Kratochvíl, Jiří 902
Kreditní Banka 466
Krejča Circle playwrights
  844
Krnka, Karel 669
Kroha, Jiří 1027
Kroutil, Josef 172
Krušné hory mountain
  range 33
Ktož sú boží bojovníci
  (Hussite battle hymn) 132
Kubelík, Rafael 1041
Kubín, Alfred 969
Kuklík, Ladislav 978
Kundera, Milan 405, 822,
  828, 834, 838, 844, 903,
  914, 916, 918, 998
  and feminism 915
  and women 915
  bibliography of works on
    and by 914-15
  criticism of the works of
    917
  literary and critical
    works of 918
  views on translations
    923
  works of 915-16, 918-19,
    920-23
Kupka, František 969
Kytice (Karel Jaromír
  Erben) 831

L

Labour 528, 640
  and legislation 516
Labyrint světa a ráj srdce
  (Comenius) 828
Lachian 959
  poetry 959-60
Lachians 809
Lachs 809
Land reform see History
Landownership see
  History
Lands of Bohemian Crown
  see History
Landscape gardening 78
Lane of Alchemists see
  Golden Lane, Prague
  Castle
Language 7, 12, 757, 1152
  Czech 7, 12, 757-59,
    809-10
  database 807
  dialects 808-09, 813,
    815
  dictionaries
    Czech-English 774,
      777-78, 783, 85,
      790-91
    English-Czech
      774-76, 778,
      780, 782, 786-91
  extraterritorial 813
  grammar 401, 760,
    792-806
  journal 1117
  language aids 1152
  linguistics 12
  orthography 757, 768
  Polish-Czech linguistic
    border 809
  relationship between
    Standard and
    'Common' Czech
    813-15
  socio-linguistics 812-
    15
  spoken and written
    814
  spoken Czech in
    literature 814
  teaching of 401, 1157
  Teschen, Czech

Republic 809
  textbooks 792-806
  Czech National Corpus
    807
  Slavic and East European
    1152
  Slavonic 757-59
  Slovak 809-10
  rights and laws 249
  see also History
Lapidarium 1149
Largo desolato (Václav
  Havel) 828
Latin America 465
Latvia 725
Laughable loves, The
  (Milan Kundera) 914,
    916-17
Law 504-15
'Law on State Enterprise
  of April 19, 1990' 507
League of Nations see
  History
Léčiva pharmaceuticals
  573
Legal materials see Law
Legenda o Sodomovi (Jiří
  Karásek ze Lvovic)
    828
Legends, Moravian 313
Legislation see Law
Lekce Faust 1008
Lepidoptera 86
Levete, Amanda 1037
Liberated Theatre of
  Prague 995
Liberec 553, 687, 689
Libraries
  guide 1132-35
  see also History
Library Act for the Unified
  System of Libraries
    1956 1136
Life is elsewhere (Milan
  Kundera) 914, 916
Linguistics see Language
Linhartová, Věra 902
Literary criticism 19,
  838-42, 845-51
Literature 12, 818-23
  Baroque 828, 895, 1013
  Church Slavonic works
    325

Literature *contd*
  Communist literary philo-
    sophical tradition 822
  Czech 7, 810, 813, 819,
    832-33, 935
  and national
    emancipation 821
  and universal literature
    821
  anthologies 895-908
    on Prague 906-08
    plays 904-05
    prose 895-96
    short stories 902, 906
    verse/poetry 896-901
  Bildungsroman
    (psychological
    novel) 848
  dissident writers 843,
    905
  émigré and samizdat
    843, 909-32
  essays/prose 854, 872,
    878, 880, 882-83
    see also Literature:
    Czech: anthologies
  exile literature 846,
    909-10
  feuilletons 883
  fiction 847-48
  for children and young
    people 843
  in English 852
  legends/fables 855, 863
  letters 873
  mediaeval 1051
  novels 856-57, 861-62,
    869-71, 884-89,
    893-94
  novels set during
    Second World War
    869-71
  on Prague 906-07
  output of exile
    publishing houses
    909, 911
  plays 860, 874-76
  poetry 909
  samizdat 843, 909-32
  science fiction 860
  short stories 854, 858,
    881, 887
  tales 863-64, 866, 887

  translations 818-19
  verse/poetry 853, 867-
    68, 877, 879, 890-92
    see also anthologies
  drama 823
  German 933-35
    German-Jewish writers
    934
    Jews in German
    literature 934
    Kafka, Franz 936-56
    history 958
    Kafka, Franz 936-56
    other nationalities 957-60
    Prague 837
    Prague German Jewish
    writers 933
    Prague German
    literature 820
    Prague German writers
    933, 935
    Prague literary life 935
    short stories about
    Prague 906-07
  reinstatement of authors
    who had fallen foul of
    the Communist régime
    843
  Slavic and East European
    962, 1152
  Slovak 810, 852
    in exile 909-10
  Soviet Union samizdat
    literature 912
    see also History
Lithuania 725
Living standards *see* History
Local administration and
  government 521-22
Loos, Adolf 1024, 1027
Luck, Ukraine *see* History
Luskačová, Markéta 984
Lustig, Arnošt 902
Lutheranism 351
Lvovic, Jiří Karásek ze 828
Łysohorský, Óndra 959

M

Má vlast (Smetana) 1041
Mácha, Karel Hynek 828,
  831, 833

Macocha chasm 36, 313
Magyars *see* History
  see also Hungary
Mahen, Jiří 900
Mahler, Gustav 72, 1063
Máj (Karel Hynek Mácha)
  828, 831
Majerová, Marie 18, 836,
  838
Makropulos (Leoš
  Janáček) 1071
Makropulos affair, The
  (Leoš Janáček) 1071
Malířová, Helena 18
Malý, Václav 349
Managers and
  management 371, 557
Mánes, Josef 964
Manufacturing *see*
  Industrial sectors
'Map of Moravia' 412
Maps and atlases 38-42
  see also History: maps
  and atlases
Mariánské Lázně 687
Marketing 1093
Marketization 461
Marriage 18, 418, 421
  statistics 418
Marshall Plan *see* History
Martinů, Bohuslav 1081-85
  bibliographies and
  catalogues 1083, 1085
Martyrs 6, 326-27
Masaryk, Alice Garrigue
  191
Masaryk, Jan 189-90
Masaryk, T. G. *see*
  Masaryk, Tomáš
  Garrigue
Masaryk, Tomáš Garrigue
  148, 174, 181-82, 185,
  189, 430, 434
  and Czech-German
  relations 284
  and history 128
  and philosophy 358
  and sociology 358
  criticism of the works of
  181, 183, 187
  interviews with Čapek,
  Karel 188
Nová Evropa 106

Masaryk, Tomáš Garrigue
  contd
  philosophy and its
    literary dimensions
    833
  religious views 186
  resentment towards 432
  works of 181, 184
Masaryk family 189-91
Masonic lodges *see*
  History
Mass media *see* Media
Matěj Čapek-Chod, Karel
  810, 836, 840
Maxová, Teresa, and
  Czech orphan adoption
  foundation 271
May (Karel Hynek Mácha)
  7, 831
Mechanica Corporation
  367
Media 460, 1091-99
Medicine *see* Health and
  health care; History
Memorandum, The
  (Václav Havel) 831
Memorial of Czech
  Literature, Prague 347,
  1141
Memorial of Liberation
  1145
Memorial of Resistance 1145
Mendel, Gregor 699-702
Mendelism 701-02
Menzel, Jiří 1005, 1009
Metamorphosis (Franz
  Kafka) 950
Migration 22
  see also History;
  International migration;
  Refugees
Military 497
  see also NATO
Military expenditure 647
Military history 1145
Military History Archives
  1145
Military History Library
  1145
Military Museum 1148
Military policy 468
Military Technical
  Museum 1145

Milk production 628
  see also Dairy industry
Milunič, Vlado 60
Ministry of Agriculture
  729
Ministry of Environment
  of the Czech Republic
  728
Ministry of Health 729
Minorities 249-50, 252,
  497
  Czech policy towards
    250
  see also History
Missing person, The
  (Franz Kafka) 939
Mnichovo Hradiště 1148
Moderní Revue see
  History
Monasteries 53, 346-47,
  1141
Moravia 1087
  see also History
Moravian Karst 36, 313
Moravská galerie, Brno
  1150
Moravský Kras *see*
  Moravian Karst
Morfill, Richard 816
Mortality and morbidity
  663
Most-Litvínov 687
Mrázková, Daisy 977
Mucha, Alfons 969-73
Mucha, Geraldine 482
Munch, Edvard 969
Munich Agreement, 1938
  see History
Munich crisis, 1930s *see*
  History
Munich Diktat *see*
  History: Munich
  Agreement, 1938
Murer, Ewald 902
Museum hlavního města
  Prahy *see* Museum of
  Capital City of Prague
Museum husitského
  revolučního hnutí *see*
  Museum of the Hussite
  Revolutionary
  Movement, Tábor
Museum of Art 1151

Museum of Capital City of
  Prague 1148
Museum of Czech
  Literature 347, 1141
Museum of Decorative
  Arts, Prague 1146, 1148
Museum of the Hussite
  Revolutionary
  Movement, Tábor 1148
Museums and galleries
  1141-51
Mushrooms 79
Music 10, 12, 995,
  1038-49, 1077
  composers 1046
  Czech musicians and
    writers abroad 1042
  directory 1042
  popular 1049
  Slavic and East European
    962
  see also History;
    individual composers
    by name, e.g.,
    Smetana, Bedřich;
    Dvořák, Antonín
Musicals 997

N

Národní museum *see*
  National Museum,
  Prague
National bibliographies
  1154-56
National Environmental
  Policy 729
National Gallery, Prague
  1015, 1142-43
National identity 3, 6
National Institute of Public
  Health, Prague 392
National Library of the
  Czech Republic 1133,
  1137
National Museum Library
  see Castle Library of
  Český Krumlov
National Museum, Prague
  1144, 1148-49
  sculpture 1149
  see also History

422

National Property Fund
617
National question 13
National Revival, 19th
century see History
National Theatre
Movement see History
National Theatre, Prague
993
Nationalism 18, 248-49,
283, 500
see also History
NATO 237, 240, 500, 502-
03, 615
and Yugoslav question 500
Czech preparations for
the membership of 576
Ostpolitik in post-Cold
War Europe 500
Natural gas 658
Natural history 699-704
Navrátilová, Martina 298,
748-52
Nehru, Indira 195
Nehru, Jawaharlal 195
Němcová, Božena 381
Neo-Nazis 268, 270
Netečný divák (Richard
Weiner) 828
Netherlands 389
see also History
Neumann, Stanislav
Kostka 899-900
Newmarch, Rosa 1077
Newspapers and
periodicals 1100-04
business 1124-31
English-language 1105-13
Nezval, Vítězslav 839,
899-900
Nietzsche, Friedrich
Wilhelm 841
Night with Hamlet
(Vladimír Holan) 831
Nikl, Petr 979
Nipponari (Bohuslav
Martinů) 1082
Nobility see History
Noc s Hamletem (Vladimír
Holan) 831
Nomura 651
'Normalization', 1968-
451

North America 298-302
North-Moravian region 35
Nova 1098
Nová Říše abbey,
southern Bohemia 347
Novák, Vítězslav 1040
Nováková, Teréza 18
Nový Jičín 553
Nuclear energy 659, 722

O

October Revolution see
History: Bolshevik
Revolution Oil 658, 665
Office for Religious
Affairs see History
Oil 658, 665
Olbracht, Ivan 838
Olomouc 687
see also History
Olomouc Picture Gallery
1151
Olympic games 739, 746
Opava 687
Opera 1038, 1047, 1053
Baroque 1048
Prague 993, 1013, 1048
productions 1043
Operation Danube, 1968
see History
Orlík 1148
Orphan adoption 271
Orten, Jiří 899-900
Ostrava 35, 553, 611, 687
Ostrava steelworks 645
Osvobozené divadlo 995
Ottoman Empire see History

P

Pachman, Luděk 756
Paedophilia 384
Painting 961-62, 1013
Palach, Jan 6
Palacký, František 164
Palivec, Josef 900
Památník národního
písemnictví (Museum of
Czech Literature) 347,
1141

Pammrová, Anna 841
Panna Marie Vítězná see
Carmelite Church of
Our Lady Victorious in
Prague
Panorthosia see History
Pan-Slavism see History
Papermaking 673
Páral, Vladimír 844, 851
Pardubice 687
Paris conference, 1918 see
History
Parliaments 505
Patent laws 510
Patočka, Jan 245
Paul, Bruno 1024
Payne, Peter 128
Peace of Westphalia, 1648
see History
Pekař, Josef 148
Pension schemes 355
Periodicals see
Newspapers and
periodicals
Pernštejn Castle 313
Pešat, Zdeněk 900
PETs see Planned
economies in transition
Pharmaceutical industries
388, 663-64
Philately 202-03, 970, 1166
Philosophy 422-23, 471,
962
Photography 265-66, 961,
979, 983-84
Physical education 735
Pilsen 32, 553, 687
see also History
Pilsener see Beer
Pinter, Harold 998
Pirandello, Luigi 998
Planned economies in
transition (PETs) 538
Planning and construction
law 513
Plants 74-79
Plastic People of the
Universe 1049
Plastics industry 674
Plečnik, Josip 67, 1024,
1029
Plzeň see Pilsen
Poborský, Karel 745

Počátek románu (Leoš Janáček) 1072
Poetism 899
Poetry 19, 263, 995
Poland
  and NATO 502
  architecture 1027
  banking and finance 602-03, 606
  Catholic Church 324
  contracts 511
  Czech émigrés 305
  economy 508, 547-48, 569, 619
  education 398
  environment 725, 727
  housing 708
  industry 638
  international relations 479
  language 809
  media 1091
  politics 467, 470
  privatization 550
  retail and consumer services 650
  Soviet Communism, collapse of 458
  transition economy 550-51
  see also History
Police Academy of the Czech Republic 396
Police Museum, Prague 54
Polish minority 252
Political parties 459, 466
  see also History
Politics 3, 23, 38, 101, 240, 361-62, 424-25, 437, 447-78, 497, 528, 560, 576, 618
  and nationalism 460, 471
  and religion 324, 471
  break-up of Czechoslovakia 467
  Central-local relations under new Czechoslovak constitutional law 522
  democratization 461, 515
  elections 457, 467, 469, 577, 615
  elites 469
  fundamentalism 471

green 722
international 479
party politics 467
post-Communist 466-67
public administration reform 464
separation of Czechs and Slovaks 449-54
Soviet Communism, collapse of 447
split of Czechoslovakia 453-54
state administration 464
transformation of elites 470
transition, 1989- 357, 447, 457, 462-63, 467, 473, 556-57
urban 714
Velvet Revolution, 1989 448
  see also History
Pollution *see* Environment
Polyxena of Lobkowicz 353
Pope John Paul II 320-22
Popes *see* History
Population 24, 29, 418, 459
  statistics 416, 418
  see also Demography
Porcelain 49, 989
Postage stamps 970
  see also Philately
Poster design 1028
Potatoes 628
Poultry 628
Poverty 356
Prague 21, 31, 709, 715, 720
  and post-Communist economy 713
  architecture 60, 63, 67, 714, 1015-25, 1029, 1031-33
  guides 60, 63
  Art Nouveau 1021
  bibliography 1163
  bookshops 1096
  cafés 65
  conservation 714, 717
  culture and society 21
  demographic changes 715
  domestic refuse collection 62
  drama 993

environment 719
fin-de-siècle 1022
flora 77
gardens 64
geography and geology 721
geopolitical situation 709
green spaces 719
housing 719
in literature 906-07
industry 643, 715
information for tourists 690
intellectual life 21
investment 714
Jewish 314
Little Quarter / Malá Strana 854
marriage 421
Old Town Square 714
passageways and arcades 1019
philosophy and heritage 714
pictures 53
place in European society 714
politics 714
pollution 715, 718-19
population 719
privatization 709, 714
public amenities 719
public transport 709
public utilities 719
recapitalization 30
renovation of historic quarters 714
society 21
sports and recreation 719
street cleaning 62
telecommunications 709
tourism 709
transport 683-84, 687, 690-91, 715, 719
urban planning 709, 719
social and economic conditions 21
stock exchange 617, 622-24
traveller's account 43
urban structure and transition 705, 713
urbanism 720

424

Prague *contd*
  Wenceslas Square 31
  see also History
Prague Castle 66, 983,
  1015-17, 1029, 1034
Prague Cathedral 967
  see also St Vitus
  Cathedral, Prague
Prague City Council 714
Prague Esperanto Club *see*
  History
Prague funicular 690
Prague Golden Lane
  see Golden Lane;
  History
Prague Lodge of the Three
  Stars *see* History
Prague Metro 690
Prague opera *see* History;
  Opera
Prague Ruzyně airport
  683-84
Prague School 793, 799, 811
Prague Slav Congress,
  1848 *see* History
Prague Spring, 1968 *see*
  History
Prague Spring
  International Music
  Festival 1041
Prague stock exchange
  567, 617, 622-24
Prague synagogues and
  old Jewish cemetery 314
Prague Zionism *see*
  History
Pražákův Palace, Brno 1150
Prehistory and
  archaeology 87-96
  art mobilier 91
  basketry 91
  bear bone accumulation,
    Upper Pleistocene 92
  Bohemia 87, 89
  carved stones 91
  Celtic religion and ritual
    practices 94
  ceramics 91
  Czech and Slovak lands
    88
  Dolní Věstonice, southern
    Moravia 90-91
  Iron Age 94

  mediaeval 95
  Moravia 90-91
  Neolithic finds 93
  palaeontology 92
  Pavlov, Moravia 91
  Pod Hradem Cave, near
    Brno 92
  pottery 93
  Samo 96
  southern Moravia 90
  textiles 91
  use of aerial photography
    89
  Venus, figurine of,
    Věstonice 91
  Viereckschanzen 94
Preisler, Jan 969
Preissig, Vojtěch 148, 974
Preissová, Gabriela 18
Prejudices 16
Premonstratensian abbeys
  347
Přemyslide dynasty *see*
  History
Presidency 459
  see also History:
  presidents
Press 1091
  expatriate 296
  see also Newspapers and
    periodicals; History
Privatization *see* Economy
Der Process (Franz Kafka)
  946
Procházka, Arnošt 148
Products and services
  524-25, 527
Profintern sources 433
Proletarian art 899
Property 513, 705
  law 520, 710
  markets 705
Prostitution 18, 384-85
Protestantism 337, 351
Proverbs 316
Psychology 703
Public health 392
  see also Health care
Public order 468
Public Procurement Act 516
Public transport 687-91
Publishing houses 1096
Pubs *see* Beer-halls

Pujmanová, Marie 838
Pump manufacturing 670
Punkva underground river
  313
Purges of academia *see*
  History
Purkinje cells 703
Purkyně, Jan Evangelista
  703-04

R

Rabbi Löw 314
Rabbits 628
Racial intolerance 259
  see also Anti-Semitism;
  Roma
Radegast 651
Radio
  statistics 416
  see also History
Railways 710, 712
Rais, Karel V. 834
Rapeseed 628
Raw materials 27
Real estate *see* Property
Recession *see* Economy
Recipes 79, 1086
Recreational homes 753
Red meat 628
Red trade unions *see*
  History
Redon, Aubrey 969
Reforms of economy,
  1989 – *see* Economy:
  reform
Refugees 480-81
Reháková, Anna 18
Religion 18, 320, 323-24,
  351, 459
  see also History
Religious orders 346-48
Religious symbolism 353
Renaissance *see* History:
  National Revival, 19th
  century
Rents 710
Republican Party *see*
  History
Republicanism *see* History
Research Institute for
  Water Management 729

425

Residential property *see*
Housing
Resource distribution 361
Retailing 528, 648-50, 710
privatization of 650
statistics 649
transition 649-50
Revolutions *see* History:
Velvet Revolution,
1989; History:
revolution, 1848
Richterová, Sylvie 902
Rilke, Rainer Maria 957
Rivers 692
Road maps 41-42
Roads 681-82, 710, 712
Rodin, Auguste 969
Roma 1, 251-52, 255, 257,
259-60, 269-70, 820, 1099
bibliography 256
children 266, 271
language and dialects 260
photographs 265-66
possible enclosure into
segregated, walled
areas 267
racial attacks against
267-68
recognition of Romany
language 1989 261
socio-economic
conditions 260
see also History
Roma database of State
Scientific Library in
Košice 261
Roman Catholic Church
349
religious orders 346
see also History
Romania
Czech émigrés 305-06
economy 619
environment 725
housing 708
politics 470
Romany *see* Roma
'Romany Holocaust and
Romany Present' project
266
Róna, Jaroslav 977
Rovno, Ukraine *see*
History

Rubber industry 664
Rudolf II 154-55, 1013
Rudolph II *see* Rudolf II
R.U.R (Čapek, Karel) 860
Russia 506, 511, 598
see also History
Russian Empire *see*
History
Russian minority *see*
History
Ruthenia *see* History

S

Šafařík, Pavel 6
Šalda, F. X. 900
Samizdat literature *see*
History; Literature
Santini-Aichel, Johann
Blasius 1014
Satire 995
Scenography 961
Schiele, Egon 969
Scholarship 11, 14
Schopenhauer 841
Science and technology
12, 693-704
see also History
Scotus Viator *see* Seton-
Watson, R. W.
Sculpture 961-62, 1149-50
see also History
Second Republic (1938-
39) *see* History
Second World War *see*
History
Secondary resources 356
Secret police 466
Security 468, 479, 497-98
Sedláček, Vojtěch 974
Seifert, Jaroslav 839, 899-
900, 903
Sellier & Bellot, a.s. 669
Services *see* Products and
services
Seton-Watson, R. W. 110-
11
Sexuality 391
Shopping 49-50, 52
Short stories *see* Literature
Show trials *see* History
Sibelius 1063

Sigma Lutín 670
Sign of power, The (Jan
Zahradníček) 831
Silovský, Vladimír 974
Síma, Josef 974
Sixty-Eight Publishers,
Toronto 222, 911
Skinheads 268, 270
Sklenář, Zdeněk 974
Škoda (car manufacturer)
573, 653, 698
history 685, 687
Škoda (engineering
company) 657
Škoda (locomotive and
trolleybus builder) 685,
687
Škvorecký, Josef 405, 902,
924-27
Slánský, Rudolf 219
Slánský trial, 1952 *see*
History
Slav Congress, 1848 *see*
History
Slav nations 6
Czech attitudes towards
18
Slavic philosophy 962
Slavic studies, journals of
1116, 1121-23, 1152-53
Slavkov 71
see also History
Slavkov, Battle of *see*
History: Austerlitz,
Battle of
Slavonic studies, journals
of 1116, 1121-23, 1152-
53
Slavs 7
see also History
Slovak language 809-10
Slovak musical composers
1046
Slovak literature 810, 852
exile literature 909-10
Slovak nation 6
Slovak National Uprising
1944 *see* History
Slovak people *see* Slovaks
Slovak Republic /
Slovakia
agricultural machinery
manufacturers 632

Slovak Republic /
  Slovakia *contd*
  art 965
  companies 710
  conservation 732
  construction industry 712
  culture 560
  economy 547, 558, 560,
    710
  effect of split of
    Czechoslovakia 454
  environment 725, 727
  film 1011-12
  fishing 754
  freedom of speech 1099
  glassworks 675
  housing 707
  hotels 710
  industry 635, 638, 710
  map 42
  migration between Czech
    and Slovak Republics
    22
  official Czechoslovak
    attitudes towards 251
  pharmaceutical industry
    388
  philosophy 422
  politics 461, 469, 560
  privatization 509, 650
  publishing houses 1096
  rents 710
  residential property 710
  retail trade and consumer
    services 648, 650, 710
  Roma 47
  steel industry 654
  sugar production 672
  theatre 999
  tourism 47-49, 51, 710
  transition 1989- 551,
    558, 648, 689, 710
  transport 710
  travel guide 47-49, 51
  unemployment 365
  Western Carpathians 27
  see also History:
    Slovakia / Slovak
    Republic
Slovaks
  contribution to world
    culture 11
  Czech relations with 14

  official Czechoslovak
    attitudes towards 251
  Slovaks abroad 12, 306
    see also History
  Slovenia 638, 725
  Smetana, Bedřich 1050-52
  Social conditions *see*
    Society and social
    conditions
  Social inequality 361
  Social mobility 359-61
  Social organizations 52
  Social policy 355, 357,
    463, 592
  Social problems 355
  Social Realism 899, 996
  Social reform 355, 357
  Social sciences 12
    bibliography 1152
    networking 414
    periodicals 1129
  Social security 357, 418,
    516
    statistics 416, 418
  Social theology 331
  Socialism *see* History
  Socialist distribution 361
  Society and social
    conditions 3, 12,
    354-71, 383, 437, 460,
    463, 556
    and politics 515
    transition period 354-56,
    366, 371, 459
    see also History: society
    and social change
  Society of Patriotic
    Friends of Art 1142
  Sociology 358
  Sofia *see* History
  Software 697
  Soils 28, 416
  Sokol movement *see*
    History
  Songbirds 84
  Songs 995
  Soros, George 443
  Sovereignty 23
  Soviet bloc *see* History
  Soviet Communism *see*
    History
  Soviet Communist period
    see History

Soviet Union
  civil resistance in East
    European and Soviet
    revolutions 1989-91
    489
  economy 546
  housing 707
  law 506
  parliaments 505
  political changes 1989-
    457
  women 374
  see also History
Spain *see* History
Spanish Room, Prague
  Castle 1015
Spectre's Bride, The 831
Speech, freedom of 1099
Split of Czechoslovak
  state 449-54, 505
Spolana Chemicals 549
Spartakiad *see* History
Sport 735-56
  statistics 416
  see also History; History:
    Sokol; History -
    Spartakiad
Šrámek, Fráňa 899-900
St Adalbert of Prague 326
St Clement Hofbauer, 326
St Clement's College 1137
St Cyril 325-26
St Georges Convent,
  Prague 1015
St John Nepomucene 6
St Ludmila 325-27
St Methodius 325-26
St Sarkander, Jan 326
St Vitus Cathedral, Prague
  130, 1015
St Vojtěch *see* St Adalbert
  of Prague
St Wenceslas 6, 127, 325-27
St Zdislava of Lemberk
  326
Stage design 997
Stalin, statue of, Prague
  1032
Stam, Mart 1024
State Jewish Museum,
  Prague 1147
State Library, Prague 1136
Statistical Office 729

Statistics 29, 34, 101, 413-21
Steam locomotives 685-86
Steel companies 558
Steel industry 576, 615, 654
Štefánik, M. 174
Stock exchanges 610, 617, 622-24
see also Prague stock exchange
Stock markets 528
Stoppard, Tom 998
Stösslová, Kamila 1067, 1074
Strahov abbey, Prague 347
Strahov Library, Prague 347, 1141
Stratil, Václav 979
Strauss 1063
Stráž nad Nežárkou 1047
Stretti, Viktor 974
Stuchlý, Vít 810
Sudeten Germans see History: German minority
Sudeten question 615
see also History: Sudeten question, 1918-
Sudetendeutsche Party see History
Sudetenland see History
Sugar production 628, 672
Suk, Josef 1040
Sukdolák, Pavel 978
Šumava forest 73
Sumín, Jiří 18
Surrealism 900
Švabinský, Max 974
Švankmajer, Jan 1008-09
Svatební košile (Karel Jaromír Erben)
Svatopluk, Josef 836
Švec, Colonel 6
Švehla, Antonín 436
Sviták, Ivan 217
Svoboda, General Ludvík 200, 204
Svobodová, Růžena 18
Switzerland 389
Synagogues 276-77

T

Taborites see History
Talmud school of Prague see History
Tatra Kopřivnice 698
Tausky, Vilém 1069
Taxation 513, 516, 610, 621-22
see also Economy: taxes
Teaching of foreign languages 400
Technical colleges see History
Technological needs of post-Communist countries 614
TEFL (Teaching English as a Foreign Language) 400
Teige, Karel 839, 1023
Television 1094, 1098
statistics 416
Tennis 748-50
Teplá abbey, western Bohemia 347
Teplice 687
Terezín, northern Bohemia see History
Territorial disputes 38
Territory 23
Tesař, Zdeněk 974
Teschen see History
Testaments betrayed (Milan Kundera) 923
Tever, Felix 18
Texas 813
Textiles industry 667-68
Theatre 10, 106, 993-99
Theer, Otakar 900
Theodoricus 966
Theology 330, 351
Theresienstadt see History: Terezín
Thunderstorm, The (Ostrovskij) 1067, 1073
Theresienstadt concentration camp see History
Third Republic 1945-48 see History
Thirty Years War see History

Thun Palace see History
Tichý, Trantišek 974
Tkadleček 828
Tomášek, František 320, 350
Tomin, Zdena 931-32
Topol, Jáchym 902
Topol, Josef 904, 998
Tourism 22, 26, 44, 528, 710, 712, 735-36
and conservation 55
Town planning see History
Towns 42, 125
Trade 528
deficit 615
foreign 639, 643
foreign debt 618
Trade Fair Palace, Prague 1031
Trade fairs 621
Trades Licensing Act 516
Trams 87, 687-89
Transition from Soviet Communism to free democracy, 1989- 20, 451-52, 461
agricultural cooperatives 551
and media 1091
changes within enterprises 566
companies / businesses 549-50
cooperatives 551
emergence of new entrepreneurs 550
foreign trade 552
management of 558
microeconomic policy framework 566
political economy of 537-38
privatization 550
recession 552
reforms of financial sector 552
regional cities 553
role of state 499
rural 630
social problems 552
see also Economy: transition, 1989- ; Politics: transition, 1989-

Translations and criticisms of the works of individual writers 19, 853-94
Transport 680-92, 710
air 710
museums 687
pan-European policy 680
Prague 683-84, 691
Prague Ruzyně airport 683-84
rail 710
roads 681, 710
steam locomotives 685-86
tramways 687-89
trolleybuses 687
underground 690
Transport and communications 112, 528
Travel guides 46-50
advice for disabled travellers 47, 50
advice for gays and lesbians 50
advice for vegetarians 47
advice on souvenir shopping 49
camping 55
history 50-51
maps 46-48
monuments from Stalinist era 54
Prague
architecture 60, 63
guide to guides 59
walking tours 49
websites 45
Roma 47
websites 45, 57
Travellers' accounts 43
Trial, The (Franz Kafka) 939, 946, 948
Troja Castle, Prague 1146
Trolleybuses 687
Tuberculosis see History
Turbína (Karel Matěj Čapek-Chod) 840
Turkish wars see History
Turn of century see History: fin-de-siècle movements
Tusa, John 482

Tyl, Josef Kajetán 831
Tyl, Oldřich 1031
Tyrolean elegies (Karel Havlíček Borovský) 831
Tyrolské elegie (Karel Havlíček Borovský) 831
Tyrš, Miroslav 737, 740

U

Ukrainian minority in former Czechoslovakia 252
Ukrainian nationalist writers 958
Umělecko-průmyslové museum see Museum of Decorative Arts
Unbearable lightness of being, The (Milan Kundera) 914, 916-17
Underground system 690
Unemployment 357, 363, 365, 540, 556
United Nations Security Council 501
Unites States see History
United States Congress 472
Unity of Czech Brethren see History
Universities see History
University of Prague see History
Uprising of Bohemian Estates 1618-20 see History
Uprisings, 1953 see History
Úprka, Jóža 974
Urban ecology 77 see also Environment
Urban life 714
Urban planning 705, 709, 713
Urbanization and housing policy 705-21
Urbanová, Eva 1047
Uruguay Round Agreement 627
USA 304, 389

USSR see History: Soviet Union; Soviet Union
Ústí nad Labem 687

V

Váchal, Josef 974
Vaculík, Ludvík 838, 844, 902
Vančura, Vladislav 834, 838
Vaněk, Ferdinand 905
VAT see Economy
Vatican 320-22
Veba Broumov 641
Vegetable growing 628
Velvet Revolution, 1989 see History
Vienna 308, 342, 709
Viennese Czechs see History
Viewegh, Michal 902
Viková-Kunětická, Božena 18
Vines 628
Višegrad Triangle 497, 547
Viticulture 628, 1087
Vladislav Hall, Prague Castle 1015
Vlk, Miloslav 350
Vojenské museum see Military Museum
Volhynia, Ukraine 307
Volhynian Czechs see History
Volkswagen 653
Voskovec, Jiří 995
Vostrá, Alena 810
Voucher privatization see Economy
Vyrozumění (Václav Havel) 831

W

Wage policies 368
Wallachians 809
Wallachs 809
Wallenstein, Habsburg General 157
Warsaw Pact see History

Warsaw Treaty
  Organization 647
Watchmaking see History
Water 661, 712
Weapons 669, 1148
Weights and measures 50
Weiner, Richard 828, 900
Wellek, René 900
Wenceslas IV 132
Wenceslas Square 31
Werich, Jan 995
Western Carpathians 27
Western Europe 464
Western European powers,
  1939-48 see History
White Mountain, Battle of,
  1621 see History
Wine 628, 1087
Winter King see
  Frederick, Elector
  Palatine, King of
  Bohemia
Winter Queen, Elizabeth
  483
Wisconsin 304
Wojtyla, Karol see Pope
  John Paul II
Wolker, Jiří 900, 903
Women 372-82
  and economic and
    political transition 375,
    378
  and politics 372, 375
  and society in transition
    376

and state 374
and Western feminist
  ideas 377
and work 373, 378
employment policies 372
political role of 372
religious rights 372
writers 18
young 382
see also History
Women's organizations
  375
Women's studies 380
'Wood turtle, The' (poem)
  1053
Woods 79
Wool industry see History
Working environments 52
World culture, Czech and
  Slovak contribution to 11
World War I see History:
  First World War
World War II see History:
  Second World War
Writers see Literature and
  individual writers by
  name
Wycliffe, John 134
  teaching of 330

Y

Young Czech Party see
  History

Yugoslavia 305, 470, 708
  see also History

Z

Zahradníček, Jan 900
Žalud-Vysokomýtský see
  History
Žatec see History
Závada, Vilém 900
Zbrojovka Brno a.s. 669
Zbrojovka Vsetín, a.s.
  669
Žďárec see History
Zelená Žába, Trenčianske
  Teplice, Slovakia
  1030
Želiv abbey, southern
  Bohemia 347
Zeman, Miloš 503
Zetor tractor 549
Zeyer, Julius 148, 836,
  850
Zionism see History
Živnostenská banka
  607
Žižka, Jan 138
Žleby 1148
Zlín 1035
Zlín-Otrokovice 687
Znamení moci (Jan
  Zahradníček) 831
Zrzavý, Jan 974
ZVU 641

430

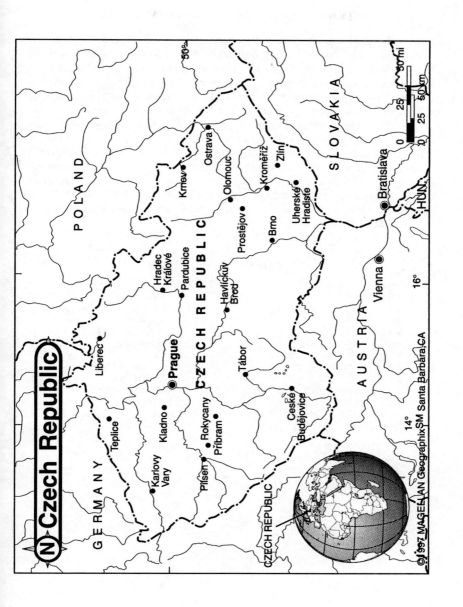

Czech Republic